Lecture Notes in Computer Science 14569

FoLLI Publications on Logic, Language and Information
Subline of Lecture Notes in Computer Science

More information about this series at https://link.springer.com/bookseries/558

Daisuke Bekki · Koji Mineshima ·
Elin McCready

Editors

Logic and Engineering of Natural Language Semantics

20th International Conference, LENLS20
Osaka, Japan, November 18–20, 2023
Revised Selected Papers

Springer

Editors
Daisuke Bekki 🄳
Ochanomizu University
Tokyo, Japan

Koji Mineshima 🄳
Keio University
Tokyo, Japan

Elin McCready
Aoyama Gakuin University
Tokyo, Japan

ISSN 0302-9743   ISSN 1611-3349 (electronic)
Lecture Notes in Computer Science
ISBN 978-3-031-60877-3   ISBN 978-3-031-60878-0 (eBook)
https://doi.org/10.1007/978-3-031-60878-0

This Springer imprint is published by the registered company Springer Nature Switzerland AG
The registered company address is: Gewerbestrasse 11, 6330 Cham, Switzerland

If disposing of this product, please recycle the paper.

LENLS 20: Twenty Years of Logic and Language

These brief remarks form the introduction to the proceedings of the 20th iteration of our workshop Logic and Engineering of Natural Language Semantics (LENLS). LENLS is an annual international conference on (mostly) formal approaches to topics at the intersection of language and logic, and so centers around linguistics, both theoretical and computational; logic; philosophy; and other sorts of formal approaches to these topics such as game theory.

The 20th LENLS conference was held November 18–20, 2023 in a hybrid format, though most talks were – at last – given in person. Each day was filled with interesting talks and thought-provoking discussion; the second day also included a conference dinner at a nearby restuarant with an amazing view over the Osaka night city. The review process for the conference was double-blind, and each paper appearing in this volume received three reviews (though some papers submitted in a 'talk-only' category had fewer); 46 papers were submitted, of which 31 were accepted; there was also one invited talk. The conference was sponsored by the Association for Logic, Language and Information (FoLLI); the "AI systems that can explain by language based on knowledge and reasoning" project (Grant Number JPMJCR20D2), funded by JST CREST Programs "Core technologies for trusted quality AI systems"; Graduate School of Humanities, Osaka University.

It is amazing to look back over the last 20 years of LENLS, especially when considering how it started. Let me reminisce a bit. I always find these sorts of stories interesting, and I hope this one will also be of interest to people in the LENLS community and even beyond it. (I am going to work with my own fallible memories here; I hope they don't diverge too far from the actual course of events.)

The main person making LENLS happen in its initial stages was Norry Ogata. Norry was a professor at Osaka University in 2002, when I happened to be visiting the Kansai area of Japan (including Kyoto, Nara and Osaka). I was working at the time on quantificational subordination and posted a query about something related on Linguist List; Norry sent me an email in response and we realized we were just down the road from each other. I went over to his office one day and we ended up going for a drink. As the alcohol flowed we started talking about the state of the Japanese semantics scene at the time – very small and without much in the way of an international presence, despite the Semantics Group in Tokyo (meeting at that time at the University of Tokyo), then organized by Makoto Kanazawa and Chris Tancredi. We somehow decided that it was time to organize a workshop and that such a thing would be really good for the Japanese community, and also might help bring that community together with the broader international semantics/logic scene. The evening ended on an excited and positive note.

Norry didn't let things end there. The first LENLS happened the following year, connected with the Japanese Society for Artificial Intelligence meeting in Kanazawa; that first LENLS had only a few long talks and lasted only a single day. I remember meeting many people there for the first time, and also the place we had the conference dinner, a very very nice fish restaurant in an old wooden building in the Kanazawa old town; this set the tradition for what became the first of many memorable conference dinners at LENLS over the years.

LENLS was held in many different places after that: Asahikawa, Tokyo, Miyazaki, Osaka, Takamatsu. Each of these iterations of LENLS had its own character, created in part by the participants and in part by the locale. I met many lifelong friends and co-authors at these conferences, as did many others, and had many interesting and exciting experiences at them, both academic and less so. And each conference venue had its own delicious local food, which we always took advantage of in organizing the conference dinners. LENLS has always been not just an academic event, but also a gourmet one. This too can be put in part down to Norry's influence, as a person who loved to eat and drink, and who applied his skills as a researcher to always finding the perfect place.

Sadly, Norry is not around to see what LENLS has become: one of (if not the) preeminent venue in Asia for the kind of logico-linguistical research that it specializes in, a part of the Association for Logic and Language (FoLLI) umbrella and publishing proceedings in the FoLLI series. He would have been so excited and happy to see the connections that our initial inspiration and all his hard work has led to. I would like to dedicate this volume to him. I would also like to thank everyone who has presented at LENLS during the past 20 years, those who have helped to organize the conference and/or make it happen and support it in other ways, and, most of all, the participants and other organizers of LENLS20 this past year in 2023.

March 2024   Elin McCready

Organization

Workshop Chair

Elin McCready   Aoyama Gakuin University, Japan

Workshop Co-chairs

Daisuke Bekki   Ochanomizu University, Japan
Koji Mineshima   Keio University, Japan

Program Committee Members

Alastair Butler	Hirosaki University, Japan
Patrick D. Elliott	Heinrich-Heine University of Dusseldorf, Germany
Naoya Fujikawa	University of Tokyo, Japan
Yurie Hara	Hokkaido University, Japan
Robert Henderson	University of Arizona, USA
Hitomi Hirayama	Keio University, Japan
Magdalena Kaufmann	University of Connecticut, USA
Yoshiki Mori	University of Tokyo, Japan
David Y. Oshima	Nagoya University, Japan
Katsuhiko Sano	Hokkaido University, Japan
Osamu Sawada	Kobe University, Japan
Eri Tanaka	Osaka University, Japan
Wataru Uegaki	University of Edinburgh, UK
Katsuhiko Yabushita	Naruto University of Education, Japan
Shunsuke Yatabe	Ochanomizu University, Japan
Kei Yoshimoto	Tohoku University, Japan

Local Organizers

Eri Tanaka   Osaka University, Japan
Akitaka Yamada   Osaka University, Japan

Contents

Putting the Argumentative Perspective Under Discussion – QUD vs.
Argumentative Goals.................................... 1
   Grégoire Winterstein

Perspective and the Self in Experiential Attitude Reports............... 17
   Kristina Liefke

Negation and Information Structure in Tree-Wrapping Grammar........... 37
   Kata Balogh

Towards a Theory of Anaphoric Binding in Event Semantics............. 55
   Oleg Kiselyov

Matrix and Relative Weak Crossover on the Level of the Individual:
An Experimental Investigation 68
   Haruka Fukushima, Daniel Plesniak, and Daisuke Bekki

Additivity in Attention Semantics 84
   Noritsugu Hayashi

Extending Abstract Categorial Grammars with Feature Structures:
Theory and Practice.. 118
   Philippe de Groote, Maxime Guillaume, Agathe Helman,
   Sylvain Pogodalla, and Raphaël Salmon

An Overt Operator Associating with Covert Focus: An *Even*-Like
Semantics for Mandarin *Gèng*.................................. 134
   Zhuang Chen and Yael Greenberg

Internal Reading and Reciprocity 155
   Ka-fat Chow

Dot-to-Dot Semantic Representation 175
   Alastair Butler

Intonational Meaning at the Limits of Grammar 191
   Lukas Rieser

Comparing Degree-Based and Argumentative Analyses of *Even* 205
   Pola Osher and Yael Greenberg

Appositive Projection as Implicit Context Extension in Dependent Type
Semantics. 224
   Daiki Matsuoka, Daisuke Bekki, and Hitomi Yanaka

On the Semantics of Dependencies: Relative Clauses and Open Clausal
Complements 244
   Philippe de Groote

Semantics of Propositional Attitudes in Type-Theory of Algorithms 260
   Roussanka Loukanova

A Structured Witness Approach to Pair-List Answers of *wh*-Questions
with Plural Definites 285
   Takanobu Nakamura

Two Places Where We Need Plug-Negation in Update Semantics:
Symmetrical Presupposition Filtering and Exclusive Disjunction 307
   Yusuke Yagi

Topology and Justified True Belief: A Baseless, Evidence-Free
(and Pointless) Approach 321
   Kohei Kishida

Semantic-Pragmatic Account of Syntactic Structures 337
   Ivan Rygaev

Author Index 353

Putting the Argumentative Perspective Under Discussion – QUD vs. Argumentative Goals

Grégoire Winterstein[✉]

Département de Linguistique, Université du Québec à Montréal, Montreal, Canada
`winterstein.gregoire@uqam.ca`

Abstract. We discuss some properties of the theory of argumentation within language (*AwL*), comparing it to QUD-based models of discourse interpretation. We begin by introducing the theory of *AwL*, its motivations and its main features. We then discuss the similarities and differences between Questions under Discussion and argumentative goals, arguing against an assimilation of the two. That discussion serves as the basis for a reevaluation of the notion of at-issueness, and its relationship to the question under which a content is said to project. We conclude with a discussion of the nature of different types of meaning, drawing on distinctions in two different domains.

Our goal in this work is to show how an approach to natural language meaning that considers the argumentative side of meaning helps to clarify certain concepts routinely used within formal theories of semantics and pragmatics, especially by comparing it with models of discourse interpretation that rely on the identification of *Question under Discussion* (QUD). In doing so, our goal is not to argue in favor of abandoning conventional semantic theories; rather we want to demonstrate the benefits of considering meaning as an object with multiple facets. Among these facets, matters of truth and reference play a role, but they are not the only factors at play, and might not be as central as modern theories take them to be.

We begin in Sect. 1 by delineating the contours of *AwL*, and provide some justification for the hypothesis that natural language meaning involves an argumentative component. We then turn our attention to the notion of *at-issueness* and highlights some issues that arise when it comes to identifying what is at issue in the QUD approach. We focus on cases in which the speaker conveys a content to which they are committed, but which stands in argumentative opposition to the argumentative goal that the speaker is aiming for (Sect. 3). In Sect. 4, we consider such examples in terms of projection, highlighting further some issues

I wish to thank the organizers and the audience at LENLS16 for their remarks and comments, in particular Elin McCready and Christopher Davis who patiently and constructively listened to several incarnations of this work. It goes without saying that all mistakes and errors in this article remain my own.

D. Bekki et al. (Eds.): LENLS 2023, LNCS 14569, pp. 1–16, 2024.
https://doi.org/10.1007/978-3-031-60878-0_1

that arise when one adopts a definition of at-issueness that is solely based on truth-theoretic considerations. We conclude in Sect. 5, where we propose an argumentative characterization of at-issueness, complemented by a new proposal for a typology of the semantic content conventionally conveyed by an utterance.

1   The Argumentative Perspective on Language

The most representative among linguistic approaches to argumentation is the theory of argumentation within language (*AwL*) initially fostered by French authors Oswald Ducrot and Jean-Claude Anscombre (D&A, see e.g. Anscombre and Ducrot 1983), though linguistic argumentative theories also borrow from works in the argumentation theory tradition and the psychology of reasoning. D&A describe *AwL* as a theory of "integrated pragmatics", which means that this is a theory of conventional meaning, but one which takes within semantics phenomena traditionally considered to belong to pragmatics. The phenomena *AwL* deals with are mostly discursive, and imply describing the conditions under which two discourse units can be articulated together to form a coherent and cohesive discourse.

The argumentative perspective on natural language interpretation takes its roots in different observations. One of its key tenets is that the coherence and cohesion conditions that bear on discourse are governed not just by the "logical" content conveyed by discourse units, but also, crucially, by their linguistic form. This is supported by contrasts such as the one between the sentences in (1).

(1)   a. Lemmy is the same height as Riley.
      b. Lemmy is as tall as Riley.

Arguably, both sentences in (1) convey the same semantic content and they appear logically equivalent: if one accepts the truth of (1b), they are bound to accept the truth of (1a) and vice-versa. Yet, in spite of this apparent logical equivalence, both sentences differ in terms of the discourse they can appear in. We illustrate it with the examples (2): while (2a) can be used to justify Lemmy being short (like Riley is), this is not true of (2b), in spite of the logical equivalence between the sentences in (1).

(2)   Riley is pretty short and. . .
      a. Lemmy is the same height as Riley, so he's short too.
      b. # Lemmy is as tall as Riley, so he's short too.

On the basis of such data, *AwL* postulates that the semantics of natural language involve an *argumentative component* which bears on whether and how a given sentence can be used to argue in favour of a certain conclusion. In the sense of *AwL*, argumentation is a pretty loose relationship. The only requirement for an utterance U to be considered an argument in favor of a conclusion C is that accepting U leads to an increased belief in C.[1] How to formally define beliefs and what an increase in belief means is beyond the goals of this paper. We will simply remark that a Bayesian interpretation of probability gives a ready-made tool to handle these aspects, and that this has been used in several works in linguistics (Merin, 1999; Winterstein, 2024), argumentative reasoning (Pfeifer and Kleiter, 2006), and psychology of reasoning (Hahn and Oaksford, 2007; Zenker, 2013).

Beyond observations as in (2), the hypothesis that natural language encodes constraints of argumentative nature can be justified at a more theoretical level. A first case in point is the prevalence of considerations about argumentation and rhetoric techniques in philosophical traditions throughout time and space, in a way that goes well beyond the confines of the tradition founded in Ancient Greece (which is often, abusively, identified as the "source" of argumentation theory, see e.g. Auer 1959). For example, *The Instruction of Ptah-Hotep*, an Egyptian document dating back to circa 3100 BCE, in the early dynastic period of ancient Egypt, is often considered to be the first known attempt to approach rhetoric in a systematic way (Kennedy, 1998; Blake, 2009). Similarly, in China, the teachings of Mozi (479-392 BCE) and the (heterogeneous) 'school of names' share an interest in language and how it can be used for argumentative purposes, sometimes prefiguring logical arguments, though with a focus on the utility of arguments rather than formal criteria of validity (Cheng, 1997). Similarly, the Nyāya school in India stands out in the Indian tradition for its interest in reasoning and the methods by which one resolves debates. Here again, the focus is on the effectiveness and utility of argumentative techniques rather than matters of logical validity (Phillips, 2018).

One can also look at argumentation from the point of view of the functions of language. For example, Jakobson (1963) distinguishes six functions of language (mapped to the components of his model of communication). Among these, the referential function, built around the relationship between a message and its (extralinguistic) context of utterance, closely corresponds to the spirit of truth-conditional approaches to natural language semantics, but this only accounts for one of the functions of language. Argumentation on the other hand falls under the conative function, centered on the relationship between a message and its audience. Under this view, meaning is not solely centered on referential aspects, a position that is getting increasingly echoed by several developments within semantics and pragmatics. Thus, Ginzburg (2012) develops an account of interactive meaning, i.e. that part of meaning which directly bears on the fact that linguistic communication typically involves an interaction between agents. The study of expressive meaning can also be seen as straying away from purely referential meaning (Davis and McCready, 2020), rather connecting it to social features, in line with work about "social meaning" (Acton, 2019; Burnett, 2019). In that sense, argumentative meaning is just one part of meaning, connected to, but also independent from other aspects of meaning.

---

[1] This contrasts with some approaches in the argumentation theory tradition that discuss additional normative considerations on what counts as an argument, see a.o. the RAS criteria of natural logic (Johnson and Blair, 1977; 2006).

A third justification for the hypothesis that natural language involves an argumentative component is rooted in considerations about testimonial reliability. Authors like Sperber et al. (2010) contend that audiences are generally epistemically vigilant, meaning that they do not readily accept and update their beliefs on the basis on the information they are presented with. Rather, audiences typically signal their acceptance of a given content, suggesting that acceptance cannot be taken for granted (Clark, 1996). Similarly, models of the speakers' perceived reliability and how it affects the assessment of their discourse moves have been proposed (Fricker, 2007; McCready, 2015; McCready and Winterstein, 2018). This contrasts with simple models of information update, e.g. based on models of Common Ground inspired by Stalnaker (1978), and suggests that speakers are actively engaged in providing evidence to their audience in order for them to accept their moves, i.e. that speakers integrate argumentative considerations in order to serve their communicative goals.

It thus makes sense to assume that the linguistic code integrates devices related to argumentative purposes.[2] In concrete terms, a theory like *AwL* postulates that the interpretation of an utterance is made relative to an argumentative conclusion that the speaker is aiming for, and which is part of their communicative goal. The speaker presents their utterance as some form of evidence that justifies increasing one's belief in that conclusion. Identifying that conclusion (when it is not made explicit) is thus also part of the interpretative process of the utterance.

Within *AwL*, the relationship between a premise and its conclusion is mediated by different aspects. First, lexical items have argumentative possibilities inscribed in their semantics. These argumentative possibilities are what helps to distinguish pairs of expressions that appear to share their denotation, but cannot reliably be substituted to each other in discourse (e.g. *being a miser* vs. *being thrifty*). Formally speaking, it has been proposed that these possibilities can be represented in the form of argumentative topoi that are present in the semantics of lexical expressions (Anscombre, 1989, 1995). These topoi are (gradable) general rules of reasoning that bridge the content of a premise to a conclusion, e.g. *the more thrifty one is, the more virtuous they are*). Rather than relying on topoi, Carel (2011) and Ducrot (2016) simply consider that the (argumentative) meaning of an expression is given by the set of discourses it can appear in, espousing an essentially distributional and structuralist (in the sense of de Saussure 1916) view on meaning.

Aside lexical meaning, the argumentative profile of an utterance is also determined by the use of argumentative operators, typically discourse markers and connectives that are analyzed as conveying constraints about the argumentative orientation of their prejacent (Anscombre and Ducrot, 1983; Winterstein,

---

[2] We do not mean that argumentation is exclusively a linguistic affair. For example Mercier and Sperber 2011 propose that human reasoning developed for argumentative purposes, i.e. as a way to formulate more cogent arguments, which in turn provides some advantage for speakers who can more effectively push their views. Their view on reasoning is not exclusively based on linguistic elements.

2024). We discuss some of these elements in the sections below, with a particular highlight on elements that put at odds the descriptive and argumentative parts of meaning. Constraints analogous to those conveyed by argumentative operators are also found in the form of general discourse laws that encapsulate various argumentative regularities, some akin to Gricean maxims (in particular that of Quantity), others related to the interplay between negation and gradable expressions (Moeschler and Reboul, 1994).

In the remainder of this paper we begin with an examination of the notion of at-issueness in the perspective of *AwL*, and in a second time use this discussion to revisit how different types are characterized in the formal semantics/pragmatics tradition.

2 QUD and Argumentative Goals

As mentioned above, a key idea within *AwL*, and one that is common to all its variants, is that utterances are oriented towards a certain conclusion. This idea parallels the role played by the *Question under Discussion* (QUD) in various works that take their roots in a long tradition that uses pairs of questions and answers to analyze rhetorical structure (Hamblin, 1970).

Among these works, the QUD-model initially developed by Roberts (1996) is especially influential. For example, it has successfully been invoked in the analysis of the semantic effect of informational focus (Büring, 1997, 2003; Beaver and Clark, 2008), and for the analysis of the projective behavior of certain types of content (Simons et al., 2010).

Like the argumentative goal, the QUD serves as the background against which a given utterance is interpreted: identifying it is part of the full interpretation of the utterance, and it is part of the required input for some phenomena. As with argumentative goals, QUD can be overt, and a given utterance can be incompatible with an explicit QUD. As an illustration, the placement of focus depends on the QUD. In (3), the focused element in Sandy's answer is *Alex*, and it would be odd to place it, e.g., on *the meal*.

(3)   a.   *Kim*: Who paid for the meal?
      b.   *Sandy*: [Alex]$_F$ paid for the meal.

Inversely, if the QUD is not explicit, e.g. if (3b) is uttered without the preceding question, one can reconstruct a QUD on the basis of the informational structure of the utterance.

Argumentative goals share this property of QUD: making one's goal explicit will forbid certain forms of discourses, and inversely, one can "abduce" the most likely goal targeted by a speaker on the basis of their utterance and assumptions about their a priori most likely communicative intentions (Zeevat and Winterstein, to appear). Argumentative goals, like QUD, are necessary for the full interpretation of a number of linguistic expressions.

Formally, there is a clear formal connection to make between QUD and argumentative goal in that one could simply turn the goal targeted by the speaker of an utterance into a polar question and consider that this is the QUD addressed by the utterance (Winterstein and Schaden, 2011), though it many cases the speaker's utterance will only indirectly address that QUD, and not in ways that would be explanatory under QUD's traditional accounts.

To illustrate the commonalities and differences between QUD and argumentative goals, let's look at example (4) from the point of view of the QUD.

(4)   *Charlie*: Should I also order you another beer?

    a.   *Alex*: Yes, I'm done with my beer.

    b.   *Alex*: Yes, I'm almost done with my beer.

In (4), Charlie's question sets the QUD. Looking at Alex's answer in (4a), one could argue that it contextually addresses the QUD if one assumes that there is a (presumptive) rule like (5) at play on the context of (4) (see e.g. definitions of addressing the QUD in Simons et al. 2010 to see why something like (5) is needed).

(5)   If a person is done with their drink, they will want to order another.

Note that in assuming (5), we are already slightly stretching regular QUD-based accounts. The rule (5) cannot reasonably be taken to hold for certain, even if only contextually (since it would entail that agents have no limit to their drinking habits). This contrasts with traditional examples of contextual knowledge which is non-defeasible (e.g. being of a certain age entailing that one can drink/drive etc.) It is thus better to see the rule (5) as something presumptive, or probabilistic, in nature, which is not straightforwardly compatible with traditional QUD-based accounts that rely on standard truth-conditional and model-theoretic relations to define notions such as "addressing the QUD".

Another observation is that besides (5), another rule such as (6) seems to be in order.

(6)   If a person is not done with their drink, they will not want to order another.

Rule (6) is motivated by the observation that a negative reply by Alex in (4) could be motivated by Alex not being done with their beer, cf. (7).

(7)   *Alex*: No, I'm not done with my beer.

Looking now at Alex's alternative answer in (4b), the picture becomes less clear. Uttering (4b) conveys two distinct pieces of information: (i) that Alex is close to finishing their beer, and that (ii) they are not yet done with their beer (Amaral, 2007; Jayez and Tovena, 2008). Each of those two pieces of information is relevant to the QUD set by Charlie, and each potentially points to a different answer to it, at least according to rules (5) and (6). Yet, overall, (4b) can only be understood as an acceptance of Charlie's offer, i.e. information (i) seems prevalent in determining what can be the use of the utterance.

This points to a difference between the QUD and argumentative goals, namely that though QUD can be biased, they leave open the possibility that any of their potential answers is true. In the argumentative perspective, speakers argue for a particular proposition, and though one can choose to see that proposition as the answer to a question, it is not necessary. Another way to see the difference is that the QUD is a descriptive, neutral, and informational-based, construct, while the argumentative goal is speaker-oriented, and partially disconnected from descriptive content. In the argumentative perspective speakers do not seek to truthfully answer a question, but rather push for a particular proposition to be accepted. In so doing, speakers choose a linguistic form that serves the goal they have in mind rather than one which attempts to give a descriptively adequate representation of the world.

3   At-Issueness and Argumentation

The discussion above leads us to question the notion of at-issueness in the context of semantics and pragmatics. Intuitively, being at-issue seems to be naturally related to argumentative concerns. Under a QUD approach, the notion is, as expected, defined relatively to a given question in the following way: "A proposition p is at-issue relative to a question Q iff the speaker intends to address the QUD via $?p$. An intention to address the QUD via $?p$ is felicitous iff $?p$ is relevant to the QUD" (i.e. if $?p$ has an answer which entails an answer to Q, Simons et al. 2010).

Let's look at example (8), simpler in some respect than the previous ones, but exhibiting the same tension between a truth-conditional and argumentative view.

(8)   a. *Alex*: Is dinner ready?
       b. *Charlie*: Yes, almost.

On the surface, the first part of Charlie's answer seems to be directly congruent to Alex's polar question Q. Under the QUD view, Alex's question is certainly "under discussion", and Charlie's answer has to be understood as addressing it, i.e. as being at-issue relative to it, and resolving the question in a positive way, i.e. by conveying that the dinner is ready (as indicated by the use of *Yes*). Yet, the second part of the utterance commits Charlie to the negation of that same content. Therefore, considering that the dinner being ready is at-issue, the negation of that same content is also at-issue relative to Q. This leads to an (undesirable) situation in which the speaker conveys two contents that are both at-issue relative to the QUD, but resolve it in opposite ways. This was also the situation in (4b), where the same speaker conveyed two contents which addressed the QUD and resolved it in opposite ways.

This is not say that a QUD approach has no way to approach a case like (8). First, it can be pointed out that speaker intentions are crucial in determining at-issueness, as mentioned in its definition. It is therefore conceivable that the negation of the prejacent of *almost* is not recognized as being at-issue precisely because it is not part of the main content of the utterance (a point we return to in the last section). Note though that this position has consequences in terms of projection (cf. next section), and that not being part of the main content does not guarantee that a given content is not at issue. In a later paper, Simons et al. (2016) develop a more nuanced to the construction of the relevant QUD (focusing on the case of factives, though their account extends to other cases). They distinguish between the Current Question (CQ), which corresponds to the question that an utterance is congruent to, and the discourse question (DQ), which is a more pragmatic one, pertaining to the larger communicative intentions of the speaker. Thus, one could argue that in the dialogue above, the Discourse Question is not about whether the dinner is ready, but whether food will be served soon (or something along those lines). With such a DQ, both parts of Charlie's answer are aligned since being almost ready resolves the DQ to a positive answer.

The distinction between CQ and DQ is intuitive enough, and again comparable in many ways to the argumentative perspective. Behind it is the idea that speakers have a certain communicative goal (the DQ, the argumentative conclusion) in mind which needs to be reconstructed to make sense of their utterance. In the case of (8), it would thus be reconstructing the real intention of Alex when they ask their question.

Yet, the question of how to interpret *Yes* in Charlie's answer somehow remains open. If one assumes that it is understood as addressing the DQ, no issues arise. But, given the semantics of *Yes*, nothing should actually prompt a hearer to accommodate such a DQ. The exchange in (8), at least without the *almost* part, is semantically congruent. But in the QUD perspective, DQ are accommodated if there is a mismatch between the information structure of an utterance and the question it apparently tries to resolve. The mismatch only happens at the content level, once the *almost* part has been uttered. This might prompt the interpreter to backtrack and come up with another interpretation by accommodating some appropriate DQ. In the argumentative perspective no such backtracking is necessary: Charlie's answer is understood as providing a positive answer to Alex's question, and the *almost* part is understood as an argument justifying that answer, even though it actually commits the speaker to the fact that the dinner is not ready. We thus come back to the foundational assumption of a theory like *AwL*: the way an utterance can be used in a discourse to justify some conclusion depends on its linguistic form, and is in great part independent from the content it commits its speaker to.

4   Projective Content in Argumentation

The notion of at-issueness has famously been put to use in order to characterize which content *projects*, i.e. which part of the conventional content of an utterance is understood to be part of the commitment of the speaker, with a particular focus on content which is found in the scope of truth-altering operators. As a (classical) example, the content conventionally triggered by some presuppositional constructions is typically found to project. If we take the verb *know* as presupposing the truth of its complement, we can see that this presupposition is triggered both in a simple declarative (9a), and in the same sentence with the addition of the possibility modal *maybe* (9b). The observation is that the modal in (9b) does not target the proposition that Riley laughed: that content projects.

(9) a. Alex knows Riley laughed.

     b. Maybe Alex knows Riley laughed.

Under the QUD view, the projective behavior of the presupposition triggered by *know* is not a consequence of its presuppositional nature. Rather, it is because both versions of (9) are seen as answering the same underlying QUD *Does Alex know that Riley laughed?*. The information that Riley laughed is not at-issue with regards to this QUD: each of the possible answers to the QUD entails that information. Therefore, the information projects equally in the two versions of (9): what projects is what is not at-issue (Simons et al., 2010, 2016)

In this section, we look at the projective behavior of the content associated with operators that involve a mismatch between some content that they conventionally convey and the argumentative properties of the utterances they appear in. Two examples of such operators are the proximal adverb *almost* (whose behavior we already discussed and exemplified with (4)), and exclusive adverbs such as English *only*. The case of *only* is illustrated in (10).

(10) *Alex*: Should we hire Riley?

      a. *Charlie*: (Yes/# No), they have a bachelor degree in computer science.

      b. *Charlie*: (# Yes/No), they only have a bachelor degree in computer science.

Both versions of Charlie's answer to Alex's question commit Charlie to Riley having a bachelor degree in computer science. But from an argumentative point of view, the addition of *only* drastically alters how the utterance is understood in the content of Alex's question in (10). The projective behaviour of the prejacent of *only* is analyzed in detail by Beaver and Clark (2008) in terms of QUD-answerhood. For a case like (10b), the explanation rests on the idea that the CQ for (10b) is about the degrees held by Riley. The import of *only* is to indicate that its prejacent is at the low end of an entailment scale (i.e. that one could have expected Riley to hold higher degrees), meaning that every other answer to the CQ entails it, making the prejacent not at-issue, and thus making it project.

This view raises some issues for examples like (11) (already discussed by Winterstein 2012).

(11) Riley only drinks the most expensive rums.

The issue with (11) has to do with the scale at play in the interpretation of *only*. Intuitively, and unlike in (10b), *only* in (11) seems to indicate that its prejacent occupies the highest point on some scale based on the price of rum. Of course, one could analyze (11) by considering a CQ and an entailment scale based on types of rum drunk by Riley, similar to the one postulated for (10b): *only* would indicate that its prejacent is low on the entailment scale, and thus that there is no other rum that Riley drinks. Beyond not doing justice to the intuition that *only* somehow indicates the top of scale in (11), such a move would entail that the prejacent projects, as for (10b). However, it is not clear that the prejacent necessarily projects out of non-veridical environment in that example, cf. (12).

(12)   a.   *Alex*: Is Riley really a rum snob?
        b.   *Charlie*: Do they only drink the most expensive rums?

Charlie's answer to Alex's query does not seem to commit Charlie to the belief that Riley drinks expensive rum. Rather, this seems to be part of Charlie's question. One way to account for the non projection of the prejacent within the QUD model would be to consider, as stated by Simons et al. (2016), that the prejacent projects if "the best explanation for the relevance of the CQ to the DQ requires attribution of the acceptance of that content to the speaker". Thus, for (12), we could assume that in the context of the conversation, Charlie is considering two mutually exclusive alternatives: either Riley drinks the most expensive rums and only those, or Riley drinks anything else (including, but not limited to, combinations of expensive rums and less expensive ones). In the first case, Riley's presumably a snob, and in the second case they are not. With such a partition, the CQ is relevant to the DQ (Alex's question), and does not commit Charlie to the belief that Riley drinks the most expensive rums. But note that this entails a different analysis of the meaning of *only*, and points to one in which scales are not relevant to its interpretation (Winterstein, 2012). In turn, this entails that either one assumes that somehow *only* works differently in (11) and (12) (one is scalar, the other one is not), or one has to come up with a different explanation for the projective behaviour of *only* in (11), namely one that does not rely on *only* marking its prejacent as being low on an entailment scale.

In addition, it is not clear that the partition we just evoked, and which is at the root of the relevance relation between CQ and DQ, is justified. In discursive terms, both (11) and its prejacent appear to have similar distributions. In particular, both versions can be used as arguments in favour of Riley being a snob (13).

(13)   Riley is really a rum snob, they (only) drink the most expensive ones [and keep raving about it.]

Again, under the QUD account, one could assume that the partition in question, which in turn determines the projection of the prejacent, is flexible, and contextually dependent. This provides a formal way to capture part of the phenomenon at hand. But it also fails to explain why *only* does not switch the argumentative orientation of its prejacent in (11), while it does in (10b), a fact which is directly related to how one can relate a DQ to a CQ, and one that deserves an explanation.

Turning to the case of proximal adverbs and projection, we first look at example (14).

(14)   a. *Alex*: Are things going well? Is the Bertier report almost finished?

      b. *Charlie*: (Yes/# No), it's actually finished.

For the same reasons we discussed about example (8) in Sect. 3, the information that the Bertier report is not finished (let's call it $\neg B$) should be considered at-issue in (14), at least from a QUD perspective (e.g. because answering Alex's questions with the information that $\neg B$ would be a coherent move, and one that can easily be interpreted as answering the DQ, and because answering that B is the case would also address the QUD). So the prediction should be that $\neg B$ does not project. Yet, that prediction is not clearly borne out. Though we cannot reasonably assume that Alex is conveying that the report is not finished, this is a situation that is compatible with their beliefs, and crucially, $\neg B$ is not part of Alex's question. Note that under the view that $\neg B$ is not at-issue (e.g. because it is not the speaker's intention to present it as such), the prediction that it should project is also problematic: one cannot impute that belief to Alex. In other words, Alex's question in (14a) is not about whether the report is close to being finished but not finished ; it is only about how close to completion the report is. Whether the report is finished or not is simply considered irrelevant with regards to Alex's question (and thus, not at-issue in the lay people's understanding of the notion).

Compare now (14) with (15).[3]

(15)   a. *Alex*: Was it a nice ride? Did you almost sweat?

      b. *Charlie*: (# Yes/No), I actually broke a sweat.

The idea behind (15) is that a nice bicycle ride (to work) is one in which one exercises enough, but not to the point where they become sweaty, which would be inconvenient when arriving at work. In (15), the content $\neg S$ (not sweating) is clearly at-issue, and is part of Alex's question, i.e. clearly does not project. What we show with such an example is that content that is not part of the main content can still be very much at-issue, and affected by the usual "family" of non-veridical operators.

In summary, those examples support in some respect the hypothesis that content that is at-issue does not project. The issues we raised are related to two aspects of the phenomenon. The first one is how to define what is at-issue. It seems that a definition based on a truth-conditional question-answer pair does not do full justice to an intuitive understanding of what it means to be at issue.

---

[3] I thank Elin McCready for providing this particular example.

Putting speaker's intention in the picture appears to be a sensible strategy, but we argue that those speaker's intention have to obey certain linguistic constraints. Such constraints are part of the empirical domain of theories like AwL. The second aspect, is about what it means to project. In the stereotypical cases discussed within the literature, projection is equated to speaker's commitment: if something projects, they are understood to be part of the beliefs of the speaker (and possibly others). But cases like (14) and (15) suggest that the picture is probably more complex, and might parallel the derivation of some conversational implicatures (we return briefly to this point in the last section).

5   A Revised Typology of Meaning

To conclude, we now move back to the argumentative perspective, and propose ways to approach the data and issues presented in the previous sections. To begin, we propose to define the notion of being at-issue in the following way:

(16)   A content p conveyed by an utterance U is at-issue iff p is positively relevant (in the argumentative sense) to the goal G targeted by the speaker of U, i.e. if learning that p positively affects belief in G.

This definition assumes that we have a proper characterization of what it means for a content to be argumentatively relevant to a conclusion. As mentioned earlier, one practical way to answer that need is to adopt a Bayesian perspective on argumentation, and to use it to forge a measure of the effect of learning a content on the process of belief update, e.g. by measuring it via Good (1950)'s weigh of evidence, as proposed by Merin (1999). Note the parallels with a QUD-based notion of at-issueness: both involve the recognition of an external element in the interpretation of an utterance (the goal/the QUD), and define at-issueness as involving a content and this external element.

At-issue content is the one that becomes affected by truth-altering operators such as the ones used in the "family of sentences" tests (negation, modals, interrogation), and is the one at play in the relation of answerhood that stands between a question and an answer. This parallels the hypothesis about projection from the QUD literature, but rather than trying to define the conditions under which a content projects (i.e. when it is not at issue), we characterize the conditions in which content does not project and is affected by various operators. When a content is not at-issue, the question of its projection remains open: it can be assigned to the speaker's beliefs or left underspecified in that regard. Here, we believe that a treatment along the lines of that of Quantity implicatures (Geurts, 2010) could prove useful. In particular, we believe that the reasoning relies on an epistemic step that involves the speaker's competence about the content under scrutiny. This step is warranted in order to attribute the content to the beliefs of the speaker. The reasoning also happens in the absence of specific discourse markers that would convey epistemic information, e.g. along the lines that the speaker believes that a certain information is shared between speakers (see Zimmermann (2011) for a discussion of such particles in German and other languages), though such content is more likely to only affect at-issue content.

In addition to the previous definition, we also propose the following generalization, following early proposals by Ducrot (1972) and Jayez (2010) about discourse attachment:

(17)   The main content of an utterance determines the argumentative orientation of the utterance.

The definition in (17) relies on the traditional distinction, dating back at least to the works of Grice (1989), between the core content of an utterance and additional contents conveyed at a different level (cf. the "conventional implicatures" distinguished by Grice within conventional meaning). We thus assume, along with much of the literature, that the linguistic code distinguishes between the main content of an utterance and secondary content.

The domain of secondary content is typically divided between presuppositions, conventional implicatures, expressive content etc. Here, we draw a simple distinction between *ancillary* content and non-ancillary one. By ancillary content, we mean secondary content that is argumentatively co-oriented with the main content (thereby doing justice to the original meaning of the term *ancillary*). Ancillary meaning is thus typically at-issue meaning, and likely to be affected by various operators.

In sum, we distinguish between three types of content (summarized in Fig. 1):

The main content of an utterance is distinguished by the grammar, and determines the argumentative orientation of the utterance, in combination with the effect of argumentative operators present in the utterance that modify the orientation of the main content. The main content is thus necessarily at-issue.

Secondary content is content that is conveyed by the utterance, usually in a conventional way, which is not distinguished as main content, and which is divided in two sub-categories.

Ancillary content is content which is argumentatively co-oriented with the main content, and is thus also at-issue. This content therefore typically does not project.

Non-ancillary content is content which is not co-oriented with the main content, and therefore not at-issue. It can project, assuming that it is consistent with what is assumed about the speaker's beliefs.

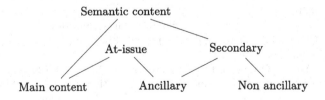

Fig. 1. A simple typology of linguistic meaning

Though the distinction between main and secondary content is linguistic and given by the grammar, the distinction between at-issue and non at-issue is contextual: it depends on the argumentative goal targeted by the speaker. To illustrate, we go back to the examples that involve *almost* that we discussed above. On the grammatical side, and in line with the literature on *almost* (Amaral, 2007; Jayez and Tovena, 2008), we distinguish two contents in the semantics of an utterance in which *almost* modifies a gradable predicate P:

- The main content, which conveys that the degree to which P stands is higher than a threshold that is indistinguishably close to the left of the standard for P
- A secondary content, which conveys that the degree to which P stands is lower than the standard for P (i.e. P does not stand)

The goals that an utterance of the form "*almost P*" can thus only be ones that require the degree of P to be at least higher than a point just below its standard. Among these goals, some are also served by higher degrees of P (as in example (14)), in which case the secondary content is not at-issue, and thus not expected to be affected by "veridicality" altering operators. On the other hand, some goals are served by the secondary content (as in example (15)), making it at-issue, and blocking any projection.

As a last word, we note that in our distinctions we mostly stay away from the distinction between conventional and non-conventional meaning. Though the main content is necessarily conventional in our approach, we want to leave open the possibility that non-conventional secondary meaning (e.g. certain conversational implicatures) can be at-issue. We leave the examination of this possibility to future work.

References

Acton, E.K.: Pragmatics and the social life of the English definite article. Language **95**, 37–65 (2019)

Amaral, P.: The meaning of approximative adverbs: evidence from European Portuguese. Ph.D. thesis, The Ohio State University (2007)

Anscombre, J.C.: Théorie de l'argumentation, topoï, et structuration discursive. Revue québécoise de linguistique **18**(1), 13–55 (1989)

Anscombre, J.C.: Topique or not topique: formes topiques intrinsèques et formes topiques extrinsèques. J. Pragmat. **24**, 115–141 (1995)

Anscombre, J.C., Ducrot, O.: L'argumentation dans la langue. Pierre Mardaga, Liège, Bruxelles (1983)

Auer, J.: An Introduction to Research in Speech. Harper and Row, New York (1959)

Beaver, D.I., Clark, B.Z.: Sense and Sensitivity: How Focus Determines Meaning. Wiley-Blackwell, Chichester (2008)

Blake, C.: The African Origins of Rhetoric. Routledge, New York (2009)

Büring, D.: The Meaning of Topic and Focus - The 59th Street Bridge Accent. Routledge (1997)

Büring, D.: On D-trees, beans, and B-accents. Linguist. Philos. **26**(5), 511–545 (2003)

Burnett, H.: Signalling games, sociolinguistic variation and the construction of style. Linguist. Philos. **42**, 419–450 (2019)

Carel, M.: L'Entrelacement argumentatif. Lexique, discours et blocs sémantiques. H. Champion, Paris (2011)

Cheng, A.: Histoire de la pensée chinoise. Éditions du Seuil, Paris (1997)

Clark, H.H.: Using Language. Cambridge University Press, Cambridge (1996)

Davis, C., McCready, E.: The instability of slurs. Grazer Philosophische Studien **97**(1), 63–85 (2020)

Ducrot, O.: Dire et ne pas dire. Hermann, Paris (1972)

Ducrot, O.: La théorie des blocs sémantiques. Verbum **XXXVII**(1–2), 53–65 (2016)

Fricker, M.: Epistemic Injustice. Power and the Ethics of Knowing. Oxford University Press, Oxford (2007)

Geurts, B.: Quantity Implicatures. Cambridge University Press, Cambridge (2010)

Ginzburg, J.: The Interactive Stance. Meaning for Conversation. Oxford University Press, Oxford (2012)

Good, I.J.: Probability and the Weighing of Evidence. Charles Griffin, London (1950)

Grice, H.P.: Studies in the Way of Words. Harvard University Press, Cambridge (1989)

Hahn, U., Oaksford, M.: The rationality of informal argumentation: a Bayesian approach to reasoning fallacies. Psychol. Rev. **114**(3), 704–732 (2007)

Hamblin, C.L.: Fallacies. Methuen, London (1970)

Jakobson, R.: Essais de linguistique générale. Minuit, Paris (1963)

Jayez, J.: Projective meaning and attachment. In: Aloni, M., Bastiaanse, H., de Jager, T., Schulz, K. (eds.) Logic, Language and Meaning. LNCS (LNAI), vol. 6042, pp. 325–334. Springer, Heidelberg (2010). https://doi.org/10.1007/978-3-642-14287-1_33

Jayez, J., Tovena, L.: Presque and almost: how argumentation derives from comparative meaning. In: Bonami, O., Hofherr, P.C. (eds.) Empirical Issues in Syntax and Semantics, vol. 7, pp. 1–23. CNRS (2008)

Johnson, R.H., Blair, J.A.: Logical Self-Defense, 1st edn. McGraw-Hill Ryerson, Toronto (1977)

Johnson, R.H., Blair, J.A.: Logical Self-Defense, 3rd edn. International Debate Education Association, New York (2006)

Kennedy, G.A.: Comparative Rhetoric: An Historical and Cross-Cultural Introduction. Oxford University Press, New York (1998)

McCready, E.: Reliability in Pragmatics. Oxford University Press, Oxford (2015)

McCready, E., Winterstein, G.: Testing epistemic injustice. Investigationes Linguisticae **41**, 86–104 (2018)

Mercier, H., Sperber, D.: Why do humans reason? Arguments for an argumentative theory. Behav. Brain Sci. **34**, 57–111 (2011)

Merin, A.: Information, relevance and social decision-making. In: Moss, L., Ginzburg, J., de Rijke, M. (eds.) Logic, Language, and Computation, vol. 2, pp. 179–221. CSLI Publications, Stanford (1999)

Moeschler, J., Reboul, A.: Dictionnaire encyclopédique de pragmatique. Seuil, Paris (1994)

Pfeifer, N., Kleiter, G.D.: Inference in conditional probability logic. Kybernetika **42**, 391–404 (2006)

Phillips, S.H.: Nyāya. In: Bilimoria, P. (ed.) History of Indian Philosophy. Routledge History of World Philosophies, pp. 175–183. Routledge, London and New York (2018). Chap. 17

Roberts, C.: Information structure in discourse: towards an integrated formal theory of pragmatics. In: Yoon, J.H., Kathol, A. (eds.) OSU Working Papers in Linguistics, Volume 49: Papers in Semantics, pp. 91–136 (1996)

de Saussure, F.: Cours de linguistique générale. Payot, Paris (1916). (réimpr. 1995)

Simons, M., Beaver, D., Roberts, C., Tonhauser, J.: The best question: explaining the projection behavior of factives. Discourse Process. **54**(3), 187–206 (2016)

Simons, M., Tonhauser, J., Beaver, D., Roberts, C.: What projects and why. In: Proceedings of Semantics and Linguistic Theory (SALT) 2010, pp. 309–327. CLC Publications (2010)

Sperber, D., et al.: Epistemic vigilance. Mind Lang. **25**(4), 359–393 (2010)

Stalnaker, R.C.: Assertion. In: Cole, P. (ed.) Pragmatics, Syntax and Semantics, vol. 9, pp. 315–322. New York Academic Press, New York (1978)

Winterstein, G.: "Only" without its scales. Sprache und Datenverarbeitung **35–36**, 29–47 (2012)

Winterstein, G.: Argumentative Semantics – Meaning with a Purpose. Oxford University Press (2024). Under contract

Winterstein, G., Schaden, G.: Relevance and utility in an argumentative framework: an application to the accommodation of discourse topics. In: Lecomte, A., Tronçon, S. (eds.) Ludics, Dialogue and Interaction. LNCS (LNAI), vol. 6505, pp. 134–146. Springer, Heidelberg (2011). https://doi.org/10.1007/978-3-642-19211-1_8

Zeevat, H., Winterstein, G.: Minimal Bayesian pragmatics. In: Oxford Handbook of the Philosophy of Linguistics. Oxford University Press (to appear)

Zenker, F. (ed.): Bayesian Argumentation. The Practical Side of Probability. Springer, Dordrecht (2013). https://doi.org/10.1007/978-94-007-5357-0

Zimmermann, M.: Discourse particles. In: Portner, P., Maienborn, C., Heusinger, K.V. (eds.) Semantics: An International Handbook of Natural Language Meaning, vol. 2, pp. 2012–2038. De Gruyter Mouton, Berlin (2011)

Perspective and the Self in Experiential Attitude Reports

Kristina Liefke[✉️][iD]

Ruhr-Universität Bochum, Universitätsstraße 150, 44780 Bochum, Germany
kristina.liefke@ruhr-uni-bochum.de
https://www.ruhr-uni-bochum.de/phil-inf/

Abstract. It is often assumed that self-directedness (i.e. *de se*-ness) and first-person perspective (1pp) can be jointly captured through individual centers (s.t. 1pp- and *de se*-contents both take the form of *centered propositions*, or properties). This assumption is challenged by instances of 'outside' (i.e. *objective*, or *observer*) remembering and imagining, which intuitively combine *de se* with a third-person [= non-actual/non-original, possibly unoccupied] perspective. My paper answers this challenge: It argues that perspective can be captured through a classical propositional account of attitudes that identifies experiential attitude content with a set of situations. Individual centers are only required to account for the *de se*-status of these attitudes. The separation of modelling mechanisms for perspectivity and *de se*-ness also enables an account of an inverse phenomenon to outside imagining, viz. first-person perspectival non-*de se* imagining.

Keywords: Attitudes *de se* · Experiential attitudes · Perspective · Imagining · Remembering · 'inside'/'outside'-ambiguity

1 Background

A whole industry in semantics and the philosophy of language has argued for the existence of *de se* content (see, e.g., [6,14,23,39,45]). This work typically starts from scenarios like the one below (based on [43]'s 'campaign watching'-example) in which an attitudinal agent fails to recognize themself [9,42].

Scenario (SINGING). The department is hosting their annual anonymous singing contest. John really wants to win; Mary wants someone else to win. (She hates the attention.) To identify the winner, all members listen to all

I thank my LENLS 20 reviewers for valuable comments and suggestions. The paper originates from discussions on imaginative perspective with Justin D'Ambrosio and Louis Rouillé. It has profited from comments by Nikola Andonovski, Alastair Butler, Patrick Elliott, Hana Filip, Jan Köpping, James Openshaw, Dolf Rami, Emil Eva Rosina, André Sant'Anna, Markus Werning, Simon Wimmer, and Yichi Zhang. Earlier versions of this paper were presented at the Cologne-Bochum Memory Workshop (April 2023) and at the SoPhA Early-Career Conference (Grenoble, July 2023).

D. Bekki et al. (Eds.): LENLS 2023, LNCS 14569, pp. 17–36, 2024.
https://doi.org/10.1007/978-3-031-60878-0_2

recordings. Upon hearing 'her' recording, Mary is impressed, thinking "I want this person to win." John is underwhelmed with the singer in 'his' recording, thinking "I do <u>not</u> want him to win."

In this scenario, neither John nor Mary self-identify with the singer in their respective recording. As a result, they each have a different relation to the content 'I want to win' (which is true of John, but false of Mary; see the a-cases below) than they have to the content 'I want the person in the recording to win' (which is false of John, but true of Mary; see the b-cases below).

(1)   a. John wants to win the contest.   (**T**)
       b. John wants {himself, the singer [= John]} to win the contest.   (**F**)
(2)   a. Mary wants to win the contest.   (**F**)
       b. Mary wants {herself, the singer [= Mary]} to win the contest.   (**T**)

In an intuitive sense, the a-cases in (1) and (2) differ from the b-cases in that, in the a-cases, the attitudinal agent self-ascribes the content [23] – they are aware that the content of the attitude is essentially about themself. The contents in (1a) and (2a) are thus self-locating [6, 45], self-directed, or *de se*.

Following Lewis [23] (see [9]), the difference between self-locating contents like (1a)/(2a) and non-self-locating contents like (1b)/(2b) is typically captured by analyzing the former as properties or, equivalently, as *centered propositions* (see the interpretation of (2a) in (3a)). Centered propositions differ from classical propositions (e.g. (3b)) in assuming that their content is dependent on an additional parameter besides the world parameter (w), viz. on an individual parameter (x) (called the *individual center*).[1] In virtue of this parameter, centered propositions are analyzed as sets of centered worlds. The members of such sets are individual-world pairs $\langle x, w \rangle$, where x is the individual center of w [40, 48].

(3)   a. $[\![\text{want}]\!](\{\langle x, w \rangle : x \text{ wins the contest in } w\})(\text{Mary})$ $\left(= [\![(2a)]\!]\right)$
       b. $[\![\text{want}]\!](\{w : \text{Mary wins the contest in } w\})(\text{Mary})$ $\left(= [\![(2b)]\!]\right)$

On the classical, Chierchia-inspired [9] account of self-locating attitude reports (see also [34, 42, 43, 48]), the 'centered proposition'-analysis in (3a) is forced by the obligatory *de se*-interpretation of the silent pronoun PRO in the analysis of (2a) (see (4)). Since (2b) contains a reflexive pronoun (or definite description) instead of PRO, its analysis uses classical, non-centered propositions (see (3b)).

(4)   [Mary wants PRO to win the contest]
       $= [\![\text{want}]\!](\lambda x_1. \{w : \text{PRO}_1 \text{ wins the contest in } w\})(\text{Mary}) \;=\; (3\text{a})$

---

[1] Classical propositions can also be represented as sets of individual/world-pairs (see the representation of (3b) in $(\star)$). I will return to such representations in Sect. 4.

$(\star)$ $[\![\text{want}]\!](\{\langle x, w \rangle : \text{Mary wins the contest in } w\})(\text{Mary})$

Historically, self-locating contents have been studied for bouletic attitudes like desire (see (2a), (5)) and for doxastic attitudes like belief/thought (see (6a), based on [19, pp. 533,537(fn. 64)], and (6b)). In (6a, b), the emphatic reflexive *he himself* has a similar effect to PRO in (2a) and (5) [7,9,18] (but see [42]).

(5)   John wants PRO to become a doctor.   ([9, p. 23])

(6)   a. Pavarotti believes that he himself has pants on fire.   ([9, p. 7])

       b. Mad Heimson believes that he himself is Hume.   ([23, p. 525])

Much recent work has extended the study of self-locating content to other attitudes – most prominently, to representational counterfactual attitudes like imagining and dreaming (see [2,31,39,42,44]) and to mnemic attitudes like episodic remembering (see [18,24,29,49]). These attitudes are special in that they allow *de se*-content to be reported both through the emphatic reflexive *he himself* (e.g. in (7a); similar to (6a)), through non-emphatic *himself* (e.g. in (8b)), and through PRO (in (8a); similar to (5)/(2a)). These pronouns are used with finite and, respectively, with gerundive (or infinitival)[2] occurrences of the verb *imagine*. Finite complements are selected by propositional uses of *imagine*, which relate the imaginer to a(n informationally poor) proposition or possibility (see (7)). Gerundive complements are selected by experiential uses of *imagine*, which relate the imaginer to a(n informationally rich) situation, event, or scene [3,18,25,49] (see (8)). In what follows, I will mark experiential uses of verbs like *imagine* through a subscript 'EXP'. Propositional uses will be marked through subscript 'PROP'.[3] I will hereafter focus on experiential attitude reports – in particular, on the two experiential imagination reports in (8).

(7)   a. Zeno imagines$_{\text{PROP}}$ that he himself is swimming in the ocean. (*de se*)
       b. Zeno imagines$_{\text{PROP}}$ that he is swimming in the ocean.   (both)

(8)   a. Zeno imagines$_{\text{EXP}}$ PRO swimming in the ocean.   (*de se*)
       b. Zeno imagines$_{\text{EXP}}$ himself swimming in the ocean.   (*de se*)

Like their bouletic counterparts (see (2a, b)), the imagination reports in (8a) and (8b) have different truth-conditions. Thus, while (8a) is intuitively only true in the EXPERIENCER-scenario below, (8b) is most obviously true in the ONLOOKER-scenario. The two scenarios are inspired by Vendler [50, p. 161].

---

[2] Some languages (e.g. German) allow experiential attitudes to be reported through a PRO-infinitival – rather than a gerundive – construction (see (†b)). They thus share the grammatical structure of their bouletic counterparts (see (†a); compare (2a)).

(†)   a. Zeno wünscht sich, PRO im Ozean zu schwimmen.
           Zeno wish-3SG.REFL PRO in-the ocean to swim-INF.
           'Zeno wants PRO to swim in the ocean.'

       b. Zeno stellt sich vor, PRO im Ozean zu schwimmen. [imagine-3SG.REFL PRO]
           'Zeno imagines PRO swimming in the ocean.'

[3] I will leave open the question whether these different uses are the result of verbal polysemy, of the (type of) semantic value of the complement, or of other factors.

Scenario (EXPERIENCER). Zeno is looking down upon the ocean from a cliff. He imagines what it would feel like to be swimming in the water: he imagines the cold, the salty taste of the water, the tug of the current, ...

Scenario (ONLOOKER). Zeno is looking down upon the ocean from a cliff. He is imagining what he / his swimming in the water would look like (to a person watching from the cliff): he imagines his scrawny body being tossed about, bobbing up and down in the foamy waste ...

In contrast to what is assumed for (2a) and (2b), the truth-conditional difference between (8a) and (8b) does not lie in the agent's failing to recognize themself. (Zeno could felicitously describe the content of either of the two scenarios by stating 'I am swimming in the ocean'.) Even in the ONLOOKER-scenario, Zeno is very much aware that it is himself whom he visualizes (see [3, 51]). The difference between these two scenarios lies rather in the perspective from which Zeno's swimming is experienced. While this perspective is the swimmer's perspective [= a 'subjective' [50] or field perspective] in the EXPERIENCER-scenario, it is the onlooker's perspective [= an 'objective' [50] or observer perspective] in the ONLOOKER-scenario (which distinguishes the perspective-taker from the experiencer/Zeno). In philosophy and psychology, these two perspectives are often described as 'first-personal' (1pp) and 'third-personal' (3pp), respectively. The two scenarios exemplify what, following Williams [52] and Peacocke [41], has been called 'imagining from the inside' and 'imagining from the outside' (see [11, 29, 38, 50]).

That (8a) receives an 'inside' reading has led some researchers to assume that, in reports like (8a), PRO simultaneously denotes the *de se*-center and the origin of the (visual, proprioceptive, emotional, or other) perspective. This assumption is captured in the common description of PRO as referring to the *perspectival* (!) *center* (see, e.g., [4, 8, 10, 20]). Based on this assumption, some researchers have even called *de se* content 'perspectival content' (cases including [14, 21, 30]). The association of PRO with the original viewpoint of the experiencer is supported by the observation that (8a) is intuitively equivalent to the overtly first person-perspectival report in (9). Since the modifier *from his own swimmer's perspective* in (9) duplicates the 1pp contribution of PRO, (9) is even slightly marked:

(9)   [(?)]Zeno imagines PRO swimming in the ocean *from his own (proprioceptive / swimmer's) perspective.*

The association of PRO with 1pp is explicit in the below passage from [49, p. 150]:

> [...] for ['John remembered feeding the cat'] to be true, John must be aware that it is his own self that is doing the feeding in his memory. But beyond being obligatorily <u>de se</u>, [it is] also obligatorily interpreted as involving imagining or remembering from the inside in the sense of Vendler [50] [...]. That is, the mental image John builds up must be from the sensory perspective of the person doing the feeding; it is not sufficient that John be able to identify this individual as his <u>de se</u> counterpart.

To capture the simultaneous first-person perspectival and *de se*-interpretation of PRO, much work on experiential attitudes identifies the 1pp perspective-taker with the *de se* center. Modulo a different interpretation of the attitude verb [26, 49],[4] (8a) then receives a fully analogous semantics to (2a) (in (10)):

(10) $[\![\text{imagine}_{\text{EXP}}]\!](\{\langle x, w \rangle : x \text{ swims in the ocean in } w\})(\text{Zeno}) \qquad (= [\![(8a)]\!])$

My paper argues that this 1pp-with-*de se* identification is a mistake. It locates the source of this mistake in the possibility of 'outside' (or observer) imagining: since observer imagining is still *de se*, its analysis along the lines of (10) would ignore the intuitive difference between 'outside' and 'inside' imagining (see above). Its alternative analysis as (11a) or (11b) would fail to capture either the self-locating or the experiential nature of the attitude (and, would hence, equate (8b) with an experiential version of (3b) or, respectively, with (7a)).

(11)   a. $[\![\text{imagine}_{\text{EXP}}]\!](\{w : \text{Zeno swims} \dots \text{in } w\})(\text{Zeno}) \ \ (\text{s.} \ [\![(7b)]\!])$
       b. $[\![\text{imagine}_{\text{PROP}}]\!](\{\langle x, w \rangle : \text{Zeno swims} \dots \text{in } w\})(\text{Zeno}) \qquad (= [\![(7a)]\!])$

This paper seeks to give an adequate semantics for imagining from the outside (as well as for related attitudes like observer remembering and dreaming about oneself) that avoids these problems. To achieve this, it proposes separate mechanisms for the modelling of *de se*- and perspectival centers that combine in the analysis of 'inside' imagining. Since these mechanisms can be independently manipulated, they enable an adequate analysis both of 'outside' imagining and of first-person perspectival, but non-*de se*, attitudes like (12) (due to [12, p. 223]).

(12)   Justin is imagining what Sally's getting home late is like to Sally's mother.

The paper is structured as follows: To support my argument against the identification of perspectival with *de se*-centers, I first describe the phenomenon of outside imagining (and remembering) and its challenges for familiar accounts of self-locating attitudes (in Sect. 2). I then develop my 'two mechanisms'-account of this phenomenon. My account assumes that perspectivity cannot be captured through reference to *de se*-centers, but requires a different modelling mechanism (familiar from picture semantics [1, 32]). Section 3 spells out this mechanism. Section 4 explains how this mechanism can be combined with the common tool for modelling self-locating contents, i.e. *de se*-individual centers. It shows that this combination gives rise to a fully compositional semantics for experiential attitude reports that accounts for the intuitive difference between (8a) and (8b). The paper closes by suggesting how this semantics can be used to account for 1pp non-*de se* attitudes like (12) and for imagining being someone else [52] (in Sect. 5).

---

[4] This difference is due to the experiential nature of the interpreted attitude verb.

2   The Challenge from Observer Experiences

When we visually perceive an event, the perspective (or 'viewpoint') from which we see this event is prescribed by our spatiotemporal location: I cannot – at least not at the original time, with my own eyes – perceive an event from a viewpoint other than my own. Experiential imagination, vivid dreaming, and episodic memory differ from visual perception in allowing us to sever the link between the perspective-taker and the experiencer. They enable a (*perspectival*) *displacement* [12, 25] of the original or actual viewpoint to a different perspective, possibly even in a different modality (see (14)) [33, 37, 46]. In imagination and dreaming, such displacement is made possible by the counterfactual nature of these attitudes. In virtue of this nature, the attitudinal agent can take any viewpoint whatsoever, including an unoccupied or impossible viewpoint (see (13)). In Anand's example (13b), this viewpoint is a cross-sectional perspective through the different layers of snow and air. In (13a), it is a (surreal) perspective on the apocalypse.

(13)   a. Ede imagines (watching) the world ending.   (see [53, p. 440])
        b. Mary imagines being buried, unconscious, under a pile of snow inches
            away from the rescue team.   [3, p. 4]

In episodic remembering (as reported by, e.g., (14)), perspectival displacement is owed to the empirical fact that the viewpoint of the original experience need not be preserved during recall [18, 33, 37, 46]. This is illustrated by Chris McCarroll's [33] autobiographical PACKING-scenario below. This scenario portrays Chris' packing from a (hovering) onlooker's perspective. This is possible although Chris originally experienced this packing – and associated emotions – himself (see the second sentence in the description of this scenario). In (14), the difference between the inside and the outside perspective on Chris' packing is reflected in the use of different embedded subjects (viz. PRO vs. *himself*) and of perception verbs (i.e. *feel* vs. *look*).

> **Scenario** (PACKING). "Here is [a] memory from my recent past: My partner, Paloma, and I are packing all our things [. . .]. We are leaving Cardiff [. . .] to fly to Sydney so that I can start my PhD. [. . .] I can see us in the remembered scene, as if from a position near the ceiling, Paloma energetically packing, me looking more than a bit bewildered."   [33, p. 2]

(14)   a. Chris experienced PRO feeling more than a bit bewildered.
        b. Chris remembers himself looking more than a bit bewildered.

An analogous example to the above can be construed for the *remember*-counterpart of (8b) (in (15)):

(15)   a. Zeno experienced PRO swimming in the ocean.
        b. Zeno remembers$_{\text{EXP}}$ himself swimming in the ocean.

As was suggested in my original discussion of (8a/b), the experiential attitudes that are reported through (8b) and (13b)–(15b) are still *de se*. This is apparent from the fact that only (15b) entails Zeno's self-identification with the swimmer in this scenario (see (16b)), i.e. Zeno's identification with "someone who has the same body that he *de se* knows he has" [3, p. 4]. It is in this respect that (15b) differs from (16a) (which does not entail (16b)).

(16)   a. Zeno remembers a man (who looked like him) swimming in the ocean.
  $\not\Rightarrow$ b. Zeno is aware that he is visualizing *himself* swimming in the ocean.

At the same time – as might already be apparent from the absence of PRO –, (8b) and (13b)–(15b) all have a salient 'outside' reading. This reading is reinforced by the observation that (14b) and (8b)/(15b) only hesitantly allow modification with a 1pp viewpoint adjunct (see the markedness of (17a)), but are very natural with a 3pp viewpoint adjunct (see the acceptability of (17b)).

(17)   a. $^{??}$Zeno {remembers, imagines} himself swimming in the ocean *from his own (proprioceptive/swimmer's) perspective.*   (vs. (9))

    b. Zeno {remembers, imagines} himself swimming in the ocean *from the (visual) perspective of someone up on the cliff.*

The modification in (17b) supports Walton's [51, p. 31] claim that "[i]magining *de se* is not always imagining from the inside [...]". However, much of the little existing work on experiential attitudes makes just the converse assumption. Thus, Stephenson [49] defines centered situations [= spatiotemporal parts of centered worlds] as "a situation experienced from the perspective of one of the individuals in that situation" (p. 151). She builds this definition into her semantics for experiential *imagine* through the following assumption (adapted from [49, p. 153] to comply with my earlier notational conventions):

(18) $[\![\text{imagine}_{\text{EXP}}]\!](\{\langle x, s\rangle : x \ldots \text{ in } s\})(z)$ iff
    (i) z forms a mental image of s as if by directly witnessing it, and
    (ii) z's imagined experience of s is from the perspective of x

But this goes against Walton's observations and my findings above.

    To enable an adequate interpretation of 'outside' imagining and remembering, I propose to separate the modelling of perspectivity from the modelling of *de se*-ness. Specifically, I assume that individual centers are only required to model *de se*-ness. The agent's adoption of a particular (i.e. original/actual or displaced) perspective can be modelled through classical (i.e. non-centered) propositions, analyzed as sets of possible worlds/situations. In virtue of my analysis, perspectival contents are compatible with propositionalism – the view that all semantic information contents are propositional (see [28]). To prepare my claim (detailed below) that perspectival content is, however, typically richer than the lexical content of the attitude complement, I precede my propositionalist treatment of perspectivity with a description of the intuitive objects of experiential attitudes.

3 Capturing Perspectivity

At a pre-theoretical level, the objects of experiential imagining and episodic remembering are not propositions, but situations, events, or scenes [16, 18, 49]. The latter are entities that may be located at a specific space and/or point in time, and that can serve as the truth- (or false-) makers of propositions. The scene-status of these objects is supported by the possibility of substituting the *-ing* construction in (8a) by an overtly situation- or event-denoting expression (see (19a)).

(19)   a. Zeno imagines *a situation/event in which he himself is* swimming . . .
       b. Zeno imagines *(the fact) that he himself* swam/was swimming . . .

Intuitively, the complement in (19a) carries much richer information than the proposition 'I swam': If this proposition were the only content of Zeno's imagining, his attitude would likely be reported through (19b), rather than (8a)/(19a).

The greater richness of the complement in (8a)/(19a) is supported by the observation that reports of experiential imagining can make explicit reference to (actual or displaced) perspective (see (9)/(20)), where perspective is commonly associated with situations (Barwise's [5] *scenes*), rather than with propositions.

(20)   Zeno imagines himself swimming *from the perspective of a fellow swimmer/from the point of view of an aquaphobiac/from up on a cliff.*

Recent work has shown that scenes[5] like the ones above have a propositional representation (intuitively: the sum of all propositions that are true of this scene; see Liefke [27]). D'Ambrosio and Stoljar [12] obtain such propositions as an answer to a concealed question of the form 'What is the scene like [to the salient experiencer]?'. For the visual scene depicted in Fig. 1a/b,[6] both approaches yield the same complex proposition, viz. (21):

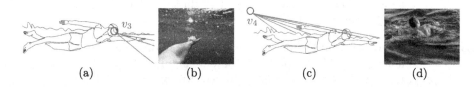

Fig. 1. 1pp (a) and 3pp swimming (b). (Color figure online)

(21)   'in a body of bubbly teal-blue water, a man's right arm with two bracelets is stretched forward, his hand is/appears smaller than his upper arm . . .'

---

[5] Unlike Barwise [5], I do not assume that scenes are restricted to the visual modality. They can also take some other (perceptual or sympathetic) perspective (see [35]).

[6] Source: Cristian Palmer. Sept. 20, 2022. https://unsplash.com/photos/RaOKzBt N8fI.

The representation in (21) is propositional as desired. However, as is suggested by the continuation '...' in (21), the scene's informational richness yields unwieldily complex propositions. Since it is further difficult to describe a scene's inherent perspectivity from a given mode of experience (e.g. vision – although this can be done by linguistic means; see the reference to proportional size in (21)), we propose to enhance our representation with tools from picture semantics (see [1,32]).

Picture semantics distinguishes a situation[7] (i.e. a small spatio-temporal part of some possible world w) from the viewpoint v from which this situation is perceived. In its simplest form, the difference between situation and viewpoint is exemplified by Fig. 2 (adapted from [15, pp. 246–248]): Subfigures 2a and 2c share the same situation (viz. a minimal situation that consists only of a (particular) Rubik's cube, ▓ , located in a white space). They differ w.r.t. the viewpoint (represented by a red circle) from which this situation/the cube is perceived (or 'projected'). In Fig. 2a, this viewpoint is straight in front of the cube (as illustrated in Fig. 2b). In Fig. 2c, the viewpoint is in front above of the top right corner of the cube (see Fig. 2d). Analogous observations hold for the situation and viewpoint in Figs. 1a and 1c (see Fig. 1b resp. 1d).

Fig. 2. Different perspectives on a Rubik's cube, based on [15]. (Color figure online)

Expectedly, the situation itself (incl. the cube, its location, and its properties) does not vary with the viewpoint from which it is perceived. However, this viewpoint has an effect on the situation's representation and representational content. This content is determined relative to the viewpoint (which determines the *perspective* of the content) and a projection function π (which collapses the situation into a two-dimensional picture plane). This function takes a world w and a viewpoint v and returns a picture p (i.e. $\pi(w, v) = p$; see (22)). It has contextually set parameters for, e.g., perspective type, edge-to-line-conversion type, and colors [32]. For the present purposes, I assume that π is linear, s.t. it represents objects that are further away from the viewpoint by smaller regions on the picture plane (analogously to visual perception; see [15, p. 239]). I will intermittently ignore any other projection parameters. For input ▓ (below: the situation w) and viewpoint v_2 (see Fig. 2c), it produces the grey picture in Fig. 2d.

---

[7] Picture semantics uses the term 'scene' instead of situation. My choice of the term 'situation' avoids ambiguating 'scene' between perspectival (see [5]) and non-perspectival world-parts (see [15]) and is in line with the established terminology from [22].

(22) $\pi(\ \blacksquare\ , v_2) =$

The above enables a definition of accuracy for pictures [15]. According to this definition, a picture accurately represents (a part of) a possible world w iff there is a viewpoint v in w from which w 'looks like' the picture [32] (see [15] for a sophisticated version of this definition). For ease of exposition, I treat accuracy as a binary notion, where '1' means accurate and '0' not accurate. $[\![\,\cdot\,]\!]$ is a function that evaluates a picture's accuracy relative to a world and viewpoint (see (23)).

(23) $\left[\!\left[\ \blacksquare\ \right]\!\right]^{v,w} = 1$ iff $\pi(w, v) =$

From (23), the picture's representational content is obtained by existentially quantifying over viewpoints and abstracting over worlds [32, p. 2]. The content of a picture is then the set of possible worlds/situations relative to which the picture is true from some viewpoint (see (24)).

(24) $\left[\!\left[\ \blacksquare\ \right]\!\right] = \left\{ w : \exists v.\ \left[\!\left[\ \blacksquare\ \right]\!\right]^{v,w} = 1 \right\}$

The above considerations are directly applicable to the two projections (or 'pictures') from Fig. 1. According to these considerations, the difference between these pictures lies in the fact that they present the same event (there: Zeno's swimming) from two different viewpoints, viz. Zeno's own eyes (v_3) and a likely unoccupied geometrical space ca. seven feet above behind of swimming Zeno (v_4). The pictures in Fig. 2 are then the values of a projection function π for a particular 'Zeno swimming' event and the viewpoint v_3 (see (25a)) resp. v_4 (see (25b)).

(25)   a. $\pi(w, v_3) =$ b. $\pi(w, v_4) =$

The content of the two 'Zeno swimming' pictures is given in (26) and (27):

(26) $\left[\!\left[\ \blacksquare\ \right]\!\right] = \left\{ w : \exists v.\ \begin{array}{l}\text{from } v, \text{ a swimmer's left arm is stretched out} \\ \text{in a large body of bubbly teal-blue water in } w, \\ \text{the left hand is smaller than the arm in } w, \ldots \end{array} \right\}$

(27) $\left[\!\left[\ \blacksquare\ \right]\!\right] = \left\{ w : \exists v.\ \begin{array}{l}\text{from } v, \text{ a swimmer's left arm is stretched out} \\ \text{in a large body of bubbly teal-blue water in } w, \\ \text{the left hand is smaller than the arm in } w, \ldots \end{array} \right\}$

Since they depict the same event, (26) and (27) share some of their content (e.g. that someone is swimming in a large body of teal-blue water, that their left arm is stretched out). However, the different viewpoints on this event also effect some significant differences. Thus, only (27) – but not (26) – contains information about the color and style of the swimmer's hair, the tan on his back, etc.

Note that, on the above account, the representational contents of pictures are just classical propositions. However, their explicit reference to a viewpoint carries substantial merit. This merit comes out in reports with overtly perspectival content (e.g. 'his left hand is [or better: appears] smaller than his upper arm'; see (26)): only by reference to the viewpoint v can we account for the fact that, in the depicted situation itself, the swimmer's hand is <u>not</u> smaller than his arm. The distortion in the picture is the product of a specific viewpoint and the particular adopted perspectival projection. In Figs. 1a and 1c, this projection is linear. The viewpoint is that of the swimmer himself – more specifically: of his eyes. It assumes that the swimmer's eyes are looking straight ahead and that his radius of vision is 60°. In virtue of this observation, (26) (which uses specifically perspectival content) is equivalent to (28) (which combines non-perspectival content with the specification of a particular viewpoint). Identifying the viewpoint thus obviates the supplementation of perspectival content.

(28) $\{w : \exists x.\, x$ swims in w & $\exists v.\, \boldsymbol{v} = \boldsymbol{x}$('s eyes, with a straight gaze & radius 60°) and, from v, x's left arm is stretched out underwater in $w\}$

Identifying v with the swimmer's eyes (see the boldfaced '$v = x$') captures the 1pp nature of (28) (and, likewise, of (12)). Dissociating v from x (see '$v \neq x$') captures the 3pp nature of (27). The underspecification of the relation between the viewpoint and the agent (s.t. either $v = x$ or $v \neq x$, as in (29)) underlies Vendler's inside/outside ambiguity (captured in (30)).

(29) $\{w : \exists x.\, x$ swims in w & $\exists v.\, \boldsymbol{v} \neq \boldsymbol{x}$, where v is ca. 7 ft above behind of x, and, from v, x's left arm is stretched out underwater in $w\}$

(30) $\{w : \exists x.\, x$ swims & $\exists v.$ from v, x's left arm is stretched underwater in $w\}$

The above examples all assume a <u>visual</u> perspective on the depicted situation, which adopts a linear visual projection function. This is explicit in the identification of v with the swimmer's eyes in (28). It is implicit in the mention of visually perceivable properties (e.g. color: teal-blue, brown; direction: left; shape: large, stretched out) in the restrictor of (30). The visual nature of the viewpoint in Figs. 1b/d is supported by the fact that (8a) (which admits (28) as its semantic complement) allows specification with a 1pp <u>visual</u> viewpoint adjunct (see (31a)).

(31) a. Zeno imagines a man swimming *from that man's own visual perspective*.

(≡ b. Zeno imagines *what a man swimming <u>looks</u> like to that man*.)

Contrary to what is suggested by my examples above, the mode of experience (or, more formally: the different projection parameters) are not tied to the visual modality. This is already apparent from (8a), which has a more intuitive specification in terms of proprioception and kinesthesia (see, e.g., [11,35,49,50]):

(32) a. Zeno imagines a man swimming *from that man's own <u>proprioceptive-kinesthetic</u> perspective*.

(≡ b. Z. imagines *what a man swimming <u>(physically) feels like for that man</u>*.)

It is also apparent from the possibility of introducing an explicit emotional or agentive perspective (8b) (see (33)), and of combining the contents that are produced by different such viewpoints (see [33, 36, 37]).

(33)   Zeno imagines a man swimming in the ocean *from the emotional perspective of someone up on a cliff.*

Since the above distinguishes the imaginer (in (12)/(34a): Justin) both from the agent in the imagined scenario (in (12): Sally) and the perspective-taker (i.e. Sally's mother), it provides a sensible account of reports like (12) (see (34b)):

(34)   a.   Justin is imagining what Sally's getting home late is like to Sally's mother.

   b. $[\![\text{imagine}_{\text{EXP}}]\!](\{w : \exists v. \, v$ is Sally's mother and, from v, Sally gets home late in $w\})(\text{Justin})$

The above notwithstanding, reference to the perspective-taker alone does not (yet) provide a satisfactory account of 'outside' imagining and remembering. I will solve this problem below.

4   *De se*-ness and Outside Imagining

I have pointed out above that my account of perspectival contents still interprets the gerundive complements of *imagine* as classical propositions (see (26)–(30)). As a result, they are still unable to capture the difference between (9) [= 1pp, *de se*] and (35) [= 1pp, NON-*de se*].

(35)   Zeno imagines {i. Zeno, ii. a man (who looks like Zeno)} swimming *from that man's perspective.*

To compensate for this shortcoming, I supplement perspectival contents of the form $\{w : \exists v. \ldots\}$ with individual centers, x. This supplementation proceeds by replacing possible worlds w by centered worlds [= sets of ordered world-individual pairs, $\langle w, x \rangle$][8] in representations like (26)–(30) and by letting the variable for the referent of the embedded subject (in (28)–(30): x) be bound by the abstractor over the individual center. The semantics for (9) that is obtained by using this approach is given in (36a).

(36)   a. $[\![\text{imagine}]\!](\{\langle w, \boldsymbol{x} \rangle : \exists v. \text{ from } v. \, \boldsymbol{x} \text{ swims in } w\})(\text{Zeno})$ (*de se*)

   b. $[\![\text{imagine}]\!](\{\langle w, \boldsymbol{x} \rangle : \exists v. \text{ from } v. \text{ a man swims in } w\})(\text{Z.})$ (non-*de se*)

To provide a uniform account of *de se*- and non-*de se* contents (that interprets both contents as centered propositions), this semantics uses Egan's [13] notion of 'boring' centered propositions. The latter are centered proposition-type representations of classical propositions whose content does not vary with the individual

---

[8] These pairs are equivalent (up to coding) to the individual-world pairs from Sect. 1. I use 'world first'-pairs since they are the output of my compositional semantics below.

center (i.e. $\forall x \forall y \forall w. p^*(w,x) \leftrightarrow p^*(w,y)$, where p^* is a centered proposition). Boring centered propositions feature in the interpretation of (35-ii) (in (36b)).

The difference between (36a) and (36b) is an experiential counterpart of the distinction between *wants* PRO *to win* and *wants herself to win* in (2) (for their familiar semantics, see (3)/(11b)). However, for our purposes, the interesting difference lies in the distinction between the (now adequately modelled) experiential (8a)/(8b) and their non-experiential (and, hence, non-perspectival) – but still *de se* – counterpart (7a). Traditional accounts of *de se* attitudes, which treat experiential attitudes as propositional attitudes and identify perspectival with *de se* centers, are unable to capture this distinction. My semantics for (8a), (8b), and (7a), which preserves these distinctions, is given below:

(37)   a. $[\![(8a)]\!] = [\![$Zeno imagines PRO swimming in the ocean$]\!]$ (1pp, *de se*)
       $= [\![$imagine$]\!](\{\langle w, \boldsymbol{x}\rangle : \exists v. \, \boldsymbol{v} = \boldsymbol{x} \, \& \text{ from } v, \, \boldsymbol{x} \text{ swims in } w\})(\text{Zeno})$
       $\equiv [\![$imagine$]\!](\{\langle w, \boldsymbol{x}\rangle : \text{from } \boldsymbol{x}, \, \boldsymbol{x} \text{ swims in } w\})(\text{Zeno})$

       b. $[\![(8b)]\!] = [\![$Z. imagines himself [/his body] swimming $\dots]\!]$ (3pp, *de se*)
       $= [\![$imagine$]\!](\{\langle w, \boldsymbol{x}\rangle : \exists v. \, \boldsymbol{v} \neq \boldsymbol{x} \, \& \text{ from } v, \, \boldsymbol{x} \text{ swims in } w\})(\text{Zeno})$

       c. $[\![(7a)]\!] = [\![$Zeno imagines that he himself swims in the ocean$]\!]$
       $= [\![$imagine$]\!](\{\langle w, \boldsymbol{x}\rangle : \boldsymbol{x} \text{ swims in } w\})(\text{Zeno})$ (non-perspectival *de se*)

Notably, the interpretations in (37a) and (37b) differ only with respect to whether the viewpoint is identified with the *de se*-center. (The latter is the case in the semantics of (8a), but not of (8b).) To make such identification possible, I treat viewpoints as a special kind of (type-*e*) individuals, i.e. as perspective-takers. Perspective-takers differ from concrete particulars like Zeno and me in that they can be non-actual [= not exist in the actual world] and, thus, abstract: viewpoints can be accidentally unoccupied (as in (17b) and the PACKING-scenario). They can even be structurally unoccupied (as in (13)). In view of the latter, some viewpoints are physically impossible.

Since my semantics for the non-experiential report (19b) (in (37c)) does not make reference to a viewpoint, it makes an identification of the viewpoint with the *de se*-center irrelevant. Observe that, since the report in (37a) is 1pp, it obviates the introduction of a separate viewpoint (that is different from the embedded subject, x). The same holds for intuitively non-*de se* 1pp reports like (38a), in which the attitude holder 'walks in someone else's shoes':

(38)   a. Justin is imagining the battle from the perspective of the poor sod on the front line.   [12, p. 223]

       b. $[\![$imagine$]\!](\{\langle w, x\rangle : \exists y. \, y \text{ is a poor sod on the front line } \&$
                           $\text{from } y, \text{ there is a battle in } w\})(\text{Justin})$

My semantics for experiential attitude reports has assumed that the complements in these reports have a largely analogous interpretation to the complements of *de se* propositional attitudes, viz. as centered propositions. To show which syntactic and morphological constituents contribute which semantic elements (e.g. the viewpoint, the individual center, their (non-)identification), I give a compositional semantics for the complements of the reports in (37). For simplicity, this semantics neglects the prepositional phrase *in the ocean*. It adopts the entry for *swim* in (39a). It assumes that gerundive *-ing* introduces eventive entities and, therewith, perspectivity. Specifically, the semantic value of *-ing* applies to the extensional semantic value, ϑ, of a TP (i.e. a truth-value) to yield the set of viewpoints v from which ϑ is true (see (39b)).

(39) a. $[\![\text{swim}]\!] = \lambda w. \{x : x \text{ swims in } w\}$
      b. $[\![\text{-ing}]\!] = \lambda \vartheta^t. \{v : \text{from } v, \vartheta\}$
      c. $[\![\text{PRO}_1]\!] = [\![\text{he}_1]\!] = x_1$

(40) $[\![\text{-self}_1]\!] = [\![\text{-self}]\!]([\![\text{he}_1]\!]) = \{v : v = x_1.\top\}$

In line with Chierchia's [9] established account of *de se*-reports, I assume that PRO/PRO$_1$ introduces an unbound variable, x_1, that is later bound by a lambda abstractor (yielding a construction of the form '$\lambda_1 [\ldots [\text{PRO}_1]\!]$'). In classical propositional *de re*-reports like (2a), which add another lambda abstractor over the

$[\![\lambda_0 [\lambda_1 [\exists\text{-closure} [\text{ID}_1 [\text{-ing} [\text{PRO}_1 \text{ swim-in-}w_0]]]]]]\!] : \langle s, \langle e, t \rangle \rangle$
$\{\langle w, x \rangle : \text{from } x, x \text{ swims in } w\}$

$\lambda_0 \quad [\![\lambda_1 [\exists\text{-closure} [\text{ID}_1 [\text{-ing} [\text{PRO}_1 \text{ swim-in-}w_0]]]]]\!] : \langle e, t \rangle$
$\{x : \exists v. v = x \ \& \ \text{from } v, x \text{ swims in } w_0\} \ (\{x : \text{from } x, x \text{ swims in } w_0\})$

$\lambda_1 \quad [\![\exists\text{-closure} [\text{ID}_1 [\text{-ing} [\text{PRO}_1 \text{ swim-in-}w_0]]]]\!] : t$
$\exists v. v = x_1 \ \& \ \text{from } v, x_1 \text{ swims in } w_0$

$[\exists\text{-closure}] : \langle \langle e, t \rangle, t \rangle \quad [\![\text{ID}_1 [\text{-ing} [\text{PRO}_1 \text{ swim-in-}w_0]]]\!] : \langle e, t \rangle$
$\lambda P \exists v. P(v) \quad \{v : v = x_1 \ \& \ \text{from } v, x_1 \text{ swims in } w_0\}$

$\text{ID}_1 \quad [\![\text{-ing} [\text{PRO}_1 \text{ swim-in-}w_0]]\!] : \langle e, t \rangle$
$\{v : v = x_1\} \quad \{v : \text{from } v, x_1 \text{ swims in } w_0\}$

$[\![\text{-ing}]\!] : \langle t, \langle e, t \rangle \rangle \quad [\![\text{PRO}_1 \text{ swim-in-}w_0]\!] : t$
$\lambda \vartheta. \{v : \text{from } v, \vartheta\} \quad x_1 \text{ swims in } w_0$

$[\![\text{PRO}_1]\!] : e \quad [\![\text{swim-in-}w_0]\!] : \langle e, t \rangle$
$x_1 \quad \{x : x \text{ swims in } w_0\}$

$w_0 : s \quad [\![\text{swim}]\!] : \langle s, \langle e, t \rangle \rangle$
$\lambda w. \{x : x \text{ swims in } w\}$

Fig. 3. Compositional semantics of the complement in (8a).

world w_0, this binding straightforwardly yields the desired semantic complement (i.e. a centered proposition; see (4)). The situation is more complicated for experiential attitude reports like (8a). This is so since the gerundive -*ing* in their complement converts the term in the scope of λ_1 (in (2a): '[PRO to win]', interpreted 'x_1 wins in w_0', type t) into a term for a set of viewpoints (type $\langle e, t \rangle$; see the semantics for '[-ing [PRO$_1$ swim-in-w_0]]' in Fig. 3). Binding the free occurrence of x_1 in this term would ultimately yield a semantic complement of type $\langle s, \langle e, \langle e, t \rangle \rangle \rangle$. While this goes against my claim that all experiential attitude complements can be interpreted as centered propositions, the bigger problem is that the resulting semantics for 'λ_1[-ing [PRO$_1$ swim-in-w_0]]' (i.e. $\{\langle x, v \rangle$: from v, x swims in $w_0\}$) would still not identify v with x, contra (37a).

To answer this challenge, I complement the lambda operator that binds x_1 in (4) by the characteristic function, ID$_1$, of the set $\{v : v = x_1\}$. ID$_1$ combines with the semantic value of '[-ing [PRO$_1$ swim-in-w_0]]', i.e. $\{v :$ from v, x_1 swims in $w_0\}$, through Heim and Kratzer's [17] rule of Predicate Modification (here analyzed as set intersection). From the result of this combination, we obtain the semantic complement in (37a) through existential quantification over v (see Sect. 3) and abstraction over x_1 (see above).

In the full compositional semantics for the complement of (8a) (in Fig. 3), the complex construction 'λ_1 [∃-closure [ID$_1$ [... [PRO$_1$ ...]]]]' might initially look undermotivated. However, the late (i.e. higher-up) binding of 'v' (which is also witnessed in the semantics for (8b), see Fig. 4) enables an easy compositional processing of locative modifiers like *from above* (see (41)) and of viewpoint adjuncts like *from the (visual) perspective of someone up on the cliff* (see (17b)).

(41)   Zeno is imagining a man swimming *from above*.   [12, ex. (1)]

I have noted in my discussion of (8b) [*imagines himself swimming*] that this report saliently receives an outside (i.e. 3pp, *de se*) interpretation (see (37b) and Fig. 4). To compositionally obtain this interpretation, I combine the semantics for *swim* and gerundive -*ing* from (39) with the entry for *he$_1$* from (39c) and the entry for -*self* in (40). To distinguish the viewpoint from the *de se*-center in (8b)/(37b), the semantics in (40) treats the identification of v with x_1 as a presupposition. (This differs from ID$_1$, where this identification is asserted.) In reports like (8b), the availability of a stronger alternative to $[\![$-self$_1]\!]$, viz. $[\![$ID$_1]\!]$, then cancels this presupposition. The full compositional semantics is given in Fig. 4.

Importantly, the semantics for -*self* from (40) can also be used in the interpretation of the complement of propositional *de se*-reports like (37c). Expectedly – like the complement in its experiential counterparts –, the complement of this report is interpreted as a centered proposition. However, in contrast to (8a)/(8b), the TP in (37c) is finite (or progressive, but not gerundive). Hence, it does not introduce a perspectival proposition (of the form '$\{v :$ from v, x_1 swims in $w_0\}$'), but a parametrized truth-value (of the form 'x_1 swims in w_0'). As a result, it does not require that the argument, v, in the semantics of *himself* be interpreted as a viewpoint. This explains the non-perspectivity of propositional [= non-experiential] *de se*-attitude reports. The compositional semantics for the complement of (37c) is given in Fig. 5.

$[\![\lambda_0\,[\lambda_1\,[\exists\text{-closure}\,[\text{-self}_1\,[\text{-ing}\,[\text{he}_1\,\text{swim-in-}s_0]]]]]]\!] : \langle s, \langle e, t\rangle\rangle$
$\big\{\langle w, x\rangle : \exists v.\,\underline{v = x}.\ \text{from } v,\ x \text{ swims in } w\big\}$

$\lambda_0\quad [\![\lambda_1\,[\exists\text{-closure}\,[\text{-self}_1\,[\text{-ing}\,[\text{he}_1\,\text{swim-in-}w_0]]]]]\!] : \langle e, t\rangle$
$\{x : \exists v.\,\underline{v = x}.\ \text{from } v,\ x \text{ swims in } w_0\}$

$\lambda_1\qquad [\![\exists\text{-closure}\,[\text{-self}_1\,[\text{-ing}\,[\text{he}_1\,\text{swim-in-}w_0]]]]\!] : t$
$\exists v.\,\underline{v = x_1}.\ \text{from } v,\ x_1 \text{ swims in } w_0$

$[\![\exists\text{-closure}]\!] : \langle\langle e, t\rangle, t\rangle\qquad [\![\text{-self}_1\,[\text{-ing}\,[\text{he}_1\,\text{swim-in-}w_0]]]\!] : \langle e, t\rangle$
$\lambda P\exists v.\,P(v)\qquad\qquad \{v : \underline{v = x_1}.\ \text{from } v,\ x_1 \text{ swims in } w_0\}$

$[\![\text{-self}_1]\!]\qquad [\![\text{-ing}\,[\text{he}_1\,\text{swim-in-}w_0]]\!] : \langle e, t\rangle$
$\{v : \underline{v = x_1}.\top\}\quad \{v : \text{from } v,\ x_1 \text{ swims in } w_0\}$
$\cdots\quad\cdots$

Fig. 4. Compositional semantics of the complement in (8b).

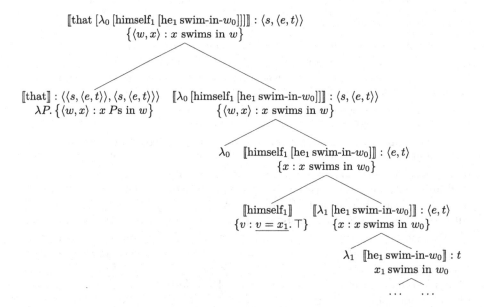

$[\![\text{that}\,[\lambda_0\,[\text{himself}_1\,[\text{he}_1\,\text{swim-in-}w_0]]]]\!] : \langle s, \langle e, t\rangle\rangle$
$\big\{\langle w, x\rangle : x \text{ swims in } w\big\}$

$[\![\text{that}]\!] : \langle\langle s, \langle e, t\rangle\rangle, \langle s, \langle e, t\rangle\rangle\rangle\quad [\![\lambda_0\,[\text{himself}_1\,[\text{he}_1\,\text{swim-in-}w_0]]]\!] : \langle s, \langle e, t\rangle\rangle$
$\lambda P.\,\big\{\langle w, x\rangle : x\,Ps \text{ in } w\big\}\qquad\quad \big\{\langle w, x\rangle : x \text{ swims in } w\big\}$

$\lambda_0\quad [\![\text{himself}_1\,[\text{he}_1\,\text{swim-in-}w_0]]\!] : \langle e, t\rangle$
$\{x : x \text{ swims in } w_0\}$

$[\![\text{himself}_1]\!]\qquad [\![\lambda_1\,[\text{he}_1\,\text{swim-in-}w_0]]\!] : \langle e, t\rangle$
$\{v : \underline{v = x_1}.\top\}\qquad \{x : x \text{ swims in } w_0\}$

$\lambda_1\quad [\![\text{he}_1\,\text{swim-in-}w_0]\!] : t$
$x_1 \text{ swims in } w_0$
$\cdots\quad\cdots$

Fig. 5. Compositional semantics of the complement in (7a).

5   Conclusion

In this paper, I have provided a semantics for experiential attitudes that accounts for cases of 'outside' imagining and remembering. To achieve this, my semantics uses individual centers only to account for *de se*-ness, but not for first person perspectivity (unlike [49]). (First- and third-person) Perspective are modelled by using tools from picture semantics [1, 15, 32] (esp. the introduction of existentially quantified viewpoints from which the world 'looks like' the picture). These tools enable the representation of perspectival content as classical propositional contents (albeit with greater informational richness). The combination of these tools enables us to distinguish between a rich taxonomy of *de se*-attitudes, including 'inside' imagining (1pp, *de se*), 'outside' imagining (3pp, *de se*), propositional non-perspectival *de se* imagining, and propositional non-*de se* imagining.

My previous discussion of this taxonomy has excluded instances of perspectival non-*de se* imagining, in which the imaginer takes a (first-person) perspective on an imaginary scene without recognizing themself in this scene (possibly because they are not an individual in this scene). An example of such perspectival, non-*de se* imagining is given in (38a) (copied in (42a)). In this example, Justin's imagined scene is *as if he himself were standing on the front line*. However, contrary to what is suggested by the emphatic reflexive in this description, Justin's imagining in (38a) is <u>not</u> self-locating. The semantics in (36b) (in particular, its equivalence to the classical proposition in (42b)) supports this observation:

(42)   a.   Justin is imagining the battle from the perspective of the poor sod on the front line.   [12, p. 223]

b. $\{w : \exists y.\, y$ is a poor sod on the ... & from y, there's a battle in $w\}$

In a pre-theoretical sense, 'bare' [= non-*de se*] perspectival contents like the one in (42b) resemble the contents of imagining being someone else (e.g. (43a); due to [52]). In imaginings like (43a), the imaginer (there: Louis) intuitively does not self-identify – not even in a pretense-kind of way – with Napoleon. Rather, he simply takes Napoleon's first-person perspective. (This is similar to the situation in Spike Jonze's (1999) movie *Being John Malkovich*, where a portal "takes you inside John Malkovitch. You see the world through John Malkovich's eyes".[9]) To capture such first person perspective-taking, my semantics still identifies the viewpoint with the individual center (s.t. the content of Louis' imagining in (43a) is an 'interesting' [= non-boring] centered proposition). However, this is only necessary to attribute Napoleon's own eyes- (1pp-) perspective on the battle of Waterloo to Louis. The impression of non-*de se*-ness then arises from the fact that Louis (and, hence, x) does not directly feature as an agent in the imagined scene, contra what is the case in (37a).

---

[9] I owe this analogy to Louis Rouillé (see [47]).

(43) a. Louis imagines PRO being Napoleon (looking out on Waterloo).

  b. $\{\langle w, x \rangle : \exists v.v = x \ \& \ \text{from } v, \ x \text{ is Napoleon looking at Waterloo in } w\}$
   $\equiv \{\langle w, x \rangle : x = \text{Napoleon} \ \& \ \text{from } x, \text{ Napol. is looking at Waterloo in } w\}$

Admittedly, my account of perspective and *de se* in imagining being someone else is still in need of much further development. Future work will moreover have to explain how semantic complements like the ones above interact with experiential uses of *imagine* (as well as of *remember*). It will also have to provide a more detailed semantic account of the distinction between 'ordinary' and emphatic reflexives (i.e. *himself* vs. *he himself*). I am convinced that these efforts will contribute to the development of a sophisticated account of imagining and remembering that combines insights from formal semantics, philosophy, and psychology.

Acknowledgements. The research for this paper is supported by the German Research Foundation DFG (as part of the research unit FOR 2812: *Constructing Scenarios of the Past*; grant 397530566) and by the German Federal Ministry of Education and Research [BMBF] through Kristina Liefke's WISNA professorship.

References

1. Abusch, D.: Possible worlds semantics for pictures. In: Matthewson, L., Meier, C., Rullmann, H., Zimmermann, T.E. (eds.) The Companion to Semantics. Wiley, Oxford (2020)
2. Anand, P.: Dream report pronouns, local binding, and attitudes *de se*. In: Semantics and Linguistic Theory (SALT), vol. 17, pp. 1–18 (2007)
3. Anand, P.: Suppositional projects and subjectivity. Ms (2011). https://web.eecs.umich.edu/~rthomaso/lpw11/anand.pdf
4. Anand, P., Toosarvandani, M.: Narrative and point of view. In: Altshuler, D. (ed.) Linguistics Meets Philosophy, pp. 176–214. Oxford University Press, Oxford (2022)
5. Barwise, J.: Scenes and other situations. J. Philos. **78**, 369–97 (1981)
6. Castañeda, H.N.: *He*: a study in the logic of self-consciousness. Ratio **8**, 130–157 (1966)
7. Castañeda, H.N.: On the logic of attributions of self-knowledge to others. J. Philos. **54**, 439–456 (1968)
8. Charnavel, I.: Logophoricity, perspective, and reflexives. Ann. Rev. Linguist. **7**, 131–155 (2021)
9. Chierchia, G.: Anaphora and attitudes *de se*. Semant. Contextual Expr. **11**, 1–31 (1989)
10. Coppock, E., Wechsler, S.: The proper treatment of egophoricity in Kathmandu Newari. In: Expressing the Self, pp. 40–57, Oxford University Press (2018)
11. D'Ambrosio, J., Stoljar, D.: Vendler's puzzle about imagination. Synthese **199**, 12923–12944 (2021)
12. D'Ambrosio, J., Stoljar, D.: Imagination, fiction, and perspectival displacement. In: Oxford Studies in Philosophy of Mind, pp. 219–240, Oxford University Press (2023)
13. Egan, A.: Secondary qualities and self-location. Philos. Phenomenol. Res. **72**(1), 97–119 (2006)

14. Garcia-Carpintero, M.: The SELF file and immunity to error through misidentification. Disputatio **5**(36), 191–206 (2013)
15. Greenberg, G.: Beyond resemblance. Philos. Rev. **122**(2), 215–287 (2013)
16. Grimm, S., McNally, L.: The *-ing* dynasty. In: Semantics and Linguistic Theory (SALT), vol. 25, pp. 82–102 (2015)
17. Heim, I., Kratzer, A.: Semantics in Generative Grammar. Blackwell, Oxford (1998)
18. Higginbotham, J.: Remembering, imagining, and the first person. In: Barber, A. (ed.) Epistemology of Language, pp. 496–533. Oxford University Press, Oxford (2003)
19. Kaplan, D.: Demonstratives. In: Almog, J., Perry, J., Wettstein, H. (eds.) Themes from Kaplan, pp. 489–563. Oxford University Press, Oxford (1989)
20. Kaufmann, M.: Who controls who (or what). In: Semantics and Linguistic Theory (SALT), vol. 29, pp. 636–664 (2019)
21. Kölbel, M.: Objectivity and perspectival content. Erkenntnis **87**, 137–159 (2022)
22. Kratzer, A.: Facts: particulars or information units? Linguist. Philos. **5–6**(25), 655–670 (2002)
23. Lewis, D.: Attitudes *de dicto* and *de se*. Philos. Rev. **88**(4), 513–543 (1979)
24. Liefke, K.: Modelling selectional super-flexibility. In: Semantics and Linguistic Theory (SALT), vol. 31, pp. 324–344 (2021)
25. Liefke, K.: Experiential attitude reports. Philos Compass **18**(6), e12913 (2023)
26. Liefke, K.: Two kinds of English non-manner *how*-clauses. In: Non-Interrogative Subordinate Wh-Clauses, pp. 24–62, Oxford University Press, Oxford (2023)
27. Liefke, K.: Experiential attitudes are propositional. Erkenntnis **89**, 293–317 (2024)
28. Liefke, K.: Intensionality and propositionalism. Ann. Rev. Linguist. **10**, 4.1–4.21 (2024)
29. Liefke, K., Werning, M.: Experiential imagination and the inside/outside-distinction. In: Okazaki, N., Yada, K., Satoh, K., Mineshima, K. (eds.) JSAI-isAI 2020. LNCS (LNAI), vol. 12758, pp. 96–112. Springer, Cham (2021). https://doi.org/10.1007/978-3-030-79942-7_7
30. Ludlow, P.: Interperspectival Content. Oxford University Press, Oxford and New York (2019)
31. Maier, E.: Parasitic attitudes. Linguist. Philos. **38**, 205–36 (2015)
32. Maier, E., Bimpikou, S.: Shifting perspectives in pictorial narratives. In: Proceedings of Sinn und Bedeutung 23 (2019)
33. McCarroll, C.: Remembering from the Outside. Oxford University Press, Oxford (2018)
34. Morgan, J.: On the criterion of identity for noun phrase deletion. In: Papers from the Sixth Regional Meeting of the Chicago Linguistic Society, pp. 380–389. CLS, Chicago (1970)
35. Nagel, T.: What is it like to be a bat? Philos. Rev. **83**(4), 435–450 (1974)
36. Nanay, B.: Multimodal mental imagery. Cortex **105**, 125–134 (2018)
37. Nigro, G., Neisser, U.: Point of view in personal memories. Cogn. Psychol. **15**(4), 467–482 (1983)
38. Ninan, D.: Imagination, inside and out. Ms (2007). https://tinyurl.com/umvuh3p
39. Ninan, D.: Imagination, content, and the self. Ph.D. thesis, MIT (2008)
40. Ninan, D.: *De se* attitudes: ascription and communication. Philos Compass **5**(7), 551–567 (2010)
41. Peacocke, C.: Imagination, experience, and possibility: a Berkeleian view defended, pp. 19–35, Clarendon Press, Oxford (1983)
42. Pearson, H.: Counterfactual *de se*. Semant. Pragmatics **11**, 2-EA (2018)

43. Percus, O., Sauerland, U.: On the LFs of attitude reports. In: Proceedings of Sinn und Bedeutung, vol. 7, pp. 228–242 (2003)

44. Percus, O., Sauerland, U.: Pronoun movement in dream reports. In: Proceedings from the North East Linguistics Society (NELS), vol. 33, pp. 265–284 (2003)

45. Perry, J.: The problem of the essential indexical. Noûs **13**(1), 3–21 (1979)

46. Rice, H.J., Rubin, D.C.: I can see it both ways: first- and third-person visual perspectives at retrieval. Conscious. Cogn. **18**(4), 877–890 (2009)

47. Rouille, L.: How much of your self do you need to imagine being someone else? Topoi 1–11 (2024).https://doi.org/10.1007/s11245-023-09992-5

48. Stephenson, T.: Control in centred worlds. J. Semant. **27**, 409–36 (2010)

49. Stephenson, T.: Vivid attitudes: centered situations in the semantics of remember and imagine. In: Semantics and Linguistic Theory (SALT), vol. 20, pp. 147–160 (2010)

50. Vendler, Z.: Vicarious experience. Revue de Métaphysique et de Morale **84**(2), 161–173 (1979)

51. Walton, K.: Mimesis as Make-Believe. Harvard University Press, Cambridge (1990)

52. Williams, B.: Imagination and the self. In: Problems of the Self: Philosophical Papers 1956–1972, pp. 26–45. Cambridge University Press, Cambridge (1973)

53. Zimmermann, T.E.: Painting and opacity. In: Freitag, W., Hans, R., Sturm, H., Zinke, A. (eds.) Von Rang und Namen: Philosophical essays in honour of Wolfgang Spohn, pp. 427–453. Brill/Mentis (2016)

Negation and Information Structure in Tree-Wrapping Grammar

Kata Balogh[(✉)]

Heinrich-Heine-Universität Düsseldorf, Düsseldorf, Germany
balogh@hhu.de
http://user.phil.hhu.de/balogh

Abstract. In this paper, we introduce a proposal towards a formal grammatical model that captures different types of negation uniformly, in terms of pragmatic structuring. The central objective of the paper is the analysis of the relation between focusing and negation, modeling both 'focus negation' and 'sentential negation'. We propose a modular grammatical model, with separate but interrelated representations for syntax, semantics and information structure. We argue for a two-level analysis of negation, such that next to semantics it operates at the level of information structure. The main concern of the paper is the formal grammatical modeling of the IS-level, where negation targets the communicative function determined by the given focus structure.

Keywords: focus negation · information structure · formal grammar modeling · formalized RRG

1 Introduction

1.1 'Types' of Negation

Dating back to the earliest discussions on negation (Aristotle, the Stoic School, [15,21]), two major 'types' are generally distinguished, which reflect the intuition that the negation operator can have a different scope: wide or narrow. In current literature, wide scope negation is often referred to as *sentential* (or *propositional*) *negation*, and the narrow scope negation as *constituent negation*.[1] While the former notion is used in a rather uniform way across languages, the use of the latter is less consistent. Nevertheless, all its uses reflect the intuition that in *constituent negation* the negation operator scopes over a single constituent instead of the whole sentence. This constituent is generally considered the narrow focus of the sentence (1), and the construction is often referred to as *focus negation*.

(1)   a.   Sam didn't kiss [JO]^F in Osaka.

b.   Sam didn't kiss Jo [in OSAKA]^F.

---

[1] Under the latter type, also affixal negation (e.g., *unhappy*) and inherent negation (e.g., *deny*) are often understood. Although they share the property of having a narrow scope, we assume that affixal and inherent negation represent different types.

D. Bekki et al. (Eds.): LENLS 2023, LNCS 14569, pp. 37–54, 2024.
https://doi.org/10.1007/978-3-031-60878-0_3

In compositional analyses, maintaining a logical semantics, the scope of the operator is the semantic content of the expression that stands in a given structural relation with it. In 'traditional' approaches to the syntax-semantics interface this relation is often captured within the LF, and in terms of c-command. For sentential negation this leads to the insertion of the logical operator above the predicate, which straightforwardly captures the core semantic contribution of negation: changing the polarity/truth-conditions of the sentence. In truth-conditional terms, however, sentences with focus negation are true under the same conditions as their corresponding sentential negation constructions. The circumstances that make example (1a) true are the same as the ones that make *Sam didn't kiss Jo in Osaka* true. This indicates that the function and contribution of natural language negation reaches beyond the (logical) semantics of the sentence.

1.2   Focus and Negation

The difference between the assumed types of *sentential negation* and *focus negation* should be captured with reference to the focus structure of the sentence and the focus sensitivity of negation. It is widely accepted that the interpretation of a range of linguistic expressions is dependent on the information structure (IS) of the utterances in which they occur [4,22,23]. This observation holds across languages and the phenomenon is often referred to as *focus sensitivity*. The discussion usually concentrates on focus sensitive particles, such as *only, also, even*, the focus sensitivity of negation has been considerably much less investigated. Only few studies deal explicitly with the issue of the focus sensitivity of negation, of which the approach by Beaver and Clark [4] is the most elaborate one.

Beaver and Clark [4] take a pragmatic view on focusing based on the Question Under Discussion (QUD) approach [30], where the focus of the utterance indicates the current question (CQ). Their theory applies to a wider range of constructions (including negation, quantificational adverbs, focus sensitive particles etc.), and they seek to answer the question whether all these cases of focus sensitivity are due to a uniform mechanism, and whether or not they are conventionalized (i.e., lexically encoded). They argue that there are multiple mechanisms at work, and propose a model, involving three distinct processes. The three types of association with focus have in common that they relate to the QUD-structure and are used to establish a coherent discourse. Negation is claimed to manifest 'Quasi Association' with focus, where the relation of the operator and the focus leads to a pragmatic implicature.

Capturing the difference between sentential negation and focus negation, Beaver and Clark point out that a negative sentence with a narrow focus gives rise to a special inference. This inference is derived by the underlying CQ, which is determined by the respective focus structure. To take a simple example, in *Sam did not kiss [JO]^F*, the CQ is the corresponding (positive) *wh*-question: *Whom did Sam kiss?* This CQ is derived by arguments regarding the possible prosodic patterns of the sentence with 'focus negation' together with the prosodic characteristics of complete versus partial answers. Taking the Hamblin-semantics of questions as a set of propositions [13], the CQ gives rise to the existential inference that *Sam kissed someone*. Together with the fact that *Sam did not kiss [JO]^F* entails that *Sam did not kiss Jo*, the inference that *Sam kissed someone different from Jo* is derived.

(2) a. focus marking $\leadsto$ $[\![CQ]\!]$ = { p | p = Sam kissed x }

  b. $[\![CQ]\!]$ $\leadsto$ $\exists x.kiss(sam, x)$

  c. (1a) $\models$ $\neg kiss(sam, jo)$

  d. b. and c. $\leadsto$ $\exists x.x \neq jo \land kiss(sam, x)$

Beaver and Clark [4] capture the interpretational effect of narrow focus and negation within pragmatics, in terms of the inference raised. Their approach is elegant and well-grounded, and it is in line with our argument that a more elaborate analysis of natural language negation should be given beyond semantics. We elaborate on this essential argument, and target additional issues from the perspective of formal grammars. We address the main question: What does natural language negation target?, and the sub-questions: How negation relates to the communicative function and whether the same mechanisms are at work in narrow and broad focus structures?

The main objective of this paper is the formal modeling of the relation between the focus structure of the sentence and the negative particle. We introduce our proposal towards a formal grammatical model that accesses the focus structure and its corresponding communicative function. We begin with the application to *focus negation*, that extends to *sentential negation* in a uniform way. The paper is structured as follows. Section 2 provides a brief introduction to the relation between focusing and negation in terms of pragmatic structuring. Section 3 forms the core of the paper with a short introduction to the theoretical framework (Sect. 3.1), followed by the proposal of the formal grammar that captures the information structural contribution of negation (Sects. 3.2 and 3.3). Section 4 briefly introduces some further applications of the proposal and Sect. 5 concludes the paper.

2 Natural Language Negation and Pragmatic Structuring

We argue for the cross-linguistic validity of the claim that negation generally has a direct access to the focus structure of the utterance [35], and it operates on the contribution by focusing in terms of communicative functions. This includes both narrow and broad focus structures. Building upon the work of Vallduví [34], we propose a two-level approach, where negation operates both at the level of semantics and at the level of information structure. Vallduví argues that at the semantic level, the negation operator in both sentential and focus negation have the same scope in the logico-semantic interpretation. In the information structure component, he proposes a focus/assertion operator, that determines the asserted content. At this level the sentences differ, as negation within information structure targets the focus operator. While building upon the essence of Vallduví's approach, we differ in its implementation. We propose a grammatical model of an essentially cognitive linguistic perspective, within the formal specification of the linguistic theory of Role and Reference Grammar (RRG) [35, 36] and Lambrecht's theory of information structure [24].

Lambrecht introduces a pragmatic approach to information structure [24]. He proposes that the contribution of focusing should be captured beyond semantics, in terms of *pragmatic structuring* into a 'pragmatic presupposition' and a 'pragmatic assertion'. This structuring reflects the *communicative function*: what information is conveyed and how this information is transferred between the discourse participants. The 'pragmatic presupposition' is the information content that is part of the discourse context shared by the discourse participants and the 'pragmatic assertion' is the newly conveyed information, in relation to the pragmatic presupposition. Importantly, both concepts are lexicogrammatically defined, hence pragmatic structuring is determined by the grammatical organization of the sentence.

Another major notion is *focus structure*, what Lambrecht [24] defines as "*the conventional association of a focus meaning with a sentence form*". He distinguishes three core focus structures based on the domain (i.e., scope) of the focus in the given sentence, and presents the systematic ways natural languages encode these structures in their morphosyntax. The core distinction is given on the basis of whether a single constituent or multiple constituents are included in the focus domain. In this respect, 'narrow focus' and 'broad focus' structures are distinguished. Broad focus is further divided into 'predicate focus', where the focus domain includes all parts except the topic and 'sentence focus', where the focus domain is the entire sentence. The predicate focus construction correlates with the topic-comment distinction, and is referred to as the unmarked focus type. According to Lambrecht, these core focus structures differ in their communicative functions as follows. Sentence focus is associated with introducing an event or a referent, predicate focus provides some information of a given topic and narrow focus signals the identification of an entity with respect to an open proposition. The 'focus' of the sentence is considered as the semantic content of the 'focus domain'. The 'focus' and the 'pragmatic presupposition' stand in a special relation, which is determined as the newly conveyed information, i.e., the 'pragmatic assertion'. Hence, this relation and the 'pragmatic assertion' depends on the focus structure. In a narrow focus construction, the pragmatic assertion is the relation between an open proposition and the content of the focus domain, such as the focus provides the specification of the 'missing' information in the open proposition (3). Lambrecht calls this relation 'identification'.

(3) *Sam kissed $[JO]^F$ in Osaka*
    $\rightsquigarrow$ pragmatic presupposition: 'sam kissed x in osaka' (open proposition)
    $\rightsquigarrow$ focus: content of the noun phrase 'Jo'
    $\rightsquigarrow$ pragmatic assertion: 'x = jo' (identification)

In 'focus negation', like (1a), the negation operator targets this 'identification' relation, which is present as a proposed pragmatic assertion by the focus structure. This is supported by the fact that for a felicitous use of sentences with focus negation the corresponding positive sentence must be at least expected as an attempt to resolve the CQ. The sentence in (1a) targets the underlying issue *Whom did Sam kiss in Osaka?* (which is implicit, indicated here by { CQ }). The statement *Sam kissed JO in Osaka* is at least expected, containing the identification relation that intends to resolve the underlying issue, and this proposed/expected identification is denied ($\sim$) by the negation.

(4) {CQ: $?x.kiss(sam, x)$ (simplified)} $\Rightarrow$ {identification: $(x = jo)$} $\Rightarrow$ denial: $\sim (x = jo)$

In the next section, we turn to the formal grammatical modeling of this analysis. This requires a grammar formalism where the semantic content and the information structural interpretation are represented at distinct, but yet related levels.

3   Formal Modeling

3.1   Role and Reference Grammar

For our two-level analysis of natural language negation, Role and Reference Grammar (RRG) [35,36] provides a theoretical suitable ground. RRG is a cognitively motivated, surface oriented grammar theory, developed from a strong typological and theoretical perspective. The general architecture of RRG (Fig. 1) is modular, with different levels of representation called 'Projections' and well-defined linking between them to model the interfaces. The syntactic representation captures universal notions in terms of predicate-argument relations, as well as language-specific aspects in terms of special syntactic positions. The syntactic representation is given in two closely related projections, the 'Constituent Projection' and the 'Operator Projection'. The semantic representations are based on the classification of predicates by Vendler [37] and adapted from the decompositional system of Dowty [8]. The center of the grammatical model is the bi-directional *linking algorithm* between the syntactic and the semantic representations, capturing both language production and comprehension.

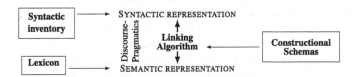

Fig. 1. The general architecture of RRG

Discourse-pragmatics contains the 'Focus Structure Projection', that influences the bi-directional linking in various ways [5,6,35]. Within this projection, RRG distinguishes the *actual focus domain* (AFD), the syntactic domain that corresponds to Lambrecht's *focus domain*, and the *potential focus domain* (PFD), where the focus can occur. Both domains include one or more *information units* (IU), which are the minimal phrasal units in the syntactic representation [24,35]. The AFD-PFD distinction is cross-linguistically relevant. Although in English, the PFD is always the entire clause, this is not generally the case in other languages. For example, in Italian, the PFD excludes any prenuclear elements [5,36], or in Hungarian, the structural topic position is clause-internal, but external to the PFD. The focus domains include one or more IUs, that are linked to syntactic domains in the constituent structure. Figure 2 briefly illustrates the RRG representation of narrow object focus and predicate focus respectively.

This representation shows the IUs, that are linked to syntactic domains in the constituent structure, and the focus domains, that each include one or more IUs. Hereby, it represents the various focus structures, as proposed by Lambrecht [24]. Although RRG's Focus Structure Projection is claimed to capture Lambrecht's theory of information structure, the link between the structural considerations of the various focus domains and the corresponding communicative functions is missing. That aspect is, however, crucial for a comprehensive analysis of negation, and asks for an extension

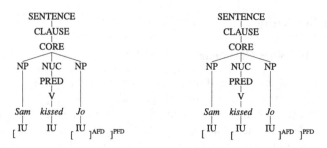

Fig. 2. RRG's Focus Structure Projection

of RRG's model of information structure. The necessary extensions will be introduced together with the formal modeling in the next section.

3.2   Formal Specification of the Grammar

The formal analysis of any linguistic phenomenon requires a two-sided approach: theoretical claims need to be verified by empirically valid and formally exact models, and formal models must be built on solid theoretical grounds. In our proposal, we build upon the theoretical base as discussed in the previous sections. For the formal modeling and the required extensions we use the formalized version of RRG as proposed by Kallmeyer and Osswald [19,27]. This facilitates the necessary two-sided approach. This formal grammar is based the solid theoretical framework of RRG, providing its formal specification in terms of *Tree-Wrapping Grammar* (TWG) [20,27], which is strongly inspired by Tree-Adjoining Grammar [16]. TWG is a tree-rewriting formalism with two basic syntactic composition rules: (wrapping) substitution and sister adjunction (Fig. 3).

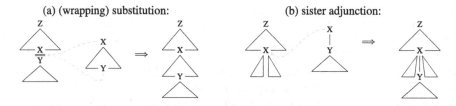

Fig. 3. Syntactic operations in TWG

In our approach, we maintain a cognitive semantic perspective, where meanings are considered mental representations,[2] in terms of *Frame Semantics* in the Düsseldorf-tradition[3] [25,26,28]. Frame Semantics follows the major claim of Barsalou [3] that

---

[2] Being cognitively oriented, our semantic representations reflect the relation between expressions and mental representations, not between expressions and the world in terms of truth conditions. The latter relation can be captured by an additional mapping.

[3] Note that our understanding of a *frame* is different from Fillmore's Frame Semantics program [11] despite the unfortunate coincidence of the names of the two approaches.

frame-representations are the universal format of semantic and conceptual knowledge. This uniform representation format is grounded at the psychological (and neural) levels, providing a cognitively plausible theory of meaning. The model introduced in this paper builds upon the formal characterization of the frame-representation of semantic concepts by Kallmeyer and Osswald [17] and Petersen [28], formally defined as *base-labelled typed feature structures*, see (5), based on [17]. Frame structures (or simply frames) can be represented as graphs or as attribute-value matrices (AVMs). We use the latter representation format. A frame structure is defined given a signature $\langle A, T, B \rangle$ where A is a finite set of *attributes*, T is a finite set of *(ordered) types* and B is a countably infinite set of *base-labels*.

(5) Given $\langle A, T, B \rangle$, a frame structure is defined as a tuple $\langle V, \beta, \tau, \delta \rangle$ where
V is a finite non-empty set of nodes ;
β is a partial function from $B \to V$ (base-labeling function);
τ is a function from $V \to T$ (typing function);
δ is a partial function $V \times A^* \to V$ (node transition function);
such that every node is reachable from a base-labeled node:
$\forall v \in V : \exists v' \in \beta(B) \land \exists p \in A^*$ such that $v = \delta(v', p)$
i. e. for each node v there is another base-labeled node v' and
an attribute path p such that v can be reached from v' via p

The nodes in the syntactic trees are supplemented with feature structures, containing interface features, which establish the link between syntax and semantics. The semantic composition is on a par with the syntactic composition, mediated by index features on the nodes (e.g., $I = e$), which point to parts in the semantic representation. The syntactic operations trigger the composition of the semantic representations, thereby deriving the meaning representation of the sentence. The semantic composition proceeds by unification. See Fig. 4 for an illustration.

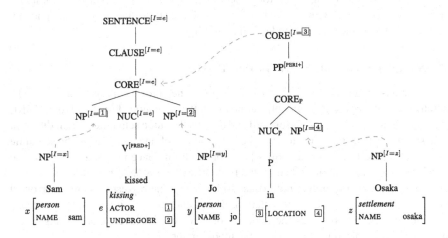

Fig. 4. Derivation in TWG

For the analysis of (1a), Fig. 4 shows the elementary structures: pairs of a tree template and its respective semantic representation. The tree template of the predicate *kissed* has two argument slots for two NPs, represented as substitution nodes. The index features I = ① and I = ② on the NP nodes link their respective semantic content: the trees that will be substituted at these nodes provide the values of the ACTOR and UNDERGOER roles. By combining the tree templates, the feature structures are unified and the values of all index features are identified (e.g., ① = x). The semantic representation of the final tree is calculated by unification of the semantic content of the participating trees, constrained by the syntactic composition (Fig. 5).

Derived semantic representation for (1a) under ① = x, ② = y, ③ = e, ④ = z:

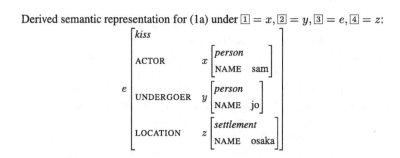

Fig. 5. Derived semantic representation for (1a)

The above example does not contain operators, that are crucial for the analysis of negation. In classical RRG, operators (e.g., negation, tense) are represented in a separate 'Operator Projection', a mirror image of the layers in the syntactic representation. The projection represents that a given element is an operator and which layer of the clause it modifies. The same can be represented without loss of information if we collapse the constituent projection and the operator projection into one tree [18]. The operator nodes are distinguished as OP with a subscript for the operator type, and they are attached by sister adjunction at the node of the layer they modify.

3.3   Negation in Formalized RRG Using TWG

At the syntax-semantics interface, natural language negation is analyzed as a CORE-operator, which targets the semantic content of the syntactic domain of the CORE (Fig. 6a,b). This is rather straightforward and derives the same semantics for all different focus structures (Fig. 6c). Considering the contribution of negation within the semantic representation we follow Jackendoff's [14] approach on conceptual structures. By the use of negation, an event described by the frame (i.e., the scope of negation) is conceptualized as non-existing in the mind (marked by ¬ ⇓). The representation is borrowed from [14]. The exact formal representation of the conceptualization of (non-)existence of events and entities requires the addition of a referential layer. Considering space limits, we cannot introduce that part of the model in the current paper.

While at the level of semantics, the scope of the negation operator is the same for each case, at the level of information structure its contribution varies according

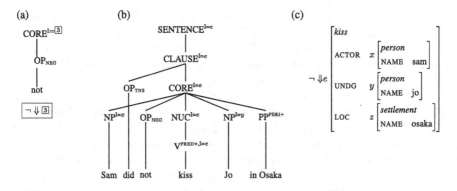

Fig. 6. Negation as a CORE-operator

to the different focus structures. As we argue, negation targets the pragmatic assertion determined by the focus structure of the sentence. Hence, it must be represented
within the 'Information Structure (IS) Projection' as well. The IS Projection is an extension of RRG's Focus Structure Projection, proposed in [1], also representing the topic-
comment division. In order to simplify the representations here, we only give the focus
structure, that is directly relevant to our proposal. The current development of the formalization of RRG in terms of TWG provides a specification of the syntax-semantics
interface, but lacks the modeling of information structure, which asks for an extension
(see also [2]).

In the representation of the IS Projection, the basic components are the *information
units* (IUs) that make up the information contained in the elements of the pragmatic
structuring. Information units correspond to the information content of the syntactic
domains of the nucleus, the core arguments and the adjunct complements in the periphery. The information content of the focus domains are derived by unification of the
semantic representation of their parts. This process respects the composition of syntax
and semantics, and as such it is subject to the same constraints on unification.

$$\begin{array}{llll}
[[[\text{Sam}]_{\text{NP}} & [\text{kissed}]_{\text{NUC}} & [\text{Jo}]_{\text{NP}} & [\text{in Osaka}]_{\text{PP-PERI}}]_{\text{CORE}}]_{\text{CLAUSE}}]_{\text{SENTENCE}} \\
\downarrow & \downarrow & \downarrow & \downarrow
\end{array}$$

$$\left\{ x\begin{bmatrix} person \\ \text{NAME} & \text{sam} \end{bmatrix}, e\begin{bmatrix} kissing \\ \text{ACTOR} & \boxed{1} \\ \text{UNDERGOER} & \boxed{2} \end{bmatrix}, y\begin{bmatrix} person \\ \text{NAME} & \text{jo} \end{bmatrix}, \boxed{0}\begin{bmatrix} \text{LOC} & z\begin{bmatrix} settlement \\ \text{NAME} & \text{osaka} \end{bmatrix} \end{bmatrix} \right\}$$

Fig. 7. Set of information units in (1a)

Information units are not simply pieces obtained by cutting up the derived semantic representation, as they possibly correspond to pieces of information that cannot be
directly pointed at in the derived frame. For example, the information content of the
NUCLEUS or the information content of a periphery PP does not correspond to a node
in the frame-representation. Nevertheless, these units are accessible via the derivation
tree, that uniquely describes the given derivation. The derivation tree contains nodes

for all elementary structures used in the derivation, edges for all syntactic compositions performed, and edge labels indicating the target node of the given syntactic operation. These edge labels are Gorn addresses [12], referring to the nodes in the given target elementary tree (i.e., at which node some other tree is substituted or adjoined). The root node of the tree has address 0 (or ϵ), and the ith daughter of the node with address n has address ni. See, for example, the derivation tree in Fig. 8a, that describes the derivation in Fig. 4. The derivation tree indicates that the trees of *Sam* and *Jo* are substituted to the tree for *kissed* at nodes 111 and 113 respectively, the tree for *in* is adjoined to the tree for *kissed* at node 11 and the tree for *Osaka* is substituted to the tree for *in* at node 112. The derivation tree describes all syntactic operations within a derivation, and furthermore it implicitly includes the respective unifications of the corresponding pieces of semantic contents. The information content of the IUs correspond to the root node of the derivation tree and its non-operator daughter nodes (see Fig. 8b).

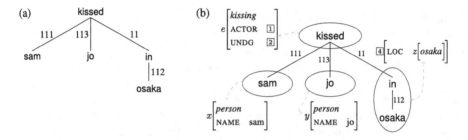

Fig. 8. (a) derivation tree for Fig. 4 and (b) derivation tree and IUs

The set of information units (Fig. 7) is partitioned into two disjoint sets, the actual focus domain and the non-focus domain, representing the given focus structure. Note that this approach has a general advantage as opposed to 'traditional' accounts based on syntactic F-marking. Crucially, the IUs are linked to syntactic domains, but the focus domains are not determined on the nodes of the constituent structure. Therefore, when the (basic) IUs are determined, any combination of them can make up the actual focus domain, and therefore discontinuous or non-constituent focus structures [7] can be captured without problems. The unification (under constraints) of the elements of these subsets correspond to the information content of the 'focus' and the 'pragmatic presupposition' respectively. See Fig. 9.[4]

The pragmatic assertion (i.e., the newly conveyed information) is defined as the relation between the pragmatic presupposition and the focus. In the above example, this relation is the specification of the value of the UNDERGOER argument in the pragmatic presupposition: $\boxed{2} = y$, which corresponds to Lambrecht's 'identification' relation. Within the IS Projection, negation generally targets this relation, the pragmatic assertion. Hence, in 'focus negation' (1), the contribution of negation is the denial of the expressed/proposed 'identification relation'.

---

[4] For a simplification of the frames, from here on we use the following abbreviations:
$$x\begin{bmatrix}person\\name\;\;sam\end{bmatrix} \rightarrow x[sam], \quad y\begin{bmatrix}person\\name\;\;jo\end{bmatrix} \rightarrow y[jo], \quad z\begin{bmatrix}settlement\\name\;\;osaka\end{bmatrix} \rightarrow z[osaka].$$

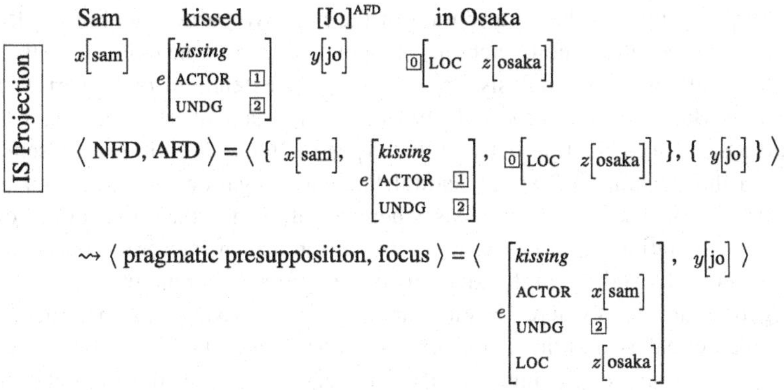

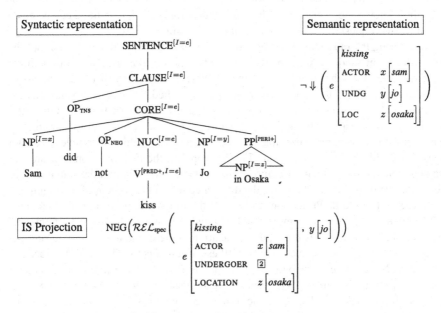

$$\langle \text{NFD, AFD} \rangle = \langle \{ x[\text{sam}], \begin{bmatrix} \textit{kissing} \\ e \begin{bmatrix} \text{ACTOR} & \boxed{1} \\ \text{UNDG} & \boxed{2} \end{bmatrix} \end{bmatrix}, \boxed{0}[\text{LOC} \; z[\text{osaka}]] \}, \{ y[\text{jo}] \} \rangle$$

$$\rightsquigarrow \langle \text{pragmatic presupposition, focus} \rangle = \langle e \begin{bmatrix} \textit{kissing} \\ \text{ACTOR} & x[\text{sam}] \\ \text{UNDG} & \boxed{2} \\ \text{LOC} & z[\text{osaka}] \end{bmatrix}, y[\text{jo}] \rangle$$

Fig. 9. IS Projection with narrow object focus

To put it all together, the formalized RRG analysis (using the TWG formalisms) of the object narrow focus construction, representing the respective projections, is given in Fig. 10. The three projections in the analysis are separate representations, that are nevertheless linked via the values of the interface features. The modules of the semantic representation and the IS Projection together capture the interpretive component of the sentence (in terms of a cognitive/conceptual view on meaning), that are related to each other, as well as to the syntactic structure.

Fig. 10. Negation with object narrow focus

This approach models the contribution of the negative particle within the IS Projection in 'focus negation' constructions: in sentences where negation targets a narrow focus constituent. The analysis straightforwardly extends to other narrow focus constructions. Based on our proposal above, an important question arises, whether we should assume a distinction between the types of 'focus negation' and 'sentential negation' in the general analysis of natural language negation. We argue for a uniform account, that leads to an analysis where negation has the same effect on the semantic representation in all cases, while the difference in interpretation lies in the IS-interpretation, depending on the given focus structure. We argue that cases of 'sentential negation' are cases where negation interacts with a broad focus construction. An important theoretical assumption is that each sentence is assigned a focus structure.

From the functional/communicative perspective, the essential contribution of focusing is providing information. This itself is not novel, a significant amount of linguistic work on focusing relies on this basic insight. What we contribute here is the direct integration of this essentially communicative view into the grammatical organization of natural languages in general. In this vein, the pragmatic assertion directly relates to the communicative function. The pragmatic presupposition is characterized as "the information already known" or "already in the common ground". The other side of the coin is that next to information already known, there is always some yet unspecified (or 'missing') information. Information we communicate is centered around eventualities. This information contains the type of the eventuality, the specification of the participants in that eventuality (i.e., its semantic arguments and optional aspects like location, time etc.). Therefore, while the pragmatic presupposition defines what is known, it also defines what is 'missing', hereby raising an issue. In order to advance or guide the communication, such issues must be resolved. A request for resolving an issue can be made explicit by overt questions, but very often it remains implicit [29,31].

Considering the pragmatic presupposition, we make a major division: (i) either the type of the event (and the roles of its arguments) and the presence of some optional aspects is given and what is missing is the *specification* of either of the arguments or optional aspects, or (ii) the type of the event is unspecified, while participants are possibly specified. The former case is expressed by narrow focus structures, and the latter one corresponds to various broad focus structures. The cases when multiple arguments are unspecified correspond to multiple focus constructions. Within this article we do not discuss these structures. Figure 11 and Fig. 12 represent the IS Projection of sentences with negation and broad focus structures. The syntactic structure and the semantic representation are the same as in Fig. 10, the difference lies in the content of the pragmatic structuring within the IS Projection. In Fig. 11, the pragmatic presupposition contains the information that there is an unspecified eventuality of which the ACTOR argument is specified. The focus provides the type specification of the event, and hereby introduces further semantic arguments, and it specifies these arguments together with the location of the event. Negation relative to this focus structure leads to the IS interpretation that it is not the case that the unspecified event under discussion of which Sam is the ACTOR is 'kissing Jo in Osaka'. In Fig. 12, none of the arguments is specified in the presupposition. Negation in this focus structures leads to the IS interpretation that it is not the case that the unspecified event under discussion is 'Sam kissing Jo in Osaka'.

Sam did not [kiss Jo in Osaka]^{AFD}.

$$\boxed{\text{IS-Projection}} \quad \text{NEG}\left(\mathcal{REL}_{\text{spec}}\left(e\begin{bmatrix} event \\ \text{ACTOR} \quad x\begin{bmatrix} sam \end{bmatrix} \end{bmatrix}, \quad e\begin{bmatrix} kissing \\ \text{ACTOR} \quad x \\ \text{UNDG} \quad y\begin{bmatrix} jo \end{bmatrix} \\ \text{LOC} \quad z\begin{bmatrix} osaka \end{bmatrix} \end{bmatrix}\right)\right)$$

Fig. 11. IS Projection for negation with predicate focus structure

[Sam did not kiss Jo in Osaka]^{AFD}.

$$\boxed{\text{IS-Projection}} \quad \text{NEG}\left(\mathcal{REL}_{\text{spec}}\left(e\begin{bmatrix} event \end{bmatrix}, \quad e\begin{bmatrix} kissing \\ \text{ACTOR} \quad x\begin{bmatrix} sam \end{bmatrix} \\ \text{UNDG} \quad y\begin{bmatrix} jo \end{bmatrix} \\ \text{LOC} \quad z\begin{bmatrix} osaka \end{bmatrix} \end{bmatrix}\right)\right)$$

Fig. 12. IS Projection for negation with sentence focus structure

4   Further Phenomena

The main contribution of the paper is the proposal of a unified account implemented in a formally specified grammar architecture. We have introduced here the basic ideas of the formal grammar modeling of the relation between negation and focusing. Needless to say, there are still essential issues to resolve at all three levels (syntax, semantics and information structure) for a comprehensive analysis of negation at the interfaces. Within the scope and the aims of the current paper, it is not possible to address all these aspects. To sketch further applications of our model, we take the issue of syntactic narrow scope of the negative particle, and the application of the proposed analysis to languages that distinguish narrow and wide scope negation in their morphosyntax.

4.1   Denial and Correction

The above analysis captures the contribution of the English negative particle in its default position, i.e., as a core-operator, that interacts with information structure targeting the pragmatic assertion. This directly leads to the question how to capture negation that is structurally tied to a constituent. For example, in English, next to its default syntactic position there is another one where the negative particle can appear: immediately preceding an argument or adjunct (6).[5]

(6)   a.   Sam kissed not Jo but Alex in Osaka.

    b.   Sam Kissed Jo not in Osaka but in Tokyo.

---

[5] Note that examples with copular constructions as in *All that jokes are not funny* or with negative quantification as in *No student met Kate in Paris* are not considered here.

In this construction, the negative particle has a narrow syntactic scope, directly attached to a constituent. This type of narrow scope negation appears in English in the '*not* XP *but* YP' construction, containing a corrective *but* (see also [33]). Corresponding sentences without '*but* YP' are not grammatical.

(7)   *Sam kissed not Jo in Osaka. / *Sam kissed Jo not in Osaka.

As [33] proposes, the '*not* XP *but* YP' construction forms one constituent in the syntactic structure. The negative particle is attached to the first element of the coordination. For our concerns in this paper the question is what the information structural contribution of this construction is. The core contribution of this special construction is the expression of an explicit denial and correction, which targets the 'identification' relation. However, this construction is more complex as it compresses the discourse process (or strategy of inquiry) in (4) and the corrective utterance into one single construction. In the complex object noun phrase in (6a), the first conjunct contributes the denial, which directly relates to the immediate discourse context, and the second conjunct contributes the correction. The sentence in (6a) is interchangeable with pairs of clauses expressing explicit correction, where the AFD in the second clause contributes the correction. The denial is expressed either within the first clause using a 'focus negation' construction (8a, b), or by *No* marking the relation between the two sentences (8c).

(8)   a.   Sam did not kiss $[JO]^F$ in Osaka, but $[ALEX]^F$.
      b.   Sam did not kiss $[JO]^F$ in Osaka. She kissed $[ALEX]^F$ (there).
      c.   Sam kissed $[JO]^F$ in Osaka. No, she kissed $[ALEX]^F$ (there).

In (8a, 8b), the positive counterpart of the negation in the first clause must be at least expected, which is an attempt to resolve the current question (CQ) (= the underlying QUD), as discussed before in (4). The second clause provides the correction on this proposed/expected identification. Example (8c) is similar, with the difference that the statement *Sam kissed JO in Osaka* is explicit. The denial by *No* at the beginning of the second sentence provides the denial of the identification as before, and the second sentence, with narrow focus, expresses the correction.

(9)   { CQ: $?x.kiss(sam, x)$ (simplified)} $\Rightarrow$ { identification: $(x = jo)$ } $\Rightarrow$
      denial: $\sim (x = jo) \Rightarrow$ correction: $(x = alex)$

All these examples express denial and correction in separate clauses. The construction in (6a) expresses the same meaning components, but using a special complex NP construction. Both conjuncts are considered narrow AFD, but in different statements within the strategy of inquiry. Nevertheless, negation targets the 'identification' relation as proposed for narrow/argument focus structures in general. The ungrammaticality of the sentences in (7) and the special meaning contribution of the '*not* XP *but* YP' construction suggest that plain 'constituent negation' (or syntactic narrow scope negation) expressed by the negative particle *not* in English is not a general strategy, but expresses a constructional meaning.[6]

---

[6] Note that this argument does not include negative quantification, e.g., *No student kissed Jo in Osaka*. These cases represent a different (though not unrelated) phenomenon.

4.2   Negation and Morphosyntactic Restrictions

Considering the issue of syntactically narrow scope negation, the applicability of the proposal to languages where different 'types' of negation are reflected in the morphosyntax should be carefully examined. Take, for example, Hungarian, where the negative particle is linearized in restricted ways. In Hungarian, the negative particle *nem* 'not' can occur in different positions in the surface structure (see also [10]): immediately preceding the verb/predicate (10a) it expresses 'sentential negation', while right before the preverbal focus (10b) it expresses 'focus negation'.[7]

(10)   a.   Samu nem csókolta meg   Kati-t.
          Sam   not   kissed   VPRT Kate-ACC

          'Sam did not kiss Kate.'

    b.   Samu nem Kati-t   csókolta meg.
          Sam   not   Kate-ACC kissed   VPRT

          'Sam did not kiss [KATE]^F. ($\approx$ It was not Kate whom Sam kissed.)

Our proposal is directly applicable to Hungarian. What makes this language special is the way the different focus structures are reflected within the morphosyntax. Hungarian is a discourse configurational language [9,32] with a designated syntactic position for the narrow focus constituent. This 'focus position' is immediately before the verb/predicate (inducing the inverse order of the verb and the verbal particle). Placement to the narrowly focused constituent is obligatory to this position. In Hungarian, the focus structure (i.e., the AFD-NFD division), and therefore the different relations that the negation operator targets in the IS Projection is syntactically marked. This effect of discourse configurationality is captured withint the syntax-IS interface in terms of information structurally driven syntactic positions. This is implemented in the elementary structures, assigning the focal status to designated tree fragments. For the Hungarian preverbal focus the pre-nuclear position (PrNUC) is assumed, which determines that its element is the (single) IU within the AFD. The positional restriction of the Hungarian negative particle is determined at the syntax-IS interface by the linearization constraint that the negative particle must immediately precede the actual focus domain. The way the negation operator works at the level of IS is the same as proposed above.

While the core examples of Hungarian negation nicely support our approach, there is a construction that needs special attention. The two positions of the Hungarian negative particle are distinct syntactic positions, which is supported by the fact that the two negation 'types' can co-occur in one clause (11).

(11)   Samu nem Kati-t   nem csókolta meg.
      Sam   not   Kate-ACC not   kissed   VPRT

      'It was not Kate whom Sam did not kiss.'

---

[7] There is a third possible position for the negation particle in Hungarian, right before the universally quantified NP. This constructions is rather peculiar, and since the characterization of negation in Hungarian is not our concern in this paper, we do not discuss it further.

This double-negative construction raises the question what the appropriate focus structure of such a clause is. In our proposal, negation is directly related to the actual focus domain. This predicts that (11) has two AFDs, which seems inappropriate at first sight. The explanation for two AFDs within one clause relies on their different discourse status: the second negation (preceding the verb) is part of the background. Therefore it is related to a second occurrence predicate focus, which is represented as an AFD at another level within the discourse. The formal modeling of this issue, and many other questions related to our initial proposal are left for further research.

5   Conclusions

In this paper, we started out with the earlier made distinction between 'sentential negation' and 'focus negation', and addressed the question what these types share in their interpretation and how to model them uniformly within a formal grammar. This issue goes beyond the semantics of the sentence, and asks for an approach where information structure, in particular the focus structure, interacts with negation at the syntax-semantics-pragmatics interface. We introduced a two-level analysis of capturing the meaning contribution of natural language negation, following the core proposal of Vallduví [34] that negation contributes both to the semantics and to the information structure of the sentence. We argued for a modular grammar architecture in the analysis of negation, where the syntactic structure, the semantic representation and the information structure are represented in separate levels, with explicit linking between them, modeling the interfaces. We implemented our analysis within the formalized version of Role and Reference Grammar [35,36], formally specified in terms of Tree-Wrapping Grammar [19,20] together with a semantic representation where meanings are taken as conceptualizations (or mental descriptions) of eventualities in terms of decompositional frames [17,25,28].

As the core contribution of the paper, we introduced the formalization of the IS Projection. We argued for a more complex meaning contribution of negation, that, next to its contribution to the semantic representation, also targets the communicative function determined by the given focus structure. The interpretational dimension of the sentence is an interplay between its semantic representation and its information structure: the former given as a decompositional frame and the latter given in terms of pragmatic structuring [24]. We argued that in general, negation has access to and operates on the pragmatic assertion. Our proposal offers a uniform analysis of the contribution of natural language negation within the information structure component of the sentence: it targets the pragmatic assertion, corresponding to the newly conveyed information, which is the relation between the pragmatic presupposition and the focus. Our model formally derives this relation in all basic focus structures by the same process. All backgrounds above contain some unspecified information that is necessary to conceptualize an eventuality (i.e., event-type and core arguments), which is provided by the focus. We build upon the theory of Lambrecht [24], however, we revise his characterization of the communicative functions of the different focus structures. We take the core function of focus being the specification of certain unspecified information in the conceptualization of an eventuality under discussion.

References

1. Balogh, K.: Additive particle uses in Hungarian: a Role and Reference Grammar account. Stud. Lang. **45**(2), 428–469 (2021)
2. Balogh, K., Kallmeyer, L., Osswald, R.: Information structure in formalized RRG. Presented at the 17th International Conference on Role and Reference Grammar, Düsseldorf, Germany, 14–16 August 2023 (2023)
3. Barsalou, L.W.: Frames, concepts, and conceptual fields. In: Lehrer, A., Kittay, E.F. (eds.) Frames, Fields, and Contrasts: New Essays in Semantic and Lexical Organization, pp. 21–74. Lawrence Erlbaum, Hillsdale (1992)
4. Beaver, D.I., Clark, B.Z.: Sense and Sensitivity: How Focus Determines Meaning. (Explorations in Semantics 5). Wiley-Blackwell, Oxford (2008)
5. Bentley, D.: The interplay of focus structure and syntax: evidence from two sister languages. In: Van Valin, Jr., R.D. (ed.) Investigations of the Syntax-Semantics-Pragmatics Interface, pp. 263–284. John Benjamins, Amsterdam (2008)
6. Bentley, D.: The RRG approach to information structure. In: Bentley, D., Mairal Usón, R., Nakamura, W., Van Valin, Jr., R.D. (eds.) The Cambridge Handbook of Role and Reference Grammar, pp. 456–487. Cambridge University Press, Cambridge (2023)
7. Büring, D.: Discontinuous foci and unalternative semantics. Linguistica **56**(1), 67–82 (2016)
8. Dowty, D.: Word Meaning and Montague Grammar. Reidel, Dordrecht (1979)
9. Kiss, K.É. (ed.): Discourse Configurational Languages. Oxford University Press, Oxford (1995)
10. Kiss, K.É.: The Syntax of Hungarian. Oxford University Press, Oxford (2002)
11. Fillmore, C.J.: Frame semantics. In: The Linguistic Society of Korea (ed.) Linguistics in the Morning Calm, pp. 111–137. Hanshin Publishing, Seoul (1982)
12. Gorn, S.: Explicit definitions and linguistic dominoes. In: Hart, J., Takasu, S. (eds.) Systems and Computer Science, pp. 77–115. University of Toronto Press, Toronto (1967)
13. Hamblin, C.L.: Questions in montague English. Found. Lang. **10**(1), 41–53 (1973)
14. Jackendoff, R.S.: Foundations of Language. Brain, Meaning, Grammar, Evolution. Oxford University Press, Oxford (2002)
15. Jespersen, O.: Negation in English and Other Languages. A. F. Høst & Søn, Copenhagen (1917)
16. Joshi, A.K., Schabes, Y.: Tree-adjoining grammars. In: Rozenberg, G., Salomaa, A. (eds.) Handbook of Formal Languages, pp. 69–123. Springer, Heidelberg (1997). https://doi.org/10.1007/978-3-642-59126-6_2
17. Kallmeyer, L., Osswald, R.: Syntax-driven semantic frame composition in lexicalized tree adjoining grammars. J. Lang. Model. **1**(2), 267–330 (2013)
18. Kallmeyer, L., Osswald, R.: Combining predicate-argument structure and operator projection: clause structure in role and reference grammar. In: Kuhlmann, M., Scheffler, T. (eds.) Proceedings of the 13th International Workshop on Tree Adjoining Grammars and Related Formalisms, pp. 61–70. ACL Anthology, Umeå (2017)
19. Kallmeyer, L., Osswald, R.: Formalization of RRG syntax. In: Bentley, D., Mairal Usón, R., Nakamura, W., Van Valin, Jr., R.D. (eds.) The Cambridge Handbook of Role and Reference Grammar, pp. 737–784. Cambridge University Press, Cambridge (2023)
20. Kallmeyer, L., Osswald, R., Van Valin, R.D.: Tree wrapping for role and reference grammar. In: Morrill, G., Nederhof, M.-J. (eds.) FG 2012-2013. LNCS, vol. 8036, pp. 175–190. Springer, Heidelberg (2013). https://doi.org/10.1007/978-3-642-39998-5_11
21. Klima, E.: Negation in English. In: Fodor, J.A., Katz, J. (eds.) The Structure of Language, pp. 246–323. Prentice Hall, Englewood Cliffs (1964)

22. König, E.: The Meaning of Focus Particles: A Comparative Perspective. Routledge, London/New York (1991)
23. Krifka, M.: For a structured meaning account of questions and answers. In: Féry, C., Sternefeld, W. (eds.) Audiatur Vox Sapientiae: A Festschrift for Arnim von Stechow, pp. 287–319. Akademie Verlag, Berlin (2001)
24. Lambrecht, K.: Information Structure and Sentence Form. Cambridge University Press, Cambridge (1994)
25. Löbner, S.: Functional concepts and frames. In: Gamerschlag, T., Gerland, D., Osswald, R., Petersen, W. (eds.) Meaning, Frames, and Conceptual Representation. Studies in Language and Cognition 2, pp. 13–42. Düsseldorf University Press (2015)
26. Löbner, S.: Frame theory with first-order comparators: modeling the lexical meaning of punctual verbs of change with frames. In: Hansen, H.H., Murray, S.E., Sadrzadeh, M., Zeevat, H. (eds.) TbiLLC 2015. LNCS, vol. 10148, pp. 98–117. Springer, Heidelberg (2017). https://doi.org/10.1007/978-3-662-54332-0_7
27. Osswald, R., Kallmeyer, L.: Towards a formalization of role and reference grammar. In: Kailuweit, R., Künkel, L., Staudinger, E. (eds.) Applying and Expanding Role and Reference Grammar. NIHIN Studies, pp. 355–378. Albert-Ludwigs-Universität, Universitätsbibliothek, Freiburg (2018)
28. Petersen, W.: Representation of concepts as frames. In: Gamerschlag, T., Gerland, D., Osswald, R., Petersen, W. (eds.) Meaning, Frames, and Conceptual Representation. Studies in Language and Cognition 2, pp. 43–67. Düsseldorf University Press (2015)
29. Riester, A.: Constructing QUD trees. In: Zimmermann, M., von Heusinger, K., Onea, E. (eds.) Questions in Discourse. Volume 2: Pragmatics, pp. 164–193. Brill (2019)
30. Roberts, C.: Focus, the flow of information, and universal grammar. In: Culicover, P., McNally, L. (eds.) The Limits of Syntax, pp. 109–160. Academic Press, New York (1998)
31. Roberts, C.: Information structure: towards an integrated formal theory of pragmatics. Semant. Pragmatics 5(6), 1–69 (2012)
32. Surányi, B.: Discourse-configurationality. In: Féry, C., Ishihara, S. (eds.) The Oxford Handbook of Information Structure, pp. 422–440. Oxford University Press, Oxford (2015)
33. Toosarvandani, M.: Corrective but coordinates clauses not always but sometimes. Nat. Lang. Linguitic Theory 31, 827–863 (2013)
34. Vallduví, E.: Information structure and scope of sentential negation. In: Hall, K., Koenig, J.P., Meacham, M., Reinman, S., Sutton, L.A. (eds.) Proceedings of the Sixteenth Annual Meeting of the Berkeley Linguistics Society, pp. 325–337. Berkeley Linguistics Society, Berkeley (1990)
35. Van Valin, Jr., R.D.: Exploring the Syntax-Semantics Interface. Cambridge University Press, Cambridge (2005)
36. Van Valin, Jr., R.D., LaPolla, R.J.: Syntax: Structure, Meaning and Function. Cambridge University Press, Cambridge (1997)
37. Vendler, Z.: Linguistics in Philosophy. Cornell University Press, Ithaca (1967)

Towards a Theory of Anaphoric Binding in Event Semantics

Oleg Kiselyov[✉]

Tohoku University, Sendai, Japan
oleg@okmij.org
https://okmij.org/ftp/

Abstract. Scope and (anaphoric) binding are tough problems for event semantics. Unlike the former, the latter has not even been attempted, it seems. The present paper makes an attempt and reports on the ongoing work, in the context of polynomial event semantics.

Polynomial event semantics is a variable-free dialect of Neo-Davidsonian event semantics originally developed as a new approach to (quantifier) scope. Extended to relative clauses, it had to face traces, which is a form of anaphora. The present paper extends the mechanism proposed for traces to (nominal) pronouns. The same mechanism happens to also apply to discourse referents. Anaphoric binding becomes oddly symmetric. Also comes to light is a close analogy of indefinites and unbound pronouns.

1   Introduction

Pronouns and in general anaphora is the elephant in the room of event semantics. From surveys such as [13] or comprehensive treatments [2], among others, one may get an impression that anaphora is subject *non grata*. At least [15] explicitly says that "pronouns are not our main focus here, so I will not pursue it further." A theory of meaning and entailment, however, rather sooner than later must confront pronouns – and, eventually, crossover, gaps, ellipsis, donkey anaphora, paycheck pronouns, etc.

In contrast, a closely related problem of scope and quantification is widely acknowledged in event semantics literature, as event quantification problem, and has received considerable attention: see [2] for survey. Dealing with quantification (and negation) in a non-traditional, variable-free way was the motivation for the polynomial event semantics [7,8,10] – a theory of meaning and entailment in a neo-Davidsonian tradition. It was later extended to relative clauses, including clauses with quantification and negation [9]. Giving denotations to traces, and paraphrasing relative clauses as independent matrix clauses linked via 'pronouns' came close to the treatment of anaphora. The present work elaborates that approach and applies to pronouns and discourse referents, including bound-variable anaphora.

As in the previous work, our goal is deciding entailments, with as few postulates as possible. As a whetstone we have been using the FraCaS textual

D. Bekki et al. (Eds.): LENLS 2023, LNCS 14569, pp. 55–67, 2024.
https://doi.org/10.1007/978-3-031-60878-0_4

inference problem set [3,12] – which includes the dedicated section just for nominal anaphora, and another section for ellipsis, gapping and related phenomena. Anaphora also appears in 'temporal reference' and other sections. The hope is that the event semantics would deliver simple, postulate-free solutions to these and other entailment problems – especially in cases of VP modification (including temporal adverbials). Before we attempt that, however, we need to build the foundation for analyzing anaphora in event semantics, which has been entirely lacking. The present paper describes the current progress.

The paper hence focuses on developing the polynomial event semantics and reproducing standard analyses of (nominal, in this paper) anaphora, including bound-variable anaphora. Still, we already obtained interesting insights. Commonly, anaphoric binding is seen as asymmetric – which is particularly noticeable in dynamic semantics, which talks about "pushing discourse referents" and that a pronoun "pulls the value out of the context" [1]. On our account, however, we see a surprisingly symmetric picture of referents and pronouns. In particular, nominal pronouns, their antecedents as well as trace are all denoted by the identity relation – with different domains. We also see a close analogy of indefinites and unbound pronouns. Unlike many other analyses, sentences with unbound pronouns in our approach have a meaning, with a clear denotation.

After a brief reminder of the polynomial event semantics, Sect. 3 describes in detail so-called 'relative denotations', which first appeared in the compositional semantics of phrases with a trace. Section 4 applies them to nominal pronouns as well as their referents. In particular, Sect. 4.1 analyses several typical examples of bound-variable anaphora.

2   Polynomial Event Semantics: Brief Reminder

As a reminder of the polynomial event semantics, (1) shows the denotation of a simple sample sentence. The denotation is clearly built compositionally, matching the structure of the sentence:

(1)   [John traveled to Paris.]
$$= (\mathsf{subj'}/\mathsf{john}) \cap \mathsf{Travel} \cap (\mathsf{toloc'}/\mathsf{paris})$$

Here john and paris are individuals (notated i) and Travel is a set of events (notated e), specifically, traveling events. Further, subj' is a relation between events and individuals, viz. 'agents'.[1] The *relational selection* (or, restriction) subj'/john is then the set of events whose 'agent' is John:

$$\mathsf{subj'}/\mathsf{john} = \{e \mid (e, \mathsf{john}) \in \mathsf{subj'}\}$$

---

[1] Since we take events in broad sense [13], including states, etc., 'agent' is to be understood as the event attribute roughly corresponding to the role played by the grammatical subject. Currently we take the events of, say, 'reading' and 'being read' as distinct, but relatable by semantic postulates.

Likewise, $\mathsf{toloc}'/\mathsf{paris}$, to be abbreviated as TP, is the set of events involving Paris as the destination. The meaning of the whole sentence is the intersection of the meaning of its constituents: viz., the set of traveling events whose subject is John and destination is Paris. The denotation of a sentence is hence a set of events that witness it – or the formula like (1) that represents it, which may be regarded as a query of the record of world events. The sentence is true in that world if the result of the query is non-empty.[2]

Simple sets do not suffice, however, when it comes to (distributive) coordination such as:

(2)   Bill and John traveled to Paris.

"Bill and John" are obviously not a single individual. Rather, they are a 'loose group', for the lack of a better word, indicating that they are both involved, but not necessarily together. We introduce the (associative and commutative) operator $\otimes$ to build such loose groups of individuals. The denotation of "Bill and John", therefore, is $\mathsf{john} \otimes \mathsf{bill}$, to be called a poly-individual. Events in which Bill and John are subjects are then denoted by $\mathsf{subj}'/(\mathsf{john} \otimes \mathsf{bill})$, which is no longer a simple event set. We call it a polyconcept; a generalization of event sets (concepts). Event sets are regarded as (trivial) polyconcepts.

Set intersection extended to polyconcepts is written as $\sqcap$. That is, if two polyconcepts d_1 and d_2 happen to be ordinary sets, then $d_1 \sqcap d_2 = d_1 \cap d_2$. The operation $\sqcap$ also applies to individuals and poly-individuals; in particular,

$$i_1 \sqcap i_2 = \begin{cases} i_1 & \text{if } i1 = i2 \\ \bot & \text{otherwise} \end{cases}$$

where $\bot$ is the empty poly-individual/polyconcept. It is the null of both $\sqcap$ and $\otimes$:

$$d \sqcap \bot = \bot \qquad d \otimes \bot = \bot$$

With thus introduced polyconcepts, the denotation of (2) can then be written as (3).

$$[\![\text{Bill and John traveled to Paris.}]\!]$$

(3) $= \mathsf{subj}'/(\mathsf{john} \otimes \mathsf{bill}) \sqcap \mathsf{Travel} \sqcap \mathsf{TP}$

(4) $= (\mathsf{subj}'/\mathsf{john} \cap \mathsf{Travel} \cap \mathsf{TP}) \otimes$

$(\mathsf{subj}'/\mathsf{bill} \cap \mathsf{Travel} \cap \mathsf{TP})$

The meaning of the operator $\otimes$ is how it behaves, or distributes. In particular, the relational selection acts as homomorphism (or, 'commutes'):

$$\mathsf{subj}'/(\mathsf{john} \otimes \mathsf{bill}) = (\mathsf{subj}'/\mathsf{john}) \otimes (\mathsf{subj}'/\mathsf{bill})$$

What Bill and John act as a subject in is a loose group of two event sets: of Bill acting as a subject and of John. Intuitively, an event from both sets must have transpired. The operator $\sqcap$ distributes over $\otimes$ in case of simple concepts:

(5) $(d_1 \otimes d_2) \sqcap j = (d_1 \sqcap j) \otimes (d_2 \sqcap j)$

---

[2] Negation requires elaboration: see [9, 10].

where j is an event set (not a group); d is an arbitrary polyconcept. See [10] for detail on equational laws, and [8] for a model.

The relational selection homomorphism and the above distributive laws give (4). The sentence (2) is hence justified by a pair of events, of John traveling to Paris, and of Bill.

For the choice "Either John or Bill" we introduce $\sqcup$ (when the choice is internal) or $\oplus$ (when external). Quantification is the generalization: "Everyone" is denoted by $\bigotimes_{i \in \mathsf{Person}} i$, to be abbreviated as $\mathcal{A}\,\mathsf{Person}$. A wide-scope existential and indefinite "a person" is $\bigoplus_{i \in \mathsf{Person}} i$ (abbreviated $\mathcal{I}\,\mathsf{Person}$) and the narrow-scope existential is $\bigsqcup_{i \in \mathsf{Person}} i$ (abbreviated $\mathcal{E}\,\mathsf{Person}$). Here Person is a set of individuals. For more detail (as well as negation, not used here), see [9,10].

3 Polyconcepts in Context: Relative Denotations

The paper [9] applied the polynomial event semantics to relative clauses. For example, for the following noun-modification phrase it *derived* the intuitive denotation:

$$(6) \qquad\qquad [\![\text{city John traveled to } \mathsf{T}]\!]$$
$$= \mathsf{City} \cap \{i \mid [\![\text{John traveled to } i]\!] \neq \bot\}$$

where T is trace. The paper [9] derived the denotation in two ways, one of which is compositional – which means giving denotation to the trace T. We now elaborate this method and, in Sect. 4, apply to pronouns and their referents.

To handle trace, [9] had to generalize denotations from poly-individuals (and polyconcepts) d to relations between contexts and poly-individuals (resp. poly-concepts): in effect, set of pairs $\{(i,d) \mid i \in C\}$, for which we now adopt a more compact notation $d|i{:}C$. We call them relative denotations. The context C at present is a set of individuals (although it may be any other set). The denotation d in $d|i{:}C$ may itself be a relative denotation $d'|i'{:}C'$. We write such nested relative denotations as $d'|(i'{:}C' \times i{:}C)$, to be understood as

$$d'|(i'{:}C' \times i{:}C) \stackrel{\Delta}{=} d'|i'{:}C'|i{:}C = \{(i,(i',d')) \mid i' \in C', i \in C\}$$

Any denotation d can be converted – or embedded, relativized – to a relative denotation:

$$d \underset{\rho}{\overset{\iota}{\rightleftarrows}} d|i{:}C$$

where ι is inclusion (or, embedding) and ρ is retract (or, projection):

$$\iota_C\, d = d|i{:}C$$
$$\rho\,(d|i{:}C) = d \qquad \text{provided } d \text{ is independent of } i$$

An alternative way to define the retract is to use the relational selection: after all, a relative denotation is a relation:

$$\rho_C\, r = d \qquad \text{where } r/C = \{d\}$$

Embeddings and projections are the inverses of each other; however, an embedding is not surjective and a projection is not total, in general. An important particular case (which we come across later) is C being a singleton. For the singleton context, the embedding is surjective and the projection is total: they form a bijection. In this case, the relative denotation is isomorphic to the non-relative one. (We shall use $\approx$ to explicate and emphasize an isomorphism.)

The relational selection $\mathsf{subj}'/\cdot$ is again homomorphism:

$$\mathsf{subj}'/(d|i{:}C) = (\mathsf{subj}'/d)|i{:}C$$

and hence commutes with ι and ρ:

$$\iota_C\left(\mathsf{subj}'/i\right) = \mathsf{subj}'/\left(\iota_C\,i\right) \qquad \rho\left(\mathsf{subj}'/i\right) = \mathsf{subj}'/\left(\rho\,i\right)$$

Polyconcept operations likewise commute:

$$(7) \qquad (d_1|i{:}C) \circledast (d_2|i{:}C) = (d_1 \circledast d_2)|i{:}C$$

where $\circledast$ stands for $\sqcap$, $\otimes$, $\oplus$ or $\sqcup$. (7) does not apply to $(d_1|i_1{:}C_1) \sqcap (d_2|i_2{:}C_2)$ with $C_1 \neq C_2$, however. To bring them to the common ground, so to speak, we may embed the two relative polyconcepts in each other contexts. Recall, embedding applies to any poly-individual or polyconcept, including a relative polyconcept.

$$
\begin{aligned}
(8) \qquad & \iota_{C_2}(d_1|i_1{:}C_1) \circledast \iota_{C_1}(d_2|i_2{:}C_2) \\
&= (d_1|i_1{:}C_1)|i_2{:}C_2 \circledast (d_2|i_2{:}C_2)|i_1{:}C_1 \\
&= (d_1|(i_1{:}C_1 \times i_2{:}C_2)) \circledast (d_2|(i_2{:}C_2 \times i_1{:}C_1)) \\
&\approx (d_1|(i_1{:}C_1 \times i_2{:}C_2)) \circledast (d_2|(i_1{:}C_1 \times i_2{:}C_2)) \\
&= (d_1 \circledast d_2)|(i_1{:}C_1 \times i_2{:}C_2)
\end{aligned}
$$

where we have used the obvious relational isomorphisms.

There is a yet another way to bring two relative concepts to the common ground (common context): narrowing. Unlike the previous approach, it does not preserve the denotation; rather, it makes it 'narrower'. First we introduce the narrowing operation

$$\Downarrow_{C_1}(d|i{:}C_2) \triangleq d|i{:}(C_1 \cap C_2)$$

Given two polyconcepts $d_1|i_1{:}C_1$ and $d_2|i_2{:}C_2$ we may try to combine them in one of the following ways:

$$(9) \qquad d_1|i_1{:}C_1 \circledast \Downarrow_{C_1}(d_2|i_2{:}C_2)$$
$$(10) \qquad \Downarrow_{C_2}(d_1|i_1{:}C_1) \circledast d_2|i_2{:}C_2$$
$$(11) \qquad \Downarrow_{C_1 \cap C_2}(d_1|i_1{:}C_1) \circledast \Downarrow_{C_1 \cap C_2}(d_2|i_2{:}C_2)$$

One may think of (9) as interpreting the right concept in the context of the left. Likewise, (10) interprets the left polyconcept in the context of the right one;

(11) is symmetric. We shall see in the next section the significance of these three different strategies for semantic analyses.

The strategies (9)–(11) may be written in an alternative form, by performing the construction (8) first, followed by the narrowing:

$$
\begin{aligned}
(12) \quad & d_1|i_1{:}C_1 \circledast \Downarrow_{C_1} d_2|i_2{:}C_2 \\
= \ & \Downarrow_{C_1} d_1|i_1{:}C_1 \circledast \Downarrow_{C_1} d_2|i_2{:}C_2 \\
= \ & \Downarrow_{C_1 \times C_1} (d_1 \circledast d_2)|(i_1{:}C_1 \times i_2{:}C_2) \\
(13) \quad & \Downarrow_{C_2} d_1|i_1{:}C_1 \circledast d_2|i_2{:}C_2 \\
= \ & \Downarrow_{C_2 \times C_2} (d_1 \circledast d_2)|(i_1{:}C_1 \times i_2{:}C_2) \\
(14) \quad & \Downarrow_{C_1 \cap C_2} (d_1|i_1{:}C_1) \circledast \Downarrow_{C_1 \cap C_2} (d_2|i_2{:}C_2) \\
= \ & \Downarrow_{(C_1 \cap C_2) \times (C_1 \cap C_2)} (d_1 \circledast d_2)|(i_1{:}C_1 \times i_2{:}C_2)
\end{aligned}
$$

In an important case $C_1 \subset C_2$, the narrowing to the left

$$
\begin{aligned}
& \Downarrow_{C_2 \times C_2} (d_1 \circledast d_2)|(i_1{:}C_1 \times i_2{:}C_2) \\
= \ & (d_1 \circledast d_2)|(i_1{:}C_1 \times i_2{:}C_2)
\end{aligned}
$$

is the identity. On the other hand, the narrowing to the right (which is the same as the symmetric narrowing in this case)

$$
\begin{aligned}
(15) \quad & \Downarrow_{C_1 \times C_1} (d_1 \circledast d_2)|(i_1{:}C_1 \times i_2{:}C_2) \\
\equiv \ & \Downarrow_{C_1} d_1|i_1{:}C_1 \circledast \Downarrow_{C_1} d_2|i_2{:}C_2 \\
= \ & d_1|i_1{:}C_1 \circledast d_2|i_2{:}C_1 \\
= \ & (d_1 \circledast d_2[i_2{:=}i_1])|i_1{:}C_1
\end{aligned}
$$

where $[i_2{:=}i_1]$ is a (meta)variable substitution. In other words, the narrowing behaves quite like binding – which is exactly how we will use it in linguistic analyses.

4   Nominal Pronouns and Referents

As the first example of pronouns, consider "It is famous". In [9], the trace was given the denotation $i|i{:}\mathcal{I}$ where $\mathcal{I}$ is the set of all individuals. Since trace is anaphoric, it is tempting to likewise make $[\![\mathsf{it}]\!] = i|i{:}\mathsf{Thing}$, relativized to the set of things (non-human individuals). Let's give in to the temptation. The whole sentence then receives the denotation:[3]

$$
\begin{aligned}
& [\![\text{It is famous.}]\!] \\
= \ & \mathsf{subj}'/ \, (i|i{:}\mathsf{Thing}) \sqcap \iota_{\mathsf{Thing}} \, \mathsf{Famous} \\
(16) \quad = \ & (\mathsf{subj}'/i \sqcap \mathsf{Famous})|i{:}\mathsf{Thing} \\
(17) \quad = \ & [\![i \text{ is famous.}]\!]|i{:}\mathsf{Thing}
\end{aligned}
$$

---

[3] We are simplifying, but only slightly: see [10] for the treatment of copular clauses.

Since "it" has a relative denotation, we need a relative denotation for $[\![famous]\!]$, obtainable by embedding. To lighten the notation, hereafter we shall apply embeddings silently as needed. One may have recognized the parenthesized expression in (16) as the denotation for "i is famous".

The sentence is grammatical and meaningful, even by itself: a listener is free to imagine a suitable referent for "it", not constrained by any prior discourse (which does not exist here). The denotation is inherently relative (ρ does not apply), which indicates it contains an unresolved anaphoric reference.

Next consider "John traveled to Paris$^\triangleright$." where Paris$^\triangleright$ is an NP creating a referent. We take its denotation to be the relativized paris:

$$(18) \qquad [\![Paris^\triangleright]\!] = \iota_{\{paris\}} \ paris = paris \,|\, i\colon \{paris\} = i \,|\, i\colon \{paris\}$$

Oddly, $[\![Paris^\triangleright]\!]$ turns out almost the same as $[\![it]\!]$; only the former is relativized to the singleton $\{paris\}$ and the latter to the set of all things. Therefore, the former can be projected to the non-relative denotation, but the latter cannot. For the whole sentence we obtain:

$$[\![John\ traveled\ to\ Paris^\triangleright.]\!]$$
$$= \iota_{paris}\ subj'/john \sqcap \iota_{paris}\ Travel \sqcap toloc'/ \ (i\,|\,i\colon\{paris\})$$
$$= (subj'/john \sqcap Travel \sqcap toloc'/i)\,|\,i\colon\{paris\}$$
$$= [\![John\ traveled\ to\ i]\!]\,|\,i\colon\{paris\}\,.$$

Combining the two sentences and using (8) gives:

$$[\![John\ traveled\ to\ Paris^\triangleright.\ It\ is\ famous.]\!]$$
$$= [\![John\ traveled\ to\ Paris^\triangleright.]\!] \otimes [\![It\ is\ famous.]\!]$$
(19)
$$= ([\![John\ traveled\ to\ i_1]\!] \otimes [\![i_2\ is\ famous]\!])\,|$$
$$(i_1\colon\{paris\} \times i_2\colon Thing)$$

After all, "it" does not have to refer to Paris.

If, from pragmatic considerations, one decides that "it" resolves to "Paris", we can carry out this decision in our formalism, by applying the (right) narrowing $\Downarrow_{\{paris\}\times\{paris\}}$ obtaining (as in (15)):

$$([\![John\ traveled\ to\ i]\!] \otimes [\![i\ is\ famous]\!])\,|\,i : \{paris\}$$

The context becomes the singleton set. Recall, a polyconcept relative to a singleton context is isomorphic to the non-relative polyconcept. Therefore, the above denotation is equivalent to the pair $[\![John\ traveled\ to\ Paris]\!]$ and $[\![Paris\ is\ famous]\!]$. It is now "context-free": with no longer any unresolved dependencies, no appeal to listener's imagination.

The narrowing we have just applied corresponds to the left-to-right interpretation (9); the opposite (10) does not affect the denotation and does not, hence, result in the pronoun resolution. On the other hand, for "John travel to it. Paris is famous." the left-to-right interpretation (9) leaves the pronoun unresolved; we would have needed the right-to-left interpretation for the resolution. The theory therefore has the mechanisms for both interpretations. It is an empirical fact that in English left-to-right interpretation is commonly observed. Right-to-left is not unheard of: "John travel to it. I mean, travel to Paris." Such right-to-left interpretation is common in scientific language: so-called 'where' clauses (or 'here' sentences). An example, claimed to require no explanation, is

$$f(b + 2c) + f(2b - c) \quad \text{where } f(x) = x(x + a)$$

from [11, §2]. Here, 'f' in the main clause is resolved by the 'f' defined in the 'where' clause; a, b and c are free.[4]

The key idea hence is that discourse is a constraint on listeners' imagination. The narrower is the context, the tighter is the constraint. In the limit, a proper noun is the anaphoric reference in the singleton context, which constrains it unambiguously. The close similarity of $[\![\text{Paris}^{\triangleright}]\!]$ and $[\![\text{it}]\!]$ should not be so surprising.

We must stress that the question of deciding which pronoun refers to which referent is in domain of pragmatics and outside the scope of our theory. What we propose is a semantic framework, in which to carry out analyses and obtain denotations *without* having committed to a particular referent resolution. Once we obtain denotations, we can see the derived context, and then apply pragmatic and other referent resolution strategies.

In other words, whether to apply a narrowing and which narrowing to apply is the matter of *policy*, and is left to pragmatics. Narrowing by itself is the *mechanism* to carry out a particular decided policy within the formalism. Allowing for both left-to-right and right-to-left narrowing is a feature: unlike many other formalisms, we do not bake-in any preferred way of resolving pronouns, leaving it to policy.

4.1   Bound Variable Anaphora

Indefinites may also bind pronouns: "John traveled to $a_W^{\triangleright}$ city. It is famous." (assuming "it" refers to the above-mentioned city), where $a_W^{\triangleright}$ is a referent-creating (wide-scope) indefinite (and therefore, it uses $\oplus$):

$$(20) \qquad [\![a_W^{\triangleright} \text{ city}]\!] = \bigoplus_{j \in \text{City}} \iota_{\{j\}} j = \bigoplus_{j \in \text{City}} i \,|\, i\colon \{j\}$$

---

[4] This sentence is itself an example of a 'here' sentence, giving the definitions for f, a, b, and c that appeared in an earlier formula.

Once again we see the identity relation $i|i{:}C$. The external choice $\oplus$ (of the city, in our case) distributes completely, giving

$$[\![\text{John traveled to a}^{\triangleright}_{W}\text{ city. It is famous.}]\!]$$

(21) $$= (\bigoplus_{j\in\mathsf{City}}[\![\text{John traveled to }i_1]\!]\,|\,i_1{:}\{\mathsf{j}\})\ \otimes$$

$$([\![i_2\text{ is famous}]\!]\,|\,i_2{:}\,\mathsf{Thing})$$

(22) $$= \bigoplus_{j\in\mathsf{City}}([\![\text{John traveled to }i_1.]\!]\otimes[\![i_2\text{ is famous.}]\!])\,|$$

$$i_1{:}\{\mathsf{j}\}\times i_2{:}\,\mathsf{Thing}$$

$\{\text{Narrowing by }\Downarrow_{\{\mathsf{j}\}\times\{\mathsf{j}\}}\}$

$$\Rightarrow \bigoplus_{j\in\mathsf{City}}[\![\text{John traveled to }i.\ i\text{ is famous.}]\!]\,|\,i{:}\{\mathsf{j}\}$$

$\{\text{Bijection: context is singleton}\}$

$$\approx \bigoplus_{j\in\mathsf{City}}[\![\text{John traveled to }j.\ j\text{ is famous.}]\!]$$

where the use of narrowing reflects the assumption that "it" refers to a city. We must stress again that narrowing in general does not preserve denotations and is not free to use at will. Narrowing has to be justified by, and is the reflection of, a resolution decision made by pragmatics.

Incidentally, [9] related the result to the denotation of the sentence with the relative clause: "A city John traveled to is famous".

A similar derivation does not work for (23):

(23) $$[\![\text{John traveled to every city. It is famous.}]\!]$$

(24) $$= (\bigotimes_{j\in\mathsf{City}}[\![\text{John traveled to }i_1]\!]\,|\,i_1{:}\{\mathsf{j}\})\ \otimes$$

$$([\![i_2\text{ is famous}]\!]\,|\,i_2{:}\,\mathsf{Thing})$$

The key transition from (21) to (22) is the distribution of $\otimes$ into $\oplus$, followed by the application of (8). The similar transition does not apply to (24) because $\otimes$ does not distribute in each other. We could have applied (8) to "John traveled to every city", obtaining

$$[\![\text{John traveled to every city}]\!]$$

$$= (\bigotimes_{j\in\mathsf{City}}[\![\text{John traveled to }i_j]\!])\,|\ \prod_{j\in\mathsf{City}}i_j{:}\{\mathsf{j}\}$$

It does not help, however, in binding "it" because the simple context $i{:}\,\mathsf{Thing}$ cannot be meaningfully intersected with the tuple $\prod_{j\in\mathsf{City}}i_j{:}\{\mathsf{j}\}$. Therefore, the narrowing cannot be applied. On the other hand, if the pronoun were "they", the binding would have worked.

The same argument shows why there is anaphoric binding of "it" in (25) but not in (26).[5]

(25)   A donkey enters. It brays.

(26)   Every donkey enters. It brays.

More interesting cases of bound variable anaphora are found in (27) and (28). (The latter is [1, (113)]).

(27)   Every boy loves his father.

(28)   A referee rejected every paper she reviewed.

For (27), we obtain

$$[\![\text{Every boy loves his father.}]\!]$$
$$= \mathsf{subj}'/\,[\![\text{Every boy}]\!] \sqcap \mathsf{Love} \sqcap \mathsf{ob1}'/\,[\![\text{his father.}]\!]$$

where (using the embedding, eventually)

$$[\![\text{Every boy}]\!] = \bigotimes_{j\in\mathsf{Boy}} j = \bigotimes_{j\in\mathsf{Boy}} (k\,|\,k\colon\{\mathsf{j}\})$$

"Father" is denoted by a set of individuals Father, which is then restricted by "his". The operator $\mathcal{E}$ denotes a choice of an individual from the resulting set:[6]

$$[\![\text{his father}]\!] = \mathcal{E}(\mathsf{Father}\cap\mathsf{of}'/\,i)\,|\,i\colon\mathsf{Male}$$

Overall, we obtain:

$$[\![\text{Every boy loves his father.}]\!]$$
$$= \bigotimes_{j\in\mathsf{Boy}} (\mathsf{subj}'/\,k \sqcap \mathsf{Love} \sqcap \mathcal{E}\,\mathsf{ob1}'/\,(\mathsf{Father}\cap\mathsf{of}'/\,i))\,|$$
$$k\colon\{\mathsf{j}\}\times i\colon\mathsf{Male}$$
$$\{\text{Narrowing } \Downarrow_{\{\mathsf{j}\}\times\{\mathsf{j}\}}, \text{ assuming "his" refers to the boy}\}$$
$$\Rightarrow \bigotimes_{j\in\mathsf{Boy}} (\mathsf{subj}'/\,k \sqcap \mathsf{Love} \sqcap \mathcal{E}\,\mathsf{ob1}'/\,(\mathsf{Father}\cap\mathsf{of}'/\,i))\,|$$
$$k\colon\{\mathsf{j}\}\times i\colon\{\mathsf{j}\}$$
$$\approx \bigotimes_{j\in\mathsf{Boy}} (\mathsf{subj}'/\,j \sqcap \mathsf{Love} \sqcap \mathcal{E}\,\mathsf{ob1}'/\,(\mathsf{Father}\cap\mathsf{of}'/\,j))$$
$$= \bigotimes_{j\in\mathsf{Boy}} [\![j \text{ loves a father of } j]\!]$$

For (28), we first compute the denotation of the relative clause clause along the lines of (6):

$$[\![\text{paper she reviewed T}]\!]$$
$$= (\mathsf{Paper}\cap\{k \mid [\![i \text{ reviewed } k]\!]\neq\bot\})\,|\,i\colon\mathsf{Female}$$
$$\triangleq P_i\,|\,i\colon\mathsf{Female}$$

---

[5] The example is due to Carl Pollard.

[6] The set of "father of i" is not necessarily singleton, if we take "father" in a broad sense, including stepfather, godfather, etc.

For conciseness, we write P_i for the parenthesized denotation. Then

$$\text{[every paper she reviewed T]} = \mathcal{A}(P_i|i\colon \mathsf{Female}) = (\mathcal{A}P_i)|i\colon \mathsf{Female}$$

If we take

$$\text{[A referee]} = \bigoplus_{j\in\mathsf{Referee}} k\,|\,k\colon \{\mathsf{j}\}$$

as in (20), we obtain for the whole sentence the denotation that can be narrowed to $\bigoplus_{j\in\mathsf{Referee}}[j$ rejected $\mathcal{A}P_j]$. On the other hand, had we chosen [A referee] to be $\mathcal{E}$ Referee and distribute it inside $\mathcal{A}P_i$:

$$\left(\bigotimes_{k\in P_i}\mathcal{E}\,\mathsf{subj}'/\,\mathsf{Referee}\sqcap\mathsf{Rejected}\sqcap\mathsf{ob1}'/\,k\right)|i\colon \mathsf{Female}$$

the narrowing cannot be applied, and "she" remains unbound. The binding of "she" to a referee hence works out only on the surface reading – the harsh referee does not vary with papers, – as was pointed in [1].

5   Related Work

Anaphora in general, and its particular approach: dynamic semantics, is an active area with enormous literature (not as far as event semantics, however). A concise overview is given in [1]. Although [1] pursues a rather different from us approach – dynamic semantics for anaphora and continuation semantics for the theory of scope – it is surprisingly related: It also represents the context as a (nested) tuple. The paper [1] is quite more precise and rigorous in its treatment of context, which we aspire to.

One contentious point in the theories of bound-variable anaphora is treating a pronoun as a bound variable. A strong argument against is given in Dekker's PLA [4]. Like [1], we side-step this argument: after all, there are no bound variables in our semantics (at least, not as conventionally understood). PLA [4], among many others, consider an unresolved pronoun as a failure to give a denotation. In contrast, we (again, as [1]) take sentences with unresolved pronouns to be meaningful, with well-defined denotations.

Since the pioneering work of Heim [6], the dynamic semantics tradition takes an individual sentence to mean its "context change potential": if discourse is a file of cards, an individual sentence is adding or modifying a card. It is the entire file rather than a sentence that has truth conditions. This seems to be too narrow a view of 'truth conditions'. In our approach, a sentence denotation is generally a relation, between context and events witnessing the truth of the sentence. A relation between context and truth conditions may still be called truth conditions.

Our denotation (17) for "It is famous" – the relation, or a set of pairs of a thing and a witness of its being famous – closely relates to the meaning of the question "What is famous?" in Hamblin theory of interrogatives [5], and to the alternative semantics [14].

6   Conclusions and Future Work

We have thus seen that anaphoric dependencies can, after all, be expressed in a variable-free event semantics, and in a surprisingly symmetric way. Both the referent and the reference have the meaning of a polyconcept relative to a context. Traces and indefinites also have the same meaning. The analogy of indefinites with unbound pronouns seems worth looking into further.

We have limited ourselves to nominal anaphora in this paper. Pronouns may also refer to events – which was one of the motivations for the (Neo-)Davidsonian semantics. The extension to event anaphora is forthcoming. Although we have not discussed FraCaS problems, many are already solvable in the approach presented here. We show details in the upcoming work.

The development of the theory of anaphoric binding in event semantics has just began. Dynamic semantics literature (including [1]) has the wealth of interesting examples of anaphora to investigate, from crossover to donkey anaphora to gaping and ellipsis – and also anaphoric references to times, worlds, degrees, events. The eventual goal is to apply our analyses to entailments.

On the implementation front, it is interesting to integrate our approach with the existing libraries for anaphora resolution.

Acknowledgement. I am very grateful to Simon Charlow for many fruitful discussions. I thank Alastair Butler and Daisuke Bekki for helpful suggestions and encouragement. Insightful comments by the reviewers and participants of the LENLS20 workshop are gratefully acknowledged.

Disclosure of Interests. The author has no competing interests to declare.

References

1. Bumford, D., Charlow, S.: Dynamic semantics with static types. lingbuzz/006884 (2022)
2. Champollion, L.: The interaction of compositional semantics and event semantics. Linguist. Philos. **38**(1), 31–66 (2015)
3. Cooper, R., et al.: Using the framework. Deliverable D16, FraCaS Project (1996)
4. Dekker, P.: Predicate logic with anaphora. In: Harvey, M., Santelmann, L. (eds.) Proceedings from Semantics and Linguistic Theory IV. Cornell University Press, Ithaca (1994). https://doi.org/10.3765/salt.v4i0.2459. http://staff.science.uva.nl/~pdekker/Papers/PLA.pdf
5. Hamblin, C.L.: Questions in Montague English. Found. Lang. **10**, 41–53 (1973)
6. Heim, I.: The semantics of definite and indefinite noun phrases. Ph.D. thesis, Department of Linguistics, University of Massachusetts (1982). http://semanticsarchive.net/Archive/Tk0ZmYyY/. http://semanticsarchive.net/Archive/jA2YTJmN/
7. Kiselyov, O.: Polynomial event semantics. In: Kojima, K., Sakamoto, M., Mineshima, K., Satoh, K. (eds.) JSAI-isAI 2018. LNCS (LNAI), vol. 11717, pp. 313–324. Springer, Cham (2019). https://doi.org/10.1007/978-3-030-31605-1_23

8. Kiselyov, O.: Polynomial event semantics: negation. In: Okazaki, N., Yada, K., Satoh, K., Mineshima, K. (eds.) JSAI-isAI 2020. LNCS (LNAI), vol. 12758, pp. 82–95. Springer, Cham (2021). https://doi.org/10.1007/978-3-030-79942-7_6

9. Kiselyov, O., Watanabe, H.: Events and relative clauses. In: Bekki, D., Mineshima, K., McCready, E. (eds.) LENLS 2022. LNCS, vol. 14213, pp. 18–30. Springer, Cham (2023). https://doi.org/10.1007/978-3-031-43977-3_2

10. Kiselyov, O., Watanabe, H.: QNP textual entailment with polynomial event semantics. In: Yada, K., Takama, Y., Mineshima, K., Satoh, K. (eds.) JSAI-isAI 2021. LNCS, vol. 13856, pp. 198–211. Springer, Cham (2023). https://doi.org/10.1007/978-3-031-36190-6_14

11. Landin, P.J.: The next 700 programming languages. Commun. ACM **9**(3), 157–166 (1966)

12. MacCartney, B.: The FRACAS textual inference problem set. https://nlp.stanford.edu/~wcmac/downloads/fracas.xml

13. Maienborn, C.: Event semantics, chap. 8, pp. 232–266. Semantics - Theories, De Gruyter Mouton (2019). https://doi.org/10.1515/9783110589245-008

14. Rooth, M.: Alternative Semantics. Oxford University Press (2016). https://doi.org/10.1093/oxfordhb/9780199642670.013.19

15. Schwarzschild, R.: Pure event semantics. lingbuzz/006888 (2022)

Matrix and Relative Weak Crossover on the Level of the Individual: An Experimental Investigation

Haruka Fukushima[1](✉), Daniel Plesniak[2], and Daisuke Bekki[1]

[1] Ochanomizu University, Tokyo, Japan
{fukushima.haruka,bekki}@is.ocha.ac.jp
[2] Seoul National University, Seoul, Republic of Korea
plesniak@usc.edu

Abstract. A variety of claims have been made about weak crossover effects in both matrix and relative clauses. In this paper, we conduct an experiment using Hoji's Language Faculty Science (LFS) methodology, focusing on a comparison and contrast between these two constructions. The results of this experiment show a clear division in the conditions under which they are acceptable.

1 Introduction

In this work, we argue that two syntactic configurations/effects, matrix weak crossover (M-WCO) and relative weak crossover (R-WCO), are fundamentally different in terms of English speakers acceptability judgements. In particular, we perform an empirical test of a prediction of the theory of Dependent Type Semantics (DTS: [1]) regarding M- and R-WCO, using the methodology of Language Faculty Science (LFS: [6]).

DTS is a proof-theoretic framework of natural language semantics. One of the main features of DTS is its fully-compositional account of anaphora and presuppositions. Recently, [2] proposed an update to the theory of DTS regarding the underspesification mechanism for anaphora in order to better capture subject-object asymmetry, and in particular, to address the question of how and why so-called "Weak Crossover (WCO: [19]) effects" obtain.

Below, (1a) and (1b) demonstrate M-WCO, i.e., WCO effects in a matrix clause.

(1) a. Every boy loves his mother.

   b. *His mother loves every boy.

In general, (1a) allows an interpretation in which each boy loves his *own* mother, namely, boy$_1$ loves boy$_1$'s mother, boy$_2$ loves boy$_2$'s mother, and so on. This interpretation is called the Bound Variable Anaphora (BVA: [15]) reading. On the other hand, many people find it impossible to accept a BVA reading in (1b), which, were it possible, would mean that each boy is loved by his own mother. Many accounts, including [2], predict the contrast between acceptability of sentences (1a) and (1b).

(2a) and (2b) are examples of *purported* R-WCO, i.e., WCO effects in a relative clause.

© The Author(s), under exclusive license to Springer Nature Switzerland AG 2024
D. Bekki et al. (Eds.): LENLS 2023, LNCS 14569, pp. 68–83, 2024.
https://doi.org/10.1007/978-3-031-60878-0_5

(2)   a. Every boy who loves his mother bought flowers.

      b. Every boy who his mother loves bought flowers.

Hypotheses in the literature as to whether BVA in these cases *should* be acceptable are far less consistent than those regarding (1). Some such as [5] and [16] predict that the BVA reading is possible in the sentence (2a), which would mean that every boy who loves his own mother bought flowers, but they predict the BVA reading is impossible in the sentence (2b), namely, it cannot mean that every boy who is loved by his own mother bought flowers. (See, e.g., the overview in [16] of this basic proposal). On the other hand, the DTS account in [2] predicts that these sentences lack a contrast, unlike the case of M-WCO, and that the sentence (2b) can mean that every boy who is loved by his own mother bought flowers. That is, there is no true R-WCO effect.

One challenge to distinguishing these two types of hypotheses is that judgements as to the acceptability of R-WCO BVA are highly variable, with many speakers disagreeing about what is and is not acceptable. The same is in fact true of M-WCO as well. However, despite this variation, the contrast of M-WCO has been substantiated using the methodology of Language Faculty Science (LFS). The basic idea of the LFS method is that people's judgements can vary based on a number of factors such as situation, time or words in the sentence, but specific correlations between judgements are invariant. These correlations can be used to assess structural hypotheses by having an individual judge multiple sentences with various interpretations so as to check whether the predicted correlation of judgements obtains. This method has yielded universally consistent results with regard to the unacceptability of M-WCO BVA, once certain non-structural "interfering factors" are eliminated.

In this project, we attempt to extend these results to R-WCO cases, in order to check the predictions of DTS regarding BVA readings. In particular, we obtain the judgements of ~100 speakers of English with regard to a number of sentences, and based on their judgements we use the LFS methodology to focus on informants whose judgements are not affected by interfering non-structural factors. This allows us to check their judgements about potential R-WCO effects, and thereby to determine whether R-WCO has a similar status to M-WCO.

We find that relative WCO has a different status from matrix WCO. Even without an individual-level analysis, it is clear that relative WCO is frequently accepted, whereas matrix WCO is frequently rejected. These differences only become more stark once we look at individuals: while applying the relevant controls results in universal M-WCO BVA *rejection*, we find universal R-WCO *acceptance* under the same conditions.

2   Background

2.1   Dependent Type Semantics

Dependent type semantics (DTS) [1–3] is a proof-theoretic framework of natural language semantics. DTS is built on underspecified dependent type theory (UDTT), a type theory extending Martin-Löf type theory (MLTT) [9] with *underspecified types* that represent lexical contributions of anaphoric expressions, presuppositions, and conventional implicatures (CIs). Inheriting the proof-theoretic semantics of MLTT, DTS assigns a type to a sentence as its meaning. Each type is a collection of proofs under a given context, and the truth value of a sentence is defined as an inhabitance of proofs.

Unlike dynamic semantics or other type-theoretic semantics, DTS allows us to uniformly analyze dynamic (or projective) aspects of natural language, such as anaphora resolution, presupposition binding/filtering, and CIs, while attaining the compositionality required in the syntax-semantics interface. This is achieved by launching the proof-search of MLTT during the UDTT's type checking algorithm [2,4]. This proof search algorithm is the same as the one that calculates the validity of inferences between sentences.

The following analysis on WCO is based on the latest version [2] of DTS, where the underspecified terms adopted in the previous version [3] are replaced with underspecified types, defined as control operators in the type checking algorithm. The type checking is defined as a function $[\![-]\!]$ that takes a UDTT judgment as input and returns a list of MLTT proof diagrams (it returns an empty list when type checking fails). Each list member is a proof diagram that shows the well-formedness of a semantic representation (a type in MLTT) that corresponds to a certain reading of the given sentence. We use the same notation $[\![-]\!]$ for type checking, type inference, and proof search algorithms, whose inputs are $\Gamma \vdash M : A$, $\Gamma \vdash M : ?$, and $\Gamma \vdash ? : A$, respectively. The following discussion presumes the type checking algorithm defined in [2].

Predictions on M-WCO. We adopt Combinatory Categorial Grammar (CCG [17]) as a syntactic theory and assume the lexical items enumerated in (3) for the following discussion.[1]

(3) $[\![\text{every} \vdash \boldsymbol{T}/(\boldsymbol{T}\backslash NP), \boldsymbol{T}\backslash(\boldsymbol{T}/NP)]\!] \stackrel{def}{\equiv} \lambda n.\lambda p.\lambda\vec{x}.\left(u : \begin{bmatrix} x : \text{entity} \\ n(x) \end{bmatrix}\right) \rightarrow$
$p\vec{x}(\pi_1 u)$

$[\![\text{boy} \vdash N]\!] \stackrel{def}{\equiv} \lambda x.\textbf{boy}(x)$

$[\![\text{loves} \vdash S\backslash NP/NP]\!] \stackrel{def}{\equiv} \lambda y.\lambda x.\textbf{love}(x, y)$

$[\![\text{his} \vdash \boldsymbol{T}\backslash(\boldsymbol{T}/NP)/(N\backslash NP)]\!] \stackrel{def}{\equiv} \lambda r.\lambda p.\lambda\vec{x}. \begin{bmatrix} u@\begin{bmatrix} x : \text{entity} \\ \textbf{male}(x) \end{bmatrix} \\ v@\begin{bmatrix} y : \text{entity} \\ r(y)(\pi_1 u) \end{bmatrix} \\ p\vec{x}(\pi_1 v) \end{bmatrix}$

$[\![\text{mother} \vdash N\backslash NP]\!] \stackrel{def}{\equiv} \lambda z.\lambda y.\textbf{motherOf}(y, z)$

$[\![\text{who} \vdash N\backslash N/(S\backslash NP), N\backslash N/(S/NP)]\!] \stackrel{def}{\equiv} \lambda p.\lambda n.\lambda x. \begin{bmatrix} nx \\ px \end{bmatrix}$

$[\![\text{bought} \vdash S\backslash NP/NP]\!] \stackrel{def}{\equiv} \lambda y.\lambda x.\textbf{buy}(x, y)$

$[\![\text{flowers} \vdash \boldsymbol{T}/(\boldsymbol{T}\backslash NP)]\!] \stackrel{def}{\equiv} \lambda p.p(f)$

---

[1] Each lexical item has the form of $[\![\textit{a surface form} \vdash \textit{a CCG syntactic category}]\!] \stackrel{def}{\equiv}$ *a raw term in DTS*. This constitutes a map from syntactic structures in CCG to semantic representations in DTS, when combined with maps defined for combinatory rules in CCG.

Then, the syntactic structures of (1a) and (1b) are respectively calculated as follows.

(4)

$$
\cfrac{\cfrac{\text{Every}}{T/(T\backslash NP)/N} \quad \cfrac{\text{boy}}{N}}{\cfrac{T/(T\backslash NP)}{}}\,{}^{>} \quad \cfrac{\cfrac{\text{loves}}{S\backslash NP/NP} \quad \cfrac{\cfrac{\text{his}}{T\backslash(T/NP)/(N\backslash NP)} \quad \cfrac{\text{mother}}{N\backslash NP}}{T\backslash(T/NP)}\,{}^{>}}{\cfrac{S\backslash NP}{}}\,{}^{<}}{S}\,{}^{>}
$$

(5)

$$
\cfrac{\cfrac{\cfrac{\text{his}}{T/(T\backslash NP)/(N\backslash NP)} \quad \cfrac{\text{mother}}{N\backslash NP}}{T/(T\backslash NP)}\,{}^{>} \quad \cfrac{\cfrac{\text{loves}}{S\backslash NP/NP} \quad \cfrac{\cfrac{\text{every}}{T\backslash(T/NP)/N} \quad \cfrac{\text{boy}}{N}}{T\backslash(T/NP)}\,{}^{>}}{S\backslash NP}\,{}^{<}}{S}\,{}^{>}
$$

These structures are mapped to the semantic representations (6) and (7) composed along (4) and (5) (where, intuitively, the variables w and v correspond to the proof terms of *his* and *his mother*, respectively).

(6)
$$
\left(u : \begin{bmatrix} x : \text{entity} \\ \mathbf{boy}(x) \end{bmatrix} \right) \rightarrow \begin{bmatrix} w@\begin{bmatrix} z : \text{entity} \\ \mathbf{male}(z) \end{bmatrix} \\ v@\begin{bmatrix} y : \text{entity} \\ \mathbf{motherOf}(y, \pi_1 w) \end{bmatrix} \\ \mathbf{love}(\pi_1 u, \pi_1 v) \end{bmatrix}
$$

(7)
$$
\begin{bmatrix} w@\begin{bmatrix} z : \text{entity} \\ \mathbf{male}(z) \end{bmatrix} \\ v@\begin{bmatrix} y : \text{entity} \\ \mathbf{motherOf}(y, \pi_1 w) \end{bmatrix} \\ \left(u : \begin{bmatrix} x : \text{entity} \\ \mathbf{boy}(x) \end{bmatrix} \right) \rightarrow \mathbf{love}(\pi_1 u, \pi_1 v) \end{bmatrix}
$$

DTS requires the semantic felicity (well-formedness) condition that every semantic representation A of a sentence should fulfill the judgment $\Gamma \vdash A : \text{type}$ under a given context Γ, thus conducts its type checking, during the process of which the underspecified type $w@\ldots$ launches the proof search shown in (8) and (9). Namely, this is a search for the antecedent of *his* that returns a set of proof diagrams, which may contain multiple elements corresponding to its potential antecedents.

Comparing the structures of (6) and (7), however, the underspecified type $w@(z : \text{entity}) \times \mathbf{male}(z)$ appears within the scope of u in (6), while it does not in (7). The underspecified types in both (6) and (7) launch proof searches of the form (8) and (9), where the structural difference leads to the difference in the contexts that are given to these proof searches.

(8) $\Gamma, u : \begin{bmatrix} x : \text{entity} \\ \mathbf{boy}(x) \end{bmatrix} \vdash_{\mathbf{UDTT}} ? : \begin{bmatrix} x : \text{entity} \\ \mathbf{male}(x) \end{bmatrix}$

(9) $\Gamma \vdash_{\mathbf{UDTT}} ? : \begin{bmatrix} x : \text{entity} \\ \mathbf{male}(x) \end{bmatrix}$

This means that, in anaphora resolution of (8), on one hand, when the underspecified $w@(z : \text{entity}) \times \textbf{male}(z)$ type calls the proof search for w, the only information it can use to construct the proof term of the type $(z : \text{entity}) \times \textbf{male}(z)$ is (i) the (implicitly defined) signature σ and (ii) the context Γ. In words, this means that co-indexation and E-type anaphora are the only options for interpreting *his*.

On the other hand, in the proof search (9) that underspecified type $w@(z : \text{entity}) \times \textbf{male}(z)$ launches for w, it can use the variable $u : (x : \text{entity}) \times \textbf{boy}(x)$ in addition to signature σ and context Γ in the proof construction. In words, this means that BVA reading with u being an antecedent is an option in addition to co-indexation and E-type anaphora.

This is the outline of the analysis of M-WCO in [2], and experiments based on LFS in [10] show that the predictions of this analysis are supported. The semantic analysis based on DTS in [2] differs from previous syntactic analyses, which rely on the c-command relation on the syntactic structure as the basic concept. The semantic analysis based on DTS uses the scope relation: whether a certain term is in the scope of a given variable. These two lines of analysis are indirectly connected since, in most cases, for an underspecified type to appear within the scope of the variable introduced by a quantifier, the phrase containing the underspecified type must be syntactically adjacent to the quantifier. A more detailed comparisons will be the subject of future research. However, here, we emphasize that the LFS methodology is not limited to minimalist syntax as a theoretical device.

Predictions on R-WCO. What prediction does this version of DTS then yield on the behaviour of R-WCO? The syntactic structures of (2a) and (2b) are (10) and (11).

(10)

(11)

These structures are mapped to the semantic representations (12) and (13).

(12)
$$\left(u : \begin{bmatrix} x : \text{entity} \\ b : \textbf{boy}(x) \\ w@\begin{bmatrix} z : \text{entity} \\ \textbf{male}(z) \end{bmatrix} \\ v@\begin{bmatrix} y : \text{entity} \\ \textbf{motherOf}(y, \pi_1 w) \end{bmatrix} \\ \textbf{love}(x, \pi_1 v) \end{bmatrix} \right) \rightarrow \textbf{buy}(\pi_1 u, f)$$

$$(13) \quad \left(u : \begin{bmatrix} x : \text{entity} \\ b : \textbf{boy}(x) \\ w@\begin{bmatrix} z : \text{entity} \\ \textbf{male}(z) \end{bmatrix} \\ v@\begin{bmatrix} y : \text{entity} \\ \textbf{motherOf}(y, \pi_1 w) \end{bmatrix} \\ \textbf{love}(\pi_1 v, x) \end{bmatrix} \right) \rightarrow \textbf{buy}(\pi_1 u, f)$$

The only difference between (12) and (13) lies in the order of the first and second arguments of the predicate **love**. And in both semantic representations, the underspecified type $w@(z : \text{entity}) \times \textbf{male}(z)$ appears inside the scope of x and b. Therefore, both (12) and (13) launch the same proof search (14).

$$(14) \quad \Gamma, x : \text{entity}, b : \textbf{boy}(x) \vdash_{\text{UDTT}} ? : \begin{bmatrix} x : \text{entity} \\ \textbf{male}(x) \end{bmatrix}$$

Thus, the proof search for this query has the option of using x and b for the construction of a proof corresponding to *his*. In other words, in the semantic representation of R-WCO constructions (12) and (13), the Σ-type brought about by the quantificational expression *every boy who* ... takes a scope over the entire relative clause. Therefore, DTS predicts that in R-WCO constructions, there will be no reason for the WCO effect to show up in either of Subject or Object relative clauses.

2.2 The LFS Method

[7] discusses M-WCO in Japanese and shows that native speakers for whom independent tests diagnose no interference of "noise" consistently reject BVA interpretations regarding the binder X and the bindee Y in sentences where X does not c-command Y. [14] succeeds in reproducing results of [7] in English. In these two previous studies, the experiments performed are divided so that there are sub-experiments and a main experiment, with sub-experiments checking things like informant attentiveness and comprehension, and the main experiment (a) diagnosing whether there is non-structural interference on individuals' judgements using interpretations other than BVA (Distributive Readings (DR) and Coreference (Coref)) and (b) checking their judgements on the BVA sentences of interest.

(15) DR SVO
Every teacher praised two students.

(16) DR WCO
Two students praised every teacher.

(17) Coref SVO
John praised his student.

(18) Coref WCO
His student praised John.

(19) BVA SVO
Every boy praised his father.

(20) BVA WCO
      His father praised every boy.

DR is the interpretation where, e.g., each teacher praised a distinct set of two students in the sentence (15), and Coref is the interpretation where, e.g., *his* is interpreted as *John's* in the sentence (17).

What has been shown is that a correlation (21) holds [7], where $[+cc]$ means that X (or X') c-commands Y (or Y'), and $[-cc]$ means that it does not.

(21) DR $(S^{[+cc]}, X, Y')$: yes $\wedge$ Coref $(S^{[+cc]}, X', Y)$: yes

$\wedge$ BVA $(S^{[+cc]}, X, Y)$: yes

$\wedge$ DR $(S^{[-cc]}, X, Y')$: no $\wedge$ Coref $(S^{[-cc]}, X', Y)$: no

$\rightarrow$ BVA $(S^{[-cc]}, X, Y)$: no

This follows from a number of factors, most crucially the potential sources of BVA, as argued for in works like [13], which gives the following list:

(22) Conditions for Sources of BVA(X, Y):

    a. FR (Formal Relation in [8]): X must c-command Y.

    b. ID (Indexical Dependency in [18]) : X must precede Y.

    c. NFS1 (Non-Formal Source 1 in [8]): (among other things) X must be understood as the "sentence topic."

    d. NFS2 (Non-Formal Source 2 in [8]): Y must be understood as "non-individual denoting."

In both [7]'s and [14]'s experiments, though many informants did accept M-WCO readings, all such informants were independently diagnosed via their DR and Coref judgements as utilizing non-FR sources. Those who were diagnosed as using only FR universally rejected M-WCO, even while still accepting BVA in other constructions such as reconstruction-based OSV. This suggests that M-WCO is indeed $S^{[-cc]}$ and reconstruction OSV is indeed $S^{[+cc]}$, as expected.

3   Design of Experiment

3.1   Forms of Sentences

In this work, in a similar way to [14], we use various BVA, DR, Coref schemata, as given in Table 1.

Table 1. C-command relation and precedence in schemata in the main experiment

Sentence Type	Abbreviation	Form	X c-commands Y	X precedes Y
Canonical BVA	SVO	X V [Y's N].	yes	yes
Matrix Weak Crossover	WCO	[Y's N] V X.	no	no
Precedence-based Spec-Binding	PSB	[X's N_1] V [Y's N_2]	no	yes
Reconstruction	OSV	[Y's N], X V.	yes	no
Subject Relative Clause	SRC	X which V_1[Y's N] V_2	yes	yes
Object Relative Clause	ORC	X which [Y's N] V_1 V_2	?	yes

In [14], OSV-type and WCO-type sentences are used in order to check whether the judgments are based on c-command relation; this experiment adds SVO, PSB (Precedence Spec-Binding), SRC (Subject Relative Clause) and ORC (Object Relative Clause), the last of which corresponds to a potential R-WCO configuration. Note that SRC is a relative clause analogue of SVO/OSV, just as ORC one of WCO. The type and the forms of schemata are all the same among BVA, DR, and Coref, except that in DR sentences, Y is not embedded in a larger nominal.

The reason for using PSB-type sentences is to check whether X preceding Y can lead to BVA, i.e., whether ID(X, Y) is possible for a given individual with a particular choice of X and Y; we discuss this aspect further in the results section.

3.2   X and Y for BVA(X, Y)

In addition, due to (22c) and (22d), what is used as X, Y, V and N in sentences affects judgements.

For example, regarding the binder, X, past experiments suggest that many people can accept WCO-type of BVA(every N, Y), but if "more than one N" is used, it is rarer for people to accept it.

Regarding the bindee, Y, according to [10], informants are sometimes confused because of gender and stylistic issues surrounding "his", "her", and "their". Therefore, we decided to use "its" as Y for BVA or Coref schemata in this work. To fit with "it", we used "school in Japan" as the N of "more than one N", and thus had "it" be the possessor of "high achieving student".

Examples of SVO sentences for the different interpretations are given in (23), (24) and (25):

(23)   BVA (more than one school in Japan, its)
       More than one school in Japan lied to its high-achieving student.

(24)   DR(more than one school in Japan, two high-achieving students)
       More than one school in Japan lied to two high-achieving students.

(25)   Coref (a school in Japan,its)
       A school in Japan lied to its high-achieving student.

Following [11], we used one choice of X and Y for BVA(X, Y), along with two choices of Y ("two high-achieving students" and "three high-achieving students") for DR(X, Y), two choices of X ("a school in Japan" and "the school in Japan") for Coref(X, Y), and two main verbs ("sued" and "lied to"), for a total of 60 sentences, in addition to sub-experiments in the style of [6] to check informants' attentiveness and comprehension).

3.3   The Method of Conveying Interpretations

In the experiment of [14], BVA, DR, and Coref interpretations were presented as para-phrases like (26).

(26)   "His student spoke to every teacher."

       a. In this sentence, "his student" can refer to each teacher's own student.

    b. In this sentence, "his student" cannot refer to each teacher's own student.

    c. This is not a sentence of English.

However, according to [12], paraphrases can sometimes be easy to misunderstand. In order to get clearer results and make it easy for informants to understand the interpretation, we used figures similar to those used in [10], adapting them when necessary to cover relative clause-type sentences, such as in Fig. 1.

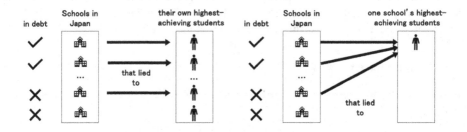

Fig. 1. Figures of interpretations of (27)

(27)   SRC-type of BVA
     More than one school in Japan which lied to two high-achieving students is now in debt.

Each sentence was paired with an image that corresponded to the relevant interpretation (BVA, DR, Coref) and one that corresponded to a contrasting "referential" interpretation. Participants were asked to indicate which interpretations were possible, choosing both or neither being options as well.

3.4 Further Details

For reliable results, in addition to providing a tutorial, we also checked whether participants understood the interpretation-conveying pictures as intended, using sub-experiments like as shown in (28)/Fig. 2

(28)   BVA Inst-Sub
     Every school in Japan lied to the same high-achieving student.

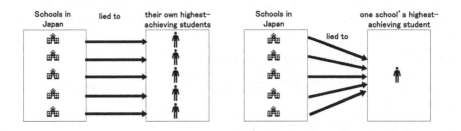

Fig. 2. Figures of interpretations about (28)

When considering sentence (28), if informants understand the BVA interpretation picture (on the left of Fig. 3), they should clearly feel it cannot be a possible interpretation of the sentence in question. As such, they are expected to choose only the option corresponding to the picture on the right (not the one on the left or the "both" option.)

Below, we include examples illustrating how different interpretations were conveyed. First, the three basic types (BVA, DR, and Coref) were as conveyed as below, corresponding to the SVO examples in (23)–(25) (Figs. 4 and 5).

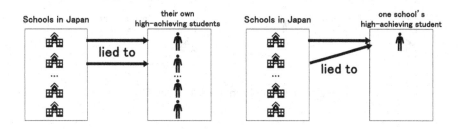

Fig. 3. Figures of interpretations about (23)

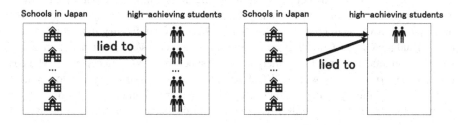

Fig. 4. Figures of interpretations about (24)

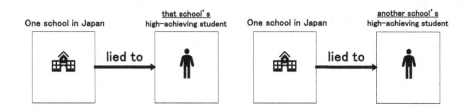

Fig. 5. Figures of interpretations about (25)

Pictures for sentences of the OSV-type were identical to those of the SVO-type, and those of the WCO-type were created simply by changing the verb in the image to a passive (e.g., "lied to" changed to "were lied to by"). The same change was used to convert between SRC and ORC pictures, which had an appearence as already shown in Fig. 1. PSB type sentences were shown as in the example below (Fig. 6):

(29)   PSB-type of BVA
       More than one school in Japan's principal lied to its high-achieving student.

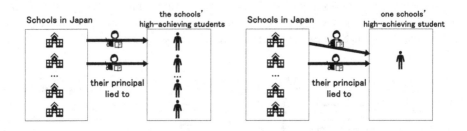

Fig. 6. Figures of interpretations about (29)

4   Results

The results of the experiment (a) replicate previous findings about matrix weak crossover (M-WCO), and (b) show a failure to replicate if we extend the domain of inquiry to relative weak crossover (R-WCO). That is, if we classify individuals based on their judgements on Coref/DR sentences and attentiveness/comprehension-checking sub-experiments, a clear pattern emerges with respect to M-WCO acceptance, whereas no such pattern emerges with R-WCO acceptance. This asymmetry would seem to undermine any theory which predicts the two to pattern identically in terms of their acceptability, though, as we will discuss at the end of this section, there is still at least one critical question remaining.

Before beginning any sub-analysis, it is often informative to look at the pattern of raw acceptability. Already there, it is clear that there are differences between M-WCO (represented by the "WCO" construction) and R-WCO (represented by the more theory-neutrally labeled "ORC" (object relative clause) construction) (Fig. 7).

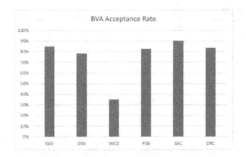

Fig. 7. BVA acceptance rates in different constructions

Across the judgements of the 107 participants, recruited on the platform Prolific to judge the relevant sentences, (M-)WCO BVA was accepted only 35% of the time, contrasting with every other construction, which were each accepted roughly 80–90% of the time. This latter group includes the ORC (R-WCO) construction, the acceptance rate of which was 84%, almost identical to that of the SVO construction (85%), which we may consider the "control" case as the SVO construction is uncontroversially acceptable with a BVA reading.

Even with no further analytical tools deployed, it is clear already that M-WCO and R-WCO do not have the same basic "status" in this dataset. However, it is possible that, after informant classification has been done, even a construction for which BVA is frequently accepted may be seen to have a non-typical status; this was the finding of [11] with regards to topicalized spec-binding sentences, for example. In that study's case, such sentences were frequently accepted, but when informant classification was applied, it became clear that all cases of individuals accepting the construction with BVA showed clear signs of making use of NFS sources to achieve said interpretations (see (22)). When focusing only on individuals who were diagnosed as clearly not making use of NFS-based BVA but only FR-based BVA, no topicalized spec-binding acceptances occurred.

In principle, the same might be true here, that i.e., R-WCO is more frequently accepted than M-WCO, but that they are both ultimately accepted due to NFS-based BVA. Performing the relevant classification, however, it becomes apparent that this is not the case. Following previous experiments, we classified individuals according to three basic criteria:

(30) Classification Criteria (conceptual):

    a. Whether the individual showed clear signs of being attentive/comprehending the questions as intended, as judged by the relevant sub-experiments.

    b. Whether the individual showed clear signs of not being able to use NFS-1 to enable BVA, as predicted based on the individual's judgement on DR sentences.

    c. Whether the individual showed clear signs of not being able to use NFS-1 to enable BVA, as predicted based on the individual's judgement on Coref sentences.

As discussed in [12], there is a degree of fine-tuning necessary in order to implement these criteria in a manner useful for the dataset in question. For example, while demanding 100% accuracy on the attentiveness/comprehension-checking sub-experiments in order to satisfy criterion (30a) might be ideal in principle, in practice, it can be needlessly eliminative, causing participants who most likely did understand the questions as intended and pay attention to be counted as "non-reliable". Indeed, if we followed such a strict procedure in this case, we would be left with only 12% of the participants counted as "reliable" in this sense, a much smaller fraction than the ones counted as reliable in any of the comparable previous experiments. As a result, following [14], we chose to use only the BVA-Inst sub, as that seems to be the one most crucial for identifying whether participants do indeed understand the questions they were being asked as intended; this leaves us with 65% of the participants being classified as reliable.

For criterion (30b), we largely followed previous experiments, counting only individuals who always rejected "WCO" DR (really inverse scope DR, given that, as mentioned in Sect. 3.1, Y is not embedded in a larger nominal) and who at least sometimes accepted OSV DR; this results in 29% of individuals being classified as clearly showing no signs of NFS-1 effects on "more than one school in Japan". However, given that precedence is not known to effect DR judgments in a relevant manner, we decided to also include individuals who failed to accept OSV DR but did sometimes accept SVO DR, the logic being that, so long as they consistently reject inverse scope DR and accept DR in some non-inverse scope cases, the test seems to conclusively show that DR is unacceptable for the individual in question specifically under inverse scope, which is the signature of NFS-1 being impossible for the choice of X of DR/BVA(X, Y) in question [7,8]. This yields about 36% of individuals meeting criterion (30b).

For criterion (30c), we faced a challenge, in that all but one individual accepted WCO Coref (more than one school in Japan, its) at least some of the time, most individuals accepting it all of the time. A significant minority, however, rejected it at least sometimes. Because of the well-known confound from Co-D indexation-based Coreference [13], and given that WCO Coref rejection of any sort was inherently noteworthy in this dataset due to its minority status, we decided to take a more relaxed approach to criterion (30c) and hold that any individual who rejected WCO Coref at least sometimes could be considered as clearly demonstrating a lack of NFS-2 effects. (As all individuals accepted SVO/OSV Coref, it was not necessary to consider acceptances of such cases as a separate requirement.) This criterion was met by 31% of individuals.

Thus, are classification criteria ultimately were:[2]

(31) Classification Criteria for M-WCO (implementational):

    a. Whether the individual always passed the BVA-Inst sub (indicating attentiveness/comprehension)

    b. Whether the individual always rejected "WCO" DR with 'more than one school in Japan' and at least sometimes accepted SVO and/or OSV DR with 'more than one school in Japan' (indicating a lack of NFS-1 effects on 'more than one school in Japan')

    c. Whether the individual ever rejected WCO Coref with 'it' (indicating a lack of NFS-2 effects on 'it')

Following previous experiments, we also divide participants based on their BVA judgements on the sentences of interest:

(32) BVA Classification (M-WCO)

    a. Individuals who accept OSV BVA(more than one school in Japan, its) at least sometimes but reject WCO BVA(more than one school in Japan, its) always (indicating clearly that the structure of WCO in particular disallows the BVA in question)

---

[2] While these were the particular criteria we felt best illuminated the patterns in the data, many other analogous criteria might have been used, and, taken as a whole, they all converged to the same basic results as the ones we present below. To forestall concerns that these criteria might have been in some way cherry-picked, and also to allow further exploration/analysis of the data, we have made our data public at Haruka Fukushima's github (https://github.com/fuyunoharu).

b. Individuals who reject both OSV BVA(more than one school in Japan, its)
and WCO BVA(more than one school in Japan, its) always (which is still
WCO rejection, but which is harder to clearly attribute to the structure of
WCO in particular)

c. Individuals who accept WCO BVA(more than one school in Japan, its)
(indicating that WCO BVA is possible for them)

Dividing individuals based on which, if any, of the criteria in (32) they meet, and using
these as the columns of the table below, set against the classification of individuals
based on their BVA judgements as in (32) as rows, we obtain the following (Table 2):

Table 2. Results of classification (M-WCO)

M-WCO	(31a)(31b)(31c)	(31a)(31b)	(31b)(31c)	(31a)(31c)	(31a)	(31b)	(31c)	None	Total
(32a)	6	11	0	5	11	5	4	2	44
(32b)	0	1	0	0	2	0	1	0	4
(32c)	0	8	3	7	18	4	7	12	59
Total	6	20	3	12	31	9	12	14	107

While much could be said here, most crucially, we see that, of the 6 individuals
who met all criteria, all were of type (32a); that is, of the individuals for whom no non-
FR factors were diagnosed, none accept WCO BVA. This result is comparable both
qualitatively and quantitatively to previous experiments (e.g., [8, 10, 11, 14]), providing
a replication of the well-established pattern for M-WCO, namely that M-WCO BVA
is sometimes acceptable, but that these times are clearly diagnosable as cases of either
NFS-1 or NFS-2 (or just poor comprehension/attentiveness). M-WCO thus differs qualitatively from other constructions, such as OSV reconstruction, where FR-based BVA
is possible, even despite the lack of X preceding Y. [11]

Turning to R-WCO, we use exact the same classification strategy, only substituting
ORC for WCO and SRC for OSV in (32). This yields the following Table 3:

Table 3. Results of classification (R-WCO)

R-WCO	(31a)(31b)(31c)	(31a)(31b)	(31b)(31c)	(31a)(31c)	(31a)	(31b)	(31c)	None	Total
(32a)	0	1	0	0	2	0	1	1	5
(32b)	0	0	0	0	1	0	0	0	1
(32c)	6	19	3	12	28	9	11	13	101
Total	6	20	3	12	31	9	12	14	107

The results have utterly flipped. Of the individuals who we can be confident use
exclusively FR-BVA (more than one school in Japan, it), all of them accept instances
of R-WCO, contrasting with their universally consistent rejection of all instances of

M-WCO.[3] That is, while M-WCO BVA acceptance can be eliminated by focusing on individuals who show no signs of non-attentiveness/non-comprehension and neither of NFS-1 nor NFS-2 effects, the same is not true of R-WCO; such individuals, in fact, universally accept R-WCO.

One possible conclusion is that BVA in R-WCO can be based on FR. However, one caveat must be observed: in M-WCO, X of BVA(X, Y) follows Y, whereas in R-WCO, X precedes Y. This opens up the possibility that ID(X, Y), rather than FR(X, Y), might be responsible for the source of BVA acceptance in R-WCO; if so, this would indicate that it is not structure but simply word order which distinguishes M- from R-WCO. We attempted to test this possibility by including PSB constructions in our experiment, intending them to serve as probes for which individuals can make use of ID (more than one school in Japan, it), as following the results in [10, 11], BVA in such constructions can only be based on ID or NFS1/NFS2. However, the rate of PSB acceptance was very high, and as such, there were too few individuals who did not accept it in order for the relevant predictions to be tested. We thus intend to perform a follow-up experiment in the future in order to answer the question of whether structure or word order is behind the M-WCO R-WCO contrast. Such an experiment could either be performed in English, making use of choices of X and Y that make ID(X, Y) less likely (e.g., [18] suggests that using a phrase quantified by 'no' may block or inhibit ID), or perhaps more simply, be performed in a language like Japanese, where relative clauses precede the nouns they modify, eliminating the possibility of ID due to X preceding Y.

In sum, at this point, we have evidence that M-WCO and R-WCO have different statuses, at least in English, and further work will have to determine the source (structure or linear word order) of that difference.

5 Conclusion

In this work, we explored the relationship between matrix weak crossover (M-WCO) and relative Weak crossover (R-WCO) thorough an experiment that allowed us to check DTS predictions regarding BVA availability in matrix clauses vs. in relative clauses. In particular, by utilizing the methodology of LFS, we were able to focus on individuals for which certain interfering factors are clearly controlled. After performing the relevant informant classification, two very different patterns emerged for M-WCO and R-WCO; the former was always rejected in the controlled cases, whereas the latter was always accepted. Further work remains to distinguish whether these results are due to differing

---

[3] Another way in which one might analyze this data might be to substitute SRC not only in (31) as well as (32). This is the strategy used in [11] for demonstrating the incorrectness of "bad hypotheses", such that reconstruction is impossible in an OSV configuration. In that case, the results obtained in this experiment mirror exactly what [11] shows should happen if ORC/R-WCO does not have the same $S^{[-cc]}$ status as M-WCO. In particular, almost no one meets the resulting criteria, and the one person who does still accepts BVA in ORC sentences. Analogous results obtain if we try to "mix and match" the OSV/WCO and SRC/ORC sentence types; only if WCO is used as the $S^{[-cc]}$ does the intended pattern of unacceptability obtain, and in fact, this can be done even if ORC is used as the $S^{[+cc]}$.

structures or differing word orders between the constructions, but results thus far are supportive of theories (like DTS in [2]) that do not predict R-WCO to have the same pattern of unacceptability as M-WCO.

Acknowledgements. We sincerely thank the participants and the anonymous reviewers of LENLS20 for their insightful comments. This work was partially supported by Japan Science and Technology Agency (JST) CREST Grant Number JPMJCR20D2.22 and Japan Society for the Promotion of Science (JSPS) KAKENHI Grant Number JP18H03284.

References

1. Bekki, D.: Representing anaphora with dependent types. In: Asher, N., Soloviev, S. (eds.) LACL 2014. LNCS, vol. 8535, pp. 14–29. Springer, Heidelberg (2014). https://doi.org/10.1007/978-3-662-43742-1_2
2. Bekki, D.: A proof-theoretic analysis of weak crossover. In: Proceedings of LENLS18, pp. 75–88 (2021)
3. Bekki, D., Mineshima, K.: Context-passing and underspecification in dependent type semantics. In: Chatzikyriakidis, S., Luo, Z. (eds.) Modern Perspectives in Type-Theoretical Semantics. SLP, vol. 98, pp. 11–41. Springer, Cham (2017). https://doi.org/10.1007/978-3-319-50422-3_2
4. Bekki, D., Sato, M.: Calculating projections via type checking. In: TYpe Theory and LExical Semantics (TYTLES), ESSLLI2015 Workshop (2015)
5. Higginbotham, J.: Pronouns and bound variables. Linguist. Inquiry **11**(4), 679–708 (1980)
6. Hoji, H.: Language Faculty Science. Cambridge University Press, Cambridge (2015)
7. Hoji, H.: Predicted correlations of judgments in Japanese. In: The Theory and Practice of Language Faculty Science. De Gruyter Mouton, Berlin and Boston (2022)
8. Hoji, H.: Detection of C-command effects. In the theory and practice of language faculty science. In: The Theory and Practice of Language Faculty Science. De Gruyter Mouton, Berlin and Boston (2022)
9. Martin-Löf, P.: Intuitionistic Type Theory, vol. 17. Bibliopolis, Naples (1984)
10. Plesniak, D.: Towards a correlational law of language: three factors constraining judgement variation. Ph.D. thesis, University of Southern California (2022)
11. Plesniak, D.: Predicted correlations of judgments in English. In: The Theory and Practice of Language Faculty Science. De Gruyter Mouton, Berlin and Boston (2022)
12. Plesniak, D.: Implementing experiments on the language faculty. In: The Theory and Practice of Language Faculty Science. De Gruyter Mouton, Berlin and Boston (2022)
13. Plesniak, D.: C-command and beyond: the emerging universe of formal and non-formal relations. Korean J. Linguist. **48**(2) (2023)
14. Plesniak, D.: Possibility-seeking experiments: testing syntactic hypotheses on the level of the individual 1. In: Studies in Generative Grammar (2023)
15. Reinhart, T.: Coreference and bound anaphora: a restatement of the anaphora questions. Linguist. Philos. **6**, 47–88 (1983)
16. Safir, K.: Weak crossover. In: The Wiley Blackwell Companion to Syntax, 2nd edn. Wiley Blackwell (2017)
17. Steedman, M.J.: Surface Structure and Interpretation. The MIT Press, Cambridge (1996)
18. Ueyama, A.: Two types of dependency. Ph.D. thesis, University of Southern California, Los Angeles (1998)
19. Wasow, T.: Anaphoric relations in English. Ph.D. thesis, Massachusetts Institute of Technology (1972)

Additivity in Attention Semantics

Noritsugu Hayashi[(✉)] [ID]

The University of Tokyo, 3-8-1 Komaba, Meguro, Tokyo 153-8902, Japan
ac@hayashi-lin.net
https://hayashi-lin.net/

Abstract. Three counterexamples are presented against the idea that obligatory additive marking is directly motivated by exhaustivity implicatures. It is argued that it is the notion of potential question that is crucial. A discourse semantic and pragmatic theory is submitted, implemented with the notion of *attention* proposed by Westera [63,64].

Keywords: additivity · Attention Semantics · Alternative Semantics · Question under Discussion · discourse management

1 Introduction

An intuitive characterization of additive markers such as *too*, *either*, and *also* in English and *auch* in German is that they indicate that the predicate predicated of the associate of the additive marker is also applicable to another entity in the context. Karttunen [30, p. 33, (51)] implemented this antecedent requirement as a presupposition. However, subsequent research has demonstrated that this view needs revision in several respects: (i) the licensing condition (when they *can* be used), (ii) the obligatory nature in certain context (when they *must* be used),[1] (iii) the semantic and pragmatic contribution of additive markers, and (iv) polarity sensitivity.

A particular point of interest pertaining to (ii) is the question of whether the obligatoriness is a direct consequence of the exhaustivity implicature. This paper presents several observations, mainly made in Japanese, which argue against implicature-driven accounts such as Krifka [34] and Sæbø [58]. Instead, a pure Question under Discussion (QuD)-driven account is more preferred, in which obligatory additive marking is a consequence of the *discourse question* [55] being "settled" by a confirmed previous answer, rather than the previous answer or the prejacent clause generating implicatures. These observations include cases in which the otherwise expected exhaustivity implicature is overtly suppressed (5), those in which an indefinite expression exempts additive marking (6), and those where the associate of the additive marker is a conjunction, which strictly entails the antecedent proposition (8).

---

[1] Note that (i) and (ii) are independent of each other. There is a middle between unlicensedness and obligatoriness, in which additive marking is purely optional (see [54, pp. 42–43, (32) vs. (34)] and [65]).

D. Bekki et al. (Eds.): LENLS 2023, LNCS 14569, pp. 84–117, 2024.
https://doi.org/10.1007/978-3-031-60878-0_6

This paper is organized as follows. Section 2 introduces basic ideas of obligatory additive marking and the relevant discourse schema. Section 3 critically reviews Krifka's [34] work, which offers a baseline of implicature-driven accounts. Attention Semantics (and Pragmatics) [63, 64] is introduced in Sect. 4. This two-dimensional semantics is then reconstructed based on state-based semantics [3, 4] for rich representations, which is to be embedded in the table model managing QuD stacks [16, 44]. Section 5 demonstrates how this framework can predict the problematic observations. Section 6 concludes and talks about several relevant areas for future research.

2   The Base Case of Obligatory Additive Marking

Kaplan [29, p. 510, (1)] discusses the following example found by Green [21], where the use of *too* appears obligatory.

(1)   Jo had fish and Mo did, *(too).

However, the obligatoriness of *too* is a fragile property. In a continual responding utterance made by a single speaker, each item of the list answer can be marked by no additive markers [65, p. 1797, (37)]:

(2)   Q: What did they eat?
       A: John had spaghetti, Bill had spaghetti and Susan had a pizza.

A more stable effect of obligatoriness can be found in the following trilogue schema:

(3)   Q: Who knows the password?
       A: John does.
       B: Exactly. Bill does, #(too).

(4) is an exact Japanese counterpart of (3) (translation omitted):

(4)   Q: dare-ga   pasuwādo-o   sit-tei-masu-ka?
            who-NOM   password-ACC know-ASP-HON-Q

       A: Hanako-ga   sit-tei-masu.
            Hanako-NOM know-ASP-HON

       B: sonotōri-desu. Tarō-{ # ga / mo }   sit-tei-masu.
            exactly-HON Taro-{ NOM / NOM.ADD } know-ASP-HON

Here, there are three participants, namely speakers Q, A, and B. The discourse consists of three utterances made by each of them: a given question raised by speaker Q, a previous answer made by speaker A, and a subsequent answer made by speaker B following an affirmative response to speaker A's previous answer. The observed obligatoriness can be described as follows: when the context provides a given question and a previous answer to that question which is confirmed by a subsequent answerer, the subsequent answerer must mark their answer with an additive marker.[2] [3]

Different factors have been proposed in the literature which motivate additive marking in such a discourse setting. Among those are conversational implicatures [34,58], QuD-related conditions [5,27], saliency of antecedents [65, p. 1791] and the existence of alternative utterances [43,56]. This paper will not attempt to adjudicate each of these proposals. Rather, this paper will focus on disproving the direct connection between obligatory additive marking and conversational implicatures and to propose an alternative theory which attributes the obligatoriness directly to discourse questions.

---

[2] A reviewer does not appreciate the additively marked variant of (4B), with the response word *sonotōri(-desu)*, as a fully natural assertion of speaker B. This reviewer finds that in contrast to other response words such as *sō(-desu)-ne* and *ē* (see also Sect. 6), this response word is an affirmation stronger than the author expects, indicating that the previous answer is exhaustive. This reviewer also finds it unusual for an additional information to follow a directly affirmative response word (even a weaker response word such as *sō-desu-ne*; see Sect. 6), and claims that it is necessary for this reviewer to add either the sentence-final particle *yo* or a clausal conjunctive (see footnote 3 below).

First, the author concurs with the reviewer in that in general, the discourse schema would become better with additional discourse particles such as the sentential particle *yo* that eventually increase the cohesion of the utterances. (Nevertheless, this subtle verbal awkwardness would not undermine the overall proposal). Secondly, there might be a variation between speakers with regard to the exhaustive implication brought about by the response word *sonotōri(-desu)*. (For speakers who interprets this word with exhaustivity, these response words are stronger ones in the sense that they *reject* any attention revision.) However, there is certainly a dialect or an idiolect in which *sonotōri(-desu)* does *not* imply uncancellable exhaustivity. Here is an attested example. If we assume that *sonotōri(-desu)* necessarily entails exhaustivity, it cannot be continued with any additional information even with the additive conjunct *ato* 'besides'.

(1)   Interviewer: So you are making it possible to bulk search three different journals of buddhism studies.

      Interviewee: sonotō-ri-desu. ato tōzen-desu-ga kikan-ripozitori-ga ari-masu.

      'Exactly. Besides, we have the institute digital repository.'

      (https://service.infocom.co.jp/das/result/infolib/bukkyo-u.html)

---

[3] *Mo* is not the only additive marker in the language. Clausal conjunctives such as *ato* 'besides' and *sorekara* 'and then' also sanction the subsequent answer:

(4B″)   sonotōri-desu. *sorekara* Tarō-{ ga / mo } sit-tei-masu.

3   Implicature-Based Accounts and Problematic Cases

Three observations is presented here in this section to argue against implicature-based accounts. First, inserting *sukunakutomo* 'at least' does not make the additive marker optional.

(5)   Q: Who knows the password?

A: (sukunakutomo) Hanako-ga   sit-tei-masu.
(at least)   Hanako-NOM know-ASP-HON

'(At least) Hanako does.'

B: sonotōri-desu. (sukunakutomo) Tarō-{ # ga / mo }
exactly-HON   (at least)   Taro-{ NOM / NOM.ADD }
sit-tei-masu.
know-ASP-HON

'Exactly. (At least) Taro does, #(too).'

Krifka [34] will face a problem here. *Sukunakutomo* 'at least', an upper-side-ignorance-marking focus sensitive marker [8,20,31,35], suppresses the exhaustivity implicature. Therefore, an incorrect prediction will be made that the additive marker is not obligatory.[4] Sæbø [58], which argues that the source of the oblig-

---

[4] The nominative case marker *-ga* has been argued to be exhaustive in certain cases [37,38]. However, this paper will not attribute any exhaustive reading to nominative case markers. First of all, the exhaustive reading is not really attached to the case marker except in limited environments such as root clauses hosting a stative or individual-level predicate. Moreover, the obligatoriness additive marking is observed even with a stage-level predicate, where the nominative case marker is considered *not* to be exhaustificational.

(1)   Q: dare-ga sono-toki te-o age-masi-ta-ka?
'Who raised their hand at that time?'

A: sono-toki Hanako-ga age-masi-ta.   'Hanako did at that time.'

B: sonotōri-desu.   'Exactly.'
sono-toki Tarō-{ # ga / mo } age-masi-ta. 'Taro did at that time, #(too).'

Another piece of evidence that it is wrong to assume that nominative case markers intrinsically bear exhaustivity is that the list answer example (2) below. Exhaustivity, if any, *emerges* from the whole answer;

(2)   Q: dare-ga pasuwādo-o sit-tei-masu-ka? 'Who knows the password?'

A: Hanako-ga sit-tei-masu\. Tarō-ga sit-tei-masu\. Zyon-ga sit-tei-masu\.
'Hanako knows it. Taro knows it. John knows it.'

where \ marks the downward tone. Eckardt [15] also found that exhaustivity might disappear depending on the type of discourse. Whatever exhaustive reading is related to the nominative case marker, it should be a consequence of the congruence between a question and an answer [25].

To avoid such complications, one can just avoid the nominative case and instead use different case markers (such as the accusative and the dative case marker) or zero case markers to replicate the same observation.

atory additive marking is the subsequent (B's) answer rather than the previous one (A's), is also problematic.[5]

Second, indefinite expressions can exempt additive marking. The subsequent answer in (6) is acceptable without additive marking.[6]

(6) Q: Who knows the password?

A: Hanako-to-dareka-ga   sit-tei-masu.
    Hanako-and-someone-NOM know-ASP-HON

    'Hanako and someone (else) do.'

B: sonotōri-desu. Tarō-{ ga / mo } sit-tei-masu.

    'Exactly. Taro does, (too).'

The optionality of additive marking should be attributed to the indefinite *dareka* 'someone (else)' in the previous (speaker A's) answer. This is corroborated by the following minimal pair (7), in which an associate plural -*tati* [39] is used to counterbalance the informative sent:[7]

---

[5] Note that either side of the ignorance implicature alone is not logically strong enough to contradict a logically consistent subsequent answer. In (1), speaker A's explicit ignorance cannot be negated by *īe, tigai-masu* 'No, it's wrong.' in speaker B's answer.

(1) Q: Who knows the password?

A: Hanako-ka Tarō-ga sit-tei-masu-ga dotiraka-wa siri-mase-n.

    'Either Hanako and Taro does, but I'm not sure which does.'

B: { Sonotōri-desu / # īe, tigai-masu }.   '{Exactly / No, it's wrong.}.
    Tarō-ga sit-tei-masu.   'Taro does.'

[6] A reviewer does not find (6) natural with either *ga* or *mo*. The author agrees with this reviewer on the point that (6B) is a response less optimal than the one using the specificational copular construction:

(6B')   sonotōri-desu. { sono-hito / mō-hitori }-wa Tarō-desu.

    'Exactly. { That person / The other person } is Taro.

The author would like to leave open the discrepancy between the author's and the reviewer's judgment on this suboptimality. Instead, the author would like to point to (6") in p. 22, §6, a variant of (6) in which a negative response word is substituted for the positive one. A clear *ga/mo* discrepancy is observed in (6"), which contrasts with the absence of, or at least the unclearness of, differences in acceptability between *ga* and *mo* in (6).

[7] A caveat must be put here that the obligatory use of *mo* does not replicate when *Hanako-tati* is understood as specific (i.e. there is a group of particular individuals including Hanako) and definite (i.e. that group is salient to both Speakers A and B). In such a context, *mo* is optional.

However, this is not a real counterexample which threatens our proposal. Considering that the definite pluralized NP refers to (the sum of) Hanako and Taro, B's answer is in fact not a distinct (or "disputable" in terms of Krifka [34]) answer, but just a restatement of an obvious consequence of A's answer.

(7) Q: Who knows the password?

    A: Hanako-tati-ga   sit-tei-masu.
       Hanako-PL-NOM know-ASP-HON
       'Hanako and her associates do.'

    B: sonotōri-desu. Tarō-{ # ga / mo } sit-tei-masu.
       'Exactly. Taro does, #(too).'

In fact, not all implicature-based accounts is problematic in this regard. Krifka [34] remains safe because exhaustivity is suppressed by the conjoined indefinite in (6A). In contrast, this example afflicts Sæbø [58]. Contrary to the fact, this theory will predict that *mo* in (6) is obligatory because exhaustivity would arise from the subsequent answer (6B), which contradicts the previous answer (6A).

Lastly, additive marking is unnecessary and even prohibited when it associates with a conjunction.[8] [9]

(8) Q: Who knows the password?

    A: Hanako-ga   sit-tei-masu.
       Hanako-NOM know-ASP-HON
       'Hanako does.'

    B: sonotōri-desu. Tarō-to-Hanako-{ ga / # mo }
       exactly-HON   Taro-and-Hanako-{ NOM / NOM.ADD }
       sit-tei-masu.
       know-ASP-HON
       'Exactly. Taro and Hanako do, (# too).'

The same prohibition can also be found in English [59, p. 353, (19b, 20)]:[10]

---

[8] The same observation as (8) can be also gained with the conjunction NP replaced with an universal quantifier *zen'in* 'everyone'. The resolution of the covert domain of that quantifier is a non-trivial issue, though. The default domain seems to be the whole set of all relevant individuals, which evidently includes Hanako, but it is defeasible by the context. When the domain is specified as *Hanako-igai-no zen'in* 'everyone except Hanako', the additive marker becomes permissible, where the covert domain to be inferred seems to have to exclude Hanako if we maintain our generalization.

[9] A reviewer does not find (8B) natural with *ga* unless either the speaker inserts the connective expression *yori sēkaku-ni-wa* 'to be more precise', or replaces the response word *sonotōri-desu* with *ie, tigai-masu* 'no, it's wrong'. The author is open-minded to the former choice, but this choice would only make the contrast in (8B) more salient. The latter option, which is acceptable (Sect. 6), is off the topic of this paper.

[10] Several apparent counterexamples are found in the literature. First, Ruys [49, pp. 346–347, (9, 10)] observes that the associate of *too* need not be distinct from the antecedent. In the following examples, the associates are part of, rather than independent of, the corresponding antecedents:

(1)   a. Surely, if *a*, *b* and *c* dominate *x*, then *a* dominates *x*, too.

      b. Surely, if all members of A are divisible by x, then the smallest member of A is divisible by x, too.

(9)   I called Alice. # I also called Alice and Mary.

(10)   I called Alice and Mary. This means in particular that I (# also) called Mary.

Technically, Krifka [34] and subsequent works ([27, §2], [7, p. 73], and [59, §3.4]) are free from such overgeneralization by resorting to a stipulation that the prejacent and the antecedent sentences must be mutually independent. However, it would be better for a stipulation to be motivated.

The first observation (5) shows that exhaustivity cannot be the sole motivation for obligatory additive marking. The obligatoriness remains even without exhaustivity. The second observation (6) suggests that it is the indefinite that is more likely responsible. Indefinites are known to open up potential questions. A potential question, induced by an expression such as (but not necessarily limited to) an indefinite, is just a question (or an alternative set) which is projected from within the clause containing the inducer. It feeds into subsequent semantics and pragmatic mechanisms, such as the free choice implicature [6, 17, 64], the interaction between indefinites and conditionals [12], and (re)calculation of the saliency of potential QuDs in discourse [41, 42, 61]. A possibility worth developing is that (i) when the information focus of an answer contains a potential question, it interacts with the discourse question; (ii) additive marking is obligatory when the given answer is not a legitimate answer to the discourse question; and (iii) confirmed previous answer removes all other answers, but an indefinite can save them from being removed. This idea will be developed in the next section.

---

(2)   The republicans all voted against the bill, { so / hence } Senator Blank did, (too).

He attributed this to "rhetorical factors". It seems to me that the argumentational discourse construction *if A then B* and markers *so* and *hence* play a crucial role here. To draw a conclusion *B* from a premise *A*, one must *pretend* that *B* is independent of *A*. Similar examples are also found in [65, p. 1789, (9)], where the discourse marker *thereby* must be a main factor.

(3)   a.   Why did Alena not come? — She broke her skis. Thereby she also lost all her means of transportation.

b.   Why did Alena not come? — She lost all her means of transportation. (?) They stole her bicycle too.

On the contrary, (8) is not about drawing a conclusion from a premise, but is about speaker B's adding a new answer.

The following example from the same paper [65, p. 1789, (9)] remains unexplained, though:

(4)   a.   Do you have three chairs? — Yes, I also have seven.

b.   Do you have seven chairs? — (?) Yes, I also have three.

.

4 Proposal

A wide coverage of data necessitates a complex architecture. Generally speaking, a semantic and pragmatic system consists of the following three layers: (i) an underlying semantic language and logic, (ii) a translation from the target natural language to the underlying language, and (iii) a discourse model which manages different participants and their utterances. As for (i), the logical foundation will be la in state-base semantics (Sect. 4.2), which proffers a rich expressive power to represent meanings and constraints. For (ii), a natural language sentence is translated into two dimensions: *the information dimension* and *the attention dimension* (Sect. 4.1). This multi-dimensionality, together with a dimensionally parallel implicature calculation mechanism (Sect. 4.5), is the essence of Attention Semantics (and Pragmatics) [63,64]. Lastly, as for (iii), utterances are embedded in a discourse structure, which is modeled by the table model [16]. Discourse moves (Sect. 4.4) construct a discourse structure, which dictates what is implicated (Sect. 4.5 again) and what a legitimate subsequent discourse move (Sect. 4.6) is.

4.1 Attention Semantics and Pragmatics

Westera's Attention Semantics and Pragmatics [63,64], designed for a proper production of the ignorance and the exhaustivity implicatures stemming from indefinite and disjunctive expressions, turns out to be also helpful to address the indefinite-*mo* example (6).[11]   Essentially, his system is just a two-dimensional variation of Alternative Semantics [45,46]. The two dimensions are called *the information dimension* and *the attention dimension*. Sometimes a speaker making an utterance does not only intend to convey information but also to "draw an audience's attention to certain things" [63, p. 52]. Both of the dimensions are "semantic" for their concreteness in terms of speaker commitment and their equivalent nature on the semantic and pragmatic interface.[12]   We denote the base logical language by $\mathscr{L}$ and the two-dimensional extension by $\mathscr{L}_{\text{ATT}}$.

4.2 State-Based Semantics

The least requirement of the underlying semantics and logic $\mathscr{L}$ is that the capability to refer a sentence to multiple propositions (i.e. alternatives) at once. This

---

[11] "Attention" here has nothing to do with recent technology of machine learning. In fact, this notion originates from Inquisitive Semantics [10].

[12] I thought that the name "Attention Semantics" was a better choice than Westera's original "Attention Pragmatics" because his framework committed itself to more than just pragmatics; it necessitated multi-dimensionality and concrete speaker commitment for all of the dimensions. His theory had one foot in the realm of semantics. On the other hand, the name "Attention Semantics" is also a bit misleading because the main contribution of his theory is on the pragmatic side. I am now unsure whether I made a fair choice. The title cannot be changed, anyway.

paper pursues the choice of state-based semantics [3,4][13] , preferring it over the Roothan alternative semantics [45,46], for its power of sufficiently expressing properties of alternatives states.

Let α, β, ..., κ, ... be constants, and φ, ψ, ... be variables, in the base logical language $\mathscr{L}$, into which a natural language (Japanese) sentence $n \in \mathcal{N}$ is translated as $[n] \in \mathscr{L}$. Let $M = [\text{DOM } D, \text{INTERPRET } I]$ be an interpretative model, where D is the sets of domains and I is an interpretation function. Let a, b, ..., s, t, u, v, ... $\in D_{\text{state}} = \text{Pow}(D_{\text{world}})$ be *states*, each of which refers to a set of worlds. Let x, y, ... $\in D_{\text{indiv}}$ be individuals. Let g be an assignment function for variables.

(11) (Support of an atomic sentence)

A structure (i.e., a model with a state and an assignment) (M, s, g) *supports* an atomic sentential constant α, written as $M, s, g \vDash \alpha$, iff $s \in I(\alpha)$. Likewise, it supports a sentential variable φ, denoted as the same, iff $s \in g(\varphi)$. If the model and the assignment are clear from the context, we may omit them and just say that a state s supports α or φ.

Complex sentences in $\mathscr{L}$ are constructed with logical connectives. These connectives can be classified into (at least) two types. *Local* connectives are those applying each supporting state of a subformula and those interconnecting each pair of supporting states of subformulae. *Global* connectives are those applying directly to the whole set of supporting states of a subformula and those applying to the whole sets of supporting states of multiple subformulae. Their conditions of support are defined as follows:

(12) (Local operators in $\mathscr{L}$)

operator	condition
$M, s, g \vDash \alpha \wedge \beta$	iff $s \in \{a \cap b \mid M, a, g \vDash \alpha, M, b, g \vDash \beta\}$
$M, s, g \vDash \alpha \vee \beta$	iff $s \in \{a \cup b \mid M, a, g \vDash \alpha, M, b, g \vDash \beta\}$
$M, s, g \vDash \top$	iff $s \neq \varnothing$
$M, s, g \vDash \bot$	iff $s = \varnothing$
$M, s, g \vDash \alpha \rightarrow \beta$	iff for all a such that $M, a, g \vDash \alpha$, there is a b such that $M, b, g \vDash \beta$ and $s \subseteq \bar{a} \cup b$
$M, s, g \vDash \neg\alpha$	iff $M, s, g \vDash \alpha \rightarrow \bot$ (i.e., for all $M, a, g \vDash \alpha$, $s \cap a = \varnothing$)
$M, s, g \vDash \forall \iota. \alpha$	iff $s \in \{\cap \mathbf{v} \mid \mathbf{v} \in \bigtimes\{\{s' \mid M, s', g[\iota \mapsto x] \vDash \alpha\} \mid x \in D_{\text{type}(\iota)}\}\}$
$M, s, g \vDash \exists \iota. \alpha$	iff $s \in \{\cup \mathbf{v} \mid \mathbf{v} \in \bigtimes\{\{s' \mid M, s', g[\iota \mapsto x] \vDash \alpha\} \mid x \in D_{\text{type}(\iota)}\}\}$

---

[13] Bilateralism is abstracted out here because no negation-related phenomena are of our interest.

(13) (Global operators in $\mathscr{L}$)

operator	condition
$M,s,g \vDash \alpha \wedge \beta$	iff $M,s,g \vDash \alpha$ and $M,s,g \vDash \beta$
$M,s,g \vDash \alpha \vee \beta$	iff $M,s,g \vDash \alpha$ or $M,s,g \vDash \beta$
$M,s,g \vDash \mathbb{1}$	always holds
$M,s,g \vDash \mathbb{0}$	never holds
$M,s,g \vDash \alpha \Rightarrow \beta$	iff $M,s,g \nvDash \alpha$ or $M,s,g \vDash \beta$
$M,s,g \vDash \dashv \alpha$	iff $M,s,g \vDash \alpha \Rightarrow \mathbb{0}$ (iff $M,s,g \nvDash \alpha$)
$M,s,g \vDash \forall\!\forall \iota.\, \alpha$	iff for all $x \in D_{\text{type}(\iota)}$, $M,s,g[\iota \mapsto x] \vDash \alpha$
$M,s,g \vDash \exists\exists \iota.\, \alpha$	iff for some $x \in D_{\text{type}(\iota)}$, $M,s,g[\iota \mapsto x] \vDash \alpha$

(14) (Uncategorized operators in $\mathscr{L}$)

operator	condition
$M,s,g \vDash \phi \alpha$	iff $M,\bar{s},g \vDash \alpha$
$M,s,g \vDash \square\, \alpha$	iff $M,s,g \vDash \alpha$
$M,s,g \vDash \diamondsuit\, \alpha$	iff $M,s,g \nvDash \neg\alpha$ (iff $M,s,g \vDash \dashv \neg\alpha$)

A logical sentence $\alpha \in \mathscr{L}$ can either inherently *closed* or be made closed by a closure operator.

(15) (Closedness)

    a. α is *downwardly closed* iff $\alpha =\!\!\models\, \downarrow \alpha$.

    b. α is *conjunction closed*[14] iff $\alpha =\!\!\models \alpha^{\wedge}$.

    c. α is *informative* iff $\neg\neg\alpha \nvDash \mathbb{1}$.

    d. α is *inquisitive* iff $\neg\neg\alpha \nvDash\, \downarrow \alpha$.

Closedness can be also defined *per model and assignment* similarly.

(16) (Closures)

name	operator	condition
upward	$M,s,g \vDash\, \uparrow \alpha$	iff there is a state t such that $s \supseteq t$ and $M,t,g \vDash \alpha$
downward	$M,s,g \vDash\, \downarrow \alpha$	iff there is a state t such that $s \subseteq t$ and $M,t,g \vDash \alpha$
(local) conjunction	$M,s,g \vDash \alpha^{\wedge}$	iff there are states t and u such that $s = t \cap u$, $M,t,g \vDash \alpha$ and $M,u,g \vDash \alpha$

An ancillary binary logical connective $\rightrightarrows$, which is called *the inquisitive projection*, is crucial for our purposes:

(17) (Inquisitive projection)

    $M,s,g \vDash \alpha \rightrightarrows \kappa$ iff $M,s,g \vDash (\uparrow \alpha) \wedge \kappa$

---

[14] Unlike Inquisitive Semantics [11], we do not presume any unconditional downward closure applied to propositions. Instead, we explicitly mark the downward closure (and any others) when necessary. Notably, Westera [64, p. 5] grounds himself on the conjunction closure instead of the downward closure; otherwise his A-Quantity would fail to work.

The meaning of $\rightrightarrows$ is evident; $\alpha \rightrightarrows \kappa$ is the *resolution* [11, pp. 166–] of a question κ by an answer α. Only alternatives in κ such that α upwardly entails will remain in $\alpha \rightrightarrows \kappa$.

The entailment relation is defined in an *exact* manner:

(18)   (Exact entailment)

$\alpha_1, \alpha_2, \ldots \models \beta_1, \beta_2, \ldots$ iff for every logical model M, s, g, if $M, s, g \models \alpha_i$ for all i, there is some j such that $M, s, g \models \beta_j$.

4.3   Lexical Specifications for the Attention Dimension

A natural language expression $n \in \mathcal{N}$ is translated into the logical language $\mathcal{L}_{\text{ATT}}$ ($= \mathcal{L} \times \mathcal{L}$). As said in Sect. 4.1, the translation of n is a two-dimensional logical sentence which consists of an information and an attention dimension. The information dimension is straightforwardly $[n]$. The attention dimension is *derived* from the information dimension. It traces the information dimension except for the following cases: (i) where the information dimension contains indefinites and disjunctions, (ii) where it contains foci and (contrastive) topics, (iii) where it contains focus-sensitive expressions including *at least* in English and *sukunakutomo* in Japanese (5), and (iv) where the attention dimension is revised by an additive marker. We denote this determination process, covering the cases (i-iii), by the function $\maltese : \mathcal{L} \to \mathcal{L}$, which is inductively defined:

(19)   (The derivation of the attention dimension)

$$\maltese(\alpha \vee \beta) \overset{\text{def}}{=} \maltese\alpha \veebar \maltese\beta$$

$$\maltese\exists\iota.\,\alpha \overset{\text{def}}{=} \exists\exists(\maltese\iota).\,\maltese\alpha$$

$$\maltese\text{Focus}(\alpha)(\beta) \overset{\text{def}}{=} (\exists\exists\iota.\,(\maltese\beta)(\iota)) \Rightarrow (\maltese\beta)(\maltese\alpha)$$

$$\maltese\text{CTFocus}(\gamma)(\alpha)(\beta) \overset{\text{def}}{=} (\exists\exists\iota.\,(\maltese\beta)(\maltese\alpha)(\iota))$$
$$\Rightarrow (\exists\exists\iota.\,(\maltese\beta)(\iota)(\maltese\gamma)) \Rightarrow (\maltese\beta)(\maltese\alpha)(\maltese\gamma)$$

$$\maltese\text{AtLeast}(\alpha)(\beta) \overset{\text{def}}{=} (\maltese\beta)(\maltese\alpha)$$
$$\veebar \left[(\maltese\beta)(\maltese\alpha) \wedge \neg \left((\exists\exists\iota.\,(\maltese\beta)(\iota)) \barwedge\dashv (\maltese\beta)(\maltese\alpha) \right) \right]$$

where α is the focus of, and β is the background of AtLeast$(\alpha)(\beta)$. Otherwise $\maltese(\alpha)$ is defined inductively.

(20)   (The Only operator)

$$\text{Only}(\alpha)(\beta) \overset{\text{def}}{=} \beta(\alpha) \wedge \neg \left((\exists\exists\iota.\,(\beta(\iota))) \barwedge\dashv\uparrow \beta(\alpha) \right) \wedge \top$$

The definition of $\maltese$AtLeast$(\alpha)(\beta)$ and Only needs explication in prose. Firstly, its information dimension vacuously defined as $\beta(\alpha)$. Attention is drawn both to $(\maltese\beta)(\maltese\alpha)$ (the attentions of the prejacent) and its exhaustified variant Only$(\maltese\alpha)(\maltese\beta) = (\exists\exists\iota.\,(\maltese\beta)(\iota)) \barwedge\dashv(\maltese\beta)(\maltese\alpha)$ ("it is only $\maltese\alpha$ that is $\maltese\beta$"). The alternatives to be exhaustified are expressed by the global existential quantification $\exists\exists\iota.\,(\maltese\beta)(\iota)$ from which the prejacent is excluded (by the $\barwedge\dashv(\maltese\beta)(\maltese\alpha)$

part). The ignorance implicature of *sukunakutomo* 'at least' is derived from this attention setting via the maxim of A-parsimony (27b) introduced in Sect. 4.5 later.[15]

(33) in Appendix A provides illustrative examples.

4.4 Discourse Management

An assumption made in this paper, which abstracts out the myriad aspects of our daily discourse behaviors, is that a discourse is just a series of inquiries, responses, and confirmations over proposition (i.e. information about what the world is like). Participants in a discourse are assumably reasonable (i.e. they comply to conversational maxims) though not necessarily cooperative.

The table model [16] is a well-recognized model to date. The particular shape of the "table" is not essential here; rather, it is the way of utterances being organized that is of importance.

(21) A discourse structure $K = [\text{PARTICIPANTS } E, \text{DC}, \text{CG}, \text{STACK } T]$ is a tuple of the following components:

    a. E is a set of discourse participants.

    b. $\text{DC} \subseteq E \to \text{Pow}(\mathscr{L}_{\text{ATT}} \times \mathscr{L}_{\text{ATT}})$ is the set of discourse commitments for each participant $e \in E$. A discourse commitment is a pair of sentences $[\text{SENT } \alpha, \text{DQ } \kappa]$, where α is the assertion and κ is the *discourse question* to which the participant e has intended α to be an answer.

    c. $\text{CG} \subseteq \mathscr{L}_{\text{ATT}}$ is the common ground.

    d. T is a stack of annotated inquires. Formally, it is a stack of tuples $[\text{ORIG } n, \text{SENT } \pi, \text{ADDR } e, \text{INQTYPE } t]$, where $n \in \mathscr{N}$ is the original

---

[15] In this connection, (the contrastive topic kind of) the marker *wa*, having similar functions to *sukunakutomo*, is yet to be located in Attention Semantics. It is said to be marking speaker's incompetence ($\neg\Box$) [23, p. 29, (26)], a marked choice of a speech act [60], and a complex thereof [51,52]. A crucial difference between *wa* and *sukunakutomo* is that only the latter commits to a full-fledged ignorance ($\neg\Box\neg$ in addition to $\neg\Box$).

(1) a. ?Mary-wa   *sukunakutomo* gohan-o tabe-ta-ga
          Mary-TOP.NOM at.least   rice-ACC eat-PST-but
          hoka-wa   tabe-nakat-ta.
          other-TOP.ACC eat-NEG-PAST

          'Mary at least ate rice, but she didn't eat others.'

  b. Mary-wa   gohan-*wa* tabe-ta-ga   hoka-wa
          Mary-TOP.NOM at.least   rice-CT.ACC eat-PST-but
          tabe-nakat-ta.
          other-TOP.ACC eat-NEG-PAST

          'Mary ate rice$_{\text{CT}}$, but she didn't eat others.'

The two certainly cannot be assimilated, but the exact formulation of *wa* under Attention Semantics remains a question.

form of utterance, $\pi \in \mathscr{L}_{\text{ATT}}$ is the logical sentence expressed by n, [16] $e \in E$ is the addresser (or the speaker) of the utterance, and t is the type of inquiry. [17]

(22)   (Possible models of a discourse structure)

A discourse structure K constraints possible models in which a participant or an observer of the discourse can use to interpret utterances. The range of possible models $\mathscr{M}_{K,e}$ for a participant $e \in E$ in K is defined as follows:

$$\mathscr{M}_{K,e} \stackrel{\text{def}}{=} \left\{ (M, s, g) \,\middle|\, \begin{array}{l} M = (D, I) \text{ is a model} \\ E \subseteq D_{\text{indiv}} \\ M, s, g \vDash \downarrow \bigwedge \{\pi.\text{INFO} \mid \pi \in \text{CG} \cup \text{DC}(e)\} \end{array} \right\}$$

The range of possible models for an external observer $\mathscr{M}_{K,\text{-}}$ is defined the same as above except that $\text{DC}(e)$ is replaced with $\varnothing$.

The state component of a possible model $s \in \mathscr{M}_{K,e}$ can be interpreted as a possible epistemic state of e in K. The state component of a possible model $s \in \mathscr{M}_{K,\text{-}}$ can be interpreted as a possible epistemic state shared by all participants in K.

Discourse participants advance the discourse with discourse moves. A notation is introduced for the sake of conciseness: $K \{\ldots\}$ is understood as a record update. For a set $A \subseteq \mathscr{A}$ and an item $a \in \mathscr{A}$, $A + a$ means $A \cup \{a\}$, and $A \stackrel{+}{\leftarrow} a$ means $A \leftarrow A + a$. Likewise, for a stack T and an item t, $T + t$ means $T.\text{push}(t)$, and $T \stackrel{+}{\leftarrow} t$ means $T \leftarrow T + a$.

(23)   (Discourse moves)

---

[16] π, originated from the translation of n, can be deviated from the original meaning $[n]$ during the development of discourse. As will be clear later, π may undergo revision in subsequent discourse moves. In fact, the main proposal of this paper is that an additive marker modifies π.attention. This is why n must be kept on track in separation of π.

[17] In the current system, it is either Question or Cfm. These two types of discourse moves are a sophisticated restatement of the sentential features [D] (standing for declarative) and [I] (interrogative) in [16, p. 91], respectively. Without these features, they cannot distinguish a question from an assertion since they remain in the realm of truth-conditional semantics.

This mechanism apparently becomes a burden rather than a benefit for us because such markings seem redundant under the expressive power of state-based semantics and, as pointed out by a reviewer, it calls for an extra mechanism to ensure the identity of the kind of a proposition/utterance and the type of the corresponding feature. As far as the data in this paper are concerned, the features can be done without. Nevertheless, they might be worthful for possible discrepancies between the syntactic forms and its actual contribution to the discourse, such as the cases of rhetorical questions and declarative questions, which occasionally happen in the syntax-semantics interface in general.

a. $\text{Question}(K, n, e) \overset{\text{def}}{=}$
$K\left[\text{STACK} \leftarrow K.\text{STACK}.push(n, ([n], \maltese[n]), e, \text{Question})\right]$

b. $\text{Assert}(K, n, e) \overset{\text{def}}{=} K \begin{bmatrix} \text{DC}(e) \overset{+}{\leftarrow} [\text{SENT}\ ([n], \maltese[n]), \text{DQ}\ \kappa] \\ \text{STACK} \overset{+}{\leftarrow} \begin{bmatrix} \text{ORIG}\ n,\ \text{SENT}\ ([n], \maltese[n]) \\ \text{ADDR}\ e,\ \text{INQTYPE}\ \text{Cfm} \end{bmatrix} \end{bmatrix}$

where $[\text{SENT}\ \kappa, \text{INQTYPE}\ \text{Question}] = K.\text{STACK}.peek()$ and $[n]$ must meet the answerability prerequisites detailed in §4.6.

c. $\text{Cfm}(K, e) \overset{\text{def}}{=} K \begin{bmatrix} \text{DC}(e) \overset{+}{\leftarrow} [\text{SENT}\ (\pi', \alpha'), \text{DQ}\ \kappa] \\ \text{stack} \leftarrow T' \end{bmatrix}$

where $([\text{SENT}\ (\pi', \alpha'), \text{ADDR}\ e', \text{INQTYPE}\ \text{Cfm}], T') = K.\text{STACK}.pop()$, κ is some question such that $[\text{SENT}\ (\pi', \alpha'), \text{DQ}\ \kappa] \in \text{DC}(e')$, and $e' \overset{\text{def}}{=} e$.

d. $\text{CfmInfoOnly}(K, mod, e) \overset{\text{def}}{=} K \begin{bmatrix} \text{DC}(e) \overset{+}{\leftarrow} [\text{SENT}\ (\pi', mod(\alpha')), \text{DQ}\ \kappa] \\ \text{stack} \leftarrow T' \end{bmatrix}$

where $([\text{SENT}\ (\pi', \alpha'), \text{ADDR}\ e', \text{INQTYPE}\ \text{Cfm}], T') = K.\text{STACK}.pop()$, κ is some question such that $\{\text{SENT}\ (\pi', \alpha'), \text{DQ}\ \kappa\} \in \text{DC}(e')$, and $e' \overset{\text{def}}{=} e$. $mod \in \mathscr{L} \to \mathscr{L}$ modifies α', the attention dimension of the previous answer.

e. $\text{CfmNone}(K, e) \overset{\text{def}}{=} K \begin{bmatrix} \text{DC}(e) \overset{+}{\leftarrow} [\text{SENT}\ (\neg\pi', \neg\alpha'), \text{DQ}\ \kappa] \\ \text{stack} \leftarrow T' \end{bmatrix}$

where $([\text{SENT}\ (\pi', \_), \text{ADDR}\ e', \text{INQTYPE}\ \text{Cfm}], T') = T.pop()$, κ is some question such that $\{\text{SENT}\ (\pi', \_), \text{DQ}\ \kappa\} \in \text{DC}(e')$, and $e' \overset{\text{def}}{=} e$.

(24) (Passively and automatically applied discourse moves)

a. $\text{IncreaseCG}(K) \overset{\text{def}}{=} K \begin{bmatrix} \text{CG}(e) \overset{+}{\leftarrow} (\pi', \alpha') \\ \text{stack} \leftarrow T' \end{bmatrix}$

where $(\pi', \alpha') \in \mathscr{L}_{\text{ATT}}$ is arbitrary proposition that for all [18] participants $e \in E$, either $[\text{SENT}\ (\pi', \alpha')] \in \text{DC}(e)$ or $[\text{SENT}\ (\pi', \alpha'), \text{ADDR}\ e, \text{INQTYPE}\ \text{Cfm}] \in K.\text{STACK}$.
T' is the result of elimination of all assertions and confirmations of the proposition (π', α') from $K.\text{STACK}$.

4.5 Conversational Maxims

The first and original function of the attention dimension is to provide a basis for the non-monotonic calculation of conversational implicatures. Westera's [63, 64] primary idea is to apply the conversational maxims to the information and the attention dimension in a separate and parallel way. In this paper we present our own formulation of the set of maxims, while preserving Westera's predictions on conversational implicatures.

First, the total discourse commitment of a participant e to a discourse question κ in a discourse structure K is denoted by (25) below:

---

[18] To make the point clearer for the reader, IncreaseCG must be severed from Cfm, as in [16, p. 99, (17)], because a proposition enters the common ground not when it is confirmed by one participant, but when it is confirmed by *all* participants.

(25) (Total commitment of participant e to question κ)

$$\tau_{e,\kappa} \overset{\text{def}}{=} \begin{bmatrix} \text{INFO} \wedge \{\pi' \mid ((\pi', \_), \kappa) \in \text{DC}(e)\} \\ \text{ATT} \wedge \{\alpha' \mid ((\_, \alpha'), \kappa) \in \text{DC}(e)\} \end{bmatrix}$$

The conversational implicatures of e arising from K restricts the range of possible models $\mathscr{M}_{K,e}$ for a participant e.[19] The more implicatures a possible model $M, s, g \in \mathscr{M}_{K,e}$ supports, the more it is preferred to other models.[20] In the following, $\{t\}$ is called the *backport* of a state $t \in D_{\text{state}}$ to a proposition in $\mathscr{L}$.

(26) (I(nformation)-maxims)

    a. I-Quality: the addresser e believes $\tau.\text{INFO}$
        $M, s, g \vDash \Box \downarrow\tau.\text{INFO}$ (i.e. $M, s, g \vDash \downarrow\tau.\text{INFO}$)

    b. I-Relation: $\tau.\text{INFO}$ is a reductive answer [1, p. 24, (21)] to κ
        $M, s, g \vDash (\tau.\text{INFO} \rightarrow \downarrow\kappa)\mathbb{W}(\neg\tau.\text{INFO} \rightarrow \downarrow mathopkkk\kappa)$

    c. I-Quantitiy: any alternative in κ that is not entailed by $\tau.\text{INFO}$ is not convincing enough to e
        For each alternative state [21] $t \in D_{\text{state}}$ such that $M, t, g \vDash \kappa$, either

        i. the alternative state backported to a proposition, $\{t\}$, is entailed by $\tau.\text{INFO}$:
          $M, t, g \vDash \tau.\text{INFO} \Rrightarrow \kappa$, or

        ii. it violates I-Quality: $M, s, g \vDash \neg\Box\{t\}$.

(27) (A(ttention)-maxims)

    a. A-Quality: e entertains the possibility of each attention alternatives
        For each alternative state t of $\tau.\text{ATT}$, $M, s, g \vDash \Diamond\{t\}$

    b. A-Parsimony: all alternatives of $\tau.\text{ATT}$ are *independently* possible
        For each alternative state t of $\tau.\text{ATT}$, either

        i. it is impossible: $M, s, g \vDash \neg\Diamond\tau.\text{ATT}$, or

        ii. is possible independently: $M, s, g \vDash \Diamond\left(\{t\} \wedge \neg(\tau.\text{ATT} \mathbb{A}\dashv\{t\})\right)$.

    c. A-Relation: at least one alternative state must be relevant to κ
        $M, s, g \vDash \Diamond(\tau.\text{ATT} \Rrightarrow \kappa)$ (i.e., $M, s, g \vDash \Diamond(\uparrow\tau.\text{ATT})\mathbb{A}\kappa$)

    d. A-Quantitiy: any alternative state in κ that is not given attention by $\tau.\text{ATT}$ has no possibility
        For each alternative state $t \in D_{\text{state}}$ of $\kappa^{\wedge}$ (the $\wedge$-closure of κ) (i.e., $M, t, g \vDash \kappa^{\wedge}$), either

        i. it is given attention: $M, t, g \vDash \tau.\text{ATT} \Rrightarrow \kappa^{\wedge}$, or

        ii. it violates A-Quality: $M, s, g \vDash \neg\Diamond\{t\}$.

---

[19] Note that an implicature arising from the discourse structure K may not survive in a subsequent discourse structure K' due to recalculation of implicatures based on speakers' changing commitments.

[20] The preference order of the maxims is too huge a topic to discuss in this paper. Readers are invited to [2, p.11, (23)].

I-Quantity and A-Quality together generate an ignorance implicature. Thus, following the derivation of the attention dimension (19), an ignorance implicature arises from the indefinite expression *dare-ka* 'someone' in (6A). The ignorance marker *sukunakutomo* 'at least', which is translated to AtLeast, introduces a special form of attention which leads to an upper-side ignorance in (5A) and (5B). A-Quantity generates an exhaustivity implicature.

This theory guarantees that the two implicatures arise independently of each other (see relevant discussions by Westera [64, §4.1]). The maxims can also be applied to cases where τ.INFO is inquisitive. Moreover, as argued by [64, §4.3], this formulation breaks off the fetters of the problematic *opinionatedness assumption* ([57, p. 534, (bii)], [62, p. 507], [50, §3], [19, §2.3]).

4.6 Answerability

There is a diversity of notions and perspectives related to what is counted as a proper answer to a question. First of all, a proper answer should be in some way *relevant* to a discourse question, ([22, p. 338, p. 353], [44, p. 21, (15)], [11, p. 17], [47]). A proper answer should also has a prosodic structure, be it syntactically or exo-syntactically specified, that is congruent to the discourse question [7, 13, 33, 36, 44, 46, 53].

Yet another kind of appropriateness of an answer, which matters here, concerns the *answerability* of a speaker adding a new answer to previous ones. It has been known in the QuD literature that a juxtaposition of answers with specific sentence-final tones has a limited way of interpretation [26]. The same kind of restriction is should be expected also in a discourse among multiple answerers, as already observed in (3) and (4). This is implemented by adding a prerequisite condition, named *the condition of respecting attention*, to the Assert discourse move (23b):

(28) (Remnant question [22,23])

   The *remnant question* for speaker e respecting previous answers to the latest discourse question κ is:

$$\rho \overset{\text{def}}{=} \tau_{e,\kappa}.\text{ATT} \rightrightarrows \kappa.\text{INFO} \quad (= \uparrow \tau_{e,\kappa}.\text{ATT} \curlywedge \kappa.\text{INFO}),$$

   where $\tau_{e,\kappa}$ is the total commitment ((25) in §4.5) of e to κ.

(29) (The condition of respecting answerability)

   Assert(K, n, e) is a valid discourse move only if $[n] \vDash \downarrow \rho$.

---

[21] The backported proposition of an alternative state of κ is, by definition, I-Relevant to κ. The ignorance implicature is sufficiently generated by κ's alternatives.

[22] The notion of remnant question here is different from that in [14], which differentiates the german additive particles *auch* and *noch*. In our theory, alternatives to an answer which are not included in the attention dimension are excluded (without recourse to the exhaustification implicature) along with that answer.

[23] Restricting the remnant question with the information dimension of the previous answer(s), i.e., imposing $\curlywedge\tau_{e,\kappa}.\text{INFO}$, would complicate the subsequent formulation

The idea is that if a discourse participant e has made a commitment [SENT (π, α), DQ κ] $\in$ DC(e), that participant can make no more answers to κ except the part reserved by the attention α. Conceptually, the attention dimension α is what the participant e leaves as unresolved possibilities for the discourse question κ.

As discussed in (5) and footnote 5, obligatory additive marking should be something that is employed to overcome the condition (29). Zeevat's [66, p. 1886] remark that "the purpose of additive marking—and presumably the explanation of the fact that additive markers are often obligatory—is to mark that both answers hold at the same time and to prevent an interpretation of the host as a correction or a restatement of the first answer" is almost correct in that additive marking avoids the correction and the restatement interpretation. However, it remains unclear what discourse-grammatical device drives such kinds of interpretation.[24]   The paper takes a deflational position that it must be a primitive condition like (29) rather than an avoidance of a potential exhaustivity implicature.

Finally, we postulate another prerequisite condition for Assert. Whenever a speaker submits a new answer, it must be more informative than what the speaker has committed before with respect to the discourse question κ.

(30)   (The informativeness condition)

Assert(K, n, e) is valid only if $\tau_{e,\kappa}$.INFO $\nvDash \downarrow([n] \rightrightarrows \rho) \wedge \dashv([n] \rightrightarrows \rho)$.

Appendix D explicates more on this condition.

---

of the answerability condition.

The current formulation formulation of remnant question causes the following potential overgeneration. In (1), the remnant question after speaker B's response is $\exists x. |x| = 5 \wedge \mathrm{came}(x) \rightrightarrows \exists\exists n. |x| = n \wedge \mathrm{came}(x)$, which is equivalent to $\exists\exists n. |x| = n \wedge n \leq 5 \wedge \mathrm{came}(x)$. (The one-sided semantics of numerals is assumed here.) This incorrectly licences the answer "Two came" as an Assert move, which would not happen if the remnant question were capped with $\wedge \tau_{e,\kappa}$.INFO.

(1)   Q: kinō-wa nan-nin ki-masi-ta-ka?   'How many person came yesterday?'
      A: go-nin ki-masi-ta.   'Five came.'
      B: sonotōri-desu. # hutari ki-masi-ta.   'Exactly. # Two came.'

The same argumentation also obtains from the disjunctive answer in (2).

(2)   Q: kinō Tarō-wa nani-o tabe-masi-ta-ka?   'What did Taro eat yesterday.'
      A: ringo-o tabe-masi-ta.   'He ate apples.'
      B: sonotōri-desu. # ringo-ka banana-o tabe-masi-ta.
           'Exactly. # He ate either apples or bananas.'

A simplistic way to circumvent this problem is to embrace the constraint (30) below.

[24] Since Jasinskaja [26, Chapter 4], following van Rooy [48], attributes the preference to the correction and the restatement interpretation of a sentence juxtaposed with an answer to exhaustivity implicatures, it is likely that Zeevat [66] as well as Jasinskaja [26] attributes obligatory additive marking to exhaustivity.

5   Predictions

5.1   The 'At Least' Case (5)

Let $K_0 = $ [PARTICIPANTS $\{Q, A, B\}$, DC $\{\}$, CG $\{\}$, STACK $[]$] be the initial discourse structure. K_A is the discourse structure after (5A) is uttered.

$$K_A = K_0.\text{Question}(\text{``(5Q)''}, Q).\text{Assert}(\text{``(5A)''}, A)$$

$$= \begin{bmatrix} \text{PARTICIPANTS } \{Q, A, B\} \\ \text{DC} \qquad\quad [Q \mapsto \{\}, A \mapsto \{(\alpha, \kappa)\}, B \mapsto \{\}] \\ \text{CG} \qquad\quad \{\} \\ \text{STACK} \qquad [(\text{``(5Q)''}, \kappa, Q, \text{Question}), (\text{``(5A)''}, \alpha, A, \text{Cfm})] \end{bmatrix}$$

where $\kappa = $ [INFO $\exists\exists\iota\,\text{knowPass}(\iota)$, ATT $\exists\exists\iota.\,\text{knowPass}(\iota)$] is the discourse question and $\alpha = $ [INFO knowPass(Hanako), ATT knowPass(Hanako)] is the proposition of the assertion speaker A has asserted.

By uttering *sonotōri-desu* 'exactly', speaker B affirmatively confirms both the assertion and the attention dimension (23c) of (5A). The resulting discourse structure is K_{B1}:

$$K_{B1} = K_A.\text{Cfm}(B)$$

$$= \begin{bmatrix} \text{PARTICIPANTS } \{Q, A, B\} \\ \text{DC} \qquad\quad [Q \mapsto \{\}, A \mapsto \{[\text{SENT } \alpha, \text{DQ } \kappa]\}, B \mapsto \{(\alpha, \kappa)\}] \\ \text{CG} \qquad\quad \{\} \\ \text{STACK} \qquad [(\text{``(5Q)''}, \kappa, Q, \text{Question})] \end{bmatrix}$$

In order for speaker B to assert the new answer $n = $ *Taro-ga sit-tei-masu*, the prerequisites of Assert (29, 30) must be met for the discourse question κ, but it is not. The new answer does not upwardly imply the remnant question (a detailed proof is in (45) in Appendix E).

To rescue, speaker B uses an additive marker to *modify* and *revise* the previous attention. A lexical assumption needs to be made first that the response word *sonotōri-desu* 'exactly' can be interpreted as CfmInfoOnly as well as Cfm:

$$K_{B1'} = K_A.\text{CfmInfoOnly}(_{-1}, B)$$

$$= \begin{bmatrix} \text{PARTICIPANTS } \{Q, A, B\} \\ \text{DC} \quad \begin{bmatrix} Q \mapsto \{\} \\ A \mapsto \{(\alpha, \kappa)\} \\ B \mapsto \{[\text{SENT } [\text{INFO } \alpha.\text{INFO}, \text{ATT } _{-1}(\alpha.\text{ATT})], \text{DQ } \kappa]\} \end{bmatrix} \\ \text{CG} \qquad \{\} \\ \text{STACK} \quad [(\text{``(5Q)''}, \kappa, Q, \text{Question})] \end{bmatrix}$$

where $_{-1}$ is a meta-theoretical hole for the attention argument of CfmInfoOnly, which is to be filled by the subsequent of the utterance. (Admittedly, this meta-theoretical hole is an awkward gimmick which is to be replaced in the future.) The additive marker *mo* takes the additive dimension of a previous answer as an argument of it and weakens it by adding the global disjunction with the prejacent. In this case, the revised attention is $mod(\alpha.\text{ATT}) = \alpha.\text{ATT} \veebar \text{knowPass(Taro)}$. The modification function mod will enter the metatheoretical hole. The remnant question, being revised accordingly, now includes knowPass(Taro), which enables speaker B to pass the prerequisites. IncreaseCG will be applied automatically.

$$K_{B2'} = K_A.\text{CfmInfoOnly}(\underline{mod}_1, B).\text{Assert}(n, B).\text{IncreaseCG}()$$

$$= \begin{bmatrix} \text{PARTICIPANTS} & \{Q, A, B\} \\ \text{DC} & \begin{bmatrix} Q \mapsto \{\} \\ A \mapsto \{(\alpha, \kappa)\} \\ B \mapsto \begin{cases} [\text{SENT } [\text{INFO } \alpha.\text{INFO}, \text{ATT } \underline{mod}_1(\alpha.\text{ATT})], \text{DQ } \kappa], \\ [\text{SENT } [\text{INFO } [n], \text{ATT } \maltese[n]], \text{DQ } \kappa] \end{cases} \end{bmatrix} \\ \text{CG} & \{\alpha\} \\ \text{STACK} & [] \end{bmatrix}$$

5.2   The Indefinite Case (6)

Let us rewind the derivation to K_{B1}, where speaker B has confirmed the assertion of speaker A before asserting another answer of his own n = "*Taro-ga sit-tei-masu*" to the discourse question κ, where $\kappa.\text{INFO} = \exists\exists\iota.\text{knowPass}(\iota)$. The total commitment of speaker B is:

$$\tau_{B,K_{B1}} = \begin{bmatrix} \text{INFO knowPass(Hanako)} \wedge \exists\iota.\iota \neq \text{Hanako} \wedge \text{knowPass}(\iota) \\ \text{ATT knowPass(Hanako)} \wedge \exists\exists\iota.\iota \neq \text{Hanako} \wedge \text{knowPass}(\iota) \end{bmatrix}$$

from which the remnant question obtains:

$$\rho = \tau_{B,K_{B1}}.\text{ATT} \rightrightarrows \kappa.\text{INFO} \not\Vdash \exists\exists\iota.\text{knowPass}(\iota)$$

The answer $[n]$ = knowPass(Taro) entails $\downarrow \rho$. Its inquisitive projection to ρ is also informative against $\tau_{B,K_{B1}}.\text{INFO}$. Therefore, speaker B's assertion n is approved without need of revising attention.

There is another option that speaker B can take: if B chooses to ignore the attentional effect of the indefinite in (6A), then the attention dimension becomes non-inquisitive and the assertion requires additive marking again.

The unacceptability of B's assertion in (7) is also accounted for; the associative plural *-tati* does not open up a question in the attention dimension.

5.3   The Conjunction Case (8)

Most of the settings are the same as the 'at least' case (5). In particular, the information dimension of the total commitment of speaker B and the remnant question are identical with those in (5). The assertion, translated to $[n]$ = knowPass(Taro) $\wedge$ knowPass(Hanako), entails the downward closure of the remnant question ρ = knowPass(Hanako). Its inquisitive projection to ρ is also informative against $\tau_{B,K_{B1}}.\text{INFO}$. Therefore n can enter the discourse structure by the Assert move without additive marking.

Moreover, the prediction has it that additive marking is even *disallowed* here. Unlike the indefinite case (6), there is no attentive effect, namely a potential question, to begin with such that by being ignored, a violation of answerbility (29) would occur, which requires an additive marker for its recovery.

6 Conclusion

It has been made clear that the attention dimension is a key component to which (obligatory) additive marking is sensitive and which mediates, but keeps intact, answerability and conversational implicatures.

This research has implications on areas other than additive marking nad its interaction with potential questions and the dimension of attention. Firstly, the choice of the response words in the examples (4–8) is crucial in a way different from previous research on response words to yes-no questions [16]. The response word *sonotō-ri(-desu)* 'exactly' and its kin (31) are distinguished from others in that only these words *publicize* the speaker's agreement to (the information dimensions of) previous answers.

(31) *sore-{ne / na}* '(colloq.) that's right',
  sore-wa sonotōri-{da / desu}-{∅ / ne} 'that is right',
  sore-wa tadasi-i-(desu)-{∅ / ne} 'that's correct.', etc.

They are contrasted with weaker affirmative response words such as *hai* 'yeah' and *sō(-desu)-ne* '(lit.) so it is'. These response words would pardon the non-use of additive markers (though the absence of additive marking renders speaker B's assertion as a *correction* to speaker A's assertion).

(32) Q: dare-ga pasuwādo-o sit-tei-masu-ka?   'Who knows the password?'
  A: Hanako-ga sit-tei-masu.   'Hanako does.'
  B: { hai / sō-desu-ne }. Tarō-{ ga / mo } sit-tei-masu.
    '{ Yeah / So it is }. Taro does(, too).

These words are weaker in the sense that they can be followed by blatant denial expressions such as *tiga-(i-masu)* 'be wrong':

(32′) B: { hai / sō-desu-ne }, tigai-masu.   'Well, you are wrong.'

This observation is in the same direction with Kitagawa [32], which observes that the uses of *hai* ranges wider than the stronger ones. Thus it is proposed there that "*hai* is a polite signal to the addressee to indicate that the speaker has *heard (and understood)* what the addressee said to him" ([32, p. 110, (9)], emphasis mine). It is also suggestive that the English interjection *yeah*, whose frequent use is described to be "acknowledge the *receipt* of information" ([28, p. 180, (9)], emphasis mine), but not necessarily the information itself [40, p. 874].

The class of negative response words is also worth investigating. Substituting *īe, tigai-masu* 'no, it's wrong' for the response word in (4–8B) yields different results.

(5″) A: (At least) Hanako knows the password.

B: īe, tigai-masu. Tarō-{ %ga / (??)mo } sit-tei-masu.

(6″) A: Hanako and someone else know the password.

B: īe, tigai-masu. Tarō-{ %ga / *mo } sit-tei-masu.

(8″) A: Hanako knows the password.

B: īe, tigai-masu. Tarō-to-Hanako-{ ga / #mo } si-tei-masu.

where % indicates correction. It is notable that additive marking is compatible with both a strong affirmative response (5) and a negative response is (5″). This suggests that the negative response word is not so much a denial of the information dimension, but rather just a denial of the attention dimension.

Finally, this paper might open up a possibility to solve the cross-linguistic conundrum that additive markers are used to construct existential quantifiers (e.g., in Ossetic [24, §7.2; A.20, (A.153)]): the aspect of additivity marker to weaken attention by $\mathbb{W}$ is exerted there.

Acknowledgements. Special thanks to Yoshiki Mori and his students for their insightful comments and discussions. Yusuke Kubota also provided valuable feedback and offered the author an opportunity of an internal presentation in his seminar, in which the author received helpful comments from the participants including Yo Matsumoto.

Gratefulness is also extended to the participants at the venue and to the anonymous reviewers for their comments and suggestions which have contributed to the improvement of the paper.

This research was supported by the GSI Caravan project "research on linguistic theory exploring the possibilities for mutual understanding in society" directed by Yoshiki Mori, the University of Tokyo.

Appendix

A Examples of Attention Derivations

(33) a. John walks.

⤳ [INFO walk(John), ATT walk(John)]

b. Does John or Mary walk?

⤳ [INFO walk(John)$\mathbb{W}$walk(Mary), ATT walk(John)$\mathbb{W}$walk(Mary)]

c. John or Mary walks.

⤳ [INFO walk(John) $\vee$ walk(Mary), ATT walk(John)$\mathbb{W}$walk(Mary))

d. Who walks?

⤳ [INFO $\exists\exists\iota.$walk(ι), ATT $\exists\exists\iota.$walk(ι)]

e. Someone walks.

⤳ [INFO $\exists\iota.$walk(ι), ATT $\exists\exists\iota.$walk(ι)]

f. [John]$_F$ walks.

$\rightsquigarrow$ [INFO Focus(John)(walk), ATT ✿Focus(John)(walk)]

= [INFO walk(John), ATT ($\exists\exists\iota$.walk(ι)) $\Rightarrow$ walk(John)]

g. [John]$_{CT}$ walks [tomorrow]$_F$.

$$\rightsquigarrow \begin{bmatrix} \text{INFO} & \text{CTFocus(tmrrw)(John)(walk)} \\ \text{ATT} & ✿\text{CTFocus(tmrrw)(John)(walk)} \end{bmatrix}$$

$$= \begin{bmatrix} \text{INFO} & \text{tmrrw(walk(John))} \\ \text{ATT} & \begin{array}{l}(\exists\exists\tau.\tau(\text{walk(John)})) \\ \Rightarrow (\exists\exists\iota.\text{tmrrw(walk}(\iota))) \Rightarrow \text{tmrrw(walk(John))}\end{array} \end{bmatrix}$$

h. [At least John]$_F$ walks.

$$\rightsquigarrow \begin{bmatrix} \text{INFO} & \text{Focus(AtLeast(John), walk)} \\ \text{ATT} & ✿\text{Focus(AtLeast(John), walk)} \end{bmatrix}$$

$$= \begin{bmatrix} \text{INFO} & \text{walk(John)} \\ \text{ATT} & (\exists\exists\iota.\text{walk}(\iota)) \Rightarrow \text{walk(J)} \mathbb{W} \text{Only(John)(walk)} \end{bmatrix}$$

where Only is defined as (20) in §4.3.

B   Corollaries of the Logical Constants

(34)   Corollary: $\alpha \wedge (\beta \mathbb{W} \gamma) =\!\!\Vdash (\alpha \wedge \beta) \mathbb{W} (\alpha \wedge \gamma)$.

Proof:

a. The forward direction: Take an arbitrary pointed model M, s, g such that $M, s, g \vDash \alpha \wedge (\beta \mathbb{W} \gamma)$. Then there are states t and u such that $M, t, g \vDash \alpha$ and $M, u, g \vDash \beta \mathbb{W} \gamma$. Either $M, u, g \vDash \beta$ or $M, u, g \vDash \gamma$. Proof by cases:

   i. If $M, u, g \vDash \beta$, then $M, s, g \vDash \alpha \wedge \beta$. Therefore $M, s, g \vDash (\alpha \wedge \beta) \mathbb{W} (\alpha \wedge \gamma)$.

   ii. If $M, u, g \vDash \gamma$, the proof is similar.

b. The reverse direction: Take an arbitrary pointed model M, s, g such that $M, s, g \vDash (\alpha \wedge \beta) \mathbb{W} (\alpha \wedge \gamma)$. Proof by cases:

   i. If $M, s, g \vDash \alpha \wedge \beta$, then there are states t and u such that $M, t, g \vDash \alpha$ and $M, u, g \vDash \beta$. From the second statement, $M, u, g \vDash \beta \mathbb{W} \gamma$. Therefore $M, s, g \vDash \alpha \wedge (\beta \mathbb{W} \gamma)$.

   ii. If $M, s, g \vDash \alpha \wedge \gamma$, the proof is similar.

(35)   Corollary: $\alpha \vDash \neg\neg\alpha$.

Proof: Take an arbitrary pointed model M, s, g such that $M, s, g \vDash \alpha$. Take an arbitrary state t such that $M, t, g \vDash \neg\alpha$. Then for any state u such that $M, u, g \vDash \alpha$, $t \cap u = \varnothing$. Applying s to u yields $s \cap t = \varnothing$. Therefore $M, s, g \vDash \neg\neg\alpha$.

(36) Corollary: $\neg\alpha$ is disjunction closed.

Proof: Take an arbitrary model M and assignment g. Take two states s and t such that $M, s, g \vDash \neg\alpha$ and $M, t, g \vDash \neg\alpha$. Take an arbitrary state u such that $M, u, g \vDash \alpha$. By the nature of s and t, $u \cap s = \varnothing$ and $u \cap t = \varnothing$. Therefore, $u \cap (s \cup t) = \varnothing$. This means $M, s \cup t, g \vDash \neg\alpha$.

(37) Corollary: $\neg\alpha$ has a unique maximum supporting state.

Proof: Proof by contradiction. Take an arbitrary model M and assignment g. Suppose that there are two distinct maximum supporting states s and t for $\neg\alpha$. By (36), $M, s \cup t, g \vDash \neg\alpha$. But $s \cup t$ is strictly a superset of the two, which contradicts the maximality of s and t in terms of $\neg\alpha$'s support.

(38) Corollary: an arbitrary sentence α is non-inquisitive iff for any model M and g, if α is supported by any state, there is a unique maximum state u in M, g such that $M, u, g \vDash \alpha$.

Note that by definition (15d), α is non-inquisitive iff $\neg\neg\alpha \vDash \downarrow \alpha$.

a. Proof of the forward direction: Proof by contradiction. Suppose that α is non-inquisitive and there is a supporting state for α. Take an arbitrary model M and assignment g. Suppose that there are two distinct maximum supporting states u and v supporting α. Then $u \cup v$ is strictly a superset of the two. By (35), $M, u, g \vDash \neg\neg\alpha$ and $M, v, g \vDash \neg\neg\alpha$. By (36), $M, u \cup v, g \vDash \neg\neg\alpha$. By the non-inquisitiveness assumption, $M, u \cup v, g \vDash \downarrow \alpha$. Then there is a state r such that $M, r, g \vDash \alpha$ and $u \cup v \subseteq r$. This means $u \subseteq u \cup v \subseteq r$ and $v \subseteq u \cup v \subseteq r$. Since $u \cup v$ is strictly a superset of u and v, so is r. Contradiction.

b. Proof of the backward direction: Take an arbitrary model M and assignment g.

If α is supported by no states in M and g, neither is $\neg\neg\alpha$. Therefore, for arbitrary state s, it is vacuously true that if $M, s, g \vDash \neg\neg\alpha$ then $M, s, g \vDash \downarrow \alpha$.

Let u be the unique maximum supporting state for α. By (37), there is a unique maximum supporting state for $\neg\alpha$, which is $\bar{u}$. Take an arbitrary state s such that $M, s, g \vDash \neg\neg\alpha$. By the outer negation of $\neg\neg\alpha$, $s \cap \bar{u} = \varnothing$. By the maximality of $\bar{u}$, $s \subseteq u$. This means that u is a state such that $s \subseteq u$ and $M, u, g \vDash \alpha$. Therefore $M, s, g \vDash \downarrow \alpha$.

(39) Corollary: if α and β is non-inquisitive in a model M and assignment g, so is $\alpha \wedge \beta$.

Proof: For any state s such that $M, s, g \vDash \alpha \wedge \beta$, there are states t and r s.t. $s = t \cap r$, $M, t, g \vDash \alpha$, and $M, r, g \vDash \beta$. By (38), there are unique maximum supporting states u_α and u_β for α and β, respectively. therefore $t \subseteq u_\alpha$ and $r \subseteq u_\beta$. This means $s = t \cap r \subseteq u_\alpha \cap u_\beta$. Hence $u_\alpha \cap u_\beta$ gives an upperbound of an arbitrary state s such that $M, s, g \vDash \alpha \wedge \beta$. Besides, $M, u_\alpha \cap u_\beta, g \vDash \alpha \wedge \beta$ for obvious reasons. Therefore, $u_\alpha \cap u_\beta$ is the unique maximum supporting state for $\alpha \wedge \beta$.

C   On the Only Operator

(20) $\text{Only}(\alpha)(\beta) \overset{\text{def}}{=} \beta(\alpha) \wedge \neg \left((\exists\exists\iota.\,(\beta(\iota))) \barwedge\exists\uparrow\beta(\alpha) \right) \wedge \top$

(40)   Assumption for the following corollaries: The arguments α and β are such that in every model M and assignment g, there is a unique state s such that $M, s, g \vDash \beta(\alpha)$.

(41)   Corollary: Given assumption (40), $\text{Only}(\alpha)(\beta)$ is non-inquisitive.

Proof: Take an arbitrary model M and assignment g. We need to look at each of the three conjuncts of the local conjunction in Only. Assumption (40) guarantees a unique supporting state s for $\beta(\alpha)$, which makes $\beta(\alpha)$ non-inquisitive. By (37) and (38), the second conjunct with $\neg$ is also non-inquisitive. $\top$ is by definition non-inquisitive as well. By (39), the whole conjunction is non-inquisitive as well.

(42)   Corollary: Given assumption (40), $\uparrow\beta(\alpha) \vDash \uparrow\text{Only}(\alpha)(\beta)$.

Proof: Take an arbitrary model M and assignment g. Let s be the unique supporting state for $\beta(\alpha)$ given by (40). Let o be the unique maximum supporting state for $\text{Only}(\alpha)(\beta)$ given by (38) and (41). Since $\beta(\alpha)$ is a conjunct of $\text{Only}(\alpha)(\beta)$, $o \subseteq s$. Therefore, for an arbitrary state t such that $M, t, g \vDash \uparrow\beta(\alpha)$, $t \supseteq s \supseteq o$, which means $M, t, g \vDash \uparrow\text{Only}(\alpha)(\beta)$.

(43)   Corollary: Given assumption (40),
for an arbitrary pointed model M, s', g, if $M, s', g \vDash \beta(\alpha')$ but $M, s', g \nvDash \uparrow\beta(\alpha)$, then $M, s', g \nvDash \uparrow\text{Only}(\alpha)(\beta)$.

Proof: Suppose that there is a pointed model M, s', g such that $M, s', g \vDash \beta(\alpha')$ and $M, s', g \nvDash \uparrow\beta(\alpha)$. Let s be the unique supporting state for $\beta(\alpha)$ in M, g given by (40). Let o be the unique maximum supporting state for $\text{Only}(\alpha)(\beta)$ in M, g ensured by (38) and (41).

Think about o. There is a state o_{excl} such that $o \subseteq o_{\text{excl}}$ and (by (37)) maximally supports $\neg((\exists\exists\iota.\,\beta(\iota))\wedge\exists\uparrow\beta(\alpha))$. Therefore, $\overline{o_{\text{excl}}}$ is an upper bound of $(\exists\exists\iota.\,\beta(\iota))\barwedge\exists\uparrow\beta(\alpha)$.

s' supports $\exists\exists\iota.\,\beta(\iota)$ for obvious reasons. s' also supports $\exists\uparrow\beta(\alpha)$ because $M, s', g \nvDash \uparrow\beta(\alpha)$. Therefore, $s' \subseteq \overline{o_{\text{excl}}}$, which means $s' \cap o_{\text{excl}} = \varnothing$.

By the meaning of Only and maximality, $o = s \cap o_{\text{excl}} \cap D_{\text{world}} = s \cap o_{\text{excl}}$, which means $o \subseteq o_{\text{excl}}$. Therefore, $s' \cap o = \varnothing$ By the maximality of o, any state o' supporting $\uparrow\text{Only}(\alpha)(\beta)$ is such that $o' \subseteq o$. Therefore $s' \cap o' = \varnothing$, which means $o' \not\subseteq s'$, for any such o'. It can be said that $M, s', g \nvDash \uparrow\text{Only}(\alpha)(\beta)$.

(44)   Corollary: Given assumption (40),
no states support $\uparrow\text{Only}(\alpha)(\beta) \barwedge((\exists\exists\iota.\,\beta(\iota))\barwedge\exists\uparrow\beta(\alpha))$.

Note: Even the empty state $\varnothing$ does not support it.

Proof: Proof by contradiction. Suppose that there is any state s' such that $M, s', g \vDash \uparrow\text{Only}(\alpha)(\beta) \wedge((\exists\exists\iota.\,\beta(\iota)) \wedge\exists\uparrow\beta(\alpha))$. By definition of $\barwedge$ and $\exists$, $M, s', g \vDash \uparrow\text{Only}(\alpha)(\beta)$, $M, s', g \vDash \exists\exists\iota.\,\beta(\iota)$, and $M, s', g \nvDash \uparrow\beta(\alpha)$.

By the global existential, there is a state α' such that $M, s', g \models \beta(\alpha')$. By (43), $M, s', g \not\models \uparrow \mathrm{Only}(\alpha)(\beta)$. Contradiction.

D   On the Informativeness Condition

(30)   (The informativeness condition)

Assert(K, n, e) is valid only if

$$\tau_{e,\kappa}.\mathrm{INFO} \not\models \downarrow([n] \Rrightarrow \rho) \wedge \dashv([n] \Rrightarrow \rho).$$

This condition compares the informativeness of the new answer n projected on the remnant question ρ to to the total commitment of the addresser e. A new answer specifies an answer in ρ. This answer cannot be less informative than the commitment the speaker has made.

E   (Incomprehensive) Proofs of the Predictions

(45)   After speaker B's affirmative response in (5), the resulting discourse structure being K_{B1}, the speaker cannot assert the new answer $n = $ "*Taro-ga sit-tei-masu*" without additive marking.

(5)   Q: Who knows the password?

A: (sukunakutomo) Hanako-ga   sit-tei-masu.
(at least)   Hanako-NOM know-ASP-HON

'(At least) Hanako does.'

B: sonotōri-desu. (sukunakutomo)
exactly-HON   (at least)
Tarō-{ # ga / mo }   sit-tei-masu.
Taro-{ NOM / NOM.ADD } know-ASP-HON

'Exactly. (At least) Taro does, #(too).'

$K_{B1} = K_A.\mathrm{Cfm}(B)$

$$= \begin{bmatrix} \mathrm{PARTICIPANTS} & \{Q, A, B\} \\ \mathrm{DC} & [Q \mapsto \{\}, A \mapsto \{[\mathrm{SENT}\ \alpha, \mathrm{DQ}\ \kappa]\}, B \mapsto \{(\alpha, \kappa)\}] \\ \mathrm{CG} & \{\} \\ \mathrm{STACK} & [(\text{``(5Q)''}, \kappa, Q, \mathrm{Question})] \end{bmatrix}$$

where

$$[n] = \text{knowPass(Taro)}$$

$$\kappa = \begin{bmatrix} \text{INFO} & \exists\exists\iota.\,\text{knowPass}(\iota) \\ \text{ATT} & \exists\exists\iota.\,\text{knowPass}(\iota) \end{bmatrix}$$

$$\alpha = \tau_{B,K_{B1}}$$

$$= \begin{bmatrix} \text{INFO} & \text{knowPass(Hanako)} \\ \text{ATT} & \text{knowPass(Hanako)} \,\text{\reflectbox{W}}\, \text{Only(Hanako)(knowPass)} \end{bmatrix}$$

Only(Hanako)(knowPass)

$$= \text{knowPass(Hanako)} \wedge \neg \big((\exists\exists\iota.\,(\text{knP})(\iota)) \,\text{\reflectbox{A}}^{\exists} \uparrow \text{knP(Hanako)} \big) \wedge \top.$$

For the derivation of $\alpha.\text{ATT}$, see (33h) in appendix 6 above.

a. Assumption: The logical sentences knowPass(Hanako), knowPass(John), ..., are non-inquisitive and *non-suggestive* in the sense that each of them has exactly one supporting state (denoted by s_h, s_j, ..., respectively, which are determined based on each model).

Justification: This assumption is reasonable considering the declarative nature of these sentences.

b. Assumption: knowPass(Taro) $\not\vDash \downarrow$ knowPass(Hanako).

The countermodel for this non-entailment may be (and in most case, is) *a departure* from what speaker B entertains as possible models $\mathscr{M}_{K_{B1},e}$. In other words, this assumption is about a *possibility* of the interpretation of the two sentences rather than the interpretation in a particular model (or a particular *context*).

This distinction is crucial because when knowPass(Hanako) is in the commitment of speaker B, the two sentences knowPass(Taro) and knowPass(Hanako) $\wedge$ knowPass(Taro) are no more distinguishable in terms of contextually restricted truthmaking, all cases being reduced to the additive-marking-repelling (8).

Justification: That being said, this assumption is reasonable for obvious reasons. One can easily construct a situation where Taro's knowing the password is independent of Hanako's knowing it. Compare it to the non-independence of Taro and Hanako's knowing the password from Hanako's knowing it. See also [9,18] for similar discussion.

Consequence: By this assumption, there is a model M and assignment g such that the only state s_t supporting knowPass(Taro) does not support $\downarrow$ knowPass(Hanako). That is, $s_t \not\subseteq s_h$.

c. *The total commitment of speaker B, $\tau_{B,\kappa}$, is identical with α* because the only commitment spaker B has ever made is Cfm(B) (rather than CfmInfoOnly), which totally confirms the answer α made by speaker A.

Note that the affirmative response *sonotōri-desu* made by speaker B cannot be yet identified as CfmInfoOnly. The CfmInfoOnly move requires an attention modifier which is not specified yet (it will be specified by an additive marker later).

d. *The remnant question* with previous answers to κ is:

$$\rho = \tau_{B,K_{B1}}.\mathrm{ATT} \rightrightarrows \kappa.\mathrm{INFO}$$

$$\dashvDash \uparrow \begin{pmatrix} \mathrm{knowPass(Hanako)} \\ \mathbb{W}\,\mathrm{Only(Hanako)(knowPass)} \end{pmatrix} \wedge \exists\exists\iota.\,\mathrm{knowPass}(\iota)$$

$$\dashvDash \begin{array}{l} \uparrow\mathrm{knowPass(Hanako)} \wedge \exists\exists\iota.\,\mathrm{knowPass}(\iota) \\ \mathbb{W}\uparrow\mathrm{Only(Hanako)(knowPass)} \wedge \exists\exists\iota.\,\mathrm{knowPass}(\iota) \end{array}$$

by (42),

$$\dashvDash \uparrow\mathrm{Only(Hanako)(knowPass)} \wedge \exists\exists\iota.\,\mathrm{knowPass}(\iota)$$

by (44),

$$\vDash \uparrow\mathrm{knowPass(Hanako)}.$$

By assumption (44a), the entailment-reversing nature of $\uparrow$, and the fact that $\mathrm{Only}(\alpha)(\beta) \vDash \beta(\alpha)$,

$$\uparrow\mathrm{knowPass(Hanako)} \vDash \uparrow\mathrm{Only(Hanako)(knowPass)}.$$

Therefore,

$$\rho \dashvDash \begin{array}{l} \uparrow\mathrm{knowPass(Hanako)} \wedge \exists\exists\iota.\,\mathrm{knowPass}(\iota) \\ \cancel{\mathbb{W}\uparrow\mathrm{Only(Hanako)(knowPass)} \wedge \exists\exists\iota.\,\mathrm{knowPass}(\iota)}. \end{array}$$

This means that the remnant question of "At least Hanako knows the password." is the same as that of "(Only) Hanako knows the password."

e. Proof: The condition of respecting answerability (29) is $[n] \vDash \downarrow \rho$, i.e.,

$$\mathrm{knowPass(Taro)}$$
$$\vDash \downarrow(\uparrow\mathrm{Only(Hanako)(knowPass)} \wedge \exists\exists\iota.\,\mathrm{knowPass}(\iota))$$
$$\dashvDash \downarrow(\uparrow\mathrm{knowPass(Hanako)} \wedge \exists\exists\iota.\,\mathrm{knowPass}(\iota)).$$

Take an arbitrary model M and assignment g. By (44a), the sentences $\mathrm{knowPass(Hanako)}$ and $\mathrm{knowPass(Taro)}$ are each uniquely supported by states s_h and s_t, respectively.

Think about $\mathrm{knowPass(Taro)} \rightrightarrows \rho$. For any state s,

$$M, s, g \vDash \mathrm{knowPass(Taro)} \rightrightarrows \rho$$

iff

$$s_h \subseteq s, s_t \subseteq s, \text{ and } M, s, g \vDash \exists\exists\iota.\,\mathrm{knowPass}(\iota).$$

By assumption (44b), $s_t \nsubseteq s_h$. Thus there is an element $w \in s_t \subseteq s$ such that $w \nsubseteq s_h$. Therefore, $s_h \subsetneq s$. This means that a supporting state of knowPass(Taro) $\rightrightarrows \rho$, if it ever exists, must be strictly less informative than that of knowPass(Hanako). Therefore, $M, s_h, g \vDash$ $\downarrow$(knowPass(Taro) $\rightrightarrows \rho$) and $M, s_h, g \nvDash$ knowPass(Taro) $\rightrightarrows \rho$. Since M and g are arbitrary, this is equivalent to

$$\text{knowPass(Hanako)} \vDash \downarrow(\text{Taro} \rightrightarrows \rho) \wedge \neg(\text{Taro} \rightrightarrows \rho),$$

which is a failure of the informativeness condition (30).

(45)   After the attention modification by additive marking in (5), speaker B can validly use the Assert.

Proof: The attention modification by the additive marker in (5B) is:

$$mod(\alpha) = \alpha \mathbb{W} \text{knowPass(Taro)}.$$

The *mod* function will affect the discourse structure via the response word *sonotōri-desu*.

To be more precise, the response word is reinterpreted as a CfmInfoOnly move, the attention argument of which is expected to be filled by *mod*.

$$K_{B1'} = K_A.\text{CfmInfoOnly}(\text{-1}, B)$$

$$= \begin{bmatrix} \text{PARTICIPANTS} \{Q, A, B\} \\ \text{DC} \begin{bmatrix} Q \mapsto \{\} \\ A \mapsto \{(\alpha, \kappa)\} \\ B \mapsto \left\{ \begin{bmatrix} \text{SENT} \begin{bmatrix} \text{INFO } \alpha.\text{INFO} \\ \text{ATT } \text{-1}(\alpha.\text{ATT}) \end{bmatrix} \\ \text{DQ} \quad \kappa \end{bmatrix} \right\} \end{bmatrix} \\ \text{CG} \quad \{\} \\ \text{STACK} \quad [(\text{``(5Q)''}, \kappa, Q, \text{Question})] \end{bmatrix}$$

Accordingly, the remnant question ρ changes to

$$\rho^+ = \begin{pmatrix} \text{knowPass(Hanako)} \\ \mathbb{W} \text{Only(Hanako)(knowPass)} \\ \mathbb{W} \text{knowPass(Taro)} \end{pmatrix} \rightrightarrows \exists\exists\iota. \text{knowPass}(\iota).$$

The condition of respecting answerability (29) is met for obvious reasons. Now the inquisitive projection of speaker B's assertion, knowPass(Taro) $\rightrightarrows \rho^+$, has s_t as a supporting state, which is not less informative than s_h. Therefore, the informativeness condition (30) is also met.

The resulting discourse structure is $K_{B2'}$ (here the applyable passive moves are not applied):

$$K_{B2'} = K_A.\text{CfmInfoOnly}(\underline{mod}_1, B).\text{Assert}(\text{"Tarō-mo sit-tei-masu"}, B)$$

$$= \begin{bmatrix} \text{PARTICIPANTS} & \{Q, A, B\} \\ \text{DC} & \begin{bmatrix} Q \mapsto \{\} \\ A \mapsto \{(\alpha, \kappa)\} \\ B \mapsto \left\{ \begin{bmatrix} \text{SENT} & \begin{bmatrix} \text{INFO} & \alpha.\text{INFO} \\ \text{ATT} & \underline{mod}_1(\alpha.\text{ATT}) \end{bmatrix} \\ \text{DQ} & \kappa \end{bmatrix}, \\ [\text{SENT} [\text{INFO} [n], \text{ATT} \, \maltese[n]], \text{DQ} \, \kappa] \end{bmatrix} \right\} \\ \text{CG} & \{\} \\ \text{STACK} & [(\text{"(5Q)"}, \kappa, Q, \text{Question})] \end{bmatrix}$$

(46) The speaker B in (6) can validly assert the new answer $n = $ "*Tarō-ga sit-tei-masu*" without additive marking.

(6) Q: Who knows the password?

A: Hanako-to-dareka-ga   sit-tei-masu.
Hanako-and-someone-NOM know-ASP-HON

'Hanako and someone (else) do.'

B: sonotōri-desu. Tarō-{ ga / mo } sit-tei-masu.

'Exactly. Taro does, (too).'

$$K_{B1} = K_A.\text{Cfm}(B)$$

$$= \begin{bmatrix} \text{PARTICIPANTS} & \{Q, A, B\} \\ \text{DC} & [Q \mapsto \{\}, A \mapsto \{[\text{SENT} \, \alpha, \text{DQ} \, \kappa]\}, B \mapsto \{(\alpha, \kappa)\}] \\ \text{CG} & \{\} \\ \text{STACK} & [(\text{"(5Q)"}, \kappa, Q, \text{Question})] \end{bmatrix}$$

where

$$[n] = \text{knowPass(Taro)}$$

$$\kappa = \begin{bmatrix} \text{INFO} & \exists\exists\iota.\,\text{knowPass}(\iota) \\ \text{ATT} & \exists\exists\iota.\,\text{knowPass}(\iota) \end{bmatrix}$$

$$\alpha = \tau_{B,K_{B1}} = \begin{bmatrix} \text{INFO} & \text{knowPass(Hanako)} \land \exists\iota.\,\iota \neq \text{Hanako} \land \text{knowPass}(\iota) \\ \text{ATT} & \text{knowPass(Hanako)} \land \exists\exists\iota.\,\iota \neq \text{Hanako} \land \text{knowPass}(\iota) \end{bmatrix}$$

Assumptions: The same assumptions as (44a) and (44b) are made here, too.

Proof: The remnant question ρ is:

$$\rho = \tau_{B,K_{B1}}.\text{ATT} \rightrightarrows \kappa.\text{INFO}$$
$$\not\Vvdash (\text{knowPass(Hanako)} \land \exists\exists\iota.\,\iota \neq \text{Hanako} \land \text{knowPass}(\iota))$$
$$\rightrightarrows \exists\exists\iota.\,\text{knowPass}(\iota)$$

by (34),

$$\nVdash (\exists\exists\iota.\,\mathrm{knowPass(Hanako)} \wedge \iota \neq \mathrm{Hanako} \wedge \mathrm{knowPass}(\iota))$$
$$\rightrightarrows \exists\exists\iota.\,\mathrm{knowPass}(\iota)$$
$$= \uparrow (\exists\exists\iota.\,\mathrm{knowPass(Hanako)} \wedge \iota \neq \mathrm{Hanako} \wedge \mathrm{knowPass}(\iota))$$
$$\mathbb{\wedge} \exists\exists\iota.\,\mathrm{knowPass}(\iota),$$

which is eventually equivalent to $\exists\exists\iota.\,\mathrm{knowPass}(\iota)$.

It is obvious that $\mathrm{knowPass(Taro)} \vDash \exists\exists\iota.\,\mathrm{knowPass}(\iota)$. Therefore, the condition of respecting answerability (29) is met.

By (44a), $\mathrm{knowPass(Hanako)}$ and $\mathrm{knowPass(Taro)}$ are each uniquely supported by states s_h and s_t, respectively.

Think about $\mathrm{knowPass(Taro)} \rightrightarrows \rho$. This is supported by the state s_t, which is, by assumption (44b), not less informative than the total commitment of B, whose unique supporting state is s_h. Therefore the informativeness condition (30) is met. The resulting discourse structure is as follows:

$$K_{B2} = K_A.\mathrm{Cfm}(B).\mathrm{Assert}(n, B)$$

$$= \begin{bmatrix} \text{PARTICIPANTS } \{Q, A, B\} \\ \text{DC} \quad \begin{bmatrix} Q \mapsto \{\} \\ A \mapsto \{[\text{SENT } \alpha, \text{DQ } \kappa]\} \\ B \mapsto \{(\alpha, \kappa), (((\lceil n \rceil), ✿\lceil n \rceil), \kappa)\} \end{bmatrix} \\ \text{CG} \quad \{\} \\ \text{STACK} \quad [(\text{``(6Q)''}, \kappa, Q, \text{Question})] \end{bmatrix}$$

If speaker B ignores the attentional effect of speaker A's use of the indefinite, then it becomes another case of obligatory additive marking seen in (5) above. The resulting discourse structure is $K_{B2'}$:

$$K_{B2'} = K_A.\mathrm{CfmInfoOnly}(\underline{mod}_1, B).\mathrm{Assert}(\text{``Tarō-mo sit-tei-masu''}, B)$$

$$= \begin{bmatrix} \text{PARTICIPANTS } \{Q, A, B\} \\ \text{DC} \quad \begin{bmatrix} Q \mapsto \{\} \\ A \mapsto \{(\alpha, \kappa)\} \\ B \mapsto \left\{ \begin{bmatrix} \text{SENT} \begin{bmatrix} \text{INFO } \alpha.\text{INFO} \\ \text{ATT } \underline{mod}_1(\alpha.\text{ATT}) \end{bmatrix} \\ \text{DQ} \quad \kappa \\ [\text{SENT } [\text{INFO } \lceil n \rceil, \text{ATT } ✿\lceil n \rceil], \text{DQ } \kappa] \end{bmatrix}, \right\} \end{bmatrix} \\ \text{CG} \quad \{\} \\ \text{STACK} \quad [(\text{``(6Q)''}, \kappa, Q, \text{Question})] \end{bmatrix}$$

(45) The speaker B in (8) can validly assert the new answer
   $n = $ "*Tarō-to-Hanako-ga sit-tei-masu*" without additive marking.

   (8) Q: Who knows the password?

A: Hanako-ga   sit-tei-masu.
    Hanako-NOM know-ASP-HON

    'Hanako does.'

B: sonotōri-desu. Tarō-to-Hanako-{ ga / # mo }
    exactly-HON Taro-and-Hanako-{ NOM / NOM.ADD }
    sit-tei-masu.
    know-ASP-HON

    'Exactly. Taro and Hanako do, (# too).'

$$K_{B1} = K_A.\mathrm{Cfm}(B)$$

$$= \begin{bmatrix} \textsc{participants} & \{Q, A, B\} \\ \textsc{dc} & [Q \mapsto \{\}, A \mapsto \{[\textsc{sent}\ \alpha, \textsc{dq}\ \kappa]\}, B \mapsto \{(\alpha, \kappa)\}] \\ \textsc{cg} & \{\} \\ \textsc{stack} & [(\text{``(5Q)''}, \kappa, Q, \text{Question})] \end{bmatrix}$$

where

$$[n] = \mathrm{knowPass(Taro)} \wedge \mathrm{knowPass(Hanako)}$$

$$\kappa = \begin{bmatrix} \textsc{info} & \exists\exists\iota.\,\mathrm{knowPass}(\iota) \\ \textsc{att} & \exists\exists\iota.\,\mathrm{knowPass}(\iota) \end{bmatrix}$$

$$\alpha = \tau_{B,K_{B1}} = \begin{bmatrix} \textsc{info} & \mathrm{knowPass(Hanako)} \\ \textsc{att} & \mathrm{knowPass(Hanako)} \end{bmatrix}$$

Proof: The remnant question ρ is:

$$\rho = \tau_{B,K_{B1}}.\textsc{att} \rightrightarrows \kappa.\textsc{info}$$
$$\dasheq\vDash \mathrm{knowPass(Hanako)} \rightrightarrows \exists\exists\iota.\,\mathrm{knowPass}(\iota)$$

The condition of respecting answerability (29) is met because the only supporting state for $\mathrm{knowPass(Taro)} \wedge \mathrm{knowPass(Hanako)}$, which is $s_t \cap s_h$, supports $\downarrow \rho$.

The informativeness condition (30) is also met. Think about $\mathrm{knowPass(Taro)} \wedge \mathrm{knowPass(Hanako)} \rightrightarrows \rho$. It can be expanded to

$$\uparrow(\mathrm{knowPass(Taro)} \wedge \mathrm{knowPass(Hanako)})$$
$$\wedge \uparrow \mathrm{knowPass(Hanako)}$$
$$\wedge \exists\exists\iota.\,\mathrm{knowPass}(\iota).$$

By assumption (44a) and the entailment-reversing nautre of $\uparrow$, it is equivalent to $\uparrow \mathrm{knowPass(Hanako)} \wedge \exists\exists\iota.\,\mathrm{knowPass}(\iota)$, which is ρ itself. Since s_h is the unique supporting state for $\mathrm{knowPass(Hanako)}$, $s_h \vDash \rho$ ($\dasheq\vDash [n] \rightrightarrows \rho$). Therefore, $\mathrm{knowPass(Hanako)} \vDash \rho$ ($\dasheq\vDash [n] \rightrightarrows \rho$), From this we can conclude that $\mathrm{knowPass(Hanako)} \nvDash \exists\rho$ ($\dasheq\vDash \exists([n] \rightrightarrows \rho)$).

References

1. Agha, O., Warstadt, A.: Non-resolving responses to polar questions: a revision to the QUD theory of relevance. In: Proceedings of Sinn und Bedeutung 24, vol. 1, pp. 17–34. Osnabrück University (2020)
2. Aloni, M.: Expressing ignorance or indifference: modal implicatures in bidirectional OT. In: ten Cate, B.D., Zeevat, H.W. (eds.) TbiLLC 2005. LNCS (LNAI), vol. 4363, pp. 1–20. Springer, Heidelberg (2007). https://doi.org/10.1007/978-3-540-75144-1_1
3. Aloni, M.: Logic and conversation: the case of free choice. Semant. Pragmat. **15**(5) (2022)
4. Anttila, A.: The logic of free choice: axiomatizations of state-based modal logics. Master's thesis, Universiteit van Amsterdam (2021)
5. Bade, N.: Obligatory implicatures and the presupposition of "too". In: Etxeberria, U., Fălăuş, A., Irurtzun, A., Leferman, B. (eds.) Proceedings of Sinn und Bedeutung 18, pp. 42–59 (2008)
6. Bar-Lev, M.E., Fox, D.: Free choice, simplification, and innocent inclusion. Nat. Lang. Semant. **28**(3), 175–223 (2020)
7. Beaver, D.I., Clark, B.Z.: Sense and Sensitivity: How Focus Determines Meaning. Wiley-Blackwell, Oxford (2008)
8. Büring, D.: The least *at least* can do. In: Chang, C.B., Haynie, H.J. (eds.) Proceedings of WCCFL 26, pp. 114–120. Cascadilla Proceedings Project, Somerville (2008)
9. Chierchia, G.: On being trivial: grammar vs. logic. In: Sagi, G., Woods, J. (eds.) The Semantic Conception of Logic, pp. 227–248. Cambridge University Press (2021)
10. Ciardelli, I., Groenendijk, J., Roelofsen, F.: Information, issues, and attention. In: Gutzmann, D., Köpping, J., Meier, C. (eds.) Approaches to Meaning: Composition, Values, and Interpretation, pp. 128–166. Brill (2014)
11. Ciardelli, I., Groenendijk, J., Roelofsen, F.: Inquisitive Semantics. Oxford University Press, Oxford (2019)
12. Ciardelli, I., Zhang, L., Champollion, L.: Two switches in the theory of counterfactuals: a study of truth conditionality and minimal change. Linguist. Philos. **41**(6), 577–621 (2018)
13. Cruschina, S.: The greater the contrast, the greater the potential: on the effects of focus in syntax. Glossa: J. Gen. Linguist. **6**(1), 3 (2021)
14. Eckardt, R.: 'Was noch?' navigating in question answer discourse. In: Späth, A. (ed.) Interfaces and Interface Conditions, pp. 77–96. de Gruyter, Berlin (2007)
15. Eckardt, R., Fränkel, M.: Particles, Maximize Presupposition and discourse management. Lingua **122**(15), 1801–1818 (2012)
16. Farkas, D.F., Bruce, K.B.: On reacting to assertions and polar questions. J. Semant. **27**(1), 81–118 (2009)
17. Fox, D.: Free choice and the theory of scalar implicatures. In: Sauerland, U., Stateva, P. (eds.) Presupposition and Implicature in Compositional Semantics, pp. 71–120. Palgrave Macmillan, London (2007)
18. Gajewski, J.R.: L-analiticity and natural language (2002)
19. Geurts, B.: Quantity Implicatures. Cambridge University Press, Cambridge (2010)
20. Geurts, B., Nouwen, R.: *At least* et al.: the semantics of scalar modifiers. Language **83**(3), 533–559 (2007)

21. Green, G.M.: The lexical expression of emphatic conjunction: theoretical implications. Found. Lang. **10**(2), 197–248 (1973)
22. Groenendijk, J.A.G., Stokhof: studies on the semantics of questions and the pragmatics of answers. Dissertation, Universiteit van Amsterdam (1984)
23. Hara, Y.: Grammar of knowledge representation: Japanese discourse items at interfaces. Ph.D. thesis, the University of Delaware (2006)
24. Haspelmath, M.: Indefinite Pronouns. Oxford University Press, Oxford (1997)
25. Heycock, C.: Japanese -*wa*, -*ga*, and information structure. In: Miyagawa, S., Saito, M. (eds.) The Oxford Handbook of Japanese Linguistics. Oxford University Press, Oxford (2008)
26. Jasinskaja, E.: Pragmatics and prosody of implicit discourse relations: the case of restatement. Ph.D. thesis, Universität Tübingen (2007)
27. Jasinskaja, K., Zeevat, H.: Explaining additive, adversative and contrast marking in Russian and English. Revue de Sémantique et Pragmatique **24**, 65–91 (2008)
28. Jucker, A.H., Smith, S.W.: And people just you know like 'wow': discourse markers as negotiating strategies. In: Jucker, A.H., Ziv, Y. (eds.) Discourse Markers: Descriptions and Theory, pp. 171–202. John Benjamins, Amsterdam (1998)
29. Kaplan, J.: Obligatory too in English. Language **60**(3), 510 (1984)
30. Karttunen, L., Peters, S.: Conventional implicature. In: Oh, C.K., Dinneen, D.A. (eds.) Syntax and Semantics 11: Presupposition, pp. 1–56. Academic Press, New York (1979)
31. Kennedy, C.: A "de-Fregean" semantics (and neo-Gricean pragmatics) for modified and unmodified numerals. Semant. Pragmat. **8**(10), 1–44 (2015)
32. Kitagawa, C.: Saying 'yes' in Japanese. J. Pragmat. **4**(2), 105–120 (1980)
33. Kratzer, A., Selkirk, E.: Deconstructing information structure. Glossa **5**(1), 1–53 (2020)
34. Krifka, M.: Additive particles under stress. In: Strolovitch, D., Lawson, A. (eds.) Proceedings of SALT 8, pp. 111–129. Cornell University, Ithaca (1998)
35. Krifka, M.: At least some determiners aren't determiners. In: Turner, K. (ed.) The Semantics/Pragmatics Interface from Different Points of View, pp. 257–291. No. 1 in Current Research in the Semantics/Pragmatics Interface, Elsevier (1999)
36. Krifka, M.: For a structured meaning account of questions and answers. In: Féry, C., Sternefeld, W. (eds.) Audiatur vox sapientiae: a Festschrift for Arnim von Stechow, pp. 287–319. Akademie-Verlag, Berlin (2001)
37. Kuno, S.: The Structure of the Japanese Language. MIT Press, Cambridge (1973)
38. Kuroda, S.Y.: Generative grammatical studies in the Japanese language. Dissertation, MIT (1965)
39. Nakanishi, K., Tomioka, S.: Japanese plurals are exceptional. J. East Asian Linguist. **13**, 113–140 (2004)
40. Norrick, N.R.: Interjections as pragmatic markers. J. Pragmat. **41**(5), 866–891 (2009)
41. Onea, E.: Potential questions at the semantics-pragmatics interface. No. 33 in Current Research in the Semantics/Pragmatics Interface, Brill, Leiden (2016)
42. Onea, E.: Specificity and questions of specification. In: Gianollo, C., Von Heusinger, K., Napoli, M. (eds.) Determiners and Quantifiers: Functions, Variation, and Change, pp. 130–185. No. 44 in Syntax and Semantics, Brill (2022)
43. Percus, O.: Antipresupposition. In: Ueyama, A. (ed.) Theoretical and Empirical Studies of Reference and Anaphora: Toward the Establishment of Generative Grammar as an Empirical Science, pp. 52–73. Report of the Grant-in-Aid for Scientific Research (B), Project No. 15320052, Japan Society for the Promotion of Science, JSPS, Tokyo (2006)

44. Roberts, C.: Information structure in discourse: towards an integrated formal theory of pragmatics. Semant. Pragmat. **5**, 6 (2012)
45. Rooth, M.: Association with Focus. Ph.D. thesis, University of Massachusetts (1985)
46. Rooth, M.: A theory of focus interpretation. Nat. Lang. Semant. **1**(1), 75–116 (1992)
47. van Rooy, R.: Questioning to resolve decision problems. Linguist. Philos. **26**(6), 727–763 (2003)
48. van Rooy, R.: Relevance and bidirectional optimality theory. In: Blutner, R., Zeevat, H. (eds.) Optimality Theory and Pragmatics, pp. 173–210. Palgrave Macmillan, London (2004)
49. Ruys, E.G.: On the anaphoricity of too. Linguist. Inquiry **46**(2), 343–361 (2015)
50. Sauerland, U.: Scalar implicatures in complex sentences. Linguist. Philos. **27**(3), 367–391 (2004)
51. Sawada, O.: The Japanese contrastive *wa*: a mirror image of *even*. In: Crane, T., et al. (eds.) Proceedings of BLS 33: General Session and Parasession on Multilingualism and Fieldwork, vol. 33, p. 374. Berkeley Linguistis Society, Berkeley (2007)
52. Sawada, O.: The scalar contrastive *wa* in Japanese. In: Bîlbîie, G., Crysmann, B., Schaden, G. (eds.) Empirical Issues in Syntax and Semantics 14, pp. 239–271. CNRS, l'Université de Paris (2022)
53. Schwarzschild, R.: Givenness, AvoidF and other constraints on the placement of accent. Nat. Lang. Semant. **7**(2), 141–177 (1999)
54. Shudo, S.: Presupposition and Discourse: Function of the Japanese Particle Mo. Routledge, New York (2002)
55. Simons, M., Beaver, D., Roberts, C., Tonhauser, J.: The best question: explaining the projection behavior of factives. Discourse Process. **54**(3), 187–206 (2017)
56. Singh, R.: Maximize presupposition! and local contexts. Nat. Lang. Semant. **19**(2), 149–168 (2011)
57. Soames, S.: How presuppositions are inherited: a solution to the projection problem. Linguist. Inquiry **13**(3), 483–545 (1982)
58. Sæbø, K.J.: Conversational contrast and conventional parallel: topic implicatures and additive presuppositions. J. Semant. **21**(2), 199–217 (2004)
59. Theiler, N.: When additive particles can associate with wh-phrases. In: Espinal, M.T., Castroviejo, E., Leonetti, M., McNally, L., Real-Puigdollers, C. (eds.) Proceedings of Sinn und Bedeutung 23, vol. 2, pp. 347–364 (2019)
60. Tomioka, S.: Contrastive topics operate on speech acts. In: Zimmermann, M., Féry, C. (eds.) Information Structure: Theoretical, Typological, and Experimental Perspectives, pp. 115–138. Oxford University Press, Oxford (2009). Section: 6
61. Tönnis, S.: It is not the obvious question that a cleft addresses. In: Özgün, A., Zinova, Y. (eds.) TbiLLC 2019. LNCS, vol. 13206, pp. 128–147. Springer, Cham (2022). https://doi.org/10.1007/978-3-030-98479-3_7
62. Van Rooij, R., Schulz, K.: Exhaustive interpretation of complex sentences. J. Logic Lang. Inform. **13**(4), 491–519 (2004)
63. Westera, M.: Exhaustivity and intonation: a unified theory. Dissertation, University of Amsterdam (2017)
64. Westera, M.: Attentional Pragmatics: a pragmatic approach to exhaustivity. Semant. Pragmat. **15**(10) (2022)
65. Winterstein, G., Zeevat, H.: Empirical constraints on accounts of too. Lingua **122**(15), 1787–1800 (2012)
66. Zeevat, H.: Objection marking and additivity. Lingua **122**(15), 1886–1898 (2012)

Extending Abstract Categorial Grammars with Feature Structures: Theory and Practice

Philippe de Groote[1], Maxime Guillaume[1,2(✉)], Agathe Helman[2],
Sylvain Pogodalla[1], and Raphaël Salmon[2]

[1] Université de Lorraine, CNRS, Inria, LORIA, 54000 Nancy, France
[2] Yseop, Paris, France
mguillaume@yseop.com

Abstract. Abstract Categorial Grammars offer a versatile framework for modeling natural language syntax and semantics. However, they currently miss a key component in grammatical engineering: feature structures. This paper introduces a conservative extension to the framework, incorporating feature structures and shows the practical advantages of this integration on a French grammar.

Keywords: Text generation · Industrial grammars · Categorial grammars · Feature structures

1 Introduction

1.1 Abstract Categorial Grammar

Abstract Categorial Grammars (ACGs) derive from the tradition of type-theoretic grammars. They were developed with the intent of being a kernel for a grammatical framework [15] capable of representing various grammatical formalisms [5,6]. This includes, but is not limited to, well-known formalisms such as context-free grammars (CFGs) and tree-adjoining grammars [9].

ACGs are based on a small set of computational primitives: typed linear λ-calculus and high-order signatures.

Definition 1 (Implicative Types). *Let A be a set of atomic types, the set of implicative types over A, $\mathcal{T}(A)$ is defined by the following BNF grammar:*

$$\mathcal{T}(A) ::= A \mid \mathcal{T}(A) \multimap \mathcal{T}(A)$$

Definition 2 (High-order Signature). *A high-order signature Σ is a triplet $\langle A, C, \tau \rangle$ where:*

- *A is a finite set of atomic types;*
- *C is a finite set of constants;*
- *$\tau : C \to \mathcal{T}(A)$ is a function that associates to each constant $c \in C$ an implicative type in $\mathcal{T}(A)$.*

D. Bekki et al. (Eds.): LENLS 2023, LNCS 14569, pp. 118–133, 2024.
https://doi.org/10.1007/978-3-031-60878-0_7

Definition 3 (Terms). *Let $\mathcal{X}$ be a countable set of variables, the set of lambda-terms defined over a signature Σ, $\Lambda(\Sigma)$, is defined by the following BNF grammar:*

$$\Lambda(\Sigma) ::= c \mid x \mid \lambda^\circ x.\Lambda(\Sigma) \mid \Lambda(\Sigma)\ \Lambda(\Sigma)$$

The variable x needs to appear free exactly once in the expression $\Lambda(\Sigma)$ for the linear lambda abstraction $\lambda^\circ x.\Lambda(\Sigma)$ to be correctly formed. We adhere to the standard conventions, employing left associativity for applications and right associativity for abstractions and implications.

Paralleling traditional compiler theory, ACG offers a clear cut between the abstract syntax and the object syntax. Both of these syntaxes are defined through high-order signatures. The connection between the two is established through the lexicon, which functions essentially as an interpreter, translating abstract structures into object ones. Fundamentally, the lexicon can be conceptualized as an abstract embodiment of the compositionality principle.

Definition 4 (Lexicon). *Let $\Sigma_1 = \langle A_1, C_1, \tau_1 \rangle$ and $\Sigma_2 = \langle A_2, C_2, \tau_2 \rangle$ be two high-order signatures, a lexicon from Σ_1 to Σ_2, $\mathcal{L} : \Sigma_1 \to \Sigma_2$ is a pair $\langle F, G \rangle$ where*

- *$F : A_1 \to \mathcal{T}(A_2)$ is a morphism that interprets atomic types of Σ_1 into implicative types over Σ_2;*
- *$G : C_1 \to \Lambda(\Sigma_2)$ is a morphism that associates to each constant of Σ_1, a lambda-term defined over Σ_2.*
- *$\hat{F}$ and $\hat{G}$ are the unique homomorphic extensions of F and G to types and terms.*
- *for all constants $c \in C_1$, the following judgment is derivable:*

$$\vdash_{\Sigma_2} G(c) : \hat{F}(\tau_1(c))$$

To simplify notations, we will use $\mathcal{L}$ instead of F or G. With the previously discussed elements, we can now define an ACG.

Definition 5 (Grammar). *An ACG $\mathcal{G}$ is a quadruplet $\langle \Sigma_1, \Sigma_2, \mathcal{L}, s \rangle$ where:*

- *Σ_1 is a high-order signature called the abstract signature;*
- *Σ_2 is a high-order signature called the object signature;*
- *$\mathcal{L}$ is a lexicon from Σ_1 to Σ_2;*
- *s is a distinguished type belonging to $\mathcal{T}(A_1)$.*

An ACG generates two distinct languages: the abstract language, specifying the underlying admissible structures, and the object language, representing the surface forms of linguistic expressions.

Definition 6 (Abstract language). *Let $\mathcal{G}$ be an ACG, the abstract language of $\mathcal{G}$, $\mathcal{A}(\mathcal{G})$, is the set of linear lambda-terms defined as follows:*

$$\mathcal{A}(\mathcal{G}) = \{t \in \Lambda(\Sigma_1) \mid\ \vdash_{\Sigma_1} t : s\}$$

Definition 7 (Object language). *Let $\mathcal{G}$ be an ACG, the object language of $\mathcal{G}$, is the set of linear lambda-terms defined as follows:*

$$\mathcal{O}(\mathcal{G}) = \{t \in \Lambda(\Sigma_2) \mid \exists u \in \mathcal{A}(\mathcal{G}).\mathcal{L}(u) = t\}$$

These generated languages of linear λ-terms generalize both string and tree languages. Strings of symbols may be encoded as function compositions. Figure 1a defines the high-order signature in which the strings: *the leverage increases* and *the leverages increase* can be represented. The parse tree of *the leverage increases*, may be represented as a term built over the high-order signature defined in Fig. 1b.

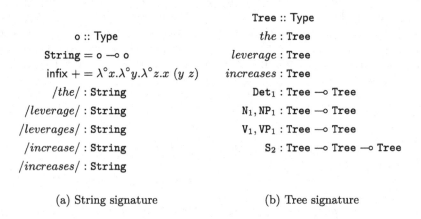

(a) String signature   (b) Tree signature

Fig. 1. Uniform representation of languages

ACGs are inherently reversible [7], they can be used in both directions, either generating or interpreting expressions. ACGs offer two primary computational paradigms. First, there is the applicative paradigm, which involves calculating the interpretation of an abstract term using the grammar's lexicon. Second, there is the deductive paradigm, which focuses on verifying whether a term u defined over the object signature belongs to the object language. This verification process depends on morphism inversion since it involves identifying the abstract terms, represented as t, for which $\mathcal{L}(t) = u$. The process of inverting morphisms for this purpose is referred to as ACG parsing.

A third paradigm, called the transductive paradigm, emerges when composing two ACGs with a shared abstract signature. It allows moving from one object language to the other object language by applying a combination of the deductive and applicative paradigms. We will use this paradigm in Sect. 4.

1.2   Morphosyntax and Grammars

The composable nature of ACGs allows for the creation of complex architectures for natural language modeling. However, modeling morphosyntactic phenomena, such as agreement, results in a substantial enlargement of grammars. To illustrate this point, suppose that we want to define the derivation structures that allow for the construction of the following sentence: *The leverage increases.* Such language may be defined using the high-order signature presented in Fig. 2a. However, if we aim to introduce the plural version of this sentence and reject the ungrammatical ones, we will need a notion of morphological number in the types, which will double the signature size, as shown in Fig. 2b.

$$S, N_{sg}, N_{pl}, NP_{sg}, NP_{pl} :: \mathsf{Type}$$

$$THE_{sg} : N_{sg} \multimap NP_{sg}$$

$$THE_{pl} : N_{pl} \multimap NP_{pl}$$

$$S, N, NP :: \mathsf{Type}$$

$$LEVERAGE : N_{sg}$$

$$THE : N \multimap NP$$

$$LEVERAGES : N_{pl}$$

$$LEVERAGE : N$$

$$INCREASES : NP_{sg} \multimap S$$

$$INCREASES : NP \multimap S$$

$$INCREASE : NP_{pl} \multimap S$$

(a) Derivation signature

(b) Derivation signature with morphological variants

Fig. 2. Derivation signatures

Although the size of this toy example is small, it demonstrates the combinatorial explosion that occurs when introducing morphosyntactic constraints. Consequently, creating and maintaining grammars becomes time-consuming. In addition, ACG parsing becomes less efficient due to the number of constants to consider.

It can get worse, especially for languages like French that have many morphological traits. ACGs lack a commonly utilized mechanism in grammatical engineering: feature structures. These structures are advantageous for succinctly describing the morphosyntactic rules of languages, such as agreement. The main goals of this paper are both theoretical and practical:

1. to introduce a conservative extension to the core ACGs that incorporates feature structures;
2. to experimentally demonstrate the benefits of the extension through a rewrite of a French grammar;
3. to empirically confirm that the size reduction impacts positively ACG parsing.

2 Proposed Extension

2.1 Modeling Feature Structures

The introductory example raises two questions: how can we effectively represent feature structures, and what are the best methods for associating these structures with atomic types? Our proposition involves the representation of feature structures by incorporating well-established constructs, namely records and enumerations. To annotate atomic types with feature structures, we advocate for the adoption of dependent types. Extending ACG with dependent types has already been explored [4,14]. However, it has been demonstrated that parsing becomes undecidable with fully fledged dependent types. Our primary objective is to propose an extension that does not augment the expressive power of the framework. Parsing in a specific class of ACGs can be reduced to the polynomial evaluation of a Datalog program [10,11], we aim to preserve this property.

Our extension, ACG with feature structures (f-ACG), utilizes typed feature structures, where the types can only be either an enumeration or a record type.

Definition 8 (Feature structure types). *The set of feature structures types, denoted as $\mathcal{F}$, is defined by the following BNF:*

$$
\begin{aligned}
&e \in E && \text{(Enumeral symbol)} \\
&l \in L && \text{(Label symbol)} \\
&\mathcal{E} := \{e_1 \mid \ldots \mid e_n\} && \text{(Enumerated type)} \\
&\mathcal{R} := [l_1 : \mathcal{F}, \ldots, l_n : \mathcal{F}] && \text{(Record type)} \\
&\mathcal{F} := \mathcal{E} && \\
&\quad\ \mid \mathcal{R} &&
\end{aligned}
$$

Definition 9 (Feature structure terms). *The set of feature structure terms, F, is defined as follows:*

$$
\begin{aligned}
&x \in \mathcal{X} && \text{(Variable symbol)} \\
&F := e && \text{(Enumeral)} \\
&\quad\ \mid x && \text{(Feature structure variable)} \\
&\quad\ \mid [l_1 = F, \ldots, l_n = F_n] && \text{(Record)} \\
&\quad\ \mid F.l && \text{(Selection)}
\end{aligned}
$$

Figure 3 introduces the typing relation for feature structures. In these rules, Γ is a context of feature structure variables.

We extend ACG types with two new constructors: type abstraction and type application. Only feature structure terms are permitted as dependencies for types. This constraint is formulated using an upper level that is above types, which is referred to as *kind*. Figure 4 introduces the kinding judgment.

$$\frac{}{\Gamma, x : \mathcal{F} \vdash_{\Sigma} x : \mathcal{F}} \text{ VAR-FEAT}$$

$$\frac{\vdash_{\Sigma} e \in \{e_1, \dots, e_n\}}{\vdash_{\Sigma} e : \{e_1 \mid \dots \mid e_n\}} \text{ ENUMERAL-FEAT}$$

$$\frac{\Gamma \vdash_{\Sigma} f_i : \mathcal{F}_i \qquad \forall i \in [1, n]}{\Gamma \vdash_{\Sigma} [l_i = f_i]_{i=1}^{n} : [l_i : \mathcal{F}_i]_{1}^{n}} \text{ RECORD-FEAT}$$

$$\frac{\Gamma \vdash_{\Sigma} f : [l_i : \mathcal{F}_i]_{i=1}^{n} \qquad l_k \in \{l_i\}_{i=1}^{n}}{\Gamma \vdash_{\Sigma} f.l_k : \mathcal{F}_k} \text{ SELECTION-FEAT}$$

Fig. 3. Feature structures typing rules

Definition 10 (Extended Types). *Let A be a set of atomic types, the set of extended types over A, $\mathcal{T}(A)$ is defined as follows:*

$$
\begin{aligned}
\mathcal{T}(A) &:= A & \text{(Atomic type or Type family)} \\
&\mid \mathcal{T}(A) \multimap \mathcal{T}(A) & \text{(Linear functional type)} \\
&\mid \Lambda x : \mathcal{F}.\mathcal{T}(A) & \text{(Type abstraction)} \\
&\mid \mathcal{T}(A) \ F & \text{(Type application)}
\end{aligned}
$$

Definition 11 (Kind). *The set of kinds, $\mathcal{K}$, is defined by the following BNF grammar:*

$$
\begin{aligned}
\mathcal{K} &:= \mathsf{Type} & \text{(Kind of proper types)} \\
&\mid \mathcal{F} \Rightarrow \mathcal{K} & \text{(Kind of families)}
\end{aligned}
$$

We avoid the full expressiveness of dependent products by enforcing them to only appear in prenex form through the introduction of a new type level, referred to as *generalized types*, and a new kind level, referred to as *generalized kinds*. Figure 5 defines the rules for the interaction between these two generalized levels.

Definition 12 (Generalized types). *The set of generalized types over A, $\mathcal{D}(A)$, and the set of generalized kind, $\mathcal{K_D}$, are defined by the following grammar:*

$$
\begin{aligned}
\mathcal{D}(A) &:= \mathcal{T}(A) & \text{(Types)} \\
&\mid \Pi x : \mathcal{F}.\mathcal{D}(A) & \text{(Dependent product)} \\
\mathcal{K_D} &:= \mathsf{DType} & \text{(Kind of proper generalized types)} \\
&\mid \mathcal{K} & \text{(Kind)}
\end{aligned}
$$

$$\frac{a :: \mathcal{K} \in \Sigma}{\Gamma \vdash_\Sigma a :: \mathcal{K}} \quad \text{ATOMIC-TYPE}$$

$$\frac{\Gamma \vdash_\Sigma \alpha :: \mathsf{Type} \qquad \Gamma \vdash_\Sigma \beta :: \mathsf{Type}}{\Gamma \vdash_\Sigma \alpha \multimap \beta :: \mathsf{Type}} \quad \text{LFUNC-TYPE}$$

$$\frac{\Gamma \vdash_\Sigma \alpha :: \mathcal{F} \Rrightarrow \mathcal{K} \qquad \Gamma \vdash_\Sigma f : \mathcal{F}}{\Gamma \vdash_\Sigma \alpha\, f :: \mathcal{K}} \quad \text{APP-TYPE}$$

$$\frac{\Gamma, x : \mathcal{F} \vdash_\Sigma \alpha :: \mathcal{K}}{\Gamma \vdash_\Sigma \Lambda x : \mathcal{F}.\alpha :: \mathcal{F} \Rrightarrow \mathcal{K}} \quad \text{ABSTR-TYPE}$$

Fig. 4. Type formation rules

$$\frac{\Gamma \vdash_\Sigma \alpha :: \mathsf{Type}}{\Gamma \vdash_\Sigma \alpha :: \mathsf{DType}} \quad \text{PROMOTION-TYPE}$$

$$\frac{\Gamma, x : \mathcal{F} \vdash_\Sigma \alpha :: \mathsf{DType}}{\Gamma \vdash_\Sigma \Pi x : \mathcal{F}.\alpha :: \mathsf{DType}} \quad \text{PI-TYPE}$$

Fig. 5. Generalized type formation rules

2.2 Extended Abstract Categorial Grammar

The notion of a signature is redefined to consider the kinding relation and generalized types.

Definition 13 (Extended signature). *An extended signature is a quadruplet* $\Sigma = \langle A, \kappa, C, \tau \rangle$ *where:*

- *A is a finite set of atomic types;*
- $\kappa : A \to \mathcal{K}$ *is a function that assigns to each atomic type a kind;*
- *C is a finite set of constants;*
- $\tau : C \to \mathcal{D}(a)$ *is a function that assigns to each constant a generalized type;*
- $\tau(c)$ *is in β-normal form and the following kinding judgment holds:*

$$\vdash_\Sigma \tau(c) :: \mathsf{DType}$$

The inclusion of dependent products leads at the term level to the introduction of feature abstractions, feature applications, and case analysis. Figure 6 defines the typing relation for terms. A second context, Δ, appears in these rules for linear assumptions. This kind of type systems where linear and dependent types coexist has already been explored in an extension of the logical framework [3].

$$\frac{c : \mathcal{D} \in \Sigma}{\Gamma; \Delta \vdash_\Sigma c : \mathcal{D}} \text{ CONST-TERM}$$

$$\frac{}{\Gamma; x : \alpha \vdash_\Sigma x : \alpha} \text{ LVAR-TERM}$$

$$\frac{\Gamma; \Delta_1 \vdash_\Sigma t : \alpha \multimap \beta \qquad \Gamma; \Delta_2 \vdash_\Sigma u : \alpha}{\Gamma; \Delta_1, \Delta_2 \vdash_\Sigma t\, u : \beta} \text{ LAPP-TERM}$$

$$\frac{\Gamma; \Delta \vdash_\Sigma t : \Pi x : \mathcal{F}.\alpha \qquad \Gamma; \vdash_\Sigma f : \mathcal{F}}{\Gamma; \Delta \vdash_\Sigma t \bullet f : \alpha[x := f]} \text{ APP-TERM}$$

$$\frac{\Gamma; \Delta, x : \alpha \vdash_\Sigma t : \beta}{\Gamma; \Delta \vdash_\Sigma \lambda^\circ x : \alpha.t : \alpha \multimap \beta} \text{ LABSTR-TERM}$$

$$\frac{\Gamma, x : \mathcal{F}; \Delta \vdash_\Sigma t : \alpha}{\Gamma; \Delta \vdash_\Sigma \lambda x : \mathcal{F}.t : \Pi x : \mathcal{F}.\alpha} \text{ ABSTR-TERM}$$

$$\frac{\Gamma, x : \mathcal{E} \vdash_\Sigma \alpha :: \mathsf{Type} \qquad \Gamma; \vdash_\Sigma f : \mathcal{E} \qquad \Gamma; \vdash_\Sigma t_i : \alpha[x := e_i]}{\Gamma; \vdash_\Sigma \mathsf{case}\ f\ \{e_i \to t_i\}_{i=1}^n : \alpha[x := f]} \text{ CASE-VAR-TERM}$$

Fig. 6. Typing rules

Definition 14 (Terms). *Let $\mathcal{X}$ be a countable set of variables, the set of lambda-terms defined over a signature Σ, $\Lambda(\Sigma)$, is defined by the following BNF grammar:*

$$
\begin{aligned}
\Lambda(\Sigma) \coloneqq\ &c && \text{(Constant)} \\
\mid\ &x && \text{(Variable)} \\
\mid\ &\Lambda(\Sigma)\ \Lambda(\Sigma) && \text{(Application)} \\
\mid\ &\Lambda(\Sigma) \bullet F && \text{(Feature structure application)} \\
\mid\ &\lambda^\circ x : \mathcal{T}(A).\Lambda(\Sigma) && \text{(Linear lambda abstraction)} \\
\mid\ &\lambda x : \mathcal{F}.\Lambda(\Sigma) && \text{(Feature structure abstraction)} \\
\mid\ &\mathsf{case}\ F\ \{e_1 \to \Lambda(\Sigma) \mid \cdots \mid e_n \to \Lambda(\Sigma)\} && \text{(Case analysis)}
\end{aligned}
$$

A noteworthy aspect of this extension lies in the interpretation of abstract feature structure terms and types. They are interpreted in types and terms as they appear in abstract expressions. As a result, the interpretation of types must preserve the kinding judgment.

Definition 15 (Extended lexicon). *Let $\Sigma_1 = \langle A_1, \kappa_1, C_1, \tau_1 \rangle$ and $\Sigma_2 = \langle A_2, \kappa_2, C_2, \tau_2 \rangle$ be two extended signatures. An extended lexicon $\mathcal{L}$ is a pair $\langle F, G \rangle$ where:*

- $F : A_1 \to \mathcal{T}(\Sigma_2)$ *is a function that interprets atomic types with types defined over the object signature.*
- $G : C_1 \to \Lambda(\Sigma_2)$ *is a function that interprets abstract constants as terms defined over the object signature.*
- *For each a in A_1, the following kinding judgment is derivable:*

$$\vdash_{\Sigma_2} F(a) :: \kappa_1(a)$$

- *For each c in C_1, the following typing judgment is derivable:*

$$\vdash_{\Sigma_2} G(c) : H(\tau_1(c))$$

where $H : \mathcal{D}(A_1) \to \mathcal{D}(A_2)$ is a morphism defined such that:
- *If $\vdash_{\Sigma_1} \alpha :: \mathsf{Type}$, then $H(\alpha) = \hat{F}(\alpha)$*
- *If $\vdash_{\Sigma_1} \alpha :: \mathsf{DType}$ and $\alpha \equiv \Pi x : \mathcal{F}.\beta$ then $H(\alpha) = \Pi x : \mathcal{F}.H(\beta)$*

Definition 16 (Extended Grammar). *An extended ACG $\mathcal{G}$ is a quadruplet $\langle \Sigma_1, \Sigma_2, \mathcal{L}, s \rangle$ where:*

- *Σ_1 is an extended signature called the abstract signature;*
- *Σ_2 is an extended signature called the object signature;*
- *$\mathcal{L}$ is an extended lexicon from Σ_1 to Σ_2;*
- *s is a distinguished type belonging to $\mathcal{T}(A_1)$ in β-normal form.*

In Fig. 7, we revisit the introductory derivation signature using an extended signature. Figure 8 provides a definition of the lexicon from this extended abstract signature to the string signature defined in Fig. 1a. The categories N and NP are interpreted as type abstractions. They accept a number but return a string type, disregarding the value of the parameter. Furthermore, the interpretation of INCREASE and LEVERAGE involves case analysis to modify the string according to its associated number.

$$\mathsf{S} :: \mathsf{Type}$$
$$Num = \{sg, pl\}$$
$$\mathsf{N} :: [n : Num] \Rightarrow \mathsf{Type}$$
$$\mathsf{NP} :: [n : Num] \Rightarrow \mathsf{Type}$$
$$\text{LEVERAGE} : \Pi x : Num.\mathsf{N}\,[n = x]$$
$$\text{THE} : \Pi x : Num.\mathsf{N}\,[n = x] \multimap \mathsf{NP}\,[n = x]$$
$$\text{INCREASE} : \Pi x : Num.\mathsf{NP}\,[n = x] \multimap \mathsf{S}$$

Fig. 7. Extended derivation signature

$$\mathcal{L}(\text{S}) = \texttt{String}$$
$$\mathcal{L}(\text{N}) = \Lambda x : Num.\texttt{String}$$
$$\mathcal{L}(\text{NP}) = \Lambda x : Num.\texttt{String}$$
$$\mathcal{L}(\text{THE}) = \lambda x : Num.\lambda^\circ n : \texttt{String}./the/ + n$$
$$\mathcal{L}(\text{INCREASE}) = \lambda x : Num.\lambda^\circ np : \texttt{String}.$$
$$\text{case } x \ \{sg \rightarrow np + /increases/ \mid pl \rightarrow np + /increase/\}$$
$$\mathcal{L}(\text{LEVERAGE}) = \lambda x : Num.$$
$$\text{case } x \ \{sg \rightarrow /leverage/ \mid pl \rightarrow /leverages/\}$$

Fig. 8. Extended lexicon

3 Theoretical Results

3.1 Expressive Power

This extension does not augment the expressive power of ACG, as it can be established that any f-ACG is transformable into a core ACG. Formally, the following proposition holds.

Proposition 1. *Let $\mathcal{G}$ be a f-ACG grammar, there exists a core ACG grammar, $\mathcal{G}'$, wherein the abstract and object languages generated by $\mathcal{G}'$ are isomorphic to those generated by $\mathcal{G}$.*

Due to space limitations, we are not presenting the proof in this paper. The intuition about the transformation from a f-ACG to a core ACG is very similar to the reduction of context-free grammars augmented with feature structures into core CFGs. Rules with feature structure variables are instantiated and duplicated with all the possible feature values, and new non-terminals are created with all the combination of the traits.

The transformation of f-ACGs utilizes the fact that feature structures are finite. This property allows for the use of a partial generation mechanism to remove feature structures from terms and types. The transformation can be achieved through a three-step construction, which is based on the dependency graph of judgments presented in Fig. 9. First, the procedure begins with the elimination of dependent products, which removes the dependency of terms on feature structures. The second step involves the elimination of type families, after which feature structures are no longer present in types. Finally, the construction concludes with the type erasure of typed linear abstractions, resulting in a core ACG.

3.2 Parsing

This transformation generates grammars whose size renders parsing inefficient for practical real-world applications due to the elimination of factorizations.

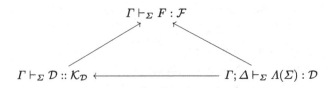

$$\Gamma \vdash_\Sigma F : \mathcal{F}$$

$$\Gamma \vdash_\Sigma \mathcal{D} :: \mathcal{K}_\mathcal{D} \longleftarrow \qquad \Gamma; \Delta \vdash_\Sigma \Lambda(\Sigma) : \mathcal{D}$$

Fig. 9. Judgment dependency graph

One potential alternative approach involves utilizing the underlying context-free barebone and subsequently filtering out inappropriate solutions. However, encoding feature structures directly into the Datalog reduction is more natural and likely more efficient.

Drawing inspiration from definite clause grammar [12], our approach to enhancing the Datalog reduction incorporates several key principles for integrating feature structures. First, atomic feature structure terms are encoded as Datalog constants. This allows for their integration into predicates corresponding to abstract types.

Since pure Datalog does not support records, they are flattened and subsequently, labels are eliminated. Additionally, feature types are encoded as extensional predicates, which allows for modeling the feature structure parameters of dependent products. The record treatment prioritizes simplicity and efficiency by reducing complex data structures to their most basic form. However, it's important to note that certain extensions of Datalog have emerged to address the need for modeling complex objects [2], such as records, without sacrificing essential properties.

Figure 10 shows the Datalog reduction of the introductory example. The construction of a noun phrase with a determiner stays factorized in its corresponding Datalog rule. In contrast, the remaining rules have been divided based on the case analysis that occurs in the extended lexicon.

```
Number(sg).
Number(pl).
S(a,c) :- NP(a,b,sg), increases(b,c).
S(a,c) :- NP(a,b,pl), increase(b,c).
NP(a,c,x) :- Number(x), the(a,b), N(b,c,x).
N(a,b,sg) :- leverage(a,b).
N(a,b,pl) :- leverages(a,b).
```

Fig. 10. Datalog reduction

4   Experimental Results

4.1   Grammar Factorization

To measure experimentally the performance and factorization gains of the overall extension in practical applications, we have developed a f-ACG compiler in Java. This proprietary compiler is designed for a company that uses ACG to automatically produce financial and pharmaceutical reports [16] from data. The extension of ACG with feature structures will, however, soon be available in the open-source Abstract Categorial Grammar Toolkit [8], ACGTK.

We've opted to explore how the extension affects the development of French grammars, given its abundance of rich morphosyntactic combinations. The grammar utilized in this experiment draws its foundations from the ACG encoding [13] of a wide-coverage French tree-adjoining grammar [1]. From an architectural perspective, the grammar is defined as the composition of two main ACGs as shown in Fig. 11. The level of derivation trees acts as the pivot between derived trees and the semantic level. The first ACG $\mathcal{G}_{\text{sem.}}$ defines the correspondence between the derivation and the semantic level, while the other, $\mathcal{G}_{\text{derived trees}}$, establishes the interpretation of derivation trees into derived trees. A third ACG, $\mathcal{G}_{\text{yield}}$, is used to flatten derived trees into strings.

The grammar employed here serves as the core component of an engine crafted for generating texts based on data. It consists of multiple unanchored, modular parts that can be dynamically assembled to suit different text generation tasks. This method enables the creation of lexicalizations in real-time, tailored to match the input. The goal of this approach is to develop extremely compact grammars for rapid text production.

The design philosophy behind the semantic level emphasizes simplicity and minimal reliance on linguistic knowledge. This approach results in a reduction in expressiveness, particularly when compared to more complex formalizations of semantics. Σ_{semantic} is defined utilizing a sole atomic type, represented by Concept. Within this high-order signature, entities are defined as Concept. Furthermore, elements such as relations, predicates, and modifiers are modeled as functions within this system. Consequently, the constructs formulated within Σ_{semantic} can be seen as elementary semantic graphs.

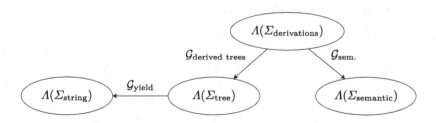

Fig. 11. French Grammar Architecture

We conducted a complete manual rewrite of the industrial French grammar within the f-ACG extension. Figure 12 shows the derivation tree families in the grammar with their associated number of derivation trees. Overall, the original high-order signature $\Sigma_{\text{derivations}}$ consists of 51,246 constants (unanchored derivation trees). The translation in f-ACG results in a grammar that is 18 times smaller, reducing the original count of 51,246 unanchored derivation trees to 2,792. The parts that are the most impacted by the addition of feature structures are the verbal, prepositional and nominal phrases. The category *other* is also significantly affected. It includes trees for various purposes, such as punctuation and linking words between sentences.

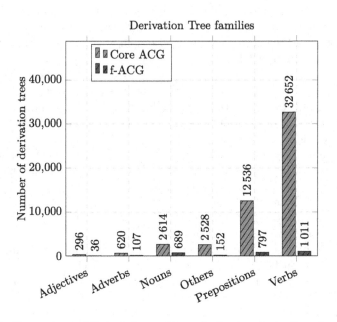

Fig. 12. Comparison of the numbers of trees in the two derivation signatures

4.2 Text Generation Performances

To evaluate the performance gains of this factorized French grammar, we have set up two distinct financial text generation scenarios, each of which has been executed 30 times to ensure reliability in our findings. Each scenario features semantic graphs of varying sizes, providing an examination of the system's performance across different complexities. Text generation for these scenarios is purely based on ACG operations from a semantic graph (a term in $\Lambda(\Sigma_{\text{semantic}})$) into texts (terms in $\Lambda(\Sigma_{\text{string}})$).

In the first scenario, called *Describe Value*, the textual content is generated based on a relatively simple semantic graph consisting of 6 nodes, as depicted in

Fig. 13. The graph contains information about NewCo's financial performance, specifically stating that: *NewCo had recorded satisfactory revenues of $921,283.5.*

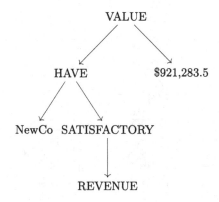

Fig. 13. Semantic graph of *Describe Value*

In the second scenario, referred to as *Describe Variation*, a semantic graph of greater complexity, consisting of 15 nodes, is employed. This graph provides historical context by describing NewCo's gross margin in 2017, which was unsatisfactory at a value of $1,463,000, and the subsequent decrease by 0.5% until 2018, signaling poor sales performance. For instance, a translation of one of the French texts generated from this graph could read: *In 2017, NewCo's gross margin of $1,463,000 was unsatisfactory and declined by 0.5% until 2018, indicating poor sales.* Text generation in this condition aims to not only convey the numerical data, but also to provide a narrative that explains the significance of these figures in the context of NewCo's business operations and sales trends.

The time spent to generate text (the latency) using this grammar heavily depends on the size of the input semantic graph and the number of used lexicalizations. However, we have found that using the compiler mentioned above, when comparing the time spent on generation with a core ACG and its factorized version in f-ACG for the two scenarios, the latency is reduced by 4 as Fig. 14a shows. In addition to having an interesting factorization power, the proposed extension also has a positive effect on performances.

When we integrate the lexicalization process and the compilation of the compact grammar tailored to the input with the text generation phase, a significant reduction in processing time is achieved. This efficiency becomes even more visible when dealing with complex syntactic structures and semantic graph inputs, as Fig. 14b shows. As these elements increase in complexity, the gains observed in the process become more pronounced.

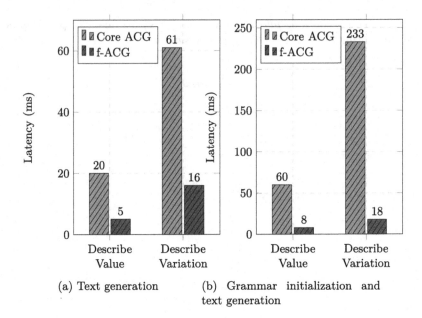

(a) Text generation   (b) Grammar initialization and text generation

Fig. 14. Benchmarks

4.3   Conclusion

In summary, the extension we've introduced provides significant advantages. It reduces the size of grammars and enhances the performance of ACG parsing. It does so while still maintaining the fundamental characteristics of the ACG formalism.

This paper has detailed the basic mathematical framework of the extension. However, it's important to note that in practice, writing grammars requires some facilities in terms of concrete syntax, notably pattern matching and modules. The incorporation of pattern matching in the ACG lexicon enables concise and clear expression of grammatical variations based on feature structure terms. Lastly, a modular system is critical for managing the complexity of grammatical systems. By structuring the ACG grammar into modular components, each responsible for a specific aspect of the language, we enhance reusability and extensibility.

It should be mentioned that our approach to feature structures is unconventional compared to most unification-based approaches to grammar. We have not explored elements like reentrancy and the f-ACG encoding of feature structures-based formalisms in this study, leaving them as potential areas for further developments.

References

1. Abeillé, A.: Une grammaire électronique du français. Sciences du langage, CNRS Éditions (2002)
2. Ceri, S., Gottlob, G., Tanca, L.: Extensions of pure datalog. In: Ceri, S., Gottlob, G., Tanca, L. (eds.) Logic Programming and Databases. SURVEYS, pp. 208–245. Springer, Heidelberg (1990). https://doi.org/10.1007/978-3-642-83952-8_11
3. Cervesato, I., Pfenning, F.: A linear logical framework. Inf. Comput. **179**(1), 19–75 (2002)
4. de Groote, Ph., Maarek, S.: Type-theoretic extensions of abstract categorial grammars. In: New Directions in Type-Theoretic Grammars (NDTTG 2007), ESSLLI 2007 Workshop, Dublin (2007)
5. de Groote, P.: Towards abstract categorial grammars. In: Proceedings of 39th Annual Meeting of the Association for Computational Linguistics, pp. 148–155 (2001)
6. de Groote, P., Pogodalla, S.: On the expressive power of abstract categorial grammars: representing context-free formalisms. J. Logic Lang. Inform. **13**(4), 421–438 (2004)
7. Dymetman, M.: Inherently reversible grammars. In: Strzalkowski, T. (ed.) Reversible Grammars in Natural Language Processing, chap. 2, pp. 33–57. Kluwer Academic Publishers (1994)
8. Guillaume, M., Pogodalla, S., Tourneur, V.: ACGtk: a toolkit for developing and running abstract categorial grammars. In: Gibbons, J., Miller, D. (eds.) 17th International Symposium on Functional and Logic Programming (FLOPS 2024), Kumamoto, Japan (2024)
9. Joshi, A.K., Schabes, Y.: Tree-adjoining grammars. In: Rozenberg, G., Salomaa, A. (eds.) Handbook of Formal Languages, pp. 69–123. Springer, Heidelberg (1997). https://doi.org/10.1007/978-3-642-59126-6_2
10. Kanazawa, M.: Parsing and generation as datalog queries. In: Proceedings of the 45th Annual Meeting of the Association of Computational Linguistics (ACL 2007), Prague, Czech Republic, pp. 176–183. Association for Computational Linguistics (2007)
11. Kanazawa, M.: Parsing and generation as datalog query evaluation. IfCoLog J. Logics Appl. **4**(4), 1103–1211 (2017). Special Issue Dedicated to the Memory of Grigori Mints
12. Pereira, F.C.N., Warren, D.H.D.: Definite clause grammars for language analysis-a survey of the formalism and a comparison with augmented transition networks. Artif. Intell. **13**(3), 231–278 (1980)
13. Pogodalla, S.: A syntax-semantics interface for tree-adjoining grammars through abstract categorial grammars. J. Lang. Model. **5**(3), 527–605 (2017)
14. Pompigne, F.: Modélisation logique de la langue et Grammaires Catégorielles Abstraites. Ph.D. thesis, Université de Lorraine (2013)
15. Ranta, A.: Grammatical framework: a type-theoretical grammar formalism. J. Funct. Program. **14**(2), 145–189 (2004)
16. Salmon, R.: Natural language generation using abstract categorial grammars. Ph.D. thesis, Sorbonne Paris Cité (2017)

An Overt Operator Associating with Covert Focus: An *Even*-Like Semantics for Mandarin *Gèng*

Zhuang Chen[✉] and Yael Greenberg

Department of English Literature and Linguistics, Bar-Ilan University,
5290002 Ramat-Gan, Israel
chenzhuangcq@gmail.com, yaelgree@gmail.com
https://sites.google.com/view/yaelgreenberglinguistics/home

Abstract. This work proposes a novel, unified *even*-like semantics for Mandarin *gèng*. *Gèng*, literally *even more*, is mostly studied regarding its combination with gradable adjectives, where it triggers a comparison with an evaluative inference in the sense of [39]. To capture this effect, *gèng* is argued by [32] a.o. to be a comparative marker with an evaluative presupposition. Intriguingly, [32] observes in passing that *gèng* can also combine with non-gradable predicates, which remains understudied. We examine [32]'s observation in detail and propose that *gèng* is an *even*-like particle à la [15]'s semantics for English *even*. This straightforwardly captures *gèng*'s combination with non-gradable predicates. Then, by adopting two independently motivated assumptions, i.e. (a) the existence of a covert comparative marker COMP in Mandarin and (b) association with covert focus, our proposal is naturally extended to *gèng*'s combination with gradable adjectives. At last, *gèng* and *shènzhì*, Mandarin unmarked *even*, are compared from a parametric variation perspective.

Keywords: Mandarin gèng · shènzhì · scalarity · even-like particles · covert focus · comparatives · evaluative presupposition · gradability · parametric variation

1 Introduction

This paper delves into Mandarin particle *gèng* which is often glossed as English *even more* in the literature. It has been widely observed (e.g. [28,32,36,56]) that *gèng*, when combined with gradable adjectives, triggers a comparative reading plus an evaluative inference in the sense of [39]. Consider (1) and (2), the most studied type of *gèng* data in the literature. In (1), *gèng* combines with the regular *bi* (than)-based comparatives. (1-a) has no evaluative inference that both John and Bill are tall, and can be felicitously continued by '*but both are short*'; however, (1-b) triggers such an evaluative inference and cannot be continued this way. In (2), *gèng* combines with the bare adjective *gao* (tall). Likewise, (2-i) has no evaluative inference that both John and Bill are tall but (2-ii) does.

D. Bekki et al. (Eds.): LENLS 2023, LNCS 14569, pp. 134–154, 2024.
https://doi.org/10.1007/978-3-031-60878-0_8

(1)   Yuehan bi   Bi'er (**gèng**) gao.
       John   than Bill   gèng   tall
       a.   Without *gèng*: John is taller than Bill.   ⤳ No evaluative inference
       b.   With *gèng*: John is even taller than Bill.   ⤳ Evaluative inference

(2)   A: Yuehan gen Bi'er yiyang gao ma?
             John   as   Bill   same   tall Q
             Is John as tall as Bill?
       B: Yuehan (**gèng**) gao.
             John   gèng   tall
             (i)   Without *gèng*: John is taller.   ⤳ No evaluative inference
             (ii)   With *gèng*: John is even taller.   ⤳ Evaluative inference

In the formal semantics literature, there have been some sporadic attempts to capture the semantics of *gèng*. For instance, [28] suggests that *gèng* is a degree intensifier akin to Japanese *motto* as studied in [3].[1] [56] suggests that *gèng* is a degree modifier that marks the existence of a presupposed comparison. Without further information, the comparison standard in this presupposed comparison is often accommodated as the general norm, as a consequence of which an evaluative inference arises. The most systematic examination of *gèng* in the formal semantics literature is perhaps [32]. [32] suggests that *gèng* is a comparative marker with an evaluative presupposition, as formalized in (3).[2]

(3) $\|gèng_{phrasal}\| = \lambda x \lambda P_{<d,et>}.\lambda y.[\iota_{max}d(P)(d)(y)] > [\iota_{max}d(P)(d)(x)] \wedge$
       the properties predicated of x and y are true in the absolute sense

A commonality such proposals share is that they all assume that *gèng* needs to syntactically combine with a gradable predicate which encodes the dimension of comparison. But intriguingly, [32] observes in a footnote that *gèng* can also combine with non-gradable predicates. Consider (4) and (5), both of which are taken from [32] ([32]'s original glosses but our translations).[3]

(4)   zhe-suo xuexiao, laoshi   shou   ren   liwu, xiaozhang **gèng** na
       this-CLF school   teacher receive people gift   president   gèng   take
       ren   hongbao.
       people cash-gift
       As for the school, teachers take gifts; the president even takes cash-gifts.

---

[1] Cf. [44] who argues *motto* is a comparative marker with an evaluative component.

[2] [32]'s entire proposal is much more sophisticated than what we show above; for space reasons, we cannot do full justice to it. But crucially, his entire proposal is based on an implicit assumption that *gèng* needs to combine, in the syntax, with some gradable predicate that encodes the dimension of comparison, which is to be challenged below.

[3] Note that some native speakers of Mandarin prefer *gèng-shì*, literally *gèng*-copula, to *gèng* in cases like (4) and (5) where *gèng* combines with non-gradable predicates. We leave the distinction between *gèng* and *gèng-shì* in such cases for future occasions.

(5)   tamen-lia, yi-ge   da-le   ren,   ling-yi-ge   **gèng** sha-le
       they-two   one-CLF hit-PERF person other-one-CLF gèng   kill-PERF
       ren.
       person
       Of them two, one guy hit persons; the other guy even killed persons.

In (4) and (5), *gèng* respectively combines with the non-gradable predicates
na ren hongbao (take cash-gift) and *sha-le ren* (killed persons). Data like (4) and
(5) pose a challenge to the aforementioned proposals given that there is simply
no gradable predicate encoding the dimension of comparison with which *gèng*
can combine. We note that *gèng* is naturally translated as English *even* in (4)
and (5); moreover, it is intuitively paraphrasable as *shènzhì*, the unmarked *even*
in Mandarin: *Gèng* can be replaced with *shènzhì* in (4) and (5) with the meaning
of the two sentences kept unchanged, as in (6) and (7) respectively.

(6)   zhe-suo xuexiao, laoshi   shou   ren   liwu, xiaozhang **shènzhì** na
       this-CLF school   teacher receive people gift   president gèng   take
       ren   hongbao.
       people cash-gift
       As for the school, teachers take gifts; the president even takes cash-gifts.

(7)   tamen-lia, yi-ge   da-le   ren,   ling-yi-ge   **shènzhì** sha-le
       they-two   one-CLF hit-PERF person other-one-CLF gèng   kill-PERF
       ren.
       person
       Of them two, one guy hit persons; the other guy even killed persons.

Our research question is what is the semantics of *gèng*. Specifically, we have
two sub-questions. **First**, how can we capture *gèng*'s combination with non-
gradable predicates ((4)–(5)), i.e. the observation that is left by [32] for future
occasions and remains understudied. To anticipate, we will argue that *gèng* is an
even-like particle in the sense of [15], and this would straightforwardly capture
gèng's combination with non-gradable predicates. **Second**, do we need two separate treatments, one for *gèng*'s combination with gradable adjectives and one for
gèng's combination with non-gradable predicates? To foresee, we would purse a
unified approach. A major motivation for this preference is that despite the lack
of any gradable predicate encoding the dimension of comparison in cases where
gèng combines with non-gradable predicates, intuitively, there is still a comparison based on a certain pragmatic/contextually supplied scale (see Sect. 4). We
will follow this intuition and show how, by integrating two independently motivated assumptions in the literature, our proposal is naturally extended to *gèng*'s
combination with gradable adjectives as well. Therefore, we will ultimately have
a unified, *even*-like account for *gèng*. If *gèng* is genuinely an *even*-like particle as
we will claim, then a natural **follow-up** question is whether *gèng* and *shènzhì*,
the unmarked *even* in Mandarin, behave identically. If not, why not? We observe
that the two expressions behave distinctly under some circumstances, and will

reduce their distinctions to the parametric variation among *even*-like particles in general cross-linguistically.

The remaining part of the paper is structured as follows. Section 2 motivates an *even*-like analysis for *gèng*'s combination with non-gradable predicates. Section 3 compares two existing accounts for English *even*. Section 4 proposes adopting for *gèng* [15]'s degree-based account for *even* and illustrates how it captures *gèng*'s combination with non-gradable predicates. Section 5 extends our proposal to *gèng*'s combination with gradable adjectives. Section 6 offers a prediction directly following our *even*-like account of *gèng*. Section 7 presents the parametric variation between *gèng* and *shènzhì*. Section 8 concludes.

2 Motivating an *Even*-Like Analysis for *Gèng*'s Combination with Non-gradable Predicates

Let's first concentrate on *gèng*'s combination with non-gradable predicates (e.g. (4)–(5)). Recall that *gèng* in such cases is naturally translated as English *even* and intuitively paraphrased as *shènzhì* ((6) and (7)), the unmarked *even* in Mandarin. This section crystallizes this intuition by observing two similarities between *gèng*, on the one hand, and English *even* and Mandarin *shènzhì* on the other hand.

The first similarity is **scalarity**. A hallmark feature of English *even*/Mandarin *shènzhì* (see e.g. [24,41] for English *even*; see e.g. [4,46] for Mandarin *shènzhì*) and *even*-like particles in general cross-linguistically (e.g. [27]) is that they are scalar in the sense that the proposition hosting the *even*-like particle (the prejacent henceforth) is stronger (in a sense to be discussed below) than its contextually relevant alternatives. We observe that this is also the case for *gèng*. Consider (5) above again. If we swap the predicate in the *gèng*-hosting proposition and the predicate in the preceding proposition, as we do in (8), then *gèng* becomes infelicitous, just like Mandarin *shènzhì* and English *even* (as given in the translation in (8)). This illustrates that *gèng* is likewise scalar, requiring its hosting proposition be stronger than its contextually relevant alternatives.

(8)   tamen-lia, yi-ge   sha-le   ren,   ling-yi-ge   (# **gèng**)/(#
       they-two   one-CLF kill-PERF person other-one-CLF   gèng
       shènzhì) da-le   ren.
       even   hit-PERF person
       Of them two, one guy killed persons; the other guy (# even) hit persons.

The second similarity is what is christened as **standard-sensitivity** by [15]. Cross-linguistically, *even*-like particles have been reported to be sensitive to the standard, that is, both the prejacent and its contextually relevant alternative proposition indicate a degree above the standard on a relevant scale (see e.g. [4,15,16,37]; cf. [57]). Let's first illustrate this observation with English *even*. Consider (9) taken from [15]. *Even* is felicitous in Seller A's reply, where the tool in the prejacent and that in the salient alternative proposition are above the standard of strength. In contrast, *even* becomes infelicitous in Seller B's reply, where the tool in the prejacent and that in the alternative proposition are both below the standard of strength, as well as in Seller C's reply, where the tool in the prejacent is above the standard of strength but that in the alternative proposition is below the standard.

(9)   Context: Both iron and steel are strong, but steel is stronger, and both plastic and aluminum are weak, but aluminum is stronger.

Client:I need a strong tool. What about the red and blue tools over there?

Seller A:The red one is made of iron and the blue one is (even) made of [steel]$_F$.

Seller B:The red one is made of plastic and the blue one is (#even) made of [aluminum]$_F$.

Seller C:The red one is made of plastic and the blue one is (??even) made of [steel]$_F$.

We observe that *gèng* is analogously sensitive to the standard when combined with non-gradable predicates. Let's demonstrate this with two examples. Firstly, the English example (9) can be straightforwardly duplicated using *gèng* with the intended effects unaltered. Due to space limits, we only duplicate Seller A's reply for illustrative purposes. Readers can duplicate the other two replies by replacing the materials in (10) with the corresponding materials and get the same effects. Note that (9) can be likewise duplicated with *shènzhì* with the intended effects unaltered, as given in the glosses.

(10)   hongse na-ge   shi yong tie zuo-de; lanse na-ge   **gèng/**
        red   that-CLF COP use   iron make-DE blue that-CLF gèng
        shènzhì shi yong [gang]$_F$ zuo-de.
        even   COP use   steel   make-DE
        The red one is made of iron; the blue one is even made of [steel]$_F$.

Secondly, *gèng*'s standard-sensitivity is reflected in its interaction with *zhǐ-bú-guò*, a Mandarin translation equivalent of English scalar *only*. Consider (11).

(11)   tamen-lia, yi-ge   **zhǐ-bú-guò** da-le   ren,   ling-yi-ge   #
        they-two   one-CLF only$_{scalar}$ hit-PERF person other-one-CLF
        gèng / # **shènzhì** sha-le   ren.
        gèng   even   kill-PERF person
        Of the two guys, one guy only$_{scalar}$/just hit persons; the other guy #even killed persons.

In (11), due to *zhǐ-bú-guò* (scalar *only*), hitting persons is portrayed as something not serious enough to make one dangerous. (cf. similar observations about scalar *only* and *just* in e.g. [1,6,17]) In this case, *gèng* is degraded, like *shènzhì* and English *even* (as in the translation). This further demonstrates that *gèng*, combined with non-gradable predicates, requires both its prejacent and the salient alternative to indicate a degree above the standard. Actually, given the wide observation that *gèng* triggers an evaluative inference when combined with gradable adjectives as introduced above, this might come as no surprise.

3 Pursuing an Analysis of *Even*-Like Particles: Two Competing Proposals of English *Even*

Given the above similarities between *gèng* and English *even* (and Mandarin *shènzhì*), we are motivated to analyze *gèng* as an *even*-like particle. Among the various existing proposals for English *even*, we examine two of them: the canonical **likelihood-based account** and Greenberg's [15] **degree-based** account (cf. [57]).

3.1 The Likelihood-Based Account

According to the **likelihood-based account** (e.g. [5,18,24,40]), English *even* does not contribute at the truth-conditional level but, crucially, carries a likelihood-based presupposition, i.e. the prejacent is less likely than all its relevant alternatives. This is often formulated, more or less, in the shape of (12) where *even* combines with a set of contextually relevant focus alternatives C and the prejacent p; *even* presupposes that p is less likely than every alternative proposition q distinct from p in C, and if this presupposition is met, *even* asserts that p is true in the world of evaluation w.[4]

(12) $\|even\|^{g,c} = \lambda C.\lambda p. : \forall q \in C q \neq p \rightarrow p <_{likely} q.\lambda w.p(w) = 1$
        where $C \subseteq \|p\|^F \wedge \|p\|^O \in C \wedge \exists q \ q \neq p \wedge q \in C$
        ($\|p\|^F$ is the focus semantic value of the prejacent p; $\|p\|^O$ is the ordinary semantic value of p, i.e. p itself; C contains at least one alternative q distinct from p)

This likelihood-based analysis has proved fruitful in accounting for a wide range of *even*-related phenomena (see e.g. [18,22,29]). To see how (12) works, consider (13-a). In (13-a), *gold* is focused and triggers an alternative set (13-b).

(13)   a.   Bill won the silver medal. John even won the [gold]$_F$ medal.
        b.   Alt. Set: {John won the gold medal, John won the silver medal}
              (the underlined alternative is the prejacent)
        c.   Bill won the gold medal; John (# even) won the [silver]$_F$ medal.

Following entry (12), (13-a) would be interpreted as follows: (i) it is presupposed that the prejacent p (*John won the gold medal*) is less likely than its

---

[4] Another often debated issue about English *even* in the literature concerns the so-called existential presupposition, i.e. whether *even* presupposes that a distinct alternative proposition in C is true in the world of evaluation w. See e.g. [14,42,51,57] for more detail. This issue is orthogonal to our discussion of *gèng* below.

alternative q (*John won the silver medal*); (ii) it is asserted that p (*John won the gold medal*) is true. This interpretation nicely captures our intuition of (13-a). Besides, entry (12) predicts that *even* would be infelicitous if it associates with *silver*: Winning the silver medal is more but not less likely than winning the gold medal. This is borne out, as in (13-c).

3.2 Greenbeg's [15] Degree-Based Account

Despite its proven usefulness, the likelihood-based account has been argued to be inadequate. Here we zero in on two of such issues as discussed in [14,15], whose relevance to us will become evident as we proceed below.

Two Issues with the Likelihood-Based Account Reported by [14,15]. The first issue concerns the **nature of the scale** *even* operates on, i.e. whether *even* necessarily operates on a scale of (un)likelihood. This issue has been debated by many (e.g. [11,21,25,42]). In particular, [14,15] shows that the presupposition that the prejacent is less likely than its alternatives is neither a necessary nor a sufficient condition to license English *even*. Consider (14) and (15), both taken from [14]. In (14), the prejacent (*the one on the left is made of steel*) is more likely than its contextually salient alternative (*the one on the left is made of strong aluminum*) given our world knowledge about what material tools are usually made of, but *even* is felicitous; this indicates that the unlikelihood-based presupposition is not necessary to license *even*. In (15), the prejacent (*the blue one has apples*) asymmetrically entails and is thus less likely than its contextually salient alternative (*the blue one has fruits*), but *even* is not licensed; this indicates that the unlikelihood-based presupposition is not sufficient to license *even*, either.

(14)   Seller to client: Both tools are strong. The one on the right is made of strong aluminum, and the one on the left is even made of $[steel]_F$.

(15)   The red box has fruits. The blue one (?? even) has $[apples]_F$ in it.

Instead, [15] convincingly illustrates that the scale *even* operates on is **context-dependent**. Consider (16). That she gave birth to a boy and that she gave birth to a girl are of equal likelihood, and both are less likely than the contextually salient alternative that she gave birth. Nonetheless, *even* is felicitous with *boy* but infelicitous with *girl*. If the context is tweaked in a such way that she becomes a queen if she gives birth to a girl, then *even* would become felicitous with *girl* but infelicitous with *boy*. This shows that the scale *even* operates on is context-dependent. And as for (16), the scale could plausibly be the importance/happiness of Princess Jane.

(16)   **Context:** Any princess who gives birth can stay in the palace. If she gives birth to a boy she becomes a queen (with the result that on average 50% of those who have given birth become queens). ([15]'s example 10) Princess Jane gave birth. She (even) gave birth to $[a\ boy]_F / \#[a\ girl]_F$.

The second issue concerns the **standard-sensitivity**. As illustrated in Sect. 2, *even* (as well as its cross-linguistic equivalents, see references above) is sensitive to the standard on the associated scale, that is, they require both the prejacent and the contextually relevant alternative to indicate a degree above the standard on that scale. The likelihood-based account (see entry (12)) has nothing to say on this issue. One may argue that perhaps the standard-sensitivity is derivable via the superlative scalar presupposition in (12). Concretely, if the prejacent is stronger than all its distinct alternatives in C, then it might be trivially above the standard. But as elaborated in [17], being the strongest alternative in a given C does not guarantee that the prejacent indicates a degree above the standard; hence, the standard-sensitivity is not derived (see [17] for details).

Greenberg's [15] Alternative Proposal: A Degree-based Account. To address the two issues above, [15] proposes a degree-based account of *even*, which is jointly inspired by [43]'s intuition that the alternatives *even* operates on are correlated with some graded property and [2]'s idea of comparative correlatives. [15]'s account can be reinterpreted as comprising four components, as in (17).

(17)   [15]'s degree-based account for English *even*: Four components

   a.   **A context-dependent scale:** The scale *even* operates on is not necessarily associated with unlikelihood but a contextually supplied gradable property G;   ⤳ (*the likelihood issue covered*)

   b.   **Comparative presupposition:** Some non-focused item/ contrastive topic x holds a higher degree on this G scale in the accessible p worlds where the prejacent holds than in the accessible $[q \land \neg p]$ worlds where the alternative q holds but the prejacent does not hold;

   c.   **Evaluative presupposition:** The degree this non-focused item/contrastive topic x holds is above the standard on this G scale in the accessible $[q \land \neg p]$ worlds (and thanks to the comparative presupposition, the degree x holds in the accessible p worlds is also above the standard);   ⤳ (*the standard-sensitivity issue covered*)

   d.   **An assertion:** The prejacent is true in the world of evaluation.

4   Our Proposal for *Gèng*'s Combination with Non-gradable Predicates: An *Even*-Like Particle à la [15]'s *Even*

As elaborated in Sects. 1 & 2, *gèng* is *even*-like when combined with non-gradable predicates. A natural question is which line of analysis for English *even* do we prefer, the likelihood-based account or the degree-based account (or neither)? For two considerations, the degree-based account is desirable for *gèng*. Firstly, as already illustrated in Sect. 2, *gèng*, like English *even* and Mandarin *shènzhì*, is standard-sensitive, which can be directly captured by the degree-based account.

Secondly, as to be illustrated immediately, we observe that the scale *gèng* operates on is also context-dependent, directly covered by the degree-based account. To see the context-dependence of the scale associated with *gèng*, we reproduce the English example (16) as in (18). As argued above, giving birth to a son and a daughter are equally likely, and both are less likely than giving birth. If adopting the likelihood-based account, we would falsely predict *gèng* to be felicitous with both *son* and *daughter*. Likewise, if the context is modified in such a way that she would become a queen if she gives birth to a daughter in lieu of a son, then *gèng* would get felicitous with *daughter* but infelicitous with *son*. In a nutshell, the argumentation up there for *even* in (16) straightforwardly applies to *gèng* in (18). Note that this argumentation also applies to *shènzhì*, the unmarked *even* in Mandarin, as given in the glosses in (18).

(18)   **Context:** Identical to (16).

Wangfei Jian sheng-le,   **gèng** / **shènzhì** sheng-le,
princess Jane give-birth-PERF, gèng   even   give-birth-PERF
ge [erzi]$_F$ / # [nüer]$_F$.
CLF son   daughter

Princess Jane gave birth. She even gave birth to [a son]$_F$/#[a daughter]$_F$.

In light of the two considerations, i.e. the standard-sensitivity and the context-dependence of the scale, we suggest analyzing *gèng* as an *even*-like particle à la [15]'s degree-based account for *even*. Formally, *gèng* is defined as (19):

(19)   For the *gèng*-hosting proposition p and all discourse-salient alternatives q ($q \neq p$) in C, $gèng(C)(p)(w)$ **asserts** $p(w)$ and **presupposes**: $\forall w1 \forall w2[w1Rw0 \wedge w2Rw0 \wedge w1 \in p \wedge w2 \in [q \wedge \neg p]] \rightarrow$

   a. $\underbrace{max(\lambda d1.G(d1)(x)(w1)) > max(\lambda d2.G(d2)(x)(w2))}_{\textbf{comparative presupposition}} \wedge$

   b. $\underbrace{max(\lambda d2.G(d2)(x)(w2)) > Stand_G}_{\textbf{evaluative presupposition}}$

(Notation: x is a non-focused element/contrative topic in p; G a contextually supplied gradable property; $w1$ is an accessible p world, $w2$ is an accessible $[q \wedge \neg p]$ world; $Stand_G$ is the standard on the G scale)

In prose, *gèng*, combining with a set of salient alternatives C, the prejacent p and a world of evaluation w, presupposes (a) that some non-focused item x is more G in the accessible p worlds than in the accessible $[q \wedge \neg p]$ worlds, and (b) that x is POS G (POS in the sense of [26]) in the accessible $[q \wedge \neg p]$ worlds (and due to the comparative presupposition x is also POS G in the accessible p worlds); if defined, *gèng* asserts that p is true in w.

Let's illustrate how (19) captures *gèng*'s combination with non-gradable predicates by applying it to (5). Here we plausibly assume the contextually supplied gradable property G to be *dangerous*, i.e. how dangerous the two guys were.

(20)   The interpretation of (5) via entry (19):
$\forall w1 \forall w2 [w1 Rw0 \wedge w2 Rw0 \wedge w1 \in p \wedge w2 \in [q \wedge \neg p] \rightarrow$

    a.   **Comparative presupposition:** $max(\lambda d1.\text{DANGEROUS}(the\ other\ guy)$
        $(w1)) > max(\lambda d2.\text{DANGEROUS}(the\ other\ guy)(w2))$

    b.   **Evaluative presupposition:** $max(\lambda d2.\text{DANGEROUS}(d2)(the\ other\ guy)$
        $(w2)) > Stand_{\text{DANGEROUS}}$

    c.   If defined, it is asserted that the other guy killed persons in w.

    where p = the other guy killed persons; q = the other guy hit persons.

In prose, the comparative presupposition (20-a) says that the other guy was more dangerous in the accessible p worlds where he killed persons than in the accessible $[q \wedge \neg p]$ worlds where he hit but didn't kill persons; the evaluative presupposition (20-b) says that the other guy was POS dangerous in the accessible $[q \wedge \neg p]$ worlds (and due to the comparative presupposition, he was POS dangerous in the p worlds as well). It is asserted that the other guy killed persons (20-c). This interpretation exactly captures our intuition. In addition, our proposal (19) also straightforwardly explains two infelicities regarding *gèng* observed above. Recall that swapping the predicate in the prejacent and the predicate in the preceding proposition as we did in (8) makes *gèng* infelicitous. This is because the comparative presupposition (19-a) is violated: Killing persons is generally considered to pose a larger danger than *hitting but not killing* persons. And as for (11) where the contextually salient alternative features *zhǐ-bú-guò* (scalar *only* in Mandarin), we derive the infelicity there from the incompatibility of *gèng*'s evaluative presupposition (19-b) with the "below the standard/expectation" inference *only*-like particles trigger (e.g. [1,17,55]).[5]

Up to this point, we have answered our first research question, i.e. how to capture *gèng*'s combination with non-gradable predicates, the type of data [32] left for future studies. Now we move on to *gèng*'s combination with gradable adjectives.

5   Extending Our *Even*-Like Proposal (19) to *Gèng*'s Combination with Gradable Adjectives

If *gèng* is an *even*-like particle as we argued, then how can we account for its combination with gradable adjectives (i.e. (1) and (2) above)? Do we need two separate treatments or can we have a unified account? This is our second research question.

In addition to its general desirability, a unified account is more preferable because we observe that *gèng*'s combination with non-gradable predicates overlaps with its combination with gradable adjectives in two crucial regards. **Firstly**, they both trigger a comparison. Take (5) and (1) for instance. In (5), the

---

[5] We are neutral on whether this "below the standard/expectation" inference is a derived effect (e.g. [17]) or a hardwired property (e.g. [55]).

two guys are compared with respect to how dangerous they were (see (20-a)); in (1), John and Bill are compared regarding height. **Secondly**, they both trigger an evaluative inference. In (5), the two guys were both implied to be dangerous (see (20-b)); in (1), John and Bill are both implied to be tall. However, there does exist a difference, which concerns how the dimension of comparison is encoded: For *gèng*'s combination with gradable adjectives, it is lexically encoded (e.g. *tall* in (1)) while for its combination with non-gradable predicates, it is contextually supplied (e.g. *dangerous* in (5)). But this difference is innocuous given that our proposal (19) does not preclude adopting a lexically encoded dimension if that happens to be the salient property. In light of such a high affinity between *gèng*'s combination with gradable adjectives vs. non-gradable predicates, we are driven to pursue a unified account. But how can that be done? As we are to show, our proposal (19) can be naturally extended to *gèng*'s combination with gradable adjectives if we adopt two assumptions independently motivated in the literature, i.e. (a) the existence of a covert comparative marker COMP in Mandarin, and (b) association with covert focus.

5.1   Two Independently Motivated Assumptions

The first assumption concerns the existence of a **covert comparative marker COMP** in Mandarin. It has been an ongoing, heated debate how the higher-than relation in Mandarin comparatives is encoded [7, 8, 12, 28, 30–32, 34, 53, 56]. Some (e.g. [7, 8, 30]) suggest that in the regular comparative constructions like (1-a), *bi* (literally, *than*) encodes the higher-than relation. For instance, [30], following [19]'s direct analysis of English comparative marker *-er/more*, formalizes the semantics of *bi* as in (21).

(21) $\|bi\| = \lambda x_{<e>} \lambda P_{<d,<et>>} \lambda y_{<e>}.[\iota max P(d)(y) > \iota max P(d)(x)]$

But this line of analysis has been questioned (e.g. [32]) because a comparative meaning arises even in the absence of *bi*. Among the various observations in this regard, a well-known one is that the most salient reading of bare adjectives in Mandarin is a comparative reading [12, 48, 56], which starkly contrasts with English where a bare adjectives like *tall* as in *John is tall* is understood to be modified by a covert modifier POS (in the sense of [26]) and takes on a higher-than-the-standard evaluative meaning. Specifically, take a look at (22) ([48]'s example (40a)). Without further contextual information, *gao* (tall) is saliently understood as taking on a comparative reading.

(22)   Zhangsan gao.
         Zhangsan tall
         Zhangsan is taller (than somebody from the context).

In order to unambiguously get an effect similar to English bare adjectives as modified by covert POS, the unstressed version of *hěn* needs to be added here, as in (23) ([48]'s example (40b)). *Hěn* literally means *very*, but its unstressed version is semantically bleached. Actually, some (e.g. [33]; cf. [12]) argue that the unstressed *hěn* is an overt realization of English POS in the sense of [26].

(23)   Zhangsan **hěn** gao.
        Zhangsan hěn tall
        Zhangsan is tall.

Given similar observations, many have argued that there is a covert comparative marker COMP in Mandarin (e.g. [12,13,31,53]) which is operative with apparently 'bare' adjectives, as in (22). Without going into more details, we will adopt this assumption. For more discussion, see the related references above.

The second assumption is **association with covert focus**. This might sound implausible to start with, because in languages like English focus is often realized as being assigned the prosodic prominence (e.g. [40,41]). If the focus is covert, how can it receive the prosodic prominence? But association with covert focus has been reported among various particles cross-linguistically. For instance, it is suggested that English additive particle *too* can focus-associate with PRO [20]. Consider (24-a). As per [20], one reading of (24-a) is that John wants it to be the case that he comes in addition to someone else. On this reading, (24-a) is analyzed as (24-b) where *too* is embedded within the small clause and associates with PRO.

(24)   a.   John wants to come, too.   ([20]'s example in footnote 13)
        b.   John wants [PRO$_F$ to come, too].

More relevantly to us, scalar particles have been reported to focus-associate with covert degree modifiers. For instance, Hebrew *only*-like particle *be-sax ha-kol* is reported to be able to focus-associate with covert degree modifier POS and triggers an approximative reading similar to English *more or less* [38]. Hebrew *even*-like particle BIXLAL is reported to be able to associate with the covert comparison class argument *C* of the degree modifier POS and triggers a range of readings traditionally not paraphrased as *even* [16] (see a similar report of Russian *even*-like particle *voobšče* by [37]). Given this cross-linguistic report, association with covert focus is not implausible.[6]

5.2   Proposal: *Gèng* Associating with Covert COMP

We adopt the two assumptions that (a) there is a covert comparative marker COMP in Mandarin and (b) association with covert focus is possible. Based upon these two independently motivated assumptions, we propose that *gèng* can associate with covert focus. More specifically, we suggest that *gèng*, combined with gradable adjectives, associates with covert COMP. Let's show how our suggested

---

[6] For more examples of association with covert focus, see [52] who argues that English exclusive *just* associates with a covert cause argument on its "unexplanatory" reading; see [23] who suggests that English scalar particle *still* associates with, for instance, the covert time variable on its aspectual reading, and see [35] for a similar suggestion for Mandarin *still*-like particle *hái*.

entry for *gèng* (19), in conjunction with this proposal of associating with COMP, naturally captures *gèng*'s combination with gradable adjectives. Take (2–ii) for illustration. Following our proposal, (2–ii) would be analyzed as (25-a). In (25-a), *gèng* associates with the covert comparative marker COMP, and plausibly has the equative as its salient alternative, as in (25-b) (the prejacent underlined).

(25)   a.   (A: Is John as tall as Bill?) B: John **gèng** COMP$_F$ gao/tall.
        b.   Alt. Set: {John is taller (than Bill), John is as tall (as Bill)}

Applying our entry (19) to (25-a), with the assumption that the most salient gradable property G is *tall* per se, returns (26):

(26)   Interpretation of (25-a)(=(2–ii)) via entry (19):
$\forall w1 \forall w2[w1Rw0 \wedge w2Rw0 \wedge w1 \in [max(\lambda d_j.TALL(d_j)(John)) > max(\lambda d_b.TALL(d_b)(Bill))] \wedge w2 \in [max(\lambda d_j.TALL(d_j)(John)) \geq max(\lambda d_b.TALL(d_b)(Bill)) \wedge \neg(max(\lambda d_j.TALL(d_j)(John)) > max(\lambda d_b.TALL(d_b)(Bill)))]] \rightarrow$

   a.   **Comparative presupposition:** $max(\lambda d1.TALL(d1)(John)(w1)) > max(\lambda d2.TALL(d2)(John)(w2)) \wedge$ **(Trivially satisfied)**
   b.   **Evaluative presupposition:** $max(\lambda d2.TALL(d2)(John)(w2)) > Stand_{tall}$ **(Non-trivial)**
   c.   If defined, it is asserted that John is taller (than Bill).

In prose, the comparative presupposition (26-a) says that John is taller in the accessible p worlds where his height exceeds Bill's height than in the accessible $[q \wedge \neg p]$ worlds where his height is equal to Bill's height. The evaluative presupposition (26-b) says that John's height is above the standard in the accessible $[q \wedge \neg p]$ worlds. If defined, it is asserted that John is taller (than Bill). The comparative presupposition is trivially satisfied, but crucially, the evaluative presupposition is non-trivial; via this evaluative presupposition, we capture the evaluative inference that both John and Bill are tall.

In addition to straightforwardly capturing the evaluative inference, our proposal of associating with covert COMP has another advantage. We observe that in cases where *gèng* combines with gradable adjectives, e.g. in (1) and (2), *gèng* is accented by default. This naturally follows our proposal: Given that COMP, the focus *gèng* associates with, is covert and thus cannot be accented, the accent shifts onto *gèng* (cf. [50]). In contrast, in cases where *gèng* combines with non-gradable predicates, the focus is overt and thus *gèng* does not bear the accent (e.g. *sha* (kill) bears the accent in (5)).

Up to this point, we have answered our second research question by extending our *even*-like analysis to *gèng*'s combination with gradable adjectives.

6   A Prediction: Superlative Force of *Gèng*

Even-like particles are argued to trigger a superlative force in that its prejacent is stronger than all its contextually relevant distinct alternatives (e.g. [10,15,17]; but cf. [25,54]). If *gèng* is a genuine *even*-like particle, then it is predicted to behave in a similar way, with both non-gradable predicates (27) and gradable adjectives (28). This prediction is borne out below. Note that as predicted, *shènzhì* behaves the same as shown in the glosses.

(27) A: "How many papers did the faculty members in your department write this year?"

 B: "tamen jin-nian dou bu-cuo. Jimu xie-le san-pian, Bi'er

 they this-year all not-bad Jim write-PERF three-CLF Bill

 xie-le liu-pian, Yadang xi-le si-pian, Yuehan #**gèng**

 write-PERF six-CLF Adam write-PERF four-CLF John gèng

 (shi) / #**shènzhì** xie-le wu-pian."

 COP even write-PERF five-CLF

 "They all did great. Jim wrote 3, Bill 6,' Adam 4, (and) John (#even) wrote 5."

(28) tamen san-ge dou hen gao. qizhong Bi'er zui gao, Yuehan hen

 they three-CLF all very tall among Bill most tall John very

 gao, Gelei bi Yuehan (#**gèng**) gao // Gelei (#**shènzhì**) bi

 tall Gray than John gèng tall Gray shènzhì than

 Yuehan gao.

 John tall

 They three are all tall. Among them, Bill is the tallest, John is very tall, and Gray is (#even) taller than John.

Gèng is infelicitous in (27), where it combines with a non-gradable predicate, because there is a contextually salient alternative stronger than the prejacent, i.e. Bill wrote 6 papers. Likewise, *gèng* is infelicitous in (28), where it combines with gradable adjectives, because a salient alternative, i.e. Bill, is taller. If *gèng* is merely a comparative marker with an evaluative presupposition, then its superlative scalar force, which naturally follows from our *even*-like analysis, would be unexplained.

7 *Gèng vs. Shènzhì*: Parametric Variation

Although *gèng* and *shènzhì*, the unmarked *even* in Mandarin, are interchangeable in many cases as demonstrated above, we observe that they behave distinctly under some circumstances. First consider (29) where *gèng* and *shènzhì* combine with the gradable adjective *gao* (tall) but trigger distinct readings.

(29) a. Zhangsan **gèng** gao.

 Zhangsan gèng tall

 Zhangsan is even taller (than some contextually salient individual).

 b. Zhangsan **shènzhì** #?(hěn) gao.

 Zhangsan even hěn tall

 Zhangsan is even tall.

With *gèng*, (29-a) means that John is taller than some salient individual; on this interpretation, the adjective *gao* (tall) is understood as taking on a comparative meaning, i.e. *taller*. In contrast, with *shènzhì*, (29-b) has a different interpretation: That *John is tall* is more noteworthy or unexpected than that John has some other contextually relevant properties, say, strong; on this interpretation, *gao* (*tall*) is understood as taking on a POS meaning. Note that the presence of the semantically bleached degree modifier *hěn*, argued by some to be the Mandarin equivalent to POS, is preferred here, which is to be captured below.

Now consider (30) where *gèng* and *shènzhì* combine with a non-gradable predicate. We observe that both *gèng* and *shènzhì* are felicitous if the contextually salient alternative to the prejacent is spelt out (30-a), but if that alternative is not spelt out, *gèng* is degraded while *shènzhì* remains felicitous, as in (30-b).

(30) a. Yuehan nanguo de   jujue shuoshuo; Bi'er nanguo de
          John   sad   EXTENT refuse speak   Bill sad   EXTENT
          gèng (shi)/**shènzhì** ku-le.
          gèng COP   even cry-PERF
          John was so sad that he refused to speak; Bill was so sad that he
          even cried.
      b. Bi'er nanguo de   ??? **gèng** (shi)/**shènzhì** ku-le.
          Bill sad   EXTENT gèng COP   even cry-PERF
          Intended: Bill was so sad that he even cried.

Does such distinct behaviors of *gèng* and *shènzhì* undermine our claim that *gèng* is genuinely *even*-like? The answer seems negative. Below we suggest this is because they differ parametrically. Parametric variation among *even*-like particles has been reported intra- and cross-linguistically. We suggest that *gèng* and *shènzhì* differ along two such parameters identified in the literature.

Parameter #1 is the **Ability to Associate with Covert Focus.** Some languages are reported to have more than one particle which assume the same semantic core but differ in the ability to associate with covert focus. For example, Hebrew *afilu* and BIXLAL are both reported *even*-like particles. However, BIXLAL can associate with the covert comparison class argument of POS and trigger readings paraphrased as English *in general*, *very*, and *at all*; in contrast, *afilu*, the unmarked *even* in Hebrew, cannot associate with covert material (see [17] for details). A similar claim has been made for Russian *daže* and *voobšče*, both of which are *even*-like particles [37]. According to [37], *voobšče* can operate on covert-based alternatives, similar to Hebrew BIXLAL in distribution and semantic effects, whereas *daže*, the unmarked *even* in Russian, cannot. Another example is Hebrew *rak* vs. *be-sax ha-kol*, both of which are claimed exclusive particles. While *be-sax ha-kol* can associate with covert POS and evoke an approximative reading paraphrased as English *more or less*, *rak*, the unmarked exclusive particle in Hebrew, cannot associate with covert focus.

Given such cross-linguistic reports, we suggest that *gèng* and *shènzhì* differ in their ability to associate with covert focus, more specifically speaking, the covert COMP here: *Gèng* is positive with respect to this parameter whereas *shènzhì* is negative. Then, the distinct behaviors observed in (29) is explained. (29-a) has a comparative reading that John is taller than some salient individual; this is because *gèng* focus-associates with the covert COMP and operates on covert alternatives like equative (see (26)). In contrast, in (29-b) *shènzhì*, unable to associate with covert COMP, has no comparative reading here, and that's why the presence of *hěn*, a claimed equivalent to English POS, is preferred here.[7,8]

Parameter #2 along which *even*-like particles are reported to vary is **contextual dependency/anaphoricity**. By contextual dependency/anaphoricity, it is meant that the particle depends on the information structure of the prior discourse context to varying extents; more specifically, whether the particle requires some contextually supplied alternative to the prejacent to be salient, or to be actually uttered in the prior context [45]. To exemplify, consider the two replies B and B' in (31). Hindi affixes *-bhii* and *-tak* are both translation equivalents for English *even*. When a contextually relevant alternative is made explicitly accessible in the discourse ((31)-B), both *-bhii* and *-tak* are felicitous; in contrast, in the absence of such an explicitly accessible alternative, *-tak* remains felicitous but *-bhii* becomes infelicitous ((31)-B') (see [45] for details).

(31) A: kis-ne bakri-kii annakhe khaayĩ?
        who goat's eyes   ate
        'Who ate goat's eyes?'

---

[7] An anonymous reviewer asked whether our analysis implies that *gèng* cannot co-occur and associate with unstressed *hěn* and, if not, why not. The answer is indeed negative: Adding unstressed *hěn* immediately before *gao* in (29-a) would make (29-a) ungrammatical. Our entry (19) can actually capture this non-grammaticality. Suppose that *gèng* associates with unstressed *hěn* which assumes the function of POS in English; then, the triggered alternatives would be other degree modifiers that indicate a degree either above POS, e.g. '*feichang*' (very), or below POS, e.g. '*bu-tai*' (literally 'negation-much', which can be paraphrased as *barely*), as in (i). With (i-a) as the alternative set, *gèng*'s comparative requirement is violated: Bill is taller in the q worlds than in the p worlds. With (i-b) as the alternative set, *gèng*'s evaluative requirement is violated: In the q worlds, Bill is below the POS level. This explains why *gèng* cannot associate with unstressed *hěn*.

(i) a. Alt. Set 1: {Bill is very tall, <u>Bill is POS/hen$_{unstressed}$ tall.</u>}
    b. Alt. Set 2: {<u>Bill is POS/hen$_{unstressed}$ tall.</u> Bill is not very/barely tall}

[8] An interesting tendency emerges out of the limited reports given above: Among the pairs of particles presented, the particle that cannot associate with covert focus is the unmarked one while the one that can associate with covert focus is marked. *Gèng* and *shènzhì* fit into this pattern: *Shènzhì* is the unmarked *even* and cannot associate with covert COMP whereas *gèng*, which is marked, can. More cross-linguistic data are needed to test this tendency, which we leave for future studies.

B: mai-ne khaayı̃ aur meri daadii-**tak**-ne/-ne-**bhii**   khaayı̃.
I   ate   and my grandma-**tak**-erg/-erg-**bhii** ate
'I ate it and even my grandma ate.'   (Hindi, [45]'s ex. 12)
B': Meri daadii-**tak**-ne/#-ne-**bhii**   khaayı̃.
My   grandma-**tak**-erg/-erg-**bhii** ate
Intended: 'Even My grandama ate it.'   (Hindi, [45]'s ex. 10)

A similar observation has been made for a pair of Spanish *even*-like particles *hasta* vs. *incluso* [45], and a pair of Russian *even*-like particles *daže* vs. *voossče* [37]: *hasta* and *voossče* have a low context-dependency while *incluso* and *daže* are highly context-dependent in this sense.

We suggest that *gèng* and *shènzhì* also align with this pattern in that *gèng* is highly context-dependent/anaphoric whereas *shènzhì* has a low degree in this regard. This explains why in (30-a) they are both felicitous but in (30-b) *gèng* is degraded whereas *shènzhì* remains felicitous. Note this parameter is also relevant for *gèng*'s combination with gradable adjectives. Out of the blue, (29-a) feels incomplete; the so-called salient individual is preferably spelt out as in (1-b) or easily retrievable as in (2–ii). We connect this to *gèng*'s context-dependency/anaphoric nature.[9]

8   Conclusion

In this work, we followed up [32]'s initial observation that *gèng*, in addition to its widely discussed combination with gradable adjectives, can also combine with non-gradable predicates; we noted that *gèng*, in its combination with non-gradable predicates, resembles English *even* and Mandarin *shènzhì*. We sharpened this intuition, and then proposed adopting for *gèng* [15]'s semantics for English *even* to capture such cases. Then, adopting two independently motivated assumptions in the literature, we extended our proposal to the much more studied cases, i.e. *gèng*'s combination with gradable adjectives. And finally, we distinguished between *gèng* and *shènzhì* by connecting their different behaviors to a broader parametric variation among *even*-like particles cross-linguistically.

---

[9] One reviewer notes that in addition to *shènzhì*, *dōu* is also considered a canonical *even*-like particle in Mandarin, and that *shènzhì* and *dōu*, though behaving similarly in some cases, have some discrepancies as well. The reviewer asks (i) whether the discrepancies between *shènzhì* and *dōu* are also a matter of parametric variation, and (ii) if the answer is affirmative, how a parametric variation between *shènzhì* and *dōu* is related to the parametric variation between *shènzhì* and *gèng*. These two inter-related questions concern a more general issue of the parametric variation among *even*-like particles intra-linguistically in Mandarin. An examination into this issue is beyond the scope of this work due to the various syntactic differences among the three particles (see e.g. [46,47] for the syntactic differences between *shènzhì* and *dōu*) and the semantic complexity especially associated with *dōu*, a particle that boasts a variety of readings. For a brief discussion of the parametric variation between *shènzhì* and *dōu*, see e.g. [4]. We leave this issue for future occasions.

There remain some open issues, one of which concerns an interesting observation offered by a reviewer. Consider (32), offered by this reviewer. The reviewer points out that in (32) a possible, contextually supplied scale is a scale of dangerous-ness where killing persons ranks higher than hitting persons. The reviewer further notes that *shènzhì*, presupposing a higher degree on this scale and associating with killing persons, and *bu-yong-shuo* (not to mention/let alone), presupposing a lower degree on this scale and associating with hitting persons, behave like 'opposites' in this sense. But interestingly, as noted by this reviewer, *gèng* can often co-occur with *bu-yong-shuo* (not to mention/let alone) (simply adding *gèng* immediately before *bu-yong-shuo* in (32)). The question is how our proposal can account for *gèng*'s co-occurrence with *bu-yong-shuo* given that *bu-yong-shuo* associates with a lower-ranked item here. We would like to explore this issue in future studies. Here we only note that to answer this question satisfactorily, the semantics of *bu-yong-shuo* itself must be taken into consideration, which itself would constitute a complex issue (see e.g. [9,49] for the discussion of the semantics of *let alone*, the English translation equivalent of *bu-yong-shuo*).

(32)   ta fanu shi **shènzhì** hui   sha ren, **bu-yong-shuo** da ren.
        he angry when shènzhì would kill person NEG-use-say   hit person
        He would even kill persons when he is enraged, not to mention/let alone hit persons.

Some other open issues are as follows. Firstly, in the presence of both the covert COMP and some overt material, does *gèng* necessarily associate with covert COMP or can also optionally associate with overt material? For instance, in (25-a) can *gèng* associate with the adjective *tall*? If not, why is this option blocked? This is perhaps an issue not confined to our case here but a general issue applied to particles reported to be able to associate with covert focus. Secondly, what are other potential parameters to differentiate *even*-like particles intra-linguistically in Mandarin (see footnote 9)? An investigation in this would, in return, contribute to a growing body of literature on the parametric variation among reported *even*-like particles cross-linguistically in general. Thirdly, a long-standing puzzle (e.g. [28,32]) is that *gèng* is incompatible with precise differentials (33); neither [32]'s proposal (3) nor ours can account for this puzzle. Then how to explain this incompatibility? Fourthly, as aforementioned in footnote 3, some native speakers of Mandarin prefer *gèng-shi* (*gèng*-copula) to *gèng* in cases where *gèng* combines with non-gradable predicates like (4) and (5); what is their difference? Should *gèng-shi* be analyzed compositionally or as a whole? We hope to address such issues in future studies.

(33)   Zhangsan bi   Lisi (* **gèng**) gao san-gongfen.
        Zhansan than Lisi gèng   tall three-centimeter
        Intended: Zhangsan is (even) 3cm taller than Lisi.

Acknowledgements. We would like to thank the two reviewers of the abstract and the full paper reviewer for the valuable feedback, as well as the audience at LENLS 20 for the lively discussion. Thanks also to the organizing committee of LENLS 20 and the editorial team of the proceedings. The research reported in this work was funded by ISF Grant 682/22 to Yael Greenberg. Any error is, of course, ours.

References

1. Beaver, D.I., Clark, B.Z.: Sense and Sensitivity: How Focus Determines Meaning. Explorations in Semantics. Wiley-Blackwell, Oxford (2008)
2. Beck, S.: On the semantics of comparative conditionals. Linguist. Philos. **20**(3), 229–271 (1997)
3. Beck, S., Oda, T., Sugisaki, K.: Parametric variation in the semantics of comparison: Japanese vs. English. J. East Asian Linguist. **13**(4), 289–344 (2004)
4. Chen, Z., Greenberg, Y.: A novel argument for an *even*-like semantics of Mandarin *dou*. In: Starr, J.R., Kim, J., Öney, B. (eds.) Semantics and Linguistic Theory, vol. 1, pp. 751–771 (2022)
5. Chierchia, G.: Logic in Grammar: Polarity, Free Choice, and Intervention. OUP, Oxford (2013)
6. Coppock, E., Beaver, D.I.: Principles of the exclusive muddle. J. Semant. **31**(3), 371–432 (2014)
7. Erlewine, M.Y.: A new syntax-semantics for the Mandarin *bi* comparative. Master's thesis, University of Chicago (2007)
8. Erlewine, M.Y.: Clausal comparison without degree abstraction in Mandarin Chinese. Nat. Lang. Linguist. Theory **36**(2), 445–482 (2018)
9. Fillmore, C., Kay, P., O'Connor, M.C.: Regularity and idiomaticity in grammatical constructions: the case of *let alone*. Language **64**(3), 501–538 (1988)
10. Francescotti, R.M.: Even: the conventional implicature approach reconsidered. Linguist. Philos. **18**(2), 153–173 (1995)
11. Gast, V., van der Auwera, J.: Scalar additive operators in the languages of Europe. Language **87**(1), 2–54 (2011)
12. Grano, T.: Mandarin *hen* and universal markedness in gradable adjectives. Nat. Lang. Linguist. Theory **30**(2), 513–565 (2012)
13. Grano, T., Kennedy, C.: Mandarin transitive comparatives and the grammar of measurement. J. East Asian Linguist. **21**(3), 219–266 (2012)
14. Greenberg, Y.: A novel problem for the likelihood-based semantics of *even*. Semant. Pragmatics **9**, 2-1 (2016)
15. Greenberg, Y.: A revised, gradability-based semantics for *even*. Nat. Lang. Semant. **26**(1), 51–83 (2018)
16. Greenberg, Y.: An overt even operator over covert-based focus alternatives: the case of Hebrew *bixlal*. J. Semant. **37**(1), 1–42 (2020)
17. Greenberg, Y.: On the scalar antonymy of *only* and *even*. Nat. Lang. Semant. **30**(4), 415–452 (2022)
18. Guerzoni, E.: *Even*-NPIs in yes/no questions. Nat. Lang. Semant. **12**(4), 319–343 (2004)
19. Heim, I.: Notes on comparatives and related issues. Ms., University of Texas, Austin (1985)
20. Heim, I.: Presupposition projection and the semantics of attitude verbs. J. Semant. **9**(3), 183–221 (1992)
21. Herburger, E.: What Counts: Focus and Quantification. MIT Press, Cambridge (2000)

22. Iatridou, S., Tatevosov, S.: Our *even*. Linguist. Philos. **39**, 295–331 (2016)
23. Ippolito, M.: On the meaning of some focus-sensitive particles. Nat. Lang. Seman. **15**, 1–34 (2007)
24. Karttunen, L., Peters, S.: Conventional implicature. In: Dineen, D., Oh, C.K. (eds.) Syntax and Semantics 11: Preuspposition, pp. 1–56. Academic Press, New York (1979)
25. Kay, P.: *Even*. Linguist. Philos. **13**(1), 59–111 (1990)
26. Kennedy, C., McNally, L.: Scale structure, degree modification, and the semantics of gradable predicates. Language **81**(2), 345–381 (2005)
27. König, E.: The Meaning of Focus Particles: A Comparative Perspective. Routledge, London (2002)
28. Krasikova, S.: Comparison in Chinese. In: Bonami, O., Cabredo Hofherr, P. (eds.) Empirical Issues in Syntax and Semantics, vol. 7, pp. 263–281 (2008)
29. Lahiri, U.: Focus and negative polarity in Hindi. Nat. Lang. Semant. **6**(1), 57–123 (1998)
30. Lin, J.W.: Chinese comparatives and their implicational parameters. Nat. Lang. Semant. **17**(1), 1–27 (2009)
31. Lin, J.W.: Chinese comparatives: commentary on clausal vs. phrasal analyses. In: New Explorations in Chinese Theoretical Syntax: Studies in honor of Yen-Hui Audrey Li, vol. 272, p. 249 (2022)
32. Liu, C.S.L.: The Chinese *geng* clausal comparative. Lingua **120**(6), 1579–1606 (2010)
33. Liu, C.S.L.: The positive morpheme in Chinese and the adjectival structure. Lingua **120**(4), 1010–1056 (2010)
34. Liu, C.S.L.: The Chinese *bi* comparative. Lingua **121**(12), 1767–1795 (2011)
35. Liu, F.H.: The scalar particle *hai* in Chinese. Cahiers Linguist.-Asie orientale **29**(1), 41–84 (2000)
36. Lu, J.: Hai he geng [Hai and geng]. In: Lu, J., Ma, Z. (eds.) Xiandai hanyu xuci sanlun [The Discussion of Function Words in Modern Mandarin] (in Chinese). Beijing University Press, Beijing (1985)
37. Miashkur, L.: A parametric comparison of two scalar particles in Russian. In: Brandel, N. (ed.) Proceedings of IATL33 & MIT Working Papers in Linguistics # 89, pp. 123-149 (2017)
38. Orenstein, D., Greenberg, Y.: Approximation derived from a scalar exclusive particle associating with covert focus: the case of Hebrew *be-sax ha-kol*. Glossa: J. Gener. Linguist. **6**(1) (2021)
39. Rett, J.: The Semantics of Evaluativity. OUP, Oxford (2014)
40. Rooth, M.: Association with focus. Ph.D. thesis, University of Massachusetts Amherst (1985)
41. Rooth, M.: A theory of focus interpretation. Nat. Lang. Semant. **1**(1), 75–116 (1992)
42. Rullmann, H.: *Even*, polarity, and scope. Pap. Exp. Theor. Linguist. **4**(40-64) (1997)
43. Rullmann, H.: What does *even* even mean. Ms., University of British Columbia (2007)
44. Sawada, O.: An utterance situation-based comparison. Linguist. Philos. **37**(3), 205–248 (2014)
45. Schwenter, S.A., Vasishth, S.: Absolute and relative scalar particles in Spanish and Hindi. In: Conathan, L.J., Good, J., Kavitskaya, D.,Wulf, A.B., Yu, A.C.L. (eds.) Annual Meeting of the Berkeley Linguistics Society, vol. 26, pp. 225–233 (2000)

46. Shyu, S.I.: (A) symmetries between Mandarin Chinese *lián... dōu* and *shènzhì*. J. Chin. Linguist. **32**(1), 81–128 (2004)
47. Shyu, S.I.: The scope of even: evidence from Mandarin Chinese. Lang. Linguist. **19**(1), 156–195 (2018)
48. Sybesma, R.: The Mandarin VP. Studies in Natural Language and Linguistic Theory, vol. 44. Springer, Dordrecht (1999). https://doi.org/10.1007/978-94-015-9163-8
49. Toosarvandani, M.D.: Association with foci. Ph.D. thesis, University of California, Berkeley (2010)
50. Umbach, C.: Comparatives combined with additive particles: the case of German 'noch'. In: Riester, A., Solstad, T. (eds.) Proceedings of Sinn und Bedeutung, vol. 13, pp. 543–558 (2009)
51. Wagner, M.: *Even* and the syntax of additivity. In: Colloquium Talk Given at the University of Chicago (2015)
52. Wiegand, M.: Exclusive morphosemantics: *just* and covert quantification. In: Bennett, W.G., Hracs, L., Storoshenko, D.R. (eds.) Proceedings of the West Coast Conference on Formal Linguistics (WCCFL), vol. 35, pp. 419–429 (2018)
53. Xiang, M.: Some topics in comparative constructions. Ph.D. thesis, Michigan State University (2005)
54. Xiang, Y.: Function alternations of the Mandarin particle *dou*: distributor, free choice licensor, and 'even'. J. Semant. **37**(2), 171–217 (2020)
55. Zeevat, H.: 'Only' as a mirative particle. In: Riester, A., Onea, E. (eds.) Focus at the Syntax-Semantics Interface, Working Papers of the SFB 73, vol. 3. University of Stuttgart (2009)
56. Zhang, L.: The semantics of comparisons in Mandarin Chinese. In: Cho, S.Y. (ed.) Proceedings of GLOW in Asia XII & SICOGG XXI: Universal Grammar and Its Cross-linguistic Instantiations, pp. 643–652 (2019)
57. Zhang, L.: The presupposition of *even*. In: Starr, J.R., Kim, J., Öney, B. (eds.) Semantics and Linguistic Theory, vol. 1, pp. 249–269 (2022)

Internal Reading and Reciprocity

Ka-fat Chow[✉]

The Hong Kong Polytechnic University, Hung Hom, Hong Kong
kfzhouy@yahoo.com
http://chowkafat.net/homee.html

Abstract. This paper first points out that the internal reading of sentences containing certain reciprocal items such as "the same" carries a reciprocal meaning. It then provides a uniform formal treatment for these items that reflects the reciprocal meaning by using the Generalized Quantifier Theory enriched by the notions of generalized noun phrases (GNPs) and raised verb phrases. The basic framework initially makes explicit use of the GNP EACH OTHER, and is then refined to make EACH OTHER implicit so as to be in line with the surface syntactic structure. The framework is further refined to handle cases that are different from the basic cases, including reciprocal items appearing in non-object positions, conjoined phrases containing reciprocal items, downward monotonic and non-monotonic quantifiers, weaker reciprocal meaning and non-NP triggers.

Keywords: internal reading · reciprocal items · Generalized Quantifier Theory · generalized noun phrases · raised verb phrases · polymorphism

1 Introduction

Sentences with "each other" in English have been treated as the canonical reciprocal expressions. However, apart from "each other", some other sentences also carry a reciprocal meaning. A typical example is the following sentence:

$$\text{John, Peter and Mary read the same books.} \tag{1}$$

The phrase with "the same" above is ambiguous with two readings: the deictic reading and the internal reading. Under the deictic reading, "same" means "same as something mentioned in the previous discourse or salient in the context", whereas under the internal reading, the sentence above is equivalent to the following (as pointed out by [12]):

$$\text{John, Peter and Mary read the same books as each other.} \tag{2}$$

meaning that any two of the three persons read the same books (here I assume the strongest reciprocal meaning as discussed in [5] and [11] by default). In this paper, I will not discuss the independence between these two readings and

D. Bekki et al. (Eds.): LENLS 2023, LNCS 14569, pp. 155–174, 2024.
https://doi.org/10.1007/978-3-031-60878-0_9

will focus on the internal reading. Note that the internal reading of sentence (1) is triggered by the plural noun phrase (NP) "John, Peter and Mary". If it is replaced by a singular NP such as "John", then the internal reading of the sentence disappears. In Subsect. 4.5, I will discuss other internal reading triggers.

In addition to "the same", some other lexical items, hereinafter called "reciprocal items" and including "different", "opposite", "similar", "related", "separate", "adjacent", "complementary", "connected", "disjoint", etc., behave similarly in that a sentence containing one of these items has an internal reading carrying a reciprocal meaning. This is best illustrated by the following example which sounds weird:

*Particles 1, 2 and 3 have different charges. (internal reading)   (3)

Under the intended (namely internal) reading, the sentence above means that the charges of the three particles are different from each other, i.e. particles 1 and 2 have different charges, particles 2 and 3 have different charges, and particles 3 and 1 have different charges. But this is impossible given that there are only two possible charges (positive vs negative).

Another evidence for the reciprocal meaning of these items is that many of them can be rendered in Chinese as words containing the morpheme "xiang" or "hu" meaning "mutual" as hown in the following table which gives the romanization and Chinese characters of the Chinese renditions of the reciprocal items, although these may not be the most colloquial Chinese renditions for these items.

Reciprocal Item	Chinese Rendition (Romanization)	Chinese Rendition (Chinese Characters)
the same	xiangtong	相同
different	xiangyi	相異
opposite	xiangfan	相反
similar	xiangsi	相似
related	xiangguan	相關
separate	xiangge	相隔
adjacent	xianglin	相鄰
complementary	hubu	互補
connected	hutong	互通
disjoint	huchi	互斥

Note that "xiang" and "hu" can in fact appear in Chinese reciprocal expressions. For instance, "xiang ai", where "ai" is the Chinese word for "love", means "love each other". The two morphemes can even combine to make the compound adverb "huxiang" or "xianghu" meaning "mutually". For instance, "huxiang bangzhu", where "bangzhu" is the Chinese word for "help", means "help each other".

In this paper, I will provide a uniform formal treatment for the internal reading of all the reciprocal items that reflects the reciprocal meaning. But first I have to point out that when I say a sentence containing a reciprocal item other than "the same" has an internal reading, I mean that the sentence carries a reciprocal meaning just like (2), and do not mean that the sentence is necessarily ambiguous in that it also has a deictic reading. In fact, sentences containing many of these reciprocal items (other than "the same") are not ambiguous. For example, the following sentence does not have a deictic reading:

$$\text{John, Peter and Mary live on separate floors.} \tag{4}$$

2 Formal Preliminaries

In this paper, I will adopt the notation in [15] which uses small cap font and boldface font for the denotations of logical and non-logical terms, respectively. If f is a characteristic function, then f' is the set of entities that f characterizes. The formal framework is mainly based on the Generalized Quantifier Theory (GQT) enriched by the notions of generalized noun phrases (GNPs) and raised verb phrases (raised VPs) developed by [18, 19, 21, 22], etc.

Before introducing the notion of GNP, I first review some basic notions of GQT. Under the classical GQT, a generalized quantifier (GQ) is a function with a number of predicates as arguments and a truth value as output. The arities of the arguments are used to name the type of a GQ. For example, a proper name such as "John" is treated as a type $\langle 1 \rangle$ GQ I_j (called "Montagovian individual" in the GQT literature) corresponding to the individual term $\mathbf{j}$ (short for "John") which requires a unary predicate as its sole argument and outputs a truth value with the following definition[1]:

$$I_j = \lambda P_{et}[P(\mathbf{j}) = 1] \tag{5}$$

A determiner such as "fewer than 3" is treated as a type $\langle 1, 1 \rangle$ GQ FEWER THAN 3 which requires two unary predicates as its arguments and outputs a truth value.

In this paper, I will also make use of the case extension operators proposed by [8]. Let Q be a type $\langle 1 \rangle$ GQ, then the nominative and accusative extensions of Q, notated Q_{nom} and Q_{acc} respectively, are functions defined as follows:

$$Q_{\text{nom}} = \lambda R_{e^2t} \lambda w_e [Q(\lambda z_e[R(z, w) = 1]) = 1] \tag{6}$$

$$Q_{\text{acc}} = \lambda R_{e^2t} \lambda z_e [Q(\lambda w_e[R(z, w) = 1]) = 1] \tag{7}$$

---

[1] In what follows, a subscript attached to a variable (such as et attached to P in (5)) is the type of that variable.

Applying any one of these two functions to a binary predicate is tantamount to filling one of the arguments (nominative or accusative) of the binary predicate with the NP represented by Q, thus obtaining a unary predicate. For example, by applying (I_j)nom and (I_j)acc to the binary predicate **hit**, we obtain the unary predicates (I_j)nom(**hit**) and (I_j)acc(**hit**), meaning "that which John hit" and "that which hit John", respectively.

Very often, we need to express conjoined phrases such as "John, Peter and Mary". In this paper, I use a polymorphic Boolean operator $\text{AND}_{n,\tau}$ to conjoin n expressions of type τ with the following recursive definition adapted from [14]:

$$\text{AND}_{n,\tau} = \begin{cases} \lambda((p_1)_t, \ldots, (p_n)_t)[p_1 \wedge \ldots \wedge p_n] & \text{if } \tau = t \\ \lambda((X_1)_\tau, \ldots, (X_n)_\tau)\lambda Y_{\sigma_1}[\text{AND}_{n,\sigma_2}(X_1(Y), \ldots, X_n(Y))] & \text{if } \tau = \sigma_1\sigma_2 \end{cases}$$
(8)

Thus, "John, Peter and Mary" can be denoted as $\text{AND}_{3,(et)t}(I_j, I_{\mathbf{p}}, I_{\mathbf{m}})^2$, where $I_{\mathbf{p}}$ and $I_{\mathbf{m}}$ are the Montagovian individuals corresponding to the individual terms $\mathbf{p}$ (short for "Peter") and $\mathbf{m}$ (short for "Mary"), respectively. It can be shown that

$$\text{AND}_{3,(et)t}(I_j, I_{\mathbf{p}}, I_{\mathbf{m}}) = \lambda P_{et}[P(\mathbf{j}) = 1 \wedge P(\mathbf{p}) = 1 \wedge P(\mathbf{m}) = 1]$$
(9)

From this we obtain

$$\text{AND}_{3,(et)t}(I_j, I_{\mathbf{p}}, I_{\mathbf{m}})' = \{S : \{\mathbf{j}, \mathbf{p}, \mathbf{m}\} \subseteq S\}$$
(10)

There are three useful notions associated with type $\langle 1 \rangle$ GQs in a finite universe, namely live-on sets, topic sets and witness sets. The definitions of these notions according to [13] are given as follows. Let Q be a type $\langle 1 \rangle$ GQ in a finite universe (which is a reasonable assumption for linguistic applications), then a set of individuals S is a live-on set of Q if the following is true for any set of individuals T:

$$T \in Q' \text{ iff } T \cap S \in Q'$$
(11)

The topic set of Q is the smallest live-on set of Q. A set of individuals W is a witness set of Q if W is a subset of the topic set of Q and $W \in Q'$. In what follows, I will use $\text{Li}(Q)$ to denote the set of live-on sets of Q, $\text{Top}(Q)$ to denote the (unique) topic set of Q, and $\text{Wit}(Q)$ to denote the set of witness sets of Q. Note that while $\text{Top}(Q)$ is a set of individuals, $\text{Li}(Q)$ and $\text{Wit}(Q)$ are sets of sets of individuals.

For example, we have $\text{Lim}(\text{AND}_{3,(et)t}(I_j, I_{\mathbf{p}}, I_{\mathbf{m}})) = \text{AND}_{3,(et)t}(I_j, I_{\mathbf{p}}, I_{\mathbf{m}})'$. To prove this, we first take an arbitrary member S of $\text{AND}_{3,(et)t}(I_j, I_{\mathbf{p}}, I_{\mathbf{m}})'$, which according to (10) is a set S such that $\{\mathbf{j}, \mathbf{p}, \mathbf{m}\} \subseteq S$, and show that S satisfies (11) for any set of individuals T where Q is instantiated as $\text{AND}_{3,(et)t}(I_j, I_{\mathbf{p}}, I_{\mathbf{m}})$. Given that $\{\mathbf{j}, \mathbf{p}, \mathbf{m}\} \subseteq S$, we have $\{\mathbf{j}, \mathbf{p}, \mathbf{m}\} \subseteq T$ iff $\{\mathbf{j}, \mathbf{p}, \mathbf{m}\} \subseteq T \cap S$. According to (10), we thus have $T \in \text{AND}_{3,(et)t}(I_j, I_{\mathbf{p}}, I_{\mathbf{m}})'$ iff $T \cap S \in \text{AND}_{3,(et)t}(I_j, I_{\mathbf{p}}, I_{\mathbf{m}})'$.

---

[2] Note that under the e-t notation, a type $\langle 1 \rangle$ GQ is a function of type $(et)t$.

We next take an arbitrary set S which is not a member of $\text{AND}_{3,(et)t}(I_\mathbf{j}, I_\mathbf{p}, I_\mathbf{m})'$ and show that S does not satisfy (11) for a particular set $T = \{\mathbf{j}, \mathbf{p}, \mathbf{m}\}$. Without loss of generality, we may assume that $\mathbf{j} \notin S$. It then follows that $\mathbf{j} \notin T \cap S$ and so $\{\mathbf{j}, \mathbf{p}, \mathbf{m}\} \not\subseteq T \cap S$. According to (10), we thus have $T \in \text{AND}_{3,(et)t}(I_\mathbf{j}, I_\mathbf{p}, I_\mathbf{m})'$ but $T \cap S \notin \text{AND}_{3,(et)t}(I_\mathbf{j}, I_\mathbf{p}, I_\mathbf{m})'$.

Since $\text{Top}(\text{AND}_{3,(et)t}(I_\mathbf{j}, I_\mathbf{p}, I_\mathbf{m}))$ is the smallest member of $\text{Li}(\text{AND}_{3,(et)t}(I_\mathbf{j}, I_\mathbf{p}, I_\mathbf{m}))$, we have $\text{Top}(\text{AND}_{3,(et)t}(I_\mathbf{j}, I_\mathbf{p}, I_\mathbf{m})) = \{\mathbf{j}, \mathbf{p}, \mathbf{m}\}$. Moreover, since $\{\mathbf{j}, \mathbf{p}, \mathbf{m}\}$ is the only set satisfying $\{\mathbf{j}, \mathbf{p}, \mathbf{m}\} \subseteq \text{Top}(\text{AND}_{3,(et)t}(I_\mathbf{j}, I_\mathbf{p}, I_\mathbf{m}))$ and $\{\mathbf{j}, \mathbf{p}, \mathbf{m}\} \in \text{AND}_{3,(et)t}(I_\mathbf{j}, I_\mathbf{p}, I_\mathbf{m})'$, we have

$$\text{Wit}(\text{AND}_{3,(et)t}(I_\mathbf{j}, I_\mathbf{p}, I_\mathbf{m})) = \{\{\mathbf{j}, \mathbf{p}, \mathbf{m}\}\} \tag{12}$$

The notion of GNP is a generalization of GQ. Instead of outputting truth values, a GNP outputs a characteristic function of ordered n-tuples of individuals (represented by ": n") or a characteristic function of type $\langle 1 \rangle$ GQs (represented by ": $\langle 1 \rangle$"). Following [19], I will treat "each other" as a GNP with a binary predicate as input and a set of type $\langle 1 \rangle$ GQs as output, and its type is notated $\langle 2 : \langle 1 \rangle \rangle$. As for the denotation of this GNP, I will adopt a modified version of the denotation of the most basic reciprocal quantifier in [10] which is given as follows:

$$\text{EACH OTHER} = \lambda R_{e^2 t} \lambda Q_{(et)t} [\exists X \in \text{Wit}(Q)[|X| \geq 2 \wedge X^2 - Id_X^2 \subseteq R']] \tag{13}$$

In the above, Q is a variable of upward monotonic type $\langle 1 \rangle$ GQs. Id_X^2 is the set $\{(x,x) : x \in X\}$ and so the statement $X^2 - Id_X^2 \subseteq R'$ means that every member x of X stands in the relation R with every other member of X except perhaps x itself. For instance, the following sentence

$$\text{John, Peter and Mary hit each other.} \tag{14}$$

will be denoted by

$$\text{EACH OTHER}(\mathbf{hit})(\text{AND}_{3,(et)t}(I_\mathbf{j}, I_\mathbf{p}, I_\mathbf{m})) \tag{15}$$

According to (13), the expression above is true if and only if there exists a plural witness set of $\text{AND}_{3,(et)t}(I_\mathbf{j}, I_\mathbf{p}, I_\mathbf{m})$ (which, as discussed above, must be the set $\{\mathbf{j}, \mathbf{p}, \mathbf{m}\}$) such that every member of that set hits every other member of that set, which is exactly what (14) means.

A consequence of the aforesaid treatment is that EACH OTHER($\mathbf{hit}$) denoting the VP "hit each other" has type $((et)t)t$ instead of et. Thus, "hit each other" is an example of raised VPs studied in [22]. The main difference between an ordinary VP (of type et) and a raised VP (of type $((et)t)t$) is that while the former serves as the argument of a type $\langle 1 \rangle$ GQ, the latter serves as a function which requires a type $\langle 1 \rangle$ GQ as its argument.

3   Basic Formal Framework for Reciprocal Items

I propose that the internal reading of sentences containing the reciprocal items should also be treated using the GNP EACH OTHER. In this section, I will first propose a formal framework that makes explicit use of EACH OTHER. Then I will refine the framework by introducing new GNPs that make EACH OTHER implicit.

Consider (1) (and its equivalent form (2)) again. I propose to denote this sentence by the expression EACH OTHER$(R)(Q)$ where Q should be the type $\langle 1 \rangle$ GQ AND$_{3,(et)t}(I_j, I_p, I_m)$, while R should be a binary predicate denoting "read the same books as". Now the question is how to determine this binary predicate.

To answer the aforesaid question, we may draw reference from [1]'s study on structured quantifiers. According to [1], the structure "the same ... as" in the sentence "The same boys sang as danced" can be seen as a type $\langle 1, 1^2 \rangle$ GQ with the following denotation:

$$\text{THE SAME AS} = \lambda A_{et}\lambda(B_{et}, C_{et})[\text{SAME}(A' \cap B', A' \cap C')] \qquad (16)$$

Note that THE SAME AS given above is an atomic logical term whose denotation contains another logical term SAME, with the following denotation (in what follows S and T are variables of sets):

$$\text{SAME} = \lambda(S, T)[S = T] \qquad (17)$$

According to [18], while the structure "the same ... as" in the phrase "read the same books as" cannot be seen as a GQ, it is one of the "generalized comparative determiners" which constitute a subtype of GNPs (and will henceforth be treated as GNPs), and include, apart from "the same ... as", such structures as "different ... than", "older ... than" (where ... stands for a noun). This subtype of GNPs satisfies a property called "argument invariance for unary determiners" (D1AI), which can be seen as a defining property of this subtype of GNPs.

In this paper, I modify [18]'s theory a bit, and propose to denote "the same ... as" in "read the same books as" as a type $\langle 1, 2 : 2 \rangle$ GNP with the following denotation:

$$(\text{THE SAME AS})_{N,2} = \lambda P_{et}\lambda R_{e^2 t}\lambda(x_e, y_e)[\text{SAME}$$
$$(P' \cap (I_x)\text{nom}(R)', P' \cap (I_y)\text{nom}(R)')] \qquad (18)$$

where the subscripts N and 2 represent the fact that the internal reading is triggered by a plural noun phrase and "the same" appears in the 2nd argument (i.e. object) position of the binary predicate R, respectively. Note that the GNP defined above satisfies a modified version of the property D1AI defined as follows: a type $\langle 1, 2 : 2 \rangle$ GNP F satisfies D1AI iff for any unary predicate P, binary predicate R and individuals a, b, c, d, if $P' \cap \{w : R(a, w) = 1\} = P' \cap \{w : R(b, w) = 1\}$ and $P' \cap \{w : R(c, w) = 1\} = P' \cap \{w : R(d, w) = 1\}$, then $F(P)(R)(a, c) = F(P)(R)(b, d)$.

Having defined the GNP above, we then apply it to the unary predicate **book** and the binary predicate **read** to obtain the denotation of "read the same books as" as follows:

$$(\text{THE SAME AS})_{N,2}(\textbf{book})(\textbf{read}) \qquad (19)$$

Finally, we can determine the denotation of (1) as follows:

$$\text{EACH OTHER}((\text{THE SAME AS})_{N,2}(\textbf{book})(\textbf{read}))(\text{AND}_{3,(et)t}(I_{\textbf{j}}, I_{\textbf{p}}, I_{\textbf{m}})) \qquad (20)$$

It can be shown that the expression above is true if and only if the following is true:

$$\{(\textbf{j},\textbf{p}), (\textbf{j},\textbf{m}), (\textbf{p},\textbf{j}), (\textbf{p},\textbf{m}), (\textbf{m},\textbf{j}), (\textbf{m},\textbf{p})\} \subseteq$$
$$\{(x,y) : \textbf{book}' \cap \{w : \textbf{read}(x,w) = 1\} = \textbf{book}' \cap \{w : \textbf{read}(y,w) = 1\}\} \,(21)$$

The expression above means that any two (different) individuals among John, Peter and Mary are such that the books that one read are the same as the books that the other read, which is exactly what (1) means.

Note that the expression above treats "the same" as having an exhaustive meaning, i.e. (1) is true if and only if the books John read, the books Peter read and the books Mary read are exactly the same, no more and no less. This is in line with the treatments adopted by a number of scholars including [7,9,12,17,20], etc., but is different from [3], which adopts a non-exhaustive treatment under which (1) would be true if there are some books that John, Peter and Mary all read, and it is possible that any one of them might have read some other books that the other have not read. As pointed out by [3,12]'s non-exhaustive treatment is incorrect. An evidence for the incorrectness is provided by the following contradictory sentence given in [20]:

*Leo and Lea read the same books and
Leo, but not Lea, read in addition *Exciting Humor*. \qquad (22)

If [3]'s non-exhaustive treatment were correct, then the first clause above would not rule out the possibility that Leo read some books that Lea did not read, and the sentence above would not be contradictory.

The internal reading of sentences containing the other reciprocal items can also be treated analogously. More specifically, I propose that all these items (each with a suitable preposition) should be treated as type $\langle 1, 2 : 2 \rangle$ GNPs. For example, "separate ... from" is denoted by the following GNP:

$$(\text{SEPARATE FROM})_{N,2} = \lambda P_{et} \lambda R_{e^2 t} \lambda (x_e, y_e)[\textbf{separate}$$
$$(P' \cap (I_x)\text{nom}(R)', P' \cap (I_y)\text{nom}(R)')] \qquad (23)$$

A justification for this treatment is that (SEPARATE FROM)$_{N,2}$ also satisfies the aforesaid modified version of D1AI. The only difference between (18) and (23) is that while SAME is a logical term with a denotation independent of models, **separate** is a non-logical term whose denotation is dependent on models, i.e. **separate**(S, T) is true in a particular model if and only if S and T are singletons and the unique members in these two singletons are separate entities in that model.

Based on the above, the denotation of sentence (4) given in Sect. 1 can be determined as follows:

$$\text{EACH OTHER}((\text{SEPARATE FROM})_{N,2}(\textbf{floor})(\textbf{live on}))(\text{AND}_{3,(et)t}(I_\textbf{j}, I_\textbf{p}, I_\textbf{m})) \tag{24}$$

It can be shown that the expression above is true if and only if the following is true:

$$\{(\textbf{j}, \textbf{p}), (\textbf{j}, \textbf{m}), (\textbf{p}, \textbf{j}), (\textbf{p}, \textbf{m}), (\textbf{m}, \textbf{j}), (\textbf{m}, \textbf{p})\} \subseteq \{(x, y) : \textbf{separate}$$
$$(\textbf{floor}' \cap \{w : \textbf{live on}(x, w) = 1\}, \textbf{floor}' \cap \{w : \textbf{live on}(y, w) = 1\})\} \tag{25}$$

The expression above means that any two of John, Peter and Mary are such that the floor on which one lives is separate from the floor on which the other lives, which is exactly what (4) means.

The remaining reciprocal items can also be treated in an analogous way. Thus, in addition to (THE SAME AS)$_{N,2}$ and (SEPARATE FROM)$_{N,2}$, we also have (DIFFERENT THAN)$_{N,2}$, (OPPOSITE TO)$_{N,2}$, (SIMILAR TO)$_{N,2}$, (ADJACENT TO)$_{N,2}$, (COMPLEMENTARY TO)$_{N,2}$, (CONNECTED WITH)$_{N,2}$, (DISJOINT FROM)$_{N,2}$, etc., which can all be shown to satisfy the modified version of D1AI. In this way, we have greatly expanded the inventory of type $\langle 1, 2 : 2 \rangle$ GNPs first studied in [18].

In the basic framework introduced above, I have been explicitly using the GNP EACH OTHER in the denotation of the sentences discussed above. However, the surface syntactic structure of (1), for instance, does not contain "each other". To further refine the framework to make it more in line with the surface syntactic structure, I propose to introduce a new GNP defined as follows:

$$(\text{INTERNAL THE SAME})_{N,2}$$
$$= \lambda P_{et}\lambda R_{e^2t}\lambda Q_{(et)t}[\text{EACH OTHER}((\text{THE SAME AS})_{N,2}(P)(R))(Q)]$$
$$= \lambda P_{et}\lambda R_{e^2t}\lambda Q_{(et)t}[\exists X \in \text{Wit}(Q)[|X| \geq 2 \wedge X^2 - Id_X^2 \subseteq$$
$$\{(x, y) : P' \cap \{w : R(x, w) = 1\} = P' \cap \{w : R(y, w) = 1\}\}]] \tag{26}$$

This new GNP is of type $\langle 1, 2 : \langle 1 \rangle \rangle$. By using this new GNP, we can now write down the denotation of (1) as follows:

$$(\text{INTERNAL THE SAME})_{N,2}(\textbf{book})(\textbf{read})(\text{AND}_{3,(et)t}(I_\textbf{j}, I_\textbf{p}, I_\textbf{m})) \tag{27}$$

Note that this expression does not contain EACH OTHER explicitly, which is in line with the surface syntactic structure of (1). Moreover, one can show that by applying the denotation of this new GNP given in (26) to the expression above, we obtain (21), which is the correct truth condition of (1).

In an analogous way, we may also introduce other type $\langle 1, 2 : \langle 1 \rangle \rangle$ GNPs such as (INTERNAL SEPARATE)$_{N,2}$, (INTERNAL DIFFERENT)$_{N,2}$, etc. In this way, we can denote sentences with internal reading by using GNPs carrying a reciprocal meaning without using the GNP EACH OTHER explicitly. For example, the denotation of (4) can now be written as

$$\text{(INTERNAL SEPARATE)}_{N,2}(\textbf{floor})(\textbf{live on})(\text{AND}_{3,(et)t}(I_{\textbf{j}}, I_{\textbf{p}}, I_{\textbf{m}})) \qquad (28)$$

4   Further Refinements of the Framework

In this section, I will further refine the basic framework formulated in the previous section to handle several cases that are different from those discussed above in one way or another.

4.1   Reciprocal Items in Non-Object Positions

The first case concerns reciprocal items appearing in non-object positions such as the following:

$$\text{The same universities admitted John, Peter and Mary.} \qquad (29)$$

in which "the same" appears in the 1st argument (i.e. subject) position of the verb "admitted". To handle this sentence, we can change the GNP (THE SAME AS)$_{N,2}$ given in (18) to (THE SAME AS)$_{N,1}$ where the subscript 1 represents the fact that "the same" appears in the 1st argument position. To define (THE SAME AS)$_{N,1}$, we only need to change (I_x)nom and (I_y)nom in (18) to (I_x)acc and (I_y)acc, respectively. Moreover, we also need to change (INTERNAL THE SAME)$_{N,2}$ given in (26) to (INTERNAL THE SAME)$_{N,1}$, with the following definition:

$$\text{(INTERNAL THE SAME)}_{N,1}$$
$$= \lambda P_{et} \lambda R_{e^2t} \lambda Q_{(et)t}[\text{EACH OTHER}((\text{THE SAME AS})_{N,1}(P)(R))(Q)]$$
$$= \lambda P_{et} \lambda R_{e^2t} \lambda Q_{(et)t}[\exists X \in \text{Wit}(Q)[|X| \geq 2 \wedge X^2 - Id_X^2 \subseteq$$
$$\{(x,y) : P' \cap \{w : R(w,x) = 1\} = P' \cap \{w : R(w,y) = 1\}\}]] \qquad (30)$$

With this GNP, we can write down the denotation of (29) as follows:

$$\text{(INTERNAL THE SAME)}_{N,1}(\textbf{university})(\textbf{admit})(\text{AND}_{3,(et)t}(I_{\textbf{j}}, I_{\textbf{p}}, I_{\textbf{m}})) \qquad (31)$$

It can be shown that the expression above is true if and only if the following is true:

$$\{(\mathbf{j}, \mathbf{p}), (\mathbf{j}, \mathbf{m}), (\mathbf{p}, \mathbf{j}), (\mathbf{p}, \mathbf{m}), (\mathbf{m}, \mathbf{j}), (\mathbf{m}, \mathbf{p})\}$$
$$\subseteq \{(x, y) : \mathbf{university}' \cap \{w : \mathbf{admit}(w, x) = 1\}$$
$$= \mathbf{university}' \cap \{w : \mathbf{admit}(w, y) = 1\}\} \tag{32}$$

The expression above is true if and only if any two of John, Peter and Mary are such that the universities that admitted one are the same as the universities that admitted the other, which is exactly what (29) means. Sentences in which the reciprocal items appear in other syntactic positions, such as the indirect object position of a ternary predicate, can be treated in an analogous manner.

4.2   Conjoined Phrases Containing Reciprocal Items

The second case concerns conjoined phrases containing reciprocal items such as the following:

John, Peter and Mary borrowed the same books and bought different magazines.
$$\tag{33}$$
with two phrases "borrowed the same books" and "bought different magazines" each containing a different reciprocal item conjoined. According to [1], there is a weak and a strong versions of "different" with the following denotations (where the subscript "w" and "s" stand for "weak" and "strong", respectively), i.e.

$$\text{DIFFERENT}_w = \lambda(S, T)[S \neq T] \tag{34}$$

$$\text{DIFFERENT}_s = \lambda(S, T)[S \cap T = \emptyset] \tag{35}$$

One may choose whichever version that fits the meaning of a particular sentence. In what follows, I arbitrarily choose the strong version. To handle (33), we have to use an appropriate version of the polymorphic $\text{AND}_{n,\tau}$ to conjoin the appropriate expressions. In this case, we can introduce the following GNP:

$(\text{INTERNAL THE SAME AND DIFFERENT}_s)_{N,2}$
$= \lambda((P_1)_{et}, (P_2)_{et})\lambda((R_1)_{e^2t}, (R_2)_{e^2t})\lambda Q_{(et)t}[\text{EACH OTHER}$
$\quad (\text{AND}_{2,e^2t}((\text{THE SAME AS})_{N,2}(P_1)(R_1), (\text{DIFFERENT}_s \text{ THAN})_{N,2}(P_2)(R_2)))(Q)]$
$= \lambda((P_1)_{et}, (P_2)_{et})\lambda((R_1)_{e^2t}, (R_2)_{e^2t})\lambda Q_{(et)t}[\exists X \in \text{Wit}(Q)[|X| \geq 2$
$\quad \wedge X^2 - Id_X^2 \subseteq \{(x, y) : P_1' \cap \{w : R_1(x, w) = 1\} = P_1' \cap \{w : R_1(y, w) = 1\}$
$\quad \wedge P_2' \cap \{w : R_2(x, w) = 1\} \cap \{w : R_2(y, w) = 1\} = \emptyset\}]] \tag{36}$

The above is a type $\langle 1^2, 2^2 : \langle 1 \rangle\rangle$ GNP because it requires an orderer pair of unary predicates P_1, P_2 and an orderer pair of binary predicates R_1,

R_2 as inputs and outputs a characteristic function of type $\langle 1 \rangle$ GQs. Note that in the expression above, I use AND_{2,e^2t} to conjoin two binary predicates $(\text{THE SAME AS})_{N,2}(P_1)(R_1)$ and $(\text{DIFFERENT}_s \text{ THAN})_{N,2}(P_2)(R_2)$[3]. This reflects the fact that what the conjunction "and" conjoins in (33) are the two verb phrases "borrowed the same books" and "bought different magazines", not just the reciprocal items "the same" and "different". With the GNP above, we can write down the denotation of (33) as follows:

$$(\text{INTERNAL THE SAME AND DIFFERENT}_s)_{N,2}(\textbf{book}, \textbf{magazine})$$
$$(\textbf{borrow}, \textbf{buy})(\text{AND}_{3,(et)t}(I_{\textbf{j}}, I_{\textbf{p}}, I_{\textbf{m}})) \tag{37}$$

It can be shown that the expression above is true if and only if the following is true:

$$\{(\textbf{j}, \textbf{p}), (\textbf{j}, \textbf{m}), (\textbf{p}, \textbf{j}), (\textbf{p}, \textbf{m}), (\textbf{m}, \textbf{j}), (\textbf{m}, \textbf{p})\} \subseteq \{(x, y) :$$
$$\textbf{book}' \cap \{w : \textbf{borrow}(x, w) = 1\} = \textbf{book}' \cap \{w : \textbf{borrow}(y, w) = 1\}$$
$$\wedge \ \textbf{magazine}' \cap \{w : \textbf{buy}(x, w) = 1\} \cap \{w : \textbf{buy}(y, w) = 1\} = \emptyset\} \tag{38}$$

The expression above means that any two of John, Peter and Mary are such that the books that one borrowed are the same as the books that the other borrowed, and the magazines that one bought are completely different from the magazines that the other bought, which is exactly what (33) means under a strong sense of "different". Sentences with conjoined phrases containing other reciprocal items can be treated in an analogous manner.

4.3 Downward Monotonic and Non-monotonic GQs

The third case concerns downward monotonic and non-monotonic type $\langle 1 \rangle$ GQs, such as the following:

Fewer than 3 persons read the same books. (39)

The denotation of EACH OTHER introduced in (13) is only applicable to cases where Q is upward monotonic such as $\text{AND}_{3,(et)t}(I_{\textbf{j}}, I_{\textbf{p}}, I_{\textbf{m}})$, AT LEAST 3 (**person**), etc. When Q is downward monotonic or non-monotonic, (13) is not adequate. For the definitions of upward monotonic, downward monotonic and non-monotonic GQs, please refer to the standard GQT literature such as [10]. To obtain the denotation applicable to all type $\langle 1 \rangle$ GQs, I propose to borrow ideas from [2] and modify (13) as follows:

$$\text{EACH OTHER}^{\#} = \lambda R_{e^2t} \lambda Q_{(et)t} \ [(\exists X \in \text{Wit}(Q)[|X| \geq 2 \wedge X^2 - Id_X^2 \subseteq R']$$
$$\vee \ \text{Top}(Q) \cap S = \emptyset) \ \wedge \ S \in Q'] \tag{40}$$

---

[3] Under the e-t notation, a binary predicate is of type e^2t.

where S is the following set denoting "individuals that enter into a mutual R relation":

$$S = \{z : \exists X [z \in X \wedge |X| \geq 2 \wedge X^2 - Id_X^2 \subseteq R']\} \qquad (41)$$

In (40), the first conjunct ($\exists X \cdots = \emptyset$) corresponds to the "witness operator" discussed in [2]. Within this conjunct, the disjunct $\exists X \cdots \subseteq R']$ is to specify the witness set whereas the disjunct $\text{Top}(Q) \cap S = \emptyset$ is to handle cases that do not require a witness set. The second conjunct $S \in Q'$ corresponds to the "counting operator" discussed in [2] and is used to count the number of individuals that enter into a mutual R relation.

The relation between (13) and (40) is given in the following proposition.

Proposition 1. *Let Q be a non-tautological upward monotonic type $\langle 1 \rangle$ GQ. Then for any binary predicate R,* EACH OTHER$(R)(Q)$ = 1 *iff* EACH OTHER$^{\#}(R)(Q) = 1$.

Proof. Let EACH OTHER$(R)(Q) = 1$, which is equivalent to $\exists X \in \text{Wit}(Q)[|X| \geq 2 \wedge X^2 - Id_X^2 \subseteq R']$. From this we can easily deduce the disjunction $\exists X \in \text{Wit}(Q)[|X| \geq 2 \wedge X^2 - Id_X^2 \subseteq R'] \vee \text{Top}(Q) \cap S = \emptyset$. Next I show that this set X satisfies $X \subseteq S$. Let $z \in X$, then it is obvious that there is an X such that $z \in X \wedge |X| \geq 2 \wedge X^2 - Id_X^2 \subseteq R'$, and so according to the definition of S, we have $z \in S$. It thus follows that $X \subseteq S$. Now from the fact that $X \in \text{Wit}(Q)$ and the definition of witness sets, we have $X \in Q'$. But then by the upward monotonicity of Q, we also have $S \in Q'$. Thus, I have shown that $(\exists X \in \text{Wit}(Q)[|X| \geq 2 \wedge X^2 - Id_X^2 \subseteq R'] \vee \text{Top}(Q) \cap S = \emptyset) \wedge S \in Q'$, which is equivalent to EACH OTHER$^{\#}(R)(Q) = 1$.

Let EACH OTHER$^{\#}(R)(Q) = 1$. Then we have $S \in Q'$ and the disjunction $\exists X \in \text{Wit}(Q)[|X| \geq 2 \wedge X^2 - Id_X^2 \subseteq R'] \vee \text{Top}(Q) \cap S = \emptyset$ both true. Suppose by way of contradiction, $\text{Top}(Q) \cap S = \emptyset$. According to the definition of topic sets, we have $\text{Top}(Q) \in \text{Li}(Q)$. So from $S \in Q'$ and the definition of live-on sets, we can deduce $S \cap \text{Top}(Q) \in Q'$, which is equivalent to $\emptyset \in Q'$. But then by the upward monotonicity of Q, we have $X \in Q'$ for any subset X of the domain of discourse, and so Q is tautological, contrary to assumption. It thus follows that $\text{Top}(Q) \cap S \neq \emptyset$, and so the disjunction $\exists X \in \text{Wit}(Q)[|X| \geq 2 \wedge X^2 - Id_X^2 \subseteq R'] \vee \text{Top}(Q) \cap S = \emptyset$ reduces to $\exists X \in \text{Wit}(Q)[|X| \geq 2 \wedge X^2 - Id_X^2 \subseteq R']$, which is equivalent to EACH OTHER$(R)(Q) = 1$. $\qquad\square$

The proposition above shows that when Q is non-tautological upward monotonic, then (40) reduces to (13) and so it is more convenient and justifiable to use the simpler expression given in (13) to denote "each other" when Q is non-tautological upward monotonic, just as we did above.

We can now write down the denotation of (39) as follows:

$$\text{(INTERNAL THE SAME)}_{N,2}(\textbf{book})(\text{FEWER THAN 3}(\textbf{person})) \qquad (42)$$

where the definition of (INTERNAL THE SAME)$_{N,2}$ given in (26) has to be modified as follows:

(INTERNAL THE SAME)$_{N,2}$

$$= \lambda P_{et}\lambda R_{e^2t}\lambda Q_{(et)t}[\text{EACH OTHER}^{\#}((\text{THE SAME AS})_{N,2}(P)(R))(Q)] \quad (43)$$

It can be shown that (42) is true if and only if the following is true[4]:

$$(\exists X \in \text{Wit}(\text{FEWER THAN 3}(\mathbf{person})))[|X| \geq 2 \wedge X^2 - Id_X^2 \subseteq$$
$$\{(x,y) : \mathbf{book}' \cap \{w : \mathbf{read}(x,w) = 1\} = \mathbf{book}' \cap \{w : \mathbf{read}(y,w) = 1\}\}]$$
$$\vee \, \mathbf{person}' \cap S = \emptyset) \wedge |\mathbf{person}' \cap S| < 3 \quad\quad (44)$$

where S is the following set denoting "individuals who read the same books":

$$S = \{z : \exists X[z \in X \wedge |X| \geq 2 \wedge X^2 - Id_X^2 \subseteq \{(x,y) :$$
$$\mathbf{book}' \cap \{w : \mathbf{read}(x,w) = 1\} = \mathbf{book}' \cap \{w : \mathbf{read}(y,w) = 1\}\}]\} \quad (45)$$

The first conjunct of (44), namely $(\exists X \cdots = \emptyset)$, consists of two disjuncts because (39) can be true in two possible ways and are thus represented by two different disjuncts. The first way is that there is a specific group (i.e. a witness set) consisting of fewer than 3 persons reading the same books, and this is represented by the disjunct $\exists X \cdots = 1\}\}]$. The second way is that no person read the same books, and this is represented by the disjunct $\mathbf{person}' \cap S = \emptyset$. The second conjunct of (44), namely $|\mathbf{person}' \cap S| < 3$, counts the number of people reading the same books. Thus, (44) gives us the correct truth condition of (39). Sentences with other downward monotonic or non-monotonic type $\langle 1 \rangle$ GQs can be treated in an analogous manner.

4.4 Weaker Reciprocal Meaning

The fourth case concerns sentences with a weaker reciprocal meaning such as the following:

John, Peter and Mary live in adjacent buildings. (46)

Using the framework developed so far, one may think that we can denote this sentence using a type $\langle 1, 2 : \langle 1 \rangle \rangle$ GNP (INTERNAL ADJACENT)$_{N,2}$ with definition similar to (43) that contains the GNP EACH OTHER$^{\#}$. However, the use of EACH OTHER$^{\#}$ is too strong for the sentence (46). Note that three buildings normally cannot be adjacent to each other in the strongest sense of "each other" given in (40) (or (13)) above because if building A is adjacent to building B and building B is adjacent to building C, then building A cannot be adjacent to building C (unless they are arranged in a circle).

---

[4] It can be shown that Top(FEWER THAN 3(**person**)) = **person**'.

To handle the sentence above, we first define a weaker version of "each other" which is notated EACH OTHER$^+$. This GNP differs from EACH OTHER$^\#$ in that the binary predicate R' in (40) and (41) is changed to $(R' \cap X^2 - Id_X^2)^+$, which represents the transitive closure of $R' \cap X^2 - Id_X^2$, i.e. the smallest transitive relation containing $R' \cap X^2 - Id_X^2$.

We then define a type $\langle 1, 2 : \langle 1 \rangle \rangle$ GNP (INTERNAL ADJACENT)$_{N,2}$ as follows:

$$(\text{INTERNAL ADJACENT})_{N,2}$$
$$= \lambda P_{et} \lambda R_{e^2 t} \lambda Q_{(et)t} [\text{EACH OTHER}^+((\text{ADJACENT TO})_{N,2}(P)(R))(Q)] \quad (47)$$

where (ADJACENT TO)$_{N,2}$ is a type $\langle 1, 2 : 2 \rangle$ GNP whose definition is similar to (23) but contains the non-logical term **adjacent** instead of **separate**. By using this GNP, we can write down the denotation of (46) as the following expression:

$$(\text{INTERNAL ADJACENT})_{N,2}(\textbf{building})(\textbf{live in})(\text{AND}_{3,(et)t}(I_\textbf{j}, I_\textbf{p}, I_\textbf{m})) \quad (48)$$

It can be shown that the expression above is true if and only if the following is true:

$$\{(\textbf{j}, \textbf{p}), (\textbf{j}, \textbf{m}), (\textbf{p}, \textbf{j}), (\textbf{p}, \textbf{m}), (\textbf{m}, \textbf{j}), (\textbf{m}, \textbf{p})\} \subseteq (\{(x, y) : \textbf{adjacent}$$
$$(\textbf{building}' \cap \{w : \textbf{live in}(x, w) = 1\}, \textbf{building}' \cap \{w : \textbf{live in}(y, w) = 1\})\}$$
$$\cap \ \{(\textbf{j}, \textbf{p}), (\textbf{j}, \textbf{m}), (\textbf{p}, \textbf{j}), (\textbf{p}, \textbf{m}), (\textbf{m}, \textbf{j}), (\textbf{m}, \textbf{p})\})^+ \quad (49)$$

In the expression above, $\{(x, y) : \cdots (\textbf{m}, \textbf{p})\}$ represents the adjacent relation (if any) between the buildings in which John, Peter and Mary live, $(\{(x, y) : \cdots (\textbf{m}, \textbf{p})\})^+$ represents the transitive closure of this relation, which is also a relation. Now if John's building is adjacent to Peter's building, which is in turn adjacent to Mary's building, then John's building and Mary's building do not in general stand in the adjacent relation. But they do stand in the aforesaid transitive closure relation. Thus, the expression above gives us the correct truth condition of (46) and this shows that EACH OTHER$^+$ gives the correct reciprocal relation associated with "adjacent".

Apart from EACH OTHER$^+$, there are other reciprocal relations studied in [5] and [11] that are also weaker than EACH OTHER$^\#$. Like "adjacent", other reciprocal items may be associated with some of these weaker reciprocal relations. A thorough understanding of the specific reciprocal relation denoted by each reciprocal item is beyond the scope of this paper and is left for future research.

4.5   Non-NP Triggers

So far in this paper I have only considered internal reading triggered by plural NPs (including conjoined NPs and plural quantified NPs). However, as pointed out by a number of scholars including [3, 4, 12, 17, 20] etc., the internal reading can also be triggered by other plural syntactic categories, as exemplified by the following sentences:

$$\text{The same boys scolded, chased and beat John.} \qquad (50)$$

$$\text{John ate different food in the morning, afternoon and evening.} \qquad (51)$$

In (50), the trigger is the conjoined verbs "scolded, chased and beat". To handle this case, we can make use of the notion of raised VP briefly introduced in Sect. 2. According to [22], from each VP of type et, one may derive a raised VP of type $((et)t)t$. For (50), we first write down the denotation of the VP "scolded John" as $(I_\mathbf{j})_{\text{acc}}(\mathbf{scold})$. For convenience, hereinafter I use $\mathbf{sj}$ (representing "scolded John") as the short form of this unary predicate. From $\mathbf{sj}$ of type et, we can derive a raised VP of type $((et)t)t$ with the following denotation[5]:

$$I_\mathbf{sj} = \lambda Q_{(et)t}[Q(\mathbf{sj}) = 1] \qquad (52)$$

Similar definitions can also be given to $I_\mathbf{cj}$ (for "chased John") and $I_\mathbf{bj}$ (for "beat John"). Note that the definition above is very similar to that of the Montagovian individual $I_\mathbf{j}$ given in (5), and can be seen as a "Montagovian VP". In this way, we are treating et as a basic type. Moreover, certain notions and functions associated with type $\langle 1 \rangle$ GQs can be extended to these Montagovian VPs.

First, the notions of live-on sets, topic sets and witness sets can all be extended to the Montagovian VPs. For example, by following similar steps for proving (12) given in Sect. 2, one can easily prove that

$$\text{Wit}(\text{AND}_{3,((et)t)t}(I_\mathbf{sj}, I_\mathbf{cj}, I_\mathbf{bj})) = \{\{\mathbf{sj}, \mathbf{cj}, \mathbf{bj}\}\} \qquad (53)$$

Second, the formal framework developed above for handling internal reading triggered by plural NPs can be extended to handle (50). But first we have to modify the GNP (THE SAME AS)$_{N,2}$ given in (18) to obtain the following GNP:

$$(\text{THE SAME AS})_{V,1} = \lambda P_{et}\lambda(F_{et}, G_{et})[\text{SAME}(P' \cap F', P' \cap G')] \qquad (54)$$

where the subscript V represents the fact that the internal reading is triggered by a plural verb phrase.

Furthermore, we also need to modify the GNP EACH OTHER$^\#$, because EACH OTHER$^\#$ given in (40) is of type $(e^2 t)((et)t)t$, whereas we now need a function of type $((et)^2 t)(((et)t)t)t$. But apart from this type change, the meaning of "each other" in fact has not changed. A solution to this problem is to change EACH OTHER$^\#$ to the following polymorphic function:

---

[5] According to [22], the raised VP derived from $\mathbf{sj}$ is notated $\mathbf{sj}^R$. In this paper, I use the notation $I_\mathbf{sj}$ instead to highlight the similarity between Montagovian individuals and raised VPs derived from ordinary VPs.

$$\text{EACH OTHER}^{\#} = \lambda R_{\tau^2 t} \lambda Q_{(\tau t)t}[\ldots] \tag{55}$$

where ... is the same as its corresponding part in (40). The function given above is of type $(\tau^2 t)((\tau t)t)t$, where τ is a generic type. By instantiating τ as e, we get our good old friend (40). By instantiating τ as et, we get EACH OTHER$^{\#}$ with the desired type for handling (50). Again, to make EACH OTHER$^{\#}$ implicit, we can define the following GNP:

$$\begin{aligned}
&(\text{INTERNAL THE SAME})_{V,1} \\
&= \lambda P_{et} \lambda V_{((et)t)t} [\text{EACH OTHER}^{\#}((\text{THE SAME AS})_{V,1}(P))(V)]
\end{aligned} \tag{56}$$

The denotation of (50) can now be written as follows[6]:

$$(\text{INTERNAL THE SAME})_{V,1}(\mathbf{boy})(\text{AND}_{3,((et)t)t}(I_{\mathbf{sj}}, I_{\mathbf{cj}}, I_{\mathbf{bj}})) \tag{57}$$

It can be shown that this expression is true if and only if the following is true:

$$\begin{aligned}
&\{(\mathbf{sj}, \mathbf{cj}), (\mathbf{sj}, \mathbf{bj}), (\mathbf{cj}, \mathbf{sj}), (\mathbf{cj}, \mathbf{bj}), (\mathbf{bj}, \mathbf{sj}), (\mathbf{bj}, \mathbf{cj})\} \subseteq \\
&\{(F, G) : \mathbf{boy}' \cap F' = \mathbf{boy}' \cap G'\}
\end{aligned} \tag{58}$$

The expression above means that any two actions among scolding John, chasing John and beating John are such that the boys engaged in one action are the same as the boys engaged in the other action, which is exactly what (50) means.

In (51), the trigger is the conjoined temporal adverbials "in the morning, afternoon and evening". To handle this case without making great changes to the existing framework, we can draw reference from [6] and introduce a new type i for time intervals and treat "morning", "afternoon" and "evening" as individual items of this new basic type (here I ignore the definite article "the"). We can then derive a "Montagovian interval" of type $(it)t$. For example, from $\mathbf{mo}$ (short for "morning") of type i, we have $I_{\mathbf{mo}}$ of type $(it)t$ with the following denotation:

$$I_{\mathbf{mo}} = \lambda P_{it}[P(\mathbf{mo}) = 1] \tag{59}$$

Similar definitions can also be given to $I_{\mathbf{af}}$ (for "afternoon") and $I_{\mathbf{ev}}$ (for "evening"). Moreover, the notions of live-on sets, topic sets and witness sets can all be extended to the Montagovian intervals. For example, it can be shown that

$$\text{Wit}(\text{AND}_{3,(it)t}(I_{\mathbf{mo}}, I_{\mathbf{af}}, I_{\mathbf{ev}})) = \{\{\mathbf{mo}, \mathbf{af}, \mathbf{ev}\}\} \tag{60}$$

---

[6] If one thinks that (57) is not in line with the surface syntactic structure of (50) by having 3 occurrences of $\mathbf{j}$, one can use λ-abstraction to abstract out $I_{\mathbf{j}}$ to obtain a function and then reapply the function back to I_j. In this way, we can replace $\text{AND}_{3,((et)t)t}(I_{\mathbf{sj}}, I_{\mathbf{cj}}, I_{\mathbf{bj}})$ in (57) by $\lambda Q_{(et)t}[\text{AND}_{3,((et)t)t}(Q\text{acc}(\mathbf{scold})^R, Q\text{acc}(\mathbf{chase})^R, Q\text{acc}(\mathbf{beat})^R)](I_j)$, which contains only 1 occurrence of I_j.

We also need to define the following function of type itt denoting the temporal preposition "in":

$$\textsc{in} = \lambda t_i \lambda p_t[p \text{ holds in interval } t] \tag{61}$$

To handle (51), we define the following GNP:

$$(\textsc{different}_s \textsc{ than})_{T,2}$$
$$= \lambda P_{et}\lambda Q_{(et)t}\lambda R_{e^2t}\lambda O_{itt}\lambda(s_i,t_i)[\textsc{different}_s(P' \cap \{w : O(s,\{z : R(z,w) = 1\} \in Q') = 1\},$$
$$P' \cap \{w : O(t,\{z : R(z,w) = 1\} \in Q') = 1\})] \tag{62}$$

where the subscript T represents the fact that the internal reading is triggered by a plural temporal adverbial. Furthermore, the GNP $\textsc{each other}^{\#}$ has to be of type $(i^2t)((it)t)t$. By instantiating the generic type τ as i in (55), we easily get $\textsc{each other}^{\#}$ with the desired type. We next define the following GNP:

$$(\textsc{internal different}_s)_{T,2} = \lambda P_{et}\lambda Q_{(et)t}\lambda R_{e^2t}\lambda O_{itt}\lambda T_{(it)t}$$
$$[\textsc{each other}^{\#}((\textsc{different}_s \textsc{ than})_{T,2}(P)(Q)(R)(O))(T)] \tag{63}$$

The denotation of (51) can now be written as follows:

$$(\textsc{internal different}_s)_{T,2}(\mathbf{food})(I_j)(\mathbf{eat})(\textsc{in})(\textsc{and}_{3,(it)t}(I_{\mathbf{mo}}, I_{\mathbf{af}}, I_{\mathbf{ev}})) \tag{64}$$

It can be shown that this expression is true if and only if the following is true:

$$\{(\mathbf{mo},\mathbf{af}),(\mathbf{mo},\mathbf{ev}),(\mathbf{af},\mathbf{mo}),(\mathbf{af},\mathbf{ev}),(\mathbf{ev},\mathbf{mo}),(\mathbf{ev},\mathbf{af})\} \subseteq \{(s,t) :$$
$$\mathbf{food}' \cap \{w : \textsc{in}(s,\mathbf{eat}(\mathbf{j},w) = 1)\} \cap \{w : \textsc{in}(t,\mathbf{eat}(\mathbf{j},w) = 1)\} = \emptyset\} \tag{65}$$

The expression above means that any two intervals among the morning, afternoon and evening are such that the food John ate in one interval is different from the food John ate in the other interval, which is exactly what (51) means. Sentences with other non-NP triggers can be treated in an analogous way provided that we introduce the appropriate basic types (like i in the previous case) and appropriate functions (like $\textsc{in}$ in the previous case).

5 Conclusion

In this paper, I have identified a number of reciprocal items and showed that the internal reading of sentences containing these items carries a reciprocal meaning. In view of this, I propose to denote such sentences by using the GNP $\textsc{each}$

OTHER as well as a number of type $\langle 1, 2 : 2 \rangle$ GNPs corresponding to the reciprocal items such as (THE SAME AS)$_{N,2}$. To refine the formal framework, I then define type $\langle 1, 2 : \langle 1 \rangle \rangle$ GNPs such as (INTERNAL THE SAME)$_{N,2}$ to make EACH OTHER implicit. In this way, sentences with internal reading can be denoted by expressions that are in line with the surface syntactic structures of the sentences. I then discuss how to further refine the framework by considering reciprocal items appearing in non-object positions, conjoined phrases containing reciprocal items, downward monotonic and non-monotonic quantifiers, weaker reciprocal meaning and non-NP triggers.

Apart from providing a uniform formal framework, this paper has also enriched the theory relating to GNPs by greatly expanding the inventory of type $\langle 1, 2 : 2 \rangle$ GNPs and introducing a new class of $\langle 1, 2 : \langle 1 \rangle \rangle$ GNPs (as well as GNPs involving basic types other than e). Moreover, by considering non-NP triggers, this paper has also enriched the notion of polymorphism by treating EACH OTHER[#] as a polymorphic function.

Before closing, I have to point out certain syntactic issues that this paper has not addressed[7]. The reciprocal items and "each other" are subject to different syntactic constraints in at least two respects. First, while "the same" (and other reciprocal items) can be triggered by a distributive plural NP, "each other" cannot, as illustrated by the following sentences:

$$\text{Both boys recited the same poems.} \tag{66}$$

$$\text{*Both boys hit each other.} \tag{67}$$

Second, while the reciprocal items can appear in subject position (as illustrated by (29)), "each other" cannot, as illustrated by the following sentence:

$$\text{*Each other hit the boys.} \tag{68}$$

Sentence (67) shows that "each other" is associated with collective (as opposed to distributive) plural NPs. Thus, to treat "each other" properly, we have to introduce notions associated with plurality/collective quantification such as those given in [2,14] and [16], to name just a few, and modify the denotation of EACH OTHER[#] (or EACH OTHER[+]) given above accordingly.

But then how can we explain the fact that "the same" can be associated with a distributive NP in (66) if we assume that the denotation of the GNP (INTERNAL THE SAME)$_{N,2}$ contains EACH OTHER[#]? A possible way is to add a distributivity operator into the denotation of (INTERNAL THE SAME)$_{N,2}$[8]. The syntactic difference between (66) and (67) can then be attributed to the presence/absence of this distributivity operator.

---

[7] My sincere thanks to an anonymous reviewer for pointing out the issues and inspiring the possible solutions.

[8] Note that this distributivity operator is not an *ad hoc* device since it is also used in the formal treatment of plurality/collective quantification as introduced in the relevant literature.

Similarly, the syntactic difference between (29) and (68) can be treated by adding certain syntactic/semantic elements into the denotations of EACH OTHER$^{\#}$ and/or (INTERNAL THE SAME)$_{N,1}$. The aforesaid syntactic difference can then be attributed to the presence/absence of these elements. As a thorough discussion of the treatment outlined above will involve introduction of new entities, notions and theories on top of those introduced in this paper, it will have to be left for future research.

References

1. Beghelli, F.: Structured quantifiers. In: Kanazawa, M., Piñón, C. (eds.) Dynamics, Polarity and Quantification, pp. 119–143. CSLI Publications, Stanford (1994)
2. Ben-Avi, G., Winter, Y.: Monotonicity and collective quantification. J. Logic Lang. Inform. **12**, 127–151 (2003)
3. Barker, C.: Parasitic scope. Linguist. Philos. **30**(4), 407–444 (2007)
4. Carlson, G.: Same and different: some consequences for syntax and semantics. Linguist. Philos. **10**(4), 531–565 (1987)
5. Dalrymple, M., Kanazawa, M., Kim, Y., Mchombo, S., Peters, S.: Reciprocal expressions and the concept of reciprocity. Linguist. Philos. **21**, 159–210 (1998)
6. de Swart, H.: Adverbs of Quantification: A Generalized Quantifier Approach. Garland, New York (1993)
7. Heim, I.: Notes on comparatives and related matters. Manuscript (1985)
8. Keenan, E.L.: Semantic case theory. In: Groenendijk, J., et al. (eds.) Proceedings of the Sixth Amsterdam Colloquium, pp. 109–132. ITLI, Amsterdam (1987)
9. Keenan, E.L., Westerståhl, D.: Generalized quantifiers in linguistics and logic. In: van Benthem, J., ter Meulen, A. (eds.) Handbook of Logic and Language, 2nd edn., pp. 859–910. Elsevier Science B.V., Amsterdam (2011)
10. Peters, S., Westerståhl, D.: Quantifiers in Language and Logic. Clarendon Press, Oxford (2006)
11. Sabato, S., Winter, Y.: Relational domains and the interpretation of reciprocals. Linguist. Philos. **35**, 191–241 (2012)
12. Solomon, M.: The compositional semantics of *same*. Manuscript (2012)
13. Szabolcsi, A.: Quantification. Cambridge University Press, Cambridge (2010)
14. Winter, Y.: Flexibility Principles in Boolean Semantics: The Interpretation of Coordination, Plurality and Scope in Natural Language. MIT Press, Cambridge (2001)
15. Winter, Y.: Elements of Formal Semantics: An Introduction to the Mathematical Theory of Meaning in Natural Language. Edinburgh University Press, Edinburgh (2016)
16. Winter, Y., Scha, R.: Plurals. In: Lappin, S., Fox, C. (eds.) The Handbook of Contemporary Semantic Theory, 2nd edn., pp. 77–113. Wiley, Chichester (2015)
17. Zuber, R.: Generalised quantifiers and the semantics of *the same*. In: Proceedings of SALT 21, pp. 515–531 (2011)
18. Zuber, R.: Some generalised comparative determiners. In: Pogodalla, S., Prost, J.-P. (eds.) LACL 2011. LNCS (LNAI), vol. 6736, pp. 267–281. Springer, Heidelberg (2011). https://doi.org/10.1007/978-3-642-22221-4_18
19. Zuber, R.: Reciprocals as higher order functions. In: Proceedings of the Ninth International Workshop of Logic and Engineering of Natural Language Semantics, vol. 9, pp. 118–129 (2012)

20. Zuber, R.: Set partitions and the meaning of the same. J. Logic Lang. Inform. **26**, 1–20 (2017)
21. Zuber, R.: On generalized noun phrases. In: Foret, A., Muskens, R., Pogodalla, S. (eds.) FG 2017. LNCS, vol. 10686, pp. 142–155. Springer, Heidelberg (2018). https://doi.org/10.1007/978-3-662-56343-4_9
22. Zuber, R.: On raised verb phrases. In: Guyris, B., et al. (eds.) K + K = 120: Papers Dedicated to L. Kálmán & A. Kornai on the Occasion of Their 60th Birthdays, pp. 561-582. MTA Research Institute for Linguistics, Budapest (2019)

Dot-to-Dot Semantic Representation

Alastair Butler[(⊠)][iD]

Faculty of Humanities and Social Sciences, Hirosaki University, Bunkyo-cho 1,
Hirosaki-shi 036-8560, Japan
ajb129@hirosaki-u.ac.jp

Abstract. This paper introduces dot-to-dot semantic representation as
an encoding for abstract dependency interpretations of natural language
data. The approach is illustrated with content created initially as syntactic tree annotations. This is transformed into construction information
for Discourse Representation Structures. This gives a basis for resolving event and entity dependencies across discourse for transformation to
Conjunctive Normal Forms with skolemization from which governor to
dependent relations arise for graph structures that are dot-to-dot semantic representations. Use of the representation approach is demonstrated
with two sample applications: database querying, and analysis feedback
for parsed corpus annotation of Old Japanese language data.

Keywords: semantic dependencies · discourse representation · event
semantics · scope · skolemization · database querying · parsed corpus
annotation

1 Introduction

This paper introduces dot-to-dot semantic representation. The aim is to have a
representation pitched at a level of abstraction that is informative about semantic argument dependencies and scope relations across discourse, only in a manner
that still allows for recovery of the represented language data (sentence fragment,
sentence, or discourse). The approach is demonstrated with two sample applications: database querying, and analysis feedback for parsed corpus annotation of
Old Japanese language data.

Inspired by the representations of the the SemR level of Meaning-Text Theory
[9], Abstract Meaning Representation (AMR; [1]), and many other approaches
relatable to semantic networks (see e.g., [14]), dot-to-dot semantic representations: are easily read when visualised as graphs, and are event semantic relation based to capture predicate-argument dependencies (which, as a reviewer

A. Butler—This paper benefited from helpful reviews from three anonymous reviewers
who are gratefully acknowledged. The work reported on Old Japanese is collaborative
work with Stephen Wright Horn and the ONCOJ annotation project. This research
was supported by the Japan Society for the Promotion of Science (JSPS), Research
Project Number: 22K00524 (Principal Investigator: Kei Yoshimoto).

D. Bekki et al. (Eds.): LENLS 2023, LNCS 14569, pp. 175–190, 2024.
https://doi.org/10.1007/978-3-031-60878-0_10

observes, is also compatible with a frame-based perspective like [13]). Another connection is to Polynomial Event Semantics [8], which offers a route to denotations for the representations.

Notable points of difference from SemR and AMR include: connections across discourse are captured, there is retention of scope and quantification restriction information to support Discourse Representation Structure readings of the assembled information, and there is less abstraction in the sense that information is retained for the represented language data to be recoverable.

The graph presentation information is collected as Datalog facts which in addition to forming the presentation information gives a way for storing and also querying the represented language analysis as database knowledge. The Datalog facts can be presented as a normalised rendering of analysis to allow for comparisons to be made on sorted fact differences. This is particularly useful for evaluating the performance of parsing systems that produce the language analysis.

The paper is organised as follows. Section 2 provides background and illustrative examples. Section 3 describes steps for reaching dot-to-dot semantic representations. Section 4 illustrates database query use of the analysis. Section 5 describes an annotation project using dot-to-dot semantic representations as feedback assisting analysis creation. Section 6 is a conclusion.

2   Background and Examples

Suppose there are **discourse entities** as references to things talked about in discourse (individuals, events, attributes, states, situations, propositions, etc.). Suppose language communication involves: (i) introducing discourse entities, and (ii) providing the means to integrate information about already introduced discourse entities. Part (ii) can include referring back to discourse entities after attention will have diverted to introducing and giving information about other newer discourse entities. Such a viewpoint underlies much natural language research in formal semantics, with, e.g., this discourse perspective articulated in Discourse Representation Theory [7] and related theories of Dynamic Semantics (e.g., [5] among many others).

We can think about both wider discourse and single sentences and even sentence fragments as being organised around discourse entities. We can picture information from discourse with a graph of connected nodes. Each node is a discourse entity. Connections leading to or from nodes gather the information content communicated by the analysed language data (sentence fragment, sentence, or discourse).

As an example, consider (1) with its representation of (2).

(1)   He has a story to tell.

(2)

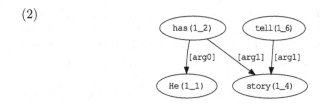

This connects four nodes, each of which is referenced to an indexed word of the analysed data. Word indexing consists of two numbers separated by an underscore character. The first number references the sentence to which the word belongs, while the second number is the position of the word in its sentence.

One node of (2) comes from the subject pronoun of (1), giving a discourse entity that references word content He(1_1) as a pronoun that remains unresolvable from the language data. Another node of (2) comes from the main verb to give a discourse entity that is an event with word content has(1_2). A connection labelled [arg0] links has(1_2) as a dependency governor to He(1_1) as its dependent. This captures the information that the He(1_1) individual is the 'have-er' of the has(1_2) event. In addition, a connection labelled [arg1] links has(1_2) to a discourse entity that is the story(1_4) individual. This captures the information that story(1_4) is what is had in the has(1_2) event. Finally, an [arg1] connection links story(1_4) and event tell(1_6) to capture that story(1_4) is content to tell for the tell(1_6) event, which has no referenced teller.

As a larger example, consider (3) and its dot-to-dot semantic representation of (4) which has seven connected nodes, including a widely scoped propositional modal operator node must(3_2) with its single [scope] dependency and an embedded every(3_9) node which is marked [quantificational] to be read as a propositional level instruction for restricted universal quantification with both [restriction] and [scope] dependencies.

(3)   He must have to tell the story to every conference attendee.

(4)

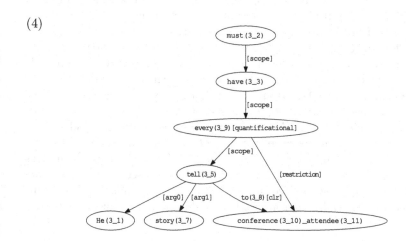

Note how the node with every(3_9) signals that conference(3_10)_attendee (3_11) is the content of the [restriction] and so can be read to gain universal quantification and be accessible to the scope of the quantification, which is seen in (4) by its contributing the to(3_8)[clr] role of tell(3_5), where tell(3_5) is the [scope] dependent and so, under a Discourse Representation Structure reading of the represented information, will be under existential quantification within the nuclear scope of the universal quantification from every(3_9).

The [clr] marking signals that the meaning of to(3_8) is closely related to the meaning of tell(3_5). With reference to a suitable predicate-argument thesaurus resource such as PropBank [2] or the Oxford Advanced Learner dictionary [4], this is information that the dependent is the indirect object.

We can also consider (1) and (3) as sentences forming a discourse which is represented with the graph of (5).

(5)

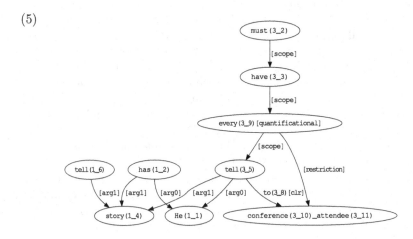

The nodes of (5) have the same sentence references (word indicies) as seen with the graphs of (2) and (4) except there is anaphoric resolution, with the He(3_1) and story(3_7) connections for tell(3_5) in (4) replaced in (5) by connections to He(1_1) (itself remaining an unresolved pronoun) and story(1_4).

The resolution of (5) has the consequence that the He(3_1) and story(3_7) connections for tell(3_5) are outside the path of scope from the must(3_2) operator and every(3_9) quantification. That is, He(3_1) and story(3_7) should be interpreted as occuring at a discourse level of existential closure, since they also link as dependencies for tell(1_6) and has(1_2) that are unreachable by following dependency paths from must(3_2) and every(3_9).

The sentence references of (5) reveal that resolved pronouns and definite descriptions have a graph presence in terms of bringing about connections to independently introduced nodes, rather than contributing nodes themselves. This is a choice of representation, as a graph with articulated nodes as intermediate connections could be adopted instead, as in [15]. The choice of direct links from resolution is especially appropriate for the database query use discussed in Sect. 4 below.

Next, consider the representation of (6) as the graph of (7).

(6)   If a farmer owns a donkey, he beats it.

(7)

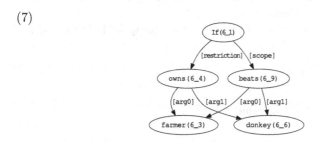

Assuming unselective universal quantification for the restriction of If(6_1) makes the discourse entities with paths leading from the [restriction] dependent (owns(6_4), farmer(6_3) and donkey(6_6)) unselectively bound with universal force, and then accessible as arguments for beats(6_9), which itself can be read as an existentially quantified event by being the [scope] dependent.

Next, consider the representation of (8) as the graph of (9).

(8)   Every farmer who owns a donkey and owns a horse beats the donkey and gives the horse carrots.

(9)

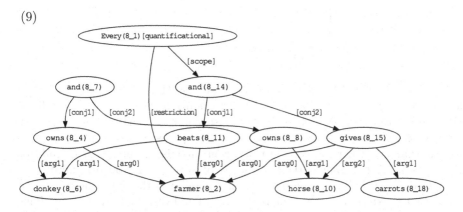

We need to capture nodes connecting with the [restriction] dependent from Every(8_1). We can do this by assuming that in addition to nodes with paths *from* the node that is linked as the [restriction] dependent (as seen with owns(6_4), farmer(6_3) and donkey(6_6) of (7)), nodes are also part of a restriction when they:

(i) have a path *to* the node that is linked as the [restriction] dependent while not having a path *from* the node that is linked as the [scope] dependent
(ii) have a path *from* a node that satisfies condition (i)

With condition (i), the discourse entities of and(8_7), owns(8_4) and owns(8_8) are found to be within the restriction of Every(8_1). With condition (ii), donkey(8_6) and horse(8_10) are found to be within the restriction of Every(8_1). In contrast, and(8_14), beats(8_11), gives(8_15) and carrots(8_18) can only be in the scope of Every(8_1).

Next, consider the representation of the discourse comprised of (10) and (11) as the graph of (12).

(10)   There was a wild donkey.

(11)   Every farmer who tried to tame it beat it.

(12)

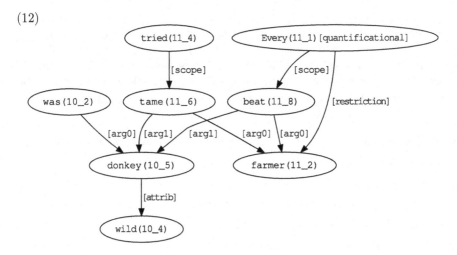

For the graph of (12), the discourse entities tame(11_6) and tried(11_4) count as part of the restriction of Every(11_1) by condition (i) above, so by condition (ii) above donkey(10_5) and wild(10_4) also count as part of the restriction. And yet donkey(10_5) and wild(10_4) also have paths from was(10_2) which is a node that is neither part of the restriction—it fails to meet either condition (i) or condition (ii)—nor part of the scope of Every(11_1). Such a link from a node that is external to scope paths is only possibly if the linked node also has scope that is external to the scope paths. We should therefore say that satisfying either condition (i) or (ii) above is information for being in the restriction of some quantification provided the node is not also linked from a node that fails to meet conditions (i) and (ii) and is also outside the scope path of the quantification.

3   Steps for Deriving the Analysis

This section sketches how the dot-to-dot semantic representation of (5) above is constructed. We start from syntactic tree annotations for the language data, as in (13).

(13)
```
/w_0001_0001/He/     (IP-MAT (NP-SBJ;{PERSON} (PRO w_0001_0001))
/w_0001_0002/has/            (HVP;~Tn w_0001_0002)
/w_0001_0003/a/              (NP-OB1;{STORY} (D w_0001_0003)
/w_0001_0004/story/                  (N w_0001_0004)
/w_0001_0005/to/            (IP-INF-REL (TO w_0001_0005)
/w_0001_0006/tell/                  (VB;~Tn w_0001_0006)
                                    (NP-OB1 *T*)))
/w_0001_0007/./       (PUNC w_0001_0007))
/w_0003_0001/He/     (IP-MAT (NP-SBJ;{PERSON} (PRO w_0003_0001))
/w_0003_0002/must/           (MD w_0003_0002)
/w_0003_0003/have/           (HV;~cat_Vt w_0003_0003)
/w_0003_0004/to/            (IP-INF-CAT (TO w_0003_0004)
/w_0003_0005/tell/                  (VB;~Tn.pr w_0003_0005)
/w_0003_0006/the/                   (NP-OB1;{STORY} (D w_0003_0006)
/w_0003_0007/story/                         (N w_0003_0007))
/w_0003_0008/to/                    (PP-CLR (P-ROLE w_0003_0008)
/w_0003_0009/every/                         (NP (Q w_0003_0009)
/w_0003_0010/conference/                        (N w_0003_0010)
/w_0003_0011/attendee/                          (N w_0003_0011))))
/w_0003_0012/./       (PUNC w_0003_0012))
```

The annotation of (13) follows the Treebank Semantics Parsed Corpus guidelines [3]. This style of analysis has projections of word class (PRO = pronoun, VB = infinitive verb, etc.) from base word references, and then further projections of function marked phrase and clause structure (IP-MAT=matrix clause, NP-SBJ = subject noun phrase, etc.).

The annotation of (13) is automatically converted into the TPTP formula of (14) which is a Discourse Representation Structure over an event semantics based information encoding, with bound variables (STATEX7, PERSONX6, STORYX8, etc.) acting as discourse referents. Constants can also act as discourse referents, which is notably the case with r_0001_0001__He in (14) referencing the instance of unresolvable *He* from (1) above.

(14)
```
fof(id__1_ex__3_ex,axiom,
    ? [STATEX7,PERSONX6,STORYX8,OPERATORX12,EVENTX13,QUANTX10,
       EVENTX11,EVENTX5,EVENTX4,ENTITYX9,STORYX1] :
    ( STATEX7 = QUANTX10
    & isA(QUANTX10,r_0003_0009__every_quantificational)
    & restriction(QUANTX10) = ENTITYX9
    & isA(ENTITYX9,r_0003_0010__conference_attendee)
    & scope(QUANTX10) = EVENTX11
    & isA(EVENTX11,r_0003_0005__tell)
    & arg0(EVENTX11) = PERSONX6
    & arg1(EVENTX11) = STORYX8
    & r_0003_0008__to_clr(EVENTX11) = ENTITYX9
    & isA(EVENTX4,r_0001_0006__tell)
    & arg1(EVENTX4) = STORYX1
    & isA(STORYX1,r_0001_0004__story)
    & PERSONX6 = r_0001_0001__He
    & STORYX8 = STORYX1
    & isA(EVENTX5,r_0001_0002__has)
    & arg0(EVENTX5) = r_0001_0001__He
    & arg1(EVENTX5) = STORYX1
    & isA(OPERATORX12,r_0003_0002__must)
    & scope(OPERATORX12) = EVENTX13
    & isA(EVENTX13,r_0003_0003__have)
    & scope(EVENTX13) = STATEX7 ) ).
```

The formula (14) is converted by the FLOTTER utility [11] into the Clause Normal Form (CNF) encoding of (15). FLOTTER implements the Optimized Skolemization of [12] and Strong Skolemization of [10].

(15)   ```
list_of_clauses(axioms, cnf).
   clause(|| -> isA(skc4,r_0001_0002__has),1).
   clause(|| -> isA(skc3,r_0001_0006__tell),2).
   clause(|| -> isA(skc5,r_0003_0002__must),3).
   clause(|| -> equal(arg0(skc4),r_0001_0001__He),4).
   clause(|| -> isA(arg1(skc3),r_0001_0004__story),5).
   clause(|| -> isA(scope(skc5),r_0003_0003__have),6).
   clause(|| -> isA(scope(scope(skc5)),r_0003_0009__every_quantificational),7).
   clause(|| -> equal(arg1(skc3),arg1(skc4)),8).
   clause(|| -> isA(restriction(scope(scope(skc5))),r_0003_0010__conference_attendee),9).
   clause(|| -> isA(scope(scope(scope(skc5))),r_0003_0005__tell),10).
   clause(|| -> equal(arg0(scope(scope(scope(skc5)))),r_0001_0001__He),11).
   clause(|| -> equal(arg1(scope(scope(scope(skc5)))),arg1(skc3)),12).
   clause(|| -> equal(r_0003_0008__to_clr(scope(scope(scope(skc5)))),
                       restriction(scope(scope(skc5)))),13).
end_of_list.
```

The CNF (15) is revealing of the dependency structure of the discourse. Thus, unembedded items (typically verbs) are associated with skolem constants (clauses 1, 2 and 3) while arguments for verbs are connected with their skolem constants under function symbols that are semantic roles (arg0, arg1, etc.). Note how clause 10 of (15) has the verb *tell* embedded as a scope(scope(scope(skc5)) dependent for *must* of skc5. This verb in turn has its arguments linked with a further layer of function symbol embedding (as seen with arg0(scope(scope(scope(skc5)))) of clause 11, arg1(scope(scope(scope(skc5)))) of clause 12, and r_0003_0008__to_clr(scope(scope(scope(skc5)))) of clause 13).

Taking the content of (15) as a series of Prolog facts and assuming the equal relation is reflexive, symmetric and transitive, we can extract dependencies as Datalog facts with the find_arc rules of (16), with G as a governor of dependent X under relation R.

(16)    ```
find_arc(arc(G,X,R)) :-
    equal(S,X), atom(X), S =.. [R,E], isA(E,G), atom(G).
find_arc(arc(G,X,R)) :-
    isA(S1,X), atom(X), equal(S,S1), S =.. [R,E], isA(E,G), atom(G).
```

The first rule of (16) will find the dependencies of (17). These are dependencies that involve a governor (G) found as content for an isA relation related to a skolem term that is under a semantic role function symbol as the relation (R) and that is equal to a constant that is the dependent (X).

(17)   ```
arc(r_0001_0002__has,r_0001_0001__He,arg0).
arc(r_0003_0005__tell,r_0001_0001__He,arg0).
```

The second rule of (16) will find the dependencies of (18). These are dependencies that involve a governor (G) found as content for an isA relation related to a skolem term that is under a semantic role function as the relation (R) and
```

that is equal to a skolem term that is in an isA relation with content that is the dependent (X).

(18)
```
arc(r_0001_0002__has,r_0001_0004__story,arg1).
arc(r_0001_0006__tell,r_0001_0004__story,arg1).
arc(r_0003_0002__must,r_0003_0003__have,scope).
arc(r_0003_0003__have,r_0003_0009__every_quantificational,scope).
arc(r_0003_0005__tell,r_0001_0004__story,arg1).
arc(r_0003_0005__tell,r_0003_0010__conference_attendee,r_0003_0008__to_clr).
arc(r_0003_0009__every_quantificational,r_0003_0005__tell,scope).
arc(r_0003_0009__every_quantificational,r_0003_0010__conference_attendee,restriction).
```

The information now gathered with the Datalog facts of (17) and (18) is the information for presenting the graph of (5) above.

Such Datalog facts also allow collections of analysis that can be presented sentence by sentence as groupings of dependency declarations, with an ordering that follows the word order of the source language data input. Exact order can follow from ordering the governors, and if a governor has multiple dependents, then from a subsequent ordering of those dependents, and if the pairing of a governor with dependent were to have multiple relation names, then from a subsequent ordering of those relation names. This sorting of results can be used for analysis performance evaluation, with matching facts as a score, and visualisations of line differences as a way to explore individual differences.

4   An Application: Querying the Text Based Encoding

This section will demonstrate how the arc Datalog facts of (17) and (18) above can be used for database querying. Each arc fact has as arguments: a governor discourse entity, a dependent discourse entity, and the name of the connection from the governor to the dependent.

Governors, dependents, and relation names are each atom values made up of optionally multiple role/function information followed by optionally multiple word information. Word information can be for the source sentence that has given rise to the fact or from prior sentences of the source language data in the case of discourse entities that result from anaphoric resolutions.

As an example of how to assemble query results from the dependency Datalog facts, consider the Prolog program of (19)–(21). The routine of (19) takes an atom value S and finds all discourse entities for which S is a sub atom and which are dependents of an arc fact, storing all found arc facts with list L1. L1 is then further grown with calls to find_governor_facts and find_dependent_facts. Finally, found facts are made unique with sort and printed as terminal output.

(19)
```
search_entity(S) :-
    setof(arc(A,B,C),(arc(A,B,C),sub_atom(B, _, _, _, S)),L1),
    find_governor_facts(L1,L1,L2),
    find_dependent_facts(L2,L2,L3),
    sort(L3,L),
    print_fact(L).
print_fact([]).
print_fact([H|T]) :- write(H), write('.'), nl, print_fact(T).
```

The `find_governor_facts` routine of (20) adds to the collection of facts all other facts where the governor of a collected fact is also the governor.

(20)
```
find_governor_facts([],L,L).
find_governor_facts([arc(A,_,_)|T],L0,L) :-
    setof(arc(A,B,C),arc(A,B,C),L1),
    append(L0,L1,L2),
    find_governor_facts(T,L2,L).
```

The `find_dependent_facts` routine of (21) recursively adds to the collection of facts all other facts where the dependent of a collected fact is the governor.

(21)
```
find_dependent_facts([],L,L).
find_dependent_facts([arc(_,A,_)|T],L0,L) :-
    setof(arc(A,B,C),arc(A,B,C),L1),
    !,
    append(L0,L1,L2),
    find_dependent_facts(L1,L2,L3),
    find_dependent_facts(T,L3,L).
find_dependent_facts([_|T],L0,L) :-
    find_dependent_facts(T,L0,L).
```

Suppose `data` is a compiled version of the `arc` facts of (17) and (18) and the Prolog program of (19)–(21) to which we can pipe queries. (22) illustrates a command line query to find facts related to any instance in the database of an unresolved `He` pronoun.

(22)
```
$ echo "search_entity('He')." | ./data
arc(r_0001_0002__has,r_0001_0001__He,arg0).
arc(r_0001_0002__has,r_0001_0004__story,arg1).
arc(r_0003_0005__tell,r_0001_0001__He,arg0).
arc(r_0003_0005__tell,r_0001_0004__story,arg1).
arc(r_0003_0005__tell,r_0003_0010__conference_attendee,r_0003_0008__to_clr).
```

While the search of (22) is for any unresolved instance of `He`, we happen to receive information about only one discourse entity individual, namely `r_0001_0001__He`, which contains reference back to the source language data. The results of (22) can be further processed to give the visualisation of (23).

(23)

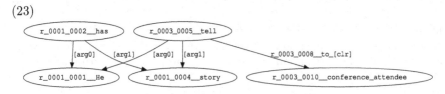

Suppose on seeing the results of (22)/(23) we are intrigued to probe deeper, and in particular we are interested to find out more about the discourse entity that is `r_0003_0010__conference_attendee`. Thus we might make the query of (24).

(24)
```
$ echo "search_entity('r_0003_0010__conference_attendee')." | ./data
arc(r_0003_0005__tell,r_0001_0001__He,arg0).
arc(r_0003_0005__tell,r_0001_0004__story,arg1).
arc(r_0003_0005__tell,r_0003_0010__conference_attendee,r_0003_0008__to_clr).
arc(r_0003_0009__every_quantificational,r_0003_0005__tell,scope).
arc(r_0003_0009__every_quantificational,r_0003_0010__conference_attendee,restriction).
```

The results of (24) can be further processed to give the visualisation of (25).

(25)

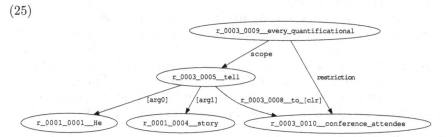

From the results of (24)/(25) we learn information about all conference attendees, namely, that they were told **r_0001_0004__story** by the unresolved **r_0001_0001__He**.

5   Another Application: Assisting Old Japanese Annotation

The Oxford-NINJAL Corpus of Old Japanese (ONCOJ; [6]) is assembling a collection of all texts from the Old Japanese (OJ) period. OJ is the earliest attested stage of the Japanese language, largely the language of the Asuka and Nara periods of Japanese history (7th and 8th century AD). As a parsed corpus, ONCOJ adds linguistic analysis to the data samples. The annotations are accessible through an on-line interface with browsing and search functionality.

To illustrate the annotation, let us consider the two sentence poem Bussokusekika.17 (BS.17) of (26) and (27) as a running example.

(26)   opomi-ato   wo mi ni   kuru pito   no   ini-si
       honorable_footprints ACC see P-CONN comes anyone GEN transpired
       kata ti-yo   no tumi sape porobu to   so   ipu
       times thousand_lives are sins even expire P-COMP P-FOC say
       'They say that even the sins that are from the times that transpired for
       a thousand lives of anyone who comes to see the honorable footprints
       expire.'

(27)   nozoku   to   zo   kiku
       takes_away P-COMP P-FOC hear
       'I hear that doing this (seeing the footprints) takes them (the sins) away.'

The format and presentation of ONCOJ parsed analysis follows the same style of analysis already seen with the analysis of English in Sect. 3 above. This provides projections of function marked phrase and clause structure from a base morphological analysis. The morphological analysis provides word segmentation marked for mode of writing (PHON(ographic) or LOG(ographic)) and linked to a dictionary database through lemma numbers (e.g., L050877 = "foot, sole of the foot") and word class information (N = noun, VB-ADC = verb ambiguous between adnominal and conclusive, etc.).

For example, the complete parse of (BS.17) is given in (28) and (29). This illustrates projection of parse structure with tag labelling: IP for clause layers; NP and PP for phrase layers. Also, label extensions are added to indicate function (SBJ = subject, ARG = argument complement, PRP = purpose clause, GEN = genitive, etc.). There are also zero elements (*arb* = pronoun with arbitrary reference, *speaker* = pronoun with speaker reference, *pro* = general pronoun, *T* = relative clause trace) and co-reference information (;{SEE}, ;{SINS}).

```
(28)    ( (IP-MAT (NP-SBJ *arb*)
                  (IP-ARG
                   (PP-SBJ
                    (NP;{SINS}
                     (PP (NP (IP-REL (NP-SBJ *T*)
                                     (IP-PRP;{SEE}
                                      (PP-OB1 (NP (N (PFX-HON (L000038 (PHON opomi))))
                                                  (N (L050877 (PHON ato)))))
                                             (P-CASE-ACC (L000534 (PHON wo))))
                                      (VB-IFC (L031712a (PHON mi)))
                                      (P-CONN (L000551 (PHON ni))))
                                     (VB-ADN (L030612a (PHON kuru))))
                             (N (L050046 (PHON pito))))
                         (P-CASE-GEN (L000520 (PHON no))))
                     (IP-REL (NP-SBJ *T*)
                             (NP-PRD (IP-REL (NP-SBJ *T*)
                                             (VB-ADN (VB-STM (L030186a (PHON ini)))
                                                     (VAX-SPST-ADN (L000015 (PHON si)))))
                                     (N (L050111 (PHON kata))))
                             (NP-QFR (N (NUM (L002013 (PHON ti)))
                                        (N (L050040 (PHON yo)))))
                             (COP-ADI (L031965 (PHON no))))
                     (N (L090401 (PHON tumi))))
                    (P-RES (L000525a (PHON sape))))
                   (VB-ADC (L031601a (PHON porobu)))
                   (P-COMP (L000530 (PHON to)))
                   (P-FOC (L000527 (PHON so))))
                  (VB-ADC (L030199a (PHON ipu))))
          (ID 28_BS;BS.17#1))
```

```
(29)    ( (IP-MAT (NP-SBJ *speaker*)
                  (IP-ARG (NP-SBJ;{SEE} *pro*)
                          (NP-OB1;{SINS} *pro*)
                          (VB-ADC (L031376a (PHON nozoku)))
                          (P-COMP (L000530 (PHON to)))
                          (P-FOC (L000527 (PHON zo))))
                  (VB-ADC (L030565a (PHON kiku))))
          (ID 29_BS;BS.17#2))
```

The annotation gives a resource of general use, but from the perspective of this paper, it is notable as content to feed the method of Sect. 3 for reaching semantic analysis and dot-to-dot semantic representations.

To further assist with creating and communicating ideas about the analysis of OJ, the ONCOJ project has started to create parsed English that provides both good translations and tight correspondences to the annotation of the OJ data. The aim is not to create a parallel corpus of English as there is some need for deviation from standard practises of English annotation to achieve close correspondences. Rather it is the purpose of the parsed English translations to act essentially as a meta level commentary on the OJ data and its analysis. This makes the OJ data and its annotation more accessible, while also providing an independent check on the OJ annotation and the dependencies that this annotation drives.

Parsed annotation for the English translation provided with (BS.17) above is shown in (30) and (31). This is annotated to include complex expressions (e.g., `honorable_footprints`) with the idea of matching where possible the topmost level of lexical analysis provided to the OJ data, so that when given as input for the steps of Sect. 3 above, the same abstract semantic dependencies will arise as with the syntactic analysis of the corresponding OJ data.

```
(30)   ( (IP-MAT (NP-SBJ (PRO They))
               (VBP;~Tf say)
               (CP-THT-OB1
               (IP-SUB
               (C that)
               (PP-SBJ (P-ROLE even)
                       (NP;{SINS}
                       (D the)
                       (NS sins)
                       (IP-REL (NP-SBJ (RPRO that))
                               (BEP;~La are)
                               (PP-PRD2 (P-ROLE from)
                                       (NP (D the)
                                           (NS times)
                                           (IP-REL (NP-SBJ (RPRO that))
                                                   (VBD;~I transpired))))
                               (PP-NIM (P-ROLE for)
                                       (NP (D a)
                                           (N thousand)
                                           (NS lives))))
                       (PP (P-ROLE of)
                           (NP (D;_nphd_ anyone)
                               (IP-REL (NP-SBJ (RPRO who))
                                       (VBP;~I comes)
                                       (PP-SCON-CNT
                                       (IP-INF;{SEE}
                                       (TO to)
                                       (VB;~Tn see)
                                       (NP-OB1 (D the)
                                               (NS honorable_footprints)))))))))))
               (VB;~I expire)))
       (PUNC .))
(ID 30_BS;BS.17#1))
```

(31)   ((IP-MAT (NP-SBJ (PRO I))
                (VBP;~Tf hear)
                (CP-THT-OB1 (IP-SUB (C that)
                                    (IP-PPL-SBJ (DAG;~Tn doing)
                                                (NP-OB1;{SEE} (D;_nphd_ this)))
                                    (VB;~Tn.p takes)
                                    (NP-OB1;{SINS} (PRO them))
                                    (RP away)))
                (PUNC .))
        (ID 31_BS;BS.17#2))

We can see the correspondences that emerge by comparing the resulting dependency graph of (32) generated from the OJ parse data of (28) and (29) with the graph of (33) generated from the English translation parse data of (30) and (31).

(32)

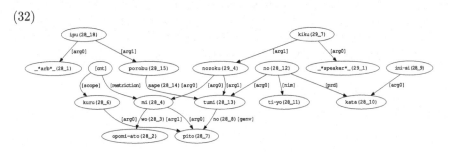

(33)

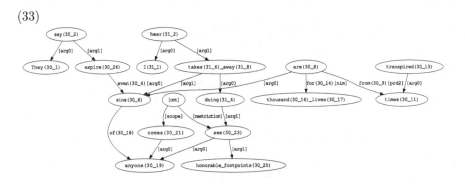

The alignments that follow from the matching structures of the graphs can be seen with the word disambiguating gloss information in the presentation of (BS.17) in (26) and (27) above.

By constructing a corpus that links the semantic interpretation of ancient Japanese texts with grammatical rules linked to translation correspondences, it becomes possible to describe the grammar of OJ more systematically. This is making possible diachronic linguistic research that contrasts ancient Japanese with modern languages and provides corpus results that are extremely accessible in terms of analysis content.

6   Conclusion

Representations capturing word and sentence syntax based analysis can have clear links to language data that consist of nested groupings, as seen with the syntactic trees above. But semantic relations necessitate more detachment from language data, with connections that have no clear counterpart from the language data as they arise from the resolution of interpretive options (e.g., picking an antecedent for a pronoun or definite description). This paper has illustrated building a discourse representation that is sufficiently disconnected from language data to capture relationships across discourse that are semantic in nature, including semantic argument dependencies and scope relations, while retaining enough information from the language data for its (partial) recovery.

The dot-to-dot semantic representations of this paper treat sentence fragments, single sentences, and wider discourse as being organised around discourse entities, where each graph node is a discourse entity. Connections leading to or from nodes gather the information content communicated by the analysed language data (sentence fragment, sentence, or discourse). We have seen that, by following paths within the graph structure, it is possible to pick out those discourse entities that have their quantificational presence introduced at the restriction level of a quantification and that are then accessible to the scope level. Similarly, it is possible to pick out those discourse entities that are limited to the internal scope of some quantification. And similarly, it is possible to pick out the discourse entities that scope with the discourse level of closure.

Key information preserved by the semantic representation includes maintaining a presence for coordination that is overtly present in the source language data. Consequently, in places, we can see a strong coupling between the contribution of syntactic and semantic information, but also, at other times, there can be wide divergence with connections. Yet always the semantic representation remains grounded with references to the content of the original source data. This use of source data connections makes the analysis output normalised when in its text Datalog fact format, so the same analysis leads to the same output, for analysis comparison to be a matter of observing matches.

Finally, this paper demonstrated uses of the representation approach with two sample applications: database querying, and analysis feedback for parsed corpus annotation of Old Japanese language data.

References

1. Banarescu, L., et al.: Abstract meaning representation for sembanking. In: Proceedings of the 7th Linguistic Annotation Workshop and Interoperability with Discourse, pp. 178–186 (2013)
2. Bonial, C., Babko-Malaya, O., Choi, J.D., Hwang, J., Palmer, M.: PropBank annotation guidelines. Center for Computational Language and Education Research, Institute of Cognitive Science, University of Colorado at Boulder, 3.0 edn. (2010)
3. Butler, A.: The treebank semantics parsed corpus (TSPC) web site (2023). Hirosaki University. entrees.github.io. Accessed December 2023

4. Cowie, A.: Oxford Advanced Learner's Dictionary, 4th edn. Oxford University Press, Oxford (1989)
5. Dekker, P.: Dynamic Semantics. Studies in Linguistics and Philosophy, vol. 91. Springer, Dordrecht (2012). https://doi.org/10.1007/978-94-007-4869-9
6. Frellesvig, B., Horn, S.W., et al: Oxford-NINJAL corpus of old Japanese (2023). oncoj.ninjal.ac.jp. Accessed December 2023
7. Kamp, H., Reyle, U.: From Discourse to Logic: Introduction to Model-theoretic Semantics of Natural Language, Formal Logic and Discourse Representation Theory. Kluwer, Dordrecht (1993)
8. Kiselyov, O.: Polynomial event semantics – non-Montagovian proper treatment of quantifiers. In: Kojima, K., Sakamoto, M., Mineshima, K., Satoh, K. (eds.) JSAI-isAI 2018. LNCS (LNAI), vol. 11717, pp. 313–324. Springer, Cham (2019). https://doi.org/10.1007/978-3-030-31605-1_23
9. Mel'čuk, I.A.: Dependency Syntax: Theory and Practice. SUNY Series in Linguistics. State University Press of New York, Albany (1988)
10. Nonnengart, A.: Strong skolemization. Technical report MPI-I-96-2-010, Max-Plank-Institut für Informatik, Saarbrücken, Germany (1996)
11. Nonnengart, A., Rock, G., Weidenbach, C.: On generating small clause normal forms. In: Kirchner, C., Kirchner, H. (eds.) CADE 1998. LNCS, vol. 1421, pp. 397–411. Springer, Heidelberg (1998). https://doi.org/10.1007/bfb0054274
12. Ohlbach, H.J., Weidenbach, C.: A note on assumptions about skolem functions. J. Autom. Reason. **15**(2), 267–275 (1995)
13. Petersen, W.: Representation of concepts as frames. In: Gamerschlag, T., Gerland, D., Osswald, R., Petersen, W. (eds.) Meaning, Frames, and Conceptual Representation. Studies in Language and Cognition, vol. 2, pp. 43–67. Düsseldof University Press (2015)
14. Sowa, J.F.: Semantic networks. In: Shapiro, S.C. (ed.) Encyclopedia of Artificial Intelligence. Wiley (1992)
15. Zeevat, H.: Semantic dependency graphs. In: Hansen, H.H., Murray, S.E., Sadrzadeh, M., Zeevat, H. (eds.) TbiLLC 2015. LNCS, vol. 10148, pp. 171–184. Springer, Heidelberg (2017). https://doi.org/10.1007/978-3-662-54332-0_10

Intonational Meaning at the Limits of Grammar

Lukas Rieser$^{(\boxtimes)}$ ⓘ

Tokyo University of Agriculture and Technology, Fuchu, Japan
`rieserl@go.tuat.ac.jp`

Abstract. In formal work on the meaning of English, intonation with expressive, or (allegedly) emotive, meaning has received little attention, and has been treated as separate from compositional meaning. I argue against this based on data from Japanese, showing that expressive intonation can be part of compositional meaning, hence "grammatical".

Focusing on intonation patterns occurring with the Japanese sentence-final particle *yo*, I propose a compositional analysis of its non-emotive meaning and argue that English intonation carries the same complex meaning—thus, it is within the scope of formal semantics/pragmatics.

Keywords: Japanese · Intonation · Particles · Pragmatics · Semantics

1 Overview

Following Xu (2019) [13], I use the term "prosody" to collectively refer to suprasegmental phonetic aspects of speech, including the instances of meaning encoded intonationally (by pitch modulation) I discuss here. Some types of prosodically encoded meaning are rather clearly classifiable as "grammatical" in that they can also be encoded by non-prosodic lexical items (*e.g.* those encoded by lexical tone, information structure, or sentence-final intonation encoding speech-act type), while others are easily classifiable as "paralinguistic" in that their meaning can be expressed by non-linguistic means (such as sounding angry, happy or annoyed, or intonationally conveyed persona).

On this background, the existence of prosodic morphemes encoding information structure or speech-act type composing linguistic meaning alongside non-prosodic counterparts is rather well-documented—this includes focus intonation as well as sentence-final falls and (question) rises. In contrast, intonation patterns with more elusive meaning, such as the rising-falling pattern discussed here, which are often distributed over various segments of an utterance, tend to be described as purely expressive in the sense of directly conveying psychological states, and are considered less "grammatical" in the sense of being part of the composition of linguistic meaning, or even "paralinguistic", *i.e.* not part of linguistic meaning at all.

While such a dichotomy between the "lexical" and "grammatical" on one side and the "elusive" and "expressive" on the other may be appealing in its apparent

D. Bekki et al. (Eds.): LENLS 2023, LNCS 14569, pp. 191–204, 2024.
https://doi.org/10.1007/978-3-031-60878-0_11

neatness, the view beyond English as the usual focus of (formal) semantics and pragmatics shows that expressive intonation is both more grammatical in the sense of being part of the composition of utterance meaning, and more lexically well-defined in the sense of encoding sharply delineable concepts, than one might assume at first glance.

Below, I offer a compositional account of Japanese prosodic morphemes occurring with sentence-final pragmatic particles, and argue that this analysis can be applied to English intonation as well, thus supporting a more "lexical", "grammatical" view of intonationally encoded expressive meaning.

2   Prosodic Morphemes in English and Japanese

This section introduces two pairs of prosodic morphemes: $\downarrow$ and $\uparrow$, and $\searrow$ and $\nearrow$, which I suggest operate on different levels of expressive meaning. $\downarrow$ and $\uparrow$ resolve a participant variable of assertive force, operating on the speech act proper, $\searrow$ and $\nearrow$ resolve participant variables in expressions such as the sentence-final particle *yo*, thus operating on speech act modifiers.

The levels are not always as neatly separate: a third contour $\nearrow\searrow$ in Japanese (obligatorily) conveys emotive meaning in addition to resolving variables within *yo*, and in English conveys all of the aforementioned meaning components (*i.e.* the emotive and non-emotive meaning of *yo* $\nearrow\searrow$, and that of assertive falling $\downarrow$) at once. This highlights the significance of the view from languages like Japanese for distinguishing types of prosodically encoded meaning that tend to be lumped together in languages like English, where paradigms of expressions encoding pragmatic meaning are less articulated.

2.1   Final Rise/Fall in English and Japanese

The prosodic morphemes $\uparrow$ and $\downarrow$ occur sentence-finally in English declaratives and interrogatives, as the following examples illustrate:

(1) a. You're coming.$\downarrow$
     b. You're coming?$\uparrow$
     c. Are you coming?$\uparrow$

In an influential analysis of sentence-final intonation, Gunlogson (2003) [3] argues that these morphemes resolve a participant variable in the speech act to the speaker ($\uparrow$) or the addressee ($\downarrow$), and offers an analysis of rising declaratives like (1-b) that differentiates them from both falling declaratives, henceforth also assertions, like (1-a), and rising interrogatives, or canonical questions, like (1-c). Davis (2009) [1] applies this analysis to Japanese, claiming that the same morphemes interact with sentence-final particles (SFPs) like *yo*, a view that is followed by Oshima (2014) [7], who's observations on intonational variants of *yo* I summarize below.

Against an analysis conflating intonational morphemes combining with bare speech acts with those occurring on sentence-final particles, I take $\uparrow$ and $\downarrow$ to be distinct from the prosodic morphemes interacting with *yo*, which I therefore write as ↗ and ↘ in order to distinguish the pairs from each other.

This is convenient for the compositional analysis of *yo* I propose, but also independently motivated: If we were to assume with the authors quoted above that ↑ and ↓ have the same function in English and in Japanese utterances with or without *yo*, we would have to assume that final rising utterances with *yo* are only concerned with addressee commitment but require none from the speaker, parallel to the rising declarative (1-b) or the canonical question (1-c) in English. Contrary to this, rising *yo*-declaratives are readily used as answers to questions and require speaker commitment to their propositional content, making it plausible that they are indeed assertions, *i.e.* semantically declaratives with a final fall (in my notation ↓), to which with a rise is added on *yo* (in my notation ↗), rather than utterances with a single final rise.

2.2 Japanese Prosodic Morphemes and Pragmatic Particles

The observations summarized in this section are due to Oshima (2014). As mentioned above, I do not take final rises and falls in bare utterances to be the same as those occurring with the particle *yo* and therefore write the final rises/falls in the following examples as ↗/↘ rather than ↑/↓. Note that I do not sperately write the final fall ↓ on the declaratives, for ease of exposition and because I claim that *yo*-declaratives cannot occur with final rising intonation ↑ as in rising declaratives, *i.e.* all of the following Japanese examples should be read as falling declaratives (assertions), with an additional morpheme ↗, ↘, or ↗↘ on *yo*.

For space, I do not provide a detailed account of the various uses of *yo*, as this paper focuses on the role of intonation. It should suffice to say that there is an extent of consensus that *yo* in assertions conveys that the speaker assumes the addressee is not duly taking the asserted proposition into consideration.[1]

Rising and Falling. *yo*. That ↑/↓ and ↗/↘ operate on different levels of pragmatic meaning is not to say that there are no parallels between them—as ↑/↓ do on the speech act proper, ↗/↘ indicate speaker- *vs.* addressee orientation within the meaning of *yo*, as the following example illustrates:

Scenario: A suggests to buy paper cups for a party.

(2)   S: kami koppu-wa mada takusan nokot-tei-ru   yo{↗/↘}
          paper cups-TOP still   plenty   left-RES-NPST SFP
       "There are still plenty of paper cups left."

The contribution of *yo* (independent of intonation) is roughly to bring to the addressee A's attention a proposition they should be, but are not aware of. In (2), it is not necessary for A to buy paper cups in light of there being plenty left, and the speaker S is making A aware of this.

As for intonation, preference for either variant of (2) depends on who A suggests buy the paper cups: When the addressee offers to do this themselves,

---

[1] Other than the work quoted throughout, Takubo and Kinsui (1997) [12] and McCready (2007) [6] provide some more detail in English.

yo ↗ is preferred as the proposition is relevant for the future actions of A. When the addressee requests the speaker to do so, *yo*↘ is preferred, as the proposition is relevant for the future actions of S (but is still shared with A to indicate that the baselessnes of the request). Thus, intonation in (2) appears to determine speaker- *vs.* addressee-orientation in terms of an action for which the asserted proposition is relevant.[2]

Note that both versions of (2) are assertions (falling declaratives) that commit the speaker to the proposition, which motivates the distinction of the final rise/fall on *yo* from that occurring on bare declaratives—if ↗ on were to be interpreted parallel to ↑, we would (assuming a compositional account) expect it to be interpreted parallel to a rising declarative or question (which in Japanese have the same word order as declaratives), rather than as an assertion.

Rising-falling *yo*. Oshima further describes a rising-falling contour ↗↘ combining with *yo*, characterizing *yo*↗↘ as a version of *yo*↘ with an additional meaning of "asking for understanding or sympathy", as illustrated in (3) and (4).

Scenario: A suggests to go outside together

(3)   S: Soto-wa   samui yo(o)↗↘
            outside-TOP cold   SFP
        "It's cold outside!"

Scenario: S is desperately looking for their own wallet

(4)   S: Saifu-ga   mitsukara-nai yo(o)↗↘
            wallet-NOM be_found-NEG SFP
        "I can't find my wallet!"

In both examples, S indicates that A is not duly considering the asserted proposition, but does not necessarily indicate that this proposition is primarily relevant for an action on A's part, as would be expected from a rising *yo*-declarative. There appears to be, however, some addresse-orientation as S is requesting sympathy for their situation from A, where in (3) this is relevant for a joint course of action, whereas in (4) this is not the case. Related to this request for sympathy, both utterances also typically also convey emotive meaning that can be characterized on the lines of indignation, exasperation or petulance.

The question arises whether these additional, emotive meaning components are purely paralinguistic, or can be compositionally derived from *yo* and ↗↘ parallel to *yo* with either ↗ or ↘, and whether the meaning of ↗↘ can somehow be derived from, or at least non-arbitrarily related to, those of ↗ and ↘.

I propose that while there is an (apparently obligatory) purely emotive component to (3) and (4), which can become apparent in intensified pitch modulation and final lengthening indicated here as *(o)*, there is expressive meaning to *yo*↗↘ that and can be analyzed in parallel to *yo*↗ and *yo*↘, if rather as an additional,

---

[2] This motivates Davis' [1] "guide-to-action" label for the rising intonation. Note, however, that the falling intonation also provides explanation about a future action, suggesting that this is a property of a particular class of examples, rather than of rising *yo* proper.

hybrid variant intonational morpheme than a composition of the two, and that the entirety of the meaning of yo↗↘ is also present in the English correspondents to (3) and (4). Furthermore, I maintain that this "grammatical" part of the constructions' meaning is, at least conceptually, if possibly not on the level of expressions, distinguishable from the emotive, "paralinguistic" part, which is expressed similarly in Japanese and English.

2.3   Expressive and Emotive Meaning in English Intonation

In a crucial observation on the universality of the meaning encoded in prosodic morphemes, English correspondents to Japanese (3) and (4), shown in (5) and (6) below, exhibit a somewhat similar intonation pattern to ↗↘, here distributed over focused (or stress-bearing) lexical items and sentence-final intonation.

(5)   "(But) it's [cold]↗ outside↘..."

(6)   "I [can't]↗ find my [wallet]↗↘..."

While the notation ↗ and ↘ is not to say that their prosodic realization is exactly the same as on Japanese yo, I argue that this is a non-coincidental similarity, as intonation marked in the English examples (5) and (6) carries the same meaning as yo↗↘ in their Japanese correspondents pagination(3) and (4). Note that this intonation is distinct from sentence-final ↑ and ↓ shown in (1)—both (5) and (6) are assertions with a final ↓.[3]

Note that emotive content conveying indignation (which is likely included in Oshima's "asking for sympathy") is encoded by amplified rises and falls throughout the utterance, as well as final lengthening, in both Japanese and English. This can be expressed by extralinguistic means, in contrast to the meaning of (yo)↗↘ proper.

Crucially, the English counterparts of the yo↗↘ do not only convey the additional meaning associated with the ↗↘ contour, but also the meaning of yo. That the lexical meaning of yo↗↘ from (3) and (4) is also present in the English correspondents (5) and (6) is remarkable not least because English correspondents to yo↗ and yo↘ are hard to come by, if they exist at all. That is, if the lexical meaning of yo↗↘ is conveyed by ↗ on focus and final ↘ in English, then English intonation is more "grammatical" than often assumed.

2.4   Compositionality of Intonation and SFPs

In addition to differentiating ↑/↓ from ↗/↘, I pursue an account of ↗, ↘ and ↗↘ as compositional in that they resolve participant variables in yo, in which ↗↘ takes meaning components from both the rising and the falling variant. Before presenting my analysis, I briefly address some objections to this view.

---

[3] ↓ is not indicated like in the Japanese examples, also because in English, there is no differentiation between ↓ and ↘, so that ↓ can be thought of as merged into ↗↘.

Oshima (2014) argues that a compositional analysis not tenable due to the variety of uses observable in the three intonational variants of *yo*-utterances in utterances with these prosodic morphemes but without particles, and in utterances where the prosodic morphemes occur with SFP other than *yo*.

While in this paper I have nothing to say about instances of $\nearrow/\searrow$ with particles other than *yo*[4], my goal is not to predict each and every instance of how particle utterances are used, but rather to capture the restrictions that each combination of particle and intonational morpheme(s) imposes on its possible uses, and shed light on some conventionalized uses based on choice of one combination over the others. I maintain that it is preferable to do this compositionally wherever possible, as viewing each construction as fully conventionalized and independent makes it excessively hard to identify connections to other expressions and natural language phenomena from the analysis.

As for the difficulty of consolidating occurrences of the prosodic morphemes in particle-less utterances within the account, it does not apply to the analysis I propose as I treat ↑ and ↓ as distinct from $\nearrow$ and $\searrow$, as stated above—the idea is that, while they are parallel in terms of encoding speaker- *vs.* addressee-orientation, they operate on different levels of meaning, the former resolving variables in the speech act (in the examples here: declarative) itself, the latter variables in the SFP when one is added to the utterance.

3 The Meaning of *yo*$\searrow$ and *yo*$\nearrow$

Most proposals of formal analyses of *yo* do not bother with prosodic morphemes. When analyzed, they are mostly treated on par with sentence-final ↑ and ↓. On my view, while both are similar in that they resolve participant variables, $\nearrow$ and $\searrow$ operate on a different level of meaning, namely that of modal thought (in the broad sense of *e.g.* Philips and Kratzer 2022 [8]), typical for pragmatic particles or other elements encoding pragmatic meaning like non-propositional negation—this is the realm where I claim the status of a given proposition as a premise or expectation, which expressions like *yo* encode, is negotiated in the discourse.

3.1 Premise and Expectation Management and *yo*

From observations in the literature on *yo*, I take it minimally necessary to make reference to speaker- and addressee orientation, to premises that the participants entertain, and to expectations that arise from these premises by modal reasoning, in order to capture what *yo*-assertions do.

To illustrate how I take the prosodic morphemes to resolve participant variables contained in *yo*, consider again the (without resolution by sentence-final intonation) ambiguous example (2), repeated here as (7).

Scenario: A suggests to buy paper cups for a party.

---

[4] I do maintain that it is not *a priori* impossible to apply similar analyses to particles like *ne* and the various intonational contours it occurs with, *cf.* Rieser (2020) [11].

(7)   S: kami   koppu-wa mada takusan nokot-tei-ru   yo{↗/↘}
          paper cups-TOP still   plenty   left-RES-NPST SFP
       "There are still plenty of paper cups left."

What both prosodic variants have in common is that in the input context, φ ("There are still plenty of paper cups left.") is not taken into account as a premise by A, to which S reacts with the *yo*-assertion.

The difference lies in whether S is sharing φ in order to adjust A's expectations about S's own behavior (*yo*↘) or whether S is sharing φ as information for A to adjust their own behavior (*yo*↗). This can be captured by assuming that a variable in *yo* is resolved to S by ↘, and to A by ↗, indicating which part of the context is targeted by the update.

3.2   Formalism

In this section, I introduce the notation for the formal sketch of *yo*-assertions as context change potentials (henceforth CCPs, *cf.* Heim (1983) [4]) constraining premises and expectation in the input and output contexts which contain participant variables resolved by the prosodic morphemes. In modeling *yo* as a modifier of CCPs, I follow both Davis' and Oshima's analyses, but propose a different view on which parts of the context *yo* constrains, and on the kind of conditions *yo* imposes on input and output contexts.

Utterances as CCPs. Any given utterance can be represented as a CCP, which is defined as a set of pairs of admissible input and output contexts. I write individual CCPs (representing utterance types differentiated by their restrictions on input and output contexts) in the following notation, which is largely continuous with previous analyses:

$\langle c, c' \rangle$ for a pair of input and output contexts

$\{\langle c, c' \rangle \mid \ldots\}$ for the set of $\langle c, c' \rangle$ pairs satisfying the elided $(\ldots)$ conditions

The conditions on input and output contexts of each utterance are derived from the characteristic conditions of the speech-act type (such as declarative, interrogative, imperative etc.), modified by elements such as SFPs or other pragmatic particles that introduce additional constraints on contexts.

Premises and Expectations. I propose that the restrictions imposed on contexts by *yo* are best captured by splitting the context set into premises and expectations.[5] The basic idea is that premises are those propositions an agent takes as the basis for further reasoning, whereas expectations are assumptions

---

[5] This is motivated by observations on and considerations regarding the formalization of varied expressions like pragmatic particles, non-propositional negation, and sentence-final expressions, among others. See Sect. 3.3 below for some more discussion of the motivation for this, and some comparison with Oshima's analysis.

made as the result of such reasoning, but which are not (yet) considered settled enough by the agent to be considered premises.

In order to capture this, and speaker- *vs.* addressee- orientation observable with *yo*, I introduce participant-specific sets of premises π and expectations ξ:

Π_x^c set of premises π in context c, which are the basis for agent x to make decisions and assumptions (modal reasoning).

Ξ_x^c set of expectations ξ which agent x assumes, under normal circumstances, to hold based on Π_x^c, but which do not (yet) have the status of premises.

While premises are directly contained in the participant-specific context sets, expectations are indirectly derived from these premises. I model this by way of relations of defeasible entailment, written with the symbol $\rightsquigarrow$, which in turn are contained in the premise set, and relate premises and expectations as follows:

$$(8) \quad \{[\pi \wedge (\pi \rightsquigarrow \xi)] \in \Pi_x^c \wedge \neg \xi \notin \Pi_x^c\} \rightarrow \xi \in \Pi_x^c$$

This is to say that when an agent's premise set contains π and a defeasible entailment relation $\pi \rightsquigarrow \xi$, this agent's premise set must contain ξ, and ξ is to be promoted to a premise unless $\neg \xi$ is already part of the premise set.

(8) does not represent the dynamic aspect of updates, as limited resources make premise revision necessarily non-instantaneous, and differences in speaker- and addressee contexts may require negations in order to resolve contradictions in shared premises and expectations, a process that is often the goal of discourse. The dynamic aspect is, however, indirectly reflected in conditions on input and output contexts, the SFP being a tool for such negotiations.

Falling Declaratives (Assertions). I give the following definition for declaratives with final falling intonation (*i.e.* canonical assertions) only, assuming on the lines of Gricean Quality (*cf.* Grice 1975 [2]) that an assertion of φ requires the speaker not to take $\neg \varphi$ to be a premise and have sufficient grounds, here represented as a premise π, to accept φ as a premise, all else being equal.

$$(9) \quad [\![\text{DECL} \downarrow (\varphi)]\!] = \{\langle c, c' \rangle \mid \exists \pi \in \Pi_S^c : \pi \rightsquigarrow \varphi \wedge \neg \varphi \notin \Xi_S^c\}$$

In the following discussion of *yo*-assertion, I ignore dynamic aspects, conflicting premises, and possible modification of required strength for assertion by pragmatic particles or modals, and assume that *yo*-assertions require the speaker to have accepted φ as a premise ($\varphi \in \Pi_S^c$).

While this would, for instance be problematic for an account of *yo* in interrogatives, which essentially narrate belief revision processes by the speaker, I maintain that *yo*-assertions require the speaker to fully accept the asserted proposition as a premise, which is a necessary condition for negotiating its acceptance, or at least consideration, by the speaker.

3.3   Remarks on the Context Model

Before moving on to the analysis of *yo* in the following section, I discuss issues regarding potential conflicting grounds for acceptance of premises and potential discrepancies between premises and expectations that are glossed over in the formalism, which is simplified to focus on the aspects that are essential to describe the basic function of *yo*-assertions with different prosodic morphemes, and briefly compare the context model I propose to that proposed by Oshima, who takes the context to contain modal bases and ordering sources.

Grounds for Acceptance. An open questions is what generally constitutes sufficient grounds to satisfy $\pi \rightsquigarrow \xi$. Generally speaking, any number of grounds to settle for ξ or $\neg\xi$ can coexist as premises. For example, an agent can see that someone's car is in the driveway, but their lights are out. Accepting both of these as premises, the agent can either expect that this someone is home (ξ), or that they are not ($\neg\xi$), but not both at the same time. The agent then needs to evaluate which of the conflicting premises is stronger, and whether there is a premise that is strong enough to settle for either ξ or $\neg\xi$.

In case the agent considers a newly accepted premise, for instance contextual evidence that has just become available, strong enough to give rise to an expectation that contradicts an extant premise, premises may be revised, but this is not necessarily the case—in the example above, the agent can see that the car is in the driveway and the lights are on, but have sufficient reason to accept that nobody is home. In this case, the conflict between expectation and reality according to the agent remains.

In sum, I take the required strength for a premise π to satisfy $\pi \rightsquigarrow \xi$ to be a relative and at times subjective judgment, but maintain that it can be defined as the strength required for a speaker to felicitously assert ξ. In discourse, this strength in itself can be the source of disagreement between participants—this is where, often, discourse particles like *yo* are used to express the speaker's stance on such disagreements, or discrepancies in premises and expectations between the speaker's and addressee's (input) contexts.

Contexts and Modality. Comparing my version of the context set with that of Oshima (2014), who takes it to contain a modal base and ordering source along with the common ground, (a) the common ground in the current proposal is the conjunct of speaker and addressee context sets, (b) the premise set closely resembles a Kratzerian epistemic and/or evidential modal base, *cf.* Kratzer (2012) [5], containing whatever propositions are taken as basic for further reasoning, the difference between individual and generic modality being represented as speaker/addressee-specific or shared context sets, and (c) expectations are derived from premises by defeasible inference, which in terms of ordering source is similar to stereotypical ordering (*cf.* Rieser (2020) [10] on Japanese *hazu*) in absence of another modal layer, and includes everything that normally follows from the content of the premise set, but has not (yet) been accepted as a basis for future reasoning.

3.4   Meaning of *yo*

Based on the basic formal framework introduced in Sect. 3.2, it is possible to sketch an analysis of *yo* in which it modifies the CCP with a condition presupposing that the asserted proposition is *not* a premise for an unresolved participant, and with a condition requiring an output context containing a premise that makes this proposition expected for an unresolved participant.

Combining this with the definition of assertion given above, simplified to requiring the speaker have accepted the asserted proposition as a premise, results in the following CCP for a *yo*-declarative:

(10) $[\![yo(\text{DECL}\downarrow(\varphi))]\!] = \{\langle c, c'\rangle \mid \varphi \in \Pi_S^c \wedge \varphi \notin \Pi_X^c \wedge \exists \pi \in \Pi_X^{c'} : \pi \rightsquigarrow \varphi\}$

While this might seem like rather weak conditions, they are necessary to cover various uses of *yo* beyond the limited cases discussed here, which are all assertions.[6] Asserting a prejacent requires it to be epistemically settled for the speaker, yielding the CCP in (8) for a *yo*-assertion. Note that this speech-act is undefined without a final $\searrow$ or $\nearrow$ which are necessary to resolve the variable X.

This puts a stronger requirement on the input context c, namely that there is a discrepancy between the speaker's premises and that of the addressee. Note that, by definition, adding φ as a premise also satisfies the output context requirement of making it expected (as $p \rightsquigarrow p$ is trivially true). Also note that premises, as grounds for expectations, can be evidential, and the assertion of φ by S can thus serve as the required π (grounds for A to expect φ, unless for A $\neg\varphi$ is epistemically settled).

Intonation resolves the part of c to be updated: $\searrow$ indicates update of the **shared** context (common ground), whereas $\nearrow$ indicates update of the **addressee**'s context only:

(11) $[\![yo \searrow (\text{DECL}\downarrow(\varphi))]\!] = \{\langle c, c'\rangle \mid \varphi \in \Pi_S^c \wedge \varphi \notin \Pi_{S,A}^c \wedge \exists \pi \in \Pi_{S,A}^{c'} : \pi \rightsquigarrow \varphi\}$

(12) $[\![yo \nearrow (\text{DECL}\downarrow(\varphi))]\!] = \{\langle c, c'\rangle \mid \varphi \in \Pi_S^c \wedge \varphi \notin \Pi_A^c \wedge \exists \pi \in \Pi_A^{c'} : \pi \rightsquigarrow \varphi\}$

The difference between the update to $\exists \pi \in \Pi_{S,A}^{c'} : \pi \rightsquigarrow \varphi$ in (11) and update to $\exists \pi \in \Pi_A^{c'} : \pi \rightsquigarrow \varphi$ in (12) is subtle, as expected for a fine pragmatic contrast— while the former indicates a speaker intention of adding a premise making φ expected to the common ground (and, in absence of epistemic settlement for $\neg\varphi$, epistemically settling for φ, with the latter the speaker indicates that φ is more relevant for the addressee than it is as common ground.

In other words, I take (12) to express a relative lack of interest in resolving the discrepancy between speaker and addressee and thereby creating a consensus on whether φ holds, which conveys a kind of "take it or leave it" attitude on part of the speaker, who remains firm in maintaining φ as a premise regardless of whether it is shared or not.

---

[6] *Cf.* Rieser (2018) [9] for some discussion of *yo* in interrogatives.

4   Prosodic Morphemes and Asking for Sympathy

What about the meaning of *yo* $\nearrow\searrow$? Can the claim that it is a variant of *yo* $\searrow$ "asking for understanding or sympathy" be supported compositionally, or is this additional meaning purely expressive, or even paralinguistic?

I propose that *yo* $\nearrow\searrow$ is a hybrid of *yo* $\nearrow$ and *yo* $\searrow$, but not in the sense of sequential application. Like the former, it focuses on φ not being a premise to the addressee, but like the latter, does not solely target addressee expectations in the output context:

Scenario: A suggests to go outside together

(13)   S: Soto-wa   samui yo(o) $\nearrow\searrow$
        outside-TOP cold   SFP
        "It's cold outside!"

(14) $[\![yo \nearrow\searrow (\text{DECL} \downarrow (\varphi))]\!] = \{\langle c, c' \rangle \mid \varphi \in \Pi_S^c \wedge \varphi \notin \Pi_A^c \wedge \exists \pi \in \Pi_{S,A}^{c'} : \pi \rightsquigarrow \varphi\}$

By choosing this marked intonation over either $\searrow$ or $\nearrow$, the speaker both decries the lack of shared awareness of φ by the speaker, and indicates that this premise is **not** directly relevant to the addressee's goals, compatible with the nuance of seeking understanding or sympathy.

Note that such an interpretation of examples like (13) is not a direct, necessary consequence of their semantically (lexically) derived meaning, but involves pragmatic reasoning—the constraints that their semantic content imposes on the context, together with the changes that they implement on it, make such utterances a tool suitable to convey the pragmatic meaning they conventionally do in both Japanese and English.

4.1   Uses of *yo* and "Pragmatic Reasoning"

It is important to note that all three intonational variants of *yo* plus prosodic morpheme are use-conditionally equivalent, as they are effectively satisfiable by the same contexts. Shouldn't this mean that they are used in the same way? I argue that this is not the case, parallel to differences arising between assertions with the same truth conditions, but different expressions, *i.e.* different paths of arriving at these truth conditions. The choice of expression, or what is proffered/foregrounded, can have an effect on utterance interpretation that arises by pragmatic reasoning. This is, for instance, often the case with differences in information structure, a kind of meaning that is also often expressed with the use of intonation.

I propose that similar mechanisms kick in on the use-conditional level of meaning. On the one hand, there are cases in which only one prosodic morpheme is compatible with a given utterance meaning and the way it is used in the specific context—these are the case in which its basic meaning can be observed by constructing minimal pairs in terms of felicity.

However, there are also uses where more than one prosodic morpheme would be felicitous with a given utterance, and the speaker has a choice of which aspects of pragmatic meaning to make explicit, and which not. From this choice, additional meaning (pragmatic enrichment) is generated in the form of an implicature on the speech-act level, in parallel to an implicature on the propositional level when there is a choice between two or more alternative propositions with the same truth conditions in a given utterance.

While a detailed attempt of accounting for this pragmatic reasoning (or applying a framework that is suitable for this) is well beyond the scope of this paper, I suggest that something like the following occurs with $yo \searrow$ vs. $yo \nearrow$, and more generally when utterances which arrive at equivalent use-conditions by different paths are interpreted. When two utterances have effectively equivalent use conditions these questions arise:

Explicitness In which variant of the utterance is the context more explicitly (lexically, *e.g.* by means of SFPs and prosodic morphemes) restricted?

Motivation For what reason would the speaker (not) make part of the effective context restrictions lexically explicit?

Falling and Rising yo. A $yo \searrow$ assertion and a $yo \nearrow$ assertion are effectively felicitous in the same contexts: the output condition of $\exists \pi \in \Pi_S^{c'} : \pi \rightsquigarrow \varphi$ made explicit by the former is also an input condition of a an assertion ($\exists \pi \in \Pi_S^c : \pi \rightsquigarrow \varphi$), which is, in absence of an explicitly contrary condition, carried over to the output context. Hence, both intonational variants map to a context where $\exists \pi \in \Pi_{S,A}^c : \pi \rightsquigarrow \varphi$ holds. Furthermore, the condition of $\varphi \notin \Pi_{S,A}^c$ is effectively equivalent to the weaker $\varphi \notin \Pi_A^c$ in assertions, as generally, φ is epistemically settled for the speaker. Expectations do not need to be consistent with actual observations ("φ should be the case, but $\neg\varphi$ is the case"), but when there is no reason to believe that something is not the case, it will be epistemically settled for. Hence, asserting φ by the speaker indicates that, indeed, φ is epistemically settled by the speaker.

On this background, I suggest that the answers to the questions of explicitness and motivation in the case of $yo \searrow$ as compared to $yo \nearrow$ go roughly as sketched below, considering both the perspective from the more marked variant and that from the less marked variant.

Explicitness The condition that $\exists \pi \in \Pi_A^{c'} : \pi \rightsquigarrow \varphi$ is weaker than $\exists \pi \in \Pi_{S,A}^{c'} : \pi \rightsquigarrow \varphi$ as it does not make explicit that the speaker is expecting φ. Similarly, the condition $\varphi \notin \Pi_A^c$ is weaker than $\varphi \notin \Pi_{S,A}^c$ as it does not make explicit that φ is not a shared premise, theoretically opening the possibility that φ is epistemically settled for the addressee, but not for the speaker—this is ruled out by the conditions on assertion, however, as they make it necessary to assume that φ is settled for the speaker, making the two conditions effectively equivalent.

Motivation for $yo \searrow$ $\varphi \notin \Pi_{S,A}^c$ and $\exists \pi \in \Pi_{S,A}^{c'} : \pi \rightsquigarrow \varphi$: the speaker's perspective is (superfluously) included in both input and output conditions, as the input conditions of an assertion already exclude the possibility that the speaker does not consider φ a premise in either input or output context. This highlights the speaker's focus on consensus building, aiming at establishing at least a shared expectation (and, eventually, a potential shared premise).

Motivation for $yo\nearrow$ $\exists \pi \in \Pi_A^{c'} : \pi \rightsquigarrow \varphi$ leaves the speaker's perspective implicit on the level of SFPs, only presenting the update of addressee expectations explicitly and highlighting the discrepancy between speaker- and addressee premises in the input context. This highlights that the speaker is not primarily concerned with consensus, but rather is informing the addressee of their epistemic stance towards the asserted proposition for their information.

Rising-Falling yo. Rising-falling yo, taken to be a hybrid of $yo\searrow$ and $yo\nearrow$, indicates mixed motivations on the speaker's side: while highlighting the discrepancy between speaker and addressee premises in the input context, consensus is sought in the output context rather than indicating mainly addressee-relevance. Along with a (negatively) emotive meaning component (on the lines of indignation, exasperation, or petulance) conveyed by para-linguistic signals, this is interpreted as the "asking for sympathy" reading observed from rising-falling yo (as well as the $\nearrow\searrow$-contour in English).

4.2 The $\nearrow\searrow$ Prosodic Morpheme in English

The "paralinguistic" meaning component in example (15), repeated from (3), expressed by an intensified pitch contour and final lengthening, also present in the English translation, repeated in (16). As noted, however, the meaning of $yo \nearrow\searrow$ appears to be present in its entirety (potentially, the optional *but* covers some of its contrastive meaning).

Scenario: A suggests to go outside together

(15)   S: Soto-wa   samui yo(o)$\nearrow\searrow$
        outside-TOP cold   SFP
        "It's cold outside!"

(16)   "(But) it's [cold]$\nearrow$ outside$\searrow$..."

There are two ways to think about this: either the intonation expressing the emotive content only is sufficient to implicate the meaning component corresponding to yo in some way, or English intonation is actually encoding "grammatical" meaning. I suggest that the latter might be the case, not least because there is no clear mechanism to derive such rather complex meaning by implicature from a mere expression of a strong emotional attitude.

It remains for future research to see whether the emotive meaning component can be separated from expressive meaning concerned with premise- and expectation management by somehow neutralizing intonational aspects such as lengthening and intensified variation in pitch. Whether this is possible or not, the case of prosodic morphemes presented here should provide some motivation to have a closer look at intonational meaning in areas that have previously been considered "paralinguistic" rather than "grammatical".

Acknowledgments. I thank three anonymous reviewers and the audience at LENLS for valuable comments. This work was supported by JSPS KAKENHI Grant-in-Aid for Early-Career Scientists Number 22K13112.

References

1. Davis, C.: Decisions, dynamics and the Japanese particle 'yo'. J. Semant. **26**(4), 329–366 (2009)
2. Grice, H.P.: Logic and conversation. In: Syntax and Semantics, Vol. 3, Speech Acts, pp. 41–58. Academic Press, New York (1975)
3. Gunlogson, C.: True to form: rising and falling declaratives as questions in English. Ph.D. thesis, UCSC (2003)
4. Heim, I.: On the projection problem for presuppositions. In: Formal Semantics: The Essential Readings, pp. 249–260. Wiley (1983)
5. Kratzer, A.: Modals and Conditionals. Oxford University Press, Oxford (2012)
6. McCready, E.: Particles: dynamics vs. utility. Jpn./Korean Linguist. **16**(6) (2007)
7. Oshima, D.Y.: On the functions of the Japanese discourse particle *yo* in declaratives. In: McCready, E., Yabushita, K., Yoshimoto, K. (eds.) Formal Approaches to Semantics and Pragmatics. SLP, vol. 95, pp. 251–271. Springer, Dordrecht (2014). https://doi.org/10.1007/978-94-017-8813-7_12
8. Phillips, J.S., Kratzer, A.: Decomposing modal thought (2022). https://doi.org/10.31234/osf.io/g6tzc
9. Rieser, L.: Doubt, incredulity and particles in Japanese falling interrogatives. In: Proceedings of the 31st Pacific Asia Conference on Language, Information and Computation, pp. 25–33 (2018)
10. Rieser, L.: Anticipative and ethic modalities: Japanese *Hazu* and *Beki*. In: Sakamoto, M., Okazaki, N., Mineshima, K., Satoh, K. (eds.) JSAI-isAI 2019. LNCS (LNAI), vol. 12331, pp. 309–324. Springer, Cham (2020). https://doi.org/10.1007/978-3-030-58790-1_20
11. Rieser, L.: Deriving confirmation and justification—an expectative, compositional analysis of Japanese 'yo-ne'. In: Proceedings of the 34th Pacific Asia Conference on Language, Information and Computation, pp. 261–269 (2020)
12. Takubo, Y., Kinsui, S.: Discourse management in terms of mental spaces. J. Pragmat. **28**(6), 741–758 (1997)
13. Xu, Y.: Prosody, tone and intonation. In: The Routledge Handbook of Phonetics, pp. 314–356. Routledge (2019)

Comparing Degree-Based and Argumentative Analyses of *Even*

Pola Osher[✉] [ID] and Yael Greenberg [ID]

Department of English Literature and Linguistics, Bar Ilan University, Max ve-Anna Webb, 5290002 Ramat Gan, Israel
{osherpo,yael.grinberg}@biu.ac.il

Abstract. This paper adds to the discussion of the nature of the scale on which *even* operates: on which dimension is such a scale based? The paper suggests a comparative analysis of two recent accounts, namely the degree-based approach proposed by Y. Greenberg and the argumentative approach proposed by G. Winterstein. Following the former, *even* operates on a scale based on a gradable property. We claim that the argumentative approach of Winterstein may be interpreted as operating on the interval argumentative scale, which we suggest in this paper. The comparative analysis of the two approaches is conducted on three different levels: the level of data that they both account for (Sect. 3.2), on the structural level (Sect. 3.3), and on the functional level (3.4). At the end of the paper (cf. Sect. 4) we present some data that we believe to be challenging for both presented approaches; Sect. 5 draws conclusions.

Keywords: Scalar Particles · Degree Semantics · Argumentative analysis · Bayesian probability

1 Introduction

The semantics and pragmatics of the scalar focus-sensitive particle *even* (and its cross-linguistic correlates) have been the center of much discussion and debates. This is due to two reasons. First, *even* seems to encode an operator whose function – comparing the strength of alternatives, as will be discussed later, – is common in natural language, and second, because *even* is assumed to play a role in several puzzling linguistic phenomena, such as biased questions, the behavior of some Negative Polarity Items, etc.

One of the debates on the semantics and pragmatics of *even* concerns the nature of the scale along which the alternatives to the 'prejacent' are ordered: whether the scale is based on the dimension of unlikelihood [1–5], informativeness [6, 7], unexpectedness [8], noteworthiness [9], etc. In the paper we compare two recent approaches to this question, namely the degree-based analyses by Greenberg [10–13] and the argumentative analysis by Winterstein [14–16].

The two accounts have been developed independently, and besides a few comments [15, 16], there was no systematic study that directly examined both in comparison of their strengths and weaknesses. Neither was there any attempt to understand how these

D. Bekki et al. (Eds.): LENLS 2023, LNCS 14569, pp. 205–223, 2024.
https://doi.org/10.1007/978-3-031-60878-0_12

approaches may interact. The current paper aims at making progress towards closing this gap.

The paper is structured as follows: Sect. 2 presents theoretical background on the degree-based and the argumentative accounts. After formulating and comparing the scalar presupposition of *even* under each account, we show the similarity between two accounts, on three levels: first, we show that both the degree-based and the argumentative accounts are equally successful in accounting for felicity contrasts with *even* (Sect. 3.2), then we draw structural parallel between the two approaches (Sect. 3.3) and, finally, we argue that the scales used in both approaches can be re-defined in terms of intervals rather than in terms of points (Sect. 3.4). Such a step has already been independently taken with respect to scales associated with gradable predicates. We develop here a similar scale for the argumentative account of *even* – the interval argumentative scale (Sect. 3.4). Section 4 presents some open questions and Sect. 5 draws conclusions.

2 Theoretical Background

2.1 Unlikelihood-Based Accounts of *Even*

The current research on *even* [1, 2, 4, 5, 10–13, 18, 22–25] agrees that it is a scalar focus–sensitive operator, i.e., one that introduces focus alternatives to its prejacent, and ranks them on a scale. More specifically, *even* is taken to trigger a 'scalar presupposition' formulated along the following lines [1, 2, 10–12, 19]:

(1) $||even||^{g,c}$: $\lambda C.\ \lambda p.\ \lambda w$: $\forall q \in C\ q \neq p \rightarrow p > q.\ p\ (w) = 1$, where $C \subseteq ||p||^F \wedge ||p||^O$ $\in C \wedge \exists q\ q \neq p \wedge q \in C$[1]

Following Rooth [2, 18], set C of focus alternatives includes at least one contextually relevant proposition that is equivalent to the prejacent except for its focused element, which is replaced by an element of the same semantic. Consider an example:

(2) Peter *even* got $[100]_F$ in the exam.
    p – the denotation of 'Peter got a100 in the exam'.
    C: { 'Peter got a 100 in the exam'; 'Peter got an 85 in the exam'; 'Peter got a 60 in the exam '; 'Peter got a 45 in the exam'…}

Given the scalar presupposition of *even* in (1), the alternatives q of the prejacent p in C are ranked on a scale such that p is placed higher than any q. For example, in (2), getting a 100 is ranked higher on the scale than getting a lower grade. More formally, it can be represented as follows:

(3) $\forall q \in C\ q \neq$ 'Peter got a 100' $\rightarrow$ 'Peter got a 100' $> q$.

In prose, (3) says that getting a 100 is stronger on the relevant scale than, e.g., getting an 85, or getting a 60.

---

[1] In fact, *even* has been traditionally taken to be a 'scalar additive' focus particle, assuming that besides its scalar presupposition, it also triggers an 'additive' one, similarly to particles like *also* and *too*. However, this assumption is under debate [26–28], [3]. In this paper we focus only on the scalar presupposition of *even*.

Notice that in both (1) and (3) the 'stronger than' relation, $>$, is unspecified. One of the popular characterizations of this relation takes the scale to be based on the notion of unlikelihood [1–4, 18]. The scalar presupposition of *even* (1) specified for unlikelihood can be rewritten like this:

(3a) $\|even\|^{g,c}$: $\lambda C.$ $\lambda p.$ λw: $\forall q \in C$ $q \neq p \rightarrow p >$ *unlikely* $q.$ $p(w) = 1$,

which, in prose, says that *even* presupposes that its prejacent p, is more unlikely than every distinct alternative q in C. In (2), for example, this would mean that getting a 100 in the exam is presupposed to be more unlikely than for getting a lower grade.

The unlikelihood-based account of *even* accounts for various observations about the use of this particle. For example, it successfully explains felicity contrasts in (4):

(4) a. John got an [85]$_F$ in the exam. Bill *even* got [100]$_F$
    b. John got a [100]F in the exam. Bill (#*even*) got [85]$_F$

Given the unlikelihood-based scalar presupposition of *even* in (3), the prejacent p is placed higher on the scale of unlikelihood, than any of its alternatives q in C, because, indeed, getting 100 in the exam is more unlikely than getting any other lower grade, which makes (4a) felicitous. As for (4b), the same requirement doesn't stand, which is why (4b) is infelicitous.

In addition, the unlikelihood-based account was argued to successfully account for semantic effects of *even* in questions [22], and the behavior of some Negative Polarity Items [4, 42, 43].

2.2   The Degree-Based Account of *Even*

However, despite the advantages of the unlikelihood account, there have also been concerns about the characterization of the scale in terms of unlikelihood. Given such concerns, some authors claimed that the scale of *even* is rather based on alternative properties, i.e., the property of informativeness [6, 7], unexpectedness [8] or noteworthiness [9].

Greenberg's degree-based account is among these alternative accounts [10–13]. She claims that there are at least three reasons to doubt that the unlikelihood-based account is a good account for *even*. In this paper, we only briefly summarize these reasons, and mention them only with the purpose of highlighting Greenberg's analysis. In general, our analysis follows the critique of the unlikelihood-based approach, both from the gradability perspective [10–13] and from the argumentative perspective [16].

First, Greenberg shows that unlikelihood is not a necessary condition for the felicity of *even p*. Consider, for example, [10]:

(5) *Client*: I need a strong tool for this work. What materials are these two tools made of?
    Seller: Both tools are strong enough for what you need. The red one is made of strong aluminum and the blue one is *even* [made of steel]$_F$

Greenberg claims that given the common knowledge on what working tools are usually made of, p in (5) (*'The blue tool is made of steel'*) is not more unlikely but, in fact, less unlikely than its focus alternative q (*'The blue tool is made of strong aluminum'*). Nonetheless, *even* is perfectly felicitous in (5).

Second, unlikelihood is not a sufficient condition for felicity of *even p* [10], as the example below illustrates:

(6) *Context*: Any princess who gives birth can stay in the palace. If she gives birth to a boy, she also becomes a queen (i.e., on average 50% of those who give birth get to be queens).
    A: What's happening with Princess Jane?
    B: She gave birth. She *even* gave birth to [a boy]$_F$ / #[a girl]$_F$

Both giving birth to a boy and giving birth to a girl are less likely than giving birth, but nonetheless in this context *even* is felicitous only with the first option. So, unlikelihood does not seem sufficient for explaining the felicity contrast here.

Third and finally, both *p* and *q* should indicate degrees which are at least as high as the contextual standard. This property will be henceforth referred to as the evaluative requirement on *even*. To illustrate, compare the responses B1, B2 and B3 in the following example [10]:

(7) *Context*: John and Bill want to join our basketball team, where the standard height is 1.90 m.
    A: Well, what about John and Bill? Should we take them?
    B1: Well, John is [1.95 m]$_F$ tall. Bill is *even* [2.10]$_F$. (We can take both).
    B2: Well, John is [1.65 m]$_F$ tall. Bill is (#*even*) [1.75]$_F$. (We shouldn't take any of them).
    B3: Well, John is [1.75 m]$_F$ tall. Bill is (#*even*) [1.95]$_F$. (We can take only Bill).

Greenberg claims that B1 is felicitous since both *p* and *q* indicate degrees above the contextual standard of height. On the contrary, B2 fails to satisfy this requirement, since both *p* and *q* indicate degrees below the contextual standard, thus, B2 is infelicitous. Response B3 is also infelicitous, since only *p* indicates a degree above the standard, but *q* doesn't. This observation cannot be accounted for by the unlikelihood-based presupposition of *even* (3) either.

These considerations led Greenberg to suggest a degree-based account[2] of *even* [10–13]. She introduces a gradable property G which underlines the scale to which *p* and its alternatives are being mapped. It is important to stress that G is a contextually salient property, and it is determined by a QUD (Question Under Discussion, cf. [17]), by a salient goal, etc.

Following the observations above, and ideas in Beck [44] on the semantics of comparative correlatives (e.g., *The taller John is, the more suitable he is for the team*), the gradability-based presupposition of *even* is composed of two components, where *x* is a non-focused element in *p* (e.g., *Peter* in (2)):

(8) a. A comparative component: *x*'s degree on a G scale in the accessible *p* worlds is higher than in the accessible *q*-and-not-*p* worlds.
    b. An evaluative component: *x*'s degree on a G scale in the accessible *p* worlds and in the accessible *q*-and-not-*p* worlds is at least as high as the standard of G.

Formally (8) can be put together as the following formulation of the scalar presupposition of *even*:

---

[2] The account was originally referred to as 'gradability-based' [10–12].

(9) $\forall q \in C q \neq p \rightarrow \forall w_1, w_2 \, [wRw_1 \wedge wRw_2 \wedge w_2 \in p \wedge w_1 \in [q \wedge \neg p]] \rightarrow$ [the max $(\lambda d2.G \, (d_2) \, (x) \, (w_2)) >$ the max $(\lambda d_1.G \, (d_1) \, (x) \, (w_1)) \wedge$ the max $(\lambda d_1.G \, (d_1) \, (x)$ $(w_1)) \geq \text{stand}_G$]

As Greenberg shows, this new definition of the scalar presupposition of *even* has three important features. First, it doesn't directly compare the propositions p and q but does that in an indirect way, by comparing degrees of non-focused entities (x) in accessible worlds where *p* holds to those where *q*-and-not-*p* holds [10]. Second, the scale on which the alternatives are ordered is not associated with the property of unlikelihood but rather with a salient property G, which helps to correctly account for a wider range of felicitous cases with *even*. Finally, the degrees indicated by *p* and *q* are compared to the standard on the *G* scale. Let's illustrate these three features by going back to example (5):

(10) (copied from 5) *Client*: I need a strong tool for this work. What materials are these two tools made of?
Seller: Both are strong enough for what you need. The red one is made of strong aluminum and the blue one is *even* [made of steel]$_F$

What is being compared here are not directly the propositions p ('*the tool is made of strong aluminum*') and q ('*the tool is made of strong aluminum*'), as in the unlikelihood-based account. Rather, there is an indirect comparison of the degrees of an element *x* in the alternatives (*the blue tool*) on a scale based on G property – which, in this case, is '*suitability*' (see Fig. 1 below):

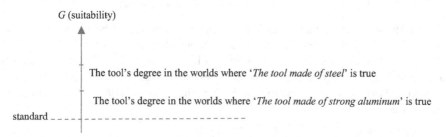

Fig. 1. A scale for example (5).

Thus, being made of the strongest material (steel), the blue tool is indeed most suitable for the purpose of the client, therefore, it gets put higher on the suitability (*G*) scale than the tool made of a different material. In addition, both tools are presupposed to be suitable, i.e., both have a degree above the standard of suitability.

2.3 The Argumentative Account of *Even*

The argumentative account offers a somewhat different analysis of *even*. The core idea of the argumentative approaches to language is that any utterance in discourse is oriented towards an argumentative goal [16, 20]. Within this group of approaches, some treat certain patterns of logical reasoning (e.g., conditionals, syllogistic reasoning) in Bayesian terms [29, 30], other make a broader use of Bayesian view and consider meaning to be probabilistic, e.g., based on degrees of belief [31, 32]. Yet another approach is more focused on certain linguistic expressions and directly applies Bayesian probability to their linguistic analysis [14, 15, 33]. The paper focuses on the latter approach.

The idea on which this argumentative approach is based goes back to the works of J-C. Anscombre and O. Ducrot [20]. These authors came up with an original interpretation of the concept of meaning: besides the truth-conditional component, an utterance contains a non-truth-conditional – argumentative – component which is crucial for the interpretation. This idea has been later applied to several expressions, e.g., *but* [34], *only* [35], *too* [16, 33], cross-linguistic analogs of *too* [36], cross-linguistic analogs of *even* [16], etc.

Following the idea of Anscombre and Ducrot [20, 37], for an utterance containing *even* to be felicitous, the prejacent must be a stronger argument for a hypothesis than the antecedent. This requirement is composed of two claims:

(11) a. Argumentative co-orientation: both the prejacent and the antecedent are arguments for the same hypothesis.
b. Argumentative superiority: the prejacent is a stronger argument than the antecedent.

Based on this account, a probabilistic interpretation of the relation 'is an argument for' was suggested by Winterstein [15]:

(12) A set of premises R is an argument for a hypothesis H iff $P(H|R) > P(H)$, i.e., the probability of H after learning that R is true (the posterior probability) is higher than it before learning that R is true (the prior probability).

We simplify this definition here by taking an argument to be a singleton-set of premises, i.e., a proposition that increases the probability of a hypothesis.

To calculate the influence that an argument has on a hypothesis (whether it leads to an increase of the prior probability or not), two steps must be made. First, one needs to calculate the posterior probability of the hypothesis, i.e., $P(H|R)$. This is done using Bayes' rule:

(13) Bayes' rule: $P(H|R) = P(R|H) \times P(H))/P(R)$,
where: $P(H|R)$ – the posterior probability, i.e., the probability of a hypothesis H given an argument R;
$P(R|H)$ – the likelihood of an argument R to be true given that a hypothesis H is indeed true;
$P(H)$ – the prior probability of a hypothesis H, i.e., the probability of H to be true without any given argument;
$P(R)$ – the marginal probability, i.e., the probability of an argument R given any hypothesis.

The second step is to compare $P(H|R)$ to $P(H)$ – to check whether an argument R supports a hypothesis H: if $P(H|R)$ is higher than $P(H)$, then an argument increases the degree of belief in the hypothesis. In other words:

(14) An argument R supports a hypothesis H iff $P(H|R) > P(H)$. If it is the case, it is reasonable to conclude that R is a suitable supporting argument for H, or, in other words, R is an argument for H.

So, the argumentative co-orientation (11a) and the argumentative superiority (11b) requirements for *even* are reformulated by Winterstein in Bayesian terms, as in (15):

(15) a. Argumentative co-orientation: $P(H|q) > P(H)$ and $P(H|p) > P(H)$, i.e., both p and q are arguments for hypothesis H.
b. Argumentative superiority: $P(H|p) > P(H|q)$. i.e., the prejacent p is a stronger argument for H than q.

The figure below captures both conditions for the felicity of *even* under the argumentative account (Fig. 2):

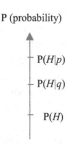

Fig. 2. Felicitous use of *even* (P is the probability scale, p is a prejacent, q is an antecedent, H is a hypothesis).

To illustrate how the argumentative analysis works, we review the following example [15]:

(16) The concert was a success. Brian played a song. Lemmy *even* [came on stage]_F.
The analysis goes as the following: '*Lemmy comes on stage*' is the prejacent p, '*Brian plays a song*' is the antecedent q (which is not a focus alternative of p). '*The concert is a success*' is the hypothesis H. $H|q$ is '*The concert is a success (if) Brian plays a song*'; and $H|p$ is '*The concert is a success (if) Lemmy comes on stage*'.

The co-orientation requirement for this example (15a) means that both p and q are arguments for the hypothesis (the success of the concert), i.e., the posterior probability $P(H|q)$, as well as the posterior probability $P(H|p)$ is higher than the prior probability of the hypothesis, $P(H)$. In other words, the fact that Brian plays a song, as well as the fact that Lemmy comes on stage, are both reasons for the concert to be a success.

Given the argumentative superiority constraint (15b), '*Lemmy comes on stage*' is a stronger argument than '*Brian plays a song*', for the hypothesis that the concert is a success, since., the former would lead to a higher posterior probability of H than the latter.

3 Comparing the Degree-Based and the Argumentative Analysis of *Even*

3.1 Methodology

In this paper we focus on comparing one difference between the degree-based and the argumentative accounts of *even*, namely the characterization of the scale on which *even* operates. Notice that there seem to be (at least) two other differences between these accounts. The first is that the argumentative account does not explicitly take two requirements (the argumentative co-orientation and the argumentative superiority) as presuppositional. In this paper, however, we follow traditional theories, and we assume that both requirements are indeed presuppositional.

Second, in the degree-based account (as well as the unlikelihood-based account) the alternatives are explicitly defined as focus alternatives, but not so in the argumentation-based account. Notice, that in both (15a) and (15b), p and q stand for the prejacent and its antecedent respectively, which, unlike what is assumed in the entry for *even* in (3) above, need not be focus alternatives. Example (16) above illustrates this difference[3]. However, to isolate just the characterization of the scale at this point, we recast Winterstein's proposal in terms of focus alternatives.

In other words, in what follows we compare the following two versions of the scalar presupposition of *even*: the degree-based scalar presupposition of *even* (17) and the argumentation-based one (18). For the prejacent of *even* p and any focus alternative q in C:

(17) A degree-based scalar presupposition: *even* (C) (p) presupposes that for any focus alternative q in C both the comparative component (8a) and the evaluative component (8b) hold.

(18) An argumentation-based scalar presupposition: *even* (C) (p) presupposes that for any focus alternative q in C both the argumentative co-orientation requirement (15a) and the argumentative superiority requirement (15b) hold.

The comparison of the degree-based and the argumentative approaches to *even* consists of the three following stages: on the first stage, we argue that both the degree-based and the argumentative accounts successfully capture felicity contrasts with *even* (see Sect. 3.2). On the second stage, we show the structural parallel between two accounts (see Sect. 3.3). Finally, in Sect. 3.4 we propose a further potential similarity between two approaches, namely the fact that in both approaches the scale, originally based on points, can be redefined in terms of intervals. Such a step can be supported for the degree-based scale by existing work on scales associated with gradable adjectives, and we will develop a parallel interval argumentative scale as well.

3.2 Accounting for the Same Data with *Even*

The first goal of this subsection is to claim that the argumentation-based approach can successfully account for the same data that the degree-based can account for. To do that,

---

[3] Indeed, in this case, q, '*Brian plays a song*', is not a member of a set C of focus alternatives to p, '*Lemmy comes on stage*'. In this case C is defined as following: { '*Lemmy comes on stage*', '*Lemmy dances*', '*Lemmy signs his favorite song*'... }.

we\proceed as follows: the first step is to show that whatever data that is accounted for by the degree-based approach, can be also accounted for by the argumentative approach. To show that we go back to two examples – one felicitous, one infelicitous, that were analyzed in terms of the degree-based approach earlier (see examples 5 and 7 in Sect. 2.2), and we will analyze them in terms of the argumentative account.

The second step would be to support the opposite: whatever data the argumentative approach accounts for can also be accounted for by the degree-based approach. To do that we take the felicitous example (16), which was analyzed in argumentative terms earlier, and show how it is analyzed in terms of the degree-based approach. Then we introduce another – infelicitous example (24) and demonstrate that the same claim still holds.

To start with the first step, and the felicitous examples, let's address example (9) which was discussed earlier when reviewing the degree-based approach. Our goal now is to show that the argumentative approach can account for this piece of data as well. Here is an example:

(19) (copied from 5) *Client*: I need a strong tool for this work. What materials are these two tools made of ?
   Seller: Both are strong enough for what you need. The red one is made of strong aluminum and the blue one is *even* made of [steel]$_F$

Here is how this example would look in argumentative terms. First, we must assume that in this case the salience of the previously uttered sentence forces the focus alternative, which are constructed based on it, into the set C (see [13]). Thus, the set of contextually supplied focus alternatives C can be taken to be { '*The blue tool is made of steel*', '*The blue tool is made of strong aluminum*', …}. Therefore, the hypothesis and the arguments can be captured as follows:

(20) *Hypothesis*: The blue tool is suitable for gardening[4].
   Argument q: The blue tool is made of strong aluminum.
   Argument p: The blue tool is made of steel.

This example is felicitous because both the argumentative co-orientation and the argumentative superiority requirements are in place: the argumentative co-orientation requirement for this example means that both being made of strong aluminum and being made of steel make this tool suitable for gardening. The argumentative superiority requirement is also met in this case: the fact that the tool is made of steel (the case of the argument p) raises the probability that it is a suitable tool for gardening, more than for the case of the argument q, where the tool is made of a less strong, and thus a less suitable, material. Since both requirements are met, the scalar presupposition (18) is satisfied and *even* is felicitous in (20).

So far, we showed that the argumentation-based account can capture the felicity of *even* in cases like (20), just as well as the degree-based account. Now, we are going to show it can also successfully capture cases where *even* is infelicitous. To illustrate this, we consider the felicity contrast in cases like (5):

---

[4] Note that there is more than one way to formulate the hypothesis for each set of arguments, since the hypotheses are contextually supplied.

(21) (copied from 7): *Context*: John and Bill want to join our basketball team, where
the standard height is 1.90 m.

A: Well, what about John and Bill? Should we take them?

B1: Well, John is 1.95 m tall. Bill is (*even*) [2.10]$_F$. (We can take both).

B2: Well, John is 1.65 m tall. Bill is (??*even*) [1.75]$_F$. (We shouldn't take them).

B3: Well, John is 1.75 m tall. Bill is (??*even*) [1.95]$_F$. (We can take Bill)

Assuming again that all alternatives here are focus alternatives to the prejacent, all of
them are about Bill. We then assume that the arguments for a hypothesis must be about
Bill as well, e.g., that Bill is eligible to join the basketball team, as in (22):

(22) *Hypothesis*: Bill is eligible to join the basketball team where the standard height is
1.90 m.

Based on (21), there are three sets of arguments, which are listed in below (Table 1):

Table 1. Felicity contrasts for example (22).

Case B1 (felicitous)	Case B2 (infelicitous)	Case B3 (infelicitous)
Argument q: Bill is 1.95 m tall *Argument p:* Bill is 2.10 m tall	*Argument q:* Bill is 1.65 m tall *Argument p:* Bill is 1.75 m tall	*Argument q:* Bill is 1.75 m tall *Argument p:* Bill is 1.95 m tall
Argumentative co-orientation: satisfied	Argumentative co-orientation: fails	Argumentative co-orientation: fails

In all three cases the argumentative superiority is satisfied: the prejacents in each case
are better arguments for the hypothesis than the antecedents. However, the argumentative
co-orientation is satisfied only in B1, where both the prejacent and the antecedent are
arguments for the hypothesis, i.e., both raise the probability of *Bill is eligible to join the
team*. In B2, neither the prejacent *p* nor the alternative *q* are arguments for the hypothesis
H. In B3 only the prejacent *p* is an argument for the hypothesis H, but the antecedent *q*
is not. Therefore, only case B1 is felicitous.

So far, we have demonstrated that our claim that the argumentative approach successfully captures felicity contrasts with *even*, same as the degree-based approach. Now
we are going to demonstrate the inverted claim, namely that the data captured by the
argumentative approach can also be captured by the degree-based approach. First, let's
take a felicitous example (16), copied below:

(23) The concert was a success. Brian played a song. Lemmy *even* [came on stage]$_F$.

The prejacent *p* here is '*Lemmy came on stage*'. Since only the focus alternatives
to *p* are taken into consideration, as was explained earlier (see Sect. 3.1), the set *C* can
be taken to be the following: {'*Lemmy came on stage*', '*Lemmy danced*', '*Lemmy sang
a song that everybody loves*', ...}. The *G* property in (23) can be taken to measure
degrees of contribution to the success of the concert: to what extent Lemmy coming on
stage/dancing/singing the song that everybody loves contributes to the success of the
concert. Thus, the degrees of *x*'s (where *x* is 'Lemmy') contribution to the success of the

concert are compared in the accessible worlds where Lemmy does these things. *Even* presupposes that (a) Lemmy's degree of contribution to the success of the concert in the accessible worlds where he comes on stage is higher that the degree of his contribution to the success of the concert in the accessible worlds where he plays a song but does not come on stage (comparative component); and (b) in both kinds of words Lemmy contributes to the success of the concert, i.e. the degree of contribution is above the standard (evaluative component). Since both requirements can be easily met in the context, *even* is correctly predicted to be felicitous in (23).

Now, when we have illustrated that our claim holds for felicitous cases, we want to demonstrate that the same claim holds for infelicitous cases. We first analyze example (24) in argumentative terms, and then we analyze the same example using the degree-based approach. Compare the following statements [16]:

(24) *Context*: I recently read a lot!
    a. For example, today I read two books. Yesterday I *even* read three.
    b. For example, today I read two books. Yesterday I (#*even*) read one.

Given the context, the hypothesis in (24) is '*I read a lot*'. In (24b) the argument q is '*Today I read two books*' and the argument p is: '*Yesterday I read one book.*' In argumentative terms, (24b) is infelicitous since the argumentative superiority requirement fails, since reading one book (argument p) is not a stronger argument for H than q. Thus, even if the argumentative co-orientation is in place, (24b) is infelicitous.

Now, in terms of the degree-based account, the G property can be taken to be 'erudition'. Thus, the degrees of erudition of an element x ('*I*') in the world where 'I read two books' is true, is compared to the degree of erudition of an element x ('*I*') in the world where 'I read one book' is true. Since the former is getting mapped on G lower than the latter, the use of *even* in (24b) is infelicitous, although reading one or two books a day signalizes a certain level of erudition (e.g., the evaluative component is met).

We have shown that both the degree-based and the argumentative approaches successfully account for the same data (see felicitous examples 20 and 22 and infelicitous examples 23 and 24). This parallel provides grounds for the following generalization, which serves as the starting point in our comparison:

(25) *Claim*: The argumentative account and the degree-based account can both successfully capture the properties of felicitous and infelicitous cases of *even*.

3.3 Structural Similarity

In the previous subsection we have shown that both approaches are equally good at capturing felicity contrasts with *even*. This subsection suggests a claim which can be generalized from the data that was analyzed: the reason for the fact that both approaches are equally successful in accounting for the same data with *even* is that both approaches have similarities on a structural level. Both approaches formulate two components that have to be satisfied for *even* to be felicitous, and there is the following structural similarity between them: the evaluative component (8b) in the degree-based account corresponds to the argumentative co-orientation requirement (11a) in the argumentative account, and the comparative component (8a) in the degree-based account corresponds to the argumentative superiority requirement (11b) in the argumentative account (Table 2).

Table 2. Structural similarity between the two accounts.

Degree-based account	Argumentative account
Evaluative component	Argumentative co-orientation requirement
Comparative component	Argumentative superiority requirement

3.4 A Final Potential Similarity: Interval-Based Instead of Points-Based Scales

In the previous subsection we have claimed that there is a structural parallel between the component of the presupposition of *even* un two approaches, e.g., that the components for felicity of *even* seem to impose similar constraints. We have also suggested that this structural parallel is the reason for the fact that the argumentation-based approach can successfully account for the same felicity contrasts with *even* as well as the degree-based account. This was done by relying on both comparative and evaluative components in the degree-based account, and on both the argumentative co-orientation and the argumentative superiority in the argumentative account.

In this subsection propose a further potential similarity between the approaches, namely the fact that in both the scale, originally based on points, can be redefined in terms of intervals.

For instance, for the degree-based approach, one can potentially redefine the comparative and evaluative components in terms of intervals: the evaluative component requires that the length of the interval measuring the difference between the degree of x on the G scale and the standard on the scale, in both accessible *p*-worlds and *q-but-not-p* worlds is a positive number. The comparative component requires that there is a positive difference between the degree of x on the G scale in the accessible *p*-worlds, and in the accessible *q-but-not-p*-worlds.

Such a potential step still needs to be precisely developed. Luckily, there are already existing theories which developed tools for doing that, and which provided independent motivation for using interval-based rather than points-based scales for various degree-based constructions, e.g. those with gradable adjectives. For example, Kennedy & Levin [45] develop a 'measure of change' function (instead of the usual measure function), which is based on differentials between degrees and standards, to account for the variable telicity of (some) degree achievements. Kennedy & McNally [21] and more recently Zhang & Ling [46] develop an interval / differential analysis of comparatives. Brasoveanu [47] develops an interval-based analysis of comparative correlatives. Finally, Greenberg [48], Thomas [49] use a differential-based analysis of incremental *more*. In future research we hope to examine the way to apply the ideas and tools in these theories, so a fully worked-out interval-based scale for *even* can be developed.

In the rest of this section we want to sketch an interval-argumentative scale for *even* as well. We start with the definition in (26):

(26) For any interval $I = [a, b]$ in the set $\mathbb{R}$ of real numbers, $\ell(I) = b - a$, where $\ell(I)$ is the *length of the interval*.

Applying this notion to the current analysis, each interval gets associated with the numeric value – the length of an interval – which represents the effect that an argument has on a hypothesis, i.e., the difference between the posterior probability and the prior probability of the hypothesis.

Both components of the argumentative scalar presupposition of *even* (18) can be easily redefined in terms of intervals. In particular, the argumentative co-orientation can be formulated in terms of intervals:

(27) a. $\ell(\mathrm{I}p) = \mathrm{P}\,(H\,|p) - \mathrm{P}(H)$ is a positive number
b. $\ell(Iq) = \mathrm{P}\,(H\,|q) - \mathrm{P}(H)$ is a positive number

And the argumentative superiority in terms of intervals is the following:

(28) $\mathrm{P}(H) < \mathrm{P}(H|q) < \mathrm{P}(H|p) \Leftrightarrow \ell(Iq) < \ell(\mathrm{I}p)$

An illustration of a scale that accommodates both (27) and (28) is presented below (where p is the prejacent, q is an alternative, Ip is the interval associated with the argument p, Iq is the interval associated with the argument q) (Fig. 3):

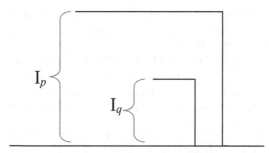

Fig. 3. Felicitous use of *even* (P is the probability scale, p is the prejacent, q in the antecedent, H is a hypothesis).

Such a scale can easily be used to distinguish between the felicitous and infelicitous cases with *even*. For example, the felicity contrast in (24), that was analyzed earlier: (29, copied from 24).

(29) *Context*: I recently read a lot!
a. For example, today I read two books. Yesterday I *even* read three.
c. For example, today I read two books. Yesterday I (#*even*) read one.

For (29a) and given the hypothesis '*I read a lot recently*' and the arguments *q:* '*Today I read two books*' and *p:* '*Yesterday I read three books*', one needs to calculate the posterior probabilities $\mathrm{P}(H|q)$ and $\mathrm{P}(H|p)$ for each argument separately. Naturally, since reading at least one whole book in a day is a lot, there is no doubt that both intervals, the one associated with p and the one associated with q, are going to be represented on the scale, i.e., the argumentative co-orientation is satisfied. Also, the more one reads, the more one can be taken for a person who reads a lot, the prejacent p would strengthen the hypothesis more than the antecedent q. Thus, the length of the interval associated with the argument p is going to be greater than the length associated with the argument q, i.e., $\ell(\mathrm{I}p) > \ell(Iq)$, which means that the argumentative superiority is satisfied.

In (29b) the hypothesis is the same, '*I read a lot recently*', but the arguments differ: argument q is '*Today I read two books*' and argument p is: '*Yesterday I read one book*'. Again, the argumentative co-orientation is satisfied, since reading even one whole book a day is a lot. However, the prejacent p fails to strengthen the hypothesis more than the antecedent q, thus, the length of the relevant interval is going to be smaller than the length associated with the argument q, i.e., $\ell(Ip) < \ell(Iq)$, which means that the argumentative superiority would fail.

In future research we hope to deepen the comparison between an interval-based analysis for the degree-based and for the argumentative-based approaches to *even*, and to examine the motivations for each of them.

4 Challenges and Open Questions

4.1 Cases with Irrelevant Alternatives

A piece of data which seems to be contradicting the suggested argumentative account, was brought up by Zhang [38]. Zhang argues that, unlike what is required in the degree-based account, given her QUD-based account, while p, the prejacent, needs to indicate a degree above the contextual standard (of G or, in terms of the QUD-based scale, G_{QUD}), no such requirement is imposed on the alternatives, q. As Zhang points out, the degree indicated by q can be either higher or lower than the standard. In her opinion, for example, this can account for the claim that *even* is felicitous in cases like the following:

(30) *Context*: Imagine Pooh and friends coming upon a bush of thistles. Eeyore (known to favor thistles) takes a bite but spits out. *Even* [Eeyore]$_F$ spit the thistles out.

Zhang claims that "from the truth of the proposition '*Eeyore spit the thistles out*', one knows that the thistles must be very prickly. On the other hand, from the truth of alternative propositions like '*Pooh spit the thistles out*', it remains rather unknown whether the thistles are prickly or not" ([38], p. 11). In other words, if Eeyore usually favors the thistles, even the relatively prickly ones, but this time he spit them out, this must be for no other reason than their unbearable prickliness. As for Pooh, there might be many different reasons for him to spit the thistles out, and it remains unknown for what reason it happens. Thus, there is a chance that he spit them out for a reason other than prickliness. If, for instance, Pooh spit the thistles out because he doesn't like them at all, this fact is irrelevant to whether the thistles are prickly or not. If this is indeed the case, according to Zhang, the degree of prickliness associated with q does not have to be above the standard.

To see whether the argumentative accounts reviewed above make the same predictions about (30), i.e., that this is a felicitous example, one needs to reconstruct the example (30) in argumentative terms now. In terms of the proposed argumentative account, the following interpretation seems valid:

(31) a. *Hypothesis*: thistles are prickly.
      b. *Argument q*: Pooh spit the thistles out (because he doesn't like them at all)
         Argument p: Eeyore spit them out (however, he likes thistles)

It turns out that argumentative accounts correctly predict the infelicity of (31a). First, in terms of two requirements by Winterstein, since the argument q is not an argument for H, it would not raise the $P(H)$ to any higher point since it would be the case where $P(H) = P(H|q)$: the argument q is irrelevant to the hypothesis H. This, in Winterstein's terms, would make the argumentative co-orientation requirement fail, therefore, leading to wrongly predicting the infelicity of (31a).

Moreover, the predictions of Zhang's analysis differ from the predictions of the interval-based point of view suggested in this paper, for the following reason: the interval that corresponds to the difference between the prior probability of the hypothesis, $P(H)$ and the posterior probability given q, would not be represented on the interval argumentative scale (since q wouldn't raise the prior probability of the hypothesis H). It means that the new superiority requirement (28) would fail, which would predict the infelicity of (31a). Therefore, the reasoning presented above reveals that Zhang's account and argumentative accounts make different predictions about the cases like (30)[5].

4.2 Cases of Mirative *Even*

As noted by Winterstein [15], there are some cases of *even* where both the argumentative co-orientation requirement and the argumentative superiority requirement are in place, but which are, nevertheless, infelicitous. Here is such an example:

(32) a. #Conference X is very attractive. You get a nice conference hat, and the organizers *even* invited interesting keynote speakers.

   b. Conference X is very attractive. The organizers invited interesting keynote speakers and you *even* get a nice conference hat.

Winterstein points out that having interesting talks is indeed a stronger argument for attending a conference, compared to receiving a hat [15], and both are clearly arguments for attending a conference. However, (32a) is infelicitous. Moreover, changing the order of the arguments (as in (32b), and, therefore, making the argumentative superiority requirement fail, would, surprisingly, make the use of *even* felicitous, thus contradicting the theory of Anscombre & Ducrot [20]).

Such uses of *even* have a 'mirative' flavor, in the sense of [40], i.e., they express 'surprise' (as originally argued in [39]). Winterstein then tries to build a finer account for *even*, which would accommodate the interpretation of such mirative uses of *even*, like (32a and 32b). As one possible interpretation of such a scale for *even*, Winterstein discusses the unlikelihood-based one. Since the mirative cases do not fit in the probability-based argumentative account, the one based on, there is a chance that they would be accounted for by a modified theory, which is closer to the unlikelihood account. This is done in the following way.

The notion of unlikelihood receives an interpretation in terms of probability: it is treated as prior probability of the prejacent and of the antecedent. Thus, the unlikelihood

---

[5] As an anonymous reviewer reasonably pointed out, one of the ways to look at it is noticing that there is no alternative proposition (e.g. '*Pooh spitting the thistles out*') uttered out in cases like (30). Further research is required to determine whether adding a constructive antecedent makes a difference to the interpretation.

requirement (3a) would mean that the prior probability of the prejacent is lower than the prior probability of the antecedent, i.e., $P(p) < P(q)$. In (32a), then, *even* is infelicitous because although indeed having keynote speakers is a better argument for the conference's success than getting nice hats, the former is less unlikely than the latter, and not more unlikely, as was required before by $P(p) < P(q)$.

Winterstein does follow the general idea of the unlikelihood-based account for such cases, but not entirely. Thus, being convinced by Greenberg's argumentation [11, 12], Winterstein rejects the 'bare likelihood' account too, as it leads to unpleasant circumstances such as over- and under-generalizations [15]. He suggests a modified version of the argumentative account [16] with the requirement for mirative cases of *even*. As it can be noticed, such version of the shares some features with both Anscombre & Ducrot's account, on one hand, and Greenberg's approach, on the other:

(33) a. $P(H|p) > P(H)$ and $P(H|q) > P(H)$, i.e., both the prejacent and the antecedent of *even* are arguments for the same hypothesis (argumentative co-orientation requirement, same as in Anscombre & Ducrot [20].
b. $P(p|H) < P(q|H)$, i.e., assuming the hypothesis is true, the prejacent is less likely to be true than the antecedent (comparative component, similar to Greenberg [11].

Such an account allows to relate an argument to a hypothesis instead of treating it in terms of 'bare likelihood'. Returning to example (32), it is now easy to explain the felicity of (32b): one would expect less of an attractive conference to offer nice hats than to be provided with good academic content. In other words, in such mirative uses of *even*, the prejacent is less likely than the antecedent. So, the felicity contrast in (32a) and (32b) might be explained by the modified argumentative account that Winterstein suggests for the mirative uses of *even*.

Besides, there might be another way to interpret the data like (32), along the following lines. One could claim that in terms of example (32b), the prejacent p by itself is not an argument for the hypothesis, i.e., getting a nice hat is not a good enough reason to attend a conference, however, it is a relevant argument. In this sense, getting a hat would be the least cause to attend a conference, which, however, being summed up with another good argument, becomes 'the straw that broke the camel's back', the last cause convincing a person to attend a conference. A similar case is analyzed by Fauconnier [41]:

(34) Georges has drunk a little wine, a little cognac, a little rum, a little calvados and *even* a little armagnac.

The hypothesis in (34) would be *'Georges got drunk'* or *'Georges drunk too much'*. This example shows that what convinces the listener at the end is the sum of the arguments, where the prejacent of *even* might be not the stronger argument, but it is a crucial one, which makes the use of *even* felicitous in such cases.

This example poses challenges for both the unlikelihood and the gradeability-based account by Greenberg: the scalar presupposition would fail, which makes (34) infelicitous. It seems to create a challenge for the argumentative account as well, since p (*'George has drunk a little Armagnac'*) is not raising the posterior probability $P(H | p)$ higher than $P(H)$ (where H is *'Georges got drunk'*), because drinking just a little armangac (and, supposedly, nothing else), would not make Georges drunk. Therefore, the argumentative co-orientation requirement is not satisfied either[6].

5 Conclusion

In this paper, we explored the ongoing debates surrounding the nature of the scalar focus-sensitive particle *even*, with the focus on the characterization of the scale. Two prominent approaches, the degree-based and the argumentative account, were examined independently, each shedding light on different aspects of the particle's behavior. Greenberg's degree-based analysis challenged the conventional unlikelihood-based perspective and introduced the degree-based scalar presupposition of *even* composed of two requirements: an evaluative and a comparative requirement. Winterstein's argumentative account followed a distinctive perspective grounded in the idea that some linguistic expressions, including *even*, are fundamentally oriented towards argumentative goals. Being formulated in terms of Bayesian probability, this approach suggests what can be called the argumentation-based scalar presupposition of *even*, which is composed of argumentative co-orientation and argumentative superiority requirements, providing a fresh lens through which to analyze the felicity of *even* in discourse.

By systematically comparing the unlikelihood-based, the degree-based, and the argumentative accounts, we identified commonalities and differences. Notably, both the degree-based and argumentative accounts demonstrated equal success in accounting for felicity contrasts with *even*, which the unlikelihood-based account failed to accomplish.

The paper analyzed specific examples, demonstrating that the degree-based and the argumentative approach can account for the same data. Moreover, a structural parallel was drawn between the two approaches, emphasizing their compatibility. Structurally, the paper identifies parallels between the evaluative and comparative components of the degree-based account and the argumentative co-orientation and superiority requirements of the argumentative account, respectively. Finally, we proposed that within both approaches the original points-based scales can be re-defined as interval-based ones.

Challenges and open questions were addressed, including cases with irrelevant alternatives suggested by Zhang, and instances of 'mirative' *even* presented by Winterstein. The paper acknowledges contradictions in predictions between the proposed accounts and these cases, suggesting modifications to resolve inconsistencies. The discussion extends to cases where the prejacent itself may not be the strongest argument but plays a crucial role in overall persuasion, introducing challenges for various theoretical accounts.

---

[6] We would like to thank an anonymous reviewer for bringing up an idea of looking at argumentative as an incremental process: Given this proposal, the previous utterances (which might be different from alternatives) are considered in the evaluation of the prejacent. This would provide grounds to interpret cases like (34): drinking a little armagnac is not a strong enough argument per se for getting drunk, but it is a legitimate positive argument in combination with all the previous mentions of drinks. As our reviewer reasonably pointed out, the argumentative standard might need to be raised up from just $P(H)$ in order to exclude the singleton discourse 'Georges has drunk # even a little armagnac' since it is a positive argument, however small it is, toward the goal that Georges is drunk/got drunk too much. We hope to develop this direction in future research.

In summary, the paper systematically compares the degree-based and the argumentative approaches to the analysis of *even*, offering insights into their respective strengths, potential modifications, and challenges in accounting for this linguistic phenomenon.

References

1. Karttunen, L., Peters, S.: Conventional Implicature. In: Presupposition, pp. 1–56. Brill (1979)
2. Rooth, M.: A theory of focus interpretation. Nat. Lang. Semant. 75–116 (1992)
3. Lahiri, U.: The semantics and pragmatics of some scalar expressions in Spanish. Anuario Seminario Filología Vasca "Julio de Urquijo" 42(2), 359–389 (2008)
4. Chierchia, G.: Logic in Grammar: Polarity, Free Choice, and Intervention. OUP, Oxford (2013)
5. Horn, L.R.: A presuppositional analysis of only and even. In: Proceedings from the Annual Meeting of the Chicago Linguistic Society, vol. 5, no. 1, pp. 98–107. Chicago Linguistic Society (1969)
6. Kay, P.: Even. Linguist. Philos. 13, 59–111 (1990)
7. Gast, V., Van der Auwera, J.: Scalar additive operators in the languages of Europe. Language 2–54 (2011)
8. Zeevat, H.: "Only" as a mirative particle (2009)
9. Herburger, E.: What Counts: Focus and Quantification. MIT Press, Cambridge (2000)
10. Greenberg, Y.: Even, comparative likelihood and gradability. In: Proceedings of the Amsterdam Colloquium, vol. 20, pp. 147–156 (2015)
11. Greenberg, Y.: A novel problem for the likelihood-based semantics of even. Semant. Pragmat. 9, 2–1 (2016)
12. Greenberg, Y.: A revised, gradability-based semantics for even. Nat. Lang. Seman. 26(1), 51–83 (2018)
13. Greenberg, Y.: On the scalar antonymy of only and even. Nat. Lang. Seman. 30(4), 415–452 (2022)
14. Winterstein, G.: Layered meanings and Bayesian argumentation: the case of exclusives. In: Zeevat, H., Schmitz, H.-C. (eds.) Bayesian Natural Language Semantics and Pragmatics. LCM, vol. 2, pp. 179–200. Springer, Cham (2015). https://doi.org/10.1007/978-3-319-170 64-0_8
15. Winterstein, G.: A Bayesian approach to argumentation within language. Semantics Archive (2018). https://semanticsarchive.net/Archive/mFkZGM0N/Argumentation.pdf
16. Winterstein, G., et al.: From additivity to mirativity: the Cantonese sentence final particle tim1. Glossa: J. Gener. Linguist. 3(1) (2018)
17. Roberts, C.: Information structure: Towards an integrated theory of formal pragmatics, volume 49 of. Technical report, OSU Working Papers in Linguistics (1996)
18. Rooth, M.E.: Association with focus (montague grammar, semantics, only, even). University of Massachusetts Amherst (1985)
19. Wilkinson, K.: The scope of even. Nat. Lang. Seman. 4(3), 193–215 (1996)
20. Anscombre, J.C., Ducrot, O.: Argumentation dans la langue. Languages, 42, Argumentation et discours scientifique, pp. 5–27 (1983). https://www.jstor.org/stable/i40078942
21. Kennedy, C., McNally, L.: Scale structure, degree modification, and the semantics of gradable predicates. Language 345–381 (2005)
22. Guerzoni, E.: Why even ask?: on the pragmatics of questions and the semantics of answers. Doctoral dissertation, Massachusetts Institute of Technology (2003)
23. Guerzoni, E.: Even-NPIs in yes/no questions. Nat. Lang. Seman. 12(4), 319–343 (2004)

24. Crnic, L.: On the meaning and distribution of concessive scalar particles. In: Proceedings of NELS, vol. 41, pp. 1–14 (2011)
25. Crnič, L.: Non-monotonicity in NPI licensing. Nat. Lang. Seman. **22**, 169–217 (2014)
26. Wagner, M.: Even and the syntax of additivity. In: Colloquium Talk Given at the University of Chicago (2015)
27. Rullmann, H.: Even, polarity, and scope. Pap. Exp. Theor. Linguist. **4**(40–64) (1997)
28. Rullmann, H.: What does even even mean. Ms., University of British Columbia (2007)
29. Oaksford, M., Chater, N.: Bayesian Rationality: The Probabilistic Approach to Human Reasoning. Oxford University Press (2007)
30. Chater, N., Oaksford, M., Hahn, U., Heit, E.: Bayesian models of cognition. Wiley Interdisc. Rev.: Cogn. Sci. **1**(6), 811–823 (2010)
31. Lassiter, D.: Measurement and modality: the scalar basis of modal semantics, p. 9. Ph. D. thesis, New York University (2011)
32. Goodman, N.D., Lassiter, D.: Probabilistic semantics and pragmatics uncertainty in language and thought. Handb. Contemp. Semant. Theory 655–686 (2015)
33. Winterstein, G., Zeevat, H.: Empirical constraints on accounts of too. Lingua **122**(15), 1787–1800 (2012)
34. Winterstein, G.: What but-sentences argue for: an argumentative analysis of but. Lingua **122**(15), 1864–1885 (2012)
35. Winterstein, G.: Only without its scales. Sprache Datenverarbeitung **35**, 29–47 (2012)
36. Winterstein, G.: The Meaning of the French additive Aussi: presupposition and Discourse Similarity. In: Talk at Journées Sémantique et Modélisation, Nancy, 25–26 March 2010 (2010)
37. Ducrot, O.: Analyses pragmatiques. Communications **32**(1), 11–60 (1980)
38. Zhang, L.: The presupposition of even. In: Semantics and Linguistic Theory, vol. 1, pp. 249–269 (2022)
39. Zeevat, H.: Expressing surprise by particles. In: Beyond Expressives: Explorations in Use-Conditional Meaning, pp. 297–320. Brill (2013)
40. DeLancey, S.: Mirativity: the grammatical marking of unexpected information (1997)
41. Fauconnier, G.: Étude de certains aspects logiques et grammaticaux de la quantification et de l'anaphore en français et en anglais. Champion, Paris (1976)
42. Lahiri, U.: Focus and negative polarity in Hindi. Nat. Lang. Seman. **6**(1), 57–123 (1998)
43. Nakanishi, K.: Even, only, and negative polarity in Japanese. In: Proceedings of SALT 2016 (2006)
44. Beck, S.: On the semantics of comparative conditionals. Linguist. Philos. 229–271 (1997)
45. Kennedy, C., Levin, B.: Measure of change: the adjectival core of degree achievements (2008)
46. Zhang, L., Ling, J.: The semantics of comparatives: A difference-based approach. J. Semant. **38**(2), 249–303 (2021)
47. Brasoveanu, A.: Comparative correlatives as anaphora to differentials. In: Semantics and Linguistic Theory, pp. 126–143 (2008)
48. Greenberg, Y.: Additivity in the domain of eventualities (or: Oliver twist's 'more'). In: Proceedings of Sinn und Bedeutung, vol. 14, pp. 151–167 (2010)
49. Thomas, G.: Incremental more. In: Semantics and Linguistic Theory, pp. 233–250 (2010)

Appositive Projection as Implicit Context Extension in Dependent Type Semantics

Daiki Matsuoka[1]([⊠])[ID], Daisuke Bekki[2][ID], and Hitomi Yanaka[1][ID]

[1] The University of Tokyo, 7-3-1 Hongo, Bunkyo-ku, Tokyo 113-8656, Japan
{daiki.matsuoka,hyanaka}@is.s.u-tokyo.ac.jp
[2] Ochanomizu University, 2-1-1 Ohtsuka, Bunkyo-ku, Tokyo 112-8610, Japan
bekki@is.ocha.ac.jp

Abstract. The content of an appositive relative clause is a type of conventional implicature, that is, secondary or supplementary information of a sentence. Focusing on discourse behaviors and scopal properties, we present an analysis of appositive relative clauses based on Dependent Type Semantics, a type-theoretical semantic framework. Our central idea is that appositive content i mplicitly extends the typing context during the process of type checking, reflecting a property of conventional implicatures, namely, that they directly update the common ground.

Keywords: Dependent Type Semantics · appositive relative clause · conventional implicature · projection · not-at-issue content

1 Introduction

Appositive relative clauses (ARCs) typically convey secondary or supplementary information apart from the *at-issue* content (i.e., the main point of the whole sentence). As such, they are highly independent of their matrix clauses. For example, the ARC in (1) is not subject to negation, considering that (1) implies the appositive content (the professor had met Kim before).

(1)   The professor did not recognize Kim, whom she had met before.

This behavior is called *projection*, which is a central topic in formal semantics. [22] argued that projective meanings triggered by specific words or constructions such as ARCs form a distinct meaning class, called *conventional implicatures* (CIs) [11]. He proposed a semantic system in which CIs and at-issue meanings are given separate semantic representations.

However, since the proposal by [22], it has been suggested that the content of an ARC can have various types of interactions with its at-issue counterpart [1,3, 24,29]. Above all, there can be anaphoric dependencies between an ARC and its matrix clause, as shown by (2), which is quite difficult to explain if we separate the two clauses completely.

© The Author(s), under exclusive license to Springer Nature Switzerland AG 2024
D. Bekki et al. (Eds.): LENLS 2023, LNCS 14569, pp. 224–243, 2024.
https://doi.org/10.1007/978-3-031-60878-0_13

(2) John$_1$, who nearly killed a woman$_2$ with his$_1$ car, visited her$_2$ in the
     hospital.   (adapted from [3])

Nonetheless, the interaction is not entirely free. For instance, pronouns inside
an ARC cannot be bound by non-referential quantifiers [8,19].

(3) #No professor$_1$ recognized Kim, whom they$_1$ had met before.

Therefore, it is not obvious how we can formally account for the extent to which
appositive and at-issue content can interact with each other.

To address this issue, we present an analysis based on *Dependent Type
Semantics* (DTS) [5,7], a type-theoretical framework of natural language semantics. The basic idea of DTS is to use types as semantic representations (SRs)
and to reduce the felicity of a sentence to the well-formedness of its SR, which
is checked through a process called *type checking*. This setup provides us with
a unified method for capturing two classes of not-at-issue meanings—CIs and
presuppositions—as well as at-issue meanings.

The remainder of this paper is structured as follows. First, we describe several
properties of ARCs (Sect. 2) and introduce the details of DTS (Sect. 3). Then,
we propose an extension of DTS (Sect. 4) and discuss what predictions it makes
(Sect. 5). After briefly discussing some related work (Sect. 6), we conclude with
future research directions (Sect. 7).

2 Properties of Appositive Relative Clauses

2.1 Discourse Properties

Not-at-Issueness. The content of an ARC is generally supplementary; it is not
the central point of an utterance. Hence, ARCs contribute to a conversational
context in a particular way, as illustrated in (4). In (4b), B's response with *no*
targets the content of the matrix clause of (4a), which is at-issue. In contrast, (4c)
shows that such a response is not possible in regard to the appositive content.

(4) a. A: Mary, who is a post-doc researcher, gave a talk at the conference.
     b. B: No, she didn't. She wasn't able to attend.
     c. B: #No, she isn't. She is still in her PhD course.

Thus, appositive content *directly updates* the common ground in a non-negotiable
manner [3,18], which is not the case with at-issue content.

Anti-backgroundedness. ARCs basically add new information to a discourse.
Thus, if an ARC repeats something that has already been established as part
of the common ground, it results in redundancy. More broadly, this property
distinguishes CIs from presuppositions, which are supposed to already be in
the common ground. As shown in (5), an ARC containing information that has
already been introduced leads to infelicity, while such repetition is not problematic with *know*, which presupposes its complement.

(5)   a. #Bob has been friends with a linguistics student for a long time, and
           says that the student, who majors in linguistics, is very diligent.

       b. Bob has been friends with a linguistics student for a long time, but
           doesn't know that she majors in linguistics.

2.2   Scopal Properties

Projection. The content of an ARC is projective, meaning that it is not subject
to entailment-canceling operators in the matrix clause. Here are examples of
negation (6a) and conditional antecedent (6b).

(6)   a. It is not the case that Ann, who danced, met John. ⇒ Ann danced.

       b. If Ann, who danced, met John, Mary was happy. ⇒ Ann danced.

Quantifier Scope. ARCs cannot scopally interact with a quantified noun phrase
(NP) unless it is referential. (7) shows that non-referential quantified NPs can
neither be modified by an ARC nor bind a pronoun inside an ARC.[1] By contrast,
referential quantified NPs can have both types of interactions, as described in (8).

(7)   a. #{Every/No} girl, who met John, danced.

       b. #{Every/No} girl$_1$ met John, who praised her$_1$.

(8)   a. {A/Some} girl, who met John, danced.

       b. {A/Some} girl$_1$ met John, who praised her$_1$.

We remark that the indefinite NPs in (8) must be interpreted as *specific indefinites* [20,29], which basically have only the widest-scope reading. This point is
illustrated by (9), where *a professor* takes wider scope than the conditional.

(9)   If a professor, who is famous, meets Ann, she will be happy. (⇒ there is
       a famous professor.)

2.3   Anaphoric Dependencies

Anaphoric links can be established between an ARC and its matrix clause in
both directions (10). Presupposition resolution, which can also be regarded as
an anaphoric process [23], shows the same behavior. (11) shows examples of the
additive particle *too*.

---

[1] Note that an ARC can be adjacent to a non-referential quantified NP [4,9,19].

(i)   Less than half the climbers, who were French nationals, made it to the summit.
       (adapted from [19])

The ARC here is not semantically in the scope of *less than half the climbers* but
rather targets the whole restrictor. Because we presently cannot ascertain what
triggers this reading, we leave the analysis for future research.

(10) a. (Appositive → matrix) John, who met a girl$_1$, praised her$_1$.

  b. (Matrix → appositive) A girl$_1$ met John, who praised her$_1$. (=(8b))

(11) a. (Appositive → matrix) John, who praised Ann, praised Mary <u>too</u>.

  b. (Matrix → appositive) John$_1$ praised Ann, who praised him$_1$ <u>too</u>.

The same pattern can be observed for inter-sentential anaphora (12).

(12) a. (Appositive → matrix) John, who met a girl$_1$, smiled. She$_1$ danced.

  b. (Matrix → appositive) A girl$_1$ danced. John, who met her$_1$, smiled.

3   Framework

3.1   Dependent Type Theory

The theoretical foundation of DTS is *dependent type theory* (DTT) [16,17], a type theory with types that may depend on terms (*dependent types*). We can use DTT as a logical framework by viewing a type and its terms as a proposition and its proofs. For instance, we can regard a product type $A \times B$ as representing the conjunction $A \wedge B$ because its proof is a pair of proofs of A and B.

We can extend this correspondence to predicates using dependent types. For example, the type come(x), representing the proposition "x comes," depends on the variable x. Here, the one-place predicate come has type e → type, where e is the type of entities and type is the (higher-order) type of types.

Because types may depend on terms in DTT, we need to handle the well-formedness of types and typing contexts with inference rules. Hence, in addition to usual typing judgments $\Gamma \vdash M : A$ (the term M has type A under Γ), DTT has judgments of the form $\Gamma \vdash A :$ type (A is a well-formed type under Γ) and Γ valid (Γ is a well-formed context). Figure 1 shows the inference rules for well-formed contexts. As we will see in the following, this object-level representation of well-formedness is useful for analyzing the felicity of natural language utterances.

$$\text{(ctx-emp)} \frac{}{\langle \rangle \text{ valid}} \qquad \text{(ctx-ex)} \frac{\Gamma \text{ valid} \qquad \Gamma \vdash A : \text{type}}{\Gamma, x : A \text{ valid}} \ (x \notin \text{dom}(\Gamma))$$

Fig. 1. Inference rules for well-formed contexts. The rule (ctx-emp) introduces the empty context $\langle \rangle$ (which is omitted when unnecessary). The rule (ctx-ex) forms a well-formed context by extending one with a well-formed type and a fresh variable.

DTT has two special types: the *dependent product type* (Σ-type) $(x : A) \times B$ and the *dependent function type* (Π-type) $(x : A) \to B$. The former corresponds to the existential quantification $\exists x \in A.B$, and the latter corresponds to the universal quantification $\forall x \in A.B$. Their inference rules are listed in Fig. 2. Central to our approach are the rules (ΣE_1) and (ΣE_2), which take the first and second elements of a pair $\langle M, N \rangle$, respectively. With these rules, we can

$$(\Sigma F) \ \frac{\Gamma \vdash A : \mathsf{type} \qquad \Gamma, x : A \vdash B : \mathsf{type}}{\Gamma \vdash (x : A) \times B : \mathsf{type}} \qquad (\Sigma I) \ \frac{\Gamma \vdash M : A \qquad \Gamma \vdash N : B[x := M]}{\Gamma \vdash \langle M, N \rangle : (x : A) \times B}$$

$$(\Sigma E_1) \ \frac{\Gamma \vdash M : (x : A) \times B}{\Gamma \vdash \pi_1 M : A} \qquad (\Sigma E_2) \ \frac{\Gamma \vdash M : (x : A) \times B}{\Gamma \vdash \pi_2 M : B[x := \pi_1 M]}$$

$$(\Pi F) \ \frac{\Gamma \vdash A : \mathsf{type} \qquad \Gamma, x : A \vdash B : \mathsf{type}}{\Gamma \vdash (x : A) \to B : \mathsf{type}} \qquad (\Pi I) \ \frac{\Gamma, x : A \vdash M : B}{\Gamma \vdash \lambda x. M : (x : A) \to B}$$

$$(\Pi E) \ \frac{\Gamma \vdash M : (x : A) \to B \qquad \Gamma \vdash N : A}{\Gamma \vdash MN : B[x := N]}$$

Fig. 2. Inference rules of the Σ-type and the Π-type. In the labels, F, I, and E each stand for *formation, introduction, elimination* (e.g., (ΣI) is the introduction rule of the Σ-type).

refer to the content of a Σ-type from outside its scope by "decomposing" pairs. For example, consider (13a) and its semantic representation (13b). We adopt the notational convention that $(x : A) \times B$ can alternatively be written as $\begin{bmatrix} x : A \\ B \end{bmatrix}$.

(13)   a. A girl came.

   b. $\begin{bmatrix} u : \begin{bmatrix} x : \mathsf{e} \\ \mathsf{girl}(x) \end{bmatrix} \\ \mathsf{come}(\pi_1 u) \end{bmatrix}$

Here, the set of girls is represented by the type $(x : \mathsf{e}) \times \mathsf{girl}(x)$, which consists of pairs of an entity x and a proof of its being a girl. The part $\mathsf{come}(\pi_1 u)$ means that the girl came, because $\pi_1 u$ is the first element of u, namely, the entity x. In this way, Σ-types show the same effect as if their scope were extended, which captures the externally dynamic nature of existential quantification [12].

3.2   Underspecified Type

DTS extends DTT with a type of the form $(x @ A) \times B$, an *underspecified type* (@-type), which represents anaphoric or presuppositional meanings. This type is characterized by the following inference rule:

$$(@F) \ \frac{\Gamma \vdash A : \mathsf{type} \quad \Gamma \vdash M : A \quad \Gamma \vdash B[x := M] : \mathsf{type}}{\Gamma \vdash (x @ A) \times B : \mathsf{type}} \ \left(\xrightarrow{@\text{-elimination}} \Gamma \vdash B[x := M] : \mathsf{type} \right)$$

Intuitively, x is a placeholder in B for a concrete term M of type A. The term M is searched for when we type check the @-type, after which we replace x with M and obtain an @-free type $B[x := M]$.

To illustrate, consider how the pronoun *she* is resolved in (14a). The condition for the second sentence to be felicitous, which we call its *felicity condition* (FC), is described as in (14b), where the SR of the first sentence is in the typing context, meaning it has already entered the common ground. Here we use the square bracket notation $[\cdots]$ for the @-type, too. We also abbreviate $(x : e) \times Px$ as P^* when P is a constant of type $e \rightarrow$ type.

(14)   a.   A girl came. She danced.

b. $v : \underbrace{\begin{bmatrix} u : \texttt{girl}^* \\ \texttt{come}(\pi_1 u) \end{bmatrix}}_{\text{A girl came.}} \vdash \underbrace{\begin{bmatrix} w @ \texttt{female}^* \\ \texttt{dance}(\pi_1 w) \end{bmatrix}}_{\text{She danced.}} : \text{type}$

To derive (14b), we need to find a term of type $\texttt{female}^*$, as required by the second premise of the rule $(@F)$. By introducing the world knowledge that every girl is female and accordingly assuming a constant $\texttt{g-to-f} : (u : \texttt{girl}^*) \rightarrow \texttt{female}(\pi_1 u)$, we can construct the term $M_v = \langle \pi_1 \pi_1 v, \texttt{g-to-f}(\pi_1 v) \rangle$ of type $\texttt{female}^*$. Substituting this term for w, we obtain $\texttt{dance}(\pi_1 M_v)$, which reduces to $\texttt{dance}(\pi_1 \pi_1 v)$. This result correctly predicts that *she* can be bound by *a girl*, because $\pi_1 \pi_1 v$ refers to the entity introduced by the first sentence.

3.3   Type Checking and @-Elimination

To completely describe the formal system, we need to specify how we can substitute a term for the variable of an @-type during the process of type checking. In a recent version of DTS [5], the type checking function $[\![-]\!]$ returns a set of derivation trees for a typing judgment, with the clause for the @-type being as follows (see [5] for the clauses of other type constructors).[2] Note that the value of $[\![-]\!]$ is not a single derivation because there may be multiple ways to construct a term of type A.

$$[\![\Gamma \vdash (x @ A) \times B : \text{type}]\!] = \left\{ \text{Norm}(\mathcal{D}_3) \left| \begin{array}{l} \mathcal{D}_1 \in [\![\Gamma \vdash A : \text{type}]\!] \text{ (Let } \mathcal{D}_1\text{'s root be } \Gamma \vdash A' : \text{type)} \\ \mathcal{D}_2 \in [\![\Gamma \vdash M : A']\!] \text{ for some term } M. \\ \mathcal{D}_3 \in [\![\Gamma \vdash B[x := M] : \text{type}]\!] \end{array} \right. \right\}$$

The derivations of the three premises of the rule $(@F)$ are internally constructed, but $\mathcal{D}_1$ and $\mathcal{D}_2$ are discarded and only $\mathcal{D}_3$ is returned (after normalization). Thus, what we obtain as a result of type checking $(x @ A) \times B$ is the normal form of $B[x := M]$, as if it were the type we wanted to check from the beginning. Hereafter, we refer to this procedure as @-*elimination*.

To see how @-elimination works, consider the FC (14b) again. Figure 3 describes a series of steps to derive it. We write in the box the premises left to prove the FC, whose derivations are constructed one by one (each step is shown with a double arrow). The first step checks the well-formedness of $\texttt{female}^*$, which is trivial. In the second step, we look for a concrete term of type $\texttt{female}^*$, and one possible answer is $M_v = \langle \pi_1 \pi_1 v, \texttt{g-to-f}(\pi_1 v) \rangle$, as we have already seen in Sect. 3.2. The result of this search is propagated to the third premise (p3), which then requires $\texttt{dance}(\pi_1 M_v)$ to be well-formed. After this final premise is

---

[2] We define Norm as a function that returns, for any derivation of a typing judgment $\Gamma \vdash M : A$, a derivation where M is reduced to its normal form.

derived (indicated as "(done)"), what is returned as a result is $\mathsf{Norm}(\mathcal{D}_3)$, whose root is the judgment $v : [\cdots] \vdash \mathsf{dance}(\pi_1\pi_1 v) : \mathsf{type}$. We can see that the original @-type has been successfully transformed to the type that corresponds to the expected interpretation of the pronoun *she*. In this way, we can simultaneously perform type checking and eliminate @-types.

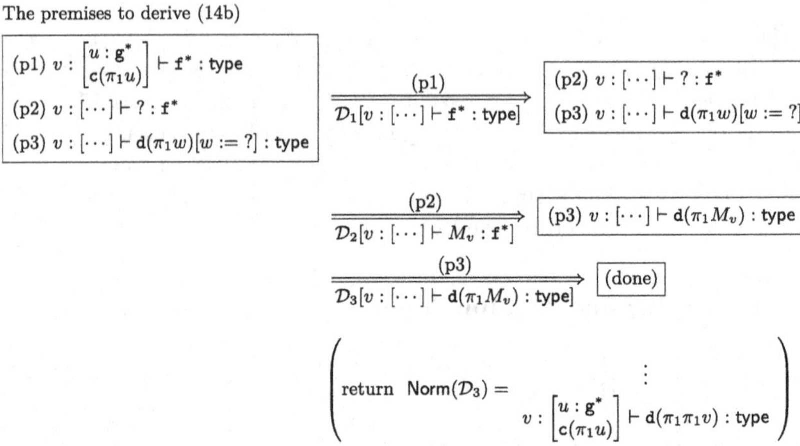

The premises to derive (14b)

Fig. 3. Process of deriving (14b). We abbreviate the names of the predicates (e.g., dance $\mapsto$ d). We also write $\mathcal{D}[J]$ for a derivation $\mathcal{D}$ with root J. M_v stands for the term $\langle \pi_1\pi_1 v, \mathsf{g\text{-}to\text{-}f}(\pi_1 v)\rangle$.

3.4   Two-Stage Validation

Before presenting our proposal, we must clarify how DTS processes discourses, which is crucial in distinguishing between at-issue and not-at-issue content. Importantly, type checking confirms only the FC of a sentence; it does not consider whether it will be accepted by the addressee. In other words, whether the SR is added to the typing context is determined after it is type checked, based on some pragmatic factors.[3] In this paper, we assume two validation stages before an SR A is added to the context Γ.

(i) **Type checking**: by calculating $[\![\Gamma \vdash A : \mathsf{type}]\!]$, we check the well-formedness of A under Γ and eliminate the @-types in A (let $\Gamma \vdash A' : \mathsf{type}$ denote the resultant judgment).

(ii) **Context extension**: we check whether A' is acceptable under Γ. If so, we extend Γ with A' by the rule (ctx-ex).

---

[3] Although it is beyond the scope of the present paper to characterize such factors, we require at least that accepting the assertion A does not contradict the preceding discourse Γ (i.e., $\Gamma, x : A \nvdash \bot$) and does not lead to redundancy (i.e., there is no M s.t. $\Gamma \vdash M : A$).

4 Proposal

The guiding intuition for our proposal is that CIs directly update the common ground, as we observed in Sect. 2.1. In light of the above-mentioned two-stage validation, this direct update should be before step (ii) (context extension); otherwise CIs would be directly challengeable (just like at-issue content), which would contradict their not-at-issueness. Thus, we must handle CIs during step (i) (type checking). @-types, which represent anaphoric or presuppositional content, are not appropriate for this purpose because CIs are anti-backgrounded. Therefore, we need a mechanism by which some content is added to, not resolved by, the context during type checking.

4.1 CI Type

We propose extending DTS with a new type $(x \triangleleft A) \times B$ (a *CI type*), characterized by the following inference rule:

$$(\triangleleft F) \quad \frac{\Gamma \vdash A : \text{type} \qquad \Gamma, x : A \vdash B : \text{type}}{\Gamma \vdash (x \triangleleft A) \times B : \text{type}} \quad \left(\xrightarrow{\triangleleft\text{-elimination}} \Gamma, x : A \vdash B : \text{type} \right)$$

As with the @-type, elimination of the $\triangleleft$-type is defined in a clause for $\llbracket - \rrbracket$.

$$\llbracket \Gamma \vdash (x \triangleleft A) \times B : \text{type} \rrbracket = \left\{ \mathcal{D}_2 \ \middle| \ \begin{array}{l} \mathcal{D}_1 \in \llbracket \Gamma \vdash A : \text{type} \rrbracket \ (\text{Let } \mathcal{D}_1\text{'s root be } \Gamma, \Delta \vdash A' : \text{type}) \\ \mathcal{D}_2 \in \llbracket \Gamma, \Delta, x : A' \vdash B : \text{type} \rrbracket \end{array} \right\}$$

Unlike the @-type, this type does not require a term of A for its well-formedness. Instead, it extends the context Γ with $x : A$ when it is eliminated after the two premises are derived. Conceptually, this context extension during type checking is *implicit* in that it leaves no room for the addressee to choose whether to accept or reject A. Such a response is possible only after step (i), namely, in step (ii) (which is, so to speak, an "explicit" context extension). This property of the $\triangleleft$-type captures the not-at-issueness and anti-backgroundedness of CIs.

With the $\triangleleft$-type, computing $\llbracket \Gamma \vdash A : \text{type} \rrbracket$ may change the original context Γ as well as the type A. Hence, we revise the two-stage validation as indicated by the underlines below (Δ is empty when A contains no $\triangleleft$-types). Figure 4 summarizes how we handle different types of content via these two steps.

(i) **Type checking:** by calculating $\llbracket \Gamma \vdash A : \text{type} \rrbracket$, we check the well-formedness of A under Γ and eliminate the @-types <u>and $\triangleleft$-types</u> in A (let $\Gamma, \underline{\Delta} \vdash A' :$ type denote the resultant judgment).

(ii) **Context extension:** we check whether A' is acceptable under $\Gamma, \underline{\Delta}$. If so, we extend $\Gamma, \underline{\Delta}$ with A' by the rule (ctx-ex).

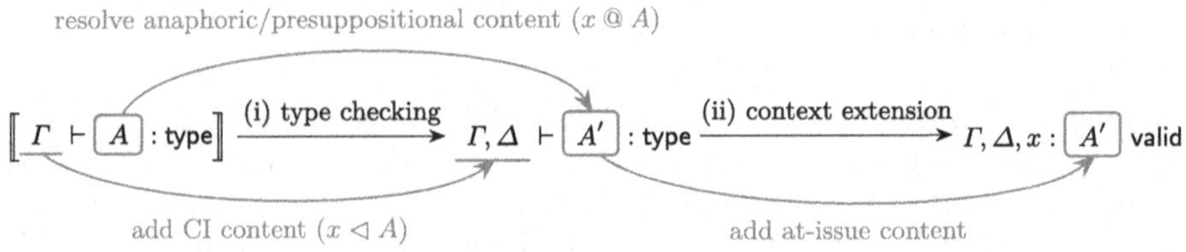

resolve anaphoric/presuppositional content ($x @ A$)

$$\left[\!\left[\; \Gamma \vdash \boxed{A} : \text{type} \right]\!\right] \xrightarrow{\text{(i) type checking}} \Gamma, \Delta \vdash \boxed{A'} : \text{type} \xrightarrow{\text{(ii) context extension}} \Gamma, \Delta, x : \boxed{A'} \; \text{valid}$$

add CI content ($x \lhd A$)   add at-issue content

Fig. 4. Overview of how each type of content is processed in DTS

4.2 Permutation

Without modification, the introduction of the $\lhd$-type clashes with other parts of the theory. Suppose that while type checking $(x : A) \to B$, we verified $\Gamma, x : A \vdash B : \text{type}$, resulting in an extended context $\Gamma, x : A, y : C$ due to a $\lhd$-type inside B. We cannot apply the rule (ΠF) in such cases because $x : A$ is not on the right end of the context.

$$(\Pi F) \; \frac{\vdots \qquad\qquad \vdots}{\Gamma \vdash A : \text{type} \quad\;\; \Gamma, x : A, y : C \vdash B' : \text{type}} \\ \times$$

To address this issue, we utilize the following structural rule (*permutation*), which is admissible in DTT.

$$(\text{perm}) \; \frac{\Gamma, x : A, y : B, \Delta \vdash M : C}{\Gamma, y : B, x : A, \Delta \vdash M : C} \; (x \notin \mathrm{FV}(B))$$

The side condition $x \notin \mathrm{FV}(B)$ is required by the property of DTT that a type can depend on terms: if $x : A$ occurs free in B, exchanging the two premises would result in an ill-formed context. We will see that this (independently motivated) restriction is important in explaining the interaction between an ARC and a quantified NP.

Now we can revise the type checking algorithm for the Π-type as follows (the same applies to the Σ-type).

$[\![\Gamma \vdash (x : A) \to B : \text{type}]\!]$

$$= \left\{ (\Pi F) \; \frac{\begin{array}{cc} \vdots \, \mathcal{D}'_1 & \vdots \, \mathcal{D}'_2 \end{array}}{\Gamma, \Delta, \Theta \vdash A' : \text{type} \quad \Gamma, \Delta, \Theta, x : A' \vdash B' : \text{type}} \; \middle| \; \begin{array}{l} \mathcal{D}_1 \in [\![\Gamma \vdash A : \text{type}]\!] \\ (\text{Let } \mathcal{D}_1\text{'s root be } \Gamma, \Delta \vdash A' : \text{type}) \\ \mathcal{D}_2 \in [\![\Gamma, \Delta, x : A' \vdash B : \text{type}]\!] \\ (\text{Let } \mathcal{D}_2\text{'s root be } \Gamma, \Delta, x : A', \Theta \vdash B' : \text{type}) \\ \mathcal{D}'_1 = \text{Extend}(\mathcal{D}_1, \mathcal{D}_2, x) \\ \mathcal{D}'_2 = \text{Arrange}(\mathcal{D}_2, x) \end{array} \right\}$$

Here, $\text{Extend}(\mathcal{D}_1, \mathcal{D}_2, x)$ simply extends the context of $\mathcal{D}_1$ with the variable declarations in $\mathcal{D}_2$ after x (Θ here). $\text{Arrange}(\mathcal{D}, x)$ is a partial function that applies the rule (perm) to $\mathcal{D}$ and returns the derivation (if any) such that its root has the variable x at the right end of the context. If there is no such derivation, type checking fails because the result of $[\![-]\!]$ is empty.

5   Predictions

In this section, we demonstrate that the $\lhd$-type correctly predicts the behavior of ARCs. To begin with, we explain the theoretical setups for the analysis.

As our syntactic framework, we adopt *Combinatory Categorial Grammar* (CCG) [25], a lexicalized grammar with a transparent syntax-semantics interface. (15) is the lexical entry for the nominative relative pronoun *who*.[4]

$$(15) \quad \underbrace{\text{who}_{\text{nom},+\text{app}}}_{\text{surface form}} := \underbrace{(NP^{\uparrow}\backslash NP)/(S\backslash NP)}_{\text{syntactic category}} : \underbrace{\lambda p.\lambda x.\lambda q.\lambda \vec{y}. \begin{bmatrix} v \lhd px \\ qx\vec{y} \end{bmatrix}}_{\text{semantic representation}}$$

$NP^{\uparrow}$ (the category of generalized quantifiers) stands for $T/(T\backslash NP)$ or $T\backslash(T/NP)$, where T is a variable ranging over categories.[5] The occurrences of T and their corresponding variables $(\vec{x}, \vec{y}, \ldots)$ are properly instantiated through a derivation. Figure 5 shows a sample CCG derivation that involves an ARC.

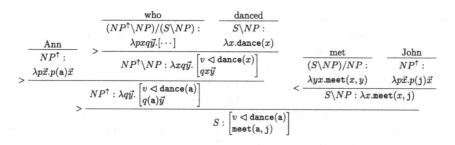

Fig. 5. CCG derivation for *Ann, who danced, met John*

Here are some details of the derivation. In the right part, the phrase *met John* is composed by instantiating the category of *John* as $(S\backslash NP)\backslash((S\backslash NP)/NP)$ (i.e., $T = S\backslash NP$). In this case, $\lambda \vec{x}.$ is realized as a single λ-abstraction ($\lambda x.$). In the part where *Ann* and *who danced* are combined, the category of *Ann* is instantiated with $T = NP^{\uparrow}$ (which means $\lambda \vec{x}. = \lambda q.\lambda \vec{y}.$). Finally, the two parts form the whole sentence after the left $NP^{\uparrow}$ is instantiated with $T = S$, in which case $\lambda \vec{y}.$ is realized as a null sequence (i.e., the SR is $\lambda q.[\cdots]$).

Next, we specify how DTS makes predictions. The felicity of an utterance is predicted through the two-stage validation: if both of the two steps succeed, then the utterance is felicitous. We define that DTS predicts inferences in the following way, based on [7] with some modifications.

---

[4] We adopt the "result-left" notation here: a phrase of category $A\backslash B$ (resp. A/B) results in an A when combined with a B on its left (resp. right).

[5] Following [25], we stipulate that T must result in S (e.g., $S\backslash NP$, S/NP, $(S\backslash NP)/NP$).

(16)   Let P, H be natural language sentences with P, H as their SRs. Suppose that there exist derivations $\mathcal{D} \in [\![\vdash P : \text{type}]\!]$ with root $\Gamma \vdash P' : \text{type}$ and $\mathcal{D}' \in [\![\Gamma, y : P' \vdash H : \text{type}]\!]$ with root $\Gamma' \vdash H' : \text{type}$.
Then, DTS predicts that P implies H if and only if there exists a term M s.t. $\Gamma' \vdash M : H'$ is derivable.

We assume that projection is a type of implication that survives when we embed the premise P into entailment-canceling operators [28].

5.1   Projection

First, we verify the projection behavior of ARCs. (17b) shows the FC of (17a), which is the premise of (6a). Negation $\neg A$ is defined as $(x : A) \to \bot$ in DTS, where $\bot$ is the empty type (i.e., the type representing contradiction).

(17)   a. It is not the case that Ann, who danced, met John.

b. $\vdash \left(v : \begin{bmatrix} u \triangleleft \text{dance(a)} \\ \text{meet(a, j)} \end{bmatrix} \right) \to \bot : \text{type}$

Figure 6 shows the process by which the FC is checked. The derivation of the premise (p1), shown in the bottom half of the figure, results in an extended context $u : \text{dance(a)}$, and this change is propagated to the other premise (p2) due to the type checking algorithm of the rule (ΠF). After (p2) is derived, we apply the rule (ΠF) and obtain $u : \text{dance(a)} \vdash (v : \text{meet(a, j)}) \to \bot : \text{type}$.

Next, we show that (17a) implies *Ann danced*, whose SR is dance(a). Let Γ be the context $u : \text{dance(a)}, s : (v : \text{meet(a, j)}) \to \bot$. We can easily confirm that dance(a) is well-formed under Γ. Moreover, $\Gamma \vdash u : \text{dance(a)}$ is derivable, which satisfies the condition (16). Therefore, DTS indeed predicts that the appositive content dance(a) projects out of the negation.

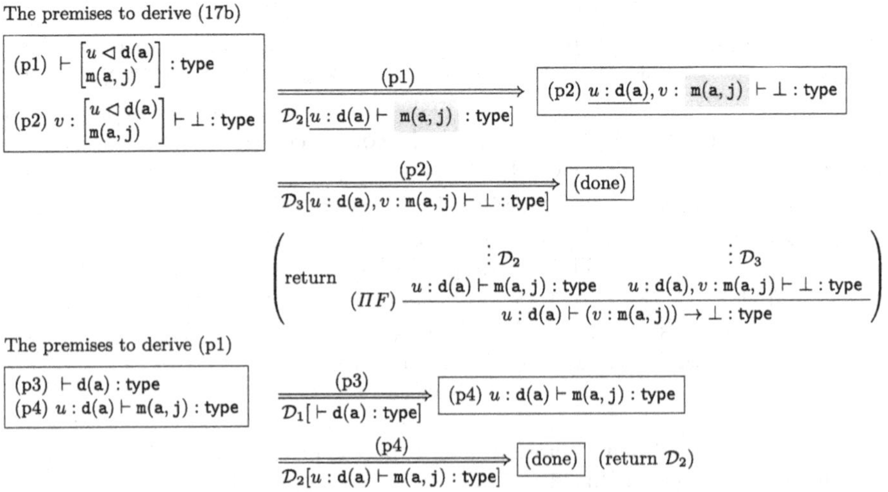

The premises to derive (17b)

The premises to derive (p1)

Fig. 6. Process of validating (17b). The underlined parts indicate the context extension, and the gray boxes show the types transformed during type checking.

5.2   Intra-sentential Anaphora

As a next step, we check how our system predicts anaphoric dependencies crossing the boundary between an ARC and its matrix clause. Here, we consider the "appositive → matrix" case (10a) (repeated as (18a)) and leave the analysis of the other direction until Sect. 5.5.

(18)   a. John, who met a girl$_1$, praised her$_1$.

b. $\vdash \begin{bmatrix} v \lhd \begin{bmatrix} u : \texttt{girl}^* \\ \texttt{meet(j}, \pi_1 u) \end{bmatrix} \\ \begin{bmatrix} w \,@\, \texttt{female}^* \\ \texttt{praise(j}, \pi_1 w) \end{bmatrix} \end{bmatrix}$: type

Figure 7 shows how the SR of (18a) is composed. We can see that the ARC first combines with the NP *John*, and then with the predicate *praised her*. This derivation results in an SR where the $\lhd$-type for the ARC takes scope over the @-type for the pronoun *her*.

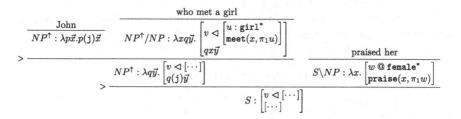

Fig. 7. CCG derivation for (18a)

Then, the FC (18b) is validated as shown in Fig. 8. The crucial point is that the @-type is type checked under the context $v : [\cdots]$, which is the appositive content. Hence, we can eliminate the @-type in the same way as in (14b): $w := \langle \pi_1 \pi_1 v, \texttt{g-to-f}(\pi_1 v) \rangle$. The resultant SR is $\texttt{praise(j}, \pi_1 \pi_1 v)$, which correctly predicts the interpretation that *her* refers back to *a girl*.

$$\begin{array}{l} \text{(p1)} \ \vdash \begin{bmatrix} u : \texttt{g}^* \\ \texttt{m(j}, \pi_1 u) \end{bmatrix} : \text{type} \\[2ex] \text{(p2)} \ v : \begin{bmatrix} u : \texttt{g}^* \\ \texttt{m(j}, \pi_1 u) \end{bmatrix} \vdash \begin{bmatrix} w \,@\, \texttt{f}^* \\ \texttt{p(j}, \pi_1 w) \end{bmatrix} : \text{type} \end{array}$$

$$\cfrac{\text{(p1)}}{\mathcal{D}_1 [\vdash [\cdots] : \text{type}]} \Longrightarrow \boxed{\text{(p2)} \ v : \begin{bmatrix} u : \texttt{g}^* \\ \texttt{m(j}, \pi_1 u) \end{bmatrix} \vdash \begin{bmatrix} w \,@\, \texttt{f}^* \\ \texttt{p(j}, \pi_1 w) \end{bmatrix} : \text{type}}$$

$$\cfrac{\text{(p2)}}{\mathcal{D}_2 [v : [\cdots] \vdash \ \texttt{p(j}, \pi_1 \pi_1 v) \ : \text{type}]} \Longrightarrow \boxed{\text{(done)}} \ (\text{return } \mathcal{D}_2)$$

Fig. 8. Process of validating (18b)

5.3   Inter-sentential Anaphora

Next, we consider anaphora between sentences. As for the "appositive → matrix" direction (12a) (here repeated as (19)), the FC of the first sentence is (20a). After it is validated, the context is (implicitly) extended with $v : [\cdots]$. After the at-issue content $\texttt{smile(j)}$ is accepted, we obtain an updated context (20b).

(19)   John, who met a girl$_1$, smiled. She$_1$ danced.

(20)   a. $\vdash \begin{bmatrix} v \lhd \begin{bmatrix} u : \texttt{girl}^* \\ \texttt{meet(j}, \pi_1 u) \end{bmatrix} \\ \texttt{smile(j)} \end{bmatrix} : \texttt{type}$

   b. $v : \begin{bmatrix} u : \texttt{girl}^* \\ \texttt{meet(j}, \pi_1 u) \end{bmatrix}, s : \texttt{smile(j)}$

Note that the appositive and at-issue content are not distinguished in the typing context: the context (20b) is identical to what we would obtain if the first sentence were replaced with *"John met a girl. He smiled."* Since the appositive content is available in the context, we can resolve the pronoun *she* in the second sentence in exactly the same way as the previous example.

The "matrix → appositive" direction (12b), which is repeated as (21), is more complicated. Supposing that the first sentence is successfully type checked and accepted, the FC of the second sentence is (22).

(21)   A girl$_1$ danced. John, who met her$_1$, smiled.

(22) $v : \begin{bmatrix} u : \texttt{girl}^* \\ \texttt{dance}(\pi_1 u) \end{bmatrix} \vdash \begin{bmatrix} z \lhd \begin{bmatrix} w \,@\, \texttt{female}^* \\ \texttt{meet(j}, \pi_1 w) \end{bmatrix} \\ \texttt{smile(j)} \end{bmatrix} : \texttt{type}$

Figure 9 shows the derivation process. In deriving (p1), we can eliminate the @-type with v,[6] and the result is propagated to the other sub-goal (p2), as indicated by the parts highlighted in gray. Finally, we obtain a context extended with $z : \texttt{meet(j}, \pi_1 \pi_1 v)$ (*John met her*), as expected.

> (p1) $v : [\cdots] \vdash \begin{bmatrix} w \,@\, \texttt{f}^* \\ \texttt{m(j}, \pi_1 w) \end{bmatrix} : \texttt{type}$
>
> (p2) $v : [\cdots], z : \begin{bmatrix} w \,@\, \texttt{f}^* \\ \texttt{m(j}, \pi_1 w) \end{bmatrix} \vdash \texttt{s(j)} : \texttt{type}$

$$\frac{\text{(p1)}}{\mathcal{D}_1[v : [\cdots] \vdash \texttt{m(j}, \pi_1 \pi_1 v) : \texttt{type}]} \Longrightarrow \boxed{\text{(p2)}\ v : [\cdots], z : \texttt{m(j}, \pi_1 \pi_1 v) \vdash \texttt{s(j)} : \texttt{type}}$$

$$\frac{\text{(p2)}}{\mathcal{D}_2[v : [\cdots], z : \texttt{m(j}, \pi_1 \pi_1 v) \vdash \texttt{s(j)} : \texttt{type}]} \Longrightarrow \boxed{\text{(done)}}\ (\text{return } \mathcal{D}_2)$$

Fig. 9. Process of validating (21)

---

[6] If we could not resolve the @-type here, then the entire SR would not be well-typed. Hence, our theory predicts that the infelicity of the appositive content leads to the infelicity of the entire utterance.

5.4   ARC + Non-referential Quantifier

Let us turn to the interaction with quantifiers. We first observe (23a), where an ARC modifies *every girl*.[7] Its FC is shown in (23b).

(23)   a. #Every girl, who met John, danced.

   b. $\vdash (u : \mathtt{girl}^*) \to \begin{bmatrix} v \lhd \mathtt{meet}(\pi_1 u, \mathtt{j}) \\ \mathtt{dance}(\pi_1 u) \end{bmatrix}$: type

Figure 10 describes how its infelicity is predicted. When the premise (p2) is derived, the context is extended with $v : \mathtt{meet}(\pi_1 u, \mathtt{j})$, in which u occurs free. This prevents the application of the rule (perm), so $u : \mathtt{girl}^*$ cannot be moved to the right end of the context, causing the type checking to fail. With the failure of type checking, DTS predicts the infelicity of (23a).

$$\begin{array}{l} \text{(p1)}\ \vdash \mathbf{g}^* : \mathsf{type} \\ \text{(p2)}\ u : \mathbf{g}^* \vdash \begin{bmatrix} v \lhd \mathtt{m}(\pi_1 u, \mathtt{j}) \\ \mathtt{d}(\pi_1 u) \end{bmatrix} : \mathsf{type} \end{array}$$

$$(\cdots)\ \frac{\text{(p2)}}{\mathcal{D}_2[u : \mathbf{g}^*, \underline{v : \mathtt{m}(\pi_1 u, \mathtt{j})} \vdash\ \boxed{\mathtt{d}(\pi_1 u)}\ : \mathsf{type}]}\ \xrightarrow{}\ (\mathsf{perm})\ \frac{\vdots\ \mathcal{D}_2}{u : \mathbf{g}^*, v : \mathtt{m}(\pi_1 u, \mathtt{j}) \vdash \mathtt{d}(\pi_1 u) : \mathsf{type}}\ \times$$

Fig. 10. Process showing the infelicity of (23a)

We can likewise handle the case of binding. Again using *every girl* as our example, we describe the FC of (24a) in (24b). We first eliminate the @-type with $u : \mathtt{girl}^*$ to obtain the reading where *her* is bound by *every girl*, which yields $(v \lhd \mathtt{praise}(\mathtt{j}, \pi_1 u)) \times \cdots$. Because u occurs free in the appositive content $\mathtt{praise}(\mathtt{j}, \pi_1 u)$, the type checking fails as in Fig. 10.[8]

(24)   a. #Every girl$_1$ met John, who praised her$_1$.

   b. $\vdash (u : \mathtt{girl}^*) \to \begin{bmatrix} v \lhd \begin{bmatrix} w\, @\, \mathtt{female}^* \\ \mathtt{praise}(\mathtt{j}, \pi_1 w) \end{bmatrix} \\ \mathtt{meet}(\pi_1 v, \mathtt{j}) \end{bmatrix}$: type

In summary, the appositive content $x \lhd A$ cannot project out if it depends on a variable introduced by Π or Σ. Importantly, this restriction derives from the side condition of the permutation rule, which is inherent in DTT.

---

[7] The prediction is the same for *no girl*, which is translated using a Π-type $((u : \mathtt{girl}^*) \to \neg(\cdots))$.

[8] Note that the type checking of (24b) succeeds if w is otherwise resolved, which corresponds to cases where the pronoun *her* is not bound by *every girl* (e.g., where it refers to a female person previously introduced in the discourse).

5.5   ARC + Referential Quantifier

Before checking the case of referential quantifiers, we introduce an auxiliary assumption that a specific indefinite NP is represented by a $\lhd$-type. This is motivated by the fact that a specific indefinite projects out of entailment-canceling environments (like definites) and is generally new to the addressee [10]: both properties can be straightforwardly captured by the $\lhd$-type.[9] Concretely, we assume the following alternative lexical entry for the indefinite determiner.

(25) $a_{\mathrm{spec}} := NP^{\uparrow}/N : \lambda n.\lambda p.\lambda \vec{x}. \begin{bmatrix} u \lhd (x : \mathbf{e}) \times nx \\ p(\pi_1 u)\vec{x} \end{bmatrix}$

Then, the sentence (26a) can be translated into (26b). Because $u : \mathtt{girl}^*$, on which the appositive content $\mathtt{meet}(\pi_1 u, \mathtt{j})$ depends, is also implicitly added to the context, we need not apply the rule (perm) and thus type checking succeeds, resulting in the judgment (26c).

(26)   a.   A girl, who met John, danced.

b. $\vdash \begin{bmatrix} u \lhd \mathtt{girl}^* \\ \begin{bmatrix} v \lhd \mathtt{meet}(\pi_1 u, \mathtt{j}) \end{bmatrix} \\ \mathtt{dance}(\pi_1 u) \end{bmatrix}$: type

c. $u : \mathtt{girl}^*, v : \mathtt{meet}(\pi_1 u, \mathtt{j}) \vdash \mathtt{dance}(\pi_1 u)$: type

The same line of reasoning shows the felicity of the binding case (8b), which also accounts for the "matrix → appositive" anaphora (10b). Likewise, our system can correctly predict that a specific indefinite with an ARC projects out of conditional antecedents, which we observed in (9).

It is noteworthy that if the indefinite is interpreted as non-specific in (26b), then the SR is $(u : \mathtt{girl}^*) \times \cdots$, which cannot be successfully type checked for the same reason as (23b). This result accounts for why an indefinite NP with an ARC does not have a non-specific reading.

5.6   Additional Analysis: Clause-Final ARCs

ARCs show peculiar properties when situated at the clause-final position. First, [2] observed and [26] experimentally confirmed that clause-final ARCs can be a target of the hearer's direct response, which suggests that they can be at-issue.

(27)   a.   Liz might be with her husband, who has prostate cancer.

b.   No, he has lung cancer.

Note that (27a) implies that Liz's husband has prostate cancer, meaning that the appositive content is not subject to the modal *might*.

Second, [21,24] showed that an ARC at the end of a subordinate clause can take narrower scope than the matrix clause. For example, the ARC in (28a) does not project out of the scope of *if* but yields an interpretation similar to (28b).

---

[9] [14] presented a similar argument, analyzing a Persian specificity marker with the system proposed by [22] (note that in his analysis, the CI content is the uniqueness of the nominal to be modified).

(28) (Adapted from [24])

[Context: someone in the department made a big mistake.]

    a. If tomorrow I called the Chair, who in turn called the Dean, then we would be in big trouble.

    b. If tomorrow I called the Chair and the Chair in turn called the Dean, then we would be in big trouble.

To capture these facts, we introduce an additional lexical entry (29) for relative pronouns appearing in clause-final ARCs.

$$(29) \quad \text{who}_{\text{cls-fin}} := ((S\backslash(S/NP))\backslash NP)/(S\backslash NP) : \lambda p.\lambda x.\lambda q. \begin{bmatrix} u : qx \\ px \end{bmatrix}$$

The SR simply conjoins the content of the matrix clause and that of the ARC with a Σ-type. The syntactic category indicates that it combines first with a relative clause predicate ($S\backslash NP$), then with an antecedent (NP), and finally with a clause missing the object (S/NP), thus forcing the ARC to be clause-final.

We can predict the projection behavior by utilizing the flexible notion of constituency in CCG. As shown in Fig. 11, the clause missing the object (*John might meet*) forms a constituent of S/NP due to the functional composition rule ($>$**B**). We can thus keep the appositive content **dance(a)** outside the scope of the possibility operator $\lozenge$.[10] We can explain the narrow scope reading of (28a) in the same way because *I called* has category S/NP.[11]

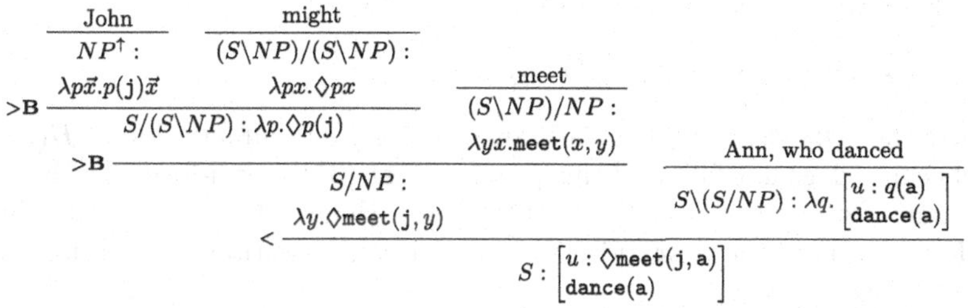

Fig. 11. CCG derivation for *John might meet Ann, who danced*. We have omitted the analysis of *Ann, who danced* for brevity.

---

[10] We leave open how to implement modal operators in DTS (see, e.g., [27] for an analysis).

[11] One crucial limitation of this analysis is that it does not correctly handle scope interactions with quantifiers. [19] observed that the following has a reading that only the interviewed climbers were French.

(i)   They interviewed less than half the climbers, who were all French nationals.

Our present analysis would predict that the ARC is in the nuclear scope of the quantifier. We need a mechanism to pass the intersection of the restrictor and the nuclear scope to the ARC, which will be the subject of future work.

6   Related Work

6.1   DTS-Based Approach

[6] presented an analysis of CIs with DTS, which is closely related to the present work. Their proposal was the *CI operator* $\mathsf{CI}(@ :: A)$, where the term $@ :: A$ (an underspecified term [7]) launches a proof search in the same way as an $@$-type. Here, a specific mechanism of their system guarantees that $@ :: A$ is never resolved by the context. In other words, the CI content A is formalized as an obligatorily accommodated presupposition. In this way, the operator correctly predicts both the projection behavior and the anti-backgroundedness of CIs.

A possible concern with this analysis is that it might not be compatible with other analyses of presuppositions with DTS. For instance, [5] recently proposed the following fallback procedure upon the failure of type checking, which is meant to reflect the distinction between *global* and *local* accommodation.

(30)   If no term M with $x_1 : A_1 \ldots x_n : A_n \vdash M : A$ is found in type checking $(x @ A) \times B$, the type checker can do either of the following:

    a.   Global accommodation: add a constant symbol of type $(x_1 : A_1) \to \ldots (x_n : A_n) \to M$ to the signature and re-run the type checking.

    b.   Local accommodation: replace the $@$-type with $(x : A) \times B$ and continue the type checking.

If we adopt this definition, the CI operator incorrectly predicts that ARCs can take scope under non-referential quantifiers. (31) is a schematized SR representing cases where an ARC is bound by *every* NP.

(31) $(u : A) \to (\ldots \mathsf{CI}(@ :: B(u)) \ldots)$

Whether the type checker performs global or local accommodation of $B(u)$, the type checking does not fail, and this predicts that (31) is well-formed. The result is the same if we replace $@$-terms with $@$-types. Hence, this justifies introducing the CI type, a new operator independent of accommodation, in addition to the existing $@$-term/type.

6.2   Dynamic Approach

[3] and several related studies analyzed ARCs with dynamic semantics, based on the same idea as ours, namely, that appositive content directly updates the common ground. Their approach utilizes discourse referents (drefs) for propositions. Appositive content constrains the dref p^{cs} representing the common ground, while at-issue content targets another dref p, which later updates p^{cs}.

Although they covered various phenomena related to ARCs, it remains unclear how to account for the fact that they do not scopally interact with non-referential NPs. One possible solution is to integrate the proposal in [19] for nominal appositives, which also employs a dynamic approach. However, [3] and [19] substantially differ in the setup of dynamic semantics. For instance, [3] treats a discourse referent as a partial function from possible worlds to entities, while [19] regards one as ambiguous between singular and plural entities. We believe further investigation is necessary to reconcile these differences.

6.3 Orphan Approach

Following [22] and many others, we posited that an ARC is locally attached to its antecedent in its surface position, with the independence of the appositive content handled at the semantic level. In contrast, some studies assume a different syntactic structure, where an ARC is viewed as an "orphan," that is, a clause that is not integrated with its antecedent but shifted to a structurally higher position.

For instance, [8] proposed that an ARC is an independent matrix clause, with the relative pronoun interpreted as an E-type pronoun. More recently, [24] extended this idea and suggested that an ARC can be attached to any propositional node dominating the antecedent.

A question that arises with this approach is why the relative pronoun of an ARC must be coindexed with the antecedent, even though it is an E-type pronoun. Consider the contrast between (32a) and (32b). The E-type pronoun *her* allows inter-sentential anaphora, whereas the relative pronoun *whom* does not. If the relative pronoun is E-type, then (32b) is predicted to be felicitous.

(32)   a. Ann_1 has been annoyed recently. The culprit is her nasty $colleague_2$. She_2 always teases her_1.

   b. Ann_1 has been annoyed recently. #The culprit is her nasty $colleague_2$, $whom_1$ she_2 always teases.

Thus, a formal procedure needs to be implemented to ensure appropriate coindexation of relative pronouns and NPs.

7 Conclusion

We proposed an extension of DTS with the CI type $(x \lhd A) \times B$, which implicitly extends the typing context during type checking. This mechanism reflects the idea that CIs directly update the common ground. Our proposal can predict the projection behavior of ARCs and the boundary-crossing anaphora between appositive and at-issue content. It also captures the (non-)interactions between ARCs and quantified NPs, based on the restriction on the permutation rule.

In future work, it would be interesting to consider *perspective shift* with CIs [13]. Although CIs generally express commitments made by the speaker, they can also be attributed to other attitude holders. For instance, the appositive content in (33) seems to describe the belief of the speaker's aunt.

(33)   My aunt is extremely skeptical of doctors in general. She says that dentists, who are only in it for the money anyway, are not to be trusted at all.   (adapted from [13])

[15] analyzed this phenomenon as a type of discourse anaphora: the contextual information determines the perspective under which a CI is interpreted. Following this idea, we could revise the lexical entry of the relative pronoun of an ARC so that it includes an @-type for an appropriate perspective. However, because the treatment of epistemic states with DTS is not well established, we leave this analysis to future work.

Another possible direction of future research is to investigate how to relate our analysis of CIs to presupposition accommodation, returning to the spirit of [6]. Although we pointed out in Sect. 6 that the recent definition of accommodation in DTS is not compatible with CIs, we might be able to revise it so that CIs and accommodated presuppositions are handled in a more unified manner. We need to further consider the discourse behavior of the two types of content to tackle this challenge.

Acknowledgements. We would like to thank the anonymous reviewers of LENLS20 for their comments and suggestions, which helped us improve this paper. This work was supported by JST, PRESTO grant number JPMJPR21C8, Japan, and JSPS KAKENHI Grant Number JP23H03452, Japan.

References

1. Amaral, P., Roberts, C., Smith, E.A.: Review of the logic of conventional implicatures by Chris Potts. Linguist. Philos. **30**(6), 707–749 (2007). https://doi.org/10.1007/s10988-008-9025-2
2. AnderBois, S., Brasoveanu, A., Henderson, R.: Crossing the appositive/at-issue meaning boundary. Semant. Linguist. Theory **20**, 328–346 (2010). https://doi.org/10.3765/salt.v20i0.2551
3. Anderbois, S., Brasoveanu, A., Henderson, R.: At-issue proposals and appositive impositions in discourse. J. Semant. **32**(1), 93–138 (2013). https://doi.org/10.1093/jos/fft014
4. Arnold, D.: Non-restrictive relatives are not orphans. J. Linguist. **43**(2), 271–309 (2007). https://doi.org/10.1017/S0022226707004586
5. Bekki, D.: A proof-theoretic analysis of weak crossover. In: Yada, K., Takama, Y., Mineshima, K., Satoh, K. (eds.) JSAI-isAI 2021. LNCS(LNAI), vol. 13856, pp. 228–241. Springer, Cham (2023). https://doi.org/10.1007/978-3-031-36190-6_16
6. Bekki, D., McCready, E.: CI via DTS. In: Murata, T., Mineshima, K., Bekki, D. (eds.) JSAI-isAI 2014. LNCS (LNAI), vol. 9067, pp. 23–36. Springer, Heidelberg (2015). https://doi.org/10.1007/978-3-662-48119-6_3
7. Bekki, D., Mineshima, K.: Context-passing and underspecification in dependent type semantics. In: Chatzikyriakidis, S., Luo, Z. (eds.) Modern Perspectives in Type-Theoretical Semantics. SLP, vol. 98, pp. 11–41. Springer, Cham (2017). https://doi.org/10.1007/978-3-319-50422-3_2
8. del Gobbo, F.: Appositives at the interface. Ph.D. thesis, University of California (2003)
9. del Gobbo, F.: On the syntax and semantics of appositive relative clauses. Parentheticals **106**, 173–201 (2007). https://doi.org/10.1075/la.106.10del

10. Geurts, B.: Specific indefinites, presupposition and scope. In: Bauerle, R., Reyle, U., Zimmermann, T. (eds.) Presuppositions and Discourse: Essays Offered to Hans Kamp, pp. 125–158. Brill, Leiden (2010). https://doi.org/10.1163/9789004253162_006

11. Grice, H.P.: Logic and conversation. In: Cole, P., Morgan, J.L. (eds.) Speech Acts, Syntax and Semantics, vol. 3, pp. 41–58. Academic Press (1975). https://doi.org/10.1163/9789004368811_003

12. Groenendijk, J., Stokhof, M.: Dynamic predicate logic. Linguist. Philos. **14**(1), 39–100 (1991). https://doi.org/10.1007/BF00628304

13. Harris, J.A., Potts, C.: Perspective-shifting with appositives and expressives. Linguist. Philos. **32**(6), 523–552 (2009). https://doi.org/10.1007/s10988-010-9070-5

14. Jasbi, M.: The suffix that makes Persian nouns unique. In: Advances in Iranian Linguistics, pp. 107–118. John Benjamins (2020). https://doi.org/10.1075/cilt.351.06jas

15. Koev, T.: Two puzzles about appositives: projection and perspective shift. In: Etxeberria, U., Fălăuş, A., Irurtzun, A., Leferman, B. (eds.) Proceedings of Sinn und Bedeutung, vol. 18, pp. 217–234 (2014)

16. Luo, Z.: Computation and Reasoning: A Type Theory for Computer Science. International Series of Monographs on Computer Science, vol. 49. Oxford University Press (1994)

17. Martin-Löf, P.: Intuitionistic Type Theory. Bibliopolis, Naples (1984). Notes by Giovanni Sambin of a series of lectures given in Padua, June 1980

18. Murray, S.E.: Varieties of update. Semant. Pragmat. **7**(2), 1–53 (2014). https://doi.org/10.3765/sp.7.2

19. Nouwen, R.: On appositives and dynamic binding. Res. Lang. Comput. **5**(1), 87–102 (2007). https://doi.org/10.1007/s11168-006-9019-6

20. Nouwen, R.: A note on the projection of appositives. In: McCready, E., Yabushita, K., Yoshimoto, K. (eds.) Formal Approaches to Semantics and Pragmatics. SLP, vol. 95, pp. 205–222. Springer, Dordrecht (2014). https://doi.org/10.1007/978-94-017-8813-7_10

21. Poschmann, C.: Embedding non-restrictive relative clauses. Proc. Sinn Bedeutung **22**(2), 235–252 (2018)

22. Potts, C.: The Logic of Conventional Implicatures. Oxford University Press (2004). https://doi.org/10.1093/acprof:oso/9780199273829.001.0001

23. van der Sandt, R.: Presupposition projection as anaphora resolution. J. Semant. **9**(4), 333–377 (1992). https://doi.org/10.1093/jos/9.4.333

24. Schlenker, P.: Supplements without bidimensionalism. Linguist. Inq. **54**(2), 251–297 (2023). https://doi.org/10.1162/ling_a_00442

25. Steedman, M.: The Syntactic Process. MIT Press (2000)

26. Syrett, K., Koev, T.: Experimental evidence for the truth conditional contribution and shifting information status of appositives. J. Semant. **32**(3), 525–577 (2014). https://doi.org/10.1093/jos/ffu007

27. Tanaka, R., Mineshima, K., Bekki, D.: Resolving modal anaphora in dependent type semantics. In: Murata, T., Mineshima, K., Bekki, D. (eds.) JSAI-isAI 2014. LNCS (LNAI), vol. 9067, pp. 83–98. Springer, Heidelberg (2015). https://doi.org/10.1007/978-3-662-48119-6_7

28. Tonhauser, J., Beaver, D., Roberts, C., Simons, M.: Toward a taxonomy of projective content. Language **89**(1), 66–109 (2013). https://doi.org/10.1353/lan.2013.0001

29. Wang, L., Reese, B., McCready, E.: The projection problem of nominal appositives. Snippets **10**(1), 13–14 (2005)

On the Semantics of Dependencies: Relative Clauses and Open Clausal Complements

Philippe de Groote[✉]

Université de Lorraine, CNRS, Inria, LORIA, 54000 Nancy, France
degroote@loria.fr

Abstract. In a previous work [4], we laid the foundations of a formal compositional semantic theory for dependency grammars. In this paper, we continue this line of research with the aim of showing that the basic principles we stated in [4] allow one to deal with more advanced syntactic phenomena. We consider two cases: the relative clauses (which depend on the acl:relcl dependency relation) and the open clausal complements (which depend on the xcomp dependency relation). This leads us to revise some of the solutions advocated in [4], while at the same time generalizing some of the principles on which our theory is based.

1 Introduction

Dependency grammars, which stem from a long linguistic tradition [9,14], have seen a resurgence of interest in recent years, especially due to the Universal Dependency project [11]. Their principle is to make explicit the dependency relations existing between the words of a sentence, these relations being identified by the syntactic functions they represent.

Dependency parsing offers an interesting alternative to constituency parsing. In particular, parsing an agrammatical sentence does not result in a failure, but in a partial dependency structure that still contains some information. For this reason, dependency parsing is considered to be more robust than constituent parsing.

Formal compositional semantics, in the tradition of Montague [10], is based on a homomorphism between syntactic structure and semantic representation. As a result, it relies heavily on the notion of constituent, which does not appear explicitly in dependency structures. For this reason, providing a dependency grammar with a Montagovian semantic interpretation is not straightforward.

Nonetheless, in recent years, several ways of adapting Montague's semantics to the case of dependency grammars have been proposed in the literature. In a series of papers, Haug and his co-authors show how to assign a formal interpretation to a dependency structure using glue semantics [5–8]. Other authors, including ourself, rely on a compositionality principle close to Montague's by exploiting a functional representation of dependency structures [12,13]. This is the path we took in a previous paper [4], in which we established possible foundations for a formal semantic theory for dependency grammars. In the present

D. Bekki et al. (Eds.): LENLS 2023, LNCS 14569, pp. 244–259, 2024.
https://doi.org/10.1007/978-3-031-60878-0_14

paper, we continue this line of thought with the intention of showing that the approach we outlined in [4] allows for the treatment of more advanced linguistic phenomena. In particular, we study the cases of two dependency relations: acl:rel, which subordinates a relative clause to a noun, and xcomp, which subordinates an open clausal complement to a control verb. This study then leads us to revise some of the positions we took in [4].

The rest of the paper is organized as follows. In the next section, we present the foundational principles underlying the semantic treatment of dependencies that we advocated in [4]. In Sect. 3, we address the problems associated with wh-extraction and the semantic interpretation of relative clauses. In Sect. 4, we discuss another linguistic construct, that of open clausal complements. These are clausal complements without their own subject, and whose semantic subject is typically provided by a complement (subject or object) of the control verb on which they depend. In Sect. 5, we discuss the solutions proposed in the previous two sections and explain why they are not entirely satisfactory. This leads us to revise our treatment of verbs in order to take into account certain elements of lexical semantics, in particular subcategorization. In Sect. 6, we bring together the various elements discussed in the previous sections and propose an integrated solution to the different problems we have addressed. We illustrate this solution with a small grammar that provides a unified treatment of the various linguistic phenomena we have considered. Finally, in Sect. 7, we conclude.

2 Foundational Principles of a Semantic Theory of Syntactic Dependencies

In [4], we laid the foundations for a possible semantic theory of syntactic dependencies. Let us synthesize and state the basic principles that outline this theory. To this end, consider the following simple sentence, together with its dependency struture:[1]

(1)   *Samuel praises Amandine*

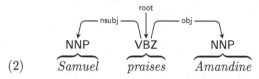

(2)   *Samuel   praises   Amandine*

In order to take advantage of structure (2) with the goal of assigning a semantic representation to sentence (1), we need to address the issue of the syntax-semantic interface. When dealing with constituency grammars (typically, phrase

---

[1] The dependency structures occurring in this paper were obtained using the Stanford parser (online version: https://corenlp.run/). In these structures, labels such as NNP or VBZ are just part-of-speech tags. They should not be confused with the syntactic categories such as NP, VP, S, ... that we will use to type terms that encode dependency structures.

structure grammars or categorial grammars), a neat solution to the syntax-semantic interface problem is to represent syntactic structures as simply typed λ-terms [15]. In order to adapt this approach to the present case, we consider dependency relations as binary functions that take as arguments the governor and the governee of the relation. This allows structure (2) to be represented by the following term:

(3)   root (nsubj SAMUEL (obj PRAISES AMANDINE))

Term (3) needs to be well-typed, and its typing derivation then corresponds to a dependency parsing of sentence (1):

$$
\frac{\text{nsubj} : \text{NP} \to \text{VP} \to \text{VP} \quad \text{SAMUEL} : \text{NP}}{\text{nsubj SAMUEL} : \text{VP} \to \text{VP}} \Bigg\} \ \Pi_0 \qquad \frac{\text{obj} : \text{VP} \to \text{NP} \to \text{VP} \quad \text{PRAISES} : \text{VP}}{\text{obj PRAISES} : \text{NP} \to \text{VP}} \Bigg\} \ \Pi_1
$$

$$
\frac{\text{root} : \text{VP} \to \text{S} \quad \dfrac{\vdots \ \Pi_0}{\text{nsubj SAMUEL} : \text{VP} \to \text{VP}} \quad \dfrac{\dfrac{\vdots \ \Pi_1}{\text{obj PRAISES} : \text{NP} \to \text{VP}} \quad \text{AMANDINE} : \text{NP}}{\text{obj PRAISES AMANDINE} : \text{VP}}}{\dfrac{\text{nsubj SAMUEL (obj PRAISES AMANDINE)} : \text{VP}}{\text{root (nsubj SAMUEL (obj PRAISES AMANDINE))} : \text{S}}}
$$

The above derivation, however, is not the only possible parsing of sentence (1). Indeed, there exists another derivation:

$$
\frac{\dfrac{\text{nsubj} : \text{NP} \to \text{VP} \to \text{VP} \quad \text{SAMUEL} : \text{NP}}{\text{nsubj SAMUEL} : \text{VP} \to \text{VP}} \quad \text{PRAISES} : \text{VP}}{\text{nsubj SAMUEL PRAISES} : \text{VP}} \Bigg\} \ \Pi
$$

$$
\frac{\text{root} : \text{VP} \to \text{S} \quad \dfrac{\dfrac{\text{obj} : \text{VP} \to \text{NP} \to \text{VP} \quad \dfrac{\vdots \ \Pi}{\text{nsubj SAMUEL PRAISES} : \text{VP}}}{\text{obj (nsubj SAMUEL PRAISES)} : \text{NP} \to \text{VP}} \quad \text{AMANDINE} : \text{NP}}{\text{obj (nsubj SAMUEL PRAISES) AMANDINE} : \text{VP}}}{\text{root (obj (nsubj SAMUEL PRAISES) AMANDINE)} : \text{S}}
$$

This second derivation yields another encoding of structure (2):

(4)   root (obj (nsubj SAMUEL PRAISES) AMANDINE)

Nonetheless, sentence (1) is not semantically ambiguous. The existence of two different parsings therefore corresponds to a spurious ambiguity. In [4], in order to overcome this difficulty, we stated a coherence principle according to which the semantic interpretation of both terms (3) and (4) must yield the same result.

As a consequence of the coherence principle, every dependency relation must be assigned a type of the form $\alpha \to \beta \to \alpha$ (or $\beta \to \alpha \to \alpha$),[2] where α is the type of the governor and β the type of the governee.

---

[2] Here, we depart slightly from [4] by accepting both type schemes for dependency relations. This allows the order of the arguments of a dependency relation to reflect the word order, which makes terms like (3) and (4) more readable.

Now that we have a type scheme for assigning a syntactic category to a dependency relation, the next question we need to answer is: what should be the semantic interpretation of the syntactic categories? With this question in mind, consider sentence (5), here below, with its dependency structure:

(5)   *a wise man praises Amandine*

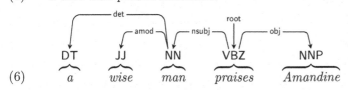

(6)

In accordance with the typing discipline we have adopted, all the phrases *man*, *wise man*, *a wise man*—or more precisely, their encodings as λ-terms, i.e., MAN, amod WISE MAN, det A (amod WISE MAN)— must be assigned the same syntactic type, namely NP, and consequently the same semantic type. This is in conflict with the usual Montagovian approach, where *man* and *wise man* are assigned the semantic type $e \rightarrow t$, while *a wise man* is assigned the semantic type $(e \rightarrow t) \rightarrow t$. The way we propose to resolve this conflict is to give to a phrase its usual Montagovian interpretation, parameterized by the interpretations of all the potential governees of the head of that phrase. Let us illustrate this principle by considering the case of noun phrases. As mentioned above, the usual interpretation of the syntactic category of noun phrases is the type $(e \rightarrow t) \rightarrow t$. Now let us consider (as a simplifying hypothesis) that the only possible governees of the head of a noun phrase are determiners (with $(e \rightarrow t) \rightarrow (e \rightarrow t) \rightarrow t$ as semantic type) and adnominal modifiers (with $(e \rightarrow t) \rightarrow e \rightarrow t$ as semantic type). Accordingly, in our setting, the semantic type we assign to the syntactic category of noun phrases is:

(7)   NP := **det** → **adnom** → **np**

where: $\begin{cases} \textbf{det} = (e \rightarrow t) \rightarrow (e \rightarrow t) \rightarrow t \\ \textbf{adnom} = (e \rightarrow t) \rightarrow e \rightarrow t \\ \textbf{np} = (e \rightarrow t) \rightarrow t \end{cases}$

That is, unfolding all the abbreviations:

(8)   NP := $((e \rightarrow t) \rightarrow (e \rightarrow t) \rightarrow t) \rightarrow ((e \rightarrow t) \rightarrow e \rightarrow t) \rightarrow (e \rightarrow t) \rightarrow t$

Using the above semantic interpretation of the category NP, we can now give a piece of grammar[3] that allows the noun phrase *a wise man* to be given a semantic interpretation.

Abstract Syntax

---

[3] We present it in the form of an Abstract Categorial Grammar [3].

ADJ, DET, NP : *type* ;
MAN : NP ;
WISE : ADJ ;
A : DET ;
amod : ADJ → NP → NP ;
det : DET → NP → NP

Object Language

e, t : *type* ;
man, wise : **e → t**

Semantic Interpretation

ADJ := $(\mathbf{e} \to \mathbf{t}) \to \mathbf{e} \to \mathbf{t}$;
DET := $(\mathbf{e} \to \mathbf{t}) \to (\mathbf{e} \to \mathbf{t}) \to \mathbf{t}$;
NP := $((\mathbf{e} \to \mathbf{t}) \to (\mathbf{e} \to \mathbf{t}) \to \mathbf{t}) \to ((\mathbf{e} \to \mathbf{t}) \to \mathbf{e} \to \mathbf{t}) \to (\mathbf{e} \to \mathbf{t}) \to \mathbf{t}$;
MAN := $\lambda da. \, d \, (a \, \mathbf{man})$;
WISE := $\lambda nx. \, (n \, x) \wedge (\mathbf{wise} \, x)$;
A := $\lambda pq. \, \exists x. \, (p \, x) \wedge (q \, x)$;
amod := $\lambda andb. \, n \, d \, (\lambda x. \, b \, (a \, x))$;
det := $\lambda dne. \, n \, d$

A few comments are in order regarding the semantic interpretation above. For the adjective (WISE) and the determiner (A), the interpretations are as usual. This is because we consider that adjectives and determiners cannot be the governors of any dependency relation.[4] The interpretation of the noun (MAN) must be of type (7). Consequently, it takes two parameters, the λ-variables d and a. The purpose of the first parameter, d, is to be eventually instantiated by the semantic interpretation of the determiner of the noun phrase whose the noun *man* is the head. As for the second parameter, a, it plays the part of a possible adnominal modifier. Accordingly, the interpretation of the dependency relation det (respectively amod) allows the first argument (respectively the second argument) of the interpretation of a noun phrase to be given an actual value. For instance, interpreting the expression det A MAN yields the following λ-term:

(9) $\lambda eaq. \, \exists x. \, (a \, \mathbf{man} \, x) \wedge (q \, x)$

---

[4] This is clearly an over simplifying assumption. In particular, we do not take into account the possible adverbial modification of an adjective as in *a very wise man*:

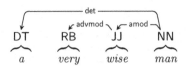

Since **det** is of type DET → np → np, the λ-term (9) must be of type (7). Thus, formally, the λ-variable e in (9) occupies the position of a determiner. But this determiner position, which is necessary for typing reasons, is in a sense fictive because the variable e does not occur in the body of (9). Similarly, the interpretation of a proper noun, which must also be of type (7), contains fictive parameters for the same typing reasons, resulting in vacuous lambda-abstractions. For instance, the interpretation of the proper noun *Amandine* is as follows:

(10)   AMANDINE := $\lambda dap. p$ **amandine**

where **amandine** is an object constant of type **e**.

Now, at some point in our semantic interpretation process, the noun phrases must be given their usual Montagovian interpretations. This can be done by providing the parameters of terms such as (9) or (10) with default values. To this end, we define the following saturating operator:

$$\text{saturate}_{np} = \lambda n. \, n \, (\lambda pq. \, \exists x. \, (p \, x) \wedge (q \, x)) \, (\lambda x. \, x)$$

Using this operator, we have that:

$$\text{saturate}_{np} \, (\lambda eaq. \, \exists x. \, (a \, \textbf{man} \, x) \wedge (q \, x)) \twoheadrightarrow_\beta \lambda q. \, \exists x. \, (\textbf{man} \, x) \wedge (q \, x)$$
$$\text{saturate}_{np} \, (\lambda dap. \, p \, \textbf{amandine}) \twoheadrightarrow_\beta \lambda p. \, p \, \textbf{amandine}$$

which corresponds to the usual Montagovian interpretation of the noun phrases *a man* and *Amandine*.

To finish this overview of the possible semantic theory whose first foundations we laid in [4], let us consider again sentence (5) and its dependency structure (6), which we repeat here as (11) and (12).

(11)   *a wise man praises Amandine*

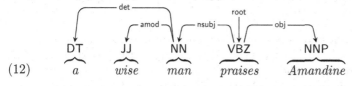

(12)   *a   wise   man   praises   Amandine*

To complete the semantic treatment of (11), it remains to settle the question of verbs and the dependency relations they govern. At the abstract syntactic level, in line with our typing discipline, we need to extend our grammar as follows:

VP : *type* ;
PRAISES : VP ;
nsubj : NP → VP → VP ;
obj : VP → NP → VP

The semantic interpretation of the syntactic category VP is then the next question to be dealt with. The answer we gave to this question in [4] is the one Champollion advocates in his treatment of event semantics [1]. It consists in interpreting verb phrases as sets of sets of events. Following this line, we extend our grammar with the following declarations and interpretations:

v : *type* ;
praise : $\mathbf{v} \to \mathbf{t}$;
agent, **theme** : $\mathbf{v} \to \mathbf{e} \to \mathbf{t}$

VP := $(\mathbf{v} \to \mathbf{t}) \to \mathbf{t}$;
PRAISES := $\lambda p.\, \exists e.\, (\mathbf{praise}\, e) \wedge (p\, e)$;
nsubj := $\lambda n v p.\, \text{saturate}_{np}\, n\, (\lambda x.\, v\, (\lambda e.\, (\mathbf{agent}\, e\, x) \wedge (p\, e)))$;
obj := $\lambda v n p.\, \text{saturate}_{np}\, n\, (\lambda x.\, v\, (\lambda e.\, (\mathbf{theme}\, e\, x) \wedge (p\, e)))$

It is interesting to note that the relations that govern the noun phrases (i.e., nsubj and obj) operate their saturation. In a similar vein, we can define the root operator as a saturation operator for verb phrases.

S : *type* ;
root : VP $\to$ S

S := $\mathbf{t}$;
root := $\lambda v.\, \text{saturate}_{vp}\, v$, where $\text{saturate}_{vp} = \lambda v.\, v\, (\lambda x.\, \mathbf{true})$

Using the apparatus we have developed so far, we can give a semantics to sentence (11) by interpreting the following term:

(13)   root (nsubj (det A (amod WISE MAN)) (obj PRAISES AMANDINE))

which results in the following formula:

$$\exists x.\, (\mathbf{man}\, x) \wedge (\mathbf{wise}\, x) \wedge (\exists e.\, (\mathbf{praise}\, e) \wedge (\mathbf{agent}\, e\, x) \wedge (\mathbf{theme}\, e\, \mathbf{amandine}))$$

Let us conclude this section dedicated to the principles underlying our semantic theory by summarizing them.

1. Dependency relations are represented as binary functions of type $\alpha \to \beta \to \alpha$ (or $\beta \to \alpha \to \alpha$), where α is the syntactic category of the governor and β is the syntactic category of the governee.
2. By virtue of a coherence principle, the different ways of encoding a dependency structure by means of a λ-term should all give rise to the same semantic interpretation.
3. The semantic interpretation of a syntactic category CAT is a type of the form $\beta_1 \to \cdots \beta_n \to \alpha$, where α is the Montagovian interpretation of CAT and $\beta_1, \ldots \beta_n$ are the Montagovian interpretations of the syntactic categories of the phrases whose heads can potentially be governed by the head of a phrase of category CAT.
4. Saturating operators allow phrases to recover their usual Montagovian interpretations.
5. Verbs and verbal phrases are semantically interpreted as sets of sets of events.

3   Relative Clauses and Wh-Extraction

In this section, we tackle the problems associated with the semantic treatment of wh-extraction, a phenomenon we did not address in [4]. As a paradigmatic example, we deal with the case of relative clauses.

Consider the following sentence together with its dependency structure and its abstract syntax.

(14)   *a man who praises Amandine speaks gracefully*

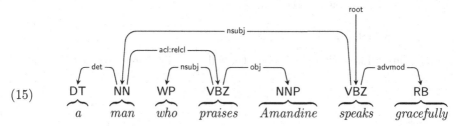

(15)

(16)   root (nsubj(det A (acl:relcl MAN (nsubj WHO (obj PRAISES AMANDINE))))) (advmod SPEAKS GRACEFULLY))

The new ingredients here are the relative pronoun WHO and the dependency relation acl:relcl.[5] According to our typing discipline, acl:relcl must be typed as follows:

$$\text{acl:relcl} : \text{NP} \rightarrow \text{WVP} \rightarrow \text{NP}$$

where WVP is the type of the relative clauses. This being established, let us take a look at what might be an appropriate semantic interpretation of the type WVP. Compared to a simple clause, a relative clause has the specificity of having undergone a wh-movement. From a semantic point of view, such a movement can be modeled as a λ-abstraction. Typically, if p is a phrase of category CAT that has undergone a wh-extraction, and if **cat** is the semantic type associated with CAT, then the semantic interpretation of p will be of type $\mathbf{e} \rightarrow \mathbf{cat}$. Applying this to our setting, we have that

$$\text{VP} := (\mathbf{v} \rightarrow \mathbf{t}) \rightarrow \mathbf{t}$$

and therefore that

$$\text{WVP} := \mathbf{e} \rightarrow (\mathbf{v} \rightarrow \mathbf{t}) \rightarrow \mathbf{t}$$

Let us now turn to the problem of interpreting acl:relcl. We expect the saturated interpretation of the relative clause *who praises Amandine* to be as follows:

(17) $\lambda x. \exists e. (\mathbf{praise}\, e) \wedge (\mathbf{agent}\, e\, x) \wedge (\mathbf{theme}\, e\, \mathbf{amandine})$

---

[5] Neither did we consider the adverbial modification of a verb phrase in the previous section. But this is not a problem, for it can be easily accommodated with the following declarations and interpretations: ADV : *type* ; GRACEFULLY : ADV ; advmod : VP $\rightarrow$ ADV $\rightarrow$ VP ; **graceful** : $\mathbf{v} \rightarrow \mathbf{t}$; ADV := $\mathbf{v} \rightarrow \mathbf{t}$; GRACEFULLY := $\lambda e.\, \mathbf{graceful}\, e$; advmod := $\lambda vaf.\, v\, (\lambda e.\, (a\, e) \wedge (f\, e))$.

On the other hand, we have that the interpretation of the noun phrase *man* is:

(18) $\lambda da.\, d\, (\lambda x.\, a\, \mathbf{man}\, x)$

and we expect the interpretation of the noun phrase *man who praises Amandine* to be:

(19) $\lambda da.\, d\, (\lambda x.\, (a\, \mathbf{man}\, x) \wedge (\exists e.\, (\mathbf{praise}\, e) \wedge (\mathbf{agent}\, e\, x) \wedge (\mathbf{theme}\, e\, \mathbf{amandine})))$

So the question is: how can we combine (17) and (18) to obtain (19)? By working it out, we get the following solution:

$$\mathsf{acl{:}relcl} := \lambda nrda.\, n\, d\, (\lambda nx.\, (a\, n\, x) \wedge (\mathsf{saturate}_{vp}\, (r\, x)))$$

In a related line of thought, we get the following interpretation of the relative pronoun:

WNP : *type* ;
WNP := $\mathbf{e} \rightarrow ((\mathbf{e} \rightarrow \mathbf{t}) \rightarrow (\mathbf{e} \rightarrow \mathbf{t}) \rightarrow \mathbf{t}) \rightarrow ((\mathbf{e} \rightarrow \mathbf{t}) \rightarrow \mathbf{e} \rightarrow \mathbf{t}) \rightarrow (\mathbf{e} \rightarrow \mathbf{t}) \rightarrow \mathbf{t}$;
WHO : WNP ;
WHO := $\lambda xdap.\, p\, x$

But then, the expression below gives rise to a type mismatch:

nsubj WHO PRAISES

which implies that term (16) is not well typed. Indeed, nsubj is of type NP $\rightarrow$ VP $\rightarrow$ VP while WHO is of type WNP. A possible way out of this problem would be to give nsubj a second interpretation that would be of the appropriate type:

NSUBJ : WNP $\rightarrow$ VP $\rightarrow$ WVP ;
NSUBJ := $\lambda nvpx.\, \mathsf{saturate}_{np}\, (n\, x)\, (\lambda x.\, v\, (\lambda e.\, (\mathbf{agent}\, e\, x) \wedge (p\, e)))$

This solution, however, is not entirely satisfactory. On the one hand, it overloads the relation nsubj, for which we would prefer to keep a unique interpretation. On the other hand, it does not obey the type scheme we have adopted for the dependency relations, which results in a violation of our coherence principle.

Another workaround is to use operators to coerce the types of the dependency relations, which is similar to the way combinators are used in combinatorial logic to simulate λ-abstraction [2]:

carg_1 : $(\mathrm{NP} \rightarrow \mathrm{VP} \rightarrow \mathrm{VP}) \rightarrow \mathrm{WNP} \rightarrow \mathrm{VP} \rightarrow \mathrm{WVP}$;
carg_1 := $\lambda rnvx.\, r\, (n\, x)\, v$

Then, the semantic interpretation of the noun phrase, *man who praises amandine*, may be computed by interpreting the following expression:

acl:relcl MAN (carg_1 nsubj WHO (obj PRAISES AMANDINE)) which results in the following λ-term:[6]

$$\lambda da.\, d\,(\lambda x.\,(a\,\mathbf{man}\,x) \wedge (\exists e.\,(\mathbf{praise}\,e) \wedge (\mathbf{theme}\,e\,\mathbf{amandine}) \wedge (\mathbf{agent}\,e\,x)))$$

To make this solution compatible with the coherence principle, we can now define another coercion operator:

$$\mathsf{carg}_2 : (\mathrm{VP} \to \mathrm{NP} \to \mathrm{VP}) \to \mathrm{WVP} \to \mathrm{NP} \to \mathrm{WVP}\,;$$
$$\mathsf{carg}_2 := \lambda rvnx.\, r\,(v\,x)\,n$$

It allows the dependency structure of sentence (14) to be encoded by another term:

$$\mathsf{acl{:}relcl}\; \text{MAN}\,(\mathsf{carg}_2\;\mathsf{obj}\,(\mathsf{carg}_1\;\mathsf{nsubj}\;\text{WHO PRAISES})\;\text{AMANDINE})$$

whose interpretation yields the following λ-term:

$$\lambda da.\, d\,(\lambda x.\,(a\,\mathbf{man}\,x) \wedge (\exists e.\,(\mathbf{praise}\,e) \wedge (\mathbf{agent}\,e\,x) \wedge (\mathbf{theme}\,e\,\mathbf{amandine})))$$

4   Control Verbs and Open Clausal Complements

In this section, we turn to another linguistic phenomenon, that of open clausal complements. Such complements are clauses that are missing their own subject and that are typically governed by a control verb or a raising verb.[7] The dependency relation between a control verb and its open clausal complement is marked by the xcomp relation, like in the following example:

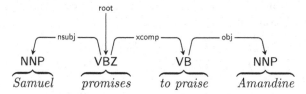

whose expected semantic interpretation is as follows:

$\exists e.\,(\mathbf{promise}\,e) \wedge$
$\quad(\mathbf{agent}\,e\,\mathbf{samuel}) \wedge$
$\quad(\mathbf{topic}\,e\,(\exists e.\,(\mathbf{praise}\,e) \wedge (\mathbf{agent}\,e\,\mathbf{samuel}) \wedge (\mathbf{theme}\,e\,\mathbf{amandine})))$

The puzzle here is that the nsubj dependency relation must provide a subject not only for *promises* but also for *praise*. This means that the interpretation of the verb phrase *to praise Amandine* must be parameterized by an entity variable that will be intantiated by a value provided by the interpretation of the verb phrase *Samuel promises*. A technical way of achieving this is based on a new interpretation of verb phrases that is obtained by type-raising the type of events not on $\mathbf{t}$ but on $\mathbf{e} \to \mathbf{t}$:

---

[6] Modulo the following elmentary logical equivalence: $\alpha \wedge \mathbf{true} \equiv \alpha$.

[7] An open clausal complement may also be the governee of an adjective.

(20) $\text{VP} = (\mathbf{v} \rightarrow \mathbf{e} \rightarrow \mathbf{t}) \rightarrow \mathbf{e} \rightarrow \mathbf{t}$

This idea, leads to the following interpretation of xcomp together with a revisited interpretation of nsubj to be used for control verbs:

$$\text{xcomp} := \lambda vcpx.\, v\, (\lambda ey.\, (\mathbf{topic}\, e\, (c\, (\lambda fz.\, \mathbf{agent}\, f\, z)\, y)) \wedge (p\, e\, y))\, x$$
$$\text{nsubj} := \lambda vnpx.\, \text{saturate}_{np}\, n\, (\lambda y.\, v\, (\lambda ez.\, (\mathbf{agent}\, e\, y) \wedge (p\, e\, y))\, y)$$

But this is not the end of the story, because it is not always the subject of the control verb that provides the open clausal complement with a semantic subject. It can also be the object, as the following sentence illustrates:

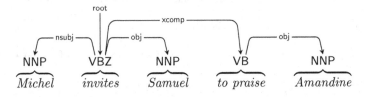

Consequently, we also need a revisited interpretation of obj to be used for control verbs akin to *invites*:

$$\text{obj} := \lambda vnpx.\, \text{saturate}_{np}\, n\, (\lambda y.\, v\, (\lambda ez.\, (\mathbf{theme}\, e\, y) \wedge (p\, e\, y))\, y)$$

But the situation is even more intricate, as it is the case that the same control verb admits both constructions:

> *Michel wants to praise Amandine*
> *Michel wants Samuel to praise Amandine*

A solution based on (20) that can account for these phenomena is possible. However, it would be rather complicated, a point we discuss in the next section.

5   Taking Stock: The Question of Lexical Semantics

In Sect. 4, we said that we prefer a dependency relation to have a unique interpretation. With the solution we discussed in the previous section, this is no longer the case. Indeed, if we adopt the solution advocated in the previous section, we would need two interpretations of the relation nsubj.

In fact the situation is even worse. In what we have developed so far, it is the dependency relations that introduce the thematic roles. However, it is not the case that there is a one-to-one correspondence between syntactic functions and semantic roles. A subject, for example, can correspond to an **agent** or an **experiencer**. Similarly, an object can correspond to a **patient**, a **theme**, a **recipient**, or even a **stimulus**. As a result, if we stick to the approach we have taken so far, we would face a combinatorial explosion of the possible interpretations of a same dependency relation. What it seems is that we have made the mistake of encoding information that is part of lexical semantics within the dependency relations.

It would be more appropriate to have for the subcategorization of a verb to appear in its lexical entry, as in the following examples:

SPEAK := $\lambda xp.\, \exists e.\, (\textbf{speak}\, e) \wedge (\textbf{agent}\, e\, x) \wedge (p\, e)$

PRAISE := $\lambda xyp.\, \exists e.\, (\textbf{praise}\, e) \wedge (\textbf{agent}\, e\, x) \wedge (\textbf{theme}\, e\, y) \wedge (p\, e)$

LIKE := $\lambda xyp.\, \exists e.\, (\textbf{like}\, e) \wedge (\textbf{experiencer}\, e\, x) \wedge (\textbf{stimulus}\, e\, y) \wedge (p\, e)$

But then, the possible problem is that we no longer have a unique semantic type for the category of verb phrases. The cure for this possible defect is to base the interpretation of the verb phrases on the same principle on which the interpretation of the noun phrases is based, that is to parameterize the semantic type of the verb phrases with the types of all the possible governees of a verb. In the fragment we are dealing with the verbs have four kinds of governees: subjects (**e**), objects (**e**), open clausal complements (**e → t**), and adverbial modifiers (**v → t**). Consequently, we obtain the following interpretation:

(21)   VP := $\mathbf{e \to e \to (e \to t) \to (v \to t) \to t}$

With this interpretation, the lexical entry of the verb *praise* becomes the following one:

PRAISE := $\lambda xycp.\, \exists e.\, (\textbf{praise}\, e) \wedge (\textbf{agent}\, e\, x) \wedge (\textbf{theme}\, e\, y) \wedge (p\, e)$

where the λ-variable c is a dummy parameter that does not occur in the interpretation of the verb and is present only for typing reasons.

Because of the presence of dummy parameters, we need to define an appropriate saturating operator for the verb phrases. We do this by using existential closures:

$$\text{saturate}_{vp} = \lambda v.\, \exists xy.\, v\, x\, y\, (\lambda x.\, \textbf{true})\, (\lambda e.\, \textbf{true})$$

Using interpretation (21) greatly simplifies the interpretations of the dependencies. For example, the interpretations of nsubj and xcomp, which are now unique, are as follows:

$$\text{nsubj} := \lambda nvxycf.\, \text{saturate}_{np}\, n\, (\lambda z.\, v\, z\, x\, y\, c\, f)$$
$$\text{xcomp} := \lambda vcxydf.\, v\, x\, y\, (\lambda x.\, \text{saturate}_{vp}\, (\lambda z.\, cx))\, f$$

It is worth noting that these new interpretations are pure combinators that do not introduce any lexical information.

In the next section, we present a grammar based on interpretation (21).

6   Bringing Everything Together

The new interpretation of the verb phrases advocated in the previous section requires a revision of the solutions we discussed in Sects. 2 and 3. We do this in this section by developing a toy grammar that integrates the various elements we have discussed. This grammar allows for the semantic treatment of a sentence like the following:

(22)   *Michel invites a wise man who likes to speak gracefully to praise Amandine*

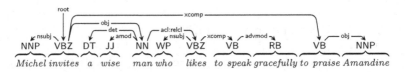

We present our integrated semantic grammar in the form of an Abstract Categorial Grammar.[8]

Abstract Syntax

ADJ, ADV, DET, NP, VP, WNP, WVP, S : *type* ;
A : DET ;
WISE : ADJ ;
MAN : NP ;
PRAISE, PROMISE, SPEAK, LIKE, INVITE : VP ;
AMANDINE, MICHEL, SAMUEL : NP ;
GRACEFULLY : ADV ;
WHO, WHOM : WNP ;
amod : ADJ $\to$ NP $\to$ NP ;
advmod : VP $\to$ ADV $\to$ VP ;
det : DET $\to$ NP $\to$ NP ;
nsubj : NP $\to$ VP $\to$ VP ;
obj : VP $\to$ NP $\to$ VP ;
xcomp : VP $\to$ VP $\to$ VP ;
acl:relcl : NP $\to$ WVP $\to$ NP ;
root : VP $\to$ S ;
wnparg1 : (NP $\to$ VP $\to$ VP) $\to$ WNP $\to$ VP $\to$ WVP ;
wnparg2 : (VP $\to$ NP $\to$ VP) $\to$ VP $\to$ WNP $\to$ WVP ;
wvparg1 : (VP $\to$ NP $\to$ VP) $\to$ WVP $\to$ NP $\to$ WVP ;
wvparg2 : (NP $\to$ VP $\to$ VP) $\to$ NP $\to$ WVP $\to$ WVP

Object Language

e, t, v : *type* ;
amandine, michel, samuel : e ;
man, wise : e $\to$ t ;
praise, promise, speak, like, invite : v $\to$ t ;

---

[8] In fact, we implemented it using the ACG toolkit:
https://gitlab.inria.fr/ACG/dev/ACGtk..

agent, theme, experiencer, recipient : $\mathbf{v} \to \mathbf{e} \to \mathbf{t}$;
topic, stimulus : $\mathbf{v} \to \mathbf{t} \to \mathbf{t}$;
graceful : $\mathbf{v} \to \mathbf{t}$;
$\text{saturate}_{np} = \lambda n.\, n\,(\lambda pq.\, \exists x.\,(p\,x) \wedge (q\,x))\,(\lambda x.\,x)$;
$\text{saturate}_{vp} = \lambda v.\, \exists xy.\, v\,x\,y\,(\lambda x.\,\mathbf{true})\,(\lambda e.\,\mathbf{true})$

Semantic Interpretation

ADJ := $(\mathbf{e} \to \mathbf{t}) \to \mathbf{e} \to \mathbf{t}$;
ADV := $\mathbf{v} \to \mathbf{t}$;
DET := $(\mathbf{e} \to \mathbf{t}) \to (\mathbf{e} \to \mathbf{t}) \to \mathbf{t}$;
NP := $((\mathbf{e} \to \mathbf{t}) \to (\mathbf{e} \to \mathbf{t}) \to \mathbf{t}) \to ((\mathbf{e} \to \mathbf{t}) \to \mathbf{e} \to \mathbf{t}) \to (\mathbf{e} \to \mathbf{t}) \to \mathbf{t}$;
VP := $\mathbf{e} \to \mathbf{e} \to (\mathbf{e} \to \mathbf{t}) \to (\mathbf{v} \to \mathbf{t}) \to \mathbf{t}$;
WNP := $\mathbf{e} \to ((\mathbf{e} \to \mathbf{t}) \to (\mathbf{e} \to \mathbf{t}) \to \mathbf{t}) \to ((\mathbf{e} \to \mathbf{t}) \to \mathbf{e} \to \mathbf{t}) \to$
$$(\mathbf{e} \to \mathbf{t}) \to \mathbf{t} ;$$
WVP := $\mathbf{e} \to \mathbf{e} \to \mathbf{e} \to (\mathbf{e} \to \mathbf{t}) \to (\mathbf{v} \to \mathbf{t}) \to \mathbf{t}$;
S := $\mathbf{t}$;
A := $\lambda pq.\, \exists x.\,(p\,x) \wedge (q\,x)$;
WISE := $\lambda nx.\,(n\,x) \wedge (\mathbf{wise}\,x)$;
MAN := $\lambda da.\, d\,(a\,\mathbf{man})$;
SPEAK := $\lambda xycp.\, \exists e.\,(\mathbf{speak}\,e) \wedge (\mathbf{agent}\,e\,x) \wedge (p\,e)$;
PRAISE := $\lambda xycp.\, \exists e.\,(\mathbf{praise}\,e) \wedge (\mathbf{agent}\,e\,x) \wedge (\mathbf{theme}\,e\,y) \wedge (p\,e)$;
PROMISE := $\lambda xycp.\, \exists e.\,(\mathbf{promise}\,e) \wedge (\mathbf{agent}\,e\,x) \wedge (\mathbf{topic}\,e\,(c\,x)) \wedge (p\,e)$;
LIKE := $\lambda xycp.\, \exists e.\,(\mathbf{like}\,e) \wedge (\mathbf{experiencer}\,e\,x) \wedge (\mathbf{stimulus}\,e\,(c\,x)) \wedge (p\,e)$;
INVITE := $\lambda xycp.\, \exists e.\,(\mathbf{invite}\,e) \wedge (\mathbf{agent}\,e\,x) \wedge (\mathbf{recipient}\,e\,y) \wedge$
$$(\mathbf{topic}\,e\,(c\,y)) \wedge (p\,e) ;$$
AMANDINE := $\lambda dap.\, p\,\mathbf{amandine}$;
MICHEL := $\lambda dap.\, p\,\mathbf{michel}$;
SAMUEL := $\lambda dap.\, p\,\mathbf{samuel}$;
GRACEFULLY := $\lambda e.\,\mathbf{graceful}\,e$;
WHO, WHOM := $\lambda xdap.\, p\,x$;
amod := $\lambda andb.\, n\,d\,(\lambda x.\, b\,(a\,x))$;
advmod := $\lambda vaxycf.\, v\,x\,y\,c\,(\lambda e.\,(a\,e) \wedge (f\,e))$;
det := $\lambda dne.\, n\,d$;
nsubj := $\lambda nvxycf.\, \text{saturate}_{np}\,n\,(\lambda z.\, v\,z\,y\,c\,f)$;
obj := $\lambda vnxycf.\, \text{saturate}_{np}\,n\,(\lambda z.\, v\,x\,z\,c\,f)$;
xcomp := $\lambda vcxydf.\, v\,x\,y\,(\lambda x.\, \text{saturate}_{vp}\,(\lambda z.\, c\,x))\,f$;
acl:relcl := $\lambda nrda.\, n\,d\,(\lambda nx.\,(a\,n\,x) \wedge (\text{saturate}_{vp}\,(r\,x)))$;
root := $\lambda v.\, \text{saturate}_{vp}\,v$;
wnparg1 := $\lambda rnvx.\, r\,(n\,x)\,v$;
wnparg2 := $\lambda rvnx.\, r\,v\,(n\,x)$;
wvparg1 := $\lambda rvnx.\, r\,(v\,x)\,n$;
wvparg2 := $\lambda rnvx.\, r\,n\,(v\,x)$

7   Conclusions

In this paper we have made explicit the principles underlying the semantic theory we began to develop in [4]. We have then shown how dependency relations involving implicit semantic arguments can be treated along these lines. This treatment, however, has necessitated a revision of the interpretation of the verb phrases. Quite satisfactorily, the new interpretation we have adopted generalizes the previous one, and is based on the principle we advocated for the interpretation of noun phrases.

It results in a semantic grammar in which the lexical semantics is encoded, as it should be, within the lexical entries. As for the dependency relations act, they act as pure combinators that assemble the meanings of the words that form a sentence. We believe that this reflects the spirit of dependency grammars and demonstrates the feasibility and adequacy of the formal theory of dependency semantics, we started to develop [4].

For future work, we intend to extend the coverage of our grammar by considering more linguistic constructs, and to conduct a real-size experiment. To this end, we will take advantage of the existence of numerous corpora annotated with dependencies, and attempt to built a semantic grammar semi-automatically from such a corpus.

References

1. Champollion, L.: The interaction of compositional semantics and event semantics. Linguist. Philos. **38**(1), 31–66 (2015)
2. Curry, H.B., Feys, R.: Combinatory Logic, vol. I, North-Holland (1958)
3. de Groote, P.: Towards abstract categorial grammars. In: Association for Computational Linguistics, 39th Annual Meeting and 10th Conference of the European Chapter, Proceedings of the Conference, pp. 148–155 (2001)
4. de Groote, P.: Deriving formal semantic representations from dependency structures. In: Bekki, D., Mineshima, K., McCready, E. (eds.) Logic and Engineering of Natural Language Semantics, LENLS 2022, LNCS, vol. 14213. Springer, Cham (2023). https://doi.org/10.1007/978-3-031-43977-3_10
5. Findlay, J.Y., Haug, D.T.T.: How useful are enhanced Universal Dependencies for semantic interpretation? In: Proceedings of the Sixth International Conference on Dependency Linguistics (Depling, SyntaxFest 2021), pp. 22–34. Association for Computational Linguistics (2021)
6. Findlay, J.Y., Salimifar, S., Yıldırım, A., Haug, D.T.T.: Rule-based semantic interpretation for Universal Dependencies. In: Proceedings of the Sixth Workshop on Universal Dependencies (UDW, GURT/SyntaxFest 2023), pp. 47–57. Association for Computational Linguistics (2023)
7. Haug, D.T.T., Findlay, J.Y.: Formal semantics for dependency grammar. In: Proceedings of the Seventh International Conference on Dependency Linguistics (Depling, GURT/SyntaxFest 2023), pp. 22–31. Association for Computational Linguistics (2023)
8. Haug, D.T.T., Gotham, M.: Glue semantics for universal dependencies. In: Proceedings of the LFG-conference, pp. 208–226. CSLI Publications (2021)

9. Mel'čuk, I.: Dependency Syntax: Theory and Practice. State University of New York Press, New York (1988)

10. Montague, R.: Formal Philosophy: selected papers of Richard Montague, edited and with an introduction by Richmond Thomason. Yale University Press, New Haven (1974)

11. Nivre, J., et al.: Universal Dependencies v1: a multilingual treebank collection. In: Proceedings of the Tenth International Conference on Language Resources and Evaluation (LREC 2016), pp. 1659–1666, Portorož, Slovenia, European Language Resources Association (ELRA) May 2016

12. Reddy, S.: Transforming dependency structures to logical forms for semantic parsing. Trans. Assoc. Comput. Linguist. **4**, 127–140 (2016)

13. Reddy, S., Täckström, O., Petrov, S., Steedman, M., Lapata, M.: Universal semantic parsing. In: Proceedings of the 2017 Conference on Empirical Methods in Natural Language Processing, pp. 89–101. Association for Computational Linguistics (2017)

14. Tesnière, L.: Eléments de syntaxe structurale. Klincksieck, Paris (1959)

15. van Benthem, J.: Essays in Logical Semantics. Reidel, Dordrecht (1986)

Semantics of Propositional Attitudes in Type-Theory of Algorithms

Roussanka Loukanova$^{(\boxtimes)}$ (iD)

Institute of Mathematics and Informatics, Bulgarian Academy of Sciences, Sofia,
Bulgaria
rloukanova@gmail.com

Abstract. In this paper, I introduce the extended type-theory of acyclic algorithms L_{ar}^λ and its version L_r^λ with full recursion. The extended theory and its reduction calculus provide algorithmic semantics of attitude expressions, including beliefs, knowledge, and statements, which are present in advanced applications requiring computational semantics of natural language. The extended type-theory of algorithms includes restrictor terms, terms of logic operators, and pure quantifiers. The restrictor terms have effects of presuppositional restrictions, requiring objects to have certain properties. I provide brief, while important information on the relation of the theory of recursion L_r^λ to the formal language LCF of λ-calculus, by Dana S. Scott and Gordon Plotkin, covering let-expressions for semantics of programming langages.

Keywords: type-theory · acyclic algorithms · full recursion · denotational semantics · algorithmic semantics · reduction calculus · recursion · restrictor · logic operators · quantifiers · attitudes · statements

1 An Overview

Human natural language (NL) is notorious for various kinds of ambiguities, e.g., lexical, syntactic, semantic. Syntactic and semantic ambiguities can be exhibited in the lexicon, across parts of speech categories, in the morphological structures of lexemes, and phrasal structures of expressions and sentences.

Often, ambiguity resolving factors are provided by the context. That can be:

(A) linguistic information provided, e.g., by linguistic expressions represented by word inflections, tenses, or by wider language context, nearest text
(B) extra-linguistic means provided by the surrounding circumstances, e.g., components of the usage, like the speaker's references, intentions, time and space locations, etc., extra-linguistics elements.

The details of modeling such linguistic and extra-linguistics factors by L_{ar}^λ and L_r^λ are outside the topic of this chapter. In it, we shall lay out the formal technique of the type-theory of algorithms of L_{ar}^λ and L_r^λ, with its higher-order

D. Bekki et al. (Eds.): LENLS 2023, LNCS 14569, pp. 260–284, 2024.
https://doi.org/10.1007/978-3-031-60878-0_15

type system and formal terms. We present syntax-semantics interfaces provided by the reduction calculi of L_{ar}^λ and L_r^λ for reducing each term to its canonical form. The canonical forms of algorithmically meaningful terms determine the distinctions between denotational and algorithmic semantics.

Among the most difficult ambiguities, for computational handling of NL, are expressions with multiple occurrences of quantifiers, which contribute to quantifier scope ambiguities and underspecification. For handling quantifier scoping, in recent developments of Type-Theory of Algorithms L_{ar}^λ, see [10, 16].

Far more difficult for computational linguistics are NL expressions having occurrences of so-called attitude components designating knowledge, beliefs, statements, and similar semantic information.

Often, some of the syntactic complements of an attitude lexeme is a sentential expression, e.g., see the examples in the following sections. The sentential complement may have subexpressions that designate semantic components, which are strictly semantic parts of the attitudinal information, i.e., in the scope of the attitude. For example, an agent a can use a sentence Φ with a major (head) word occurring in it, which is an attitude lexeme L having attitudinal syntactic arguments, e.g., subexpressions Ψ_1 and Ψ_2. The expression Ψ_1 can designate an agent a_1. On its turn, Ψ_2 can have a syntactic component B that designates a semantic object b. The expression B can be:

(1) a_1's description of b: thus, the semantics of B is in the semantic scope of L; or

(2) a's, i.e., the user's, description of b: thus, while b is a semantic component of the semantic information designated by Ψ_2, the relevant semantics of B is outside of the semantic scope of L.

Furthermore, the attitude expressions create the so-called oblique text in context, in which the attitude expressions do not preserve semantic equivalence under replacement of equivalent attitude components. The first solution was informally proposed by Frege [4], by introducing ideas of semantic distinctions between notions of reference and sense. In the approach of the type-theory of algorithms, by acyclic recursion in L_{ar}^λ and its version with full recursion L_r^λ, we preserve the classic notion of intensional sense, at least for the NL expressions.

Thus, we render, i.e., translate NL expressions into terms A of the type-theory L_{ar}^λ and L_r^λ, by a focus on acyclic versions of L_{ar}^λ. For every meaningful term A, the Carnap intension $CI(A)$ of A is a function which maps every state s to the denotational value, $den(A)(s)$, of A in s. The states in both L_{ar}^λ and L_r^λ correspond to Carnap indices, e.g., each index can represent a possible world, time, space, linguistic and extra-linguistic components like user agents, etc. Thus, L_{ar}^λ and L_r^λ introduce denotational semantics of their terms A rendering NL expressions, by denotational functions $den(A) = CI(A)$, as Carnap intensions. Importantly, in addition to denotational semantics, L_{ar}^λ and L_r^λ introduce also algorithmic semantics determined by their formal language and reduction calculi.

Montague [20] introduced his intensional logic IL for formal semantics of NL. He provided formal representation of NL attitudes, along with the quantifier scope ambiguities, by the notions of *extension* and *Carnap intension* CI, and using extra levels of syntactic disambiguation of NL expressions. That solution was adopted by some generalisations of Montague grammars. The problem has been largely open, due to its purely semantic nature, without direct syntactic ambiguities in phrasal structures and even in expressions without phrasal syntactic analyses. Significant semantic information, including semantic underspecification, of such language expressions is highly dependent on context of usage.

In addition, opting to simultaneous deriving of all, or even some, of the possible alternative interpretations, often called possible "readings", results in explosion of complexity, especially when more sentences are combined into texts.

By the work presented in this chapter, I shall extend the type-theory L_{ar}^{λ} of algorithms, to cover algorithmic semantics of some of the major attitude expressions, their semantic underspecification, and to derive reductions of specifications in contexts.

2   Some Other Approaches to Propositional Attitudes

Here I shall give a small selection of approaches to propositional attitudes, as a source of possible grasp of the possibilities in compare to utilising L_{ar}^{λ}.

Dowty et al. [3] and Gamut [6] continue to provide a classic introduction to formal semantics, including semantics of propositional attitudes, in the tradition of Montague [20]. Both books provide transitions from using First Order Logic (FOL) and modal logic, by showing weakness and inadequacy, on the way to the Montague's Intensional Logic (IL).

Muskens [25] was the first who introduced Gallin [5] intensional logic by the type system generalizing the Montague IL. He moved to a valuable generalisation of Montague Grammar, by representing semantic partiality at semantic level. He also introduced relational type-theoretic logic, in contrast to functional encoding by the technique of currying.

Loukanova [8,9] introduced Situation Theory as mathematical structures and applied it to Situation Semantics of attitudes and quantifiers in NL. The mathematical, semantic models introduced in that work of Situation Theory are mathematical structures that include situated, dependent types. Situated types are defined hierarchically, from primitive and complex types constructed by abstractions and recursion on situated propositions. The mathematical structures are based on relations, without coding them by one-argument functions, i.e., without currying encoding. That work introduced also restricted parameters as typed, semantic objects of Situation Theory, at the semantic level, in contrast to the restrictor terms of L_{ar}^{λ}, which are at the syntactic level of L_{ar}^{λ}. Loukanova [14] initiated generalizing that approach to Dependent-Type Theory of Situated Information, by recursion terms of relational type system without currying.

De Groote [1] and De Groote et al. [2] introduce technique of continuation, similarly valuable in programming, for analysis of scope ambiguity in NL.

3   Syntax of Type-Theory of Algorithms

The untyped formal languages of algorithms, covering full-recursion, were introduced as the formal languages of recursion (FLR) by Moschovakis [21–23]. The sets of untyped terms of the form (4a)–(4d) properly extend the λ-calculus.

The simply-typed theory of acyclic recursion L_{ar}^{λ}, i.e., of acyclic algorithms, was introduced by Moschovakis [24]. The type-theory L_{ar}^{λ} formalises algorithms that end, i.e., close-off, after finite number steps of calculations. Moschovakis [24] focused on demonstrating potential applications to computational semantics of NL, by approaches that are similar to the ones used for semantics of programming languages. The language L_{ar}^{λ} introduced in [24] has terms of the form (4a)–(4d), which satisfy the Acyclicity Constraint (AC) in Definition 3. The formal language L_{ar}^{λ} suffice for representing significant fragments of NL.

For introductions to type-theory L_{ar}^{λ} of algorithms, its syntax, denotational and algorithmic semantics, and reduction calculi, e.g., see Moschovakis [24], and, for recent developments of extended syntax-semantics interfaces of the computational systems of L_{ar}^{λ}, see detailed introductions by Loukanova [11–13,16,17]. The sets Types of L_{ar}^{λ} are as introduced by Gallin [5] in the logic TY_2. We define them by the recursive rules (1) in Backus-Naur Form (BNF).

Notation 1. *The symbols $\equiv$ and $:\equiv$ are meta symbols, i.e., not strictly in the formal languages of L_{ar}^{λ} and L_r^{λ}. We use the symbol $\equiv$ for literal identity between expressions and types, e.g., in definitions and abbreviations. The symbol $:\equiv$ is for the replacement operation, including for substitution of variables, and sometimes for definitions, e.g., of the generating grammar of the set Types by BNF (1) rules. The symbol $:=$ is used in overloaded ways:*

(1) In the syntax of the terms: as a component of the recursion terms in the sequences of recursion assignments in Definition 2 (4d)

(2) In the denotational semantics of L_{ar}^{λ} and L_r^{λ}: as a meta symbol for updating variable valuations by setting values of some variables

Definition 1 (Gallin Types). *See logic TY_2 introduced by [5]:*

$$\tau :\equiv e \mid t \mid s \mid (\tau_1 \to \tau_2) \qquad\qquad \text{(Types)} \quad (1)$$

The type t is for truth values: 0 for false, 1 for true, *er* for erroneous values. The following are abbreviations for the types of state-dependent objects and for the types of the state dependent truth values, i.e., for propositions:

$$\widetilde{\tau} \equiv (s \to \tau), \ \tau \in Types \qquad \text{(for state-dependent objects of type } \widetilde{\tau}) \quad (2a)$$

$$\widetilde{t} \equiv (s \to t) \qquad\qquad \text{(abbreviation for the type of propositions)} \quad (2b)$$

The classes of the formal languages of L_r^{λ} and L_{ar}^{λ}, have, for all $\sigma \in$ Types, denumerable sets of:

$$K_\sigma = \text{Consts}_\sigma \qquad\qquad\qquad\qquad \text{(constants)} \quad (3a)$$

$\wedge, \vee, \rightarrow \ \in \text{Consts}_{(\tau \rightarrow (\tau \rightarrow \tau))}, \ \tau \in \{\, t, \tilde{t} \,\}$ (logical constants)   (3b)

$\neg \in \text{Consts}_{(\tau \rightarrow \tau)}, \ \tau \in \{\, t, \tilde{t} \,\}$ (logical constant for negation)   (3c)

$\text{Vars}_\sigma = \text{PureV}_\sigma \cup \text{RecV}_\sigma$ (two kinds of variables)   (3d)

where PureV_τ is for binding by λ-abstractions and logic quantifiers, and RecV_τ is for saving calculated values of terms.

For the typed sets Terms of the type-theory of algorithms L_{ar}^λ in Definition 2, we shall use a typed Backus-Naur Form (TBNF) style, with the types of the assumed terms given as superscripts, and the newly formed terms having the types after the colon. In general, we use the typical notations for type assignments, $A : \tau$, and A^τ, to express that A is a term of type τ.

Definition 2. Terms $= \bigcup_{\tau \in \text{Types}} \text{Terms}_\tau$ *is the set of the terms of* L_r^λ, *where, for each* $\tau \in \text{Types}$, Terms_τ *is the set of the terms of type* τ, *which are defined recursively by* (4a)–(4h), (4j), (4i), *in a typed style of Backus-Naur Form (TBNF):*

$A :\equiv c^\sigma : \sigma \mid x^\sigma : \sigma$ ($c^\sigma \in \text{Consts}_\sigma$, $x^\sigma \in \text{PureV}_\sigma \cup \text{RecV}_\sigma$)   (4a)

$\mid B^{(\sigma \rightarrow \rho)}(C^\sigma) : \rho$ (*application terms*)   (4b)

$\mid \lambda(v^\sigma)(B^\rho) : (\sigma \rightarrow \rho)$ (*λ-terms*)   (4c)

$\mid \big[A_0^{\sigma_0} \text{ where } \{\, p_1^{\sigma_1} := A_1^{\sigma_1}, \dots, p_n^{\sigma_n} := A_n^{\sigma_n} \,\} \big] : \sigma_0$ (*recursion terms*)   (4d)

$\mid (C_0^{\sigma_0} \text{ such that } \{\, C_1^{\tau_1}, \dots, C_m^{\tau_m} \,\}) : \sigma_0'$ (*restrictor terms*)   (4e)

$\mid \wedge(A_2^\tau)(A_1^\tau) : \tau \mid \vee(A_2^\tau)(A_1^\tau) : \tau \mid \rightarrow(A_2^\tau)(A_1^\tau) : \tau$

     (*conjunction /   disjunction   /   implication terms*)   (4f)

$\mid \neg(B^\tau) : \tau$ (*negation terms*)   (4g)

$\mid \forall(v^\sigma)(B^\tau) : \tau \mid \exists(v^\sigma)(B^\tau) : \tau$ (*logic, pure quantifier terms*)

         (4h)

$\mid \mathcal{C}(B^{\tilde{\sigma}}(s)) : \tilde{\sigma}, \ s \in \text{Vars}_s$ (*closed scope $B^{\tilde{\sigma}}$*)   (4i)

$\mid \text{ToScope}(B^{\tilde{\sigma}}) : (s \rightarrow \tilde{\sigma})$ (*unspecified, open scope $B^{\tilde{\sigma}}$*)   (4j)

given the following assumptions:

(1) $c \in K_\sigma = \text{Consts}_\sigma$

(2) $\wedge, \vee, \rightarrow \ : (\tau \rightarrow (\tau \rightarrow \tau)), \ \neg : (\tau \rightarrow \tau), \ \tau \in \{\, t, \tilde{t} \,\}$, *as in* (3b), (3c)

(3) $x^\sigma \in \text{PureV}_\sigma \cup \text{RecV}_\sigma$ *is a pure or memory (recursion) variable,*

(4) $B, C \in \text{Terms}$ *of respective types*

(5) $v^\sigma \in \text{PureV}_\sigma$ *is a pure variable*

(6) $A_1^\tau, A_2^\tau, A_i^{\sigma_i} \in \text{Terms}$ *($i = 0, \dots, n$) are terms of the respective types*

(7) In (4d), *for* $i = 1, \dots, n$, $\sigma_i \in \text{Types}$:

    (a) $p_i^{\sigma_i} \in \text{RecV}_{\sigma_i}$ *are pairwise different recursion (memory) variables*

    (b) each term $A_i^{\sigma_i} \in \text{Terms}_{\sigma_i}$, *assigned to* $p_i^{\sigma_i}$, *is of the same corresponding type* σ_i

(8) $C_0^{\sigma_0} \in \text{Terms}_{\sigma_0}$ *and, for each* $j = 1, \dots, m$ *($m \geq 1$),* $C_j^{\tau_j} \in \text{Terms}_{\tau_j}$

(9) In (4e), (4f)–(4h), the types $\tau, \tau_j \in \{\mathsf{t}, \widetilde{\mathsf{t}}\}$ (for $j = 1, \ldots, m$) are for state-independent and state-dependent truth values, respectively
$\widetilde{\mathsf{t}} \equiv (\mathsf{s} \to \mathsf{t})$ is the type for propositions

(10) In (4e), the type σ_0 of the restrictor's "head" $C_0^{\sigma_0}$ may need to be lifted to its state-dependent version $\sigma_0' \equiv (\mathsf{s} \to \sigma_0)$, in the type of the entire restrictor term $A^{\sigma_0'}$, in case $\tau_i \equiv \widetilde{\mathsf{t}}$, for some $i \in \{1, \ldots, m\}$, and σ_0 is state independent, i.e., $\sigma_0 \not\equiv (\mathsf{s} \to \sigma)$, for all $\sigma \in$ Types. Otherwise $\sigma_0' \equiv \sigma_0$. See Loukanova [17], i.e.:

$$
\sigma_0' \equiv
\begin{cases}
\sigma_0, & \text{if } \tau_i \equiv \mathsf{t}, \text{ for all } i \in \{1, \ldots, m\} & (5a) \\
\sigma_0 \equiv (\mathsf{s} \to \sigma), & \text{if } \tau_i \equiv \widetilde{\mathsf{t}}, \text{ for some } i \in \{1, \ldots, m\}, \text{ and} & (5b) \\
& \text{for some } \sigma \in \text{Types}, \sigma_0 \equiv (\mathsf{s} \to \sigma) \\
\widetilde{\sigma_0} \equiv (\mathsf{s} \to \sigma_0), & \text{if } \tau_i \equiv \widetilde{\mathsf{t}}, \text{ for some } i \in \{1, \ldots, m\}, \text{ and} & (5c) \\
& \text{there is no } \sigma, \text{ s.th. } \sigma_0 \equiv (\mathsf{s} \to \sigma)
\end{cases}
$$

(11) ToScope : $(\widetilde{\sigma} \to (\mathsf{s} \to \widetilde{\sigma}))$, $\mathcal{C} : (\sigma \to \widetilde{\sigma})$
The type $\widetilde{\sigma} \equiv \widetilde{t} \equiv (\mathsf{s} \to \mathsf{t})$ is for propositions, in the special cases when $\sigma \equiv \mathsf{t}$, i.e., σ is for the state dependent truth values. See Notation 1 and (2b).

(A) The sequence of assignments $\{p_1^{\sigma_1} := A_1^{\sigma_1}, \ldots, p_n^{\sigma_n} := A_n^{\sigma_n}\}$ in (4d) is acyclic, in case it satisfies the Acyclicity Constraint (AC) in Definition 3. Then, the terms of the form in (4d) are called acyclic recursion terms

(B) The set Terms, in Definition 2, without requiring (AC) in Definition 3, for all terms, determines the type theory L_r^λ of algorithms including full recursion

(C) In case Definition 2 is restricted to acyclic terms in (4d), i.e., to recursion terms satisfying the Acyclicity Constraint (AC) in Definition 3, then all terms in Terms defined by Definition 2 are acyclic. In this case, Terms determines the type-theory L_{ar}^λ of acyclic algorithms.

We shall focus primarily on the type-theory L_{ar}^λ of acyclic algorithms.

Definition 3 (Acyclicity Constraint (AC)). For any $A_i^{\sigma_i} \in$ Terms$_{\sigma_i}$ and pairwise different memory (recursion) variables $p_i \in$ RecV$_{\sigma_i}$, $i \in \{1, \ldots, n\}$, the sequence (6):

$$\{p_1^{\sigma_1} := A_1^{\sigma_1}, \ldots, p_n^{\sigma_n} := A_n^{\sigma_n}\} \quad (n \geq 0) \tag{6}$$

is an acyclic system of assignments iff there is a function rank

rank: $\{p_1, \ldots, p_n\} \to \mathbb{N}$, such that, for all $p_i, p_j \in \{p_1, \ldots, p_n\}$,
if p_j occurs freely in $A_i^{\sigma_i}$, then rank$(p_j) <$ rank(p_i)
$\hfill$ (AC)

Note 1. The type assignments by Definition 2 allow the types of the terms to be derived from type assignments of the term components. The types are not per se orthographical components of the actual appearance of the terms. Sometimes, we shall skip displaying the types of the terms or of some of the sub-terms.

Notation 2. *We shall use the typical infix notation of logic terms:*

$$(A_1^\tau \wedge A_2^\tau) \equiv \wedge\, (A_2^\tau)(A_1^\tau) \tag{7a}$$

$$(A_1^\tau \vee A_2^\tau) \equiv \vee\, (A_2^\tau)(A_1^\tau) \tag{7b}$$

$$(A_1^\tau \to A_2^\tau) \equiv\, \to (A_2^\tau)(A_1^\tau) \tag{7c}$$

Notation 3. *Abbreviations of sequences are useful for sake of space and clarity:*

$$\overrightarrow{p} := \overrightarrow{A} \equiv p_1 := A_1,\ \ldots,\ p_n := A_n \quad (n \geq 0) \tag{8a}$$

$$H(\overrightarrow{u}) \equiv [\ldots H(u_1) \ldots](u_n) \quad (n \geq 0) \tag{8b}$$

$$\lambda(\overrightarrow{v})(H(\overrightarrow{u})) \equiv \lambda(v_1)\big(\ldots \lambda(v_m)\big([\ldots H(u_1) \ldots](u_n)\big)\ldots\big)$$

$$\equiv \lambda(v_1)\ldots(v_m)(H(u_1)\ldots(u_n)) \tag{8c}$$

$$\equiv \lambda(v_1,\ldots,v_m)(H(u_1,\ldots,u_n)) \quad (n, m \geq 0)$$

$$C_0 \text{ such that } \{\, \overrightarrow{C^\tau}\, \} \equiv C_0 \text{ such that } \{\, C_1, \ldots, C_m\, \} \tag{8d}$$

We shall assume, unless otherwise stated, that all replacements of variables in terms are applied on their free occurrences, without causing variable clashes.

Definition 4 (Free Occurrences and Replacement Operation). *For more details, see Loukanova [13].*

Assume that A, C, $X \in$ Terms and that, for some $\tau \in$ Types, $C : \tau$ and $X : \tau$.

1. *For any given terms X and A, an occurrence of X in A is free (in A) if and only if it is not in the scope of any binding operator (e.g., λ and where operators) that binds some variable having free occurrences in X. In case X is a variable, an occurrence of X is free in A, if it is not in the scope of any binding operator that binds X.*

2. *The result of the simultaneous replacement of all free (unless otherwise stated) occurrences of X with C in A is denoted by $A\{\, X := C\, \}$.*

3. *The replacement $A\{\, X := C\, \}$ of X with C in A is free if and only if no (free) occurrence of X in A is in the scope of any binding operator (e.g., $\xi \in \{\lambda, \exists, \forall\}$ and the recursion operator where) that binds some variable having free occurrences in C: i.e., no variable that is free in C becomes bound in $A\{\, X := C\, \}$. In such a case, we also say that X is free for C in A. We usually use free replacements applied to all free occurrences of the specified variables, unless otherwise stated.*

$X \in$ PureV $\cup$ RecV $\cup$ Consts *are special cases of $X \in$ Terms, often used in replacements, but not always.*

Note: The replacement operation can be defined formally by induction on term structure. We do not include such details here.

The immediate terms of Definition 5 are specialised terms, that do not have algorithmic meanings, i.e., they get their values directly by the variable valuation $g \in G^{\mathfrak{A}}$ and the denotation function.

Definition 5 (TBNF Style Notation). *The set* ImT *of immediate terms consists of the terms defined as follows:*

$$T^\tau :\equiv X^\tau \mid R^{(\tau_1 \to \cdots \to (\tau_m \to \tau))}(v_1^{\tau_1}) \ldots (v_m^{\tau_m}) \qquad \text{(ImAppT)}$$

$$T^{(\sigma_1 \to \cdots \to (\sigma_n \to \tau))} :\equiv \lambda(u_1^{\sigma_1}) \ldots \lambda(u_n^{\sigma_n}) R^{(\tau_1 \to \cdots \to (\tau_m \to \tau))}(v_1^{\tau_1}) \ldots (v_m^{\tau_m}) \quad \text{(Im}\lambda\text{-T)}$$

for $n \geq 0$, $m \geq 0$; $u_i \in \mathsf{PureV}_{\sigma_i}$, *for* $i = 1, \ldots, n$; $v_j \in \mathsf{PureV}_{\tau_j}$, *for* $j = 1, \ldots, m$; $X \in \mathsf{PureV}_\tau$, $R \in \mathsf{RecV}_{(\tau_1 \to \cdots \to (\tau_m \to \tau))}$.

Definition 6 (Proper Terms). *A term* A *is* proper *if and only if it is not immediate, e.g., the set* PrT *of the proper terms of* L_{ar}^λ *consists of all terms that are not in* ImT:

$$\mathsf{PrT} = (\mathsf{Terms} - \mathsf{ImT}) \qquad (10)$$

4 Gamma-Star Reduction Calculus of L_{ar}^λ

I designate the logic operators in L_{ar}^λ and L_r^λ as a set of specialised categorematic, logic constants. In this way, I classify the reduction rules for the logic terms formed by (4f)–(4g) as special cases of the reduction rule for application terms, see (3b), (3c) and (7a), (7b), (7c). For more details, see [16].

In this section, I extend the set of the L_{ar}^λ-reduction rules introduced in [24], by adding:

(1) the reduction rules (ξ) for the quantifier terms (4h) together with the λ-abstract terms, $\xi \in \{\lambda, \exists, \forall\}$
(2) an additional reduction rule, the (γ^*) rule, (20a)–(20b), which extends the corresponding rule in [12]

4.1 Extended Congruence Relation Between Terms

For a full, formal definition of the congruence relation, see also [16]. Informally:

Definition 7. *The* congruence *relation is the smallest equivalence relation between terms* $\equiv_c \subseteq \mathsf{Terms} \times \mathsf{Terms}$, *that is closed under:*

(1) reflexivity, symmetricity, transitivity
(2) operators of term-formation:
  – *application terms*
  – *logic operators of conjunction, disjunction, implication, and negation, as a special case of categorematic constants forming application terms*
  – *λ-abstraction and pure, logic quantifiers*
  – *acyclic recursion*
  – *restrictor terms*
(3) renaming bound pure and recursion variables without variable collisions, i.e., by free replacements, see Definition 4

(a) renaming pure variables bound by λ-abstraction and pure quantifiers

(b) renaming memory locations (variables) bound by where, in the assignments in the recursion terms

(4) (a) re-ordering of the assignments within the recursion terms

(b) re-ordering the restrictions within the restrictor terms

4.2   Reduction Rules of Extended L_{ar}^{λ}

In this section, we define the set RedR of the reduction rules of TTA, which are the same for its variants of full and acyclic recursion L_r^{λ} and L_{ar}^{λ}, respectively.

Congruence	If $A \equiv_c B$, then $A \Rightarrow B$	(cong)
Transitivity	If $A \Rightarrow B$ and $B \Rightarrow C$, then $A \Rightarrow C$	(trans)

Compositionality. Replacement of sub-terms with correspondingly reduced ones respects the term structure by the definition of the term syntax:

$$\text{If } A \Rightarrow A' \text{ and } B \Rightarrow B', \text{ then } A(B) \Rightarrow A'(B') \qquad \text{(ap-comp)}$$

$$\text{If } A \Rightarrow B, \text{ and } \xi \in \{\lambda, \exists, \forall\}, \text{ then } \xi(u)(A) \Rightarrow \xi(u)(B) \qquad \text{(lq-comp)}$$

If $A_i \Rightarrow B_i$, for $i = 0, \ldots, n$, then

$$A_0 \text{ where } \{p_1 := A_1, \ldots, p_n := A_n\} \qquad \text{(rec-comp)}$$
$$\Rightarrow B_0 \text{ where } \{p_1 := B_1, \ldots, p_n := B_n\}$$

Compositionality of the Restrictor Terms (in the extended L_r^{λ} and L_{ar}^{λ})

If $C_i \Rightarrow R_i$ $(i = 0, \ldots, n)$, then

$$C_0 \text{ such that } \{C_1, \ldots, C_n\} \qquad \text{(st-comp)}$$
$$\Rightarrow R_0 \text{ such that } \{R_1, \ldots, R_n\}$$

Compositionality of Scope Operators (in the extended L_r^{λ} and L_{ar}^{λ})

$$\text{If } A \Rightarrow A' \text{ then } \mathsf{ToScope}(A) \Rightarrow \mathsf{ToScope}(A') \qquad \text{(S-comp)}$$

$$\text{If } A \Rightarrow A' \text{ then } \mathcal{C}(A) \Rightarrow \mathcal{C}(A') \qquad \text{(}\mathcal{C}\text{-comp)}$$

Head Rule. Given that, for all $i = 1, \ldots, n$, $j = 1, \ldots, m$, $p_i \neq q_j$ and p_i does not occur freely in B_j:

$$\left(A_0 \text{ where } \{\overrightarrow{p} := \overrightarrow{A}\}\right) \text{ where } \{\overrightarrow{q} := \overrightarrow{B}\}$$
$$\Rightarrow A_0 \text{ where } \{\overrightarrow{p} := \overrightarrow{A}, \overrightarrow{q} := \overrightarrow{B}\} \qquad \text{(head)}$$

Bekič-Scott Rule. Given that, for all $i = 1, \ldots, n$, $j = 1, \ldots, m$, $p_i \neq q_j$ and q_j does not occur freely in A_0, A_i

$$A_0 \text{ where } \{\, p := (B_0 \text{ where } \{\, \overrightarrow{q} := \overrightarrow{B} \,\}), \overrightarrow{p} := \overrightarrow{A} \,\}$$
$$\Rightarrow A_0 \text{ where } \{\, p := B_0, \overrightarrow{q} := \overrightarrow{B}, \ \overrightarrow{p} := \overrightarrow{A} \,\} \tag{B-S}$$

Recursion-Application Rule. Given that, for all $i = 1, \ldots, n$, p_i does not occur freely in B

$$(A_0 \text{ where } \{\, \overrightarrow{p} := \overrightarrow{A} \,\})(B) \Rightarrow A_0(B) \text{ where } \{\, \overrightarrow{p} := \overrightarrow{A} \,\} \tag{recap}$$

Application Rule. Given that $B \in$ Terms is proper and $b \in$ RecV is fresh, i.e., $b \in \big[$RecV $-$ $\big($FreeV$\big(A(B)\big) \cup$ BoundV$\big(A(B)\big)\big)\big]$,

$$A(B) \Rightarrow A(b) \text{ where } \{\, b := B \,\} \tag{ap}$$

λ and Quantifier Rules. Let $\xi \in \{\, \lambda, \exists, \forall \,\}$

$$\xi(u)\,(A_0 \text{ where } \{\, p_1 := A_1, \ldots, p_n := A_n \,\})$$
$$\Rightarrow \xi(u)\, A_0' \text{ where } \{\, p_1' := \lambda(u)\, A_1', \ldots, p_n' := \lambda(u)\, A_n' \,\} \tag{ξ}$$

given that, for every $i = 1, \ldots, n$ $(n \geq 0)$, $p_i' \in$ RecV is a fresh recursion (memory) variable, and A_i' $(0 \leq i \leq n)$ is the result of the simultaneous replacements of all the free occurrences of $p_1, \ldots, p_n$ in A_i with $p_1'(u), \ldots, p_n'(u)$, respectively, i.e., each A_i' is as in (14):

$$A_i' \equiv A_i\{p_1 :\equiv p_1'(u), \ldots, p_n :\equiv p_n'(u)\} \equiv A_i\{\overrightarrow{p} :\equiv \overrightarrow{p'(u)}\} \ (0 \leq i \leq n) \tag{14}$$

Restriction / Restrictor Rules of L_{rar}^λ \hfill (st1) / (st2)
Given that, $A_0 \in$ Terms, and for $j = 1, \ldots, m$ $(m \geq 0)$, $i = 1, \ldots, k$ $(k \geq 0)$:
(1) Each $C_j^{\tau_j} \in$ Terms is proper
(2) Each $R_i^{\sigma_i} \in$ Terms in $\overrightarrow{R^\sigma}$ is immediate

(3) $C_j^{\tau_j}$ and $R_i^{\sigma_i}$ have types of truth values, i.e., $\tau_j \equiv$ t or $\tau_j \equiv \tilde{\mathsf{t}}$; and $\sigma_i \equiv$ t or $\sigma_i \equiv \tilde{\mathsf{t}}$

there are two reduction rules for the restrictor (restricted) terms:
(st1) A_0 is an immediate term, $m \geq 1$

$$(A_0 \text{ such that } \{\, C_1, \ldots, C_m, \overrightarrow{R} \,\}) \tag{st1}$$
$$\Rightarrow (A_0 \text{ such that } \{\, c_1, \ldots, c_m, \overrightarrow{R} \,\})$$
$$\text{where } \{\, c_1 := C_1, \ldots, c_m := C_m \,\}$$

for fresh $c_j \in$ RecV $(j = 1, \ldots, m)$

(st2) A_0 is a proper term

$$(A_0 \text{ such that } \{\, C_1, \ldots, C_m, \overrightarrow{R}\,\}) \tag{st2}$$
$$\Rightarrow (a_0 \text{ such that } \{\, c_1, \ldots, c_m, \overrightarrow{R}\,\})$$
$$\text{where } \{\, a_0 := A_0, \ c_1 := C_1, \ \ldots, c_m := C_m\,\}$$

for fresh $a_0, c_j \in \mathsf{RecV}$ $(j = 1, \ldots, m)$

Note 2. The restriction parts in (st1)/(st2) are proposition terms.

Scope Rule Closure of Unspecified, Open Scope

$$\mathsf{ToScope}\,\underbrace{(B_0 \text{ where } \{\, \overrightarrow{c} := \overrightarrow{C}, \underbrace{\overrightarrow{q} := \overrightarrow{B}}\,\})}_{\text{unspecified, open scope}}(s_c) \tag{17a}$$

$$\Rightarrow \tag{ScopeR}$$

$$\mathcal{C}\,\underbrace{\left(B_0(s_r) \text{ where } \{\, \overrightarrow{c} := \overrightarrow{C}\,\}\right)}_{\text{specified, closed scope}} \text{ where } \{\ \underbrace{\overrightarrow{q} := \overrightarrow{B}}_{\text{outside } \mathcal{C} \text{ scope}}\ \} \tag{17b}$$

given that $s_c, s_r \in \mathsf{RecV_s}$, $B_0 \in \mathsf{Terms}_{\widetilde{\sigma}}$, and thus, $B_0(s_r) : \sigma$

Note 3 (Explanation of the (ScopeR) *rule).* By (11) of Definition 2, $\mathsf{ToScope} : (\widetilde{\sigma} \to (\mathsf{s} \to \widetilde{\sigma}))$, $\mathcal{C} : (\sigma \to \widetilde{\sigma})$

Thus, the term (18) is underspecified and needs a specifying state, e.g., a context, designated by the free, recursion variable s_c. A variable valuation g in a semantic domain $\mathfrak{A}$ can provide a state representing a context $g(s_c) \in \mathbb{T_s}$.

$$\mathsf{ToScope}\,\underbrace{(B_0 \text{ where } \{\, \overrightarrow{c} := \overrightarrow{C}, \underbrace{\overrightarrow{q} := \overrightarrow{B}}\,\})}_{\text{unspecified, open scope}} : (\mathsf{s} \to \widetilde{\sigma}) \tag{18}$$

The (ScopeR) rule reduces the term (17a) to the specified scope (17b), expressed in (19a) by its type.

The relation between the states denoted by $(s_c$ and $(s_r$, can be expressed, e.g., by a *reference function* Ref, providing specification of $s_c \in \mathsf{RecV_s}$ to $s_r \in \mathsf{RecV_s}$, by extending the term (19a) to (19b). Note that we have not made (19b) part of the (ScopeR).

$$\mathcal{C}\,\underbrace{\left(B_0(s_r) \text{ where } \{\, \overrightarrow{c} := \overrightarrow{C}\,\}\right)}_{\text{specified, closed scope}} \text{ where } \{\ \underbrace{\overrightarrow{q} := \overrightarrow{B}}_{\text{outside } \mathcal{C} \text{ scope}}\ \} : \widetilde{\sigma} \tag{19a}$$

$$\mathcal{C}\,\underbrace{\left(B_0(s_r) \text{ where } \{\, \overrightarrow{c} := \overrightarrow{C}\,\}\right)}_{\text{specified, closed scope}} \text{ where } \{\ \underbrace{\overrightarrow{q} := \overrightarrow{B}}_{\text{outside } \mathcal{C} \text{ scope}}\ ,$$

$$s_r := \mathsf{Ref}(s_c)\,\} : \widetilde{\sigma} \tag{19b}$$

γ^*-Rule

$$A \equiv_c A_0 \text{ where } \{ \overrightarrow{a} := \overrightarrow{A}, \, p := \lambda(\overrightarrow{u})\lambda(v)P, \, \overrightarrow{b} := \overrightarrow{B} \} \tag{20a}$$

$$\Rightarrow_{\gamma^*} A_0' \text{ where } \{ \overrightarrow{a} := \overrightarrow{A}', \, p' := \lambda(\overrightarrow{u})P, \, \overrightarrow{b} := \overrightarrow{B}' \} \tag{γ^*}$$

$$\equiv A_0\{ p(\overrightarrow{u})(v) :\equiv p'(\overrightarrow{u}) \} \text{ where } \{$$

$$\begin{aligned} \overrightarrow{a} &:= \overrightarrow{A}\{ p(\overrightarrow{u})(v) :\equiv p'(\overrightarrow{u}) \}, \\ p' &:= \lambda(\overrightarrow{u})P, \\ \overrightarrow{b} &:= \overrightarrow{B}\{ p(\overrightarrow{u})(v) :\equiv p'(\overrightarrow{u}) \} \} \end{aligned} \tag{20b}$$

given that:
- the term $A \in$ Terms satisfies the γ^*-condition in Definition 8, for the assignment $p := \lambda(\overrightarrow{u})\lambda(v)P : (\overrightarrow{\vartheta} \to (\vartheta \to \tau))$
- $p' \in \text{RecV}_{(\overrightarrow{\vartheta} \to \tau)}$ is a fresh recursion variable
- for each part X_i of $\overrightarrow{X}$ in (γ^*) (i.e., for each $X_i \equiv A_i$ in $\overrightarrow{X} \equiv \overrightarrow{A}$, and each $X_i \equiv B_i$ in $\overrightarrow{X} \equiv \overrightarrow{B}$), X_i' is the result of the free replacements $X_i' \equiv X_i\{ p(\overrightarrow{u})(v) :\equiv p'(\overrightarrow{u}) \}$ of all occurrences of $p(\overrightarrow{u})(v)$ by $p'(\overrightarrow{u})$ (in the free occurrences of p), modulo renaming the variables $\overrightarrow{u}, v$, for $i \in \{0, \dots, n_X\}$, i.e.:

$$\overrightarrow{X'} \equiv \overrightarrow{X}\{ p(\overrightarrow{u})(v) :\equiv p'(\overrightarrow{u}) \} \tag{21}$$

Definition 8 (γ^*-**Condition**). *Assume that, for all $i = 1, \dots, n$ ($n \geq 0$), $\tau, \vartheta, \vartheta_i \in$ Types, $v, u_i \in$ PureV, $p \in$ RecV, $P \in$ Terms, are such that $v : \vartheta$, $u_i : \vartheta_i$, $p : (\overrightarrow{\vartheta} \to (\vartheta \to \tau))$, $P : \tau$, and thus, $\lambda(\overrightarrow{u}^{\,\overrightarrow{\vartheta}})\lambda(v^\vartheta)(P^\tau) : (\overrightarrow{\vartheta} \to (\vartheta \to \tau))$.*

A recursion term $A \in$ Terms satisfies the γ^*-condition for an assignment $p := \lambda(\overrightarrow{u}^{\,\overrightarrow{\vartheta}})\lambda(v^\vartheta)(P^\tau) : (\overrightarrow{\vartheta} \to (\vartheta \to \tau))$, with respect to $\lambda(v)$, if and only if A is of the form (22)

$$A \equiv A_0 \text{ where } \{ \overrightarrow{a} := \overrightarrow{A}, \, p := \lambda(\overrightarrow{u})\lambda(v)P, \, \overrightarrow{b} := \overrightarrow{B} \} \tag{22}$$

with the sub-terms of appropriate types, such that the following holds:

(1) $P \in$ Terms$_\tau$ does not have any free occurrences of v, i.e., $v \notin$ FreeV(P)
(2) All occurrences of p in $A_0, \overrightarrow{A}, \overrightarrow{B}$:

    (a) are free, i.e., not in the scope of where-recursion assignments (by renaming bound occurrences of recursion variables)
    (b) are occurrences in sub-terms $p(\overrightarrow{u})(v)$, which are in binding scope of $\xi(v)$, for $\xi \in \{ \lambda, \exists, \forall \}$, modulo renaming the bound variables $\overrightarrow{u}, v$, $i = 1, \dots, n$ ($n \geq 0$).

Note: the latter requirement (b) maintains the sets of the free variables of the terms A, by the γ^* reductions.

Motivation of the (γ^*) *Rule.* The additional reduction rule (γ^*) is introduced in [12] and extends the reduction calculus of L_{ar}^λ of Moschovakis [24], by reducing the complexity of the terms and their algorithmic semantics.

The more simple γ-rule introduced in [11] is a special case of the (γ^*) rule. Both rules are very useful for simplifying terms, by reducing sub-terms that have superfluous λ-abstractions, $p := \lambda(v)P$, for $v \notin \mathsf{FreeV}(P)$, and corresponding functional applications $p(x)$ that have constant values.

The (γ^*) rule is more versatile and more useful than the γ-rule for such algorithmic simplifications. A sequence of multiple consecutive λ-abstractions in an assignment part $p := \lambda(\overrightarrow{u})\lambda(v)P$ of a recursion term A, for $u_i \in \overrightarrow{u}$, $v \notin \mathsf{FreeV}(P)$, can be such that $\lambda(\overrightarrow{u}) \in \mathsf{FreeV}(P)$. This prevents application of the simple γ-rule with respect to $\lambda(v)$ in $p := \lambda(\overrightarrow{u})\lambda(v)P$. The (γ^*) rule provides reducing A by removing the vacuous $\lambda(v)$ with respect to $p := \lambda(\overrightarrow{u})\lambda(v)P$.

The (γ^*) rule does not alter algorithmic semantics of L_{ar}^λ and L_r^λ, in any other way.

It does not affect the denotational semantics of L_{ar}^λ and L_r^λ, i.e., for every term A, it preserves $\mathsf{den}^{\mathfrak{A}}(A)$ in any semantic structure $\mathfrak{A}$ having denotation function $\mathsf{den}^{\mathfrak{A}}$.

See detailed motivations, examples, and properties of the (γ^*) and γ-rule in the papers that are devoted to these rules and the corresponding extended reduction calculi Loukanova [11,12,16]. Further motivations and examples of the utility of the (γ^*) rule are provided in Loukanova [10,13,15,16].

4.3   Derived Reduction Rules

The Bekič-Scott rule (B-S) of L_{ar}^λ and L_r^λ is generalized by the Lemma 1:

Lemma 1 (Bekič-Scott Closure of Propositional Scope). *Assume that, for all $i = 1, \ldots, n$, $j = 1, \ldots, m$, $p_i \neq q_j$ and q_j does not occur freely in A_0, A_i. Then:*

$$A \equiv A_0 \text{ where } \{ p := \mathsf{ToScope} \underbrace{\big(B_0 \text{ where } \{ \overrightarrow{c} := \overrightarrow{C}, \overrightarrow{q} := \overrightarrow{B} \} \big)}_{unspecified,\ open\ scope}(s_c),$$

$$\overrightarrow{p} := \overrightarrow{A} \}$$

$$\Rightarrow A_0 \text{ where } \{ p := \mathcal{C} \underbrace{\big(B_0(s_r) \text{ where } \{ \overrightarrow{c} := \overrightarrow{C} \} \big)}_{specified,\ closed\ scope}, \qquad \text{(B-S-prC)}$$

$$\underbrace{\overrightarrow{q} := \overrightarrow{B},}_{outside\ \mathcal{C}\ scope} \overrightarrow{p} := \overrightarrow{A} \}$$

Proof. By the reduction rules of L_{ar}^λ and L_r^λ, the following reductions can be performed:

$$A \equiv A_0 \text{ where } \{\, p := \mathsf{ToScope}\, \underbrace{(B_0 \text{ where } \{\, \overrightarrow{c} := \overrightarrow{C}, \overrightarrow{q} := \overrightarrow{B} \,\})}_{\text{unspecified, open scope}}(s_c),$$

$$\overrightarrow{p} := \overrightarrow{A} \,\} \tag{23a}$$

$$\Rightarrow A_0 \text{ where } \{\, p := \Big[\mathcal{C}\, \underbrace{\big(B_0(s_r) \text{ where } \{\, \overrightarrow{c} := \overrightarrow{C} \,\}\big)}_{\text{specified, closed scope}}$$

$$\text{where } \{\, \underbrace{\overrightarrow{q} := \overrightarrow{B}}_{\text{outside } \mathcal{C} \text{ scope}} \,\} \Big], \tag{23b}$$

$$\overrightarrow{p} := \overrightarrow{A} \,\}$$

$$\Rightarrow A_0 \text{ where } \{\, p := \mathcal{C}\, \underbrace{\big(B_0(s_r) \text{ where } \{\, \overrightarrow{c} := \overrightarrow{C} \,\}\big)}_{\text{specified, closed scope}},$$

$$\underbrace{\overrightarrow{q} := \overrightarrow{B}, \quad \overrightarrow{p} := \overrightarrow{A}}_{\text{outside } \mathcal{C} \text{ scope}} \,\} \tag{23c}$$

(23b) follows from (23a) by (1)–(3):

(1) (ScopeR) applied to the assignment to p:

$$p := \mathsf{ToScope}\, \underbrace{\big(B_0 \text{ where } \{\, \overrightarrow{c} := \overrightarrow{C}, \overrightarrow{q} := \overrightarrow{B} \,\}\big)}_{\text{unspecified, open scope}}(s_c) \tag{24a}$$

$$\Rightarrow p := \Big[\mathcal{C}\, \underbrace{\big(B_0(s_r) \text{ where } \{\, \overrightarrow{c} := \overrightarrow{C} \,\}\big)}_{\text{specified, closed scope}} \tag{24b}$$

$$\text{where } \{\, \underbrace{\overrightarrow{q} := \overrightarrow{B}}_{\text{outside } \mathcal{C} \text{ scope}} \,\} \Big] \tag{24c}$$

(2) compositionality of recursion (rec-comp)

(3) Then, (23c) follows from (23b) by the Bekič-Scott Rule (B-S).

□

The (head) rule of L^λ_{ar} and L^λ_r is generalized by the Lemma 2 for Head Closure of Propositional Scope:

Lemma 2 (Head Closure of Propositional Scope). *Assume that, for all* $i = 1, \ldots, n$, $j = 1, \ldots, m$, $p_i \neq q_j$ *and* p_i *does not occur freely in* B_j. *Then:*

$$\big(A_0 \text{ where } \{\, p := \mathsf{ToScope}\, \underbrace{\underbrace{\big(B_0 \text{ where } \{\, \overrightarrow{c} := \overrightarrow{C}, \overrightarrow{p} := \overrightarrow{A} \,\}\big)}_{\text{unspecified, open scope}}(s_c) \,\} \big)}_{\text{head part}}$$

where $\{\ \overrightarrow{q} := \overrightarrow{B}\ \}$

$\Rightarrow \left(A_0 \text{ where } p := \mathcal{C}\ \underbrace{(B_0(s_r) \text{ where } \{\ \overrightarrow{c} := \overrightarrow{C}\ \})}_{\text{specified, closed scope}}\right)$ \hfill (head-prC)

$\underbrace{\phantom{A_0 \text{ where } p := \mathcal{C}\ (B_0(s_r) \text{ where } \{\ \overrightarrow{c} := \overrightarrow{C}\ \})}}_{\text{head part}}$

where $\{\ \underbrace{\overrightarrow{p} := \overrightarrow{A}}_{\text{outside } \mathcal{C} \text{ scope}},\ \ \overrightarrow{q} := \overrightarrow{B}\ \}$

Proof. By the reduction rules of L_{ar}^λ and L_r^λ:

- (ScopeR)
- compositionality of recursion (rec-comp)
- the head rule (head) \hfill $\square$

4.4   On the Denotational Semantics

In this paper, for sake of space, I do not provide the full formal definition of the denotational semantics of L_{ar}^λ. For detailed defintion, see, e.g., Moschovakis [24] and Loukanova [11–13,17], and in particular, [16,17].

Assume that we have a given, fixed semantic structure $\mathfrak{A}$ of the formal language of L_{ar}^λ, providing typed semantic domains $\mathbb{T}_\sigma$, $\sigma \in$ Types, an interpretation function of the non-logical constants, and the set of all variable valuations G, for all variables Vars.

A *denotation function* $\mathrm{den}^{\mathfrak{A}}$ in the semantic structure L_{ar}^λ,

$$\mathrm{den}^{\mathfrak{A}}: \text{Terms} \to (G \to \bigcup \mathbb{T}) \tag{25}$$

is defined by induction on the term structure by the Definition 2, i.e., (4a)–(4h), for all $g \in G$. Here, we shall extend the definition of $\mathrm{den}^{\mathfrak{A}}$ for the terms of the form (4d). and then for new ones (4i).

D4 *Recursion:*

$$\mathrm{den}^{\mathfrak{A}}(A_0 \text{ where } \{\ \overrightarrow{p} := \overrightarrow{A}\ \})(g) = \mathrm{den}^{\mathfrak{A}}(A_0)(g\{\ \overrightarrow{p_i} := \overrightarrow{\overline{p}_i}\ \}) \tag{26}$$

where $\overline{p}_i \in \mathbb{T}_{\tau_i}$ are computed by recursion on $\mathrm{rank}(p_i)$, i.e., by (27):

$$\overline{p}_i = \mathrm{den}^{\mathfrak{A}}(A_i)(g\{\ p_{i,1} := \overline{p}_{i,1}, \ldots, p_{i,k_i} := \overline{p}_{i,k_i}\ \}) \tag{27}$$
$$\text{for all } p_{i,1}, \ldots, p_{i,k_i}, \text{ such that } \mathrm{rank}(p_{i,k}) < \mathrm{rank}(p_i)$$

D9 *Closed Scope:* $\mathcal{C}(B^{\widetilde{\sigma}}(s)) : \widetilde{\sigma},\ s \in \text{Vars}_s$

$$\mathrm{den}^{\mathfrak{A}}(\mathcal{C}(B^{\widetilde{\sigma}}(s)))(g) = H, \tag{28a}$$

$$\text{for the function } H \colon \mathbb{T}_s \to \mathbb{T}_\sigma \text{ defined by (28c)} \tag{28b}$$

$$H(s') = \text{den}^{\mathfrak{A}}(B^{\widetilde{\sigma}}(s)), \quad \text{for all } s' \in \text{Vars}_s \tag{28c}$$

Note that we have the closure of the scope with respect to a specific, but underspecified state represented by the variable $s \in \text{Vars}_s$. The function H "lifts" the dependence on states by (28b).

D10 *Unspecified, Open Scope:* $\text{ToScope}(B^{\widetilde{\sigma}}) \colon (s \to \widetilde{\sigma})$

For any given $s_c, s_r \in \text{RecV}_s$, $B_0 \in \text{Terms}_{\widetilde{\sigma}}$ (and thus, $B_0(s_r) \colon \sigma$), $\overrightarrow{B}, \overrightarrow{C}$ such that there is a reduction as in (29):

$$B \Rightarrow \underbrace{B_0 \text{ where } \{\, \overrightarrow{c} := \overrightarrow{C}, \overrightarrow{q} := \overrightarrow{B} \,\}}_{\text{unspecified, open scope}} \tag{29}$$

The denotation $den^{\mathfrak{A}}(\text{ToScope}(B^{\widetilde{\sigma}})(s_c))$ can be as in (30a):

$$den^{\mathfrak{A}}(\text{ToScope}(B^{\widetilde{\sigma}})(s_c)) \tag{30a}$$

$$= den^{\mathfrak{A}}(\text{ToScope}(\underbrace{B_0 \text{ where } \{\, \overrightarrow{c} := \overrightarrow{C}, \overrightarrow{q} := \overrightarrow{B} \,\}}_{\text{unspecified, open scope}}(s_c))) \tag{30b}$$

$$= den^{\mathfrak{A}}(\mathcal{C} \underbrace{\left(B_0(s_r) \text{ where } \{\, \overrightarrow{c} := \overrightarrow{C} \,\} \right)}_{\text{specified, closed scope}} \text{ where } \{\, \underbrace{\overrightarrow{q} := \overrightarrow{B}}_{\text{outside } \mathcal{C} \text{ scope}} \,\}) \tag{30c}$$

given that, for every $s_c \in \text{RecV}_s$, we associate not more than one "split" of the assignments in (29).

5   Algorithmic Syntax-Semantics in $\text{L}^\lambda_{\text{ar}}$

In this section, we present the algorithmic semantics in the type-theory of acyclic recursion L^λ_{rar}, informally, with respect to its significance for the denotational semantics. For details, see, e.g., Moschovakis [24] and Loukanova [11–13,16,17]. This section is a brief overview of the corresponding section of Loukanova [17].

Immediate Terms In case A is an immediate term of $\text{L}^\lambda_{\text{ar}}$, see Definition 5, (ImAppT)–(Imλ-T) i.e., of the form $\lambda(u_1)\ldots\lambda(u_n)(p(v_1)\ldots(v_m))$ $(m, n \geq 0)$, it has no algorithmic sense. The value $\text{den}(A)(g)$ is given by the valuations $g(p)$ and $g(v_i)$.

Proper Terms. For every proper (non-immediate), i.e., algorithmically meaningful $A \in \text{Terms}$, its canonical form $\text{cf}(A)$ (31) determines the algorithm $\text{alg}(A)$ for computing $\text{den}(A)$.

$$\text{cf}(A) \equiv A_0 \text{ where } \{\, p_1 := A_1, \ldots, p_n := A_n \,\}$$
$$\text{for some explicit, irreducible } A_i \in \text{Terms}, i = 1, \ldots, n (n \geq 0) \tag{31}$$

The following points describe informally how the canonical form $\text{cf}(A)$ (31) obtained, in comparison to its denotational value $\text{den}(A)$:

- The denotational semantics of L^λ_{rar} (L^λ_{ar}) is by induction on term structure
- The type theories L^λ_{ar} and L^λ_{rar} have *effective reduction calculi*, see, e.g., Moschovakis [24] and Loukanova [11–13].

  For every $A \in$ Terms, there is a canonical form $cf(A)$, which can be obtained from A, by a finite number of reductions using the reduction rules of L^λ_{ar}, including the extended ones in this paper:

$$A \Rightarrow_{cf} cf(A) \tag{32}$$

- For a given, fixed semantic structure $\mathfrak{A}$ and valuations G, for every *algorithmically meaningful* $A \in$ Terms$_\sigma$, the algorithm $alg(A)$ for computing $den(A)$ is determined by $cf(A)$, so that:

$$den(A)(g) = den(cf(A))(g), \text{ for } g \in G \tag{33a}$$
$$alg(A) = alg(cf(A)) \tag{33b}$$

The denotation $den(A)(g) = den(cf(A))(g)$ of a proper term A is computed stepwise, iteratively from $cf(A)$, which is a term of the form (31). The steps follow the ranking $rank(p_i)$, $i = 1, \ldots, n$ ($n \geq 0$). By starting with the lowest rank value among $rank(p_1) \ldots, rank(p_n)$, and proceeding in increasing order. The algorithm $alg(cf(A))$ computes the denotational values of the parts $den(A_i)(g)$ and saves them in the corresponding memory variables p_i. Then, these values are used for computing the denotation of the head part, i.e., the subterm $den(A_0)(g)$:

$$den(A_0)(g) = den(cf(A))(g) = den(A)(g) \tag{34}$$

Figure 1 gives the general scheme of the *computational syntax-semantics interface* within L^λ_{rar} (L^λ_r), i.e., the relation between the syntax of the terms of L^λ_{rar} (L^λ_r) and their algorithmic and denotational semantics.

Syntax of L^λ_{ar} (L^λ_r) $\implies$ Algorithms for Iterative Computations: $cf(A)$ $\implies$ Denotations

Canonical Computations

Computational Syn-Sem: Algorithmic and Denotational Semantics of L^λ_{ar} / L^λ_r

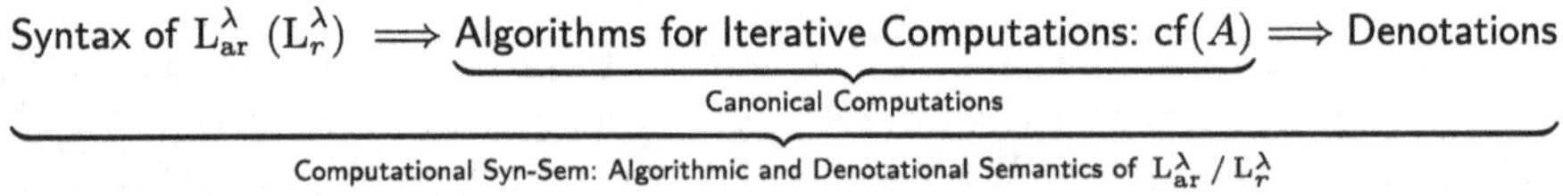

Fig. 1. Computational Syntax-Semantics Interface in L^λ_{ar} (L^λ_r)

6   Algorithmic Syntax-Semantics of Propositional Attitudes

In this paper, I disregard rendering verbal inflections, e.g., for event time, since that is outside of its major topic.

I shall present a possibility for algorithmic syntax by L_{ar}^{λ} of verbs designating propositional attitudes. It is with respect to their corresponding algorithmic semantics. I shall consider only verbs taking sentences as complements, e.g.:

$$\text{ToScope} : (\widetilde{t} \rightarrow (s \rightarrow \widetilde{t})), \quad \mathcal{C} : (t \rightarrow \widetilde{t}) \quad \text{(operator constants)} \tag{35a}$$

$$\tau_{pa} \equiv (\widetilde{t} \rightarrow (\widetilde{e} \rightarrow \widetilde{t})) \tag{35b}$$

$$\text{claim (that)} \xrightarrow{\text{render}} claim : \tau_{pa}, \quad \text{state (that)} \xrightarrow{\text{render}} state : \tau_{pa},$$

$$\text{believe (that)} \xrightarrow{\text{render}} believe : \tau_{pa}, \quad \text{know (that)} \xrightarrow{\text{render}} know : \tau_{pa}, \ \dots \tag{35c}$$

At first, I shall express the concepts of the algorithmic semantics of sentential attitudes, by an example, as a representative of a large class of verbal attitudes.

I present the concept of verbal attitudes, which are context dependent. The scope of the semantic components is underspecified without any specific context.

$$\text{Jim believes that Mary's sister is happy.} \xrightarrow{\text{render}} A \tag{36a}$$

$$A \equiv believes\Big(\text{ToScope}(happy[mary's(sister)])(s_c)\Big)(jim) : \widetilde{t} \tag{36b}$$

$$\Rightarrow believes(q)(j) \text{ where } \{\, q := \text{ToScope}(happy[mary's(sister)])(s_c), \\ j := jim \,\} \tag{36c}$$

The syntax-semantics interface for analyses of possessive expressions of NL are outside of the topic of this chapter. However, we shall use the nominal possessive determiner "Mary's", as an example of a moderately complex L_{ar}^{λ} term abbreviated in the following compositional renderings. Let's assume the following constants and variables, and some more of suitable types, which are needed for the renderings below:

$$mary \in \text{Consts}_{\widetilde{e}}, \ mary : \widetilde{e} \tag{37a}$$

$$m, m_s, m_s' \in \text{RecV}_{\widetilde{e}} \tag{37b}$$

$$sister \in \text{Consts}_{(\widetilde{e} \rightarrow (\widetilde{e} \rightarrow \widetilde{t}))}, \ sister : (\widetilde{e} \rightarrow (\widetilde{e} \rightarrow \widetilde{t})) \tag{37c}$$

$$m_s := [m_s' \text{ such that } \{\, relationTo(mary)(sister)(m_s') \,\}] \tag{38d}$$

Then:

$$\text{Mary's} \xrightarrow{\text{render}} H_0 \tag{38a}$$

$$H_0 \equiv \underbrace{mary's}_{\text{abbreviation}} \equiv relationTo(mary) : ((\widetilde{e} \rightarrow \widetilde{t}) \rightarrow (\widetilde{e} \rightarrow \widetilde{t})) \tag{39b}$$

In the following sequence of renderings, the term assignment in (38d) to m_s is a restricted parameter, i.e., free, but restricted memory variable, restricting m_s to be assigned to any individual who is having the property of being Mary's syster. That is, the term $relationTo(mary)(sister)(m_s')$ designates the proposition that an object denoted by the restricted variable m'_s is in the relation denoted by the constant $sister \in$ Consts to the object denoted by $mary \in$ Consts. In case this proposition is not true, the value $\mathsf{den}(m_s)$ is the error er. Thus, also $\mathsf{den}(H_2) = \cdots = \mathsf{den}(H_8) = $ er.

Note 4. Here, $s_c \in \mathsf{RecV_s}$ is a variable for states, and $\dot{s}_c \in \mathbb{T_s}$ is a state of a context of using the given sentence. In this work, we do not consider what is the structural composition of these states. That is a subject of forthcoming work.

Then:

$$\text{Mary's sister is happy} \xrightarrow{\text{render}} H_2 \tag{39a}$$

$$H_2 \equiv happy[m'_s \text{ s.t. } relationTo(mary)(sister)(m'_s)] \tag{39b}$$

$$\equiv happy[(mary's)(sister)] \qquad \text{(meta-abbreviation)} \tag{39c}$$

$$\Rightarrow happy(m_s) \text{ where} \tag{39d}$$
$$\{\, m_s := [m'_s \text{ s.t. } \{\, relationTo(mary)(sister)(m'_s) \,\}] \,\} \equiv H_3$$
$$\text{from (39b) by (ap)}$$

$$\Rightarrow happy(m_s) \text{ where} \tag{39e}$$
$$\{\, m_s := [[m'_s \text{ s.t. } \{\, r \,\}] \text{ where}$$
$$\{\, r := relationTo(mary)(sister)(m'_s) \,\}] \,\} \equiv H_4$$
$$\text{from (39d) by (st1), (rec-comp)}$$

$$\Rightarrow happy(m_s) \text{ where } \{\, m_s := [m'_s \text{ s.t. } \{\, r \,\}], \tag{39f}$$
$$r := relationTo(mary)(sister)(m'_s) \,\} \equiv H_5$$
$$\text{from (39e) by (B-S)}$$

$$\Rightarrow_{cf} happy(m_s) \text{ where } \{\, m_s := [m'_s \text{ s.t. } \{\, r \,\}],$$
$$r := relationTo(m)(p)(m'_s), \tag{39g}$$
$$m := mary, \ p := sister \,\} \equiv H_6$$
$$\text{from (39f) by 2 x (ap), 2 x (recap), 2 x (B-S), (rec-comp)}$$

$$\equiv happy(m_s) \text{ where } \{\, m_s := m's(p),$$
$$m := mary, \ p := sister \,\} \equiv H_7 \tag{39h}$$
$$\text{from (39g), by conventional abbreviation}$$

of meta-constant $'s$ for a posessive relation $p$between m and m'_s (39i)

$$m's(p) \equiv [m'_s \text{ s.t. } \{\, r \,\}], \ r := relationTo(m)(p)(m'_s)$$

$$\equiv H_8 \equiv \mathsf{cf}(H_2) \tag{39j}$$

By a tradition from Situation Semantics, situations and states of using NL expressions are called *utterances*, as a generic technical notion. It provides a context by a valuation function $g \in G$ applied on the state variable s_c, $g(s_c) = \dot{s}_c$, or by a function called the agent's (e.g., the speaker's), references, in (40a), by using the sentence, in written or spoken NL:

$$\langle \dot{s}_c, \text{Jim believes that Mary's sister is happy.} \rangle \xrightarrow{\text{render}} A_1 \tag{40a}$$

$$A_1 \Rightarrow believes(q)(j) \text{ where } \{\, q := \mathsf{ToScope}\Big(happy[mary's(sister)]\Big)(s_c),$$
$$j := jim \,\} \tag{40b}$$

$$\Rightarrow believes(q)(j) \text{ where } \{$$
$$q := \mathsf{ToScope}\Big(happy(m) \text{ where } \{\, m_s := mary's(sister) \,\}\Big)(s_c), \tag{40c}$$
$$j := jim \,\} \equiv A_2$$

The scoping operator ToScope applies to the term rendering the sentence complement of the attitude verb. There are two ways to apply ToScope, each creating its own scope of the algorithmic closure $\mathcal{C}$:

$$A_2 \Rightarrow_{\mathsf{cf}} A_3 \equiv believes(q)(j) \text{ where } \{ \hspace{3cm} \text{(de-dicto)}$$
$$q := \mathcal{C}\big(happy(m)(s_r) \text{ where } \{\, m_s := m's(p),$$
$$m := mary, \ p := sister \,\}\big), \tag{41a}$$
$$j := jim \,\}$$

$$A_2 \Rightarrow_{\mathsf{cf}} A_4 \equiv believes(q)(j) \text{ where } \{ \hspace{3cm} \text{(de-re)}$$
$$q := \mathcal{C}\big(happy(m)(s_r)\big), \tag{41b}$$
$$m_s := m's(p), \ m := mary, \ p := sister, \ j := jim \,\}$$

In A_3, (41a), the operator ToScope has been applied in q of (40c) by keeping the assignment $m_s := mary's(sister)$ in the scope of $\mathcal{C}$, and thus, in the scope of the attitude $believe$. The result is A_3, which is the de-dicto meaning, i.e., in j's belief, j refers to the individual m_s as Mary's syster, represented by $m_s := mary's(sister)$ inside the believe scope.

The term A_4, in (41b), is the de re meaning of the NP "Mary's sister". The user of the sentence (40a) provides the reference to m_s, by $m_s := mary's(sister)$, and the belief of j does not provide this description of m_s, by referring directly to the individual m_s.

Note that the context of use s_c provides the state s_r, in which the attitude proposition is supposed to, i.e., believed to hold.

By the following pattern example (42a), I demonstrate the anaphoric pronouns with respect to the attitude scope in the algorithmic semantics of $\mathrm{L}_{\mathrm{ar}}^{\lambda}$:

$$\langle \dot{s}_c, \mathrm{Jim}_j \text{ claims that Mary robbed him}_j \rangle \xrightarrow{\text{render}} A \tag{42a}$$

$$A \equiv \mathfrak{c}\Big(\mathsf{ToScope}[robbed(j)(mary)](s_c)\Big)(j) \text{ where } \tag{42b}$$
$$\{\, j := jim, \ \mathfrak{c} := claims \,\}$$

$$\Rightarrow \ldots \Rightarrow \mathfrak{c}(q)(j) \text{ where } \{\, q := \mathsf{ToScope}[robbed(j)(mary)](s_c), \tag{42c}$$
$$j := jim, \ \mathfrak{c} := claims \,\} \equiv T$$

$$\Rightarrow \mathfrak{c}(q)(j) \text{ where}$$
$$\{\, q := \mathsf{ToScope}[robbed(j)(m) \text{ where } \{m := mary\}](s_c), \quad (42\text{d})$$
$$j := jim, \ \mathfrak{c} := claims \,\} \equiv T_0$$
$$\Rightarrow_{\mathsf{cf}} \mathfrak{c}(q)(j) \text{ where } \{\, q := \mathcal{C}[robbed(j)(m)(s_r) \text{ where } \{m := mary\}],$$
$$j := jim, \ \mathfrak{c} := claims \,\} \equiv T_1 \tag{42e}$$

In (42d)–(42e), ToScope keeps all assignments of the sentential term (which is the complement of the attitude) inside the scope expressed by $\mathcal{C}$. By (42e), the reference to the individual m, by the name and the corresponding constant $mary$, is in the claim of Jim.

In (43a)–(43b), the operator ToScope moves the assignments $m := mary$ outside the attitude closure by $\mathcal{C}$. By the alternative reductions (43b), Jim's claim does not include the assignment, which is in the term, but outside of the sub-term representation of the claim itself, e.g., the proper name "Mary" refers to the individual $mary$ by the user of the sentence (42a):

$$A \Rightarrow \mathfrak{c}(q)(j) \text{ where}$$
$$\{\, q := \mathsf{ToScope}[robbed(j)(m) \text{ where } \{m := mary\}](s_c), \quad (43\text{a})$$
$$j := jim, \ \mathfrak{c} := claims \,\} \equiv T$$
$$T \Rightarrow_{\mathsf{cf}} \mathfrak{c}(q)(j) \text{ where } \{\, q := \mathcal{C}[robbed(j)(m)(s_r) \text{ where } \{\}],$$
$$m := mary, \ j := jim, \ \mathfrak{c} := claims \,\} \equiv T_2 \tag{43b}$$

7 Relation of the Type-Theory of Algorithms with Other Type-Theories for Semantics of Programming Languages

The theories of recursive algorithms, in untyped versions Moschovakis [21–23] and typed versions Moschovakis [24], have been extended with sets of terms of the form (4e), by corresponding reduction rules and calculus. Details of properties and theoretical results have been introduced by Loukanova [17].

The type-theory $\mathrm{L}_{\mathrm{ar}}^{\lambda}$ is extended in [16], by including terms of the form (4f)–(4h) for logic operators, pure quantifiers, and respective reduction rules. Furthermore, [16] provides a proof that the recursion operator "where" in $\mathrm{L}_{\mathrm{ar}}^{\lambda}$, and thus of L_{r}^{λ}, is not algorithmically equivalent to the let-operator in λ-calculi, only denotationally.

Several theoretical characteristics of L_{r}^{λ} contribute to the algorithmic distinctions and significance of $\mathrm{L}_{\mathrm{ar}}^{\lambda}$ and L_{r}^{λ}, most significantly:

(1) The devision of the sets of the variables, in all types, into two kinds, pure variables for λ-abstraction and logic quantification, and recursion variables, for saving calculation data in memory
(2) The recursion operator "where" provides binding of recursion variables, i.e., memory slots, by instantiating, i.e., saving, in them calculation values provided by corresponding assignment terms

(3) Then corresponding reduction rules define reduction calculus of L_{ar}^λ and L_r^λ. The reduction calculus provides the algorithmic distinction between where-expressions and let-expressions. The reduction calculus of L_r^λ reduces each term A to its canonical form $\mathsf{cf}(A)$.

For every algorithmically meaningful term A, its canonical form $\mathsf{cf}(A)$ determines the algorithm $\mathsf{alg}(A)$ for computing $\mathsf{den}(A) = \mathsf{den}(\mathsf{cf}(A))$.

The let-operator is originally introduced by Dana S Scott [28] by the LCF language of λ-calculus, which has been implemented by the functional programming languages, e.g., ML, see e.g., Milner [19], Scheme,[1], Haskell,[2] e.g., see Marlow [18], OCaml, etc. In the classic imperative languages, e.g., starting with ALGOL and Pascal, the let-expressions provide the definitional scopes of functions.

Recently, a λ-calculus with a formal language that includes binding terms of let-instantiations, is presented by Nishizaki [26]. Historically, a constant where is used in the formation of terms in Landin [7], which are similar to let-expressions, but is also different from the recursion operator where in L_{ar}^λ / L_r^λ.

The formal language of full recursion L_r^λ, see Definition 2, (4a)–(4d), without the acyclicity (AC), is an extension of the language LCF introduced by Plotkin [27]. Scott and Plotkin λ-calculus of LCF have been having a grounding, fundamental significance in Computer Science, for the distinctions between denotational and operational semantics.

The algorithmic significance of L_r^λ for fine semantic distinctions of formal and programming languages, provides algorithmic distinctions for computational semantics of NL.

In this chapter, we introduce them for attitudes and statements expressed by NL.

8   Conclusion: The General Algorithmic Pattern

In this section, I shall present a general pattern for algorithmic semantics of attitude verbs via a memory (recursion) variable $\mathfrak{c}$ that can be instantiated by any specific representative of a suitable set of attitude expressions. Note that, ϕ, ψ are meta-variables for NL expressions, while A, B can be recursion variables, and thus, the rendering expression in (44b) is an underspecified L_{ar}^λ term; A, B can be suitably instantiated:

$$\text{For any } \phi \xrightarrow{\text{render}} A : \widetilde{\mathsf{t}}, \quad \text{attitude expression } \psi \xrightarrow{\text{render}} B : \tau_{pa} \tag{44a}$$
$$\text{and fresh variables } \mathfrak{c} \in \mathsf{RecV}_{\tau_{pa}}, s_c \in \mathsf{RecV_s}$$

$$\psi \text{ (that) } \phi \xrightarrow{\text{render}} \mathfrak{c}\big(\mathsf{ToScope}(A)(s_c)\big) \text{ where } \{\, \mathfrak{c} := B \,\} \tag{44b}$$

The algorithmic syntax-semantics of the operator $\mathsf{ToScope}$ is via reductions calculus:

---

[1] https://www.scheme.com/tspl4/start.html#./start:h4,.
[2] https://www.haskell.org.

(1) ToScope allows the term in its argument to be reduced, e.g., to its canonical form

(2) In its final stage (e.g., in (41a) or (41b)), the operator ToScope closes an attitude scope, by selection of some of the assignments in its propositional argument, depending on the state s_c. Simultaneously, ToScope transforms the selected scoping into an algorithmically closured term, by the operator $\mathcal{C}$ of algorithmic closure

(3) Simultaneously, ToScope moves the other assignments into the external recursion.

Conclusion: Assume that A, X are such that:

(1) $A \equiv A_0$ where $\{ \overrightarrow{p} := \overrightarrow{A} \} \equiv A_0$ where $\{ p_1 := A_1, \ldots, p_n := A_n \}$ $(n \geq 0)$
(2) $X(Y)$ is an attitude expression, e.g., $X \in \mathsf{Consts}$, or $X \equiv p \in \mathsf{RecV}$ for such
(3) $X(Y)$ occurs in A_0 or $\overrightarrow{A}$, Y is the scope-creating argument Y of X.

It holds that: If $Y \xrightarrow{\text{render}} T$ and $p_i := \mathsf{ToScope}(T)(s)$,
then p_i $(p_i \in \mathsf{RecV})$ occurs in the scope-creating argument Y.

9   Future Work

In forthcoming work, I shall add syntax-semantics interface between syntactic analyses of natural expressions involving propositional attitudes and their semantic representations by $\mathrm{L}_{\mathrm{ar}}^{\lambda}$.

It will be interesting to investigate the relations between the work introduced in this paper by that in De Groote [1] and De Groote et al. [2], especially on underspecified scope representations.

Acknowledgements. I am grateful to anonymous readers of a draft of this paper for their valuable comments and corrections.

References

1. De Groote, P.: Type raising, continuations, and classical logic. In: Proceedings of the Thirteenth Amsterdam Colloquium, pp. 97–101. ILLC Amsterdam (2001)
2. De Groote, P., Pogodalla, S., Pollard, C.: About parallel and syntactocentric formalisms: a perspective from the encoding of convergent grammar into abstract categorial grammar. Fundamenta Informaticae **106**(2-4), 211–231 (2011). https://doi.org/10.3233/FI-2011-384
3. Dowty, D.R., Wall, R., Peters, S.: Introduction to Montague semantics, vol. 11. Springer (1981). http://link.springer.com/book/10.1007%2F978-94-009-9065-4
4. Frege, G.: Über Sinn und Bedeutung. Zeitschrift für Philosophie und philosophische Kritik **C**, 25–50 (1892)
5. Gallin, D.: Intensional and higher-order modal logic: with applications to montague semantics. North-Holland Publishing Company, Amsterdam and Oxford, and American Elsevier Publishing Company (1975). https://doi.org/10.2307/2271880

6. Gamut, L.T.F.: Logic, Language, and Meaning: Volume 1 and 2. University of Chicago Press, Hyde Park (1991)

7. Landin, P.J.: The mechanical evaluation of expressions. Comput. J. **6**(4), 308–320 (1964). https://doi.org/10.1093/comjnl/6.4.308

8. Loukanova, R.: Generalized quantification in situation semantics. In: Gelbukh, A. (ed.) Computational Linguistics and Intelligent Text Processing, CICLing 2002, LNCS, vol. 2276, pp. 46–57. Springer, Berlin (2002). https://doi.org/10.1007/3-540-45715-1_4

9. Loukanova, R.: Quantification and Intensionality in Situation Semantics. In: A. Gelbukh (ed.) Computational Linguistics and Intelligent Text Processing. CICLing 2002, LNCS, vol. 2276, pp. 32–45. Springer, Berlin (2002). https://doi.org/10.1007/3-540-45715-1_3

10. Loukanova, R.: Relationships between specified and underspecified quantification by the theory of acyclic recursion. ADCAIJ: Adv. Distrib. Comput. Artif. Intell. J. **5**(4), 19–42 (2016). https://doi.org/10.14201/ADCAIJ2016541942

11. Loukanova, R.: Gamma-reduction in type theory of acyclic recursion. Fundamenta Informaticae **170**(4), 367–411 (2019). https://doi.org/10.3233/FI-2019-1867

12. Loukanova, R.: Gamma-star canonical forms in the type-theory of acyclic algorithms. In: J. van den Herik, A.P. Rocha (eds.) Agents and Artificial Intelligence. ICAART 2018, LNCS, book series LNAI, vol. 11352, pp. 383–407. Springer, Cham (2019). https://doi.org/10.1007/978-3-030-05453-3_18

13. Loukanova, R.: Type-theory of acyclic algorithms for models of consecutive binding of functional neuro-receptors. In: A. Grabowski, R. Loukanova, C. Schwarzweller (eds.) AI Aspects in Reasoning, Languages, and Computation, vol. 889, pp. 1–48. Springer, Cham (2020). https://doi.org/10.1007/978-3-030-41425-2_1

14. Loukanova, R.: Algorithmic dependent-type theory of situated information and context assessments. In: Omatu, S., Mehmood, R., Sitek, P., Cicerone, S., Rodríguez, S. (eds.) Distributed Computing and Artificial Intelligence, 19th International Conference, vol. 583, pp. 31–41. Springer, Cham (2023). https://doi.org/10.1007/978-3-031-20859-1_4

15. Loukanova, R.: Eta-reduction in type-theory of acyclic recursion. ADCAIJ: Adv. Distrib. Comput. Artif. Intell. J. **12**(1), 1–22, e29199 (2023). https://doi.org/10.14201/adcaij.29199

16. Loukanova, R.: Logic operators and quantifiers in type-theory of algorithms. In: D. Bekki, K. Mineshima, E. McCready (eds.) Logic and Engineering of Natural Language Semantics, pp. 173–198. Springer, Cham (2023). https://doi.org/10.1007/978-3-031-43977-3_11

17. Loukanova, R.: Restricted computations and parameters in type-theory of acyclic recursion. ADCAIJ: Adv. Distrib. Comput. Artif. Intell. J. **12**(1), 1–40 (2023). https://doi.org/10.14201/adcaij.29081

18. Marlow, S.: Haskell 2010, Language Report. Technical Report, https://www.haskell.org, https://www.haskell.org/onlinereport/haskell2010/ (2010)

19. Milner, R.: A theory of type polymorphism in programming. J. Comput. Syst. Sci. **17**(3), 348–375 (1978). https://doi.org/10.1016/0022-0000(78)90014-4

20. Montague, R.: The proper treatment of quantification in ordinary English. In: Hintikka, J., Moravcsik, J., Suppes, P. (eds.) Approaches to Natural Language, vol. 49, pp. 221–242. Synthese Library. Springer, Dordrecht (1973). https://doi.org/10.1007/978-94-010-2506-5_10

21. Moschovakis, Y.N.: The formal language of recursion. J. Symbolic Logic **54**(4), 1216–1252 (1989). https://doi.org/10.1017/S0022481200041086

22. Moschovakis, Y.N.: Sense and denotation as algorithm and value. In: J. Oikkonen, J. Väänänen (eds.) Logic Colloquium '90: ASL Summer Meeting in Helsinki, LNL, vol. 2, pp. 210–249. Springer, Berlin (1993). https://projecteuclid.org/euclid.lnl/1235423715

23. Moschovakis, Y.N.: The logic of functional recursion. In: M.L. Dalla Chiara, K. Doets, D. Mundici, J. van Benthem (eds.) Logic and Scientific Methods, vol. 259, pp. 179–207. Springer, Dordrecht (1997). https://doi.org/10.1007/978-94-017-0487-8_10

24. Moschovakis, Y.N.: A logical calculus of meaning and synonymy. Linguist. Philos. **29**(1), 27–89 (2006). https://doi.org/10.1007/s10988-005-6920-7

25. Muskens, R.: Meaning and Partiality. Studies in Logic, Language and Information. CSLI Publications, Stanford, California (1995)

26. Nishizaki, S.: Let-binding in a linear lambda calculus with first-class continuations. IOP Conf. Ser. Earth Environ. Sci. **252**(4), 042011 (2019). https://doi.org/10.1088/1755-1315/252/4/042011

27. Plotkin, G.D.: LCF considered as a programming language. Theoret. Comput. Sci. **5**(3), 223–255 (1977). https://doi.org/10.1016/0304-3975(77)90044-5

28. Scott, D.S.: A type-theoretical alternative to ISWIM, CUCH, OWHY. Theor. Comput. Sci. **121**(1), 411–440 (1993). https://doi.org/10.1016/0304-3975(93)90095-B

A Structured Witness Approach to Pair-List Answers of *wh*-Questions with Plural Definites

Takanobu Nakamura$^{(\boxtimes)}$ (iD)

Institute for Logic, Language and Computation, University of Amsterdam,
Science Park 107, 1098 XG Amsterdam, The Netherlands
t.nakamura@uva.nl
https://takanobunakamura.github.io/home.html

Abstract. [14] shows that *wh*-questions with plural definites semantically induce pair-list answers contra [17,30] and proposes an analysis in which plural definites may perform distributive quantification. However, this analysis blurs a boundary between distributive quantifiers and plural definites, making a wrong prediction about the number sensitivity of the pair-list answers of *wh*-questions with the latter. I propose an alternative in which *wh*-questions with plural definites may induce pair-list answers without distributive quantification. I offer an implementation with a simple question semantics with *Dynamic Plural Logic* [1], and its extension with *Dynamic Plural Inquisitive Semantics* [6,26].

Keywords: natural language semantics · question semantics · dynamic semantics · quantificational dependencies · plurality · distributivity

1 Introduction

Questions with plural arguments allow *pair-list* responses (1) exemplifies.

(1) a. Who do the students like?
     b. Ann likes Professor Jones and Ben likes Professor Smith.

It is controversial whether this is semantically defined 'answer' or pragmatically enriched 'response'. [17,30] took the latter path, claiming that the denotation of (1a) is *cumulative*, i.e. (1a) asserts that there exists a correspondence between the students and those who they like, but does not specify which correspondence holds in the actual situation. (2) shows the denotation of (1a), where Prof. Jones and Prof. Smith are the ones that the students like. (2) is too weak to request pair-list answers: it does not discriminate different correspondences.

(2) $[\![(1a)]\!] = \{\forall x \in \{z : z \in [\![$the student$]\!]\} \rightarrow \exists y \in \{$Jones, Smith$\} [R(x)(y)]$
     $\& \, \forall y \in \{$Jones, Smith$\} \rightarrow \exists x \in \{z : z \in [\![$the student$]\!]\} [R(x)(y)]\}$

D. Bekki et al. (Eds.): LENLS 2023, LNCS 14569, pp. 285–306, 2024.
https://doi.org/10.1007/978-3-031-60878-0_16

And yet, the addressee may offer more information than is required, e.g., clarification of who likes whom is over-informative, but still natural.

Although this cumulation-and-elaboration approach is theoretically parsimonious, [14] convincingly argues that this should not be the case: one can ask such a question even when the context entails an existence of such correspondence.

(3)   Context: The head coach of a basketball team had five jerseys made, numbered 1–5, for the five players on the team. Each player chose a jersey. The assistant coach knows all five players on the team, knows the numbers that were available, and believes that each of those players chose exactly one jerseys. However, the assistant coach was not present for the choosing, and so doesn't yet know which player selected which jersey.

    a. #Who are the players?

    b. Which numbers did the players pick?   [14]

Since the context already tells who the players are, (3a) is infelicitous. Importantly, this context already supports a cumulative relation between the players and the numbers as well. Thus, if (3b) only induces a cumulative reading, then (3b) should be infelicitous, just like (3a). However, this is not the case. Thus, a pair-list answer should be semantically enabled in the denotation of (3b). [14] achieves it in a straightforward way: plural definites may perform distributive quantification with a covert distributivity operator, *Dist*. This derives a pair-list reading on a par with a pair-list reading with distributive quantifiers. As Dist is necessary anyways to capture covert distributivity, his analysis is still parsimonious. However, his analysis raises a problem with respect to difference between distributive quantifiers and plural definites. Especially, [14] himself mentions the number sensitivity of pair-list readings of *wh*-questions with plural definites.

(4)   Which **professors** do the students like?

    a. They like Professor Jones and Professor Smith.

    b. Ann likes Professor Jones, and Ben likes Professor Smith.   [14]

(5)   Which **professor** do the students like?

    a. They like Professor Jones.

    b. # Ann likes Professor Jones, and Ben likes Professor Smith.   [14]

In contrast, *wh*-questions with distributive quantifiers do not show such number-sensitivity: it allows pair-list readings with a singular *wh*.

(6)   Which **professor** does every student like?

    a. Every student likes Professor Jones.

    b. Ann likes Professor Jones, and Ben likes Professor Smith.   [14]

I aim to maintain a fine distinction between distributive quantifiers and plural definites while maintaining [14]'s claim that *wh*-questions with plural definites may semantically induce pair-list readings. As an alternative, I propose a *structured witness approach*: the speaker requests the witness of *wh*-expressions, considering the dependencies its value participates to. The idea is that pair-list answers may arise from pluralities or quantification, which contribute to quantificational dependencies via different paths. In the first half of this paper, I offer a proof of concept under a question semantics with *Dynamic Plural Logic* (DPlL) [1, *et seq*]. The other half offers its subclausally compositional implementation in *Dynamic Plural Inquisitive Semantics* [6, 26] and discusses its consequences.

2 Background

This paper adopts versions of Dynamic Plural Logic (DPlL) [1], an extension of *Dynamic Predicate Logic* [10] with pluralities of variable assignments.[1] I call variables $u_1, u_2, \ldots$ in the domain of variable assignments *discourse referents* (drefs) [15]. *Plural assignments* $G, H, \ldots$ are sets of variable assignments $g, h, \ldots$. I model singular individuals with singleton sets, e.g., $a = \{a\}$, and plural individuals with non-singleton sets, e.g., $a + b = \{a, b\}$. One may obtain plural individuals by summing up the values spread across a plural assignment.[2]

(7) $G(u_n) = \{x : g \in G \,\&\, g(u_n) = x\}$

u_m is *dependent* on u_n iff their values *co-vary* as defined in (8b) [1].

(8) a. $G_{u_n=d} = \{g : g \in G \,\&\, g(u_n) = d\}$
     b. In a plural assignment G, u_m is dependent on u_n iff
       $\exists d, e \in G(u_n)\,[G_{u_n=d}(u_m) \neq G_{u_n=e}(u_m)]$

I adopt a definition of assignment extension that allows new drefs to be dependent to old drefs [3, a.o.]. Plural assignment extension $G[u]H$ is defined as the point-wise generalisation of assignment extension $g[u]h$ as shown in (9b).

(9) a. $g[u]h \Leftrightarrow \forall u'\,[u' \neq u \rightarrow g(u') = h(u')]$
     b. $G[u]H \Leftrightarrow \forall g \in G\,\exists h \in H\,[g[u]h]] \,\&\, \forall h \in H\,\exists g \in G\,[g[u]h]$

For example, (9b) may produce all the plural assignments exemplified in Table 1, 2 and 3. Note that u_2 is dependent to u_1 in I and J, but not in K.

I take a context as a set of *possibilities*, which are pairs of a possible world and a plural assignment. A formula denotes a function from an input context to the output context. (10) defines assignment extension refined for c.

(10) $c[u] = \{\langle w', H \rangle : \exists \langle w, G \rangle \in c\,[w = w' \,\&\, G[u]H]\}$

The sequencing operator ; signals dynamic conjunction.

(11) $c[\phi; \psi] = c[\phi][\psi]$

---

[1] I disregard subclausal compositionality until Sect. 4.
[2] I assume that the range of variable assignments contains both atomic and non-atomic individuals, but this is not important until Sect. 5.

Table 1. Dependent

G	u_1
g_1	a_1
g_2	a_2

$\xrightarrow{G[u_2]I}$

I	u_1	u_2
i_1	a_1	b_1
i_2	a_2	b_2

Table 2. Dependent

$\xrightarrow{G[u_2]J}$

J	u_1	u_2
j_1	a_1	b_1
j_2	a_1	b_2
j_3	a_2	b_2

Table 3. Independent

$\xrightarrow{G[u_2]K}$

K	u_1	u_2
k_1	a_1	b_1
k_2	a_1	b_2
k_3	a_2	b_1
k_4	a_2	b_2

I take evaluation of lexical relation to be cumulative [6, 26].[3]

(12) a. $c[R(u_1, ..., u_n)] = \{\langle w, G \rangle : \langle w, G \rangle \in c \,\&\, \langle G(u_1), ..., G(u_n)\rangle \in I_w(*R)\}$

      b. where (i) $R \subseteq *R$, (ii) if $\langle a_1, ..., a_n \rangle \in *R$ and $\langle b_1, ..., b_n \rangle \in *R$, then $\langle a_1 + b_1, ..., a_n + b_n \rangle \in *R$, and (iii) Nothing else is in $*R$.

The (non-)atomicity condition is defined collectively [3].

(13) a. $\text{atom}(x) \Leftrightarrow \forall y [y \subseteq x \to y = x]$

      b. $c[\text{At}(u)] = \{\langle w, G \rangle : \langle w, G \rangle \in c \,\&\, \text{atom}(G(u))\}$

      c. $c[\text{non-At}(u)] = \{\langle w, G \rangle : \langle w, G \rangle \in c \,\&\, \neg\text{atom}(G(u))\}$

The dynamic distributivity operator δ [1, 3, a.o.] is defined in (14). δ_{u_n} evaluates ϕ with respect to $G_{u_n = d}$ for each $d \in G(u_n)$.

(14) $c[\delta_{u_n}(\phi)] = \{\langle w', H \rangle : \exists \langle w, G \rangle \in c \,[w = w' \,\&\, G(u_n) = H(u_n) \,\&\, \forall d \in G(u_n) \,[\langle w, G_{u_n=d}\rangle \in c \,\&\, \langle w', H_{u_n=d}\rangle \in c[\phi]]\}$

I build a question semantics on it with the *witness requesting operator* $?u$ [6, 26]. In [6]'s words, it asks "which individual has the properties ascribed to u?".[4]

(15) $c[?u] = \{s : s \subset c \,\&\, \exists x_e \,\forall \langle w, G \rangle \in s \,\exists \langle w', G' \rangle \in c \,[w = w' \,\&\, \forall g' \in G' \,[g'(u) = x]]\}$

---

[3] This assumption is not important for the main data, but it is crucial in Sect. 5.

[4] For each s in $c[?u]$, the possibilities in s do not necessarily agree in the value of u if they share the world: for $\langle w, G \rangle$ and $\langle w', G' \rangle$, if $w = w'$, then $\exists s \subset c \,[\langle w, G \rangle \in s \,\&\, \langle w', G' \rangle \in s]$. Consider "who^{u_1} ran?" in the following toy context.

(i) a. $I_{w_1}(*\text{ran}) = \{\text{Ann}\}$, and $I_{w_2}(*\text{ran}) = \{\text{Ann, Belle}\}$.

     b. $G_1 = \{\langle u_1, \text{Ann}\rangle\}$ and $G_2 = \{\langle u_1, \text{Ann}\rangle, \langle u_1, \text{Belle}\rangle\}$

     c. $c[u_1] = \{\langle w_1, G_1 \rangle, \langle w_1, G_2 \rangle, \langle w_2, G_1 \rangle, \langle w_2, G_2 \rangle\}$

     d. $c[u_1; \text{run}(u_1)] = \{\langle w_1, G_1 \rangle, \langle w_2, G_1 \rangle, \langle w_2, G_2 \rangle\}$

Here, $s_1 = \{\langle w_1, G_1 \rangle, \langle w_2, G_1 \rangle, \langle w_2, G_2 \rangle\}$, where $x = \text{Ann}$, and $s_2 = \{\langle w_2, G_2 \rangle\}$, where $x = \text{Ann} + \text{Belle}$. Importantly, $\langle w_2, G_2 \rangle \in s_1$: $G_1(u_1) \neq G_2(u_1)$, but $\langle w_2, G_1 \rangle \in s_1$. This ensures that $?u$ itself just requires mention-some answers.

$?u$ splits c into sets of possibilities based on the values of u, e.g., a set of possibilities in which $x = a$ and a set of possibilities in which $x = b$. I call such a set s of possibilities *inquisitive states* or simply *states*. An *issue* I is defined as a non-empty, *downward closed* set of states, i.e. if $s \in I$, then for all $s' \subset s$, $s' \in I$.[5] A state s *resolves* an issue I iff $s \in I$ [4, a.o.]. For now, I assume that $?u$ is evaluated at the end of dynamic conjunctions [6,26], but see Sect. 4 for discussions.

The question is how the δ operator and plural definites contribute to pair-list answers. At this point, the $?u$ operator is only sensitive to the values of u and does not discriminate possibilities that involve the same values, but different dependencies.[6] For example in (3), there can be only one set of possibilities in which x is the sum of Numbers 1–5. However, the intuition is that (3b) can specify the exact correspondence between the numbers and the players that holds in the actual world. To express it, I make $?u$ not only sensitive to the values of u, but also to the dependencies that u participates to. I call it a *structured witness approach*: pair-list readings come from the structured anaphoric information.

3 Proposal: The Structured Witness Requesting Operator

I propose a version of the $?u$ operator that is sensitive to dependencies as given in (16). Here, $?u*$ is dependent to another dref u_n.

(16) $\quad c[?u*_{u_n}] = \{s : s \subset c \,\&\, \exists f_{\langle e,e \rangle} \,\forall \langle w, G \rangle \in s \,\exists \langle w', G' \rangle \in c \,[w = w' \,\&\, \forall d \in G'(u_n) \,[f(d) = G'_{u_n=d}(u)]]\}$

(16) partitions c based on a function f. If u is not dependent on u_n in G', it behaves the same as (15). If u is dependent on u_n in G', however, (16) distinguishes possibilities that agree on the value of $G'(u)$ but disagree on how its values are spread across G'. Thus, each $s \subset c$ expresses different dependencies between the values of u_n and u. There are two ways to introduce dependencies between u_n and u: the δ operator and plural assignment extension. However, they differ in distributivity: the former performs a distributive discourse update while the latter does not. This explains the difference between wh-questions with quantifiers and wh-questions with plural definites in terms of number (in)sensitivity.

Let's revisit the core examples. I use the superscript ^{u_n} for an assignment of new values to u_n and the subscript $_{u_n}$ for anaphoric reference to u_n. Throughout this paper, I put aside the issue of the displacement of wh-expressions.

---

[5] $?u$ is originally defined in the setting of *Inquisitive Semantics* [4] and (15) is refined in a non-inquisitive setting, i.e. a context stores a set of states only after $?u$ is evaluated. Accordingly, c is downward closed only after $?u$ is evaluated.

[6] Note that if the members of a plural assignment H assign different values to u, there is no such x that $\forall g' \in G' [g'(u) = x]$. In this sense, application of (15) is quite limited for plural assignments that store dependencies which involve a wh-dref.

(17)   Which professors do the students like?

    a. the students^{u_1} like which^{u_2} professors

    b. $c[u_1;\text{student}(u_1);\text{non-At}(u_1); u_2,\text{professor}(u_2);\text{non-At}(u_2);\text{like}(u_1, u_2);$
       $?u_2*_{u_1}]$

(17b) partitions c based on possible functional dependencies between the students and the professors. The output context is a set of states that match not only in the values of u_1 and u_2, but also in the dependencies between them. For example, consider four possibilities in Table 4: $c = \{s_1, s_2\}$ such that $s_1 = \{\langle w_1, G\rangle, \langle w_2, G'\rangle\}$ because they share $f_1 = \{\langle \text{Ann, Jones}\rangle, \langle \text{Ben, Smith}\rangle\}$, and $s_2 = \{\langle w_3, G''\rangle\}$ with $f_2 = \{\langle \text{Ann, Smith}\rangle, \langle \text{Ben, Jones}\rangle\}$. Note that $\langle w_4, G'''\rangle$ is discarded through this update because the collective value of u_2 is singular and thus it violates the non-atomicity condition 'non-At(u_2)'.

Table 4. Dependencies stored in possibilities

$\langle w_1, G\rangle$	u_1	u_2
g_1	Ann	Jones
g_2	Ben	Smith

$\langle w_3, G''\rangle$	u_1	u_2
g_1''	Ben	Jones
g_2''	Ann	Smith

$\langle w_2, G'\rangle$	u_1	u_2
g_1'	Ben	Smith
g_2'	Ann	Jones

$\langle w_4, G'''\rangle$	u_1	u_2
g_1'''	Ann	Smith
g_2'''	Ben	Smith

Here, $\{\langle \text{Ann, Jones}\rangle, \langle \text{Ben, Smith}\rangle\}$ and $\{\langle \text{Ann, Smith}\rangle, \langle \text{Ben, Jones}\rangle\}$ are distinct answers, i.e. they are stored in different states. Thus, (17b) semantically derives pair-list answers. Crucially, $?u*$ does not perform distributive quantification, but (17b) derives pair-list answers by virtue of pluralities.

In contrast, consider the example (18). Here, ⟦which professor⟧ is singular and thus only introduces a singular value to u_2. As a result, there is no possibility that u_2 co-varies with u_1, by definition.

(18)   Which professor do the students like?

    a. the students^{u_1} like which^{u_2} professor

    b. $c[u_1;\text{student}(u_1);\text{non-At}(u_1); u_2;\text{professor}(u_2);\text{At}(u_2);\text{like}(u_1, u_2);$
       $?u_2*_{u_1}]$

Take the four possibilities in Table 4 again. The condition At(u_2) is only satisfied in $\langle w_4, G'''\rangle$ and the other three possibilities are discarded. Accordingly, only $\{\langle w_4, G'''\rangle\}$ qualifies as an answer in this toy context.

The situation is different if the subject is a distributive quantifier because it involves δ. Consider the example (19). For an expository sake, I simplify the content of dynamic generalised quantification. See [1,2] for more details.

(19)   Which professor does every student like?

   a.   every student^{u_1} like which^{u_2} professor

   b. $c[u_1;\text{non-At}(u_1); \delta_{u_1}(\text{student}(u_1); u_2;\text{professor}(u_2);\text{At}(u_2);$
        $\text{like}(u_1, u_2)); ?u_2{*}_{u_1}]$

In (19b), the value of u_2 is constrained to be singular just like it is in (18b).
However, it is under the scope of δ in (19b). As a result, this atomicity constraint
is evaluated with respect to subset $G_{u_1=d}$ for each $d \in G(u_1)$, and its collective
value, i.e. $G(u_2)$, may still be plural. Note that this 'neutralisation' of atomicity
is reminiscent of DPlL-accounts of *quantificational subordination* [1, *et seq*]. In
Table 4, all the four possibilities are compatible with this requirement and thus all
of $\{\langle w_1, G\rangle, \langle w_2, G'\rangle\}$, $\{\langle w_3, G''\rangle\}$ and $\{\langle w_4, G'''\rangle\}$ may resolve the issue raised
by (6). This means that (19b) has pair-list answers by virtue of distributive
quantification. Note that $\{\langle w_4, G'''\rangle\}$ is not discarded in this case, unlike the
case with (17b). It predicts that "Ann likes Prof. Smith and Ben likes Prof.
Smith, too." is a legit answer to this question.

   Summing up, the $?u{*}_{u_n}$ operator semantically derives pair-list readings if
the context stores dependencies between its antecedent u_n and the *wh*-dref u,
which can be achieved with plural assignment extension or with the δ operator.
Since this analysis does not need δ to derive pair-list readings of *wh*-questions
with plural definites, its number sensitivity naturally follows.[7] Before closing this
section, let me discuss an issue that seems problematic for my analysis and [14].
When a singular indefinite sits below a plural definite, [14]'s covert Dist approach predicts that its co-varying reading is readily available. In contrast, plural
definites do not perform quantification in my analysis. As co-varying readings
of singular indefinites are harder with non-quantificational plural arguments in

---

[7] [35] has a similar criticism on [14] and proposes an alternative with the covert Resp
operator [7]. Here, g is a pragmatically given sequencing function and the n-th part
of P holds for the n-th part of x. She proposes that Resp occurs between the trace
of a plural definite and the predicate combined with the functional trace of *wh*.

(i)   a. $\text{Resp}_g = \lambda P \lambda x \forall n [1 \le n \le |g| \rightarrow [g(P)(n)](g(x)(n))]$
      b.   [which numbers λi [λw the players λj [x_j **Resp** picked$_w - f_i(x_j)$]]]

However, it is not obvious when insertion of the Resp operator is justified. Originally,
this operator is proposed for *respective predication* exemplified in (ii).

(ii)   Tolstoy and Dostoyevsky wrote Anna Karenina and The Idiot, respectively.   [7]

Two plural definites cannot enter into respective predication unless their cardinalities
are specified, and most importantly, a plural *wh* and a plural definite cannot enter
into respective predication.

(iii)   a.   The five players picked the five numbers, respectively.
        b.   *The players picked the numbers, respectively.
        c.   *Which numbers did the players pick, respectively?

This is problematic for [35] if Resp is taken as a covert version of "respectively.".

general [5,8,22,33], the proposed analysis predicts that the co-varying reading of a singular indefinite in a *wh*-question with a definite plural is as hard as it is in a vanilla sentence with a plural definite and a singular indefinite. (20a) shows that the co-varying reading is hard or unavailable in *wh*-questions with plural definites. Compare it with (21a) and (22a). At the first sight, this seems to disfavour the covert Dist approach.

(20)   Which cities did the guides recommend to a customer?

    a.   # Guide A recommended Amsterdam to Ann, Guide B recommended Utrecht to Bill and Guide C recommended Leiden to Chris

    b.   All the guides recommended a city to Ann. Guide A recommended Amsterdam to Ann, Guide B recommended Utrecht to Ann and Guide C recommended Leiden to Ann.

(21)   a.   A: Which cities did the guides recommend to customers?

    b.   B: Guide A recommended Amsterdam to Ann, Guide B recommended Utrecht to Bill and Guide C recommended Leiden to Chris

(22)   a.   A: Which city did every guide recommend to customers?

    b.   B: Guide A recommended Amsterdam to Ann, Guide B recommended Utrecht to Bill and Guide C recommended Leiden to Chris

However, note that (20) and (21) are degraded if the questioner already knows which cities were recommended.[8]

(23)   Context: This travel agency employs three guides Ann, Bill and Chris. One day, the manager noticed that three customers just came out from the office, and found three pamphlets of the tour to Amsterdam, the tour to Utrecht and, the tour to Leiden. The manager understood that the three guides recommended the three cities to the three customers, but does not know which guides recommended which cities. The manager asked the receptionist: ??(20) / ??(21a) / ^{ok}(22a)

It is expected if the pair-list readings of (20) and (21) are pragmatically derived. For [14], this means that insertion of Dist is harder if its scope contains indefinites. He conjectures that singular marking on *wh* may hinder insertion of Dist and/or plural marking on *wh* may facilitate it. This is compatible with (20), but not with (21): a plural indefinite hinders insertion of Dist despite its plural marking. For my analysis, this is problematic unless indefinites independently interfere with ?*u*∗. Hence, both [14]'s analysis and my analysis need further elaboration to accommodate with this kind of cases with an additional indefinite.

Note that my claim is that insertion of Dist is a dispreferred option and not that it is impossible. In this sense, my analysis is compatible with [14]'s analysis.

---

[8] However, the caveat is that the informants I consulted with reported that it is quite hard to parse these questions in this context, and judgements vary. Thus, testing this type of complex questions might not produce robust enough results to check this prediction concerning co-variation readings of singular indefinites.

Indeed, [14] reports that a handful of speakers accept a pair-list reading of (24) in the context (3).

(24)   % Which number did the players pick?   [14]

Considering that Dist is 'costly', this is exactly what [14] should predict. Then, my analysis is motivated for a question with a plural wh and a plural definite, whose pair-list reading is easier to obtain. In any case, more work is called for to see when insertion of Dist is motivated.[9]

4   Subclausal Compositionality in the Inquisitive Setting

In this section, I offer a subclausally compositional implementation of the proposed analysis, which emulates the $?u*$ operator without anaphoricity.

[14] observes a subject-object asymmetry in pair-list readings of wh-questions with plural definites. Precluding the possibility of cumulative questions with the context (3), [14] shows that pair-list answers are unavailable with a subject wh.

(25)   Which players picked the numbers? (# pair-list answer)   [14]

In [14], this asymmetry follows because the plural definite does not c-command the trace of wh in (25). As an alternative, I derive this asymmetry from evaluation order.[10] The idea is that $?u$ emulates $?u*$ if a distributivity operator scopes over it and nothing else, and it may induce pair-list readings only when the context already stores dependencies. I implement it with *Dynamic Plural Inquisitive Semantics* [6,26], which comes with full subclausal compositionality in the style of [3,23].[11] I refine a context c as a downward closed set of inquisitive states s.[12] Assignment extension, lexical relations and (non-)atomicity are refined in (26), (27) and (28). I maintain the definition of the sequencing operator; in (11).

(26) $c[u] = \{s : \exists s' \in c \, [\forall \langle w, G \rangle \in s' \, \exists \langle w', H \rangle \in s \, [w = w' \, \& \, G[u]H] \& \\ \forall \langle w', H \rangle \in s \, \exists \langle w, G \rangle \in s' \, [w = w' \, \& \, G[u]H]]\}$

(27) $c[R(u_1, ..., u_n)] = \{s : s \in c \, \& \, \forall \langle w, G \rangle \in s \, \langle G(u_1), ..., G(u_n) \rangle \in I_w(*R)]\}$

---

[9] There are cases in which Dist is rather preferred, e.g., (i) is true if Child 1 and Child 2 are singing, and Child 3 is dancing. I thank Patrick Elliot for data and discussions. I leave this issue for future research.

(i) The children are singing or dancing.

[10] In the earlier version of this work, I argue that this asymmetry comes from dynamic binding: wh-expressions introduce $?u*$ and its antecedent has to occur at its left.

[11] A dynamic plural question semantics is independently needed for dependency sensitive anaphora across conjoined questions. I thank to Patrick Elliot for bringing it to my attention. See also [21] for relevant data and a different dynamic plural approach. Comparison between my analysis and [21]'s analysis is left for future work.

[12] See Sect. 6 for discussion on a definition of the δ operator in the inquisitive setting.

(28)   a. $c[\mathrm{At}(u)] = \{s : s \in c \,\&\, \forall\langle w, G\rangle\,[\mathrm{atom}(G(u))]\}$

   b. $c[\text{non-At}(u)] = \{s : s \in c \,\&\, \forall\langle w, G\rangle[\neg\mathrm{atom}(G(u))]\}$

The $?u$ operator is refined in (29). It differs from [6,26]'s definition in that (i) it partitions c based on the collective value of u, and (ii) any $s \in c[?u]$ has to be an *enhancement* [4] of some $s' \in c$. This allows one to place $?u$ one after another as long as the outer one does not break the partition already established by the inner one. I call this property *issue-preserving*. If the input context does not contain any unresolved issue, this difference is inert, i.e. c is a singleton set of a state s and any state s' in the output context is trivially an enhancement of it.

(29) $c[?u] = \{s : s \in c \,\&\, \exists x_e \,\exists s' \in c\,[s \subseteq s' \,\&\, \forall\langle w, G\rangle \in s\,\exists\langle w', G'\rangle \in s'\,[w = w' \,\&\, G'(u) = x]]\}$

I define an 'unselective' distributive operator [3] refined in this setting and call it the Δ operator as defined in (30). The parametrised function f_H takes members of a plural assignment G, and returns a subset of H.

(30) $c[\Delta(\phi)] = \{s : \exists s' \in c\,[s \subseteq s' \,\&\, \exists f\,\forall\langle w', H\rangle \in s\,\exists\langle w, G\rangle \in s'\,[w = w' \rightarrow \forall h \in H\,\exists g \in G\,[g \subseteq h \,\&\, h \in f_H(g)]] \,\&\, \forall g \in G\,\forall\langle w'', K\rangle \in s\,\exists s'' \in c[\phi]\,[\langle w, \{g\}\rangle \in s' \,\&\, \langle w', f_H(g)\rangle \in s'' \,\&\, \langle w'', f_K(g)\rangle \in s'']]]\}$

Its most important feature is that two possibilities $\langle w', H\rangle$ and $\langle w'', K\rangle$ belong to the same $s \in c[\Delta(\phi)]$ iff $\langle w', f_H(g)\rangle$ and $\langle w'', f_K(g)\rangle$ belong to the same $s \in c[\phi]$ for each $g \in G$. Its interaction with $?u$ ensures that the issue raised under the scope of Δ is preserved beyond its scope. To see this, consider a plural assignment G and three possibilities illustrated in Table 5. Suppose that $\langle w, G\rangle, \langle w', G\rangle, \langle w'', G\rangle \in \cup c$, and no issue has been raised in c, i.e. $c = \cup c$.

Table 5. Two possibilities with different dependencies

G	u_1
g_1	d_1
g_2	d_2

$\langle w,$

H	u_1	u_2
h_1	d_1	e_1
h_2	d_2	e_1
h_3	d_2	e_2

$\rangle$

$\langle w',$

I	u_1	u_2
i_1	d_1	e_1
i_2	d_1	e_2
i_3	d_2	e_2

$\rangle$

$\langle w'',$

J	u_1	u_2
j_1	d_1	e_1
j_2	d_1	e_2
j_3	d_2	e_1
j_3	d_2	e_2

$\rangle$

Consider $?u_2$ in this toy context. Since it partitions c based on the collective value of u_2, and $H(u_2) = I(u_2) = J(u_2)$, these possibilities belong to the same state. Next, consider $\Delta(?u_2)$. For each $g \in G$ and each plural assignment K, it evaluates $?u_2$ with respect to $f_K(g)$. First, taking g_1, $f_H(g_1) = \{h_1\}$, $f_I(g_1) = \{i_1, i_2\}$, and $f_J(g_1) = \{j_1, j_2\}$. $?u_2$ is evaluated against these subsets. Since $f_H(g_1)(u_2) = \{e_1\}$, $f_I(g_1) = \{e_1, e_2\}$, and $f_J(g_1)(u_2) = \{e_1, e_2\}$, there is $s_1 \in c[?u_2]$ such that $\langle w, f_H(g_1)\rangle \in s_1$ and there is $s_2 \in c[?u_2]$ such that $\langle w', f_I(g_1)\rangle \in s_2$ and $\langle w'', f_K(g_1)\rangle \in s_2$. Second, taking g_2, $f_H(g_2) = \{h_2, h_3\}$, $f_I(g_2) = \{i_3\}$, and $f_J(g_3) = \{j_3, j_4\}$. $?u_2$ is evaluated against these subsets. Since $f_H(g_2)(u_2) =$

$\{e_1, e_2\}$, $f_I(g_2) = \{e_2\}$, and $f_J(g_2)(u_2) = \{e_1, e_2\}$, there is $s_3 \in c[?u_2]$ such that $\langle w, f_H(g_2) \rangle \in s_3$ and $\langle w'', f_J(g_2) \rangle \in s_3$, and there is $s_4 \in c[?u_2]$ such that $\langle w', f_I(g_2) \rangle \in s_4$. As a result, none of these possibilities belong to the same state. For example, $\langle w', f_I(g_1) \rangle$ and $\langle w'', f_J(g_1) \rangle$ both belong to s_2, but they differ with respect to g_2: $\langle w', f_I(g_2) \rangle \in s_4$ and $\langle w'', f_J(g_2) \rangle \in s_3$. Since two possibility belong to the same $s \in c[\Delta(\phi)]$ iff they belong to the same $s'' \in c[\phi]$ in each step of distributive update, $\langle w', I \rangle$ and $\langle w'', J \rangle$ belong to different states. This means that $\Delta(?u)$ distinguishes states based on dependency patterns and thus semantically derives pair-list answers just like $?u*$.

Now, I offer a subclausally compositional implementation of this analysis. I adopt four types: t for truth values, w for possible worlds, e for individuals, π for drefs. Variable assignments are modelled as functions of type $\langle \pi, e \rangle$ and plural assignments are modelled with type $\langle \langle \pi, e \rangle, t \rangle$. Following [6,26], I abbreviate type $\langle \langle \pi, e \rangle, t \rangle$ with m. Accordingly, $\langle w \times m \rangle$ models a possibility and $\langle w \times m, t \rangle$ models a state. I further abbreviate type $\langle \langle \langle w \times m, t \rangle, t \rangle, \langle \langle w \times m, t \rangle, t \rangle \rangle$ as T [6,26], which models functions from a context to a context.

Heim and Kratzer-style subclausal compositionality can be emulated by replacing e and t in their translations with π and T. (31) gives examples.[13]

(31) a. ⟦professor⟧ $= \lambda v_\pi \, [\text{At}(u);\text{professor}(v)]$

  b. ⟦professors⟧ $= \lambda v_\pi \, [\text{non-At}(u);\text{professor}(v)]$

  c. ⟦like⟧ $= \lambda R_{\langle \pi T, T \rangle} \, \lambda v_\pi \, R(\lambda v' \, [\text{like}(v')(v)])$

  d. ⟦a⟧ $= \lambda P_{\langle \pi T \rangle} \, Q_{\langle \pi T \rangle} \, [u;P(u);Q(u)]$

[6,26] define wh-expressions analogously to indefinites. They assume that $?u$ comes from the Foc head in the left-periphery.[14]

(32) a. ⟦who⟧ $= \lambda Q_{\langle \pi T \rangle} \, [u;\text{Person}(u);Q(u)]$

---

[13] I adopt an oversimplification: plural noun denotations should be number-neutral, e.g., "I just have one." is a good answer to "how many **children** do you have?", and the non-atomicity condition should come from the number distinction of "which" itself. See also Sect. 5. Furthermore, plural "which" gives rise to *partial plurality inferences*, i.e. the value of wh-dref is plural in at least one, but not in every pair. Partial plurality inferences have been observed for bare plurals [12,13,19,27–29,31, a.o.] and plural pronouns [24], and researchers suggest that plurality inferences are derived via pragmatic competition. In this sense, (i) may suggest that the non-atomicity inference with plural "which" is due to dynamic pragmatic competition [31]. I thank to Patrick Elliot for the data and discussion.

(i) a. Which professors does every student like?

  b. Johannes likes Ad and Hans, Deborah likes Klaus and Hans, Matthew likes **Nathan**.

See also [26] for cases in which the non-atomicity of plural "which" is obviated, which also suggests that the non-atomicity condition is not hard-wired to plural "which.".

[14] In this paper, I put aside issue-cancelling and presuppositional closure. However, see Sect. 6 for maximisation.

   b. [[which]] = $\lambda P_{\langle \pi T \rangle} Q_{\langle \pi T \rangle} [u;P(u);Q(u)]$

Here, I differ from [6,26]. I hard-wire $?u$ to wh-expressions themselves.[15] Again, I put aside the issue of the displacement of wh-expressions.

(33)   a. [[who$_{u_n}$]] = $\lambda Q_{\langle \pi T \rangle} [u;Person(u);Q(u) \,\&\, \Delta(?u_n)]$
       b. [[which$_{u_n}$]] = $\lambda P_{\langle \pi T \rangle} Q_{\langle \pi T \rangle} [u;P(u);Q(u); \Delta(?u_n)]$

Now, (34b) shows the translation of the felicitous case with the object wh and (35b) shows one for the infelicitous case with the subject wh.

(34)   a. Which numbers did the players pick?   (^{ok}pair-list answer)
       b. u_1;non-At(u_1);player(u_1); u_2;non-At(u_2);number(u_2); $\Delta(?u_2)$

(35)   a. # Which players picked the numbers?   (# pair-list answer)
       b. u_1;non-At(u_1);player(u_1); $\Delta(?u_1)$; u_2;non-At(u_2);number(u_2)

In (34b), u_1 precedes $\Delta(?u_2)$. Thus, $?u_2$ is evaluated against each $g \in G$ such that $\langle w, G \rangle \in s$ and each g stores a different player. Accordingly, each $s \in c[\Delta(?u_2)]$ stores different player-number correspondences. Thus, it semantically derives a pair-list answer, echoing the analysis with $?u*$. In contrast, in (35b), $\Delta(?u_1)$ precedes u_2. Recall that two possibilities $\langle w, I \rangle$ and $\langle w', J \rangle$ belong to the same $s \in c[\Delta(?u_1)]$ iff there is a possibility $\langle w, G \rangle \in c$ such that $\forall g \in G\,[f_I(g)(u_1) = f_J(g)(u_1)]$. Here, c only stores the value of u_1 at this point. Thus, this requirement is trivially met. Later, u_2 establishes new dependencies between u_1 and u_2, but it does not contribute to partition of c because $?u_2$ has already been evaluated. As a result, states in $c[(35b)]$ are only distinguished based on the collective value of u_1, i.e. it does not semantically derive a pair-list answer. Hence, the asymmetry follows: $\Delta(?u_n)$ may semantically derive a pair-list answer with respect to u_n and u_m only if $[u_m]$ is evaluated before $\Delta(?u_n)$.[16]

---

[15] In Sect. 5, I minimally extend the scope of Δ so that it also includes the wh-restrictor.

[16] In this formulation, it should be possible for $\Delta(?u)$ to retrieve dependencies already given in the discourse. This predicts that plural anaphora may obviate the subject-object asymmetry, i.e. (i) may induce a pair-list reading even if the questioner already knows which players picked five numbers. I thank to Yusuke Yagi for pointing it out.

(i) We have numbers 1–5^{u_1}. Which players^{u_2} picked them$_{u_1}$?

I have not consulted with enough number of informants about the acceptability of its pair-list reading, but one of the two informants I have consulted with reported that a pair-list reading is fine with (i) but not with (25). The other informant also reported that (i) is slightly better than (25) under a pair-list reading. This may suggest that the proposed analysis indeed makes a right prediction about the discourse sensitivity of pair-list readings of a wh-question with a plural definite. However, much more work is necessary to see how robust this pattern is, and whether this effect is indeed due to retrieval of dependencies, i.e. whether this effect comes from something else.

5   Cardinals and Distributivity Within the *wh*-Restrictor

This section discusses distributivity in the *wh*-restrictor. [14] shows that the cardinal modifier within the *wh*-restrictor is distributively evaluated if it semantically induces pair-list readings and non-distributively evaluated if it is parsed as a cumulative question. First, consider the context (36).

(36)   Context: A basketball team's head coach had ten jerseys made, numbered 1–10. From these, each of the team's five players chose exactly two jerseys, an even-numbered jersey for home games and an odd-numbered jersey for away games.

(37) is a scenario in which the questioner already knows that there are exactly ten numbers. It excludes the possibility that (37a) is parsed as a cumulative question. In this case, the cardinal modifier "two" is distributively evaluated.

(37)   Scenario 1: The assistant coach (the questioner) knows all five players, knows the numbers that were available, and believes that each player chose exactly two jerseys.

   a. Which **two** numbers did the players pick?

   b. Ann picked 1 and 10, Ben picked 2 and 3, Chris picked 4 and 7, Dan picked 5 and 6, Emma picked 8 and 9.   [14]

On the other hand, (38) is a scenario in which the questioner does not know about the identity of ten numbers. This context allows a cumulative question. In this case, the cardinal modifier "ten" can be collectively evaluated.

(38)   Scenario 2: The assistant coach (the questioner) knows all five players and believes that each player chose exactly two jerseys, but has no information about what jersey numbers were available.

   a. Which **ten** numbers did the players pick?

   b. i.   They picked numbers 1–10.

       ii. Ann picked 1 and 10, Ben picked 2 and 3, Chris picked 4 and 7, Dan picked 5 and 6, Emma picked 8 and 9.   [14]

To account for the interpretive difference, I modify the denotation of *wh* so that the scope of Δ includes the restrictor property as well. Importantly, the (non-) atomicity condition is outside the scope of Δ. I take it as the reflection of the number-marking on a *wh*-expression itself.

(39)   a. $[\![\text{which}^{SG}_{u_n}]\!] = \lambda P_{\langle \pi T\rangle}\, Q_{\langle \pi T\rangle}\, [u; \Delta(P(u); ?u); \text{At}(u); Q(u)]$

   b. $[\![\text{which}^{PL}_{u_n}]\!] = \lambda P_{\langle \pi T\rangle}\, Q_{\langle \pi T\rangle}\, [u; \Delta(P(u); ?u); \text{non-At}(u); Q(u)]$

I define the cardinality condition analogously to the (non-)atomicity condition.

(40) $c[\text{two}(u)] = \{s : s \in c \,\&\, \forall\langle w, G\rangle\, [|G(u)| = 2]$

Now, $[\![\text{which}^{PL}_{u_n}\text{ two numbers}]\!]$ is given in (41).

(41) $Q_{\langle\pi T\rangle}\,[u;\,\Delta(\text{two}(u);\text{non-At}(u);\text{number}(u);\,?u);\text{non-At}(u);Q(u)]$

On this point, it becomes crucial that the range of variable assignments includes non-atomic individuals. Thus, one may consider plural assignments such as one in Table 6. In an extreme case, one may put the maximal sum of individuals in a singleton set of variable assignment as exemplified in Table 7.

Table 6. Distributive

H	u_1	u_2
h_1	$x_1 + x_2$	y_1
h_2	$x_3 + x_4$	y_2
h_3	$x_5 + x_6$	y_3

Table 7. Non-distributive

H	u_1	u_2
h_1	$x_1 + x_2 + ... + x_{10}$	$y_1 + ... + y_5$

These cases respectively correspond to the distributive parse and the collective parse. First, consider Table 6. In this case, $\Delta(\text{two}(u))$ requires that the value of u comes in twos for each member of $H = \{h_1, h_2, h_3\}$ in Table 6. This is satisfied in Table 6, but not in Table 7. This corresponds to the distributive reading of the cardinal modifier. Second, consider Table 7. Here, the contribution of Δ is neutralised because $H = \{h_1\}$, i.e. it looks like being collectively evaluated. This corresponds to the collective reading of the cardinal modifier. Here, recall that evaluation of lexical relation is cumulative: although there is no quantificational dependency between u_1 and u_2 in Table 7, their values are still cumulatively related. Essentially, this emulates the original cumulation analysis in [17,30]: $*R(x_1 + ... + x_{10})(y_1 + ... + y_5)$ is true iff there is at least one way to pair $x_1, ..., x_{10}$ and $y_1, ..., y_5$ so that each pair satisfies R. This is on a par with [14], who preserves the possibility of a genuine cumulative parse of wh-questions with plural definites besides a parse with the covert Dist. Seeming pair-list responses are due to pragmatic follow-up.

6   Issue-Preservation and Distributivity

This section discusses some extensions and open issues with the proposed analysis. First, the proposed analysis can be applied to pair-list readings of multiple plural wh-questions. [6,26] defines a generalised witness requesting operator $?u_1...u_{n-1}, u_n$, which is equivalent to $?u$ if $n = 1$. (42) is necessary to analyse multiple wh-questions, but its virtue is lost in my analysis because I hard-wire $?u$ to wh-expressions.

(42) $c[?u_1...u_{n-1}, u_n] = \{s \,:\, s \in c\,\&\,\exists f_{(e^{n-1},e)}\,\forall\langle w, G\rangle \in s\,\exists\langle w', G'\rangle \in$
$\cup c\,[w = w'\,\&\,\forall g \in G\,[g(u_n) = f(g(u_1), ...g(u_{n-1}))]]\}$

Thus, I aim to emulate $?u_1...u_n$ with an n-sequence of $?u$. For this, the issue-preserving property of $?u$ plays the central role. Consider the example (43).

(43) Which students^{u_1} likes which professors^{u_2}?

First, $\Delta(?u_1)$ partitions $c = \cup c$ based on the collective value of u_1. The resultant context is exemplified in Table 8.[17]

Table 8. Raising issue with the first witness requesting operator

$$
\left\{
\begin{array}{|c|c|}
\hline
\langle w_1, G \rangle & u_1 \\
\hline
g_1 & \text{Ann} \\
\hline
g_2 & \text{Ben} \\
\hline
\end{array}
\quad
\begin{array}{|c|c|}
\hline
\langle w_2, G \rangle & u_1 \\
\hline
g_1 & \text{Ann} \\
\hline
g_2 & \text{Ben} \\
\hline
\end{array}
\right\} = s_1
\qquad
\left\{
\begin{array}{|c|c|}
\hline
\langle w_3, G' \rangle & u_1 \\
\hline
g_1' & \text{Chris} \\
\hline
g_2' & \text{Dan} \\
\hline
\end{array}
\quad
\begin{array}{|c|c|}
\hline
\langle w_4, G' \rangle & u_1 \\
\hline
g_1' & \text{Chris} \\
\hline
g_2' & \text{Dan} \\
\hline
\end{array}
\right\} = s_2
$$

Then, $\Delta(?u_2)$ raises another issue. The resultant context is given in Table 9.

Table 9. Raising issue with the second witness requesting operator

$$
\left\{
\begin{array}{|c|c|c|}
\hline
\langle w_1, I \rangle & u_1 & u_2 \\
\hline
i_1 & \text{Ann} & \text{Jones} \\
\hline
i_2 & \text{Ben} & \text{Smith} \\
\hline
\end{array}
\right\} = s_1'
\qquad
\left\{
\begin{array}{|c|c|c|}
\hline
\langle w_3, J \rangle & u_1 & u_2 \\
\hline
j_1 & \text{Chris} & \text{Freeman} \\
\hline
j_2 & \text{Dan} & \text{Carcassi} \\
\hline
\end{array}
\right\} = s_3'
$$

$$
\left\{
\begin{array}{|c|c|c|}
\hline
\langle w_2, I' \rangle & u_1 & u_2 \\
\hline
i_1' & \text{Ann} & \text{Smith} \\
\hline
i_2' & \text{Ben} & \text{Jones} \\
\hline
\end{array}
\right\} = s_2'
\qquad
\left\{
\begin{array}{|c|c|c|}
\hline
\langle w_4, J' \rangle & u_1 & u_2 \\
\hline
j_1' & \text{Chris} & \text{Carcassi} \\
\hline
j_2' & \text{Dan} & \text{Freeman} \\
\hline
\end{array}
\right\} = s_4'
$$

Since $?u_2$ is issue-preserving, $c[\Delta(?u_2)]$ does not break the partition already made in c. Furthermore, Δ also preserves issues raised under its scope. Accordingly, $c[\Delta(?u_2)] = \{s_1', s_2', s_3', s_4'\}$. Readers may confirm that (i) s_1', s_2' are enhancements of s_1 and s_3', s_4' are enhancements of s_2, and (ii) these states are distinguished based on the 'distributive' values of u_2, i.e. its value under each member of a plural assignment in this case. Thus, it derives a pair-list answer, just like it does in cases of wh-questions with plural definites. This way, pair-list readings of a multiple plural wh-question can be analysed with a sequence of $?u$ operators.

Furthermore, there is a case that is difficult to capture with the generalised $?u$: one may answer conjoined single-wh-questions with a pair-list answer.[18]

(44)   a.   Who^{u_1} ate lunch in the cafe? And what^{u_2} did **they**$_{u_1}$ eat?

   b.   Tom ate bitterballen, Émile ate boterham and Giorgio ate pizza.

It is not obvious how $?u_1...u_n$ derives pair-list answers to a conjunction of two single wh-questions, but the issue-preserving $?u$ can derive pair-list answers with (44a) in parallel with pair-list answers with wh-questions with plural definites.

---

[17] I disregard maximisation until the discussion on multiple singular wh-questions.

[18] See [21] for more data and a dynamic plural approach to it with a different setting.

Issue-preservation plays a role to analyse pair-list answers of wh-questions with quantifiers as well. [6, 26] leave wh-questions with a quantifier to future research. In their definition, $?u$ seeks for x such that $\forall g' \in G'\,[g'(u) = x]$. This means that if u stores different values across G, one may not find such x. Thus, this definition of $?u$ cannot be applied to wh-questions with quantifiers. The $?u*$ operator can analyse them if $?u*$ is introduced in the left-periphery so that it is evaluated outside the scope of δ. In the analysis proposed in Sect. 4, $?u$ is introduced in-situ with a wh-expression. Thus, it is evaluated under the scope of δ. This calls for an issue-preserving definition of δ. To see that a pair-list reading arises with an issue-preserving δ, recall the sample context given in Table 4. First, consider issue-raising with respect to $G_{u_1=Ann}$ as exemplified in Table 10. If the issue-raising with respect to $G_{u_1=Ben}$ preserves this partition, the resultant context c' is $\{s_1', s_2', s_3'\}$ as illustrated in Table 11.

Table 10. Issue raising with one subset from different plural assignments

$\langle w_1, G_{u_1=A}\rangle$	u_1	u_2
g_1	Ann	Jones

$\langle w_2, G'_{u_1=A}\rangle$	u_1	u_2
g_2'	Ann	Jones

$= s_1$

$\langle w_3, G''_{u_1=A}\rangle$	u_1	u_2
g_2''	Ann	Smith

$\langle w_4, G'''_{u_1=A}\rangle$	u_1	u_2
g_1'''	Ann	Smith

$= s_2$

Table 11. Issue raising with another subset from different plural assignments

$\langle w_1, G_{u_1=B}\rangle$	u_1	u_2
g_2	Ben	Smith

$\langle w_2, G'_{u_1=B}\rangle$	u_1	u_2
g_1'	Ben	Smith

$= s_1'$

$\langle w_3, G''_{u_1=B}\rangle$	u_1	u_2
g_1''	Ben	Jones

$= s_2'$

$\langle w_4, G'''_{u_1=B}\rangle$	u_1	u_2
g_2'''	Ben	Smith

$= s_3'$

Thus, $?u$ under the scope of δ may derive a pair-list answer if δ is also issue-preserving. (45) defines an issue-preserving δ.

(45) $c[\delta_{u_n}(\phi)] = \{s' : \exists s \in c\,[\forall \langle w', H\rangle \in s'\, \exists \langle w, G\rangle \in s\,[w = w'\,\&\,G(u_n) = H(u_n)\,\&\,\forall d \in H(u_n)\,\exists s'' \in c[\phi]\,\forall \langle w'', K\rangle \in s'\,[\langle w, G_{u_n=d}\rangle \in s\,\&\,\langle w', H_{u_n=d}\rangle \in s''\,\&\,\langle w'', K_{u_n=d}\rangle \in s'']]]\}$

The universal quantification over $\langle w'', K\rangle \in s'$ ensures that for any two possibilities in s', their subset possibilities with respect to each value d of u_n belong to the same $s'' \in c[\phi]$. It interacts with $?u$ in the same way as Δ does: states in $c[\delta_{u_n}(?u_m)]$ are distinguished based on the distributive values of u_m.

However, a pair-list reading with multiple singular wh poses a problem.

(46) Which student^{u_1} read which book^{u_2}?

(46) has a pair-list answer despite the atomicity condition with the singular wh. This is not a problem for [6, 26] because they define atomicity as (47): it just requires that u does not store a mereological plural in each member g of G, and does not require that the collective value $G(u)$ is atomic.

(47) $c[\text{Atom}(u)] = \{s : s \in c \,\&\, \forall \langle w, G \rangle \in s \,\forall g \in G \, [\neg \exists y \subset g(u)]\}$

Although this atomicity condition derives pair-list readings of multiple singular wh-questions, (47) makes a wrong prediction about pair-list readings of wh-questions with plural definites: it predicts that a singular wh-question with a plural definite, e.g., (5), allows a pair-list answer without even inserting the covert Dist operator. This is obviously too strong. Thus, as long as the pair-list readings of wh-questions with plural definites are number sensitive, one has to derive the pair-list reading of (46) without assuming (47). I leave precise exploration for future research, but I will sketch a possible way to derive pair-list readings multiple singular wh without assuming (47).

First of all, I adopt the maximisation operator defined in (48).[19]

(48) $c[max(u)] =$
$\{s : s \in c \,\&\, \forall \langle w, G \rangle \in s \,\forall \langle w', G' \rangle \in s \, [w = w' \rightarrow G(u) = G'(u)]]\}$

Second, I adopt a short-hand notation to say that s is an *alternative* [4].

(49)   A state s is an *alternative* in c, i.e. $Alt(s)$, iff $s \in c$ and $\forall s' \in c \, [s \not\subset s']$.

Now, I define a *state-aggregation* $\oplus$ as (50). It returns a set of states each of which aggregates the plural assignments that are paired with the same world.[20] I call the restriction for the set of I in (50) the *aggregation condition*.

(50) $c[\oplus] = \{s : \exists s' \in c \, [Alt(s') \,\&\, \forall \langle w, G \rangle \in s \,\exists \langle w', G' \rangle \in s' \, [w = w' \,\&\, G =$
$\cup \{I : \exists s'' \in c \, [Alt(s'') \,\&\, \forall \langle w'', J \rangle \in s'' \, [\langle w'', G \rangle \in s' \,\&\, \langle w, I \rangle \in s'']]\}]]\}$

In general, each state in c stores possibilities with a singleton plural assignment after evaluating a multiple singular wh-question, i.e. both wh-expression

---

[19] This is weaker than [6, 26]'s maximality operator, which is defined below.

(i) $c[max(u)] = \{s : s \in c \,\forall \langle w, G \rangle \in s \,\forall \langle w', G' \rangle \in \cup c \, [w = w' \rightarrow G'(u) \subseteq G(u)]\}$

It requires s to contain maximal plural assignments for each world across the context, while (48) only requires that each state agrees with the collective value of u. This makes mention-some answers unable to settle an issue. See also Footnote 4. This difference is important to derive pair-list readings of multiple singular wh-questions while adopting the collective atomicity condition, which is necessary to derive the number sensitivity of pair-list readings of wh-questions with plural definites.

[20] [20, 21] analyse pair-list readings of multiple singular wh-questions with a dynamic version of *family-of-question approaches* [11, 16, 18, 25, 32, 34]. He defines a pair-list answer generating operator, through which a set of dynamic Hamblin propositions is shifted to one dynamic Hamblin proposition. The $\oplus$ operation is inspired by it, but its implementation is less transparent in the setting of Inquisitive Semantics.

constrain their drefs with the atomicity condition. In such cases, each state supports a single-list answer. Then, (50) returns states each of which is the sum of such states compatible with a particular world w and supports the conjunction of single-list answers compatible with w. Thus, (50) may derive a pair-list answer with a multiple singular wh-question despite the collective atomicity condition.[21]

I assume that the interrogative C introduces this operator.

(51) $\llbracket C \rrbracket = \lambda p_T \, [p; \oplus]$

Consider the example (52a), whose translation is given in (52b).

(52) a. Which student^{u_1} likes which professor^{u_1}?

     b. $u_1;At(u_1);student(u_1); \Delta(?u_1); max(u_1); u_2;At(u_2);professor(u_2);$
        $\Delta(?u_2); max(u_2);like(u_1)(u_2); \oplus$

Suppose that there are two worlds w_1 and w_2 given in (53). Here, I disregard $*R$ for an expository sake. This does not affect the following discussion.

(53) a. $I_{w_1}(student) = I_{w_2}(student) = \{Ann,Ben\}$

     b. $I_{w_1}(professor) = I_{w_2}(professor) = \{Jones,Smith\}$

     c. $I_{w_1}(like) = \{\langle Ann,Jones\rangle, \langle Ben,Smith\rangle\}$

     d. $I_{w_2}(like) = \{\langle Ann,Smith\rangle, \langle Ben,Jones\rangle\}$

$?u_1$ partitions c based on the value of u_1. Recall that $?u$ does not require two possibilities in the same state to agree with the value of u as long as they share the world. However, $max(u_1)$ requires that each state agrees with the collective value of u_1. The resultant context is given in Table 12.

Table 12. The first witness requesting with maximisation

$$\left\{ \begin{array}{|c|c|}\hline \langle w_1, G\rangle & u_1 \\\hline g_1 & Ann \\\hline\end{array} \;\; \begin{array}{|c|c|}\hline \langle w_2, G\rangle & u_1 \\\hline g_1 & Ann \\\hline\end{array} \right\} = s_1 \quad \left\{ \begin{array}{|c|c|}\hline \langle w_1, H\rangle & u_1 \\\hline j_1 & Ben \\\hline\end{array} \;\; \begin{array}{|c|c|}\hline \langle w_2, H\rangle & u_1 \\\hline j_1 & Ben \\\hline\end{array} \right\} = s_2$$

Then, $?u$ raises another issue, preserving the previously raised issues. Here, each state in the context stores a particular single-list answer in a world (Table 13).

---

[21] One has to ensure that multiple singular wh-questions support subsequent plural anaphora as exemplified in (i). $\oplus$ is one way to achieve it without adopting (47).

(i) a. Which^{u_1} boy bought which^{u_2} book and who^{u_3} will they$_{u_1}$ send them$_{u_2}$ to?

     b. Max bought *Moby Dick*, Kyle *The Great Gatsby*, and Sam *War & Peace*. These boys will send the books to Ada.   [21]

Table 13. The second witness requesting

$$\left\{ \begin{array}{|c|c|c|} \hline \langle w_1, G' \rangle & u_1 & u_2 \\ \hline g_1' & \text{Ann} & \text{Jones} \\ \hline \end{array} \right\} = s_1' \qquad \left\{ \begin{array}{|c|c|c|} \hline \langle w_1, H' \rangle & u_1 & u_2 \\ \hline h_1' & \text{Ben} & \text{Smith} \\ \hline \end{array} \right\} = s_2'$$

$$\left\{ \begin{array}{|c|c|c|} \hline \langle w_2, G'' \rangle & u_1 & u_2 \\ \hline g_1'' & \text{Ann} & \text{Smith} \\ \hline \end{array} \right\} = s_3' \qquad \left\{ \begin{array}{|c|c|c|} \hline \langle w_2, H'' \rangle & u_1 & u_2 \\ \hline h_1'' & \text{Ben} & \text{Jones} \\ \hline \end{array} \right\} = s_4'$$

For s_1', s_1' itself trivially meets the aggregation condition, s_2' also meets this condition: $s_2' = \{\langle w_1, H' \rangle\}$ and $\langle w_1, G' \rangle \in s_1'$, and no other states meet this condition. Thus, the new state s_1'' contains $\langle w_1, G' \cup H' \rangle$. For s_3', s_3' itself meets the aggregation condition, s_4' also meets this condition: $s_4' = \{\langle w_2, H'' \rangle\}$ and $\langle w_2, G'' \rangle \in s_3'$, and no other states meet this condition. Thus, the new state s_2'' contains $\langle w_2, G'' \cup H'' \rangle$.[22] The result of $\oplus$ is given in Table 14.

Table 14. Aggregation

$$\left\{ \begin{array}{|c|c|c|} \hline \langle w_1, K \rangle & u_1 & u_2 \\ \hline k_1 = g_1' & \text{Ann} & \text{Jones} \\ \hline k_2 = h_1' & \text{Ben} & \text{Smith} \\ \hline \end{array} \right\} = s_1'' \qquad \left\{ \begin{array}{|c|c|c|} \hline \langle w_2, K' \rangle & u_1 & u_2 \\ \hline k_1' = g_1'' & \text{Ann} & \text{Smith} \\ \hline k_2' = h_1'' & \text{Ben} & \text{Jones} \\ \hline \end{array} \right\} = s_2''$$

In this way, a pair-list reading of a multiple singular *wh*-question is derived without assuming a distributive atomicity condition.

This analysis does not derive pair-list readings of *wh*-questions with indefinites. For example, (54a) has a *choice reading* [9]: it asks to choose a student and specify the professor the student likes, but not a pair-list reading.

(54)   a. Which professor^{u_2} does one of the students^{u_1} like?

   b. u_1;At(u_1);student(u_1); u_2;At(u_2);professor(u_2); $\Delta(?u_2)$; $max(u_2)$; like$(u_1)(u_2)$

The update with the indefinite results in the context given in Table 15.[23]

---

[22] In the easiest case, this holds if all the alternatives in c are singleton sets of possibilities just like in this toy example. More generally, this holds for a subset of alternatives in c that share the same set of worlds and do not overlap in the value they assign to drefs. Then, $\oplus$ maps each of those subsets to a new state.

[23] In this toy context, both worlds agree with who are students. Thus, the results of $?u_1$ without $max(u_1)$ and u_1 look the same. However, if who are student is not known, then $?u$ splits c into states each of which contains possibilities that are compatible with a particular value of u. In contrast, a singular indefinite does not partition c.

Table 15. Plural assignment extension with a singular indefinite

$$\left\{ \begin{array}{|c|c|} \hline \langle w_1, G\rangle & u_1 \\ \hline g_1 & \text{Ann} \\ \hline \end{array} \quad \begin{array}{|c|c|} \hline \langle w_2, G\rangle & u_1 \\ \hline g_1 & \text{Ann} \\ \hline \end{array} \quad \begin{array}{|c|c|} \hline \langle w_1, H\rangle & u_1 \\ \hline j_1 & \text{Ben} \\ \hline \end{array} \quad \begin{array}{|c|c|} \hline \langle w_2, H\rangle & u_1 \\ \hline j_1 & \text{Ben} \\ \hline \end{array} \right\} = s_1$$

Note that (54b) lacks maximisation on u_1 unlike (52a), i.e. indefinites may not come with max unlike wh-expressions. Then, $?u_2$ and $max(u_2)$ apply. The resultant context is illustrated in Table 16. One may resolve this issue by answering "(A student likes) Professor Smith/Jones."[24] or choosing one student-professor pair, e.g., "Ann likes Professor Jones." The latter corresponds to a choice reading: whichever single-list answer may resolve the issue.

Table 16. Raising issue with the second witness requesting operator

$$\left\{ \begin{array}{|c|c|c|} \hline \langle w_1, G'\rangle & u_1 & u_2 \\ \hline g_1' & \text{Ann} & \text{Jones} \\ \hline \end{array} \quad \begin{array}{|c|c|c|} \hline \langle w_2, H''\rangle & u_1 & u_2 \\ \hline h_1'' & \text{Ben} & \text{Jones} \\ \hline \end{array} \right\} = s_1'$$

$$\left\{ \begin{array}{|c|c|c|} \hline \langle w_2, G''\rangle & u_1 & u_2 \\ \hline g_1'' & \text{Ann} & \text{Smith} \\ \hline \end{array} \quad \begin{array}{|c|c|c|} \hline \langle w_1, H'\rangle & u_1 & u_2 \\ \hline h_1' & \text{Ben} & \text{Smith} \\ \hline \end{array} \right\} = s_2'$$

Importantly, $\oplus$ does not derive a pair-list answer in this case. For s_1', s_1' itself meets the aggregation condition, but s_2' does not: $s_2' = \{\langle w_2, G''\rangle, \langle w_1, H'\rangle\}$, and $\langle w_1, G'\rangle \in s_1'$, but $\langle w_2, G'\rangle \notin s_1'$. As a result, $\oplus$ is trivialised: $c[\oplus] = c$. In general, $\oplus$ is trivial unless there are two states s and s' in which all the plural assignments in s are compatible with all the worlds in s'.[25]

Lastly, $\oplus$ does not affect the way how the proposed analysis derives pair-list readings of (i) multiple plural wh-questions, (ii) wh-questions with quantifiers, and (iii) wh-questions with plural definites. These questions may store various values to a wh-dref from atomic values to the maximal plural value, and the weak definition of $max(u)$ makes each state agree with the collective value of u. As a result, even if an aggregation is defined for states with non-maximal value of u in w, their result is identical to the state with the maximal value of u in w. However, this is not trivial: in effect, $\oplus$ removes states with non-maximal values of u. Thus, $\oplus$ and $max(u)$ together emulate the maximality operator in [6,26]. However, more work is necessary to fully work out this approach with $\oplus$. I leave elaboration of it and discussion of remaining issues for future research.[26]

---

[24] [20] take a short answer to provide a specific value of the wh-dref and implements it under *Dynamic Hamblin Semantics*. His idea would equally work in this case.

[25] Here, it is crucial that $\oplus$ targets alternatives: if one compares $\{\langle w_1, G'\rangle\} \subset s_1'$ and $\{\langle w_1, H'\rangle\} \subset s_2'$, they meet the aggregation condition for each other.

[26] Applying $\oplus$ to a wh-question with a plural definite and a singular indefinite may predict that a co-varying reading of the singular indefinite is possible without the covert Dist operator. I leave examination of this prediction for future research.

7 Conclusion

I proposed a structured witness approach to *wh*-questions with plural definites: a *wh*-expression partitions the context based on not only its value but also the dependencies it participates to. As a proof of concept, I proposed a DPlL-based question semantics with the ?*u*∗ operator, and offered a subclausally compositional implementation with Dynamic Plural Inquisitive Semantics. Both versions derive pair-list answers if the context involves dependencies, which can be done with distributive quantification or plural predication. The proposed analyses still agree with [14]'s claim that *wh*-questions with plural definites may semantically derive pair-list readings.

Acknowledgement. I would like to thank to Maria Aloni, Patrick Elliott, Floris Roelofsen, and Yusuke Yagi for insightful comments. I also thank to the participants and the anonymous reviewers of LENLS20 for the valuable feedback. The remaining errors are all mine. This work benefited from support from the Dutch Research Council (NWO) as part of project 406.18.TW.009 *A Sentence Uttered Makes a World Appear - Natural Language Interpretation as Abductive Model Generation.*

References

1. van den Berg, M.: Some aspects of the internal structure of discourse: the dynamics of nominal anaphora. Ph.D. thesis, University of Amsterdam (1996)
2. Brasoveanu, A.: Structured nominal and modal reference. Ph.D. thesis, Rutgers University Newark, New Jersey (2007)
3. Brasoveanu, A.: Donkey pluralities: plural information states versus non-atomic individuals. Linguist. Philos. **31**, 129–209 (2008)
4. Ciardelli, I., Groenendijk, J., Roelofsen, F.: Inquisitive Semantics. Oxford University Press, Oxford (2018)
5. Dotlačil, J.: Anaphora and distributivity: a study of same, different, reciprocals and others. Ph.D. thesis, Utrecht University (2010)
6. Dotlačil, J., Roelofsen, F.: A dynamic semantics of single-wh and multiple-wh questions. Semant. Linguist. Theory **30**, 376–395 (2021)
7. Gawron, J.M., Kehler, A.: The semantics of respective readings, conjunction, and filler-gap dependencies. Linguist. Philos. **27**, 169–207 (2004)
8. Godehard, L.: Plurals. In: von Stechow, A., Wunderlich, D. (eds.) Semantik: Ein internationales Handbuch der zeitgenössischen Forschung, pp. 418–440. De Gruyter, Berlin (1991)
9. Groenendijk, J., Stokhof, M.: Studies on the semantics of questions and the pragmatics of answers. Ph.D. thesis, University of Amsterdam (1984)
10. Groenendijk, J., Stokhof, M.: Dynamic predicate logic. Linguist. Philos. **14**, 39–100 (1991)
11. Hagstrom, P.: Decomposing questions. Ph.D. thesis, Massachusetts Institute of Technology (1998)
12. Ivlieva, N.: Multiplicity and non-monotonic environments. In: Crnič, L., Sauerland, U. (eds.) The Art and Craft of Semantics: A Festschrift for Irene Heim, vol. 1, pp. 245–251. MITWPL, Cambridge (2014)

13. Ivlieva, N.: Dependent plurality and the theory of scalar implicatures: remarks on Zweig 2009. J. Semant. **37**, 425–454 (2020)
14. Johnston, W.: Pair-list answers to questions with plural definites. Semant. Pragmat. **16**, 1–23 (2023)
15. Karttunen, L.: Discourse referents. In: Proceedings of the 1969 Conference on Computational Linguistics, pp. 1–38 (1969)
16. Kotek, H.: Composing questions. Ph.D. thesis, Massachusetts Institute of Technology (2014)
17. Krifka, M.: Definite NPs aren't quantifiers. Linguist. Inq. **23**, 156–163 (1992)
18. Krifka, M.: Quantifying into question acts. Nat. Lang. Semant. **9**, 1–40 (2001)
19. Križ, M.: Bare plurals, multiplicity, and homogeneity. Ms. Institut Jean Nicod (2017)
20. Li, H.: A dynamic semantics for *wh*-questions. Ph.D. thesis, New York University (2020)
21. Li, H.: Reference to dependencies established in multiple-wh questions. Semant. Linguist. Theory **31**, 262–282 (2021)
22. Moltmann, F.: Reciprocals and "same/different": towards a semantic analysis. Linguist. Philos. **15**, 411–462 (1992)
23. Muskens, R.: Combining montague semantics and discourse representation. Linguist. Philos. **19**, 143–186 (1996)
24. Nakamura, T.: Partial plurality inferences of plural pronouns and dynamic pragmatic enrichment. Semant. Linguist. Theory **33**, 151–171 (2023)
25. Nicolae, A.: Any questions? Polarity as a window into the structure of questions. Ph.D. thesis, Harvard University (2013)
26. Roelofsen, F., Dotlačil, J.: Wh-questions in dynamic inquisitive semantics. Theor. Linguist. **49**, 1–91 (2023)
27. Sauerland, U.: A new semantics for number. Semant. Linguist. Theory **13**, 258–275 (2003)
28. Sauerland, U., Anderssen, J., Yatsushiro, K.: The plural is semantically unmarked. In: Kepser, S., Reis, M. (eds.) Linguistic Evidence: Empirical, Theoretical and Computational Perspectives, pp. 413–434. Mouton de Gruyter (2005)
29. Spector, B.: Aspects of the pragmatics of plural morphology: on higher-order implicatures. In: Sauerland, U., Stateva, P. (eds.) Presupposition and Implicature in Compositional Semantics, pp. 243–281. Palgrave Macmillan, London (2007)
30. Srivastav, V.: Two types of universal terms in questions. North East Linguist. Soc. **22**, 443–457 (1992)
31. Sudo, Y.: Scalar implicatures with discourse referents: a case study on plurality inferences. Linguist. Philos. **46**, 1161–1217 (2023)
32. Szabolcsi, A.: Quantifiers in pair-list readings. In: Szabolcsi, A. (ed.) Ways of Scope Taking, pp. 311–347. Kluwer Academic, Dordrecht (1997)
33. Williams, E.: Reciprocal scope. Linguist. Inq. **22**, 159–173 (1991)
34. Willis, P.: The role of topic-hood in multiple-wh question semantics. In: Proceedings of the 27th West Coast Conference on Formal Linguistics, pp. 87–95 (2008)
35. Xiang, Y.: Quantifying into wh-dependencies: multiple-wh questions and questions with a quantifier. Linguist. Philos. **46**, 429–482 (2023)

Two Places Where We Need Plug-Negation in Update Semantics: Symmetrical Presupposition Filtering and Exclusive Disjunction

Yusuke Yagi$^{(\boxtimes)}$

University of Connecticut, Storrs, CT 06269, USA
yusuke.yagi@uconn.edu

Abstract. This study investigates the projection problem of presuppositions, focusing on projection from disjunctions. I argue that we need what I call *the plug-negation*, the negation that filters presuppositions in two places. One is within the definition of disjunction that validates the symmetrical presupposition filtering effect [13], and the other is within the definition of exclusive disjunction. Without the plug-negation, a presupposition of a disjunct in those cases is wrongly predicted to project unconditionally, which would cause a violation of genuineness [22]. The violation is avoided with the plug-negation. I also propose that the appearance of the plug-negation is conditioned as a last-resort option.

Keywords: disjunction · presupposition projection · symmetry · exclusivity · update semantics

1 Background

This study investigates two observations that have posed issues for theories of presupposition projection from disjunctions. Below, I notate a proposition ϕ with a presupposition p as ϕ_p. Exclusive disjunction is noted with $\bar{\vee}$. The primary concerns of this study are disjunctions $\phi \vee \psi_p$, $\phi_p \vee \psi$, and $\phi\bar{\vee}\psi_q$.

The presupposition p in $\phi \vee \psi_p$ becomes the presupposition of the entire disjunction (i.e., the presupposition *projects*) except when $\neg\phi$ entails p [14]. For example, the presupposition $[_p$ *John used to smoke*$]$, triggered by the verb *stop*, projects and is presupposed by the entire disjunction in (1a), where the disjuncts are logically independent of each other. On the other hand, p is not presupposed by the disjunction in (1b), where $\neg\phi$ entails p.

(1)   a.   Either $[_\phi$ John is out of money] or $[_\psi$ he **stopped** smoking].
            Presuppose: John used to smoke.

      b.   Either $[_\phi$ John never used to smoke] or $[_\psi$ he **stopped** smoking].
            No presupposition

D. Bekki et al. (Eds.): LENLS 2023, LNCS 14569, pp. 307–320, 2024.
https://doi.org/10.1007/978-3-031-60878-0_17

This study addresses two issues. One is due to the presupposition filtering effect observed above is *symmetrical*. Although the symmetry had only been sporadically noted in the literature since [14], a recent experimental study confirms this point [13]. Thus, the presupposition is filtered when the order of disjuncts in (1b) is swapped, as in (2). In general, $\phi_p \vee \psi$ does not presuppose p when $\neg \psi$ entails p.

(2)   Either [$_\phi$ John **stopped** smoking] or [$_\psi$ he never used to smoke].
No presupposition

The other issue is presupposition projection from exclusive disjunction, which has yet to receive attention in the literature on presupposition projection (except for [18]). Some natural language disjunctions are obligatorily interpreted exclusively. English *either...or...*, French *soit...soit...* [20], and Japanese *ka...ka...dochiraka* are a few examples. Notice that the disjunctions in (1) and (2) are formed with *either...or...*. If they are obligatorily interpreted exclusively, the generalization by [14] should be restated so that the presupposition $\phi \veebar \psi_p$ does not presuppose p except when $\neg \phi$ entails p.

Any theory of presupposition projection should predict the symmetrical behavior and the filtering effect in exclusive disjunction. As I demonstrate below, the currently available theories fail to do so. I discuss two such theories: Strong Kleene trivalent logic and Update Semantics [10]. To overcome the issues, I propose to extend Update Semantics by augmenting it with the *plug-negation*, a negation that filters the presupposition of its prejacent. It is further proposed that the plug-negation is conditioned as a last-resort option: it only appears to avoid undefinedness that would occur otherwise.

The rest of this paper is organized as follows. Sections 2 and 3 discuss the Strong Kleene logic and Update Semantics, respectively, to show the empirical issues these theories face. Section 4 is devoted to demonstrating how the plug-negation resolves the issues. In Sect. 5, I show that *Innocent Exclusion* [6] alone does not resolve the issue either, and how the proposal can be extended as a dynamicized floating-A theory [2]. A remaining issue is also discussed there. Section 6 concludes.

2   Strong Kleene Trivalent Logic

The Strong Kleene logic is a trivalent logic that has three values for propositions: 1 for *true*, 0 for *false*, and * for *undefined*. I assume propositions receive the * value only when their presupposition is false. The disjunction is defined as:

Definition 1. *Strong Kleene Disjunction*

ϕ

$\vee$	1	0	$*$
1	1	1	1
0	1	0	$*$
$*$	1	$*$	$*$

ψ labels the rows.

The presupposition of a proposition is the prerequisite for the proposition to be bivalent (i.e., 1 or 0). Consider the case of $\phi \vee \psi_p$ under this definition. The disjunction is bivalent when $\phi \vee p$ holds, or equivalently, $\neg\phi \rightarrow p$ holds. Thus, the disjunction presupposes $\neg\phi \rightarrow p$.

When $\neg\phi$ entails p in $\phi \vee \psi_p$, the presupposition of the disjunction is a tautology. Ignoring exclusivity for now, (1b) is predicted to presuppose [$_{\neg\phi}$ *if John used to smoke*], [$_p$ *he used to smoke*], which is tautologically true in any worlds. Hence, the disjunction does not presuppose anything.

The Strong Kleene disjunction predicts (1a) to presuppose [$_{\neg\phi}$ *if John is not out of money*], [$_p$ *he used to smoke*], which is weaker than the presupposition observed there. This issue is dubbed as the *Proviso problem* [7]. The proviso problem is inherited by almost any theories of presupposition projection, notably except for versions of *Discourse Representation Theory* [8,16,19]. I ignore the Proviso problem in this study, but see [17] for an overview of proposed solutions.

The Strong Kleene disjunction correctly predicts the symmetrical filtering effect. Consider the case of $\phi_p \vee \psi$. The disjunction is bivalent when $\neg\psi \rightarrow p$ holds. Therefore, (2) is predicted to presuppose a tautology, hence filtering the presupposition.

However, the Strong Kleene logic does not predict the projection behavior of exclusive disjunction. Exclusive disjunction is defined as Definition 2 by [18]. $\phi \bar{\vee} \psi$ is bivalent when both ϕ and ψ are bivalent. Thus, $\phi \bar{\vee} \psi_p$ and $\phi_p \bar{\vee} \psi$ presupposes p, i.e., the presupposition of a disjunct projects unconditionally.

Definition 2. *Strong Kleene Exclusive Disjunction*

ϕ

$\bar{\vee}$	1	0	$*$
1	0	1	$*$
0	1	0	$*$
$*$	$*$	$*$	$*$

ψ labels the rows.

Consider again (1a) and (1b) then. *Either...or...* marks that the disjunction is exclusive. The Strong Kleene exclusive disjunction predicts the presupposition p to project. This is a welcome result for (1a), and it is indeed proposed by [18] that the Proviso problem is solved by interpreting the disjunction exclusively. However, it is a wrong prediction for (1b), not only because (1b) does not presuppose p, but also because the projection of p necessarily leads to a violation of *genuineness* [22]. Genuineness states that natural language disjunction is felicitous only if all the disjuncts are 'live possibilities.' Notice that, in (1b), $\phi \wedge p = \bot$. If p projects, it necessarily entails that ϕ is false and renders ϕ

not a live possibility, hence violating genuineness. The exclusive interpretation, which is obligatory because of *either...or...*, predicts (1b) to be an infelicitous disjunction, which is again contrary to fact.

3   Update Semantics

Dynamic semantics also has been developed aiming at accounting for presupposition projection since [12]. In this section, I discuss a version of dynamic semantics – *Update Semantics* [2,10,21]. Although Update Semantics is formulated to account for presupposition filtering in (1b), the symmetrical filtering and the projection from exclusive disjunction are not adequately analyzed.

In Update Semantics, sentences are translated into *context change potentials* (CCPs). A CCP takes a context (often called a *state*) s, a set of possible worlds, and updates it to a new state s'.

Definition 3. Let s be a state, a set of possible worlds, ϕ a proposition, a function from possible worlds to truth values. The update of s with ϕ is recursively defined as follows:

- $s[\phi] = \{w \mid \phi(w) = 1\}$
- $s[\neg\phi] = s/s[\phi]$
- $[\phi \wedge \psi] = s[\phi][\psi] = (s[\phi])[\psi]$
- $[\phi \vee \psi] = s[\phi] \cup s[\neg\phi][\psi]$

If ϕ has presupposition p, $s[\phi_p]$ should be defined only if p is true in every world in s. That is, the presupposition p is a prerequisite that must be satisfied for the update with ϕ to be defined. When the update is undefined, it returns $\star$ for *undefinedness*.

Definition 4. Let ϕ_p be a proposition with a presupposition p. The update of a state s with ϕ_p is defined as

- $s[\phi_p] = \begin{cases} \{w \mid \phi(w) = 1\} & \text{if } s[p] = s \\ \star & \text{otherwise} \end{cases}$

For the discussion that follows, suppose that $s/\star = \star$, $s \cup \star = \star \cup s = \star$. Then, the presupposition of a proposition ϕ is a condition for $s[\phi] \neq \star$.

The update with a disjunction in Definition 3 is designed so that it accounts for the presupposition filtering in (1b). For any s, $s[\phi \vee \psi_p] = s[\phi] \cup s[\neg\phi][\psi_p]$, and for it to be defined, $s[\neg\phi][\psi_p] \neq \star$. This is the case (for any s) if $\neg\phi$ entails p, because then p is true in every world in $s[\neg\phi]$. Since $\neg\phi$ indeed entails p in (1b), the disjunction presupposes nothing. For (1a), the definition predicts the weaker, conditional presupposition, $\neg\phi \rightarrow p$. Thus, Update Semantics also faces the Provio problem, although the issue is ignored here.

However, the definition does not predict the symmetrical filtering effect. For any s, $s[\phi_p \vee \psi] = s[\phi_p] \cup [\neg\phi_p][\psi]$. $s[\phi_p] \neq \star$ only if p is true in every world in s. But then the presupposition projects whatever ψ is, contrary to fact. In order to predict the filtering effect in $\phi_p \vee \psi$, we need another definition of disjunction, namely:

(3) $s[\phi \vee \psi] = s[\neg\psi][\phi] \cup [\psi]$

It predicts p in $\phi_p \vee \psi$ to be filtered when $\neg\psi$ entails p. The two definitions differ in presupposition projection behaviors. To predict the presupposition filtering in (1b) and (2), we need to define an update by a disjunction as:

(4) $s[\phi \vee \psi] = s[\phi] \cup s[\neg\phi][\psi]$ $\text{ or } s[\neg\psi][\phi] \cup [\psi]$

However, the disjunctive definition faces conceptual and empirical doubt. Conceptually, the disjunctive definition makes disjunction ambiguous, which is an unwelcome consequence. A more general definition must be pursued. One may wonder if the update defined as (5) is general enough.

(5) $s[\phi \vee \psi] = s[\neg\psi][\phi] \cup s[\neg\phi][\psi]$

This is not the case. Notice that in this definition, the disjunction is exclusive. As expected from the discussion in the previous section, (5) unconditionally projects a presupposition of the disjuncts. Suppose that ψ has a presupposition p. $s[\neg\psi_p] = s/s[\psi_p]$, and since $s/\star = \star$, $s/s[\psi_p] \neq \star$ only if $s[\psi_p] \neq \star$. But then p must be true in every world in s, hence projecting p. The same reasoning holds for the cases where ϕ has a presupposition.

Empirically, the definition in (5) is insufficient to account for projection behaviors of disjunction fully. So far, we have seen that a presupposition of one disjunct is filtered if the negation of the other disjunct entails it. Another pattern of presupposition filtering in disjunction is observed by [11]: in $\phi_p \vee \psi_q$, neither p nor q projects if p and q are inconsistent, i.e., $p \wedge q = \bot$. This is exemplified in (6) (which is supposed to be interpreted with the world knowledge that no country has both a king and a president).

(6)   Either [$_\phi$ **the king** of Buganda is now opening a parliament], or [$_\psi$ **the President** of Buganda is conducting the ceremony].
Not presuppose: There is a (unique) king in Buganda
Not presuppose: There is a (president) in Buganda.

The definitions available so far predict (6) to be always undefined. Consider the definition in Definition 3. $s[\phi_p \vee \psi_q] = s[\phi_p] \cup s[\neg\phi_p][\psi_q]$, and $s[\neg\phi_p]$ is defined if p is true in every worlds in s. Suppose it is defined, and $s[\neg\phi_p] = s'$. $s'[\psi_q]$ defined only if q is true in every world in s', but it cannnot be the case. Since $s' \subseteq s$, p is true in every world in s' as well, and since $p \wedge q = \bot$, q is false in every world in s'. Therefore, $s[\neg\phi_p][\psi_q] = \star$, and $s[\phi_p \vee \psi_q] = \star$ in the case of (21). The same reasoning holds for the other definitions considered so far.

The above discussion shows that symmetrical filtering calls for the disjunctive definition of disjunction, but more is needed for full generality.

So far, we have ignored the obligatory exclusive interpretation of *either...or....* If the disjunction is exclusive, the current Update Semantics also makes a wrong prediction. This is already shown in the above discussion. Defining $s[\phi \bar{\vee} \psi] = s[\neg\psi][\phi] \cup s[\neg\phi][\psi]$, it is clear (as shown above) that a presupposition of disjuncts projects unconditionally, contrary to fact.

4   Proposal

The starting point of the current proposal is to take the exclusive interpretation of *either...or...* disjunction seriously. I posit that the disjunctions in (1) and (2) induce updates by exclusive disjunction, defined as (7).

Definition 5. Update s with exclusive disjunction

- $s[\phi \bar{\vee} \psi] = s[\neg\psi][\phi] \cup s[\neg\phi][\psi]$

In the previous section, we observed that this definition predicts a presupposition of the disjuncts to project unconditionally. The unconditional projection is due to the definition of negation. The negation defined in Definition 3 captures the projection behavior of natural language negation, exemplified in (7): $\neg\phi_p$ presupposes p.

(7)   John did**n't stop** smoking.
       Presuppose: John used to smoke.

The definition is also designed to replicate the prediction made by the negation defined as (8) in trivalent logic. There, $\neg\phi$ is defined only if ϕ is defined, projecting the presupposition of ϕ.

(8)

ϕ	$\neg\phi$
1	0
0	1
*	*

However, negation can also be defined as (9), which I call the *plug-negation* (after *presupposition plug* in [14]). $-\phi$ is always bivalent even when ϕ is undefined (in such cases $-\phi = 1$). Hence, it always voids the presupposition of its prejacent.

(9)

ϕ	$-\phi$
1	0
0	1
*	1

The plug-negation is defined as follows in Update Semantics.

Definition 6. The plug-negation in Update Semantics

- $s[-\phi] := s/\bigcup_{t_n \subseteq s \wedge t_n[\phi]=t_n} (t_n[\phi])$

Each t_n is a subset of s such that $t_n[\phi] = t_n$, that is, the presupposition of ϕ and ϕ itself are true in all worlds in t_n. The generalized union collects $t_n[\phi]$ (which is t_n itself by definition) and subtracts it from s. Thus, it subtracts all worlds where ϕ is defined and true. The resultant state contains the worlds in s where ϕ is undefined, or defined and false.

The proposal is to interpret the disjunctions in (1) and (2) exclusively and adopt the plug-negation when necessary (the exact formulation of when it is used follows shortly). A similar proposal is pursued by [3] within the trivalent logic, although they didn't consider the problem caused by obligatory exclusivity. I formulate the idea in Update Semantics.

Consider the case of (2), $\phi_p \bar{\vee} \psi$. The presupposition filtering is correctly accounted for if the induced update is (10).

(10) $s[(2)] = s[\neg\psi][\phi_p] \cup s[-\phi_p][\psi]$

Notice that $s[-\phi_p]$ never results in $\star$. Thus, the right-hand side of the union does not induce any presuppositions. The left-hand side of the union is computed in the same way as above. $s[\neg\psi][\phi_p] \neq \star$ as long as p is true in all the $\neg\psi$-worlds in s, that is, as long as $\neg\psi$ entails p. This is indeed the case in (2); there is no presupposition.

By swapping $\neg$ and $-$ in (10), we also correctly predict the projection behavior in (1b).

(11) $s[(1b)] = s[-\psi_p][\phi] \cup s[\neg\phi][\psi_p]$

Furthermore, if no plug-negation is involved, the fact that (1a) presupposes p is also accounted for, as attempted by [18], avoiding the Proviso problem.

(12) $s[(1a)] = s[\neg\psi_p][\phi] \cup s[\neg\phi][\psi_p]$

4.1 Constraining the Plug-Negation

The plug-negation should be used only when necessary as a last-resort option. We encounter the proviso problem otherwise: if (1a) is interpreted as inducing the update $s[-\psi_p][\phi] \cup s[\neg\phi][\psi_p]$, for example, the disjunction should only presuppose $\neg\phi \rightarrow p$.

I propose that the normal negation, $\neg$, in a formula α is replaced by the plug negation, $-$, only when $s[\alpha] = \star$ for any s. That is, $-$ is used when the formula will necessarily result in undefinedness.

To formulate the proposal, I follow [9] and assume that disjunction (inclusive or exclusive) presupposes *genuineness* [22]. Suppose that $s' = s[\phi \vee \psi]$. Genuineness states that the utterance of disjunction in s is felicitous only if there is a world $w \in s'$ such that $\phi(w) = 1$, and a world w' such that $\psi(w') = 1$. In words, $\phi \vee \psi$ requires that both disjuncts are 'live possibilities.' Formally, genuineness requires that the left-hand side and the right-hand side of the union in Definition 5 be non-vacuous. Borrowing the idea from [1], I formulate the non-vacuity requirement with the formula NE (for *non-empty*). Since the non-vacuity is a presupposition for disjunction, $s[\text{NE}]$ returns $\star$ if $s = \emptyset$.

Definition 7.

$$- s[\text{NE}] = \begin{cases} s \text{ if } s \neq \emptyset \\ \star \text{ otherwise} \end{cases}$$

The update by exclusive disjunction, augmented with genuineness, is defined as follows.

Definition 8. Update s with exclusive disjunction (with genuineness)

$$- s[\phi \bar{\vee} \psi] = s[\neg \psi][\phi][\text{NE}] \cup s[\neg \phi][\psi][\text{NE}]$$

I propose the *replacement condition* for the plug-negation in (13).

(13)   *Replacement Condition*
Suppose that α is a proposition translated from a natural language sentence S, and that α contains one or more negation $\neg$. α^- is obtained by replacing some $\neg$ in α by the plug-negation. S is interpreted as α^- instead of α only if:
$s[\alpha] = \star$ for any s, and there is s' such that $s'[\alpha^-] \neq \star$.

Consider the case of (1b), $\phi \bar{\vee} \psi_p$, where $\phi \wedge p = \bot$. Observe:

(14) $s[\phi \bar{\vee} \psi_p] = s[\neg \psi_p][\phi][\text{NE}] \cup s[\neg \phi][\psi_p][\text{NE}] = \star$ for any s, if $\phi \wedge p = \bot$.

This is because of the left-hand side of the union. $s[\neg \psi_p] \neq \star$ as long as p is true in all worlds in s. Suppose then that $s[\neg \psi_p] = \star$, and $s[\neg \psi_p]$ is not empty. But then $s[\neg \psi_p][\phi] = \emptyset$, because $\phi \wedge p = \bot$ by assumption. Then $s[\neg \phi_p][\phi][\text{NE}] = \star$, and the update results in $\star$. This is the case for any s.

Thus, the negation $\neg$ can be replaced with the plug-negation to avoid undefinedness. What should be replaced is the negation in the left-hand side of the union. Thus, we obtain (15), which correctly predicts the presupposition projection behavior.

(15) $s[-\psi_p][\phi][\text{NE}] \cup s[\neg \phi][\psi_p][\text{NE}]$

The same reasoning holds for the case of (2), $\phi_p \bar{\vee} \psi$:

(16) $s[\phi_p \bar{\vee} \psi] = s[\neg\psi][\phi_p][\text{NE}] \cup s[\neg\phi_p][\psi][\text{NE}] = \star$ for any s, if $\psi \wedge p = \bot$.

In this case, the undefinedness is due to the right-hand side of the union. Thus, the negation should be replaced with the plug-negation, obtaining (17). Again, it correctly predicts the presupposition projection behavior.

(17) $s[\neg\psi][\phi_p][\text{NE}] \cup s[-\phi_p][\psi][\text{NE}]$

The current replacement condition does not allow the plug-negation to be involved in the case of (1a). Since ϕ and p are consistent there, there is some s such that $s[\neg\psi_p][\phi][\text{NE}] \cup s[\neg\phi][\psi_p][\text{NE}] \neq \star$. Therefore, the disjunction should be interpreted with the canonical negation ($\neg$), and as a result, the presupposition projects in the non-conditional form, avoiding the Proviso problem.

The proposed replacement condition thus eliminates the arbitrariness of updates by disjunction. By default, the update with disjunction is as defined in Definition 5 and a presupposition of the disjunct projects. By taking the exclusivity of *either...or...* conditional seriously and encoding it within the definition of the update, the Proviso problem is avoided, as proposed by [18]. The replacement condition allows the plug-negation to cancel a presupposition if the update by disjunction would necessarily lead to undefinedness otherwise.

5   Discussions and a Remaining Issue

5.1   Discussion 1: Innocent Exclusion Does Not Avoid the Problem

There is accumulated literature that proposes to derive the exclusivity of disjunction by the operation *exhaustification* [4–6]. Exhaustifying a proposition ϕ, $\text{EXH}(\phi)$, results in asserting ϕ and negating certain *alternatives* to ϕ. The alternatives for disjunction $\phi \vee \psi$ is argued to be ϕ, ψ, and $\phi \wedge \psi$. Negating all of the alternatives with asserting $\phi \vee \psi$ results in a contradiction:

(18) $(\phi \vee \psi) \wedge \neg\phi \wedge \neg\psi \wedge (\phi \wedge \psi)$

Thus, exhaustification only negates *innocently excludable alternatives* [6], $\text{EXH}(\phi)$, which is defined as follows.

Definition 9. Exhaustification and Innocent Exclusion

- $\text{EXH}(\phi) := \phi \wedge \forall\psi \in IE(\phi, \text{ALT}_\phi) : \neg\psi$

- $IE(\phi, \text{ALT}) := \cap \left\{ A \left| \begin{array}{l} A \subseteq \text{ALT}_\phi \ \& \ A \text{ is a maximal subset of } \text{ALT}_\phi \text{ such that} \\ \{\neg p \mid p \in A\} \cup \phi \text{ is consistent} \end{array} \right. \right\}$,

  where ALT_ϕ is the set of alternatives of ϕ, and a set of propositions is *consistent* if and only if there is a world w in which all the propositions in the set are true.

For disjunction $\phi \vee \psi$, $\text{ALT}_{\phi \vee \psi} = \{\phi \wedge \psi, \phi, \psi\}$. The maximal subsets of $\text{ALT}_{\phi \vee \psi}$ that meet the consistency condition is $\{\phi \wedge \psi, \phi\}$ and $\{\phi \wedge \psi, \psi\}$, because $\{\phi \vee \psi, \neg(\phi \wedge \psi), \neg\phi\}$ and $\{\phi \vee \psi, \neg(\phi \wedge \psi), \neg\psi\}$, are consistent. The set of innocently exclusive alternatives is the intersection of these two sets, $\{\phi \wedge \psi, \phi\} \cap \{\phi \wedge \psi, \psi\}$, hence $\{\phi \wedge \psi\}$. The exhaustification of the disjunction negates the proposition in this set, which results in $(\phi \vee \psi) \wedge \neg(\phi \wedge \psi)$, exclusive disjunction.

One may wonder if the sophisticated definition of *innocent exclusion* hinders the projection of a presupposition when it leads to a violation of genuineness and the plug-negation is unnecessary. This is not the case. Suppose that $\text{ALT}_{\phi \vee \psi_p} = \{\phi, \psi_p, \phi \wedge \psi_p\}$. The set of innocently excludable alternatives is determined as in (19). $\{\phi \vee \psi_p, \neg\psi_p\}$ is never consistent. For $\neg\psi_p$ to be true, p must be true and ψ must be false (recall the truth table of negation above). Since $\phi \wedge p = \perp$, in any world where p is true, ϕ is false. There is no world where both propositions in the set are true, which means that ψ_p is not in the innocently excludable set. On the other hand, $\{\phi \vee \psi_p, \neg\phi\}$ is consistent when ϕ is false and ψ_p is true, and so are $\{\phi \vee \psi_p, \neg(\phi \wedge \psi_p)\}$ and $\{\phi \vee \psi_p, \neg\phi, \neg(\phi \wedge \psi_p)\}$. Therefore, $\{\phi, \phi \wedge \psi_p\}$ is the maximal subset of $\text{ALT}_{\phi \vee \psi_p}$ which meets the consistency condition.

(19)   a. $\{\phi \vee \psi_p, \neg\psi_p\}$: inconsistent. $p = 1$ for $\neg\psi_p = 1$. By the assumption that $\phi \wedge p = \perp$, $\phi = 0$.

   b. $\{\phi \vee \psi_p, \neg\phi\}$: consistent if $\phi = 0$ and $\psi_p = 1$ (hence $p = 1$)

   c. $\{\phi \vee \psi_p, \neg(\phi \wedge \psi_p)\}$: consistent if $\phi = 0$ and $\psi_p = 1$.

   d. $\{\phi \vee \psi_p, \neg\phi, \neg(\phi \wedge \psi_p)\}$: consistent if $\phi = 0$ and $\psi_p = 1$.

Then $\text{EXH}(\phi \vee \psi_p)$ will results in (20), which *entails* ψ_p. Thus, it still violates genuineness and predicts the unwanted presupposition projection. Exhaustification with innocent exclusion, therefore, does not provide a solution.

(20) $(\phi \vee \psi_p) \wedge \neg\phi \wedge \neg(\phi \wedge \psi_p)$
       $\leadsto \psi_p$

5.2   Discussion 2: The Case of Conflicting Presuppositions and the Floating-A Theory

Recall that $\phi_p \bar{\vee} \psi_q$ presupposes neither p nor q when p and q are inconsistent.

(21)   Either [$_\phi$ **the king** of Buganda is now opening a parliament], or [$_\psi$ **the President** of Buganda is conducting the ceremony].
       Not presuppose: There is a (unique) king in Buganda
       Not presuppose: There is a (president) in Buganda.

The default definition of updates by disjunction results in $\star$.

(22) $s[\phi_p \bar{\vee} \psi] = s[\neg\psi_q][\phi_p][\text{NE}] \cup s[\neg\phi_p][\psi_q][\text{NE}] = \star$ for any s, if $p \wedge q = \bot$.

The undefinedness ensues on both sides of the union in (22). Thus, the replacement condition allows us to interpret the update as (23).

(23) $s[-\psi_q][\phi_p][\text{NE}] \cup s[-\phi_p][\psi_q][\text{NE}]$

However, this update is defined only when the disjunction is not informative, that is, only when the disjunction is true in all worlds in s. To see this, consider $s = \{w_{1,\phi p}, w_{2,\psi q}, w_{3,p}, w_{4,q}\}$, where the subscripts show the propositions that are true in a world. As shown in (24), both sides of the union still result in undefinedness.

(24)   a. $s[-\psi_q] = \{w_{1,\phi p}, w_{3,p}, w_{4,q}\}$

b. $s[-\psi_q][\phi_p] = \star$

c. $s[-\phi_p] = \{w_{2,\psi q}, w_{3,p}, w_{4,q}\}$

d. $s[-\psi_q][\phi_p] = \star$

In fact, the update is defined only when $s = \{w_{1,\phi p}, w_{2,\psi q}\}$, where the update by the disjunction is uninformative. This, in turn, means that an update by the negation of the disjunction always results in an empty state. Since $s[\neg(\phi_p \vee \psi_q)]$ is defined only if $s[(\phi_p \vee \psi_q)]$, the input s for $s[\neg(\phi_p \vee \psi_q)]$ should be $\{w_{1,\phi p}, w_{2,\psi q}\}$. But then $s[\neg(\phi_p \vee \psi_q)] = \emptyset$, as long as it is defined. That is, in no world is $\neg(\phi_p \vee \psi_q)$ true.

This problem also arises for the Strong Kleene disjunction, as pointed out by [2]. Consider $\phi_p \vee \psi_q$ $(p \wedge q = \bot)$ under Definition 1 and Definition 2. If the disjunction is interpreted exclusively, both p and q must be presupposed, resulting in a contradiction. If it is interpreted inclusively, the disjunction is never false. This is because ϕ_p and ψ_q cannot be simultaneously false. If ϕ_p is defined and false, for instance, ψ_q is undefined for the inconsistency of the presuppositions. Then, the disjunction as a whole is undefined. The same reasoning holds when ψ_q is defined and false.

Thus, both Update Semantics and Strong Kleene trivalent logic face the same issue. One way to solve this problem is to incorporate the *floating-A* theory in [3]. The floating-A theory states that the *assertion operator* (A) defined as follows can be inserted into a formula to cancel (i.e., *locally accommodate*) the presupposition of its prejacent.

Definition 10. Assertion Operator in trivalent logic

ϕ	$A\phi$
1	1
0	0
*	0

The effect of the A-operator is replicated with the following definition in Update Semantics:

Definition 11. Assertion Operator Update Semantics

$$- s[A\phi] := \bigcup_{t_n \subseteq s \wedge t_n[\phi]=t_n} (t_n[\phi])$$

Consider then the update in (25), where $s = \{w_{1,\phi p}, w_{2,\psi q}, w_{3,p}, w_{4,q}\}$. The union of (25b) and (25d) results in the intuitively correct result.

(25) $s[-\psi_q][A\phi_p][\text{NE}] \cup s[-\phi_p][A\psi_q][\text{NE}]$

    a. $s[-\psi_q] = \{w_{1,\phi p}, w_{3,p}, w_{4,q}\}$

    b. $s[-\psi_q][A\phi_p] = \{w_{1,\phi p}\}$

    c. $s[-\phi_p] = \{w_{2,\psi q}, w_{3,p}, w_{4,q}\}$

    d. $s[-\psi_q][\phi_p] = \{w_{2,\psi q}\}$

Moreover, the negation of the disjunction in question, $\neg(\phi_p \vee \psi_q)$, can also be defined and non-empty.

(26) $s[\neg(\phi_p \vee \psi_q)] = s/(s[-\psi_q][A\phi_p][\text{NE}] \cup s[-\phi_p][A\psi_q][\text{NE}]) = \{w_{3,p}, w_{4,q}\}$

The plug-negation motivated in the last section can be defined in terms of the A-operator and the canonical negation $\neg$.

(27) $-\phi \equiv \neg A\phi$

Therefore, the update considered above can be equivalently represented as (28).

(28) $s[\neg A\psi_q][A\phi_p][\text{NE}] \cup s[\neg A\phi_p][A\psi_q][\text{NE}]$

What we need, then, is a more general condition on the use of the A-operator. Recall that, as discussed in the previous section, the insertion of A is necessary to avoid undefinedness. In this section, we saw that the A-operator should be inserted in two other cases. One is when the update would be otherwise trivial, as in the case of (21). The other case is when the update necessarily results in an empty set, as in the case of the negation of (21). To cover these cases, the constraint on the A-operator should be stated as (29).

(29) A inserted to arbitrary positions in the formula ϕ if and only if

    a. $s[\phi] = \star$ for any s, or

    b. $s[\phi] = s$ for any s, or

    c. $s[\phi] = \emptyset$ for any s.

That is, the A-operator is inserted to avoid *undefinedness*, *triviality*, and *inconsistency*. The proposal is in the same spirit as the one of [19], although avoiding undefinedness was not discussed there.

5.3 A Remaining Issue

I conclude this section by pointing out one remaining issue. Observe that (30) has a conditional presupposition [15].

(30)   Either [$_\phi$ John is not a scuba diver], or [$_\psi$ he forgot to bring his wet suit]
    Presuppose: If John is a scuba diver, he has a wet suit.

In the current theory, the conditional presupposition arises if the A-operator is inserted as:

(31) $s[\neg A\psi_q][\phi][\text{NE}] \cup s[\neg\phi][\psi_q][\text{NE}]$

What motivates the insertion of the operator, however? Even if we presuppose that John has a wet suit, that would not contradict the claim that John is not a scuba diver. Thus, the left-hand side of the union could be defined and non-vacuous without A. The triviality is also absent here. Therefore, the proposed analysis does not predict the conditional presupposition.

One possibility is that undefinedness still arises here. This is the case if the speaker firmly believes that everyone who has a wet suit is a scuba diver. Then, the presupposition that John has a wet suit would contradict John's not being a scuba diver, and the A operator is motivated. I leave this issue open for future work.

6   Conclusion

In this study, it is observed that the symmetrical filtering and the obligatory exclusive interpretation of disjunction pause empirical problems for the prediction made by Update Semantics. I proposed to take the exclusive interpretation of *either...or...* as the default interpretation, which avoids the Proviso problem. The presupposition filtring effect is accounted for by the plug-negation, or the A-operator ultimately, which is constrained as a last-resort option to avoid undefinedness, triviality, and/or inconsistency.

References

1. Aloni, M.: Logic and conversation: the case of free choice. Semant. Pragmatics **15**, 1–60 (2022). https://doi.org/10.3765/sp.15.5
2. Beaver, D.: Presupposition and Assertion in Dynamic Semantics. CLSI, Stanford (2001)
3. Beaver, D., Krahmer, E.: A partial account of presupposition projection. J. Logic Lang. Inform. **10**, 147–182 (2001)
4. Chierchia, G.: Scalar implicatures, polarity phenomena and the syntax/pragmatics interface. In: Belletti, A. (ed.) Structures and Beyond: The Cartography of Syntactic Structures, vol. 3, pp. 39–103. Oxford University Press (2004)
5. Chierchia, G.: Broaden your views: implicatures of domain widening and the "Logicality" of language. Linguist. Inquiry **37**(4), 535–590 (2006). http://www.jstor.org/stable/4179384
6. Fox, D.: Free choice disjunction and the theory of scalar implicature. In: Sauerland, U., Stateva, P. (eds.) Presupposition and Implicature in Compositional Semantics, pp. 71–120. Palgrave Macmillan, New York (2007)
7. Geurts, B.: Local satisfaction guaranteed: a presupposition theory and its problems. Linguist. Philos. **19**(3), 259–294 (1996). http://www.jstor.org/stable/25001627
8. Geurts, B.: Presuppositions and Pronouns. Elsevier, Amsterdam (1999)
9. Goldstein, S.: Free choice and homogeneity. Semant. Pragmatics **12**(23), 1–47 (2019). https://doi.org/10.3765/sp.12.23
10. Groenendijk, J., Stokhofand, M., Veltman, F.: Coreference and modality. In: Lappin, S. (ed.) Handbook of Contemporary Semantic Theory, pp. 179–216. Blackwell (1996)
11. Hausser, R.R.: Presuppositions in Montague grammar. Theor. Linguist. **3**(1–3), 245–280 (1976). https://doi.org/10.1515/thli.1976.3.1-3.245
12. Heim, I.: The semantics and definite and indefinite noun phrases. Ph.D. thesis, Umass Amherst (1982)
13. Kalomoiros, A., Schwarz, F.: Presupposition projection from disjunction is symmetric. In: Proceedings of the Linguistic Society of America, vol. 6, pp. 556–571. Linguistic Society of America (2021). https://doi.org/10.3765/plsa.v6i1.4989
14. Karttunen, L.: Presuppositions of compound sentences. Linguist. Inquiry **4**, 169–193 (1973)
15. Katzir, R., Singh, R.: Two restrictions on possible connectives. In: Theories of Everything In Honor of Ed Keenan, pp. 154–162 (2012). UCLA Working Papers in Linguistics, Theories of Everything
16. Krahmer, E.: Presupposition and Anaphora. CSLI, Stanford (1998)
17. Mandelkern, M.: A note on the architecture of presupposition. Semant. Pragmatics **9**, 1–24 (2016). https://doi.org/10.3765/sp.9.13
18. Mayr, C., Romoli, J.: Satisfied or exhaustified: an ambiguity account of the proviso problem. In: Proceedings of SALT, vol. 26, pp. 892–912. Linguistic Society of America (2016). https://doi.org/10.3765/salt.v26i0.3961
19. van der Sandt, R.A.: Presupposition projection and anaphora resolution. J. Semant. **9**, 333–377 (1992)
20. Spector, B.: Global positive polarity items and obligatory exhaustivity. Semant. Pragmatics **7** (2014). https://doi.org/10.3765/sp.7.11
21. Veltman, F.: Defaults in update semantics. J. Philos. Logic **25**(3), 221–261 (1996). http://www.jstor.org/stable/30226572
22. Zimmermann, T.E.: Free choice disjunction and epistemic modality. Nat. Lang. Seman. **8**(4), 255–290 (2000). https://doi.org/10.1023/a:1011255819284

Topology and Justified True Belief: A Baseless, Evidence-Free (and Pointless) Approach

Kohei Kishida(✉)

University of Illinois, Urbana-Champaign, Urbana, IL 61801, USA
kkishida@illinois.edu

Abstract. Topological spaces and their interior operators provide semantics for modal logic S4. This semantics has recently attracted an epistemic interpretation as a model of epistemic logic, on the basis of the idea that the generating of a topology from a "base" can be interpreted as the justifying of knowledge with evidence. This is called the evidence-based approach. This paper proposes an alternative approach that may be called evidence-free, in the sense that a topology or knowledge is generated from something other than a base or evidence. (We also use the algebraic, "pointless" formalism of topology, so as to more perspicuously present the structural essence of the correspondence between semantics and logic.) The new semantics provides a logic that describes the relationship between belief and a notion of justified true belief.

Keywords: epistemic logic · knowledge · belief · justification · topology

1 Introduction

As demonstrated by the seminal result of McKinsey and Tarski [9], topological spaces and their interior operators provide a semantics for propositional modal logic S4. This semantics has recently attracted an epistemic interpretation, thereby modelling S4 as epistemic logic. This epistemic reading of topology is the topic of this paper.

Epistemic logic is a branch of modal logic that is driven by the question of what it means to say that "... knows that ...". A logician can approach this question either axiomatically or semantically. Let us write $\Box$ for the modal operator "α knows that ..." for an agent α. On the one hand, axiomatically, the logician can entertain various inference rules and axioms governing $\Box$, such as[1]

---

[1] $\top$ stands for truth or a tautology. (A4) and (A5) are normally called 4 and 5, but I adopt the labels (A4) and (A5) to avoid confusion.

© The Author(s), under exclusive license to Springer Nature Switzerland AG 2024
D. Bekki et al. (Eds.): LENLS 2023, LNCS 14569, pp. 321–336, 2024.
https://doi.org/10.1007/978-3-031-60878-0_18

$$\frac{\varphi \vdash \psi}{\Box\varphi \vdash \Box\psi}, \tag{M}$$

$$\vdash \Box\top, \tag{N}$$

$$\Box\varphi \wedge \Box\psi \vdash \Box(\varphi \wedge \psi), \tag{C}$$

$$\Box\varphi \vdash \varphi, \tag{T}$$

$$\Box\varphi \vdash \Box\Box\varphi, \tag{A4}$$

$$\neg\Box\varphi \vdash \Box\neg\Box\varphi. \tag{A5}$$

Adding these except (A5) to classical propositional logic gives modal logic S4. Further adding (A5) to S4 gives S5. On the other hand, semantically, if the logician uses Kripke semantics, they can entertain various constraints on the accessibility relation R among possible worlds: with $\Box$ for "α knows that ...", a pair of worlds w, v having wRv means that, when α is in w, v is an open possibility to α. On this relation, typical constraints include

- Reflexivity: wRw for every world w.
- Transitivity: wRv and vRu imply wRu.
- Euclideanness: wRv and wRu imply vRu.

The model theory of modal logic establishes that, while (M), (N), (C) give the modal logic of all Kripke semantics, (T), (A4), (A5) correspond respectively to reflexivity, transitivity, and Euclideanness of R. Therefore, for instance, the logician has to either endorse both of (T) and reflexivity at the same time or endorse neither. Nonetheless, when justifying formalism, the logician typically takes either an axioms-first approach, in which they first argue for or against axioms and then extend endorsement or rejection to the corresponding semantics, or a semantics-first approach, in which they first argue for or against semantics and then extend endorsement or rejection to the corresponding axioms. typical case of an axioms-first approach is philosophical reflection on axioms. When Hintikka [5] founded epistemic logic, he provided philosophical argument for the axioms of S4 but against (A5). This then commits Hintikka to endorsing a reflexive, transitive, but not Euclidean R. It would be harder to reflect upon transitivity or Euclideanness and discuss its philosophical cogency directly, than to discuss (A4) or (A5). In a similar example, Williamson [11] argued against (A4) rather than against transitivity. A prevalent case of a semantics-first approach is a "partition model" that is often used in multi-agent systems and distributed computing. It partitions the set of worlds into cells of ones that cannot be distinguished from α's perspective—which amounts to taking an accessibility relation R that is an equivalence relation, i.e., is reflexive, transitive, and Euclidean.[2] The use of this model then commits the logician to S5. But a crucial point is that the logician can justify the semantic structure as a reasonable model of epistemic situations they want to model—in the current example, features

---

[2] The combination of reflexivity and Euclideanness entails transitivity. It also entails the condition of symmetry: wRv implies vRw.

of multi-agent systems or distributed computing make it reasonable to use α-indistinguishability—quite independently of to which axioms of modal logic the structure corresponds.

In this dichotomy between axioms-first and semantics-first approaches, the recent application of topology to epistemic logic is a semantics-first one. A logician models epistemic situations in which an agent not only believes a proposition but also has some justification of it. Assumptions on how to formalize a notion of justification within the model then entail that the family of justified propositions forms a topology. This means, on the one hand, that the modal logic of the model is S4. On the other hand, and importantly, the logician can argue that the topological structure they have derived from a notion of justification is a reasonable model of epistemic situations surrounding justified belief, quite independently of modal logic. The primary goal of this paper is to provide a new way of deriving a topological structure from a notion of justification.

A preceding approach to topological semantics of epistemic logic can be called the *evidence-based* approach. This approach stems at least from two schools: One is evidence logic [3,4] on the basis of neighborhood semantics of modal logic, which led to the topological development comprehensively presented in Baltag et al. [2]. Another is the use of topology in expressing verifiability, falsifiability, and other properties of propositions, that was made in formal learning theory [6] or in logic in computer science [1,10]; a modal-logical rendering of this topological semantics was given in Kishida [7] (which predated [3,4]). In both schools, an essential component of formalism is a set of propositions called a *base*. One reads these propositions as representing pieces of *evidence*, and then, taking advantage of the conception of knowledge as *justified true belief*, generates a topology from the base to represent the justifying of knowledge with evidence.

This paper proposes an alternative approach that may be labelled *baseless* and *evidence-free*: this approach also takes advantage of the conception of knowledge as justified true belief, but it generates a topology or knowledge from something other than a base or evidence, thereby providing an alternative way of deriving a topological structure from a notion of justification. One advantage of the new approach is that the resulting logic has a modal operator for belief as well as one for knowledge, in such a way that it can explicitly describe the relationship between belief and justified belief.

As a matter of methodology, this paper uses an algebraic, "pointless" formulation of semantics and topology. In the point-set formulation of possible-world semantics, a model is given by a set X of worlds w along with an assignment of a subset $[\![\varphi]\!] \subset X$ to each proposition φ, so that $w \in [\![\varphi]\!]$ means that φ is true at the world w. For the sake of logic, however, the more essential feature of the model is not the relation $w \in [\![\varphi]\!]$ but the subset relation among (the interpretations of) propositions, $[\![\varphi]\!] \subseteq [\![\psi]\!]$, representing entailment $\varphi \vdash \psi$. The pointless formulation therefore abstracts away worlds w and the relation $\in$ from semantics and focuses on the algebra of propositions with $\leqslant$ for $\subseteq$. This enables us to more perspicuously present the essence of the correspondence between the semantic structure and its logic.

The paper proceeds as follows. We first review the basic concepts of topologies and interior operators in a pointless formulation in Sect. 2, and then review the evidence-based approach in Sect. 3. We propose an alternative approach, which we call baseless and evidence-free, in Sect. 4. We briefly discuss an application of our new formalism to the notion of common knowledge in Sect. 5 before concluding the paper.

2   Topologies and Interior Operators

Let us first review a definition of some of the most basic concepts in topology, namely, topologies and their interior operators, using a pointless formalism. We give the most general version of our definition in Subsect. 2.1, but discuss less general cases with more algebraic structures in Subsect. 2.2.

2.1   Definition and Basic Facts

In point-set topology, a topology is a certain subfamily of the powerset $\mathcal{P}X$ of a set X, and an interior operator is a certain map on $\mathcal{P}X$. Our pointless formulation, in full generality, uses a complete lattice L instead of $\mathcal{P}X$. This cannot be more general: the concept of topology makes essential use of joins of arbitrary size; therefore the definition needs a complete join-semilattice, but any complete join-semilattice is a complete lattice.

Definition 1. *Let L be a complete lattice. A* topology *on L is a subfamily of L that is closed under arbitrary joins. Note that $\bot$, the bottom element, is the empty join. Elements of a topology O are called* opens *of O. Given a topology O, its* interior operator *is a map*

$$\mathrm{int}_O : L \to L :: x \mapsto \bigvee_{u \in O, u \leqslant x} u.$$

This definition is unlike the usual one, in which a topology is closed under finite meets as well as arbitrary joins. Since the closure under finite meets plays a less crucial role in this paper, we use terminology in which a topology is required to be closed under arbitrary joins but not necessarily under finite meets, while we say that a topology is *proper* if it is also closed under finite meets.

Note that the definition of $\mathrm{int}_O\, x$ as a join characterizes int_O as follows: it is the map on L such that, for each $x \in L$, its value $\mathrm{int}_O\, x$ is the unique element of L satisfying the following two-way entailment for any $y \in L$.[3]

$$\frac{u \leqslant y \quad \text{for all } u \in O \text{ such that } u \leqslant x}{\mathrm{int}_O\, x \leqslant y} \tag{1}$$

---

[3] The definition of join used here is that, given a subset $I \subseteq L$ of a poset L, its join in L—if it exists—is a unique element $\bigvee_{x \in I} x$ of L satisfying

$$\frac{x \leqslant y \quad \text{for all } x \in I}{\bigvee_{x \in I} x \leqslant y}$$

for every $y \in L$.

Fact 1. *Let* $\text{int}_O : L \to L$ *be the interior operator of a topology O. Then*

i. int_O *satisfies the following rule and axioms.*

$$\frac{x \leqslant y}{\text{int}_O\, x \leqslant \text{int}_O\, y}, \tag{2}$$

$$\text{int}_O\, x \leqslant x, \tag{3}$$

$$\text{int}_O\, x \leqslant \text{int}_O \text{int}_O\, x. \tag{4}$$

We say that int_O *is* monotone *to mean that it satisfies* (2).

ii. int_O *satisfies the following axioms if O is a proper topology. Note that $\top$, the top element, is the empty meet.*

$$\top \leqslant \text{int}_O\, \top, \tag{5}$$

$$\text{int}_O\, x \wedge \text{int}_O\, y \leqslant \text{int}_O(x \wedge y). \tag{6}$$

iii. For each $x \in L$, we have $x \in O$ iff $x \leqslant \text{int}_O\, x$.

By (3) and (4), int_O is idempotent, *meaning that* $\text{int}_O \circ \text{int}_O = \text{int}_O$. By (3) and (iii), we have $x \in O$ iff $\text{int}_O\, x = x$.

(i) means that a modal operator $\square$ interpreted by int_O satisfies the rule and axioms corresponding to (2)–(4), i.e. (M), (T), (A4). Moreover, by (ii), $\square$ also satisfies (N) and (C) corresponding to (5) and (6), and therefore has modal logic S4 sound, if O is a proper topology.

Let us observe further that (2)–(4), or (2)–(6), characterize the interior operators of topologies or proper topologies. Indeed, topologies and interior operators are two expressions of the same information.

Definition 2. *Let L be a complete lattice. By an* interior operator *on L, we mean a map* $\text{int} : L \to L$ *satisfying* (2)–(4). *Given an interior operator* int, *we call $u \in L$ an* open of int *if $u \leqslant \text{int}\, u$, and we define the* topology of int *as the family of opens of* int, *i.e.,*

$$\mathcal{O}_{\text{int}} = \{\, u \in L \mid u \leqslant \text{int}\, u \,\}.$$

$\mathcal{O}_{\text{int}}$ for an interior operator int on L is indeed a topology on L, and proper iff int satisfies (5)–(6) as well; so let us say that int is proper to mean that it satisfies (5)–(6).

Fact 2. *Write* $\text{Top}(L)$ *and* $\text{Int}(L)$ *for the families of topologies and interior operators on L, respectively. The mappings* $\text{int}_- : \text{Top}(L) \to \text{Int}(L)$, *which maps a topology to its interior operator, and* $\mathcal{O}_- : \text{Int}(L) \to \text{Top}(L)$, *which maps an interior operator to its topology, are inverse to each other, making the following diagram commute.*

$$\text{Top}(L) \underset{\text{int}_-}{\overset{\mathcal{O}_-}{\rightleftarrows}} \text{Int}(L)$$

2.2 Some Algebraic Remarks

Although Definition 1, in full generality, works for any complete lattice L, it is often useful to consider less general cases with more algebraic structures. In particular, to provide semantics for modal logic that has implication $\Rightarrow$ and negation $\neg$, we need L to have corresponding structure. Let us therefore add $\Rightarrow: L \times L \to L$ satisfying

$$\frac{x \wedge y \leqslant z}{\overline{\overline{y \leqslant x \Rightarrow z}}}.$$

This means that the monotone map $x \wedge - : L \to L$ is a left adjoint (to $x \Rightarrow - : L \to L$) and hence preserves all joins, i.e.,

$$x \wedge \bigvee_{y \in I} y = \bigvee_{y \in I} (x \wedge y). \tag{7}$$

This makes L a *frame* or *locale*, i.e., a complete lattice satisfying the infinite distributive law (7). Now, a locale is a Heyting algebra, in which $\neg x = x \Rightarrow \bot$. Indeed, the locales are precisely the complete Heyting algebras. To model classical modal logic, however, one moreover needs the locale L to be Boolean. The Boolean locales are precisely the complete Boolean algebras.

By duality, the complete Boolean algebras L are exactly the powersets $\mathcal{P}X$, where an atom w of L corresponds to a singleton in $\mathcal{P}X$ and it has $w \leqslant x$ in L iff its element lies in the subset x of X. This connects our point-free formalism to the point-set possible-world semantics: an atom having $w \leqslant x$ can be read as $w \vDash x$, i.e., the proposition x being true at the possible world w. In this paper, instead of the notion of atoms, we use that of *tiny* elements, which is generally weaker but equivalent when L is a Boolean algebra.

Definition 3. *We say that an element w of a complete lattice L is* tiny *to mean that, if $w \leqslant \bigvee_{x \in I} x$ for any I (including $I = \varnothing$), then $w \leqslant y$ for some $y \in I$.*

When L is a Boolean algebra, $w \in L$ is tiny iff it is atomic. We therefore read $w \leqslant x$ for a tiny w as $w \vDash x$.

Since frames or locales are the structure used in one of the standard approaches to pointless topology, it may be helpful (even though it will play little role in the remainder of this paper) to note

Fact 3. *Let L be a frame. The proper topologies on L are precisely the subframes of L.*

More generally,

Fact 4. *Let L be any complete lattice. The topologies on L are precisely the sub-complete join-semilattices of L. The interior operator* $\mathrm{int}_O : L \to L$ *of a topology O on L factors through O as* $\mathrm{int}_O = i \circ r$ *for the inclusion map*

$i : O \to L :: u \mapsto u$ *and its right adjoint* $r : L \to O :: x \mapsto \mathrm{int}_O\, x$, *with* $r \circ i = 1_O$.

$$\mathrm{int}_O \; \circlearrowright \; L \underset{r}{\overset{i}{\underset{\perp}{\rightleftarrows}}} O$$

3   The Evidence-Based Approach: A Review

In this section we review the preceding, evidence-based approach to topological semantics of epistemic logic. Subsection 3.1 lays out how formally to generate a topology from a base, and Subsect. 3.2 observes how this formalism can be read epistemically.

3.1   From a Base to an Interior Operator

Let us illustrate how formally a base generates a topology and its interior operator. This formal idea plays crucial roles in the evidence-based approach to topological semantics, in which evidence generates a sort of knowledge modality.

Definition 4. *Let L be a complete lattice and B be any subset of L. Then, by the topology with base B we mean the family $\mathcal{O}_B$ of joins of elements of B, and by the interior operator with base B we mean the map*

$$\mathrm{int}_B : L \to L :: x \mapsto \bigvee_{u \in B,\, u \leqslant x} u.$$

We say that B generates $\mathcal{O}_B$ and int_B.

$\mathcal{O}_B$ and int_B are indeed a topology and an interior operator on L, and they are proper if B is closed under finite meets; so let us call B a proper base if it is closed under finite meets. Moreover, observe

Fact 5. *Write $\mathrm{Sub}_{\mathbf{Sets}}(L)$ for the family of all subsets of L. Then the following diagram commutes.*

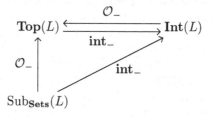

Thus, $\mathcal{O}_B$ is the topology $\mathcal{O}_{\mathbf{int}_B}$ of $\mathbf{int}_B$, and $\mathbf{int}_B$ is the interior operator $\mathbf{int}_{\mathcal{O}_B}$ of $\mathcal{O}_B$. It also follows from this fact and (iii) of Fact 1 that, for each $x \in L$, we have $x \leqslant \mathbf{int}_B x$ iff x is a join of elements of B. Also observe that, just the same way as we had (1), we can characterize $\mathbf{int}_B$ as follows: it is the map on L that assigns, to each x, the unique $\mathbf{int}_B x$ that satisfies the following two-way entailment for any $y \in L$.

$$\frac{u \leqslant y \quad \text{for all } u \in B \text{ such that } u \leqslant x}{\mathbf{int}_B x \leqslant y} \tag{8}$$

3.2   Evidence-Based Topological Semantics

The evidence-based approach interprets a base B as a set of pieces of evidence. Then the generating of an interior operator $\mathbf{int}_B$ from B constitutes a formal expression of the justifying of a sort of knowledge with evidence. This interpretation relies on

Fact 6. *Given any base B, its interior operator* $\mathbf{int}_B : L \to L$ *satisfies the following for every* $w, x \in L$.

$$w \leqslant \mathbf{int}_B x \iff w \leqslant u \leqslant x \text{ for some } u \in \mathcal{O}_B.$$

This fact has the following special case for tiny elements w (Definition 3); recall that a tiny w corresponds to a possible world, so that $w \leqslant y$ means that the proposition y is true at w.

Corollary 1. *Given any* $\mathbf{int}_B : L \to L$ *and* $w, x \in L$, *when w is tiny we have*

$$w \leqslant \mathbf{int}_B x \iff w \leqslant u \leqslant x \text{ for some } u \in B. \tag{9}$$

We then write $\square x = \mathbf{int}_{\mathcal{O}_\triangle} x$ and read it as "the agent knows that x" in a sense of knowing that gives us a cogent reading of (9). Baltag et al. [2], for instance, read (9) as the following truth condition: the proposition "the agent has factive evidence that x": is true at the world w iff there is some piece of evidence corresponding to a proposition that is true at w and entails x. In a slightly different reading, Kishida [7] reads the same as follows: x is verifiably true at w iff there is some observable proposition that is true at w and entails x.

Let us take an example scenario from [7].

Example 1. The agent makes an infinite series of coin tosses. The series is represented by taking the Cantor space $2^{\mathbb{N}}$ as the set of worlds: for the world $w : \mathbb{N} \to 2$, $w(n) = 1$ means that the $(n+1)$st toss comes up heads in w. In the scenario, what we can directly observe is the outcome of each toss and finite combinations thereof—which is to set $u \in B$ iff u is a finite intersection of $\{\, w \in 2^{\mathbb{N}} \mid w(n) = i \,\}$ for $n \in \mathbb{N}$ and $i \in 2$. By contrast, when we write x for the proposition that some toss comes up heads, we have $x \notin B$ since x is an existential proposition and not directly observable. Nonetheless, $\mathbf{int}_B$—which is exactly the interior operator of the Cantor space—has $\mathbf{int}_B\, x = x$, so that x is verifiably true if true at all: if x is true in w, there is some toss, say the $(n+1)$st, that comes up heads in w, so you can verify x by directly observing that outcome.

Another example of how the evidence-based semantics works will be discussed in Subsect. 4.3, when we compare the semantics and the one we are about to propose.

4 Our Evidence-Free Approach: A Proposal

In Sect. 3 we reviewed the evidence-based approach to topological semantics of epistemic logic, which generated a topology from a base and thereby represented the justifying of knowledge with evidence. In this section, we propose an alternative approach, which generates a topology from something else and which we therefore call *baseless* and *evidence-free*. We first lay out a new way of generating a topology formally in Subsect. 4.1, and then read this formalism as a semantic structure in Subsect. 4.2. After comparing the new semantics with the evidence-based one in Subsect. 4.3, we will provide an axiomatization of the modal logic of the new semantics in Subsect. 4.5.

4.1 From a Monotone Map to a Topology

A key formal idea behind the generating of a topology and interior operator from a base may be that the mapping $\mathbf{int}_-\,:\,\mathbf{Top}(L) \to \mathbf{Int}(L)$, which obtains an interior operator on L from a topology on L, makes sense not just for topologies but for any subfamilies of L, as one can see by comparing Definitions 1 and 4. In a similar (though orthogonal) fashion, one can reflect upon Definition 2 and observe that the mapping $\mathcal{O}_-\,:\,\mathbf{Int}(L) \to \mathbf{Top}(L)$, which obtains a topology from an interior operator, makes sense not just for interior operators but for any monotone maps, since the notion of opens makes sense for monotone maps in general. This observation, encapsulated in the following Definition 5, enables us to generate a topology and an interior operator from a monotone map $\triangle : L \to L$, rather than a subfamily $B \subseteq L$, as a primitive component of semantics.

Definition 5. *Let L be a complete lattice and $\triangle : L \to L$ be any monotone map on L. We call $u \in L$ an open of $\triangle$ if $u \leqslant \triangle u$, and we define the topology of $\triangle$ as the family of opens of $\triangle$, i.e.,*

$$\mathcal{O}_\triangle = \{\, u \in L \mid u \leqslant \triangle u \,\}. \tag{10}$$

Fact 7. *$\mathcal{O}_\triangle$ in Definition 5 is indeed a topology, and proper topology if $\triangle$ satisfies (5)–(6) (in place of $\mathbf{int}_O$).*

It is worth observing how the new, extended mapping $\mathcal{O}_-$ extends the diagram of Fact 5. Let us write $\mathbf{Pos}(L, L)$ for the family of all monotone maps on L. Then we have the following commutative diagram.

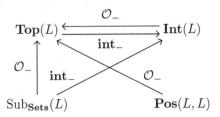

On the one hand, interior operators and topologies are in one-to-one correspondence and carry the same information. On the other hand, subsets B and monotone maps $\triangle$ carry more information: once we generate interior operators or topologies from them, this information is lost. Indeed, the information carried by B and that by $\triangle$ are generally not comparable: we cannot extract the information carried by a subset (or, respectively, a monotone map) to the format of a monotone map (or a subset) without generating an interior operator (or a topology) and thereby losing some information.

4.2   Evidence-Free Topological Semantics

The evidence-based approach to topological semantics provides conceptually cogent readings for an interior operator $\mathbf{int}_B$ generated from a base $B \subseteq L$. Our aim in this subsection is to demonstrate that an equally cogent reading is available to an interior operator $\mathbf{int}_{\mathcal{O}_\triangle}$ generated from a monotone $\triangle : L \to L$.

By the definition of $\mathcal{O}_\triangle$, Fact 6 entails

Corollary 2. *Given any monotone map $\triangle : L \to L$ and the interior operator $\mathbf{int}_{\mathcal{O}_\triangle} : L \to L$ it generates, for every $w, x \in L$ we have*

$$w \leqslant \mathbf{int}_{\mathcal{O}_\triangle} x \iff w \leqslant u \leqslant x \text{ for some } u \text{ such that } u \leqslant \triangle u. \tag{11}$$

Read epistemically, (11), like (9), stipulates that $\Box x = \mathbf{int}_{\mathcal{O}_\triangle} x$, "the agent knows that x" (in whatever suitable sense of "know" that we need to figure out), is true at the world w iff there is some proposition u that is true at w and entails both x and $\triangle u$. Here the significance of the condition that $w \leqslant u \leqslant x$ (i.e. u is true at w and entails x) can be the same as in the evidence-based approach. Therefore the crucial step in finding a suitable reading of (11) is to provide the other condition on the right-hand side, that $u \leqslant \triangle u$ (i.e. u entails $\triangle u$) or that u is an open for $\triangle$, with a suitable significance.

Here is a proposal: let us read $\triangle$ as "the agent believes that", and read the condition $u \leqslant \triangle u$ as stating that the proposition or fact that u, if true, induces the agent's belief that u. A typical case of belief induction would be the formation of belief by observation. Go back to the example of infinite coin tosses, and let u be "the second toss comes up heads", so that $\triangle u$ is "the agent believes that the second toss comes up heads". By calling "the second toss comes up heads" an observable proposition, we may assume that its truth would lead the agent, or the observer, to form the belief that it is true. The condition $u \leqslant \triangle u$ is supposed to express this assumption.

Given this interpretation of the condition $u \leqslant \triangle u$ as u being belief-inducing, we may take the induction of belief—e.g. by observation—as providing some sort of justification for the belief. We can then read (11) epistemically as follows, taking advantage of a conception of knowledge as justified true belief:

– "the agent has justified true belief that x" is true at the world w iff there is a belief-inducing proposition u that is true at w and entails x.

The "justified" part is due to the entailment by a belief-inducing proposition. For "true", observe that $w \leqslant u \leqslant x$ (u is true at w and entails x) implies $w \leqslant x$ (x is true at w). And for "belief", observe that $w \leqslant \triangle x$ (the agent believes that x at w) since the monotonicity of $\triangle$ with $u \leqslant x$ implies $\triangle u \leqslant \triangle x$ and therefore $w \leqslant u \leqslant \triangle u \leqslant \triangle x$.

4.3   Comparison to the Evidence-Based Approach

One advantage of our evidence-free approach over the evidence-based one is that a monotone map $\triangle : L \to L$ from which we generate an interior operator $\mathrm{int}_{\mathcal{O}_\triangle}$ can be taken as a modal operator itself. The logic with two modal operators, $\mathrm{int}_{\mathcal{O}_\triangle}$ and $\triangle$, can then describe the primitive component of the semantics, i.e. $\triangle$, whereas from the logic of the evidence-based approach one cannot uniquely recover the primitive component of the semantics, i.e. the base—unless one adds more vocabulary to the logic such as the global necessity operator.

Let us compare how the two approaches work using a simple example scenario.

Example 2. The agent is looking out at their backyard. There are three possibilities: in w_0, a cat ran across the yard; in w_1, the wind blew a plastic bagk accross the yard; and in w_2, nothing crossed the yard. The agent may or may not know that a cat ran across the yard in these possibilities. Let us write φ for "a cat ran across the yard", so that $[\![\varphi]\!] = \{w_0\}$, and assume that it is an observable proposition—an assumption that the two approaches formally implement in different ways.

a. The evidence-based semantics works as follows. In this semantics, our assumption that φ is observable means that $[\![\varphi]\!] \in B$. Then

$$w_i \in u \subseteq [\![\varphi]\!] \text{ for some } u \in B$$

is the case for $i = 0$ with $u = [\![\varphi]\!]$ but not for $i = 1, 2$. Therefore $\Box\varphi$, "the agent knows that a cat ran across the yard", is true at w_0 but not at w_1, w_2.

b. Our evidence-free semantics works as follows. In this semantics, our assumption that φ is observable means that the proposition $\triangle\varphi$, "the agent believes that a cat ran across the yard", is true whenever φ is, i.e., $[\![\varphi]\!] \subseteq [\![\triangle\varphi]\!] = \triangle[\![\varphi]\!]$. Let us take $[\![\triangle\varphi]\!]$ to be $\{w_0, w_1\}$—i.e., the agent believes that a cat ran across the yard when one actually did, but they believe the same when the wind blew a plastic bag across the yard. Now,

$$w_i \in u \subseteq [\![\varphi]\!] \text{ for some } u \text{ such that } u \subseteq \triangle u$$

is the case for $i = 0$ with $u = [\![\varphi]\!]$, but not for $i = 1, 2$. Therefore $\Box\varphi$, "the agent knows that a cat ran across the yard", is true at w_0, while not at w_1 or w_2. Observe the following difference between w_1 and w_2, however: For w_1, on the one hand, $u = [\![\varphi]\!]$ fails to work because $w_1 \notin u$: even though the agent believes the observable proposition φ at w_1, it is not true at w_1—i.e., they incorrectly believe that a cat ran across the yard, when it was actually a plastic bag. At w_2, on the other hand, the agent does not believe it in the first place. Thus, while the the justified true belief that φ fails to hold at both w_1 and w_2, it does in the two worlds for quite different reasons.

The comparison between (a) and (b) should make clear what each semantics can and cannot express. In particular, our evidence-free semantics can express the agent's belief as well as knowledge, and therefore it can distinguish two ways in which the agent can fail to know something: one is where the agent does not believe it in the first place, and the other is where, although the agent believes it, it is not true belief. In general, justified true belief can fail in three ways: either it is not justified, it is not true, or it is not belief. Our evidence-free semantics is expressive enough to distinguish these three. (The failure due to the lack of justification will be the highlight of Example 3 in the next subsection.) By contrast, the evidence-based semantics cannot express belief, and its notion of justified true belief therefore cannot fail for the reason that the agent does not believe it—in this sense, what the evidence-based semantics really models is the idea that something is justified and true, so that it is a justified true belief of the agent *if* they believe it.

4.4   Induced Belief and Justified True Belief

The goal of Subsect. 4.3 was to compare our semantics to the evidence-based one, and we took a simpler example there to highlight the contrast more clearly. Let us now expand the example to illustrate some other important features of our semantics.

Example 3. To the three possibilities w_0, w_1, w_2 of Example 2, let us add three more, w_3, w_4, w_5, in each of which a fox ran across the yard. Let us write ψ for "a fox ran across the yard", so that $[\![\psi]\!] = \{w_3, w_4, w_5\}$, while we keep $[\![\varphi]\!] = \{w_0\}$ for φ being "a cat ran across the yard". As to the agent's belief, let $[\![\triangle\varphi]\!] = \{w_0, w_1, w_4\}$ and $[\![\triangle\psi]\!] = \{w_3\}$—i.e., in w_3, they correctly believe that a fox ran across the yard; in w_4, they believe that a cat did although it was a fox; and in w_5, they neither believe that a cat did nor that a fox did, although a fox in fact did. Let us introduce χ for "an animal ran across the yard", with

$[\![\chi]\!] = [\![\varphi]\!] \cup [\![\psi]\!] = \{w_0, w_3, w_4, w_5\}$ and $[\![\triangle\chi]\!] = [\![\triangle\varphi]\!] \cup [\![\triangle\psi]\!] = \{w_0, w_1, w_3, w_4\}$. The question we now consider is at which worlds the agent has the justified true belief that χ.

Observe that φ is belief-inducing, i.e. $[\![\varphi]\!] \subseteq [\![\triangle\varphi]\!]$, but that ψ and χ are not, since $w_4, w_5 \in [\![\psi]\!] \setminus [\![\triangle\psi]\!]$ and $w_5 \in [\![\chi]\!] \setminus [\![\triangle\chi]\!]$. The situations at w_0, w_1, and w_2 are similar to Example 2:

- At w_0, there the agent believes that φ, a belief induced by the truth of φ. This implies, since φ entails χ, that the agent has the justified true belief that χ, i.e., $\square\chi$ is true.
- At w_1, $\square\chi$ is false because χ is false.
- At w_2, $\square\chi$ is false since the agent does not believe that χ (as well as because χ is false).

Similarly to w_2,

- At w_5, $\square\chi$ is false since there the agent does not believe that χ (though χ is true).

Thus, the justified true belief in χ fails at w_1 because it is not true, and at w_2 and w_5 due to the lack of belief. On the other hand, they also fail at w_3 and w_4, but it is due to the lack of justification.

- At w_3, the agent correctly believes that χ. This belief is however not justified, i.e., there is no belief-inducing true proposition entailing χ: although ψ and χ are true and entail χ, they are not belief-inducing.
- At w_4, the agent correctly believes that χ. This belief is however not justified. Although φ is belief-inducing and entails χ, but it is not true: in other words, the agent's belief in the belief-inducing proposition φ at w_4 is not a belief induced by the truth of φ. To spell out the situation, the agent correctly believes that an animal ran across the yard, but his justification fails because he believes it for a wrong reason: he believes he saw a cat, but it was a fox.

The most significant aspect of this example may be the failure of $\square\chi$ at w_4. In our semantics, justification means entailment by a belief-inducing proposition *that is true*. This rules out a case in which a purportedly justified true belief is justified by a *false* belief while it happens to be true.

Another important aspect to highlight is the crucial role of w_5. If we removed w_5 from the model, then χ, that an animal ran across the yard, would be a belief-inducing proposition. It would then be able to justify the agent's true belief that χ at w_4, even though their belief that they saw a cat is incorrect. To give a model in which χ is belief-inducing is to assume that, even if the agent's observation is unreliable as to whether the animal was a cat or a fox, their observation of an animal reliably leads to their correct belief that they saw an animal—so that this observation justifies beliefs. Put contrapositively, if we understand a proposition χ to be un-observable or non-justifying, then we need to provide a model with at least one world at which χ is true but $\triangle\chi$ is not, so that χ is not belief-inducing.

4.5   Logic of Belief and Justified True Belief

As stated above, one advantage of our evidence-free approach over the evidence-based one is that its language has a modal operator for belief in addition to one for knowledge or justified true belief. This enables the logic of the semantics to explicitly describe the relationship between belief and justified true belief.

Combining (8) and (10) gives the following characterization of $\text{int}_{\mathcal{O}_\triangle}$: it is the map on L such that, for each $x \in L$, its value $\text{int}_{\mathcal{O}_\triangle} x$ is the unique element of L satisfying the following two-way entailment for any $y \in L$.

$$\frac{u \leqslant y \quad \text{for all } u \in L \text{ such that } u \leqslant \triangle u \text{ and } u \leqslant x}{\text{int}_{\mathcal{O}_\triangle} x \leqslant y} \tag{12}$$

Then here is the principal theorem of this paper:

Theorem 1. *Let* $\triangle : L \to L$ *be any monotone map on* L. *Then* $\text{int}_{\mathcal{O}_\triangle}$ *is the unique function* $\square : L \to L$ *satisfying the axioms*

$$\square x \leqslant x, \tag{13}$$
$$\square x \leqslant \triangle \square x, \tag{14}$$

and the rule

$$\frac{u \leqslant \triangle u \qquad u \leqslant x}{u \leqslant \square x}. \tag{15}$$

In other words, given a belief operator $\triangle$ that satisfies (M) (in place of $\square$), the axioms and rule corresponding to (13)–(15) axiomatize the justified true belief $\square$. (M) and (A4) for $\square$ are derivable in this logic. So is

$$\square x \leqslant \triangle x. \tag{16}$$

(15), (13), and (16) respectively state that $\square$ means justified, true, and belief.

In addition, if $\triangle$ satisfies the axioms (N) and (C) (in place of $\square$) then $\mathcal{O}_\triangle$ is a proper topology and hence $\square = \text{int}\,\mathcal{O}_\triangle$ satisfies (N) and (C), so that modal logic S4 is sound with respect to the proper subversion of the semantics.

Finally, we have

Theorem 2. *For this logic of belief and justified true belief, we have soundness and completeness, both with respect to complete lattices equipped with a monotone map and with respect to powersets equipped with a monotone map.*

5   Common Knowledge

The formalism introduced in this paper is applicable to axiomatization and semantics of common knowledge. Axiomatically speaking, when we read $\triangle$ as distributed knowledge—assumed to satisfy $\triangle \leqslant 1_L$—of all agents, (13)–(14) and (16) along with the monotonicity of $\triangle$ mean that $\square$ satisfies $\square x = \triangle(\square x \wedge x)$, the fixed-point characterization of common knowledge. A similar point is made semantically by

Fact 8. *Let $\triangle$ be the necessity operator of an accessibility relation R. Then $\square$ satisfying (13)–(15) is the necessity operator of the reflexive and transitive closure of R.*

It is beneficial to compare this application with a similar work by Lismont and Mongin [8]. Lismont and Mongin use the condition $u \leqslant \triangle u$—which they call "belief-closure" whereas we call it belief-inducing—to generate common belief from distributed belief, albeit in the point-set rather than point-free setting. The core difference between the work of Lismont and Mongin and ours is that the former generates common *belief* $\square$ from distributed belief $\triangle$, while our primary goal is to generate, even from belief $\triangle$, knowledge or justified *true* belief $\square$. (Or, put more formally, topological *interior* operators are the target of our work but not Lismont and Mongin's.) Instead of (11), Lismont and Mongin have

$$w \leqslant \square x \iff w \leqslant \triangle u \text{ and } u \leqslant x \text{ for some } u \text{ such that } u \leqslant \triangle u.$$

This results in a logic that is the same as ours except that (13) is missing, and, instead of Fact 8, the fact that $\square$ is the necessity operator of the transitive (as opposed to reflexive and transitive) closure of R.

6   Conclusion

This paper has introduced a new approach to topological semantics of epistemic logic, viz., the evidence-free approach to justified true belief as an alternative to the evidence-based approach. The core idea is to take advantage of the belief-inducing property of a proposition u—i.e. that u entails an agent's belief that u—by interpreting it as providing a criterion of u being justified. This idea has given rise to a new logic of belief and justified true belief.

As an example of future work in this new approach, one may investigate what additional restrictions on the semantics would make $\square$ behave more suitably as justified true belief. For instance, one may argue that it is reasonable to assume an agent's belief to satisfy the axioms (N) and (C) so that the logic of justified true belief is (at least) the modal logic S4. One may look for more axioms and rules that an agent's belief should satisfy in a similar fashion. Or one may look for reasonable conditions or assumptions that make it more plausible to interpret $u \leqslant \triangle u$ as belief induction.

Acknowledgments. I thank the anonymous reviewers for their thoughtful comments. While the originally submitted version contained Fact 8 and suggested its connection to common knowledge, it was one of the reviewers who referred me to Lismont and Mongin [8]. Section 5 has been added in response to this reference. Another reviewer's comments have also led to the addition of Subsect. 4.4.

References

1. Abramsky, S., Vickers, S.: Quantales, observational logic and process semantics. Math. Struct. Comput. Sci. **3**(2), 161–227 (1993)
2. Baltag, A., Bezhanishvili, N., Özgün, A., Smets, S.: Justified belief, knowledge, and the topology of evidence. Synthese **200**(512), 1–51 (2022)
3. Van Benthem, J., Pacuit, E.: Dynamic logics of evidence-based beliefs. Stud. Log. **99**(1), 61–92 (2011)
4. Van Benthem, J., Fernández-Duque, D., Pacuit, E.: Evidence logic: a new look at neighborhood structures. In: Bolander, T., Braüner, T., Ghilardi, S., Moss, L. (eds.) Advances in Modal Logic, vol. 9, pp. 97–118. College Publications, London (2012)
5. Hintikka, J.: Knowledge and Belief: An Introduction to the Logic of the Two Notions. Cornell University Press (1962)
6. Kelly, K.: The Logic of Reliable Inquiry. Oxford University Press, Oxford (1996)
7. Kishida, K.: Generalized topological semantics of first-order modal logic. Ph.D. dissertation, University of Pittsburgh (2010)
8. Lismont, L., Mongin, P.: Belief closure: a semantics of common knowledge for modal propositional logic. Math. Soc. Sci. **30**(2), 127–153 (1995)
9. McKinsey, J.C.C., Tarski, A.: The algebra of topology. Ann. Math. **45**(1), 141–191 (1944)
10. Vickers, S.: Topology via Logic. Cambridge University Press, Cambridge (1996)
11. Williamson, T.: Knowledge and Its Limits. Oxford University Press, Oxford (2000)

Semantic-Pragmatic Account of Syntactic Structures

Ivan Rygaev[(✉)]

Institute for Information Transmission Problems, Russian Academy of Sciences,
Moscow, Russia
irygaev@gmail.com

Abstract. In this paper, I propose a unified account of backgrounded constituents within the framework of Discourse Representation Theory. Building upon van der Sandt (1992) and Geurts (2010), I expand the scope of presupposition resolution in DRT to encompass other forms of backgrounded expressions, such as specific indefinites and conventional implicatures (in terms of Potts 2005). Each backgrounded expression constitutes a certain instruction to find, create, or update a discourse referent in the common ground. Dependent on one another, these instructions form a tree-like structure, which is subsequently realized as a syntactic tree during the process of utterance production. Among other aspects, this approach suggests a potential answer to why backgrounded constructions are islands, as articulated by Goldberg (2006).

Keywords: DRT · information structure · common ground · backgrounding · syntactic structures · presupposition · specific indefinites · conventional implicature

1 Introduction

It is well known that the syntactic structure of a natural language sentence constitutes a tree. On the other hand, its semantic representation (and even more so the semantic representation of an entire discourse) is better approximated by a semantic graph, which does not necessarily have a single root and may contain cycles. Many knowledge representation formalisms go beyond tree-like structures (or do not assume them in the first place). Apparently, this is a requirement for any sufficiently rich semantic representation. We can safely assume that our mental representations also extend beyond trees and form more complex structures.

Given this assumption, the question arises: how do these more complex structures transform into trees during the process of speech production? In this work, I will attempt to show that communicative organization of the utterance plays a crucial role in this. The speaker's intentions to convey certain information to the hearer split their mental content into a number of instructions to modify the common ground. Dependent on one another, these instructions form a tree-like

© The Author(s), under exclusive license to Springer Nature Switzerland AG 2024
D. Bekki et al. (Eds.): LENLS 2023, LNCS 14569, pp. 337–352, 2024.
https://doi.org/10.1007/978-3-031-60878-0_19

structure, which is subsequently realized as a syntactic tree during the process of utterance production.

I address the question within the established framework of Discourse Representation Theory (Kamp et al. 2011) and propose an extension of the theory that elucidates the relationship between semantic representation and syntactic structures.

2   Background

2.1   Discourse Representation Theory

Discourse Representation Theory (Kamp 1981, Kamp & Reyle 1993, Kamp et al. 2011), abbreviated as DRT, is a dynamic semantics theory. Dynamic semantics takes into account dependencies between utterances in discourse and interprets each sentence in the context of what was said before. It emphasizes a procedural meaning of the sentence, i.e. how it changes the common ground[1]. Heim, in her brilliant file cards metaphor, formulated the following rules for the meaning of noun phrases: *"For every indefinite, start a new card; for every definite, update a suitable old card"* (Heim 1982:179)

DRT utilizes a semantic representation layer known as DRS (discourse representation structure). DRS encapsulates the common ground and includes all information communicated up to the current moment. DRS is composed of discourse referents (variables) and conditions on them (predicates). When the next sentence is processed, its representation is incorporated into the main discourse DRS with the resolution of pronouns. A pronoun is resolved (bound) to a previously established discourse referent.

(1)   A farmer bought a car

$$
\begin{array}{|l|}
\hline
x, y \\
\hline
\text{farmer } (x) \\
\text{car } (y) \\
\text{buy } (x, y) \\
\hline
\end{array}
$$

(2)   A farmer bought a car. It was pink.

$$
\begin{array}{|l|}
\hline
x, y \\
\hline
\text{farmer } (x) \\
\text{car } (y) \\
\text{buy } (x, y) \\
\text{pink } (y) \\
\hline
\end{array}
$$

In classical DRT, a sentence does not possess an independent logical form distinct from the context. Truth conditions and model-theoretic interpretation

---

[1] Hereinafter, I use the terms 'context' and 'common ground' interchangeably.

do not apply to individual sentences; instead, these belong to the updated main DRS, which represents the entire discourse. The meaning of a sentence lies in its context change potential, indicating the changes it introduces to the common ground.

A DRS can contain sub-DRSs, which serve to express complex conditions like implication, negation, disjunction, and so on. Nested DRSs form a hierarchy of subordination and accessibility. When seeking the antecedent of a pronoun, the search is limited to the current or superordinate DRSs. Subordinate DRSs are not accessible.

(3)   Every farmer owns a donkey. *It is grey.

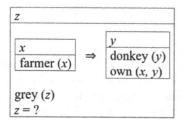

DRT explains extension of the scope of existentially quantified noun phrases beyond the sentence boundaries and the binding of pronouns that lack syntactic binding (as illustrated in donkey sentences).

2.2   Binding Theory of Presupposition

Van der Sandt & Geurts (1991) suggested that presupposition is a phenomenon very similar to anaphora. These ideas were further elaborated in van der Sandt (1992). Like a pronoun, a presuppositional expression requires resolution by being bound to an antecedent. However, in contrast to pronouns, presuppositions contain descriptive content that should be matched with a potential antecedent. To represent such content, a dedicated sub-DRS named A-DRS is introduced. The theory was subsequently termed the binding theory of presupposition by Geurts (1999:53).

Presupposition resolution unfolds in two stages. Initially, a separate sentence DRS is created. It contains (yet unresolved) A-DRSs for each presupposition from the sentence. A-DRSs can be nested if presuppositions depend on one another. Subsequently, the sentence DRS is merged with the main DRS and A-DRSs are resolved by finding antecedents for them through the accessibility hierarchy. Once the presuppositions are resolved, the A-DRSs are eliminated and the main DRS becomes a proper DRS, ready to be interpreted in a model.

(4)   John has a cat. His cat purrs.

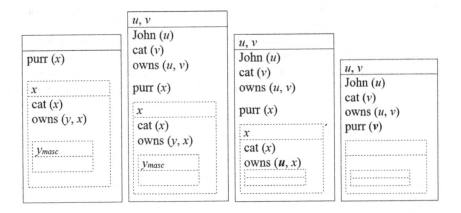

If an antecedent cannot be identified, the presupposition can be accommodated, meaning it is added at some level of the accessibility hierarchy. Unlike a pronoun, a presupposition typically contains enough descriptive content to convey meaningful and relevant information on its own. An A-DRS ascends the projection line of the accessibility hierarchy in search of a suitable antecedent. Once found, the discourse referents of the A-DRS can be bound to (identified with) the relevant discourse referents at the binding site. If the root of the accessibility hierarchy is reached without finding a suitable antecedent, the contents of the A-DRS can be accommodated there. If accommodation is not possible due to a constraint violation (see below), then we can descend one level down the projection line in an attempt to accommodate there, and so on. If no suitable site for binding or accommodation is found, presupposition failure ensues.

Binding and accommodation are subject for certain constraints, among which are the following:

1. The resolved A-DRS should not include nested unresolved A-DRSs.
2. Along the projection line, no DRS should have unresolved A-DRSs.[2]
3. Following resolution, no discourse referents should occur free in any DRS.
4. The new main DRS should be consistent and informative relative to the previous main DRS.
5. Each DRS should be both consistent with and informative relative to its higher-level superordinate DRSs.

The initial two constraints specify that A-DRSs are resolved in a left-to-right and deep-to-surface order. The third constraint prohibits an embedding presupposition from ascending beyond the resolution site of the embedded one resolved earlier. The final two constraints indicate that the updated main DRS must maintain both global and local consistency and informativeness.

---

[2] It seems that there must be an exception for the lowest non-anaphoric DRS in the projection line. There can be multiple A-DRSs in it, and since they are processed sequentially, the first should be able to be processed while the others are still present.

The merit of the binding theory lies in its natural solution to the presupposition projection problem. If a presuppositional expression is bound or accommodated at an intermediate level within the hierarchy and does not reach the top level, where discourse referents are interpreted existentially, the presupposition is effectively 'cancelled,' and the sentence as a whole does not carry the presupposition.

2.3   Specific Indefinites and Backgrounding

Specific indefinites are akin to presuppositions in that they are interpreted not at the location where they appear in a sentence but rather at a higher point in the structure. In this regard, they resemble definite noun phrases. Some languages feature morpho-syntactic markers that apply to both definites and specific indefinites while excluding non-specific indefinites (e.g., refer to Givón (1978) for Bemba or Lyons (1999) for Samoan).

The following sentence (from Karttunen 1976) has at least three different readings depending on the level where 'a museum' is interpreted:

(5)   Bill intends to visit a museum every day

Some researchers have suggested that specificity should be treated on a par with presupposition projection (Cresti 1995, Yeom 1998). Van Geenhoven (1998) provided an account of specific indefinites in terms of the binding theory of presupposition in DRT. The only difference from presuppositions is that specific indefinites are normally accommodated rather than bound.

However, Geurts (2010) proposed unifying specificity and presupposition not by reducing the former to the latter, but by encompassing them under a broader term - backgrounding. He emphasizes that accommodation is a repair strategy and it would be strange to use it normally as specific indefinites do. Instead, he puts forth the Buoyancy Principle:

• Backgrounded material tends to float up towards the main DRS.

This transition opens the door for other types of backgrounded constituents to be incorporated and processed by a similar mechanism, without reducing them to presuppositions. Indeed, Geurts proposes extending backgrounding to two phenomena: non-restrictive relative clauses and felicity conditions on speech acts. While I will not delve into the latter in this paper, I will treat the former under the term conventional implicature (CI), as defined by Potts (2005).[3] Per Potts, only two groups of expressions can be considered CIs: supplemental (appositive) expressions (including non-restrictive relative clauses) and expressives (words like *damn*).

---

[3] Geurts also suggests depriving certain expressions of their presuppositional status, such as lexical presuppositions or factive verb complements. Although those expressions pose some challenges for the theory advocated here, I leave their treatment open for now.

3 Instructional DRT

In this section, I will elaborate on Geurts' theory of backgrounding and offer a formal treatment for three types of backgrounded expressions: presuppositions, specific indefinites and conventional implicatures, following the spirit of the binding theory of presupposition.

3.1 DRSs as Instructions

In accordance with the Buoyancy Principle, every backgrounded constituent can ascend to a different level in the accessibility hierarchy. This requires that the content of each backgrounded expression must be segregated within the DRS. We can continue using something like A-DRSs for this purpose, but now they have to be marked with their respective type, as their processing differ. For instance, specific indefinites are processed differently from presuppositions; the latter seek to be bound while the former do not.

The type of a backgrounded expression corresponds to the function it plays in the process of common ground update. They act as instructions executed against the common ground. Presuppositions serve to identify a discourse referent, specific indefinites aim to introduce a new one, and conventional implicatures contribute to updating a discourse referent that has been previously established. Correspondingly, I will label them as 'find', 'create' or 'update' instructions. In addition, following Bos (2003), I adopt his notion of the principal discourse referent to indicate the distinguished discourse referent with respect to which an instruction is executed.

An A-DRS provided with its function and the distinguished discourse referent will be referred to as I-DRS (Instructional DRS). Consider the example:

(6)   The king, who was happy, rewarded a certain person

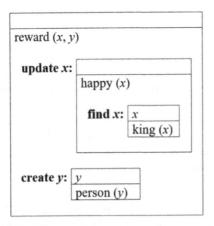

When processing this sentence DRS, we first handle the presupposition 'the king' by executing the corresponding find instruction, incorporating 'the king'

into the main DRS. Then we update it with the CI 'who was happy,' performing the update instruction.[4] Next, we treat the specific indefinite 'a certain person,' adding a new discourse referent via the create instruction.

What remains to be accounted for is the foregrounded part (that the king rewarded the person). In van der Sandt's theory, this aspect was automatically addressed by the merge of the sentence DRS into the main DRS. As a result of the merge, the main DRS is updated with the foregrounded material (not embedded into any A-DRSs).

In my theory, it is natural to introduce a separate instruction, whose purpose is to update the topic discourse referent of the sentence. Thus, the sentence DRS will be also prefixed with 'update x', similar to the CI, and will become an I-DRS as well.[5] In some sense, in van der Sandt's theory, the foreground update was performed the first, preceding any resolution of backgrounded presuppositions. In my approach, it will be the last instruction carried out.

3.2   Syntactic Structures

As we have seen, a sentence DRS is construed as a number of nested instructions arranged in a tree-like structure. The I-DRS hierarchy reflects dependencies between instructions. When the execution of one instruction relies on the result of another, then the former includes the latter as its sub-DRS.

From a syntactic perspective, each I-DRS corresponds to a constituent, and the I-DRS hierarchy aligns with the phrase-structure tree of the sentence. I propose that this correlation is not coincidental; it precisely explains the emergence of the syntactic tree. The speaker intent to communicate certain information to the hearer results in breaking down their knowledge into a set of instructions for finding, creating or updating discourse referents in the common ground. Dependent on one another, these instructions form a tree structure. This tree is then lexicalized and realized as the syntactic tree of the sentence.

I am not the first to observe the parallels between syntactic structures and the communicative organization of a sentence. For instance, Mel'čuk (2001) introduces a notion of communicative dependency, in addition to syntactic and semantic dependencies. The same semantic configuration of two nodes, such as "population being the argument of growth" can be expressed in two different ways depending on what we want the configuration to refer to - either the growth or the population - resulting in "the population growth" or "the growing population," respectively. He further notes that while the communicatively dominant node can be either semantically dominant or semantically dependent (as illustrated above), the syntactic head of the phrase always corresponds to the

---

[4] I assume that a non-restrictive relative clause is attached to at the DP level as in Toribio (1992).

[5] The need for a separate instruction type for foreground updates, distinct from CIs, is a matter of debate. Currently, I assume that CIs are represented by embedded updates, while the foreground update is always a topmost instruction, representing the whole sentence DRS.

communicatively dominant node. *"Comm-dependency is, so to speak, a way of 'foreseeing,' on the semantic level, the future syntactic dependencies"* (Mel'čuk 2001:32).

The principal discourse referent of the instruction is precisely the Comm-dominant node within the semantic structure of the particular I-DRS. It will be expressed lexically as the head of the corresponding constituent.

It can be argued[6] that this matching of information structure and syntax cannot be perfect, as it is well known that a single syntactic structure admits different information structures. Depending on the question the sentence addresses, the division into topic and focus may vary, even though the syntactic structure is generally presumed to remain the same:

(7)   What did John do? [John]$_T$ [bought an apple]$_F$.

(8)   What did John buy? [John bought]$_T$ [an apple]$_F$.

However, generative grammar permits the movement of the focus constituent to the beginning of the sentence, either overtly or covertly in LF. Indeed, covert focus movement was proposed by several researchers (see e.g. Wagner 2006). Should this occur, the resulting syntactic structure of (8) would reestablish its alignment with the information structure:

(9)   [an apple]$_F$ [John bought __]$_T$.

In addition, it must be noted that the tree manifested by a sentence DRS corresponds to the deep syntactic structure rather than the surface structure. When transitioning to a surface structure, it can potentially undergo additional transformations.

3.3   Utterances as Programs

The idea to represent the meaning of a sentence in procedural terms is not new either and can be traced back to Winograd (1972). Davies & Isard (1972) proposed a two-step process for natural language understanding, similar to the way computers "understand" programming languages - namely, through compilation and execution. There is a distinction between understanding an utterance and actually carrying it out.

These two steps correspond to two stages in the DRS resolution process. In the first step, we generate instructions, constructing a sentence I-DRS that incorporates the backgrounded I-DRSs. The second step involves executing the I-DRS instructions against the common ground, resulting in the updated main DRS of the discourse.

---

[6] As indeed was argued by one of the anonymous reviewers. I am grateful to them for this remark.

Hence, we have two levels of representation. The sentence DRS represents the procedural meaning of the sentence, capturing both the information structure and the syntactic structure. The construction of the sentence DRS does not rely on information from the common ground, rendering it context-independent. However, it remains context-sensitive, as executing it in different contexts can yield different results. The ability to preserve context sensitivity and maintain syntactic and information structures in a language-independent manner at a semantic level makes a sentence DRS a good interlingua for translating between different languages.

On the other hand, the main proper DRS represents the knowledge generated after the execution of the instructions. It captures truth conditions, supports model-theoretic interpretation, and serves as a suitable candidate for representing mental content.

Although it was demonstrated by de Groote (2006) and de Groote & Lebedeva (2010) that dynamic phenomena, and particularly the DRT-style presupposition resolution, can be accounted for in a purely static framework, I believe that the dynamic procedural approach has an advantage. This approach not only offers abstract tools for analyzing the meaning of sentences but also is likely to bring us closer to understanding of what actually happens in the process of communication (though more experimental support is needed here).

3.4   Formal Theory

The formalization mostly follows (van der Sandt 1992) with some modifications.

The vocabulary of the DRS language now additionally includes a set T of instruction types with three members: 'find', 'create' and 'update'.

There are now two types of DRSs: a bare DRS, which does not have an instruction type and a principal discourse referent attached to it, and an instructional DRS (I-DRS), which includes them.

A bare DRS K is a triple $\langle U(K), Con(K), I(K) \rangle$. $U(K)$ and $Con(K)$ are defined in the usual way as a set of discourse referents and a set of DRS conditions, respectively. The definition of (simple and complex) DRS conditions is standard and does not change in my theory. $I(K)$ is an I-structure, which is a set of I-DRSs.

An I-DRS J is a triple $\langle t, u, K \rangle$, where t is an instruction type, u is a discourse referent (called the principal discourse referent of J), and $K = B(J)$ is a bare DRS.

Merging two bare DRSs is not required anymore. It is always a sentence I-DRS that is merged with the bare DRS of the discourse. The merge consists of a simple addition of the I-DRS to the I-structure of the bare DRS.

The definition of subordination remains the same, except for a new rule for I-structure. If an I-DRS $J = \langle t, u, K_1 \rangle$ belongs to the I-structure of a bare DRS K_2, then K_1 is immediately subordinate to K_2. Accessibility is defined in the usual way through subordination. The definition of the projection line also does not change.

Resolution of an I-DRS $J = \langle t, u, K_1 \rangle$ into a bare DRS K_2 consists of adding the discourse referents and conditions of K_1 into K_2. In case of binding, it additionally includes adding an identity condition for each discourse referent from the universe of K_1 to its corresponding antecedent. Once resolved, the I-DRS is removed from its parent DRS I-structure rather than emptied, as per van der Sandt.

A bare DRS is considered proper when both its I-structure and the I-structures of all its subordinate DRSs are empty, meaning they do not contain any I-DRSs. The interpretation of a proper DRS in a model follows standard DRT. A non-proper DRS lacks an interpretation in a model. Instead, it is interpreted in terms of instructions that require execution, i.e. the resolution of their I-DRSs. Upon resolving all I-DRSs, the main DRS becomes proper and ready for interpretation.

In a proper DRS, the content created by different types of instructions is combined, and the original instruction type is lost. Yet, sometimes the subsequent discourse may depend on how the material was introduced into the common ground. For instance, foregrounded content can be denied in a straightforward way, while backgrounded content normally cannot (cf. the 'wait a minute' test for presuppositions). However, that does not imply that we should preserve instructions with all their dependencies in the main DRS. Instead, something like Layered DRT (Geurts & Maier 2003) can be employed for this purpose.[7]

3.5   Resolution Rules

Presupposition I-DRSs adhere to the resolution principles outlined in van der Sandt's theory for A-DRSs. They can either be bound or accommodated at a higher level within the projection line, subject to resolution constraints.

Specificity I-DRSs cannot be bound and require 'accommodation' at higher level, subject to the same constraints.

Conventional implicature I-DRSs are somewhat different. They attach new content to a previously established discourse referent, relying on a find or create instruction for the introduction of this referent. Therefore, their binding site is fixed to be aligned with the binding site of the corresponding find or create instruction.

Constraints on resolution remain intact, with one notable modification. Van der Sandt highlights that "anaphoric markers will thus always be resolved outside an A-structure" (van der Sandt 1992: 356). This requirement needs to be relaxed. Previously, the foregrounded material was not a part of any A-DRS and, therefore, was available to be bound to. With the introduction of the foregrounded update instruction, it is now enclosed in an I-DRS. However, we still want to keep it available for binding. Consider the sentence:

---

[7] Thanks to Gregoire Winterstein for this suggestion.

(10)   The cat caught a mouse and is eating it

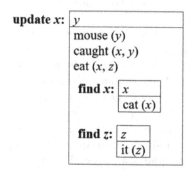

If we consider 'a mouse' as non-specific, it does not create a separate instruction but rather constitutes a part of the foregrounded update instruction. Yet we want to be able to resolve 'it' (z) to 'a mouse' (y), i.e. to another I-DRS before it is executed.

However, it is easy to construct a similar example featuring a find instruction instead of an update. This example may seem somewhat artificial, incorporating an unusually lengthy restrictive relative clause. However, in special settings where the speaker has been explicitly prompted to identify a specific cat, it is perfectly felicitous.

(11)   Here is the cat that caught a mouse and is eating it

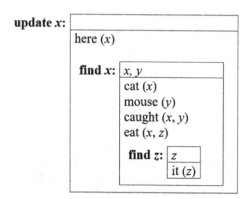

In this example, 'it' (z) also should be able to be bound to 'a mouse' (y). This indicates that the initial constraint was overly restrictive. Find instructions correspond to A-DRSs, and there was an (erroneous) prohibition against resolution into A-DRSs.

On the other hand, in expressions such as 'her sister,' we do not want to permit the identification of 'her' with 'sister.' However, this situation appears

348   I. Rygaev

more akin to Chomskian Condition B constraint (Chomsky 1993), which may not be effectively addressed in terms of the DRS structure, and probably should be accounted for elsewhere. Thus, I assume that an I-DRS can be resolved into any higher DRS, including I-DRSs.

Lifting this requirement also brings about another advantage. Up until now, in my theory, non-specific indefinites have been handled differently from specific ones. The latter introduce a separate create instruction, while the former do not. This presupposes that indefinites are inherently ambiguous between specific and non-specific readings, either in the grammar, following Geenhoven (1998), or in the pragmatics, following Geurts (2010). This perspective is quite prevalent and is supported by the presence of specificity markers in certain languages. Nonetheless, is it possible for us to treat them uniformly, eliminating ambiguity?

I believe that it is feasible. Non-specific indefinites are special in that they are interpreted in situ and directly contribute to the content of the higher syntactic constituent. However, given that we have allowed I-DRSs to be resolved into other I-DRSs, we can achieve the same outcome by resolving a create instruction into its parent I-DRS. To illustrate, the representation in (10) can be obtained from the DRS in (12) if we resolve the 'create y' instruction into its parent update I-DRS, essentially interpreting it in situ.

(12)   The cat caught a mouse and is eating it

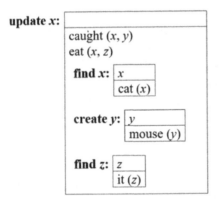

This way, all indefinite noun phrases will be handled consistently as create instructions. Only those that project higher than their parent I-DRS will be considered specific and backgrounded (and not vice versa).

Notably, the capacity to 'dissolve' into the parent I-DRS is not exclusive to indefinites. Definites, at times, appear to manifest the same behavior. Haddock (1987) highlights that, in the scenario depicted in Fig. 1, the rabbit R2 can be successfully referred to by the phrase in (13)[8].

---

[8] I am grateful to Linmin Zhang for pointing out this example.

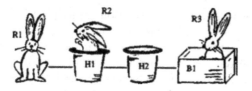

Fig. 1. The illustration for 'the rabbit in the hat' example.

(13)   The rabbit in the hat

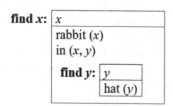

What is peculiar in this scenario is that the latter part of the NP, 'the hat,' does not single out a unique hat on the picture. The 'find y' instruction is expected to identify an existing hat, but it cannot do so because there are two equally salient hats. Typically, such a situation would lead to presupposition failure, but that is not the case here.

I suggest that what happens in this case is the local accommodation of 'the hat' into the context of the parent I-DRS, resulting in the following configuration, which is selective enough to identify the relevant rabbit:

(14)

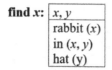

The resulting DRS is identical to that of the expression 'rabbit in a [non-specific] hat'. Intuition appears to align with this observation.

4   Discussion

4.1   Syntactic Islands

The theory presented in this paper can potentially shed some light to the nature of island constraints. An island is a syntactic construction that contains an element that cannot be extracted out of it. The communicative perspective on the island phenomena relies on information structure for explanation. It was first presented by Erteschik-Shir (1973), who proposed that islands arise due to a conflict in the information structure of the sentence. She postulated that extraction can occur only from a dominant part of the sentence, one that is not presupposed and lacks a contextual reference. Later, Goldberg (2006) formulated a simple rule:

- Backgrounded constructions are islands (BCI)

Though this observation is quite insightful, the question remains: why are they islands? The current approach offers an explanation. Each backgrounded constituent corresponds to an individual instruction, executed separately. At the moment of execution, all discourse referents that the instruction depends on must have already been identified or created by other instructions. If this is not the case, for instance, if the set of instructions is inconsistent due to vicious circles in instruction dependencies, the set becomes non-executable. Consequently, the sentence is uninterpretable. Consider an example:

(15)   ***Who** did Bill see [the picture of _]?

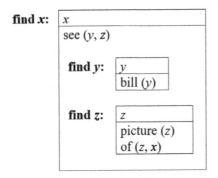

Since the definite noun phrase serves as a presupposition trigger, it introduces its own find instruction. However, this instruction cannot be executed immediately as it relies on the value for the gap, which is yet undefined. This value is requested by the topmost instruction, which, in turn, depends on the definite NP for its execution. This creates a circular dependency, rendering the set of instructions non-executable, thereby explaining the unacceptability of this sentence.

Exploring whether a similar explanation can be offered for other types of islands remains a subject for further research.

4.2   Further Issues

Several aspects remain unexplored in this paper. For example, it is necessary to demonstrate how non-anaphoric presuppositions, as described in (Kamp et al.

2011), are addressed within this framework. An example of such a presupposition trigger is the particle 'too'. In situations with multiple potential antecedents, it neither introduces ambiguity nor leads to presupposition failure. What we are seeking here is not binding to a specific antecedent but rather a general entailment by the preceding discourse:

(16)   One man entered. Then another man entered. A woman entered, too.

Certainly, one of the most challenging issues is the treatment of quantified noun phrases. If it can be demonstrated that they have the capability to float up the accessibility hierarchy similar to backgrounded constituents, this would potentially explain the quantifier raising and the quantifier scope ambiguity found in sentences such as the following:

(17)   Somebody loves everybody

Yet, the way quantifiers are represented in DRT does not align well with their syntax in the sentence. Furthermore, quantified noun phrases do not appear to fit smoothly into the instructional paradigm. The interpretation of phrases such as "all students" in terms of instructions is not straightforward.

Addressing those and numerous other open questions is a topic for further research.

5   Conclusions

In this paper, I presented a unified account of backgrounded constituents in the spirit of van der Sandt's binding theory of presupposition. The resulting representation offers a perspective on how syntactic structure of a sentence emerges from the knowledge in our mind during the process of sentence production. Additionally, it provides an explanation for why backgrounded constructions behave as islands.

References

Bos, J.: Implementing the binding and accommodation theory for anaphora resolution and presupposition projection. Comput. Linguist. **29**(2), 179–210 (2003)

Chomsky, N.: Lectures on Government and Binding: The Pisa Lectures. Walter de Gruyter (1993)

Cresti, D.: Indefinite topics. Ph.D. diss, Massachusetts Institute of Technology (1995)

Davies, D.J.M., Isard, S.D.: Utterances as programs. Mach. Intell. **7**, 325–339 (1972)

De Groote, P.: Towards a Montagovian account of dynamics. In: Semantics and Linguistic Theory, vol. 16, pp. 1–16 (2006)

De Groote, P., Lebedeva, E.: Presupposition accommodation as exception handling. In: Proceedings of the SIGDIAL 2010 Conference, pp. 71–74 (2010)

Erteschik-Shir, N.: On the nature of island constraints. Ph.D. diss, Massachusetts Institute of Technology (1973)

Givón, T.: Definiteness and referentiality. Univ. Hum. Lang. **4**, 291–330 (1978)

Geurts, B.: Presuppositions and pronouns. In: Presuppositions and Pronouns. Brill (1999)

Geurts, B.: Specific indefinites, presupposition and scope. In: Presuppositions and Discourse: Essays Offered to Hans Kamp, pp. 125–158. Brill (2010)

Geurts, B., Maier, E.: Layered DRT. Ms., University of Nijmegen (2003)

Goldberg, A.E.: Constructions at Work: The Nature of Generalization in Language. Oxford University Press, Oxford (2006)

Haddock, N.J.: Incremental interpretation and combinatory categorial grammar. Department of Artificial Intelligence, University of Edinburgh (1987)

Heim, I.R.: The semantics of definite and indefinite noun phrases. University of Massachusetts Amherst (1982)

Kamp, H.: A theory of truth and semantic representation. Form. Semant. Essential Read. 189–222 (1981)

Kamp, H., Reyle, U.: From Discourse to Logic: Introduction to Modeltheoretic Semantics of Natural Language, Formal Logic and Discourse Representation Theory (1993)

Kamp, H., Van Genabith, J., Reyle, U.: Discourse representation theory. In: Gabbay, D., Guenthner, F. (eds.) Handbook of Philosophical Logic, vol. 15, pp. 125–394. Springer, Dordrecht (2011). https://doi.org/10.1007/978-94-007-0485-5_3

Karttunen, L.: Discourse referents. In: Notes from the Linguistic Underground, pp. 363–385. Brill (1976)

Lyons, C.: Definiteness. Cambridge University Press, Cambridge (1999)

Mel'čuk, I.: Communicative organization in natural language, pp. 1–405 (2001)

Potts, C.: The Logic of Conventional Implicatures, vol. 7. OUP, Oxford (2005)

Toribio, A.J.: Proper government in Spanish subject relativization, pp. 291–304 (1992)

Van der Sandt, R.A.: Presupposition projection as anaphora resolution. J. Semant. **9**(4), 333–377 (1992)

Van der Sandt, R.A., Geurts, B.: Presupposition, anaphora, and lexical content. In: Herzog, O., Rollinger, C.R. (eds.) Text Understanding in LILOG. Lecture Notes in Computer Science, vol. 546, pp. 259–296. Springer, Heidelberg (1991). https://doi.org/10.1007/3-540-54594-8_65

Van Geenhoven, V.: Semantic incorporation and indefinite descriptions: semantic and syntactic aspects of noun incorporation in West Greenlandic (1998)

Wagner, M.: Association by movement: evidence from NPI-licensing. Nat. Lang. Semant. **14**, 297–324 (2006)

Winograd, T.: Understanding natural language. Cogn. Psychol. **3**(1), 1–191 (1972)

Yeom, J.-I.: A Presuppositional Analysis of Specific Indefinites: Common Grounds as Structured Information States. Routledge (1998)

Author Index

B
Balogh, Kata 37
Bekki, Daisuke 68, 224
Butler, Alastair 175

C
Chen, Zhuang 134
Chow, Ka-fat 155

D
de Groote, Philippe 118, 244

F
Fukushima, Haruka 68

G
Greenberg, Yael 134, 205
Guillaume, Maxime 118

H
Hayashi, Noritsugu 84
Helman, Agathe 118

K
Kiselyov, Oleg 55
Kishida, Kohei 321

L
Liefke, Kristina 17
Loukanova, Roussanka 260

M
Matsuoka, Daiki 224

N
Nakamura, Takanobu 285

O
Osher, Pola 205

P
Plesniak, Daniel 68
Pogodalla, Sylvain 118

R
Rieser, Lukas 191
Rygaev, Ivan 337

S
Salmon, Raphaël 118

W
Winterstein, Grégoire 1

Y
Yagi, Yusuke 307
Yanaka, Hitomi 224

© The Editor(s) (if applicable) and The Author(s), under exclusive license
to Springer Nature Switzerland AG 2024
D. Bekki et al. (Eds.): LENLS 2023, LNCS 14569, p. 353, 2024.
https://doi.org/10.1007/978-3-031-60878-0

Printed in the United States
by Baker & Taylor Publisher Services